ABOUT THE AUTHORS

Frank Kusy is a professional travel writer. Born in England, the son of Polish-Hungarian immigrants, he first travelled abroad at the age of four and has been wandering ever since. He left Cardiff University for a career in journalism and worked for a while with the *Financial Times*. He has also written a successful guide book to India in the Cadogan Guide series.

Frances Capel is a novelist, freelance journalist and travel writer. She has had the unique opportunity to spend several months in Burma researching this guide.

CADOGAN GUIDES

CADOGAN GUIDES

THAILAND
&
BURMA

FRANK KUSY & FRANCES CAPEL

Illustrations by Pauline Pears

CADOGAN BOOKS
LONDON

Cadogan Books Ltd
(Holding Company – Metal Bulletin PLC)
16 Lower Marsh, London SE1

Cover design by Keith Pointing
Cover illustration by Povl Webb
Maps by Thames Cartographic Services Ltd

Series Editors: Rachel Fielding and Paula Levey
Editor: Janey Dalrymple

First published in 1988

British Library Cataloguing in Publication Data

Kusy, Frank
   Thailand & Burma.—(Cadogan Guides).
   1. Burma—Visitors' Guides   2. Thailand—Visitors' Guides
   I. Title   II. Capel, Frances
   915.91′045

ISBN 0946–313–77 6

Photoset in Ehrhardt on a Linotron 202
Printed and bound in Great Britain by Redwood Burn Ltd, Trowbridge, Wiltshire

PLEASE NOTE

Every effort has been made to ensure the accuracy of the information in this book at the time of going
to press. However, practical details such as opening hours, travel information, standards in hotels and
restaurants and, in particular, prices are liable to change.

We will be delighted to receive any corrections and suggestions for improvement which can be
incorporated into the next edition, but cannot accept any responsibility for consequences arising from
the use of this guide.

We intend to keep this book as up-to-date as possible in the coming years, so please do write to us.
Writers of the best letters will receive a free copy of the Cadogan Guide of their choice.

CONTENTS

THAILAND

Introduction

CONTENTS

BURMA

Introduction *Page 245*

CONTENTS

LIST OF MAPS

THAILAND

BURMA

ACKNOWLEDGEMENTS

THAILAND

It is impossible to mention everybody who has contributed to this guide, but special thanks go to: Trailfinders (especially Gail Randall and Beth Hooson); Ian Pollack and 'Swit' Prasertpont (Chiang Mai); Sukhum, Mongkon and T T Guest House (Bangkok); Mr Virat, K. Kultida and Korakoat Jitrapiriom (Bangkok); Poo & Tangsukjai restaurant (Chiang Mai); Vanna and Yoothapong Kunateerachadalai (UK); Miss Tassanee Bhikul (Songkhla National Museum); Sue Wild and Toss Putsorn (Koh Samet); Dr Sally Meecham-Jones, Anne Edwards and Bridget Crampton (UK); Dave Glynn-Thomas (Canada); Stephen ('Wherever I lay my hat, that's my home . . .') Merchant, Rosie Targett, Anna Donovan, Georgia and Tony; to Jessica Kent (who was there when it all began), and to my parents.

For cordial service, friendly assistance and lots of information, I should like to thank TAT (Tourism Authority of Thailand), especially offices in London, Bangkok, Phuket, Pattaya, Hua Hin, Kanchanaburi and Chiang Mai.

Finally, a special *sabai! sabai!* to the following, for sharing the joys of Thailand with me: BANGKOK: John Runcie, Kate Burton (UK); Romy de Weerdt (Belgium); Lynn Cote (Canada), Anek Chitrbandh, 'Froggy' and Roof Garden Guest House. CHIANG MAI: Jill and Jane (NZ), Poo and Boon Tean; BAN CHIANG: Thadsanee Kanyarat (and National Museum); CHIANG RAI: 'Chat'; HAT YAI: Adrian Dale, Tim and Tracey (UK), Alfred and Stefano (US); HUA HIN: Tipawan Thampusana (TAT); KANCHANABURI: Jos Aarts (Holland), John Richards, Tina and Jill (UK), Berni Koppe (Canada), Sunya Koohamongkol; KHAO YAI: 'Po'; KOH PHI PHI: Leonard, Johann, Anna and Katrina (Sweden); Clare and Fiona (UK), Ann and Herb (US), Donna (NZ) and Ann (Canada); KOH PHANGAN: Alistair and Debbie (UK); KOH SAMET: Janine and Jenny (Australia), Anya (Germany), Eileen and Katrina (UK), Judy & Nuan Kitchen; KOH SAMUI: Raewyn Annas, Karen and Pete Lloyd (NZ), Karen and Frank (Australia), Dominic and Colin (UK), Poh, Sak, Kai and Moon Bungalow; KOH SI CHANG: Toom & Tiewpai Hotel, Alison Campbell (UK), Andrea Nidhof (Germany); KRABI: Jate and PP Guest House, Hans Carlsson (Sweden), Erica (UK), Mark (Switzerland), Philip and Larry, Mary and Joom; LAMPHUN: Duang Chan Longlai; MAE HONG SON: Helmut and Julia (Germany), Caroline Lander (UK), Florence and Michelle (France), and 'Nok' Anan; MAE SARIANG: Peter Charlesworth (UK), Pai Toon; NAKHON PATHOM: Boon Khong Luksapol, Siammit and Supap; NAKHON RATCHASIMA: Nikki & 'La Ploy'; NONG KHAI: Wolfgang Marik (Germany) and Boonthom ('Prem') Natenee; PAI: Willi (Switzerland), Duang, Kim and 'Jungle Joe'; PATTAYA: Scott Fisher (Australia); PHANG NGA: Sayan Tamtopol; PHUKET: Didden Alex (Belgium); SOPPONG: Albert (Malaysia), Elbe, Rob and Tracy (UK); SUKHOTHAI: Lakana & Chinawat Hotel.

ACKNOWLEDGEMENTS

BURMA

This book is for my dear friends in Burma, without whom it could not have been written. I would also like to thank: my daughter Mary, for her meticulous work in situ, updating the facts; Paula Levey for letting me write the book and nursing me through it and Janey Dalrymple for her tactful editing and encouragement.

THAILAND
by Frank Kusy

To my grandfather, László Hunor, with gratitude. Nam-myoho-renge-kyo.

INTRODUCTION

Thailand, formerly known as Siam, is a small, friendly Southeast Asian kingdom where 20th-century modernity exists alongside a unique culture developed over 700 years. The country has a population about the same as the UK (60 million in an area about the size of France (500,000 sq km), and is bounded—proceeding counterclockwise from the south—by the Gulf of Thailand, Kampuchea, Laos, Burma and Malaysia. It divides into four distinct regions—the mountainous north, the sprawling northeast plateau, the long, narrow isthmus of the south, and the central plain commonly known as the 'Rice Bowl of Asia'.

What makes Thailand so special is that it is the only nation in Southeast Asia which has never really been colonized by a foreign power. Parts of it have been occupied by Burma and Laos, or lost outright, but never for long enough to rob the Thais of their cherished national character, customs or traditions. As a people they are very proud of this fact, and commonly refer to their country as 'Muang Thai' or 'Land of the Free'. Steered into the 20th century by a remarkable succession of kings—beginning with King Mongkut (of *The King and I* fame)—Thais today remain Third World enough to compete favourably in Third World markets (especially in fabrics and high-quality 'fake' goods) yet progressive enough to borrow Western ideas without sacrificing their individuality. Despite great poverty in certain areas—notably the northeast—and long-standing border disputes with neighbouring Burma and Laos, the Thais have managed to avoid internal revolution. Two things hold them together through thick and thin—their devotion to their king and their belief in Buddhism. Both symbols of national unity are richly reflected in their art and culture. More than anything else, Thailand is a country of royal palaces and Buddhist temples—thousands of them!

As a tourist destination, Thailand has much to offer. It combines beautiful beaches, remote islands, tropical jungles, mountain valleys, ancient sites, and bargain shopping in one convenient package. And it's still remarkably cheap. Here you can stay in an international-class hotel for £20, buy a complete new fashion wardrobe for £50 and enjoy a top-quality gourmet meal for less than £10 a head. The country appeals to a broad spectrum of people—from the backpacker living on a shoestring to the affluent business couple who prefer air-conditioning and all mod cons. It especially appeals to single men, who comprise some 70% of tourists arriving in the country. Thailand's image as sex capital of the world has been slow to change—though the raunchy beach resort of Pattaya is now to losing out to family-style resorts like Phuket, and sightseeing and trekking is certainly the chief preoccupation of visitors to Chiang Mai and the north. Over the past five years or so, the kind of traveller coming here has perceptibly changed—from hippie to yuppie, from beach-bum to culture-vulture, from backpacker to package tourist. But Thailand, the 'Land of Smiles', happily accommodates everyone. In 1987, over 3 million tourists visited the country. And it now has only one official tourist season—all year round!

Part I

GENERAL INFORMATION

A Tuk-Tuk

Preparing to Go

Thailand has a lot more to offer than shopping in Bangkok, trekking in Chiang Mai, beachcombing on Phuket, or 'entertainment' at Pattaya. If these increasingly touristy attractions are all you want or have time for, then a number of good package-tour companies will be delighted to plan your trip for you. If however, you want a holiday away from the tourist centres, and can make the time to explore the country properly, travel independently and plan your own itinerary. While the ideal length of stay—for a comprehensive tour of Thailand—would be around 3 months, you could cover most of its highlights in just 8 weeks. This would allow two weeks in and around Bangkok, two weeks in the north, three weeks in the south, and a week exploring the neglected northeast.

There is no 'traveller's trail', as such, in Thailand. Most travellers arrive by air in Bangkok, from where they generally head north to Chiang Mai or south to the beaches. People entering the country overland from Malaysia have a straight run up the southern isthmus to Bangkok, while those entering overland from India or Nepal drift down to the capital from the far north. In general, the best way to plan your Thailand holiday is to decide what it is you want—and then choose two or three centres which fit the bill. To help you, Bangkok and Chiang Mai have the best shopping and sightseeing, Phuket and Pattaya the best water-sports and 'upmarket' beach resort facilities, Koh Samui and

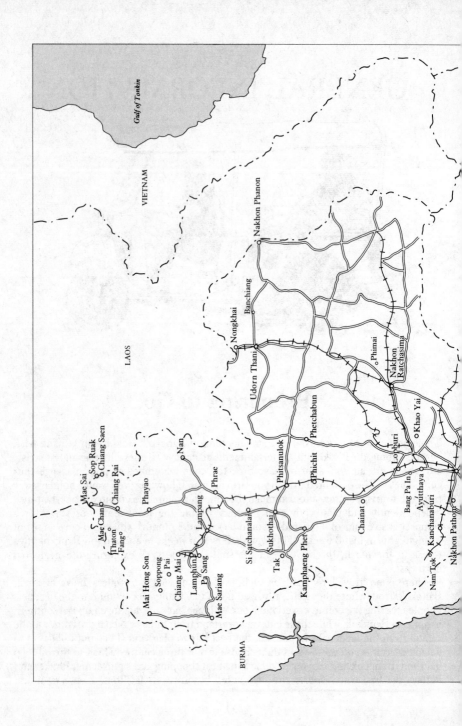

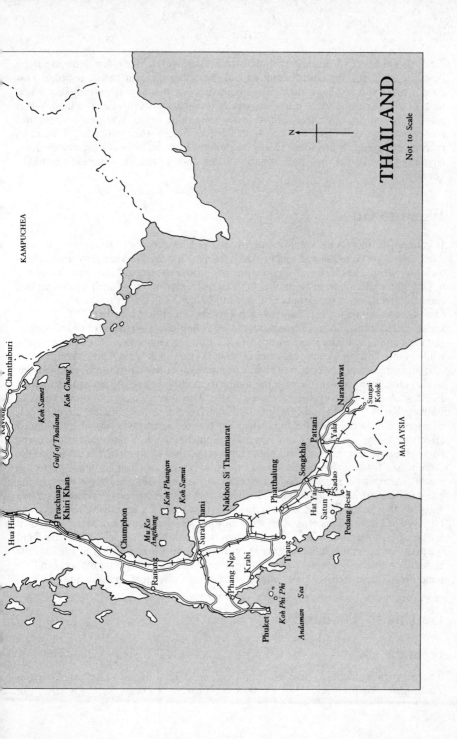

KAMPUCHEA

THAILAND

Not to Scale

N

Chanthaburi

Koh Samet

Koh Chang

Gulf of Thailand

Prachuap
Khiri Khan

Hua Hin

Chumphon

Mu Ko
Angthong

Koh Phangan

Koh Samui

Ranong

Surat Thani

Nakhon Si Thammarat

Phang Nga

Krabi

Phatthalung

Songkhla

Pattani

Trang

Hat Yai

Yala

Narathiwat

Satun

Sadao

Sungai
Kolok

Phuket

Koh Phi Phi

Pedang Besar

MALAYSIA

Andaman
Sea

Krabi the best coral-diving and offshore islands, Chiang Rai, Mae Hong Son and Pai the best hill-tribe trekking, and Sukhothai and Ayutthaya the best ruined temples. Few people make the northeast their prime objective, but this area is nevertheless a real magnet to anyone interested in archaeology, lost civilizations and 'real' Thailand. When planning your trip, don't feel obliged to see everything in one visit—and, if you find somewhere you really like, don't rush off in order to 'see' something else. Thailand's relaxed, easygoing nature doesn't really encourage hectic, high-pressure travel. Besides, anything you miss the first time around, you can always catch on your next visit to the country!

When to Go

In general, the most comfortable months to visit Thailand are from October to February. After this, it gets very hot and sticky (March to June) and then very wet and humid (June to September). The three main seasons are: hot, from February to May; rainy, from June to October; and cool, from November to January. Europeans may find these distinctions rather blurred, since temperatures rarely fall below 33°C (90°F) in the rainy season (when several short showers may fall each day) and are seldom less than 24°C (75°F) in the so-called 'cool' season. Throughout the year, the climate is generally hot and humid. Bangkok's temperatures range from 16°C (62°F in December to 35°C (96°F) in April; while cooler Chiang Mai ranges from 20°C in January to 28°C in April/May.

If planning a beach holiday, you should be aware of the *two* separate monsoon seasons of the south. From May to October the southeast monsoon comes up from the Andaman Sea and sweeps right up the southwest coast. This means heavy rains and winds at Phuket, Krabi, Phi Phi and Phang Gna. From November to February, the northeast monsoon comes over from Kampuchea and hits the southeast coast of the isthmus affecting resorts like Samui and Songhkla. Sometimes these monsoons come early, sometimes late, but the good thing about them is that they rarely hit both coastlines at the same time. Thus, if the weather breaks down at Samui, you'll often find it perfect at Krabi (a shortish bus-ride away), or vice versa. I've only met one couple who got the worst of both worlds—they arrived at Koh Phangan when monsoons were raging on *both* sides of the peninsula. All the beaches are best visited a month or two *after* the rains—when infestations of sandfleas and mosquitoes have died down. March and April are nice practically everywhere—which is why the Thais have their school holidays then! Thailand in general is busiest between November and April, which is its high tourist season. Visiting in September and October, when rains are only intermittent, can be a good idea—fewer tourists, more empty beaches, and discounts on many hotels!

Getting to Thailand

From the UK

There are direct flights to Bangkok from London on **Thai Airways, British Airways, Philippine Airlines** and **Qantas**. Booking through a cheap flight specialist like

Trailfinders (tel 01–603 1515) or **Hann Overland** (01–834 7367), you can get low-season discount return fares of £536 (Thai Airways International) or £528 (Philippine Airlines). If you don't mind a change of planes, then even cheaper low-season returns can be obtained—from **Kuwait Airlines** (£396), **Gulf Air** (£402) and **Royal Jordanian** (£407).

If you buy a **one-way ticket** from London to Bangkok (currently around £220 from bucket-shop agencies), you'll almost certainly be able to pick up a cheap return flight in Bangkok (cf. Banglampoo/Soi Ngam Dupli, Bangkok section).

Thai Airways offer attractive international and domestic flight discounts during the low season (May to October), also (if you book the London/Bangkok long-haul flight through them) a £30 discount on the short-haul Bangkok/Rangoon flight. This is good news to anyone seeking to combine Thailand with Burma.

Since cheap flights out of London are often heavily booked (especially from July to December), it's advisable to book two months before your intended departure date. Check travel sections of magazines like *Time Out*, *LAM* and *TNT* for current cheap-fare deals.

The **Miracle Bus Co**, 408 Strand, London (tel 01–373 3024) offers overland travel by coach from London to Bangkok for £199 single, £399 return.

From the US

Thai International, Korean Airlines, Pan Am, Canadian Airlines and **China Airlines** all offer budget or 'Super Apex' flights to Bangkok from US$900 to US$1150 round-trip (from Los Angeles, Seattle, San Francisco); from US$1000 to US$1300 (from New York, Chicago). There are great deals from **Sunbeam Travel**, 330 North Michigan Ave, Chicago—they sell Korean Airlines round-trip tickets (Chicago/Bangkok) for just US$850. New Yorkers often find it cheaper to fly to London, and pick up cheap onward tickets there. Californians can fly to Bangkok on Bangladesh Airlines for just US$350, one-way. Again, finding a cheap ticket home in Bangkok is no problem.

While discounted tickets are something of a rarity in the US, American travellers can sometimes find cut-price fares advertised in local newspapers.

From Canada

In October 1987, **Canadian Airlines** began operating direct-flight services from Toronto to Bangkok. But it's still **Korean Airlines** that have the best budget deals—their popular 'milk run' ticket (Vancouver–Los Angeles–Seoul–Bangkok) costs just C$569, one way.

From Australia

Flying to Bangkok, one-way economy tickets cost around AUS$1100 from Sydney/Melbourne, around AUS$950 from Perth. Buying advance-purchase tickets (must be booked and paid for 21 days before departure date), one-way fares are only AUS$600–700 from Sydney/Melbourne (AUS$900–1100 return) and AUS$450–500 from Perth (AUS$750–800 return). Further reductions may be obtained by shopping around at cheap-flight specialists in Sydney like **Travel Specialists,** 7 Picadilly Arcade, 222 Pitt St (tel 2679122), **Sydney Flight Centre**, Martin Place (tel 2212666) and **Student Travel Australia**, 1a Lee St, Railway Square (tel 2126744).

Many Australians are now entering Thailand on the overland route from Bali or Singapore (both around AUS$400–450 from Sydney) or via Denpasar (about AUS$215 by air from Darwin).

Package Holidays

These are best booked in the UK, where several tour companies are now offering Thailand at ridiculously low prices. A good example is **Jetset Tours**, 74 New Oxford St, London WC1 (tel 631 0501)—10 days in Bangkok at just £475 (less than a cheap return air-fare!), and a 17-day *Thailand Discovery* tour at £880, taking in Bangkok, Kanchana-buri, Chiang Mai and Pattaya. Several other operators, like **Travelbag**, 12 High St, Alton, Hampshire (tel 0420 89521) and **Poundstretcher**, Hazelwick Ave, Three Bridges, Crawley (tel 0293 518060) offer generous three-weeks-for-the-price-of-two deals. And **Oriental Magic**, Preston New Rd, Blackpool (tel 0253 791100) has a good-value *Jade Tour* costing £892 and including Hong Kong, Bangkok and Pattaya. Finally, there's **Kuoni**, Kuoni House, Dorking, Surrey (tel 0306 885044), which features Thailand in both its Worldwide and Kuoni 3 programmes—13- to 19-day packages in Bangkok and Pattaya from £560 to £580. In general, the more you pay for a package-tour, the more 'plastic' is the environment. Also, while sightseeing trips—plus English-speaking guides—are often laid on, they are not included in the price. You have to pay for these yourself—allow about £10 a trip.

Package tours don't appeal to everybody—especially freedom-lovers—but Thailand is a large country, and if you want to cover a lot of it in a short time, some form of organized holiday is actually not a bad idea. Recently, a few London-based companies have begun to offer semi-organized tours geared to the budget-conscious independent traveller. The best is **Trailfinders**, based at 42–48 Earls Court Rd, London W8 (tel 938 3444, 603 1515). This company provides a complete travel service—insurance, in-noculations, information, visas and cut-price air tickets. It also offers the *North Thai Rover*—an excellent 10-day tour of Bangkok, Tha Ton, Chiang Mai, Chiang Rai, Ayutthaya and Khao Yai National Park. This leads in at £219, and includes chartered transport, an experienced tour-leader, and decent accommodation—real value for money! Trailfinders also do a *Bangkok-Bali Rover* for £325—this, a 20-day tour of Thailand, Malaysia, Singapore and Indonesia. Again, a well-structured and flexible programme, allowing freedom to see or do only what interests you. Two other companies offering the same kind of deal are **Explore**, 7 High St, Aldershot, Hants. (tel 319448) and **Topdeck Travel**, 133 Earls Court Rd, London W8 (tel 373 8406).

Passport & Visas

A valid passport and a **visa** is required by all foreign nationals arriving in Thailand. However, transit passengers with confirmed onward air tickets are allowed to stay in Thailand for up to 15 days without visas. Staying longer than 15 days, you've a choice of three kinds of visa: a 30-day **transit visa** (£5.50 or US$5), a 60-day **tourist visa** (£8 or US$10), or a 90-day **non-immigrant visa** (£13.50 or US$15). All visa applications should be accompanied by three passport photos, and (in the case of the non-immigrant visa) by a letter of financial guarantee from a reliable referee (e.g. bank manager). Visas are obtainable from all Thai embassies and consulates. In the UK, apply to the Thai Embassy, 30 Queen's Gate London SW7 (tel 01–589 0173) between 9.30 am and 12.30 pm, Monday to Friday. Collect visa (and passport) the next working day, between 2 and 4 pm.

All visas of entry into Thailand are valid for 90 days from the date of issue. Visas are officially non-extendable (as my embassy quipped: 'Thailand is the land of the lotus-eaters—who wants to leave?'), but the Thai Immigration office at Soi Suan Phlu, Sathorn Tai Rd, Bangkok, sometimes grants extensions—here, it helps to have a big smile on your face and a very good reason for staying. Possibly the best place to extend visas is on Koh Samui (cf. p 194). Where you can get a 30-day extension on a tourist visa with no problem. But it's highly unlikely you'll get more than 15 days extension on a transit visa.

If you want to stay over 60 days in Thailand—and don't want the hassle involved in getting a non-immigrant visa, or of extending a transit or tourist visa—then your best bet is to buy a **two-entry tourist visa** (£16 or US$20). This gives you two lots of 60 days in the country. To claim the second lot, you've got to go out of the country and come back in again. The simplest place to do this is Pedang Besar (cf. Hat Yai, Getting There) just across the Malaysian border. You can also get a **dual-entry non-immigrant visa** (£27 or US$30), which allows a stay of 120 days—again, provided you leave and re-enter the country.

Burma visas can be obtained in Thailand from the Burmese Embassy's visa office at 132 North Sathorn Rd, Bangkok. Applications are received (with three passport photos) between 8 am and 12 noon, Mondays to Fridays. The cost of a visa is 110B.

Customs

You can bring into Thailand 200 cigarettes (or 250 grams of tobacco), a quart of wine or alcohol, and up to 2000B in Thai currency. You can't bring in any drugs or pornographic literature. You can take out up to 500B in Thai currency, and any amount of gems and jewellery. You can't take out any Buddha images (except pocket-size ones), antiques or art objects, unless you've got permission from the Fine Arts Department (ring Bangkok National Museum on 224–1370 for further details). Visitors leaving Thailand are also prohibited from taking out over US$10,000, unless declared on arrival, or permission has been granted by the Bank of Thailand.

Jabs & Tabs

No vaccinations are required for Thailand, unless you are coming from a contaminated area. This said, jabs are strongly recommended against cholera, typhoid, tetanus, polio and infective hepatitis. A single dose of Hepatitis A vaccine will give you 60–70% protection only, so it's still wise to stick to bottled or purified water in Thailand.

Malaria pills are essential. You'll need to start taking these a week before you set off, and to keep on taking them for four weeks after your return. Since certain brands can cause unpleasant side-effects (nausea, vomiting etc), it's wise to order them from your doctor a good two weeks before your departure—that way you've got time to change your prescription if they don't agree with you. Currently, most doctors recommend a combination of Maloprim and Novoquine tablets. But it's worth ringing up the London Hospital of Tropical Diseases (tel 01–387 4411) for up-to-date information, or contacting Trailfinders' excellent medical centre. The WHO (World Health Organisation) are said to be developing the 'perfect prophylactic' against malaria—called Meflaquine—which may shortly be available on general prescription. In a country like Thailand, where malarial mosquitoes are said to be resistant to 90% of current chloroquine-based preventives, this is welcome news indeed.

Diarrhoea tablets are also recommended for 'emergencies'. The most widely prescribed are Imodium and Lomotil (Codeine-Phosphate is also okay, but can be toxic). In general, diarrhoea is best left to run its natural course. Use tablets only if you're on a busy schedule, and simply can't afford to be sick.

An excellent guide to health abroad—both readable and informative—is Dr Richard Dawood's *Travellers' Health* (Oxford University Press, UK). It's also available in the States, published by Viking under the title *How to Stay Healthy Abroad*. Also worth obtaining (UK only) are the DHSS leaflets SA35 (Protect your Health Abroad) and SA30 (Medical Costs Abroad). Your doctor should stock these.

Money

Prices are rising all the time, but Thailand is still a fairly cheap place to live. The cost of a two-week holiday—including food, accommodation, transport, tours and entertainment (but excluding shopping!)—is currently around £250 (on a shoestring), £400 mid-range comfort) and £750–1000 (living in style). Cutting out alcoholic drinks and staying away from expensive tourist centres will reduce the above estimates substantially!

Travellers' cheques are the safest means of carrying your money. They normally have automatic insurance and are easy to replace. Since Thailand has no currency black market (unlike say, India or Burma) there is no advantage in taking lots of cash. Especially since travellers' cheques command a better exchange rate at Thai banks than hard currency. For safety, order your cheques in small denominations, keep them separate from your sales receipt (record of purchase) and keep a note of the refunding agent's address in Thailand (vendor should supply this) in a safe place. At the time of writing, Sterling cheques are the best buy, but Dollar cheques are equally acceptable.

Major **credit cards** such as American Express, Visa, Diners Club, Carte Blanche and Master Charge are accepted in many large hotels, restaurants and department stores. A credit card can be a lifesaver if, for any reason, your travellers' cheques and money go missing. It's also very handy for shopping—especially when, as happened to me, a bargain silk sale comes up on your last day in Bangkok, and you're clean out of cash!

Travel insurance is essential. If your bank or travel company can't suggest a good policy, check out the comprehensive schemes offered by Trailfinders or Topdeck Travel (cf. Package Tours). Your policy should cover lost luggage, money and valuables, personal liability and travel delay. It should also supply a 24-hour number to contact in the case of a medical emergency.

For currency exchange see 'Changing Money' on p. 24.

What to Take

In general, the less you take the better. You can buy all you need—clothes, baggage, toiletries etc—in Bangkok, and often a good deal cheaper than at home. But don't bring *too* little! I've seen smug repeat visitors arriving in Thailand with nothing but the clothes they stand up in. They stop smiling when they have to spend their first day in Bangkok's heat shopping for basics like toothpaste and sun-cream. The message is—travel light, but bring all essentials. Make up a short but comprehensive packing list, and leave a copy at home with someone reliable—this will assist insurance claims, should your luggage be lost or stolen.

Luggage

Don't take more luggage than you can easily carry—toting heavy bags around in Thailand's humid heat can be very tiring. Try and pack everything in one large soft bag (Globetrotter and Samsonite do a good range) or in a frameless rucksack with top carrying-handle and plenty of pockets. All small items—camera, newspaper, books etc—can go in a small shoulder bag or day sack—useful not only for travelling on the plane, but also for sightseeing and day-outings within Thailand. Inside the country, it's a good idea to wear shoulder bags diagonally across the body—this prevents theft. If you're going to be doing a lot of travelling between towns, consider leaving the inevitable accumulation of presents and souvenirs in store—most of the larger hotels and major rail/bus stations have left-luggage rooms. This leaves you free to get around without the encumbrance of excess luggage. Check with your airline regarding luggage allowance—if it looks like you're going to go seriously over weight on your return flight (and this is *very* common!) consider freighting a few kilos home prior to departure, or posting parcels home by sea or air-mail. The main Bangkok post offices have an excellent packing service.

Clothing

Cool, cotton clothes are your best bet—and you should pack at least one smart, casual outfit. The Thais are smooth dressers. Nobody can look cooler than the hip young Thai leaning lazily on his Japanese motorbike in his designer disco-jacket, his personalized cufflinks, his Levi jeans, and his custom-made shoes. Even ordinary Thai housewives are decked out like fashion models! While you can kit yourself out in the latest styles at Bangkok's numerous department stores and boutiques, it's worth bringing a jacket and tie if you're going to be staying at a plush hotel, or intend visiting high-class restaurants or nightclubs.

For the rest, you can get away with just two T-shirts, (or cotton shirts), a pair of trousers (or jeans), a skirt or dress, two sets of socks and underwear, a comfy pair of flat

9

shoes, swimwear, a towel, a sun hat, a pair of shorts, and perhaps a pair of sandals (or thongs/flip flops). If you're going during the rainy months, also include a light water-proof, and a small, folding umbrella. If you're visiting northern Thailand from Novem-ber to January (when it gets quite cold at night) take a warm sweater—and a sleeping bag.

Because clothes tend to dry quickly, bring only a few and wash them regularly. Many hotels and guest houses, for a modest fee, will wash them for you—or will be able to recommend a laundry service nearby.

Equipment

Things worth taking are a money-belt (or security wallet), sunglasses and sun-cream, a small torch and spare batteries, a roll of toilet paper, a water bottle and some water-purification tablets (Puritabs are best), personal toiletries (including a mirror and a sewing kit), a washing line and soap powder, a penknife with openers (useful for peeling fruit etc), a personal medical kit (should include mosquito repellent, antiseptic mouth-wash etc), reading and writing matter, playing cards or travel-scrabble (good for whiling away long train journeys), perhaps a walkman (pirate cassettes are cheap in Bangkok and Chiang Mai), a camera and *lots* of film. You can buy film in Thailand (Fuji is best), but it's pricey, and you need to check the expiry date before purchasing.

Other useful inclusions are a small alarm clock (for catching early trains), a combi-nation padlock (for securing baggage etc), snorkelling equipment (the stuff hired out on Thai beaches is seldom good quality), a half-sheet with attached pillowcase (for budget lodges with dirty linen, or for trek huts with no linen at all!) and, of course, a mosquito net (large single, or double, size is best—most Thai accommodation has vast beds!). An inflatable pillow always comes in handy, especially on long and arduous bus journeys. Spectacle and contact lens wearers should take spare glasses/lenses, and should have their prescriptions noted down somewhere safe, in case replacements are required. Finally, consider taking along a few small presents for the Thai friends you'll be making. Photos of yourself and your family go down well. So do postcards of your home town or of the English royal family (Thais especially like ones of the Queen on horseback!). Small foreign coins make good gifts for children, while Thai women like Max Factor make-up! It's difficult to know what to give Thai men—though a bottle of Scotch whisky generally goes down a treat, as do English or American cigarettes. When presenting gifts to Thais, you should do so with both hands—giving a slight bow called a *wai*.

Most equipment you can pick up from a good camping shop. In the UK, two good ones are **Blacks Camping and Leisure**, 53 Rathbone Place, London W1, tel 01–636 6645/6 and **Survival Aids**, West Colonnade, Euston St, London, tel 388 8353. Ring ahead to check availability of sleeping bags and mosquito nets—these are popular items, and are often out of stock!

Books & Information

The more you read about Thailand—both before going and whilst there—the more you're likely to enjoy the country. Visit your local library, scout around the larger bookshops, and (if in the UK) drop in on Trailfinders, who issue free handouts on

Bangkok, Thailand and Southeast Asia. They also have an excellent little reference library, full of useful guides, maps and travel mags.

Tourist Information

For general information, plus a decent map of Thailand, visit your nearest TAT (Tourism Authority of Thailand) office. TAT has overseas offices at:
Australia: 12th Floor, Royal Exchange Bldg., 56 Pitt Street, Sydney NSW 2000 (tel 277549, 277540).
France: 90 Avenue des Champs Elysées, 75008 Paris (tel 45 62 86 56, 45 62 87 48).
Japan: Hibiya Mitsui Bldg., 1–2 Yurakucho 1-Chome, Chiyoda-ku, Tokyo 100 (tel 5806776–7)
UK: 49 Albemarle St, London W1 (tel 01–499 7679)
USA (East): 5 World Trade Center, Suite No. 2449, New York, NY 10048 (tel: 4320433)
USA (West): 3440 Wilshire Blvd., Suite 1101, Los Angeles, California 90010 (tel 3822353–5)
In Thailand, TAT has a head office at Bangkok, and local offices at Kanchanaburi and Pattaya (central), at Chiang Mai and Phitsanoluke (north), Nakhon Ratchasima (northeast), and Phuket, Songkhla and Surat Thani (south). All are helpful, efficient and hand out masses of useful material.

Maps

Two good country maps of Thailand, published by APA and Nelles, sell in the UK for £4.95, and in Bangkok (e.g. The Bookseller, Patpong) for only £1! If you're into serious map-reading, visit Bangkok's TAT head office on Ratchadamneon Nok—this offers a remarkably detailed 4-map set (covering central, northeast, north and south regions) for 65B.

City maps of Bangkok and Chiang Mai, compiled by Nancy Chandler, sell both in Thailand (60B) and at major travel bookshops abroad. Packed with useful information, these are actually better city guides than maps! TAT do a reasonable map of Bangkok (free), and their provincial offices issue complimentary town/city maps. Most bookstores in Bangkok sell the essential 'bus map' (35B), which is a bus map, an excellent city map, and a country map all rolled into one.

Books

Western bookshops don't tend to stock many books on Thailand, and you may be better off waiting till you get to Bangkok and Chiang Mai. Here you can pick up some excellent titles, including Carol Hollinger's *Mai Pen Rai means Never Mind* (Asia Book Co, Bangkok), a wry, witty, and well-observed account of Thai manners and cultural conflicts; the perceptive *Siam in Crisis* by Sulak Sivaraksa (DK Books, Bangkok); and the absorbing *Everyday Life in Thailand—an Interpretation* by Dr. Niels Mulder (another one from DK), which is a first-class analysis of Thai customs, society and religion.

If you want to know more about Buddhism, and don't want to wade through vast tomes on the subject, look out for *Understanding Thai Buddhism*, a short, readable study of M. L. Manich Jumsai (DK, Chiang Mai), or *A Meditator's Diary* by Jane Hamilton-Merritt (Pelican, UK), an interesting account of one Western woman's experiences in Thai monasteries.

For history and archaeology, there's still nothing to touch A. Clerac's *A Guide to Thailand* (OUP, UK). The author was French ambassador to Thailand, travelled the country by limo, and is generally spot on. Also worth a read is *Thailand, a Short History* by David K. Wyatt (Yale University Press, London). Two good introductions to the northern hill-tribes of Thailand are *Peoples of the Golden Triangle* by Paul and Elaine Lewis (Thames and Hudson, UK) and *People of the Hills* by Preecha Chaturabhand (DK Bookshop). A few modern Thai novels have recently appeared in English translation. Two recommended ones are *Rice without Rain* (Andre Deutsch, UK) by Min Fong Ho—a racy little story about the City of Angels, Bangkok; and *A Child of the North East* by Kampoon Boon Tawee (DK Bookshop, Bangkok/Chiang Mai)—an award-winning novel about a year in the life of a northeastern village in the 1930s. Finally, if you want to know more about Thai food, there's *Thai Cooking* by Jennifer Brennan (Futura, Mc-Donald & Co, Sydney), probably the best all-round introduction; also *Cooking Thai food in American Kitchens* by Malulee Pinsuvana, full of well-illustrated recipes.

Newspapers

Bangkok has two morning papers, the *Bangkok Post* and the *Nation*, and one in the afternoon called *Bangkok World*. Most travellers favour the *Bangkok Post*. It's a real gossip rag, with all kinds of wry, humorous pokes at life in Thailand and in the UK. It goes in for sensational headlines like 'Monk gored to death by rogue elephant', and it prints some really outrageous letters from foreign tourists. Half of these, I'm convinced, are fictitious!

On Arrival

Orientation

Most visitors enter Thailand via Bangkok, and have few problems adapting to the capital city's busy, yet relaxed, modernism. Much of the rest of the country isn't anything like as developed, but wherever you go the people are just the same—easygoing, friendly and hospitable. Unlike many Asian countries, Thailand has no history of Western colonialism. It's a poor country, yet proud and independent. The Thai people aren't into hassling tourists for money, gifts or favours. Instead, they aim to make foreign guests feel relaxed and at ease. This they do as a matter of courtesy, with no expectation of reward. What they do expect however, is that you show the same kind of respect yourself—particularly to their king, their religion and their customs. Wandering around like a colonial overlord, treating the Thais like second-class citizens, won't win you any friends. Unless you're polite, respectful and ask for things nicely, you'll certainly run up against *mai pen rai* (no worry, no hurry) in its severest form. The Thais can be remarkably slow, forgetful and awkward when they've a mind to be! In recent years, as they've witnessed tourists skinny-dipping on their beaches, scaling sacred monuments for photographs, and displaying physical affection in public places, they've lost quite a lot of respect for Europeans. The tendency of a growing minority of Thais is to take grasping foreigners—especially those who are here for sex and sin—for as much money as they can.

Getting along with the Thais is easy, just as long as you observe a few *dos* and *don't*s: *do* dress neatly when visiting temples and religious shrines (i.e. no shorts, sarongs, or sleeveless tops), *do* remove shoes when entering Thai houses, temple chapels and mosques, and *do* smile a lot and learn a few Thai courtesy phrases. *don't* insult the royal family—unless you want a bad accident. *don't* get caught with drugs—unless you want a long spell in prison. *don't* touch Thai adults on the head (the most sacred part of the body) or slap them heartily on the back—unless you fancy being slapped about in return. You *don't* have to *wai* (bow, with hands together in prayer, the standard Thai greeting) to younger people, only to elders or important people. The Thais *don't* go in for open, lavish displays of affection (except to children), and frown on foreigners groping each other out of doors. Thai guys *don't* take kindly to prolonged eye contact (it often invites a fight) and Thais in general *don't* kiss with the mouth (kissing with the nose is the custom!). A very big *don't* is pointing your feet at people (or Buddha images)—the sole of the foot, being in contact with the earth, is considered the most degraded part of the body. In Thai temples or houses, either kneel, or sit crosslegged, or perfect the 'Asian squat'. Anything will do, just so long as your feet are tucked out of sight. The biggest *don't* of all is to lose your temper. Normally, the Thais are the nicest, smiliest people you can imagine. You can kid around with them, and they'll always pick up on it. The Thais have a good sense of joy. But if provoked, they also have a less noble side, which you should be aware (but not paranoid) of. The Thais may not often show anger ('they don't have the energy', was one wry comment, 'it's too hot!')—but when they get mad, they get *very* mad!

TAT publish a short guide to *Dos* and *Don't*s in Thailand', which is well worth picking up from their airport desk, on arrival in Bangkok.

Thailand must be one of the few countries in the world where it's more hassle to travel as a man than as a woman! Okay, women travellers may have to fend off the occasional over-amorous trek guide or monk, but in general they are treated with the highest respect by Thai men. Over-familiarity, however, can be misinterpreted as a come-on, and as a woman on your own you'll have to be careful about how open and friendly you are. As one girl reported:

> I received three separate offers of marriage from Thai men. They thought I must be rich and would be able to support them. Thai guys have a definite thing about Western women—they want to marry them and come to the West.

Male travellers don't get off so easy. Thailand is essentially a country for men, and a foreign man on his own is a prime target for enterprising Thai prostitutes. Sometimes it's impossible even to get a quiet cup of tea, without an endless procession of touts turning up to offer 'big boy' massages or short-time rental of their daughter, sister or even grandmother. The main 'hit' spots are Bangkok, Pattaya and Koh Samui. Here, as one guy related, prostitutes are now ensnaring travellers by the most ingenious means:

> I'd been down to Koh Samui, and my ears were blocked up from swimming. So I decided to visit a local doctor and have them syringed. Well, I was waiting at the

bus-stop and a very smart-looking Thai lady beckoned me over. She had a map of Bangkok, and wanted me to recommend a good hotel since she was from Malaysia (she said) and would be quite lost in the busy capital. We chatted for a bit, and then I happened to mention that I was off to the doctor to have my ears syringed. 'What luck!' she announced, '*I'm* a doctor actually!' I looked at her sideways and said 'Oh, *are* you?' And she replied, 'Yes, I could make you feel *much* better!!'

Getting Around

Thailand is a very easy country to travel round. Air, rail and bus services are modern and efficient—everything usually runs on time. Out of Bangkok, most towns are fairly small and manageable, which makes sightseeing easy. In town, you often have a choice of local transport—usually *tuk-tuks* and *songthaews*, sometimes taxis and buses too. Some beach resorts are conveniently explored by motorbike, and some ancient temple towns are best toured by bicycle, or even on foot. In a few places (e.g. Krabi, Sukhothai) air-conditioned minibus tours are an excellent way of getting round the sights.

By Air

Thai Airways, flies to all major centres in Thailand. Fares are very cheap—with 20% discounts on certain night flights—and some examples are as follows:

From Bangkok to	Chiang Mai	1275B (1020B night-flight)
	Hat Yai	1760B (1410B night-flight)
	Nakorn Ratchasima	1340B
	Phitsanoluke	730B
	Phuket	1545B (1240B night-flight)
	Surat Thani	1380B
	Udorn Thani	1010B
From Chiang Mai to	Chiang Rai	300B
	Hat Yai	2580B
	Phitsanoluke	505B
	Phuket	2400B
	Surat Thani	2260B
	Udorn Thani	1945B

Addresses of Thai Airway offices are:

Bangkok: Head Office, 6 Larn Luang Rd (tel 2800090–110); Reservations, (tel 2800070, 2800080); Don Muang Airport (tel 5238271–3).

Chiang Mai	240 Prapokklao Road	(tel 211541, 211420, 211044–7)
Chiang Rai	870 Phaholyotin Road	(tel 711179, 713663)
Hat Yai	166/4 Nipat Utit 2 Road	(tel 245851–2, 243711, 246165, 233433)

Khon Kaen	183/6 Maliwan Road	(tel 236523, 239011, 238835)
Lampang	314 Sanambin Road	(tel 217078, 218199)
Mae Hong Son	71 Sinhanatbamrung Road	(tel 611297)
Nan	34 Mahaprom Road	(tel 710377, 710498)
Nongkhai	453 Prachak Road	(tel 441530)
Pattani	9 Preeda Road	(tel 349149)
Phitsanulok	209/26–28 Bromtrailoknart Road	(tel 258020, 251671)
Phrae	42–44 Rasdamner Road	(tel 511123, 511977)
Phuket	78 Ranong Road	(tel 211195, 212499, 212946)
Songkhla	2 Soi 4 Saliburi Road	(tel 311012)
Surat Thani	3/27–28 Karoonrat Road	(tel 272610, 273355, 273710)
Trang	199/2 Viseskul Road	(tel 218066, 210863)
Ubon	292/9 Chayanggoon Road	(tel 254431, 255959)
Udorn	60 Makkang Road	(tel 221004, 243222)

By Train

Thailand's State Railway has four trunk routes, running to the north, northeast, east and south. All long-distance trains have sleeping cars and/or air-conditioned coaches. Train reservations can be made at the Advance Booking Office of Bangkok's Hualamphong station (tel 2233790, 2233762) from 8.30 am to 6 pm weekdays, 8.30 am to 12 noon weekends. Schedules and fares are available from the State Railways of Thailand (tel 2230374, 2237010, 2237020). In addition to the regular passenger fares quoted throughout this guide (cf. Getting There sections), there are surcharges for Rapid (20B) and Express (30B) trains, for sleeping berths (1st class air-con, 210B; 1st class non air-con, 130B; 2nd class air-con, upper berth 150B, lower berth 180B; 2nd class non air-con, upper berth 70B, lower berth 100B per person), and for air-con 2nd class coaches (40B).

Trains are usually a little slower than buses, but they compensate by being safer and a lot more comfortable. I would recommend them for all long-distance travel. Unlike in a bus, where you're pinned to your seat, you can stroll around and stretch your legs. Buying a sleeping berth on an overnight train to Chiang Mai or to Surat Thani (for Samui) from Bangkok, you'll arrive refreshed and relaxed—not (as on a bus) a limp rag. The Express trains are the quickest form of rail transport—they reach destinations a lot quicker than Rapid trains (not rapid at all) or languishing Ordinary trains. Travelling 3rd class is okay on short journeys (say, up to 3–4 hours), but I wouldn't suggest it for long overnight trips. One person, travelling south from Hua Hin to Surat Thani, reported 3rd class compartments so crowded that people were sleeping under seats and even in hammocks strung up between luggage racks! I believe him. One journey I made—from Nong Khai down to Bangkok—was a 3rd class nightmare. A whole family occupied my seat while I was in the toilet. I hadn't the heart to kick them out, and spent 14 hours eating peanuts and tossing back Mekong in the gangway with local youths. Most of the Thai language I ever learnt, I picked up that night! Overnight trains like this always serve meals and drinks. The vendors are often young boys, who eat, sleep and live on these trains. 'Where is your home?' I asked one of these lads. 'Train 41 to Chiang Mai!' was the bright response. And then, as an afterthought, 'Oh, and on train 42, going back to Bangkok!' His name was Vishu, and he earnt just 10B (25p) for each 12-hour journey he

15

made—plus 10% commission on every beer he sold. His father, his two uncles, and his ten brothers and sisters also lived on trains.

By Bus

Here you have a choice between public state-run buses and private 'tour' buses. Both are cheap, uncomfortable, and subject to accidents—which is why many drivers wear Buddha amulets and charms. Government buses are cheap, and travel throughout the country. Private buses mainly run between major tourist centres like Bangkok, Pattaya, Phuket, Koh Samui and Koh Samet. They are a little more expensive, but offer 'civilized' comforts like free meals, pillows and blankets (for overnight journeys) and, more ominously, videos. I once travelled up to Bangkok from Hua Hin on one of these 'video' buses—never again! The only functional speaker in the bus was directly above my head, and I had to strap my sleeping bag over it in order to block out the loud orgasmic moans of 'Lovely Young Tracy', an awesomely explicit pornographic film which somehow lulled every Thai passenger aboard to sleep!

On the whole, I would recommend ordinary (non air-con) buses for short point-to-point trips of 4 hours or less. Anything over that, it's worth paying a little extra for an air-con bus. If you've got long legs, either sit right at the front, or in the conductor's seat by the rear entrance (he won't minding sharing). Overnight bus journeys are notorious for theft—I've even heard of whole busloads of people being ripped off, after phoney 'waitresses' put them to sleep with drugged drinks. The introduction of video cameras onto prime-risk routes (like Bangkok–Chiang Mai and Bangkok–Surat Thani) has reduced such incidents dramatically. But you should still never accept food, drinks or sweets from strangers. Buy your own food on buses—there's no shortage of it! The amount of food that descends on the average public bus in the course of an average journey is quite phenomenal. At each stop (and there are several) an endless procession of baseball-hatted youths—mainly grinning young girls wearing lumberjack shirts and 'I love Coke' T-shirts—mount the bus hawking bottles of Fanta, boiled eggs in a basket, Chinese dim-sums, barbecued chicken on sticks, iced drinks in plastic bags, carved pineapples, trays of sweets, and even girlie mags! Round and round they go, entering the bus at one exit and leaving it by the other, rather like a continually revolving mobile restaurant. As often as not, the bus only leaves this scene of culinary delights at all because a biblical plague of wasps—drawn by the sweet and sticky food within—has spurred the driver into action. And when he finally gets going, just watch out!

By the way, don't worry about finding your bus at crowded terminals. In Bangkok and Chiang Mai at least, someone will nearly always materialize to shove you on the right bus. Often, your *deus ex machina* will be a young girl with a tray of chewing gum. The deal is, she guides you to your bus, and you buy some of her chewing gum!

Local Buses

These operate in many larger cities, notably Bangkok and Chiang Mai, and are very cheap. They can also (cf. Bangkok section) be very slow. You'll need a town map or English-speaking assistance to use local buses—their destinations are usually posted only in Thai.

16

Taxis & Tuk-Tuks

You'll find taxis and motorized *tuk-tuks* (the noisy 3-wheeled vehicles locally known as *samlors*) in Bangkok and several regional centres. Both forms of transport have meters, and neither use them. They have a 'local' and a 'tourist' price. If a local TAT tourist office tells you that the in-town *tuk-tuk* fare is 5B, that will be the local price. As a tourist, you'll probably be charged 20B. If you bargain hard—and this is essential—you should arrive at a mutually satisfactory fare of POB. Fares differ from town to town, but since taxis are air-conditioned, they charge 5–10B more than *tuk-tuks*. If you're not sure what the fare should be, ask a local person. *Never* set off in a taxi or a *tuk-tuk* without agreeing the cost of your journey in advance. And *always* insist that they take you to the hotel or guest house of your choice—not to one of their own 'recommendations'. Outside of Bangkok, you'll often come across bicycle *samlors*—similar to the 3-wheeled cycle rickshaws found elsewhere in Asia—which are a slow but relaxing way of getting around town. You should hardly ever have to pay more than 5B on one of these.

Songthaews

These small pickup trucks have two rows (*songthaews*) of seats, and pursue a more or less fixed route round Chiang Mai and other regional centres. They are sometimes known as *bemos* (in the Indonesian fashion) and have established themselves as the main form of local transport on islands like Phuket and Koh Samui. You flag them down as you would a taxi, and pay 5B or less to go anywhere on their route. If you don't like their route, you can hire out the whole vehicle. Late at night, when all other forms of transport may be off the road, this can be a very good idea. And in a group, quite cheap.

Cars & Motorbikes

Self-driving a **car** in Bangkok's mad traffic is strictly for the brave. I would only advise it to people who've had a full, rich life and don't mind leaving it behind. Cars can be rented from agencies like Hertz (Bangkok, tel 2524918; Chiang Mai, tel 235925) or Avis (Bangkok, tel 2330397; Chiang Mai, tel 222013). Many top hotels at major centres can also arrange car rentals.

Motorbikes are very popular as a means of touring Chiang Mai and island resorts like Phuket and Koh Samui. In general, you're much safer on a solid road-bike (150–250B a day) than on a rickety moped (80–100B a day). When hiring, don't be fooled by bike-shop signs like: 'Please give us serve you! With responsibility prices and free for helmet!' None of them will insure against breakdown or accidents, so you should check your machine very carefully before signing any hirer's agreement. In many cases, if the bike packs up, you may be liable for full repair costs. Many people prefer to hire **bicycles**, which are available at several tourist centres. The average daily hire rate is 20B.

You're supposed to have an international drivers' licence to use cars, motorbikes and jeeps in Thailand. Personally, I've never been asked to produce one. But I have heard of unlicensed travellers being stopped by the police and charged exorbitant fees for so-called 'temporary' licences!

Where to Stay

There's a wide range of accommodation in Thailand, from opulent super-luxury hotels to simple beach bungalows on remote islands. Places to stay are most abundant in Bangkok, Chiang Mai, Pattaya and Phuket, where the tourist boom has produced an excess of hotels offering attractive discounts in low season. **Luxury hotels** cost around 1000B for a single room, 1200B for a double. They are air-conditioned, they have swimming pools, bars, restaurants, coffee shops and various recreations. Some offer sporting facilities, entertainments (e.g. a Thai dinner-dance show) and a night-club/disco. Service is generally excellent, and the 10% service charge (and 11% government tax) which is politely added to your bill is usually worth it. Luxury hotels, like the Manohra in Bangkok, will often give 20% discounts between May and September. Sometimes, if you book through a hotel's travel agency, you get *another* 20% off your bill! **Mid-range hotels** have single rooms about 400–500B, doubles around 500–600B, and are generally very good value. You get the same deal as at a luxury hotel, though there will be far fewer facilities. Several middle-bracket hotels offer 50% discounts in the low season. From November to February (high season), it's wise to book in advance at both luxury and mid-range hotels—they're often full up at this time of year.

Cheaper **Thai-style hotels** generally offer a choice between air-conditioned (around 300B) and fan-cooled (around 150B) rooms. Because of the humidity, many travellers pay the extra for air-con comfort. There's often a party going on next door to cheap 'fan' rooms, and they sometimes have a few resident cockroaches. Rooms without a bathroom (and no roaches) cost in the region of 100B. Cheap budget accommodation is found mainly in **guest houses** (some with meals and laundry services), which charge between 40B and 80B per person. Rooms are fairly basic, but have a fan, a shower and a toilet and are perfectly adequate. There are also a few **Youth Hostels**—at Bangkok, Chiang Mai, Kanchanaburi, Lopburi, Nakhon Pathom and Phitsanoluke. On the beach, you normally have a choice between cheap bamboo huts (50–80B per person) and swanky bungalows with modern comforts (300–500B).

If travelling alone, it's a good idea to make a friend with whom you can share accommodation costs. This is because most places to stay cater primarily for couples—and charge more or less the same for one as for two people. Single rooms often have two beds! In cheaper hotels or guest houses, you should check a) toilets and waste bins for cockroaches; b) bed-linen for cleanliness; c) under mattresses for bedbugs; d) mosquito-netting on windows for holes; e) door-locks for security; f) fans and air-conditioning units for controllability—some have only one speed, very fast or very cold! Finally, you need offer tips only to staff of major hotels—5 or 10B should cover most individual services, including porterage.

Eating Out

Food

There's a standing joke about the Thais, that they only have one meal a day—it starts at 8 am and it finishes at 8 pm! This may be an exaggeration, but Thai people certainly love their food. And they do prefer to pick at things (a bowl of this, a bag of that) all day long, rather than sitting down to a 'proper' meal in the Western sense. No foreign visitor need every worry about going short on food here—it's on offer practically round the clock! As a friend of mine, a Dutch restauranteur in Bangkok, said:

> Finding places to eat is never a problem, because half of Thailand is constantly cooking for the other half! If you're hungry, you can close your eyes, wander a minute or so in any direction, and be pretty sure of walking into some good, hot food. I've friends here in Bangkok who go out every night, and who—in two or three years— have never yet dined at the same place twice. That's quite something, isn't it? And the quality of food in Thailand is just superb. Every street vendor throughout the country is sold out of what he has cooked every day. Again, quite amazing.

Thai cuisine—a cross between Indian and Chinese food, with a dash of inspiration from Portugal, Indonesia and France—is hot and spicy (yet delicate) encompassing a whole spectrum of flavours. A typical Thai meal uses fresh coriander (the soul of Thai cookery), garlic and chilli as springboards for a carnival of tastes. Other characteristic flavourings are tamarind juice, ginger, coconut milk and lemon grass called *makroot*. The hottest, most lethal ingredient is *phrik kii noo*, a small green chilli pepper which has foreigners diving for water and beer when they should be reaching for a far better antidote—rice! If you don't want fiery food, then ask for something *mae pet* (not hot) or stick to readily available Chinese food, which is often less spicy. Traditionally, the Thai dinner comprises five dishes—including curries, soups, salads and vegetables—serve around a central bowl of rice. It is accompanied by a hot, pungent sauce known as *nam prik*, and by a fish sauce called *nam plaa*, made from anchovies or shrimp paste, which is used in the place of salt. The meal is washed down with whisky or brandy (by the men) or with fruit juice or iced jasmine tea (by the women). Thai food is for most *farangs* (foreigners) an acquired taste. An easier introduction is in the north, where the cuisine is fairly mild, or in the south, which is famous for its tasty seafood and its Muslim-style sweet and mild curries. It's hardest to acquire in the northeast, notorious for its incandescent 'specialities' and salads.

Local fare ('street food') can be sampled at the numerous noodle shops, night markets, and pavement food-stalls found in most tourist centres. Most dishes are around 10B, and include *tom yum* (a spicy soup flavoured with lemon grass, lime juice, shrimp, chicken or pork), *tom yam kung* (the standard Thai soup, with shrimp, lemon grass and mushrooms), *pat thai* (fried noodles with onions, peanuts, vegetables and egg), *mee krob* (fried noodles plus anything the cook has on hand), *hor mok* (fish in chilli, onion, and garlic sauce), *kai yang* (spicy barbecued chicken), *kang kiew wan kai/nua* (chicken/beef curry), *kao pat* (fried rice with onions, vegetables, sometimes an egg), and *kao pat kai/mu/gung* (chicken/pork/shrimp fried rice). If you want something else, look to see what the locals are eating and—if it looks edible—point to it. Street food is safe enough, just so long as you can see it's been freshly cooked. Things like stir-fried vegetables, seafood omelettes, and anything that comes out of a sizzling wok, you just can't go wrong with!

When eating out in restaurants, it's best to go in a group and to order as a 'family' rather than as individuals—the Thais are used to communal eating. A good restaurant meal can be had for around 100B a head, including a drink. Normally, each Thai restaurant has its own specialities, and it's a good idea to ask the waiter 'what's special?' (*Mee arai phe set?*). Outside of Bangkok, you may have no other option, since fewer restaurants will have English menus. Mind you, the tourist boom has produced some marvellous attempts to make Thai dishes intelligible to the *farang* diner. While you're waiting for your meal (it won't be long), puzzle over items like 'Pog Leg in gravy sauce, with Bread as side order', or 'Bean curd with Hom's Bowel Soup', or 'Pig Legs in Hot and Sour soup'. The beach restaurants of Koh Samui proudly advertise 'Barbecued Crap', while the floating restaurants of Kanchanaburi tempt travellers with 'Yum Bean', 'Pork Stomach with Salted Butter soup', and 'Bucket of Ice'. Pee Pee islands have their 'Two choices of fried egg—one sunny side up, two over easy', and Pattaya offers something very special—'Horse Balls'! Thais are also fond of skinned frogs, crunchy insects, serpent's heads and (a Chinese delicacy) birds' nests. Don't be alarmed—there's some really good stuff in there, if you're prepared to experiment! If you want to play safe, stick to Thai favourite dishes like *Kai ho bai toei* (seasoned fried chicken in leaf wrappers), *Pla Brio Wan* (snapper fish, with ginger and garlic sauce), *Thotman plak-rai/kung* (Thai-style fish/shrimp balls), *Gaeng Mussaman* (Thai Muslim curry), various kinds of *Yam* (Thai salad); curry and *Nam Prik* dipping sauce, with fresh vegetables. Delicious sticks of satay and fat omelettes stuffed with pork and stir-fried vegetables also appeal to the Western palate.

Thai restaurants don't do much in the way of desserts—unless you like sweet, sticky coconut items—but there's a vast choice of fruits. For your fruit salad, there's mangoes, pineapples, watermelons, papayas (great for stomach upsets), pomegranates, oranges, jackfruits, durians (okay, if you can bear the smell!), lychee-like rambutan (jokingly referred to by Thais as 'white man's balls'), longans (similar to lychee, but without a prickly skin), strawberries and over 20 varieties of banana. If you're into ice-cream, look out for the famous Foremost ice-cream parlours, in Bangkok and some provincial towns.

To get service in a Thai restaurant, beckon waiters with a wave of the hand (preferably as the locals do, with fingers waving downwards, in towards the palm). Clapping, hissing, and snapping fingers is bad manners—and a sure way of being left to starve! Only waiters in middle to high-class restaurants expect a tip, which should be around 10B or 10% of the bill. If you want a change from Thai/Chinese food, larger hotels and coffeeshops serve an approximation of European food. And all the major beach resorts and tourist centres are now gearing themselves to Western gourmets. In Bangkok and Chiang Mai, you can now choose from around a dozen international cuisines!

Drinks

Thai-style coffee is unpalatably sweet to most Westerners. It's heavily laced with sticky condensed milk, which lurks like treacle at the bottom of the glass, and is best left there. If you don't want milk/sugar, ask for your coffee *mai sai nom* or *mai sai naam taan*. Alternatively, ask for *Nescafe*, which comes with little packets of Coffeemate—very civilized. But there's just no pleasing some people. One coffee connoisseur travelled the length and breadth of the country, before discovering that 'Thai Airways do just about the only drinkable cup of black coffee in Thailand'. This unique brew came to his attention while he was flying 3000 feet above Chiang Mai province. Thai coffee, whether good, bad or indifferent, is often accompanied with a weak, but refreshing, glass of free

Chinese tea. Coffee shops are very popular in Thailand—especially among young 'groovy' Thais, who hang around them much in the same way that pre-Beatles teenagers in the West used to patronize 'milk bars'. Several coffee shops style themselves 'disco cafes', and have entertainments ranging from live music and talent shows, to transvestite cabarets (in Trat) and can-can dancers (in Krabi). They constitute a whole new sub-culture in Thai society, and deserve a book all to themselves.

The brand of whisky favoured by most Thais is *Mekong*. This local firewater is very cheap (110B a bottle) and very strong. Taken with Coke, it tastes pleasantly like Bacardi rum. Taken in excess, it predicts a violent hangover. It's worth paying a little extra (140B a bottle) for *Sangsom* whisky, which is far smoother. Thai beer is strong, but pleasant. It reminds many Westerners of high-quality German lager. The two main brands are *Singha* ('Happiness you can drink') and *Kloster*, and the cost of a bottle is around 45B in a restaurant, 36B in a Bangkok supermarket.

Bottled drinks are even sweeter than coffee. Personally, I always drink Thai lemonade or Coke with a glass of ice—far more thirst-quenching, and you get two drinks for the price of one (provided, of course, you can wait for the ice to melt!). The Thais are especially fond of 'fortified' drinks with health-inspiring names like 'Lipo-Vitan E' and 'Electrolyte Beverage'. These drinks abound in northern trekking areas, where people often need all the fortification they can get! Sample delicious milkshakes, *lassis* and fruit juices at ice-cream parlours or cheap guest-house restaurants in Bangkok or Chiang Mai. But don't drink local tap water, unless boiled. Bottled mineral water—usually *Polaris* ('ozonated artesian well-water')—is cheap and widely available.

Health

People can get sick in Thailand although it's a very clean country, and food is generally freshly cooked on the spot. The sudden change in diet can sometimes cause tummy problems ('Bangkok Boogie') and it's wise to avoid spicy food, raw vegetables and ice for the first few days of your stay. Thereafter you can avoid sickness by drinking only boiled or bottled water, and by eating only peeled fruit. If you do get a stomach upset, the best cure is bland food (boiled rice, bananas etc) and warm tea. To prevent dehydration and dizziness, drink plenty of fluids and take extra salt with food. Also, ease slowly into the heat—the most common affliction amongst European visitors to Thailand is sunburn! Use sun-cream for protection, and don't doze off at the swimming pool!

There are so many stray dogs in the country, especially round temples, that rabies is a risk. In certain areas (e.g. Pai, Mae Sariang) it's highly inadvisable to go strolling around at night on your own. When Siamese dogs take it into their heads to attack, they really mean business! If bitten (by dogs or rats), wash the wound immediately—with clean water or alcohol, soap or detergent—and go immediately to the nearest doctor or hospital (your hotel will always be able to recommend one). You may need a rabies vaccination.

Malarial mosquitoes inhabit beach resorts like Koh Samet and the hilly, forested areas of northern Thailand. If following visits to these regions you develop a fever, get an immediate blood check for malaria. If there isn't a local malaria centre or a provincial hospital nearby, head straight for the Hospital of Tropical Medicine in Bangkok (tel

2460056–8, ext OPD, 24-hour service) or ring Bangkok's Malaria Division (tel 2816650) for advice.

While it's worth visiting your dentist and optician for a check-up before coming to Thailand, you can get excellent (often cheaper) dental/optical services in Bangkok and Chiang Mai. The cost of a pair of smart, fashion spectacles—at a reliable optician like Universal Optical, 138 New Rd, Bangkok—is just £35, inclusive of lenses. And an hour of private dental work in Chiang Mai could cost you just 60B! People with contact lenses will be pleased to learn that Thailand's high humidity makes lens wear extremely comfortable.

Hospitals
In Bangkok: Ramathibodi Hospital, Rama IV Rd, (tel 2813566; 2811364, 2819110).
Bangkok Christian Hospital, 124 Silom Rd, (tel 2336981–9)
Sumitivej Hospital, Soi 49, Sukhumvit Rd.

In Chiang Mai: McCormick Hospital, Nawarat Rd.
Ariawongse Clinic, Changmoi Rd.
Chiang Mai Hospital, Suan Dawk Rd.

Security

Thailand is a relatively safe country—most of the population are good Buddhists, to whom the thought of theft or violence on foreign guests is alien. But some visitors do let their guard down—lulled into a false sense of security by Thai friendliness—and there are always a few horror stories going the rounds from travellers who've been ripped off, doped on buses, or stuck with huge bills in restaurants. Even a good barrel like Thailand has a few rotten apples! As anywhere, your best security is you yourself. Wandering around with an exposed money belt bulging with cash is like wearing a sign saying 'Please rob me!'. If you must wear a belt, keep it out of sight (under a shirt or skirt is best) and take note, many belts—especially on crowded Bangkok buses—have been slit by expert razor-thieves. Personally, I keep all money, travellers' cheques and air tickets in a cloth wallet, which straps comfortably inside the upper arm by means of an elasticated tubigrip. There's no way this can be infiltrated—especially when you sleep on it! On the streets, you should never carry more cash than you need for daily expenses. Surplus cash and all valuables should be stored in hotel safe deposits. But *never* leave your credit card in a hotel safe (cf. Chiang Mai, Trekking)—it may be copied during your absence. In transit (i.e. when travelling from town to town), *never* leave your bags unattended. And, as one experienced tour leader suggested. 'Always keep 1000B handy, to give someone if you do happen to be held up—they'll usually take it and run, without checking you for the rest.' Also, watch out for pickpockets and street touts, who often pose as friendly 'students'. These students say they want to practise English with you, and then invite you to an expensive restaurant, nightclub or 'government shop'. One couple accepted such an offer from a 'nice young man' outside the Grand Palace, Bangkok. They had to pay a horrendous 1400B lunch tab, after their host 'went to the toilet' and never came back. If dark streets, crowded markets and public buses are prime risk areas for theft, you can at least relax in your room. Apart from beach bungalows, practically every place I've stayed at in Thailand (even the cheapest guest houses) have their rooms secured by the same reliable push-button door lock, which locks from the inside. But bring a combination lock anyway—for your bags, and for often insecure beach huts. And though rooms are generally safe, don't leave cash or valuables in them.

If travelling on your own, take extra care. Especially when—and this is common—you find yourself booked into a seat right at the back of a night bus. In the course of the long, long journey, you may well be offered food, drinks or sweets by 'kindly' strangers. Don't accept them—you may be drugged. One guy spent hours of friendly travel with a charming old man (who appeared totally incapable of deceit) before accepting a cigarette. He woke up on the boat pier at Surat Thani with the rest of the cigarette pack, and nothing else.

In the case of theft or loss, you can report to the **Tourist Police** (phone numbers are posted at all hotels, and at the airport) or dial 195 for TAT's English-speaking assistance service. Don't expect too much sympathy. This is, remember, a Buddhist country—your safety and security are considered to be your own individual responsibility. So, if you have your own ways of protecting your interests, stick to them. Don't, as one poor traveller did, break the habits of a lifetime and stick all your money under your pillow at night. He was halfway to a different city before he remembered about it!

Communications

Postal Services
Postal Services in Thailand are excellent. Bangkok's **Central GPO** in New Road, Silom, is open from 8 am to 8 pm Mondays to Fridays, from 9 am to 1 pm at weekends. It has a **24-hour telegram service** and a **parcel-packaging** counter. Outside Bangkok, most post offices are closed at weekends, and are open only till 4.30 pm during the week. The **Poste Restante** service is generally very reliable—though you'll need to insist that friends and family writing to you print your surname in block capitals, and underline it. This ensures that a letter addressed to say, Joe E. *Bloggs* is correctly filed under 'B'. Anything carelessly addressed to Joe E Bloggs, on the other hand, could well be filed under 'J' or even under 'E'. You'll generally be charged 1B for every letter or postcard you collect.

Phone Services
Phone Services, in the cities at least, can be amazingly efficient. In general, it's best to make international phone calls from large hotels—it costs more (about 80B per minute, to anywhere in the world) but is really worth it. One traveller, used to the vagaries of Asian phones, requested an overseas call at the Oberoi Hotel, Bangkok, and then sat down to plough through *Gone with the Wind*. To her astonishment, she was connected in two minutes flat! Bangkok and Chiang Mai post offices have international call facilities too, and you can either direct-dial or get an operator to dial for you. If phoning overseas yourself, just pick up the receiver, ask the operator for your number, put down the phone, and wait a few minutes for it to ring. This means you've been connected. Local (in town) calls cost 4B for an unlimited amount of time, and you can phone from most hotels and

23

many guest houses. Using the domestic phone service to call from town-to-town (i.e. from Bangkok to Chiang Mai), you'll often get better results by asking hotel operators to dial for you. Most provincial towns have local telephone exchanges, but their service isn't all that good.

Electricity
Electricity is 50 cycle, 220 volt AC, in Bangkok and most of Thailand. The better hotels supply their guests with adaptors for electrical appliances.

Time
Time in Thailand is 7 hours ahead of London GMT. Therefore, when it's 12 noon in Bangkok, it'll be 5 am in London, 1 am in New York and 3 pm in Sydney. Bear this in mind when making long-distance telephone calls!

Changing Money

The Thai Baht (B) divides into 100 Satang. Notes are 10B (brown), 20B (green), 50B (blue), 100B (red) and 500B (purple). Coins are 5B, 2B and 1B (silver); 50 Satang and 25 Satang (copper). The new 5B coins, worth noting, have a copper edge—this is the only real way of telling them apart from the near-identical 1B coin! The approximate exchange rates at the time of writing are:

£1 = 45B
US$ = 25B
AUS$ = 18B

It's not necessary to change any foreign currency prior to arrival. Exchange facilities are readily available on a 24-hour basis at Bangkok airport—rates here are often better than those quoted abroad. In Thailand, you can exchange foreign currencies at banks (open 8.30 am to 3.30 pm, Monday to Friday), currency-exchange counters at main banks (open 8.30 am to 10 pm daily) and authorized money-changers (24-hour service, daily). Use hotels to change money only in emergencies—their rates are usually poor.

Embassies

See page 80.

Shopping

Thailand is a shopper's paradise, full of temptingly cheap bargains. There's quality silk, jewellery, antiques, bronzeware, nielloware (silver inlaid with black alloy), copy designer goods and modern fashion clothes in Bangkok. There are ethnic hill-tribe crafts and silver in Chiang Mai. There's *mudmee* tie-and-dye silk at Pakchongchai; precious gems at Chanthaburi and Kanchanaburi; cultured pearls at Phuket; beautiful cotton fabrics at Hua Hin, Songkhla and Nong Khai; and even cheap hi-fi equipment (mostly smuggled in from Singapore) at Hat Yai. The list of attractions is endless—nearly every Thai centre has some 'local' speciality worth buying! And throughout the country, shopping is so very convenient. If there's one shop selling leather boots, there'll be a whole cluster of shops selling boots all around it. So, not only can you do all your shopping in one place, but you can wander easily from one shop to another, comparing prices and quality. If a shop hasn't got just what you want in stock, it can generally produce it for you overnight. The same goes for tailors, who can run up any garment to your precise specifications within 24 hours. Bulky purchases, such as teakwood furniture or heavy antiques, can be shipped home for you. Expensive jewellery can be verified at Bangkok's reliable gem-testing laboratory. Large hotels have their shopping emporia, and Bangkok department stores have their fashion boutiques. These are the places to shop in air-conditioned comfort. Outside, on the streets, there's invariably a market in full swing—offering a wide variety of fabulous goods at knock-down prices. The markets, and various smaller shops, often stay open till late evening (including weekends). Most tourist shops however, are open Monday to Friday only, from 8 am to 9 pm (and department stores, from 10 am to 7 pm). For an idea of what's available, and how much it should cost, pick up the TAT's *Official Shopping Guide* from their airport desk, on arrival. This handy publication lists some 200 shops in Bangkok, Phuket, Chiang Mai and Pattaya where the quality of goods (mainly silk, leather, jewellery and handicrafts) is guaranteed. These shops display the TAT-approved sticker—the logo is a woman hawker with carrier baskets.

All prices quoted throughout this guide are the result of hard bargaining—an integral part of shopping in Thailand! The Thais love bargaining, especially if you show you're enjoying it too. Smile a lot while haggling, and never lose your cool. If the first price asked is too high (it nearly always is), use some local lingo to bring it down. Say *Mai! Ma dai!*' (No! Too much!) and make some absurdly low counter-offer. Now it's their turn to cry *Ma dai! Ma dai*! (No way, José!). Let them calm down, and then offer 30% to 50% of the first asking price—they'll generally accept it. As a rule, the longer you bargain for something, the cheaper it gets. I once met a girl in Chiang Mai who'd spent *six days* negotiating over a beautiful hill-tribe coat—she got the price down from 2000B to 850B. But the good old 'walkaway' technique only works if you've lots of time to spare, and don't mind if the article is sold in the meantime to someone else. Besides which, the Thais have got wise to tourists—they just know if you really want something. You can walk away as far as you like, and it won't bother them. They just know you're going to be back soon! On the other hand, they're not unreasonable. Just as soon as you've given them a good battle, they'll give you a decent price! Finally, I wouldn't suggest doing all your shopping in one or two cities. Shop around, and try to buy at source. Looking for, say, northeastern silk (the best in Thailand) at Khorat, or blue sapphires (from the local mines) at Kanchanaburi, you'll not only get a better choice of produce, but often better prices too!

Festivals

Thai festivals are a combination of joyful, colourful merriment and solemn religious ritual. The temples are the focal points of all local celebrations, which are connected either with Buddhism, animals, the crops or honouring past kings. Many events feature

Flower Festival Float

folk/classical dancing, percussion music, competitions, beauty contests, fireworks and Thai boxing. There are festivals throughout the year, primarily in the early summer (before it gets too hot to celebrate anything), in the early autumn (just after the rains), and at year-end. There are no fixed dates for many festivals (the timing of which varies from year to year, in accordance with the lunar calendar) though by October, TAT has usually published its annual listing of events for the forthcoming year (with dates), and you can pick this up from your nearest tourist office. Major festivals include:

January
New Year's Day (January 1st)—Public holiday.
Winter Fair (one week)—Chiang Mai.

February
Magha Puja (Full Moon day)—Nationwide. Commemorates the 'spontaneous' gathering of 1250 of Buddha's disciples.
Flower Festival (three days)—Chiang Mai.

March
Seafood Festival (two weeks)—Phuket.

April
Chakri Day (April 6th)—Public Holiday. Commemorates Rama I, founder of the Chakri dynasty.
Songran Festival (April 12th–15th)—Nationwide. Celebrates the lunar New Year. Much liberation of birds and fish, lots of water-throwing. Everybody gets very wet. Great fun.
Pattaya Festival (10 days)—Pattaya
Glory of Ayutthaya (10 days)—Ayutthaya. Spectacular sound-and-light show.

May
Coronation Day (May 5th)—Nationwide. Best in Bangkok, where the King and Queen commemmorate their 1946 coronation at Wat Phra Keo.
Visakha Puja (Full Moon)—Nationwide. Wat-based celebrations, commemorating the date of Buddha's birth, death and enlightenment.

July
Asalha Puja (Full Moon)—Nationwide. Held in remembrance of Buddha's first sermon.

August
Queen's Birthday (August 12th)—Public holiday for Queen Sikrit's birthday.

October
Vegetarian Festival (nine days)—Phuket.
Chulalongkorn Day (October 23rd)—Public holiday in honour of King Chulalongkorn (Rama V).

October/November
Tod Kathin (one month)—Marks the 'official' end of the rainy season. King presents robes to the monks of the Temple of the Dawn, Bangkok. Monks nationwide receive new robes. Spectacular royal barge procession (Bangkok).

November
Loi Krathong (Full Moon)—Nationwide, but best in Sukhothai and Chiang Mai. Myriad banana-leaf boats, prettily illuminated by candles, are floated on rivers, lakes and canals. Perhaps the most 'typically Thai' festival—masses of happy-happy people, lots of spectacle and atmosphere.
Elephant Round-up (two days)—Surin. Up to 200 elephants playing soccer and tug o' war, 'walking over men in the ground', and parading in 'full battle dress'. Touristy, but photogenic.

November/December
River Kwai Bridge Week (November 28th–December 5th)—Kanchanaburi. Historical exhibitions, folk performances and amazing sound-and-light show nightly.

December
King's Birthday (December 5th)—Nationwide, but best in Bangkok. Boat races, illuminations, and royal troops parade.

Creepies & Crawlies

As a hot, humid country, Thailand has its fair share of insects, reptiles and rodents. It also has some pretty weird animals, including the pink dogs of Ayutthaya—painted with red antiseptic—and the pink (albino) water-buffaloes of Koh Samui, which are nicknamed *farangs* by the islanders because they look so strange and anaemic!

27

Open-billed Storks

Cockroaches hang out in bathrooms mainly, and are found in all but the best hotels. They're a smaller variety then say, India's, but they get everywhere! If you're having a shower, they'll pop out of sinks and toilets to join you. If you're lying on your bed feeling lonely, they'll pop up on your shoulder to keep you company. If you really can't stand them, get a room *without* an attached bathroom, or splash out on a decent hotel. Many travellers keep their light on overnight to deflect roaches, but the surest guarantee of an uninterrupted night's sleep is still a mosquito net. This keeps *all* crawlies at bay!

Mosquitoes come out mainly after dark, and seem to dine exclusively on foreigners. The best preventive is a generous application of *Skeetolene* (the local Thai repellent) to arms, ankles and face when going out in the evening. Mozzies are worst during the damp months of June to November. The malarial variety are restricted to certain areas like Koh Samet, Kanchanaburi and Mae Hong Son province. In these places, you'll need to take extra precautions—including sleeping under a mosquito net. Throughout the country, you'll find hotels and guest houses that are prepared to spray your room against mosquitoes while you're out sightseeing. On your return, keep all doors and windows closed until the morning!

Lizards come in three main varieties—the small chin-chuck (don't toss these out— they eat mosquitoes) to the medium-size gecko and the large talkay. On Koh Samet, I found a talkay squatting on my bungalow toilet (yes, it was that big!). Later, it took up residence in the roof, stomping over the ceiling and clucking to itself all night. Lizards are a chatty lot, and do nobody any harm.

The same can't always be said for **spiders**, especially the huge fanged variety found up in the north. Koh Samui has some whoppers too—one traveller discovered a spider the size of a dinner-plate on his bungalow bed. Mind you, Koh Samui is famous for its 'wildlife' in general—during my stay, I received visitations from ants, lizards, baby scorpions, spiders and snakes. I was apparently 'lucky'. A friend of mine had her underwear taken away and eaten by rats! Another had her toothpaste devoured by a tribe of cockroaches! A couple I came across on Koh Phangan had left a bunch of bananas out at night—very unwise. Their bungalow was invaded at night by a flock of giant bats!

Snakes in Thailand get a really bad press—well, 90% of them are supposed to be poisonous. Travellers rarely encounter them, except when trekking in the northern hills. Even then, local guides walk on ahead and root them out. Poisonous snakes are usually small and green—the smaller they are, and the less they move, the more lethal they're supposed to be. Most snakes in this country end up as handbags or cowboy boots.

Drugs

Up until quite recently, Thailand was a major narcotics centre and a favourite 'hippy hangout'. But them came international pressure against heroin production, large-scale package tourism, and the 1987 Visit Thailand Year—all of which convinced the Thai government that it was time for a big clean-up. By the end of 1987, over 70 kgs of narcotic drugs—mostly marijuana—had been incinerated in public bonfires in and around Bangkok. And stiff new drug laws were introduced, making possession and sale of narcotics punishable by hefty fines and severe prison terms.

At the time of writing, there are some 700 *farangs* languishing in Thai jails on drugs-related charges. Many of them are there on the evidence of local street-dealers who turned out to be police-informers. Few of them receive any other visitors except the few sympathetic backpackers who respond to guest-house notices in Bangkok's Banglampoo district. None of them have been able to afford to 'buy' themselves out of trouble. Fines are so high that one guy, caught with just three sticks of dope, had to fork out 22,000B (£500) to escape a minor possession charge which could have imprisoned him for *five years*!

The simple message with drugs is—*don't*! Be especially careful with 'fun drugs' on Koh Samui—there are no measurements involved, you don't know how much you're taking, and what you expect to be an hour or two of harmless fun can well turn out to be 12 hours of unmitigated hell which you'll just have to sit out patiently. Anyone crossing the border from Thailand to Malaysia should watch their bags—in case 'extra luggage' is smuggled into them by drug-dealers looking for innocent tourists to take on their risk. Importation of drugs into Malaysia carries the death penalty. Finally, even if you're sensible about drugs, never travel with someone who isn't. Be warned—you only have to *accompany* someone possessing narcotics to be implicated yourself!

Part II
BACKGROUND INFORMATION

Dancer

People & Society

Thailand is a synthesis of numerous different racial and ethnic groups—mainly Thai, Chinese, Mon, Khmer, Lao, Malay, Indian and Persian—who have either been assimilated by right of conquest, or who have arrived as migrants. If Thailand has an indigenous people at all, it's probably the old Mon-Khmer stock who inhabited the country before the Thais arrived, though even before them there was an aboriginal negroid population, all traces of which have now disappeared.

While there is no 'typical' Thai physiognomy or physique, the Thai people—especially the women—are generally considered the most attractive in Southeast Asia. This probably has less to do with their physical attributes than with their disarmingly charming national temperament. Thai society places great value on polite speech and polite smiles. The Thais have got smiling down to a fine art; it has been said that they have a smile for every emotion. They are also masters of relaxation, with a national motto of *mai pen rai* which loosely translates as 'no hurry, no worry'. On the surface, they appear a happy, optimistic people who—having maintained their independence and freedom through several centuries—exude a self-confidence and a deep trust in their own ways which enables them to tolerate other people, and to get along with each other with the minimum of overt conflict. All of which makes Thailand one of the easiest, most pleasant countries in the world to travel around.

The 'land of smiles' is, on the whole, a land of genuine smiles—smiling makes everyone feel comfortable, secure and welcome. Behind the smiles however, Thailand has one of the highest murder rates of any country, as well as escalating drug addiction and some one million prostitutes. The Thai character is enigmatic, and highly unpredictable: because there is no allowance for criticism or for resolution of negative feelings through discussion, when anger comes to the fore, it often does so very suddenly and often very violently.

Such violence, in a general sense, lies at the heart of current social problems in the country, and it derives much from the impact of modernity. The Thais are fundamentally a conservative people who have raced into the modern age at breakneck speed. During the 1932 revolution, the power of the nobility transferred overnight to a new class of educated commoners. Suddenly, money and power—two things that the Thais greatly respect—came within the reach of the general population. A mass migration began to provincial centres like Bangkok and Chiang Mai, swelling these capitals with a multitude of peasants looking for money and work. Few of them found what they came for. But even fewer return to certain poverty in the fields.

Today, while roughly half of Thailand's population—mainly the new class of provincial capitalists and those living off tourism—can now make ends meet, the remainder still live a hand-to-mouth existence. A consequence of this has been the alarming growth of prostitution amongst girls from the poorer rural areas. They migrate to the cities and to the tourist beaches in search of work. The minimum monthly wage for any job stipulated by the government is 2200B a month, but jobs are so scarce they will accept wages of 600B a month or even less. Many of them start out as waitresses, and then, when they see their friends report getting a month's pay in a day from 'entertaining' rich foreigners, they turn to prostitution themselves. There is no moral stigma attached to this profession. Money is so highly respected that, as long as a prostitute cares for her parents she can still present herself as a 'good' person and may—after enough cash has been stashed—return home and be accepted as a good marriage bet.

Almost too late, Thailand is waking up to the sobering reality that tourism and 'progress' have their price—time-honoured customs, traditions, folklore, even national identity, are being eroded and undermined. The current trend in Thai society—popularly described as 'modernization without development'—indicates that the brakes have already been applied. But have they been applied too late?

History

Origins

For a number of reasons, early Thai history is very obscure. Firstly, the Thais—or Siamese—had no written language until the 13th century, and the little we know of them prior to this time has been gleaned from the journals of various Chinese travellers. Secondly, the high humidity of Thailand's climate has destroyed most of its art treasures and deserted cities, leaving few clues as to the glories of past civilizations. Thirdly, and most disastrously, the powerful Thai capital of Ayutthaya was completely sacked by the Burmese in 1767, and a vast treasurehouse of precious records and archives literally went up in smoke. Painstaking efforts to reassemble pre-Ayutthayan history have only been partially successful. The yawning gaps that remain may never be filled by anything but myth and legend.

Until quite recently, it was believed that the Thai people originated in southern China, Burma and Mongolia, and that they were forced down into present-day northern Thailand following Kublai Khan's capture of Nanchao (their capital in south-central China) in 1253. Recent archaeological discoveries, however, have completely upturned this theory. During the 1960s a series of prehistoric sites was located—at Kanchanaburi, at Mae Hong Son, and finally at Ban Chiang—which suggest that Thailand was probably the home of the world's oldest Bronze Age civilization, dating back some 5000 years. The Thais are very keen to substantiate this—it would mean that their civilization predates that of China, whose own Bronze Age began around 2000BC. It would also suggest that the original Thais migrated *to* China, rather than—as popularly supposed—the reverse.

Sukhothai – Ayutthaya

Whatever, the early 13th century witnessed a large-scale migration of Sino-Thai peoples southward from China, and down into the hill country of present-day northern Burma, Thailand and Laos. In 1238 Thai armies captured the Khmer garrison-town of Sukhothai in north-central Thailand, and the various Thai tribes came together to form their first major kingdom. From this capital, they expanded rapidly outwards to displace the Mons (who'd entered central Thailand from southern Burma, and founded a major empire from the 6th to the 11th centuries) and the Khmers (who'd driven westward into Thailand from present-day Kampuchea). The previous name of Sukhothai ('happy Thai') was Sayam, and it was during this period that Siam became a nation with a culture and character all of its own. Well, not *quite* all its own—selective borrowing did take place. For instance, the Sukhothai Thais soon came into contact with the already ancient civilization of India, with enduring effect on their cuisine, calligraphy and complexions.

In 1275 King Ramkhamhaeng, Sukhothai's most notable ruler, began his 40-year reign. The cultural and military *paterfamilias* of the country, he gave the Thais—already united in speech and in customs—their first written language. He borrowed from the Cambodian Khmers to establish the first Thai alphabet. A wise and enlightened ruler, he also abolished slavery, codified the law, and established Buddhism as the national religion. Sukhothai had three more kings after Ramkhamhaeng, but none equalled his talents. The capital was intermittently attacked by the Burmese and was finally abandoned when Ramatibodi, Prince of Utong, captured the Khmer strongholds of Chanthaburi and Lopburi—establishing in 1350 a far safer and more central government at Ayutthaya, 40 miles up the Chao Phya River from modern Bangkok.

Ayutthaya was capital of Siam for more than four centuries. Its power stretched from Luang Prabang in the north all the way to Johore and Singapore, even including (under King Naresuan) the Shan states and Kampuchea. Ramatibodi, considered the first Thai king, was a progressive ruler who devised a new code of laws and received the emissary (Portuguese) from the West in the early 16th century. Soon the city was receiving regular visitors (mainly traders) from Japan, France, Holland, Spain and England. The word *farang*—a corruption of *feringhi*, used by Indian immigrants to denote the French—appeared around this time, and was used by Thais to describe white people in general.

By the end of the 17th century, Ayutthaya had clinched important trade deals with the Dutch and English, and was—at least as far as Europe was concerned—the most consequential capital in Southeast Asia. Then came the wooden horse that was to wreck its fortunes—an ambitious Greek adventurer named Constantine Phaulkon. King Narai first employed him as his interpreter with *farangs*, but it wasn't long before he became the king's Prime Minister. This appointment, and his clear French sympathies, aroused much envy amongst the Thai nobles. In 1688—following his conspiracy to replace Narai with a French-controlled puppet-king—the nobles were forced to unite in self-defence. The French garrison at Bangkok which Phaulkon had helped to establish, was ousted and he was arrested and publicly executed on July 5 1688. For the next 150 years, the Thais kept contact with the West to the barest minimum.

Much of Ayutthaya's history had been spent fighting the Khmers in the east and the Burmese in the west. Under King Narai's successors—a generally poor bunch—the capital became progressively weaker. Burma returned to the attack in 1758, commencing a 9-year siege which ended—in 1767—with the total destruction of Ayutthaya. Ironically, one of the few survivors (albeit brief) of the ensuing holocaust was the debauched King Ekatat—the last of Ayutthaya's rulers—who in true Nero fashion dallied with girls and executed a 'favourite' general while his capital went up in flames. So frustrated were the Burmese conquerors by the city's years of stubborn resistance that it slaughtered or sold into slavery all but 10,000 of its one million inhabitants. Palaces, buildings and even temples were left smoking ruins. The city's precious histories and records were destroyed, and all its treasures taken away as war booty. The effect on the Thai nation has been compared to that of a nuclear bomb.

Thonburi

If the Burmese thought Thai power crushed along with Ayutthaya, they were wrong. Shortly before the capital fell, a brilliant young general called Taksin fled southeast with a few hundred followers to the area of Rayong. Here he reorganized his forces, and returned to the fight. Within a few short months, he had rallied the Thai people, ousted the Burmese from the country, and re-established the Thai kingdom almost to the size it had been before Ayutthaya's capture—a remarkable accomplishment. Taksin proclaimed himself king, and established a new capital farther down the Chao Phya River at Thonburi. After seven years of rule, he decided to stay put in the capital and sent trusted generals out on campaign in his stead. The most notable of these, General Chao Phya Chakri, repelled the Burmese and subdued the Lao kingdoms of Vientiane, Luang Prabang and Chiang Mai. In 1778, Chakri found the legendary Emerald Buddha in Vientiane, and sent it back to Thonburi.

Near the end of his reign, King Taksin developed an anti-social form of megalomania. Convinced that he was a reincarnation of Buddha, he began flogging Buddhist monks, Christians, Chinese and anyone else who crossed him, and put some of his wives to death on trumped-up charges. A revolt broke out in Thonburi, and General Chakri hurried back to the capital to find himself declared the new king by the army and nobility in April 1782. There was some difficulty in knowing what to do with Taksin. In the end, recognizing his many achievements on behalf of the state, his ministers had him tied in a velvet bag and beaten to death with sandalwood clubs. This rather drastic rite—which we are told was 'painless'—had been instituted by King Trailok in 1450 for those of royal descent and avoided the shedding of royal blood. Taksin was the last—perhaps the only—reigning Thai monarch to die in this fashion.

Bangkok

General Chakri, now Rama I, moved his capital across the Chao Phya river from Thonburi to the village of Bangkok. He named the new city Krung Theb Ratanakosin, and supervised its construction with his Grand Palace at the centre. It was Rama I who founded the Chakri dynasty (of which King Bhumibol Aduldej is the ninth and present ruler) which was to transform and modernize the state, both by overhauling Thai forms of government and by borrowing from the West.

Rama I was a broadminded reformer who spent much of his long reign (1782–1809) in governmental consolidation and reconstruction. He devised a new code of law, tightened up the Buddhist priesthood, and did much to recover the religious and secular knowledge lost at Ayutthaya. He is also credited with writing at least part of the *Ramakien*— Thailand's definitive literary masterpiece—which is based on the Indian *Ramayana* epic. Under Rama I, the nation began at last to enter a period of peace and prosperity.

Rama II (1809–24) is chiefly remembered as a poet, but he also made a number of positive legal and administrative reforms. His major shortcoming was in not designating an heir. When he died suddenly, Prince Mongkut—his eldest son by the queen—had just entered the priesthood at the age of 20. The nobles were left with no option but to appoint Prince Chesda—the son of a consort—as Rama III (1824–1851). The new king was a devout Buddhist, who constructed some fine temples (including Wat Arun and additions to Wat Po), as well as supporting the work of Prince Mongkut, who had wisely elected to stay put in the Sangha (the monastic order) out of his brother's way. When Rama III died in 1851, having also failed to designate a successor, the nobles sought out Mongkut in his temple sanctuary and elected him Rama IV.

King Mongkut was a gifted, enlightened ruler who successfully ushered Thailand into the modern world. That he is chiefly remembered as the light-hearted libertine of the film *The King and I*—based on the fanciful recollections of Anna Leonowens, the English governess hired as tutor to his children—is indeed unfortunate. The sybaritic demagogue portrayed in the film bore little resemblance to the austere, venerated monarch who had spent 27 years in a Bangkok monastery. Significantly, the king's voluminous state papers contain just one brief reference to Anna—as an appendix to a shopping list!

Mongkut's domestic achievements were impressive—he restored the beautiful palace at Bang-Pa-In, he reformed the Buddhist priesthood (founding the new ascetic Thammayut sect), he introduced minted coins, and he began to reorganize his army along modern European lines. But it was as an international diplomat that he really excelled. As the other nations of Southeast Asia fell one by one under Western colonial control, losing their culture and traditions in the process, Mongkut took steps to avoid the same fate for Thailand. In 1864, he wrote to his ambassador in France of his dilemma:

Siam is being harassed by the French on one side, with the British colony on the other

34

. . . It is for us to decide what we are going to do; whether to swim up river to make friends with the crocodile or to swim out to sea and hang on to the whale.

In the event, by negotiating a series of clever trade treaties with Britain, France and the United States (he once even offered Abraham Lincoln some war-elephants to help him win the American Civil War!), Mongkut kept all these powers at bay and established the principle of Thailand as an independent buffer-state between all the colonial powers in Southeast Asia. A keen astronomer, in 1868 he calculated the time for a total eclipse of the sun, and moved his entire court (plus several Thai and foreign scientists) out to the best viewing point. The eclipse took place exactly as predicted, disproving ancient Thai myths about a giant obscuring the sun, and Mongkut returned home in triumph. Sadly, the spot he'd chosen for his camp contained fever, and he died shortly after of severe malaria.

His able son and successor, King Chulalongkorn (1868–1910) was appointed as Rama V. Despite an inauspicious start to his reign—his first queen fell from a royal barge and drowned—Chulalongkorn went on to become the only king of Thailand to earn the prefix 'the Great'. He finally abolished slavery as well as prostration by Thais before the monarch, he modernized the army and administration, he opened up the land with railways, and he was the first reigning Thai monarch to travel abroad. Above all, he was a great humanitarian and it was he who raised Thailand from a feudal to a modern 20th-century state.

Chulalongkorn's greatest achievement was to preserve Thailand's precarious independence as a 'buffer' betwen the British (India, Burma, Malaya) and French (Indo-China) colonial states. True, he was forced to make concessions—ceding his claim to Kampuchea and part of Laos to the French in 1904, and four minor Malay states to Britain in 1909—but he nonetheless kept his country free from colonial rule. A much-loved monarch, the date of his death (23rd October, 1910) is now a national holiday.

Chulalongkorn was succeeded by his son, King Vajiravudh (1910–25), who became Rama VI. He was a noteworthy poet, who patronized literature and the arts. He is also remembered for launching the Boy Scout movement, and for passing a law requiring all Thais to 'acquire' last names (before 1916, they all had just one name). But the most spectacular act of his reign was to enter World War I, dispatching a token force of Thai troops to support the Allies in France.

Next on the throne was King Prajadhipok, who as Rama VII (1925–32) was the last of Thailand's absolute monarchs. An amiable, cosmopolitan young man, Prajadhipok faced first the international financial depression of the 1920s—which forced him to make a series of unpopular governmental cutbacks—and then growing dissatisfaciton from the class of European-educated junior officials, who resented being passed over for senior appointments by 'old guard' princes. On 24th June 1932, a junta of 27 army officers styling themselves the Promoters seized the government in Bangkok in a bloodless 'revolution'. They sent the king an ultimatum demanding he accept constitutional status under their leadership. He agreed so promptly, that they sent a second letter apologizing for the rudeness of the first one!

Shortly after the Promoters (now the People's Party) launched their new constitution (December 10th 1932), King Prajadhipok decided to abdicate (1935) in favour of his ten-year-old nephew, Anan da Mahido, or Rama VIII, who could adapt better to the challenge of a constitutional monarchy. The 'cold *coup d'etat*' of 1932 set the scene for a long series of similarly bloodless coups and counter-coups, new constitutions, elections and unsuccessful attempts to overthrow the government by force. It soon became aparent that the Thais didn't care much who actually governed the country, just as long as the king was safe on the throne. The stability of the Crown as a counter-balance to the coup meant that nothing much really changed from one government to the next—especially since each new government since 1932 sought the king's approval. Further, until 1957 at least, those politicos who mounted the successive coups were mainly the same 'Promoters' who had led the first coup group. Bound by a gentlemanly oath of mutual loyalty, they overthrew each other with as little violence as possible—an example not followed by the younger politicians who came after them.

World War II faced Thailand with a major dilemma. When the Japanese arrived on December 7th 1941, the government had little option but to welcome them in. Later, when an Axis victory looked probable, the Thai government even declared war on Britain and the US. In return, it gained from Japan the 'reward' of the four northern provinces of Malaya. But Thailand's involvement with the Japanese was never anything more than tepid—beneath the surface, she remained sufficiently aligned to her Western 'adversaries' to provide them with an active Free Thai underground. Somehow (a diplomatic *tour de force*!) Thailand emerged at the end of the war stronger than before—no longer bound by cumbersome treaties which previously gave foreigners in Thailand special privileges.

In December 1945, King Anan Mahidol returned from his studies in Switzerland to take up the throne as Rama VIII. Just a few months later, on 9th June 1946, he was found shot through the forehead in the Grand Palace. Accident or foul play? Nobody has ever known for certain. His younger brother, King Bhumibol Aduldej, succeeded him in 1950 as Rama IX. Though arriving on the throne under the most difficult circumstances, he has since handled the job with commendable skill and diligence.

Political power meanwhile, was largely in the hands of one man—Field Marshal Pibul Songgram—who held the prime ministership of the country for much of the period before and during World War II. He fended off a number of attempts to unseat him, but was finally toppled in 1957/8 (two successive coups) by Field Marshal Sarit Thanarat. A tough army man, Sarit exercised sole government over the country (which he placed under martial law) until his death in 1963. Stability returned to government, and Thailand entered a period of unprecedented social and material well-being. Sarit's main domestic concern was the impoverished northeastern regions of the country, which he saw as prime targets for Communist propaganda. Despite major electrification and irrigation schemes, aimed at relieving the problems of the drought-stricken northeast, Sarit's successor, Field Marshal Thanom Kittikachorn, soon discovered that the Communists had already got a firm foothold in this region. This (and other reasons) delayed the much-anticipated democratic constitution and the holding of free elections until 1969. Democracy lasted just two years. In late 1971, Marshal Thanom abolished it in a bloodless coup. This did not go down well with Thai students however, and they staged a mass demonstration in October 1973. This devolved into a bloody revolution, resulting in the death of some 100 students at the hands of the military.

In 1975, a free democratic election resulted in a right-wing coalition government led by M. R. Kukrit Pramoj. The following year, following Kukrit's unpopular alignment with Communism (following the collapse of Vietnam and Cambodia), renewed student riots gave the military its required excuse to resume control of the country. The new premier, Thanin Kraivichien was unseated by General Kriangsak in October 1977, and by General Prem in 1980. Each new incumbent has promised the same strong checks on Communism and the same liberalization of the constitution. In recent years, this has resulted in a semi-open political system known as the 'half-way democracy'. This also means a half-way dictatorship, which has turned political parties already plagued by factional struggles into weak organizations. Opposition parties fare poorly whenever they attempt to topple the present government. In fact, they are merely waiting in the wings to join the coalition should there be a reshuffle. However, though Thailand's political situation is still far from clear, it is essentially a stable country, united both by its religion and by its strong and respected king.

Monarchy

The importance of the king in Thailand cannot be overemphasized. The Sukhothai ideal of the king was as 'father of the people'. The Khmer ideal, adopted by Ayutthaya, was of the king as *devaraja* or 'Lord of Life'. Until quite recent times, Thai monarchs were—at least in theory—the most absolute in the world. They were credited with possessing near-divine powers, and the penalty for touching one (or even whispering during a royal audience) was death. Today, Thailand is the only country in Southeast Asia (apart from Brunei) still to have a hereditary monarch as its head of state. And while King Bhumibol, the present ruler, is only a constitutional monarch, he still remains the spiritual and temporal head of the nation, the lynchpin of Thai unity.

Bhumibol, together with his lovely Queen Sikrit, is a 'working royal' who has earned the respect of other nations and the love (almost worship) of his own subjects through his active sponsorship of innumerable public projects—land reclamation, irrigation, dams, cottage industries and rice cultivation—aimed primarily at helping the poor and under-privileged in remote rural areas of his kingdom. He is, in many respects, a thoroughly modern monarch, and a man of many talents. Not only an artist, composer, and award-winning sailor, he is also a talented musician. Recently, a UK newspaper carried this story:

> King Bhumibol of Thailand is a keen jazzman who blows up a storm on clarinet and trumpet. So much so that he sat in with a band led by the legendary New Orleans trumpeter, Kid Sheik Cola, 79, during a jam session at his Bangkok palace. After-wards a bemused Sheik said: 'It was strange for the musicians when the King, Queen and Princess were waited on by chamberlains crawling on their knees, but the King got right into it.' Indeed, he enjoyed himself so much that he presented Sheik with a French-made trumpet.

Even by Thai standards, Bhumibol's popularity is impressive. Every household, every bus and train, every restaurant and hotel, every museum, temple and village hut, has a garlanded or gilt-framed picture of the King (and often his Queen) in a prominent place, usually next to a Buddhist altar or a spirit shrine. And at 6 pm each evening, when the national anthem blares forth from every tinny tannoy or transistor in the country, everything grinds to a halt as the Thais acknowledge with silent respect their powerful and popular king. Never, it seems, has a Thai monarch been so venerated and so valued by his people. Certainly, this is much to do with Bhumibol himself—a hard-working, gifted and caring man if there ever was one—but is there another reason? I've asked several Thais why they *really* value the king's presence, and the following answer is fairly typical:

> The military has so much power now. If we don't have the king, the military is sure to take over the government, and many problems are going to happen. The king is so important. He's a really good guy—much better than the government!

Religion

The professed religion of 95% of Thais is *Theravada* Buddhism. The greatest of all Thai institutions, Buddhism is the single most important unifying force in the country. It preserves and perpetuates the Thai nation and its traditions, and it moulds the Thai character and personality. The politeness, modesty and tolerance of the Thai people stem directly from their belief in Buddhism, which extends its influence to every aspect of daily life.

The Buddha

The historical Buddha, known as Gautama or Shakyamuni, lived about 2500 years ago in India. A royal prince, he spent his early life surrounded by wealth and luxury. At the age of 19 (29 according to some sources) he became preoccupied with the questions of birth, old age, sickness and death, and set off on a long quest for the Truth. Finally, at the age of 30 (or 35) he achieved his enlightenment under the Bo tree at Bodhgaya, in North India. The remaining 45 years of his life, he spent teaching his new philosophy to as many people as possible, irrespective of their status. His teaching incorporated the Hindu doctrines of *karma* and reincarnation, but he reinterpreted them in a far more dynamic form. Karma could be changed. Enlightenment could be achieved by anyone, and in this lifetime. It was a simple, optimistic message which spread in time to Sri Lanka, China, Nepal, Tibet, Central Asia, Southeast Asia and Japan. In India, about a century after the Buddha's death, a schism appeared in the *Sangha* (community of monks), causing a division into two major schools. The conservative *Theravada* school (later termed *Hinayana* or 'lesser vehicle') clung to the earlier, provisional teachings of the Buddha, and held that enlightenment was an individual pursuit, achieved by meditation and by self-denial. The progressive *Mahayana* school (or 'greater vehicle') taught that enlightenment was a collective altruistic pursuit with the ultimate aim of bringing all humanity to salvation. This school was based on the Buddha's later teachings—principally, the Lotus Sutra (*Myoho Renge Kyo*) taught by the Buddha in the last eight years of his life, and revealed as his supreme teaching by the 13th-century Japanese monk Nichiren. While the *Theravada* (*Hinayana*) sect always refers to the Buddha in terms of external symbols (e.g. *stupas*, pagodas, temples), the growing realization of the *Mahayana* sect is to look for the Buddha nowhere else but in themselves, and in every living thing.

Buddhism in Thailand

Buddhism arrived in Thailand from India and Ceylon, probably around the 3rd century BC. The country's former religion—animism or spirit worship—was not so much replaced by Buddhism as integrated with it. The same process of integration took place when Brahmanism arrived (also from India) in the 11th century AD. Thai religion then became a fascinating blend of different elements: *Theravada* Buddhist (though with traces of *Mahayana*), Hindu Brahmanist, and animist. Thai Buddhism was, therefore, a form of 'popular Buddhism', which later evolved into an institutionalized 'civic' Buddhism. It is—as evinced by the profusion of Hindu gods and beliefs represented in Buddhist temples, and by the Thai fascination with animistic 'lucky' charms—an extremely flexible religion!

In Thai Buddhism, negative *karma* (present sufferings caused by past errors) is erased, and *nirvana* (perfect enlightenment) made possible, by making merit. A very popular way for ordinary people to make merit is to free captured birds, tortoises and fish. These are often sold outside temples, freed by devout Buddhists, and captured again to give more devotees a chance to make merit. Even kings must make merit, and the present monarch, Bhumibol, made a great deal of merit in 1957 by becoming a monk for 14 days. For a Thai man, becoming a monk is the best possible way of making merit. He not only makes merit for himself (monkhood turns him from a 'raw' into a 'ripe' man, and makes him a suitable marriage prospect), but he also makes merit for his parents. Most Thai men spend at least a few months serving in a Buddhist monastery, and some 350,000 monks, novices and nuns currently support Thailand's 28,000 or so Buddhist temples. Monks make merit because they live an austere life, eating only twice a day (after noon, they can only take drinks), owning nothing but an umbrella, a razor and maybe a few books, wearing simple yellow robes, and sleeping in bare, spartan cells. Each morning around 6 am, they walk the streets collecting their first meal of the day. This gives each Thai family who gives a spoonful of food a chance to make some merit too.

There are two main sects in the general community of monks called the *Sangha*. The *Thammayut*, founded by the ascetic King Mongkut in the mid-19th century, are in the minority. This sect enjoins its monks (*bhikkus*) to spend most of their day studying, to avoid touching even paper money, and to live as austerely as possible. Several *Thammayut* are 'forest-dwelling' monks, who spend their time exclusively in prayer and meditation. The other main sect, the *Mahanikaya*, comprise the vast majority of Thai monks. They are ordained for a period from five days to three months, usually during the rainy season, when all monks stay put inside their monasteries. Most *Mahanikaya* are poor country boys who, having taken advantage of the educational advantages of monkhood (the temple is the traditional intellectual centre of the community), leave the *wat* to become lorry drivers, soldiers, kick-boxers and tourist guides. Only a small percentage of monks stay in the *Sangha* for more than a few years.

Underlying orthodox Buddhism is the pervasive influence of Thai animism. This religious system deals primarily with *phis* or nature spirits, who must be constantly appeased if life is to run smoothly and happily. To gain their favour or protection, Thais commonly wear sacred amulets or holy water, often imbued with 'power' by Buddhist monks. Furthermore, in almost every Thai house compound, there is a 'spirit house' erected to appease the *chao thi* or 'lord of the land'.

As animistic symbols of power continue to multiply—magically gifted monks and charms included—concerned critics within the *Sangha* have begun to argue strongly for a revitalized Buddhism which is relevant to modern times. They point out that temple education—which concentrates much on arid rules and ceremonies, and little on Buddhism's deeper wisdom or goal—prepares its young monks far better for life outside the *Sangha* than for any meaningful contribution within it.

But a growing section of the population just isn't interested in religion any more. As the *Bangkok Post* recently reported:

> Most Thais are paying less attention to religious activities, and are spending more time watching television. A survey of 20,000 families throughout the country showed that only 4.5% of those living in municipal areas went to Buddhist temples regularly to listen to sermons; 20% said they went occasionally; and 75% said not at all. In municipal areas, 11% offered alms to monks regularly, 46% occasionally, and 41% never.

Survival, not spiritual growth, now seems to be people's main concern. And while Thailand's minority religions—the Muslims of the far south, the Christians of the north, the Indian Hindus, Chinese Confucianists, Taoists and *Mahayana* Buddhists—have all made a few converts, the new gods of materialism and money look set to claim very many more.

Culture

Thai art and culture is basically a compound of three separate influences—Khmer from the east, Burmese from the north, and Srivijaya from the south—together with selective borrowing from India and China. In historic times, art in Thailand has been exclusively **religious** art. The main impetus behind the creation of buildings, paintings, sculpture and dance is to create merit. Not for self-glorification or personal self-expression, but to create beautiful things—often incorporating Buddhistic and Brahmanic symbols (e.g. the Wheel of Law, the Tree of Enlightenment, Vishnu and Shiva)—to ensure beautiful circumstances in the life to come. So, sculptures are mostly of the Buddha and of the Hindu gods. Architecture is mostly temples and *stupas* (often containing 'relics' of the Buddha) and worshipping places of Brahmanic deities. Paintings are mainly linear-form murals on stucco temple walls (mostly destroyed by Thailand's humid climate), depicting mainly the 547 **Jakarta** stories of Buddha's life or the *Ramayana* epic of Hinduism. Literature follows a uniformly religious theme, and culminated in the Thai version of the *Ramayana*, called the *Ramakien* (most other Thai writings, apart from a few 17th- and 18th-century romantic stories were lost at Ayutthaya in 1767). Music and classical dance drama also has a rich religious and historical heritage, and is still mainly performed in temples, in celebration of the power of Buddha.

Art periods fall into the following styles—**Dvaravati** (6th to 11th centuries), **Srivajaya** (8th to 13th), **Lopburi** (7th to 14th), **Chiang Saen** (11th to 18th), **Sukhothai** (13th to 14th), **U-Thong** (12th to 15th), **Ayutthaya** (14th to 18th), and **Bangkok** (late 18th century to the present day). The overlap of the various styles of art and architecture are the result of the co-existence of two or sometimes three major kingdoms in the country at various points in its history.

Sculpture

As the main artistic impetus in Thailand has been Buddhism, Thai sculptors have concentrated mainly on building Buddha images for worship. All representations of Buddha are strictly stylized. In theory, they are all copies of an 'ideal' image based on portraits made of the Buddha during his lifetime. Sculptors of the Buddha image were not expected to be original or experimental, merely to copy earlier (presumably more authentic) images. The 'ideal' Buddha image is generally tall, slim and willowy, with an asexual body (no muscles, no bones). His eyebrows are like drawn bows, his nose like a parrot's beak, and his chin like a mango stone. Around the 5th–6th century AD, it was decided that Buddha had been born with 33 'extraordinary signs'. These included tightly-curled hair, a topknot (*usnisha*) on the head, and long earlobes (an indication of princely rank; princes wore heavy ear jewellery from birth). Further stylization of these images, which varied in size from the miniature to the colossal, derived from their depiction of Buddha in four prescribed postures or 'attitudes'—standing, sitting, reclining or walking. In the course of time, inevitable variations in style took place, which serve as a guide to the period in which they were composed.

The historical Buddha regarded himself as an ordinary (albeit enlightened) man, and not supernatural or godlike. He did not wish to be worshipped in his lifetime, nor to have images and statues built to him after his death. But all prophets tend to become objects of worship, and around 500 years after the Buddha's death the first image of him appeared in present-day Afghanistan. Influenced by Grecian settlers (remnants of Alexander the Great's army), this prototype image was in the Greco-Roman style, with a halo, classical features and simple, flowing robes. By the 5th century, the art of Buddha-building had spread to India. During the famous Gupta period (the Golden Age of Indian art) images began to acquire their 'extraordinary signs', and to be coated with (or made of) gold—this being the purest metal, symbolic of the Buddha's purity.

The earliest Buddha images fashioned in Thailand appeared in the Mon kingdom of **Dvaravati**, which flourished in central Thailand between the 6th and 11th centuries. This style has an idealized Mon face—broad, with well-formed features, bulging eyes, and a large, sensitive mouth—with the *usnisha* as a round knob. Standing figures usually have hands raised in the gesture of exposition; seated ones (often under a *naga* or sacred serpent) are usually in the attitude of giving the first sermon, or of subduing Mara (symbol of earthly desires). Between the late 7th and 13th centuries, the empire of **Srivijaya** in the south was heavily influenced by India with whom it did a lot of trading. The Srivijaya style of Buddha (and *Mahayana*-type Bodhissatva) images derives from Indian types, mainly Gupta and Pala. Srivijaya figures are typically well-proportioned, naturalistically modelled, and often backed by a backslab or *mandala* surmounted by a parasol.

The **Lopburi** style of the Khmers, who ruled much of northeast and central Thailand between the early 11th and late 13th centuries, continued to portray Buddha as an ascetic. Typical images are small, with realistic proportions and a masculine appearance. Features are gentle, benign and refined, with bulging eyelids, flat nose and thick lips. Figures are usually seated on the *naga* in the attitude of dispelling fear. By the 12th century, the god-king culture of the Khmers led to the creation of Buddhas wearing crowns, jewelled earrings and rather stern, lawgiving expressions.

The **Sukhothai** period, commencing in the 13th century, is considered the Gold Age of Thai art. It re-interpreted traditional models—giving its Buddha images graceful curves, a flamelike *ushnisha*, pointed features and an oval face—and it invented the 'walking Buddha', for which there was no prototype. The pre-Ayutthayan style of **King Uthong** favoured the square-faced Buddha with thick lips, smiling mouth, connected eyebrows and cone-shaped *usnisha*, seated on a plain base, subduing Mara. During the **Ayutthaya** period (14th–18th centuries), early delicacy and craftsmanship deteriorated as the concept of divine kingship inevitably affected religious art. Buddha images became mass-produced and very ornate, often heavily bejewelled and dressed in royal finery. Some say Ayutthaya created a Buddha in its own image—materially rich, spiritually corrupt—which foretold its own ruin.

The present **Bangkok** period has produced little fresh art. After Ayutthaya's destruction, it became practice for sculptors to tour the country resurrecting and renovating old Buddha images, producing nothing new themselves except poor, hackneyed copies of earlier styles. With the loss of Buddhism's vitality at Ayutthaya, religious art went into steep decline. Even today, art students in Bangkok are principally engaged in copying murals from the walls of the Grand Palace. But though some advances have been made in painting and in the minor arts a definitive Bangkok style of art and architecture has yet to emerge.

Architecture

Architecture is synonymous with temples. These are usually typically Thai, though the larger examples often display Indian-style *stupas*, or Cambodian and Burmese elements. The standard Thai temple is called a **wat**, and contains within its compound various buildings and structures. The most notable are the *bot*, the main chapel and ordination hall containing the temple's main Buddha image; one or more *viharns*, or secondary chapels, used for public worship and housing lesser Buddha images; one or more *chedis* (*stupas*, pagodas), either Thai-style with bell-shaped dome tapering into a spire, or Khmer-style (*prang*) with an elliptical spire, and often containing relics of the Buddha or of royal personages; and the *sala*, an open-sided rest house or pavilion, used for visitors, and pilgrims.

The most conspicuous architectural feature of Thai temple buildings are their roofs—generally steeply sloping (for quick run-off of rain), many-tiered, and covered with cheerfully-coloured glazed tiles. The motifs of the *naga* (holy serpent) and *chopha* (Brahma's carrier, the swan) turn up as horn or beak-shaped finials on the ridge ends of temple roofs. On Chinese temples, the motif is a dragon. Many Thai temples, especially in Bangkok, have a number of stone Chinese figures (usually mandarins or *singha* lions) dotted around their compounds. These were brought into Thailand by Chinese junks, who used them as ballast to weigh down very light cargoes of ceramics. The male variety of the *singha* has a stone ball in its mouth. It is believed that anyone who can remove the ball without damaging the figure or the ball will live for ever. Hindu deities feature prominently in Thai art—notably blue-faced Rama (often bearing a bow and arrow), and the Naga snake (Hindu god of the underworld, said to have saved the Buddha from drowning while he was meditating), which often lead the way up the entrance of temples. Many Thai temples also have a mirrored or reflecting-glass façade, an animist influence designed to deflect or frighten away evil spirits.

Music & Dance

Classical Thai **music** shows influences of Indian, Javanese, Chinese, Burmese, Malay and Khmer musical traditions. It is customarily played by a *piphat* woodwind and percussion band comprising between five and twenty players. The principal woodwind instrument is called a *pi*, and both looks and sounds like an oboe. Percussion instruments are divided between xylophone-like instruments called *ranad* and a semi-circle of gongs called the *gong wong yai* (both of which provide the melody), and an assortment of drums, cymbals and lesser gongs (which provide the rhythm). The intricacies of Thai music, which has defeated transposition for play by Western bands, arise from its complex musical scale, in which seven full tones (and no semi-tones) separate an eight-note octave. Thai musicians play seated on the floor before their instruments, and they generally perform at festivals, funerals and weddings. 'Modern' Thai music, as played in low-lit jazzy 'disco cafes', leans heavily on '60s R & B, Country & Western, and soulful Western-style ballads. There is either a 'Cliff Richard and the Shadows'-type band with twanging guitars and a stock of summery 'happy-happy' songs; or there is a female vocalist rendering plaintive, wistful Western-copy tunes, with droning, dirge-like accompaniment on keyboards. You'll love it to pieces!

Thai classical **dance** is heavily influenced by Indian temple dancing, on which it is modelled. The two major dance-drama forms are the *khon*, where the performers (originally all men) wear masks, and the *lakhon*, usually performed by women dancing both male and female roles. Both dramas are commonly based upon stories from the *Ramakien*—the Thai version of the Hindu *Ramayana* epic poem. Briefly, this tells of the great prince Rama (a reincarnation of Vishnu) who is sent to earth by Brahma, creator of the world, to destroy the demon king Ravana. He wins the beautiful princess Sita, but is banished by his earthly father, the king of Ayodhya, and wanders around in the forest for 14 years accompanied by Sita and his younger brother Lakshman. Then Ravana, who wants Sita for himself, steals her away and a powerful monkey-king called Hanuman deserts Ravana's army and decides to help out Rama instead. Many battles ensue, before Rama finally kills Ravana, recovers Sita, and returns to Ayodhya to reclaim his throne. It's a long, long story never performed today in its entirety. Most classical dinner-dances at major hotels in Bangkok and most tourist-oriented 'cultural shows' depict only a few selected scenes—a far cry from the marathon performances of the courts of old Siam, which used to run for days on end. Both *khon* and *lakhon* are highly stylized forms of dance, with prescribed hand and feet movements to indicate subtle changes in mood and feeling. Of the two, the *Khon* is more visually striking, with the performers wearing ornate traditional masks and costumes (deep green for Rama, gold for Lakshman, white for Hanuman etc). A third form of Thai drama, the *nang* or **shadow-play** in which the story is told by means of large, elaborate silhouettes cut out of buffalo hide, is little seen nowadays, even in the south where it was once most popular. The dance which tourists are most likely to come across in Thailand is the notorious *Ramwong* or circle-dance. This is one of those embarrassing audience participation affairs where unsuspecting dinner-dance guests are suddenly plucked onto the stage and shuffle around looking horribly ill-at-ease, while their friends take lots of unkind photographs!

Part III

BANGKOK

Royal Barge

Despite its trappings of progressive modernism—high-rise hotels, fast-food restaurants and *haute couture* boutiques—Bangkok remains distinctly Thai and is one of the friendliest, liveliest cities in the East. 'It's unique', was one typical comment, 'the kind of place where you can arrive and feel at home right away!' Others say the city is like getting used to a strong cheese—the heat, the noise, the pollution and the mind-numbing traffic may overwhelm you at first, but once you've acquired the taste, all other cities seem dull and bland by comparison! The key to Bangkok's provocative, intriguing Asian mystery is that it has no centre. It's not like a city at all. Rather, it's a country town gone wild—a series of self-contained villages loosely strung together to make up a 'city'. Bangkok's veneer of urban sophistication is never more than paper-thin. One-fifth of its population still live a totally traditional life on its waterways and *klongs* (canals); white-collar company directors still sing happy folk songs on their way to work; barefoot groups of orange-robed monks still tour the grey city pavements each dawn, begging for alms; students still bound up to lost tourists at crowded traffic intersections, offering help; and everybody (I mean everybody!) gives you a smile and a cheery *Sawatdee*!, no matter how busy they are. It's not just that Bangkokites like tourists (which they do)—they are simply country people, living in a big city.

So, welcome to 'Krungthep Manakhon Bovorn Ratanakosin Mahintharayutthaya Mahadilokpop Noparatratchathani Burirom Udomratchanivetmahasathan Avatarn-sathit Sakkathattiya-visnukarmrasit'—or simply 'Krungthep', as the locals call it. This short title means 'City of Angels' (Los Angeles!), and is just one of many sobriquets that Bangkok has earned over the years. Current favourites include 'Venice of the East' (a reference to its many canals), 'Bargain Basement of Asia' (you can save, and spend, a

45

fortune here!) and 'Sex Capital of the World' (men, watch out!). But the name Bangkok, an abbreviation of Tumbol Bangmakok, simply means 'Village of Wild Plums'—and that's just how it started out.

History

When Rama I moved his capital here from Thonburi in 1782, Bangkok was a tiny mosquito-infested village (with plums), overlooking the Chao Phya River. His vision was to rebuild Ayutthaya, the old capital gutted by the Burmese in 1767, in a new setting. To this end, he used artisans, advisers, and even building materials from the ruined ex-capital, and even cut canals to the eastern side of Bangkok to surround it (like Ayutthaya) with water. For the first century of its life as a capital city, Bangkok's only form of transportation was by water—and when King Mongkut cemented new trade agreements with the West in the late-19th century, the numerous *klongs* fanned out even further to accommodate a large influx of new merchants, traders and shippers. Road transport only became a prominent feature after WW II, and even as recently as the early 1960s, Bangkok was still a charming, leisurely city with sparse motorized traffic and a few tree-lined roads. By this time, it had acquired a skyline of glittering spires and steep orange and green roofs—evidence of its many temples (more than 300). Looking upon this colourful vista from his convalescent bed at the Oriental Hotel, Somerset Maugham expressed his wonderment: 'It makes you laugh with delight to think that anything so fantastic could exist on this sombre earth . . . The artists who developed [these temples] step by step from the buildings of the Ancient Khmers had the courage to pursue their fantasy to the limit.'

In 1960, Bangkok had a population of just 1½ million. In 1965, it became a designated venue for American troops on R & R (Rest & Recreation) from Vietnam. The result was a boom in bars, cinemas, hotels, restaurants and massage parlours. The city became a magnet for poor rural people—especially young girls—seeking to escape a life of hopeless poverty in the country provinces. The consequent migration was dramatic. By the early '80s, the lure of employment, money and bright lights had flooded Bangkok with 6 million people—40 times the population of the second largest city, Chiang Mai. One in ten Thais now live in Bangkok, and more than half of these are of Chinese descent. One million of the capital's inhabitants own and drive cars—the result is a traffic nightmare, and the lowest oxygen level of any city in the world. An order has gone out to ban the production of any new *tuk-tuks* (the main offenders) but they just keep on appearing.

Bangkok Today

Despite the frequent clouds of smog, Bangkok maintains an incredibly clean 'front'— waste-bins and street cleaners everywhere! No longer is it a drab, malarial city of canals and waterways—many of these have now been filled in—but a bright, fast-moving and optimistic metropolis of broad, neon-lit avenues, behind which—in a labyrinthine maze of narrow *sois* (streets)—traditional life goes on in hundreds of street markets, floating markets and tiny temple courtyards converted into yet more markets. If one thing holds the jigsaw of Bangkok together, it must be its markets—which seem to have no beginning and no end. And if one place holds the nation together—socially, politically, and commercially—it must be Bangkok. In all respects, it's a city-state—Thailand's only really modern, developed centre. The bewildering contrasts between rich and poor, beauty and ugliness, spirituality and materialism, may unsettle—even shock—you, but Bangkok still has more variety, more charm and more character than any other capital city in the East. A big statement? Well, just spend a few days here and you'll surely agree!

WHEN TO GO

Bangkok is most comfortable from December to February—during these months, humidity is low and temperatures are often comparable to a pleasant English summer. Hotels have their high season from October to April (the big ones are often full, so book in advance!) and their low season from May to September (when it is possible to get a discounted 3-star double room for as little as £15).

Festivals

Festivals take place throughout the year, though apart from Lumpini Park and Chao Phya River, there's nowhere really to hold them! The best riverside festival is **Loi Krathong** (October/November), when flotillas of boats put out from the Oriental pier to launch gaily-decorated candlelit floats. Street festivals happen daily in Bangkok, especially in and around the temples. Check out Chinatown—the Chinese really know how to hold a party!

GETTING TO AND FROM BANGKOK

By Air

Perfectly placed for stopover traffic, Bangkok benefits from the ease with which it can be combined with other Asian destinations, such as Hong Kong, Bali, Delhi and Rangoon. It's a great place to pick up cheap airline tickets (especially in the discount centres of Banglampoo and Soi Ngam Dupli) and to obtain visas.

   Don Muang Airport, 25 km north of the city, is one of the busiest airports in the world, serving over 30 international airlines. Small, modern and efficient, it has a tourist information centre, a hotel-booking desk, two currency-exchange points, a left-luggage office (20B a day, per piece) and a Thai International restaurant up on the observation deck (the only place to enjoy a civilized cup of coffee!). **The Airport Hotel** (tel 5661020) is directly connected to the airport (very handy), has good rooms from 1600B single, 1700B twin, and offers complimentary transfers from the airport and into town.

   From Don Muang, there are several choices of transport into the city:

Air-con limo direct to hotel—the most comfortable option. **Thai Limousine** sells tickets for 300B in the International Lounge, and for only 200B in the Domestic Lounge!

Air-con minibus, dropping off at individual hotels. **Thai Limousine** sells 100B tickets, from 9 am to midnight only.

Private taxi, hired at the airport exit. Bargain hard for the 150B minimum fare.

Public bus, from the street-stop outside the airport. Two useful buses are No. 59, which goes to Victory Monument (continue on No. 39 for Democracy

Monument/Banglampoo); and No. 29, which goes to Phetburi Rd (change here for Democracy Monument), Rama I Rd (for Siam Square, change here for Sukhumvit), and Hualamphong station (for Silom-Surawong). The fare is just 5B. Two comfy **air-con buses**, Nos. 4 and 29, head into town from the airport for 15B.

Train, from Don Muang rail station (connected to the airport via Airport Hotel). Trains leave for Hualamphong station every 20 minutes or so, from 5.05 am to 11.20 pm. Fare is 5B, 3rd class.

From airport to town takes between 45 minutes (at night) to 1$\frac{1}{2}$ hours (at rush hour). If travelling by public transport (i.e. bus or train), keep an eagle eye on your bags and wallet—the airport route is plied by expert thieves.

Airport Tax
When leaving, or flying within the country, have your **Airport Tax** handy—150B for international flights, 20B for domestic flights. If in transit (i.e. if you haven't left the airport building) you don't have to pay this—but you do need to fill in a declaration form.

    Domestic flights on Thai Airways, servicing several destinations within the country, also leave from Don Muang airport—see General Information section.

Airlines with offices in Bangkok are as follows:

International

Aeroflot	7 Silom Rd	233–6965–7
Air Canada	1053 New Rd	233–5900–9 Ext11–14
Air France	942/51 Charn Issara Tower, Rama IV Rd	2341330–9
Air India	Amarin Tower, 500 Phloenchit Rd	256–9614–9
Air Lanka	942/51 Charn Issara Tower, Rama IV Rd	2364981
Alitalia	Boonmitr Bldg, 138 Silom Rd	233–4000–1, 234–5253
American Airline	Maniya Bldg, 518/2 Phloenchit Rd,	251–1393, 252–3520–2
Bangladesh Biman	Chongkolnee Bldg, 56 Surawong Rd	235–7643–4
British Airways	2nd Fl, Charn Issara Tower, Rama IV Rd	236–8655–8
Burma Airways	208/1 Surawong Rd	233–3052, 234–9692
CAAC (China)	134/1–2 Silom Rd	235–1880–2, 235–6510–1
Canadian Airlines	518/2 Maniya Bldg, Phloenchit Rd	251–4521, 252–8842
Cathay Pacific	5th Fl, Charn Issara Tower, Rama IV Rd	235–4330–9
China Airline	4th Fl, Peninsula Plaza, Ratchadamri Rd	253–5733–7
Dragonair	46/1 Sukhumvit 3	253–0681–4
Eastern Airlines	20/10–11 Soi Bangkok Bazaar, Ratchadamri Rd	253–9097–8
Egypt Air	120 Silom Rd	233–7601–3, 233–7599
Finnair	518/2 Maniya Bldg, Phloenchit Rd	251–5012, 251–5075
Garuda	944/19 Rama IV Rd	233–0981–2, 233–3873
Gulf Air	9 Decho Rd	233–5039, 233–1111, 233–1123
Indian Airlines	2/1–2 Decho Rd	233–3890–2
Iraqi Airways	325–329 A.S.C. Bldg, Silom Rd	233–3271–4, 235–5950–5
Japan Airlines	Wall Street Tower, 33/33–34, Surawong Rd	233–2440
KLM	2 Patpong Rd	235–5150–9

Korean Air	Room 306 Dusit Thani Bldg, Rama IV Rd	234–9283–9
Kuwait Airways	159 Ratchadamri Rd	251–5855
Lot-Polish	485/11–12 Silom Rd	235–2223–7, 235–7092–4
Lufthansa	Pilot Bldg, 331/1–3 Silom Rd	234–1350–9
Malaysian Airlines	98–102 Surawong Rd	234–9790–4, 234–9795–9
Northwest Orient	153 Peninsula Plaza, Ratchadamri Rd	253–4423–5
Pakistani International	52 Surawong Rd	234–2961–5, 234–2352
Pan Am	518/2 Maniya Bldg, Phloenchit Rd	251–4521, 252–8842
Philippine Airlines	56 Chongkolnee Bldg, Surawong Rd	233–2350–2, 234–2483
Qantas Airways	942/51 Charn Issara Tower, Rama IV Rd	236–7493–4
Royal Brunei	2nd Fl, Charn Issara Tower, Rama IV Rd	234–0007
Royal Jordanian	56 Yada Bldg, Silom Rd	236–0030
Royal Nepal Airlines	Sivadon Bldg, 1/4 Convent Rd	233–3921–4
Sabena	CCT Bldg, 109 Surawong Rd	233–2020
SAS	412 Rama Rd	253–8333
Saudia	CCT Bldg, 109 Surawong Rd	236–9395–9403, 236–0112
Singapore Airlines	Silom Center, 2 Silom Rd	236–0440, 236–0303
Swissair	IBM Bldg, 1 Silom Rd	233–2935–7, 233–2930–4
Tarom	89/12 Soi Bangkok Bazaar, Ratchadamri Rd	253–1681–5
Thai Airways International	89 Vibhavadi-Rangsit Rd	513–0121
	485 Silom Rd	233–3810, 234–3100
TWA	12th Fl, Charn Issara Tower, Rama IV Rd	233–7290–1
United Airlines	Regent House, 183 Ratchadamri Rd	253–0558–9

Domestic

Bangkok Airways	144 Sukhumvit 46	253–4014–6, 253–8942–7
Thai Airways	6 Lan Luang Rd	280–0070, 280–0080, 280–0090
	4th Fl, Charn Issara Tower, 942/136 Rama IV Rd	236–7884–5

Airports

Bangkok International Airport	523–6201, 531–0022–59
Bangkok Domestic Airport	523–6201, 523–7222

By Rail

Bangkok's central railway station **Hualamphong** is at the western end of Rama IV Rd. It covers all routes north and northeast, plus many southern destinations. The Advance Booking office at Hualamphong (open 8.30 am to 6 pm weekdays, 8.30 am to noon weekends) has a tourist information desk, and hands out rail timetables. Trains for Kanchanaburi leave from Bangkok Noi railway station, across the river.

By Bus

Regular air-conditioned (air-con) and non air-conditioned (non air-con) buses leave for most tourist centres from three main bus-stations in Bangkok. These are the **Northern Bus Terminal**, Phahonyothin Rd (tel 271010), which services Ayutthaya, Chiang Mai, Chiang Rai, Lamphun, Lopburi, Phitsanoluke, Sukhothai, Khorat, Nong Khai and Udorn Thani; the **Eastern Bus Terminal**, off Soi 42, Sukhumvit Rd (tel 3912504), which covers Pattaya, Rayong, Si Racha and Chanthaburi; and the **Southern Bus Terminal**, Charansanitwong Rd (tel 4110511), which runs out to Hat Yai, Hua Hin,

Kanchanaburi, Krabi, Nakhon Pathom, Phang Nga, Phuket, Koh Samui and Surat Thani. The Northern and Eastern bus-stations have baggage-deposit facilities (10B per piece)—very useful if you're heading north, and want to fly straight out on your return to Bangkok (the Northern terminal is close to Don Muang airport).

GETTING AROUND BANGKOK

With its high humidity, broken pavements and traffic-choked streets, Bangkok is not a city conducive to walking. Apart from a stroll to the local shops, you'll nearly always have to take some form of transport. This usually means travelling by bus, taxi, *tuk-tuk* or hired car—and a head-on encounter with Bangkok's diabolical traffic. Well, is it really that bad? One of the city's leading newspapers, *The Nation*, evidently thinks so:

> We believe that no system in the world could improve the traffic in Bangkok. The reason is simple: there are too many vehicles in the city. The conventional wisdom is that if you line up all motor vehicles registered in Bangkok Metropolis on the city streets, there will not be enough road space for any vehicle to move . . . Every time it rains the city grinds to a halt and many a motorist is ready for the psychiatric ward.

The *Bangkok Post* adds an optimistic footnote:

> Within the next 10 years, the population in Bangkok could well exceed 11 million . . . You can imagine how chaotic it would be for Bangkok traffic without expressways and the sky train which we are going to build. If no obstacles arise, the ETA will commence the construction of three routes for the 'Sky Train' late next near (1988).

Every major paper ran an editorial ridiculing the new city police chief's promise to 'solve Bangkok's traffic problem'. Everyone knows it's quite insoluble. At rush hour, the highways are jammed solid all the way up from Sukhumvit to Silom, and vendors casually wander from car to car, selling newspapers and puzzle games to keep the drivers from dozing off at the wheel. Traffic is particularly slow from 7.30 am to 9.30 am, and between 4 pm and 7 pm—these are the rush (crush!) hours, and you'll need to allow for extra travelling time (especially if you've a plane or train to catch). But traffic jams in Bangkok are never dull. If stuck in a stationary bus or taxi, you'll be constantly entertained by close encounters with mad-cap motorcyclists (their bikes often stacked high with carpets, hi-fi equipment, toilet brushes and—when there's an inch of spare room—a baby or two!). And wherever you stop, there'll always be enough colourful street-action to keep you amused, and your camera clicking!

By Bus

Public buses are the cheapest form of transport. They'll take you virtually anywhere in the city for just 2B (after 10 pm, 3B). But they're often hot and crowded, and have a poor reputation for pickpockets and slit-bag thieves. Every route has at least one air-con option (5B for the first 10 km)—take it if you can. Last bus services are around 11 pm, though a few services run through the night. Check with your hotel regarding route numbers and bus-stops—Thai buses rarely have English-language destination boards. An essential buy is a **Bus Map** (35B) listing routes and numbers—available from most bookshops and stationers. The two clearest maps (at present) are those printed by M. Suwanchai and K. S. Thaveepholchar.

By Taxi

Taxis are plentiful, air-conditioned, and the easiest way of getting around—especially if you're short on time. Taxis stopped on the street tend to be cheaper than those on standby outside hotels. But none of them use meters. It's essential to agree a fare (20–30B for short journeys, 50–70B across town) before setting off.

By Tuk-Tuk

Tuk-tuks (motorized *samlors*) are a little cheaper than taxis (i.e. 15–20B short trips, 40–50B long hauls) and are often manned by manic drivers who know every short-cut going in their part of town. Few of them speak or understand English though, and many get lost outside their 'beats'. Ask your hotel to write your destination in Thai, and to give you one of their own cards, so that you can get home again! With *tuk-tuks*, you need to bargain very hard to get a fair price—and this must be agreed *before* you set off!

By Boat

River-transport is the ideal way of beating Bangkok's traffic, and is very cheap. The Chao Phya River snakes through the capital, and not only affords a completely different view of the city, but connects many of its sightseeing attractions. The main form of public river-transport is the **Chao Phya Express** (*rua duan*)—a large, long river-taxi with a red roof, a large number board, and usually a little guy aboard frantically blowing a whistle. You can't miss it!

Express boats are very cheap (from 3B to 7B, depending on distance) and very regular (one ever 20 minutes or so, from 6 am to 6 pm). There are about 40 stops on the route, including some really useful ones like the GPO, the Grand Palace, the National Museum, Prannok Rd (for the Southern Bus Terminal) and Banglampoo. Many people take the rewarding one-hour trip all the way up from the Oriental Pier to Nonthaburi, taking lunch at the nice little restaurant (English menu and good local food) 100 yards below the Nonthaburi pier.

Slower **cross-river ferries** (*rua kham fak*) operate from several jetties, and simply go back and forth across the river. **Long-tail taxis** (*rua hang yao*) zip up the Chao Phya and through the narrow *klongs* at incredible speeds. They are a good bet if you're in a hurry, or want to travel in style. You can charter one in a group (100B one-way) from the Oriental Hotel to the Grand Palace, or vice versa. For something special, go to Tha Tien pier (behind Wat Po), where share-fare longtail boats leave every half-hour from 6.30 am to 6 pm for the picturesque side-*klong* trip down **Klong Mon**. This outing features canalside temples, fruit orchards, orchid farms, and fascinating scenes of waterborne life. On Sundays, you can hire a whole long-tail boat (for a group of up to 20 people) to see all the major temples, the floating market, the royal barges and the *klongs*, for just 400B. This is a 7-hour excursion, offered by **No 1 Siam Tour** (tel 2330581) at Oriental Hotel pier. Any other day, the best deal like this you can get is a short 3-hour speedboat trip (10 persons only) costing 500B. To arrange this, get a small group together and bargain for your own boat. If there's only one or two of you, consider an organized river trip out of an hotel. There's a good one offered by **Narai Hotel**, Silom Rd, running from 7 am to 12 noon daily and priced at 270B.

By Car

Cars can be hired at around 300B a day from **Avis** (tel 2341010), **Asoke** (3924422),

BANGKOK
Not to scale

N

PRADIPAT

Chaophraya River

SANTIWONG RD

CHARAN

RD

SAMSEN

AMNUI SONG

KHRAM RD

NAKHON CHAISI

RD

RAMA V RD

RATCHAWITHI RD

SI AYUTHAYA RD

RAMA V RD

RATCHA

PHITSANULOK RD

RAMA VI RD

SI AY

SWANKHALOK

PETCH

PHRANNOK RD

PHRACHAN RD

BONGSE RD

WISUTKASAT RD

RACHATHIP-ATAI RD

Boxing Stadium

KRUNG KASEM RD

PHRASUMEN RD

RATCHADAMNOEN

● Southern Bus Terminal

NAPHRALAN RD

NAPHRATHAT RD

CHAKRA RD

Royal ● KLANG

DIN SO RD

AVE

BAMRUNG

MUANG RD

RD

Thor H

NAPHRALAN RD

● Grand Palace

RACHINI RD

SANAMCHAI RD

ATSADANG RD

TI THONG RD

CHAROEN KRUNG RD

LUANG RD

RAMA I RD

RAMA VI

RONG MUANG RD

● Wat Arun

● Wat Po

PAHURAHT RD

CHINA TOWN

Hualumphong Railway Station

CHAROEN MUANG RD

YAOWARAJ RD

● Trimit

CHAKRAPHET RD

RATCHAWONG RD

Empire ●

Chaophraya River

MAHA PLUETHARAM RD

SI PHRAYA RD

Plaza ● R

● Floating Market

Royal Orchid Sheraton ●

G.P.O.

SURAWONG

Narai ● R

● Manohra

SILOM

Sing En

● Talatphlu Railway Station

Swan ●

NEW RD

● New Fuji

RAMA IV RD

Pan

TAKSIN RD

Oriental ●

Shangri-La ●

Burm
Embas

SATHON

SATHON

CHAROEN KRUNG RD

First (2523877) and **Hertz** (2524903). Consider hiring a hotel limousine with driver (fixed rates)—much safer than driving yourself!

TOURIST INFORMATION

TAT (Tourist Authority of Thailand) main office is at Ratchadamnoen Rd (tel 2821143–7). Very good at handing out information, pretty poor at handling individual enquiries (just try asking about say, scuba-diving facilities on Phuket!). Beautiful wall-posters on Thailand are sometimes available from the small Distribution Office, round the side of the main building. TAT also has a desk in Don Muang airport arrival lounge.

WHAT TO SEE

Sightseeing in Bangkok takes time and dedication—this is a large city, about the size of London or Paris, and its sights are widely spread. To see everything at leisure, ideally you need two weeks. Most visitors however, allow only 4 or 5 days, and this really puts the pressure on! Enervating heat, snarled traffic, and the barrier of language mean that lightning tours are simply not possible. Independent travellers often have difficulty covering more than one or two sights in a day. The old city is completely camouflaged by modern business blocks, cinemas, shopping centres and hotels, making quick orientation impossible. To make best use of your time, you have to be organized. First, aim to be out and about as early as possible—see as much as you can in the cool of the morning. Second, only use public transport between 10 am and 4 pm (thus avoiding the rush hours). Third, spend your first free morning or afternoon on the Chao Phya River (cf. Getting Around). Go armed with a good city map (the 35B 'bus' map is adequate) and get a quick overview of the city sights and layout. Fourth, alternate individual sightseeing with organized tours. Many hotels and guest houses offer half/full-day tours by air-con minibus or coach at around 120–220B (50B extra, if booking through a big hotel!). These are very useful, if you've a lot to see in a short time. Fifth, don't take on too much—in Bangkok, the visitor must slow down to the Thai pace, or perish! Finally, make a list of the sights you *must* see, and do as much advance preparation for them as possible (e.g. arrange early-morning call, advance-book taxi, check opening and closing times of various sights—they vary greatly!). If you need an English-speaking guide, contact **World Travel Service**, 1053 Charoen Krung Rd, Silom (tel 2335900) or the **Professional Guides Association** (tel 2513504). They provide badge-carrying guides at around 1000B a day—quite cheap, if you're in a large group! Freelance guides are in very short supply. I've only ever come across them at the Grand Palace and at Wat Pho. Often, your best bet is to tack onto a package tour—every sight has one, and they always seem to have the best guides!

Grand Palace & Major Temples
(by river-boat, on foot; full day)

Wat Arun – Wat Po – Grand Palace – Wat Phra Keo – Vivanmek Palace

For this suggested tour, go down to the pier below the Oriental Hotel and take a public express boat up to **Wat Arun**, then across to **Wat Po**. From here, it's a short walk to the **Grand Palace and Wat Phra Keo**, and then a short 20–30B ride by *tuk-tuk*/taxi over to **Vivanmek**. Set out early, and dress reasonably well—you won't be allowed in the Grand Palace in shorts or sleeveless tops.

Wat Arun

Wat Arun, or the Temple of the Dawn, lies on the west (Thonburi) bank of the river, and is perhaps Bangkok's most striking landmark. Formerly a 16th-century temple called Wat Chang, it was repaired for use as a royal temple by King Taksin during the early 1800s. Its main claim to fame is that it once housed the famous Emerald Buddha—in fact, this was the last home of the venerated image before Rama I founded Bangkok across the river, and moved it over to the Grand Palace. He compensated the monks for their loss by instructing his son (later Rama II) to make this wat 'more glorious than the others'. Rama II obliged by elevating the central spire (*prang*) from 15 metres to a staggering height of 79 metres, leaving the four smaller *prangs* around it to be completed by Rama III. All five *prangs* are in the Cambodian style, inviting comparisons with Anghor Wat (the famous Khmer sanctuary in present-day Kampuchea), and their stucco exterior is completely covered with colourful pieces—some whole, some broken—of glazed Chinese porcelain and crockery. Each of the *prangs* is surmounted with Shiva's trident, and each rests on a series of terraces, 'supported' by rows of angels and demons. The lower terrace has four small pavilions, depicting the four main events in Buddha's life: birth, enlightenment, first sermon, and death. The central *prang*—which you can climb for great views of the river and city—has four niches, each with an image of the Hindu god Indra, seated on his three-headed elephant, Erawan. The niches of the smaller *prangs* contain figures of the Moon god, riding a white horse.

Wat Po

Wat Po, a few river-boat stops upriver from Wat Arun, and on the Bangkok side of the Chao Phya, is one of the capital's largest and oldest temples. Built over an older monastery called Wat Potharam, it was begun by Rama I in 1793, and later added to by Ramas III and V. It's open 8 am to 5 pm daily, admission is 10B, and guides can be hired at the entrance (120B for one or two persons). Look out for Guide No. 5—a real performer! His tour often starts with an inspection of two giant statues, of Chinese

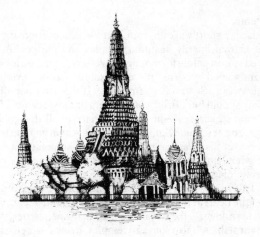

Wat Arun

55

mandarins wearing European dress. 'Hat like Johnny Walker', is his opening gambit, 'They have stick! Look like Johnny Walker . . . a bit!' If you want to wander round on your own, turn right inside the entrance (then left, past a brace of bronze lions) to find the *bot*, which lies in a private courtyard. This enclosure is surrounded by double galleries, containing 394 seated Buddha images. The three-tiered roof of red and yellow tiles is supported by a colonnade of square pillars. The huge teakwood doors at the east and west walls, beautifully inlaid with mother-of-pearl, are examples of superb work-manship. The substructure of the main chapel features bas-relief marble panels—recovered from Ayutthaya's ruins—showing scenes from the *Ramayana* epic. The *bot* itself contains an ancient bronze Buddha and, in the altar, some of Rama I's remains. Moving on, you'll spot the 'Four Great Chedis' in another private courtyard. Rama I built the green *chedi*; Rama II, the white and yellow *chedis*, and Rama IV, the highly elaborate blue one.

Wat Po's main attraction, located in the western courtyard, is its enormous Reclining Buddha. This measures 46 m long and 15 m high, and represents the Buddha entering Nirvana. Built of brick, covered in gold leaf, it was commissioned by Rama I and donated to the monastery by Rama III. The soles of the feet are of special interest—covered with mother-of-pearl. They are inscribed with the 108 'extraordinary signs' by which a true Buddha is recognized.

Wat Po was Thailand's first open university, and today it offers courses in acupuncture, herbalism and massage. Its traditional 'medical massages' are famous. They are given in a small hall near the main entrance, last one, glorious hour, and cost 120B. If you're here *just* for the massage, there's no need to pay the 10B entrance to the temple—just slip in the side-door, always left slightly ajar, on the eastern side of the compound. The best time to show up is 7 am—by 10 am, all the masseurs are usually booked. Wat Po also has an amazing night market—fizziest between 7 pm and 9 pm—with hundreds of foodstalls selling cheap, tasty meals. It's a great place to hang out in the evening.

The Grand Palace

The Grand Palace, a short walk up from Wat Po, and overlooking the river, is a whole square mile of extraordinarily beautiful temples and palaces. A vast, glittering Dis-neyland of gilded spires, colourful mosaics, jewel-encrusted shrines, gargoylish Chinese figures, and landscaped gardens, it's an absolute sensory overload—and not to be missed! As one awestruck traveller remarked, 'If this isn't one of the wonders of the world, it certainly should be!'. Bring your camera or movie camera (8 mm only), and lots of film. Also bring sunglasses—the reflected glare of all this gold and glitter is quite blinding! There are a few guides knocking around, whom you can bargain down to 100B an hour. Otherwise, just wander round in dazed stupefaction like most people do. There's a free guidebook given on admission, which few people can follow. Still, who cares. It's all quite magnificent!

The Grand Palace was built by the early kings of the Chakri dynasty, and was—in Rama I's time—the heart of the capital. Its wide compound of high white walls contained the King's private residence, the Royal Secretariat, the Ministries, the army barracks and the royal elephant stables—also some 50 temples, many covered with dazzling sheets of gold leaf. It was, effectively, a city within a city, which could be defended in times of

56

trouble. Even up until recently, it remained the residence of the king and the governing centre of the country.

Tours of the palace generally start at the **Royal Coins and Medals Pavilion**, just inside the entrance. This is an air-conditioned mini-museum of coins (including Ayutthayan pebble-coins gathered from the sea-shore, polished, and carefully carved on each side), gold-encrusted spittoons, uniforms, photos, and various other royal paraphernalia. Within the compound, track down the two beautiful halls of audience—the **Amarinda Vinichai Hall** (used for coronations) and the traditional Thai-style **Dusit Maha Prasad** which is considered the finest building here. It contains a famous stone 'throne seat' slab hewn by Ramkhamhaeng, King of Sukhothai, in 1292. Both halls date to around 1783, and are closed on weekends. Don't miss the **Chakri Palace**, an impressive structure built in the Italian Renaissance style in 1876.

Wat Phra Keo (The Temple of the Emerald Buddha)

The centrepiece of the Grand Palace—the one thing that everybody comes to see—is **Wat Phra Keo**. This is the king's personal chapel, the only wat situated inside the royal palace itself, and the most important temple in Thailand. It was built by Rama I (completed 1785) to house the country's most sacred object—the **Emerald Buddha**. This tiny image, just two feet high, is made of fine green jade—not emerald at all. It is believed to be over 1000 years old, and to have originated from Ceylon or Northern India. It first came to light in Thailand in 1436, when a large plastered Buddha image in Chiang Mai revealed a crack—and its hidden treasure! It later travelled from one Lao capital to another, depending on the power of each, and came to Vientiane. From there, it was brought to Thonburi by Chakri (later Rama I) in 1778. The present king changes the Buddha's robes three times a year—dressing it in blue for the rainy season, gold for the cool season, and in diamond-studded finery for the hot season. Protocol is very strict at this temple—shoes must be left outside, photographs are not allowed inside, and pointing your feet at the altar is taboo. These preliminaries observed, you can relax and gaze up in awe at the tiny figurine perched up on a high dais, lit by a single spotlight, and enjoy the beautiful friezes running round the walls, which tell the story of Buddha's life.

The Grand Palace and Wat Phra Keo are open 8.30 am to 11.30 am, 1 pm to 3.30 pm daily. The audience rooms are closed on Saturday and Sunday. The 100B admission ticket also includes entrance to Vivanmek Palace. To get your money's worth, see both places the same day—Grand Palace first, Vivanmek second. Doing it the other way round, you'll have to pay twice!

Vivanmek Palace

Located at Uthong Nai Rd (off Rajavithi Rd, next to Dusit Zoo), Vivanmek—or 'Paradise on the Cloud'—is a beautiful L-shaped teakwood palace, built at the turn of the century as the home of Rama V. Packed with royal regalia, period furniture, worldwide *objets d'art*, 'magic' carpets and interesting old photos, it's quite possibly the best sight in Bangkok. Novelty exhibits include the first typewriter used in Thailand, the country's first shower (in the king's bathroom) and a quaint porcelain pig nestling in a velveted black box which was a present from Rama V to a queen born in the year of the pig. Vivanmek is open 9 am to 4 pm daily—though you should arrive at 3 pm at the latest, to catch the last guided tour in English. These tours, which run every hour (on the hour) are excellent. The guide concludes her commentary with 'Now, ladies and gentlemen, you can take photographs at the backside . . .' She's referring to the rear of the palace, which is the **only** place where photography is allowed. Having wound on your camera, enjoy the scenery. Vivanmek lies within beautiful gardens, surrounded by canals, and is the ideal picnic-spot to relax after a hard day's sightseeing! Admission is 50B—but free, if you arrive with a 'combination' ticket from the Grand Palace.

National Museum & More Temples
(by boat, taxi, and on foot; full day)

Wat Benchamabopit – National Museum – National Art Gallery & National Theatre – Wat Mahathat – Wat Suthat – Wat Traimit

Wat Benchamabopit
Wat Benchamabopit, the popular **Marble Temple**, is located on Si Ayutthaya Rd—between Chitralada Palace (sometime residence of King Bhumibol) and the National Assembly building, This beautifully symmetrical temple was built in 1899 by Rama V over a smaller earlier structure called Wat Thai Tong (Wat of Five Peers). Made of Italian Carrera Marble, it is considered one of the finest examples of modern Thai architecture. It's certainly far less glitzy and gaudy than most Bangkok temples, and Westerners find its restrained charm and elegance very satisfying. It overlooks a peaceful *klong*, full of fish and turtles, with pretty little bridges guarded by laughing Chinese statues. The white *bot* covered with red glazed tiles (also from China), is flanked by rustic Javanese pavilions, each containing a Buddha image (one in bronze, seated on a *naga*; the other is Burmese, in white alabaster). The chapel interior is very subdued—the walls look papered, and all the decoration is on the ceiling. Behind the *bot*, there's an enclosed courtyard with a gallery of 51 Buddha images—mostly copies—from various styles and periods. This has examples from India, Burma and Japan, and is the perfect place to bone up on Buddhas before doing any serious *wat*-spotting! The resident Buddha image inside the *bot* is itself a copy—being modelled on the Buddha Chinaraj in Phitsanoluke.

The Marble Temple is home to some of the Buddhist world's most intellectual monks. If here at the weekends, you'll often witness an ordination ceremony. Best time of day to visit is early morning (around 7–8 am), when the monks are chanting in the chapel. Several monks here speak good English, and enjoy talking to foreigners. Admission to the temple is 10B, and it's open till 5 pm daily.

The National Museum
This lies on the far side of the Pramane Ground (if coming in by river boat, get off at Grand Palace pier), and is open 9 am to 12 noon, 1 pm to 4 pm daily—except Monday and Friday. Admission is 20B, and free guided tours in English are given on Tuesday (Thai Art and Culture), Wednesday (Buddhism), and Thursday (Pre-Thai Art). You'll need to leave the Marble Temple at 9 am at the latest to catch them—all tours start at 9.30 am sharp.

The National Museum, formerly the Palace of the Front (built 1783 as the residence of the *upraja* or deputy king), is one of the largest and best-presented museums in Asia—it contains over 1000 exhibits ranging from neolithic times up to the present

58

Bangkok period. A very extensive complex with several well-stocked exhibition halls, you'll need the guided tour to cover it comprehensively in under two hours. There are three main galleries—Thai History (to the rear), History of Art and Archaeology, and Minor Art and Metals (in the old palace building). The museum's most famous item is the **Phra Buddha Singh**—one of three such in Thailand—which, next to the Emerald Buddha, is the most venerated Buddha in the country. It originated from Sukhothai, and lives in the small Buddhaisawan chapel, formerly used by the *upraja* for his devotions. Elsewhere, there's a large collection of Buddhas from various periods (including a lovely 9th-century Padmapani—Bodhissatva—reminisicent of a truncated Venus de Milo), displays of dance masks, puppets and costumes, a weapons room (with elephant war apparel), and—in the Coronation Room—a whole hall of royal funeral chariots, the largest of which is 40 feet high, weighs 20 tons, and took 290 men to move!

The National Theatre
The National Theatre is next to the museum, on Na Phra That Rd. It's a modern building, which stages the most authentic Thai dramas and performances of classical dance in Bangkok (tel 2215861 for programme details). The **National Art Gallery** on Chao Fa Rd, opposite the National Theatre, shows traditional and modern exhibits by Thai artists. Admission is free, and it's open the same times as the museum (tel 2812224 for details of current exhibitions).

Wat Mahathat
Wat Mahathat is a short walk south of the museum, at the Pramane Ground. Also known as the 'temple of the great relic', it's a famous meditation *wat* where instruction classes are given to the public. The unusually austere *bot* is said to be the largest in Bangkok, and contains a sacred relic of the Buddha. Most times of the day, Wat Mahathat is a positive hive of activity—there's a pleasant courtyard here, beautifully laid out, full of students dying to practise English on foreigners, and to show them round their classrooms. At the weekends, the temple has a wonderful vegetable and food market—come in the afternoon, and bring your camera!

Wat Suthat
Wat Suthat, Dinso Rd, is a short 15B *tuk-tuk* ride from Mahathat. Commenced by Rama I (completed by Rama III), this large temple is mainly notable for its fabulous 18th-century murals—witty scenes of animals, nature and everyday life, full of zest and vitality. These are inside the *bot*, which features a unique double-roof and a covered gallery full of seated Buddhas. In the grounds, there's the usual assortment of Chinese ballast figures (mandarins, dogs, lions, etc), also a lot of original stuff you won't find at any other *wat*. Worthy of special mention are the lovely, low-key gardens with bonsai trees and exotic flowers, and the two beautiful pavilions, with majestic standing Buddhas and leaping bronze horses. There's a great atmosphere here too, enhanced by myriad monks, chanting or meditating.

Wat Traimit
Wat Traimit (Temple of the Golden Buddha) is near Hualamphong railway station on Traimit Rd, and is a nice spot to wind up a day's tour. This is a small, modest *wat* with

one big attraction—the solid-gold Buddha image, 3 metres high and weighing 5½ tons which resides in a small private chapel. When first discovered upcountry, this 'Golden Buddha' was believed to be just a concrete image. But then, when it was being transferred to Bangkok, it fell from a crane, lost some of its thick plaster coating, and revealed its true nature.

An exceedingly fine piece (in the Sukhothai style, probably 13th century), the Buddha sits in a tacky bathroom-pink room, surrounded by plastic lotuses and fairground paraphernalia. The kitsch donation box with 'the covered cement parts from Golden Buddha' is a masterpiece of tat! Still, there's no denying the simple power and dignity of the image itself. Included on nearly every city tour itinerary, the Golden Buddha is open to view from 8.30 am to 5 pm daily.

Other Sights

Jim Thompson's House – Suan Pakkard Palace – Rose Garden Resort – Kamthieng House – Snake Farm – Floating Market – Ancient City

Jim Thompson's House

Jim Thompson's House (Soi Kasemsong, off Rama I Rd) is a traditional Thai-style dwelling containing one of the finest private collections of Oriental art in Thailand. The building comprises six old houses, five of which were floated downriver from Ayutthaya. Jim Thompson himself was an American who settled in Thailand after WWII, and who contributed substantially to the revitalization of the Thai silk industry—primarily, by replacing vegetable dyes with colour-fast artificial dyes. He lived in Bangkok until 1967, when he went on holiday in the Cameron Highlands of Malaysia, and disappeared without trace. Jim Thompson was a great collector of (now priceless) antiques, and his house has now been turned into a private museum, of great interest to anyone interested in Thai art. There's an exquisite collection of Sino-Thai *Bencharong* (five-colour) pottery, a wooden palace full of china mice, the front door of a Chinese pawn shop, and all manner of weird and wonderful curiosities. He was also a great interior decorator and you can see the use of his Thai silk fabrics throughout the house. Jim Thompson's is open 9 am to 5 pm, Mon to Sat. Admission is 80B (students under 25, only 30B), and includes a good one-hour guided tour. Photography is not allowed.

Suan Pakkard

Suan Pakkard Palace is near the junction of Sri Ayutthaya and Phayati roads, opposite New Amarin Hotel. This is similar to Jim Thompson's House—i.e. five traditional Thai houses in an attractive garden setting, housing Asian art treasures—but is different enough to make a visit worthwhile. The centrepiece of this palace 'museum'—lovingly assembled by the late Princess Chumbot of Nagar Svarga—is the delightful **Lacquer Pavilion** which she received from her husband on her 50th birthday. It is said to have once graced a royal residence in Ayutthaya, and has been beautifully restored. Elsewhere, look out for bronze geese, chinese lions, a model of a royal barge, prehistoric Ban Chiang artefacts and huge carp in the pond. The Japanese-style semi-enclosed gardens make a perfect, tranquil retreat from the noise and bustle of the city. Admission to Suan Pakkard is 50B, and it's open from 9 am to 4 pm, Mon to Sat.

Kamthieng House
Kamthieng House at Soi 21 (Asoke) off Sukhumvit Rd is open 9 am to 4 pm, Tues to Sat, admission 25B. This attractive northern-style house has interesting displays of hilltribe costumes and farming implements. From Suriwong, it's a No. 16 bus to Siam Centre—then another bus (Nos. 25, 40, 48 or 71) along Sukhumvit.

Snake Farm
Red Cross Snake Farm on Rama IV Rd (corner of Henri Dunant Rd) is the world's second-largest snake farm, established in 1923 to produce vaccines and sera to treat snake-bites. There's an hour-long 'venom extraction' show daily at 11 am. Admission to the 'farm' is 10B (an extra 10B for camera-users!), and it's open 8.30 am to 4 pm, Mon to Fri.

Thonburi Floating Market
The Floating Market at Wat Sai (Thonburi) is now very commercialized. Most of the genuine traders have now moved elsewhere to do business, and the few Thai ladies still paddling around selling their wares are being paid 20B a day (by the mass of souvenir shops here) just to show up! Unless you want to see boatloads of Japanese tourists photographing other tourists, forget it. The best bet for getting to Thonburi floating market is to take one of the tour boats that leave from the Oriental Pier—otherwise you will have to hire your own boat. The alternative floating market, at Damnoen Saduak (100 km (60 miles) west of Bangkok), is also firmly on the tourist map but is still worth a visit—for the time being. Independent travel there from Bangkok is difficult—and many people either go from Nakhon Pathom (see p 85 for full details) or take a set tour from a hotel.

Rose Garden Resort
Rose Garden Resort is situated some 30 km southwest of Bangkok. This is plastic Thai

Floating Market

culture for package tourists—a snippet of a wedding ceremony, a snatch of Thai boxing, a bamboo-pole dance, an elephant trooping up and down collecting rides, and a few women in traditional costumes charging fat fees for photos. Few travellers get much out of this kind of 'instant Thailand'. The long bus journey (3 hours return, minimum) and the stiff admission fee (140B—shows start 3 pm daily) are further deterrents. Rose Garden is best done on a conducted tour, and is only worth doing at all if you haven't time to look for real Thai culture elsewhere.

Ancient City

Ancient City (Muang Boran), 33 km southeast of Bangkok, is 200 acres of land imaginatively landscaped into a map of Thailand and filled with impressive replicas and reconstructions of famous monuments and temples from all over the country. It was built between 1962 and 1967, for the benefit of Thai people who couldn't afford to tour their country or to see its beautiful sights. Since then, it has become a tourist attraction of sorts—though surprisingly few people go there. Ancient City is an excellent way of seeing Thailand in miniature in the shortest possible time. Most of its buildings are half to two-thirds actual size, and include a number of sights that just don't exist any more. A classic example is the reconstructed **Samphet Prasat Palace**, a richly ornate 14th-century Ayutthayan building, the original of which was destroyed two centuries ago. It cost 10 million Baht to build, and was the private donation of just one man. Elsewhere, there are reconstructions of a Thai village (complete with opium shop) and an Ayut-thayan floating market. Ancient City is best visited on a set tour, being too far from Bangkok for easy independent travel. Tour operators often combine it with the nearby **Crocodile Farm**, which has 30,000 crocodiles, disco-dancing elephants and so-called 'friendly' tigers ('you can pat them like dogs', joked my guide). Most of the crocs end up as handbags, belts or shoes, or as 'crocodile curry' (the speciality dish here). Admission is 80B.

RECREATION

Bangkok's major hotels offer a wide range of sports and recreational activities, including golf, tennis, bowls, health clubs, massage parlours, gymnasiums and swimming pools. Horse-racing takes place every Saturday (from 12.15 pm) at the **Royal Bangkok Sports Club**, Henri Dunant Rd (tel 250181), and every Sunday (from 12.15 pm) at the **Royal Turf Club of Thailand**, 183 Phitsanoluke Rd (tel 2823770).

Dance

Thai Classical Dance is best seen at one of the city's Thai-style restaurants, which lay on special shows in with the cost of a set 'traditional Thai' dinner. Two of the best places are **Baan Thai**, Soi 32 Sukhumvit Rd (tel 3913013) and **Piman**, Soi 49 Sukhumvit Rd (tel 3918107)—both restaurants have dance shows from 7.30 pm to 9 pm nightly (250B a head). Other good bets are **Bussaracum** and **Silom Village** in Silom, and **D'Jit Pochana** in Sukhumvit. Some large hotels, like the **Oriental**, the **Indra Regent**, and the **Dusit Thani** (Rama IV Rd), also offer classical dance shows as part of an evening meal. To see professional dance and drama, without the culinary trappings, visit the **National Theatre** (see p. 59). This has shows most days at 10 am and 3 pm.

Thai Boxing

Thai Boxing is an exceptionally popular spectator sport in Bangkok. Unlike Western-style boxing, contestants can use almost any part of their body—even knees and elbows—to inflict damage on their opponents. Each fight is preceded by much bowing, prayer and ritual by both boxers, and a live band (or screeching tannoyed music) whips up the baying crowd to a fever-pitch of excitement. The Thais really get into it, though many Westerners don't—all the preparatory ceremony, plus all the dancing about for the first few rounds, tends to leave bored tourists staring into their popcorn just when the *coup de grace* (often the only kick, or rabbit-punch, of the match) is administered. Quite incredible amounts of money are won and lost at these tournaments, and the audience reaction is correspondingly delirious. Best Thai boxing is at **Ratchadamnoen Stadium**, Ratchadamnoen Ave (next to TAT tourist office). Bouts run from 6 pm to 10 pm every Monday, Wednesday and Thursday, and from 5 pm on Sundays. **Lumpini Stadium**, on Rama IV Rd is more centrally located. There's boxing here from 6 pm every Tuesday, Friday and Saturday. Seats cost between 80B and 200B. For any atmosphere at all, get a ringside seat.

Thai Massage

Traditional Thai Massage is a marvellous experience. It lasts between one and two hours, costs between 120 and 150B an hour, and totally relaxes you in mind, body and spirit.* The spiritual home of Thai massage is **Wat Po**, near Bangkok's Grand Palace. Here you can get a wonderful medicinal massage for 120B an hour, or learn the art yourself. Courses last two and three weeks, and cost between 2000 and 3000B. There are several good places offering ancient massage' (i.e. no monkey business!) in Bangkok. Try **Marble House**, in the Pizza Hut lane at the Rama IV end of Suriwong Rd (tel 2353519, open 10 am to midnight). Or—for therapeutic Japanese-style massage—**Chiropractic Massage**, Soi 44 Charoen Krung, near Shangri-La Hotel (open 8.30 am to 7 pm, Mon to Sat). For an adventurous 'bath massage'—perfectly safe, and enjoyable for both men and women—try **Takara** on Patpong 2 (6 am to midnight). A very good, cheap going-over (only 80B an hour) is given at the parlour next to New Fuji Hotel, Silom. Genuine massages like this are often found attached to, or near, the better hotels. Beware of 'body' massages offered on the street—these are, as one tout delighted in telling me, 'where lady lie on you and massage your body with hers!' Intrigued, I asked him for his card. It said 'Put yourself in our hands. After this massage, you'll think you're dead and gone to *heaven!*' 'Nuff said?

NIGHTLIFE

Bangkok has the liveliest, least inhibited nightlife in the East. It also has a growing reputation as the 'Brothel of the World'. With an estimated 500,000 of the city's female population now engaged in 'entertainment-related activities', the capital is now being accused of sitting on an AIDS time-bomb. Whether one believes the figures or not (one-third of the three million tourists who visited Thailand in 1987 are said to have spent time with a prostitute) there is no doubt that Bangkok's nightlife is aimed specifically at the unaccompanied male tourist. Prostitution is illegal in Thailand, and AIDS is said not to exist in this country, yet every morning sees a flood of 'ladies of night'

---

* If you've a weak back, or don't want your knuckles cracked, you have to tell the masseur in advance. Just point at any sensitive areas you don't want touched and say *Mai*, and they'll leave those bits alone.

pouring out of the city's hotels. And as the target area of prostitution, Patpong, becomes included in more and more package-tour itineraries, worldwide concern is mounting.

Most travellers, of course, have little interest in 'sandwich' massages, painted transvestites, or child prostitutes. They can enjoy various other forms of after-dark entertainment—fun discos and coffee bars, live jazz and Western music etc—and even hit the red-light areas without either losing their dignity or taking home a nasty disease. The trick is to go in a group—far safer and more enjoyable than wandering around on your own—and to look 'poor'. I spent five nights researching Patpong's bars and clubs—the first four nights, I dressed casually and received no hassle whatsoever. The last night however, I wore a smart 100B shirt, and was bodily assaulted within 30 seconds of arrival! It's generally a good idea to have no more than 500B in your pockets—that way, even if you get talked into trouble (bar girls can be *very* persuasive!), you won't be able to afford it!

Patpong is the original red-light area of Bangkok, first patronized by American troops on leave from Vietnam, and now kept just as busy by plane-loads of foreign tourists. Named after a Thai-Chinese millionaire who owns most of the district, Patpong divides into four parallel streets—Patpong 1 & 2 (girlie bars), Patpong 3 (gay bars/ transvestite shows) and Patpong 4 (Japanese restaurants and massage parlours). By day Patpong is mainly a business district; around 6 pm the bars open and the area takes on a whole new face. Dotted between airline offices, travel agents, bookshops and restaurants, are scores of girlie and go-go bars. They're all pretty much the same—thinly-disguised pick-up joints for unattached males, with loud disco music, smiling girls bopping around on a stage wearing numbers, and customers sitting apprehensively in swivel-seats waiting for the inevitable tap on the shoulder and a low, purring 'Herrrro Sir, you like me?' A couple of bars have a small dance floor where you can bop around yourself—quite fun in a group—while the go-go dancers look on, applaud or even join in. Western men are often asked to buy colas for the girls (they get 15B for every 40B drink you buy). To avoid confusion, and possible bill-padding, pay for each round of drinks as it comes. The cost of a beer is 45/50B, and you'll need to make sure there's no cover charge before entering. Many bars have a 'Happy Hour' between 8 and 9 pm, when drinks are half-price.

Some of the bars have 'live shows'. These are illegal, and are usually held upstairs—giving the performers a chance to vanish when the police arrive. Bizarre props are used in these shows, and visitors quickly learn to expect only the unexpected—feathered darts whistling past their ears, airborne bananas plopping into their drinks, and girls opening Coke bottles and playing mouth organs in the most unorthodox fashion! Few people find the acts erotic or a turn-on—some even find them boring. Western women and couples need feel no apprehension entering these places—the Thais are a very tolerant lot! Certainly, being inside a bar is often far safer than being on the street, running a gauntlet of persistent touts offering all kinds 'services'. You're also safe in places like **Bookseller**, between Patpong 1 and 2 (a great bookshop, stocking maps, guides, fiction etc), **Trattoria da Roberto** in Patpong 2 (mellow Italian restaurant), and the nearby **Napoleon restaurant** (fantastic live jazz nightly). Shopping is good at Patpong market—fake watches at knockdown prices of 250B to 400B, and novelty gifts of mounted tarantulas!

For a tour of Patpong, start at the cosy **Toby Jug** pub at 185 Silom Rd. This has darts, cheap draught lager, and steak 'n' chips. From here, it's a short stroll down to Patpong 1, where you can drop into the **Safari Bar**, for a quick bop on their small dance-floor. Good sounds here, and minimal hassle. After this, if you're curious to see a show, cross over to **Queen's Castle**, a good 'straight' place with drink prices written on the wall. For something less tame, try **Pussy Alive** ('Happy Pussy Hours 6–9 pm')—the most outrageous bar in Patpong, guaranteed to mist up your spectacles. The more sedate **Firecat** ('We are not just another typical go-go bar—we are Upstairs.') has an incredible magician show—if you want to see a guy stick a boathook in his eye, jam two screwdrivers up his nose, and swallow a sword (then lift a 50 lb weight with his teeth) go no further. Before the bars close (around 1 am), pop over to the excellent **Rome Club** in Patpong 3. This is a great disco, with a highly professional transvestite cabaret at 1 am nightly. Admission is 160B (two free drinks) on Friday and Saturday, 80B (one drink) other days. If you're still raring to go after Rome's (closes 2 am), just hop in a *tuk-tuk* and ask your driver to take you to the nearest late-night hotspot—he'll always know one!

Soi Cowboy, a small bar-street located behind Sois 21/23 Sukhumvit Rd, is 'easy man's Patpong'. None of the bars have girlie shows, and the atmosphere is far less 'hard sell'. Drinks at all bars are around 40B, and there's no hassle to buy the girls one. Bars come and go, but current favourites are **Tilac** (new, Patpong-style), **Jukebox** (professional, pleasant) and **Ruby Star** (small, friendly). The popular **Sweetheart** bar is run by Kob, who knows all the late-night coffee shops—important, since all Soi Cowboy's bars close at 11 pm. In Soi 23, there's a delightful Dutch-British pub called **Lord Mike O'Henry**. 'I do nothing special', says manager Henk, 'just make food for hungry people!' He does that, and much more. Henk cooks superlative Dutch, European and Thai dishes, stocks some of the best draught beer in Bangkok, and provides bar games, soothing classical music, and even free handrolling tobacco!

Washington Square between Sois 22 and 24 Sukhumvit Rd, is another pleasant night scene—with a small cluster of bars and restaurants, a couple of cinemas, and lots of cheap foodstalls. There's a definite American flavour to Washington Square—the busy **Texxan** restaurant-bar has New Orleans-style soul food and Creole dishes like shrimp and crabmeat gumbo as well as charcoal-grilled burgers and marinated steaks. The Swiss-run **Happy Night** has a free barbecue every Friday, from 3 pm onwards. The **Hole In One**, run by Klaus from Sweden, is a popular ex-pat bar. As is the **Ex-Pats Retreat**, with wholesome pub grub, European-Thai dishes, darts, snooker, games and videos.

Discotheques in Bangkok are absolutely amazing. Take for instance, the **Nasa** at 999 Ramkamhaeng Rd—on a Saturday night, a capacity crowd of 4000 people can be boogying-on-down here! If the wild atmosphere, giant wall-videos, and laser-lighting fail to impress you, then the 'sci fi show' (where a spaceship emerges to the music from *2001 A Space Odyssey* and showers the dancers with balloons) certainly will! Nasa even has a rest-room, where burnt-out revellers are revitalized with hot face towels and back massages! Admission here is 140B (two free drinks) on weekdays, 180B (three drinks) at weekends. There are many Thai-style discos like this, catering mainly for the very agile Thai youth—average age 19, girls wearing high fashion, guys posing in padded-shoulder jackets and dark shades. The fabulous **Paradise** disco, in Arun Amarin Rd, (just across the river in Thonburi) is where the classiest Thais go. It's supposed to have the 'sexiest' sound system! Several big hotels have European-style discos, but they're not half as much fun.

SHOPPING

Bangkok's reputation as the Bargain Centre of Asia is well-deserved. The only problem with shopping here is choice—there's too much of it! There are seven main shopping areas used by tourists in the capital. Broadly speaking, there's little difference in price between them—though the range of products does vary from area to area. Thus, Chinatown is known for its gold jewellery, Silom for its silk, Sukhumvit for its leather goods and tailors, Siam Square for its high-fashion boutiques, Banglampoo for its hippy hilltribe ware, and markets like Pratunam and the Weekend Market for everything rolled into one! The best general buys in the capital are silk, jewellery and fake designer goods.

Designer Copy

Bangkok is the Capital of Copy, famous for its cheap fake watches, leather goods, clothes and accessories—all expert rip-offs of famous designer names. Unrestrained by Western copyright laws, Thai entrepreneurs produce copies of every luxury product known: fake Rolex Oyster watches (only 500–700B—the real thing costs £1400!), imitation Lacoste T-shirts, Gucci leather purses and bags (complete with 'Made in Italy' stamp), and Christian Dior perfumery. All the big brand-names—Ralph Lauren (the current favourite), Hugo Boss, Yves St Laurent, Benetton and Giorgio Armani—are represented, and with prices this low, it takes real willpower to keep your credit card from going over the limit! Hard bargaining will buy you brand-marked underwear and socks for 30B (75p), 100% cotton T-shirts for 120B (£3), 60% cotton T-shirts (They shrink, and the crocodiles fall off!) for 45B, designer leather belts from 100B, Louis Vuitton suitcases and briefcases for (respectively) 600B and 800B, and all manner of Cartier, Charles Jourdan and Givenchy copy accessories at very low prices—handbags at 300B, wallets at 120B, cigarette cases and key holders less than 80B. In Bangkok, you can buy an entire new wardrobe for less than £50—three cotton T-shirts (£8), jeans (£3), trousers (£3), sweatshirt (£10), track shoes (£10), underwear (£2) and two pairs of black plimsolls (£7). You should check the quality of every item, but in general all copy goods are of a pretty high standard. Bangkok's vast range of imitations can be found all over the city—primarily in Silom Rd, Sukhumvit Rd, Siam Shopping Centre, and Pratunam Market.

Silk

Thai silk is among the best in the world—strong, lustrous and very durable. It is dyed in rich colours which hold very well and woven in beautiful designs. Thick in texture, light in weight, it is both warm in the winter and cool in the summer. Silk usually comes in bright colours (often *too* bright for Western tastes, though subtler shades are also usually available), and costs anything between 180B and 280B per yard, depending on grade and quality. You can test silk for quality by giving a handful of the material a good, hard squeeze. If it settles quickly back into shape without a wrinkle, you've got top quality silk. The Silom-Surawong area is the best general hunting ground for superior Thai silk at reasonable prices. You can't go wrong at well-established places like **Design Thai** on Silom Rd, or **Jim Thompson's Silk House** on Surawong Rd. Jim Thompson's sells a lot of original designs not found anywhere else. Thus the high prices—380B for silk ties, 275 to 320B for scarves, 380–450B a yard for dress/suit material. Two or three times a year though (usually in August and mid-December), there's a clear-out sale in J. T.'s car park—and you can pick up top-quality silk at half the usual retail price. A couple of excellent tailors—**Julie Thai Silk**, 1279 New Rd (tel 2358197), and **Bon 3 Ltd** (opposite Julie's), offer much cheaper silk (180B a yard for dress material) and can make up the latest fashion in dresses (from 2500B), lined men's jackets (from 3000B), trousers (silk 700B; cotton 500B) and silk shirts (from 750B)—all within 24 hours. Also good for readymade or made-to-measure silk is **Thai Silk Shop**, just below Central Department Store, Silom. But if you're into serious silk shopping, get a list of silk factories from your embassy, and do the rounds—factory prices are wholesale, often 20% cheaper (if you buy in bulk) than in the shops.

Tailors

It's generally better to go to a proper, well-established tailor than cheapie places which may produce inferior work. While men are fairly easy to fit out (men's suits made in Bangkok are classic), women should really visit a dressmaker or tailor with a picture of the design they want, or even a whole pattern. That way, they get exactly what they want. People generally buy their suit and shirt material in Silom or Chinatown, and bring it to the tailors of Sukhumvit (concentrated down Sois 4 and 11) for making up. A first-class Tailor, like **Raja** in Soi 4, will make silk shirts for 250B, suits for 2000B, and dresses for around 700B. Lots of places, like **Siam Suits** near The Trocadero Hotel, Silom, will produce a good-quality men's wool suit, along with two shirts and a tie, for £45. However such 'package deals', most commonly offered in the Sukhumvit area, are not necessarily a good thing—the quality of the tailoring often suffers.

Gems & Jewellery

Many of the finest sapphires and rubies mined in Thailand make their way to Bangkok, and are good buys whether of the clear, or star, variety. Jade, star sapphires and rubies are especially good value. So are the popular 9-stone Princess rings (set with topaz, garnet, zircon, emerald, cat's eye, ruby, sapphire, garnet and diamond), which are worn by Thai classical dancers. The quality of all gems and jewellery is generally excellent. Bangkok is now one of the gem-cutting capitals of the world. Prices are rising fast, but at present a fine-quality ruby can be purchased from between US$200 and US$5000 per carat, depending on size and clarity, while a Grade A sapphire will cost somewhere between US$20 and US$500. Beware of synthetic stones though, peddled by expert con-artists. Always buy from a reputable, well-established dealer who provides written guarantees with quality stones, and who gives a receipt. There are many such reliable places round Silom-Surawong area (e.g. **Associated Lapidaries**, 5th floor Jal Building, 1 Patpong Rd), and some in Sukhumvit (e.g. **Tawat Gems**, corner of Soi 3 Sukhumvit Rd). Receipts should clearly state the carat, the percentage of precious metal, and the size and weight of stones. If the item was expensive, and the valuation back home doesn't correspond with what's on the receipt, send the details with a photocopy of the receipt to your local TAT tourist office. Gems can be valued at the **Asian Institute of Gemology**, 987 Rama Jewelry Building, 4th floor, Silom Rd (tel 234930–1). This place also offers an excellent gemology course—just the thing, if you're in Thailand to study or to buy precious stones. To buy top-quality 18K and 22K gold (N.B. 18K Thai gold is only 9K to 14K International) go to **Chinatown**—and be sure to take a Thai or Chinese friend along with you! Gold here is sold by the weight, and the price is pretty standard (currently, around 6000B per 15 grams). It's best to buy it in chain or bracelet form, because you pay only for the gold content—all the workmanship comes free!

Leather

The best bargains in leather are briefcases and large suitcases or bags. Leather boots, shoes and coats have a near-European price—though having them made to order can certainly save you some money. Go to Sukhumvit for leather—this area is famous for its many 'booteries'. Of these, **Chao Phya Bootery** on Soi 11 has the best quality produce, at reasonable prices—pure leather jackets from 3000B, cowboy boots from 1500B, briefcases and handbags from 1000B, women's shoes from 250B to 3000B—you can bargain all these prices down. **Tony Bootery**, opposite Soi 19, also specializes in cowboy boots and ladies' shoes (dyed every colour of the rainbow!). **Siam Bootery** at Soi 12 is a useful place, catering for extra-large or extra-small foot sizes. **Anan Shoes**, between Sois 1 and 3, has well-priced leather shoes, boots and jackets—readymade, or made-to-measure in just two days. Cheap leather goods can be found in most street markets—notably Sukhumvit and Pratunam. But be careful—don't be fobbed off with plastic posing as leather! If you're not sure, hold a lighted match to the item. If the dealer snatches it away, then it's plastic (which will burn) rather than leather (which won't).

Antiques & Bronzeware

Some of the best fake antiques and allegedly old Thai bronzes come out of Bangkok. Take great care that you aren't sold inferior merchandise—lots of fake antiques are sold outside temples. Go to a reputable antique dealer, insist they supply the obligatory permit for exporting genuine articles, and don't pay until you've seen the certificate. Old temple bells and bronze cutlery are popular buys, and you can pick up high-quality Thai art works (pricey, but good investments) at the galleries within the **Oriental** and **Siam Intercontinental Hotel** shopping complexes. The amulet market at **Wat Tachanada**, near Golden Mount, does a nice line in cheap 'lucky charm' souvenirs. Forget about buying antique Buddha heads or *garudas* though—there's a law banning their export for souvenirs. You can apply for an export licence from the Fine Arts Department, but that takes weeks to obtain. Trying to smuggle them out is not a good idea—penalties are particularly stiff.

Woodwork—Bamboo

Beautiful rosewood and teakwood furniture can be found at **Gold Bell Furniture Ltd**, between Sois 28 and 30 Sukhumvit (tel 2586286). Quality buys include elegant Chinese-style dining suites in rosewood, inlaid with mother-of-pearl (40,000B), hand-carved teakwood secretary tables (12,000B), and exquisite Chinese cabinets (from 8000B). Most pieces made here are coated with durable Chinese lacquer—this brings a natural finish to the wood, brings out the best in the grain, and won't scratch or burn. A one-kilo pot of this lacquer costs 1000B—treated furniture is therefore expensive, but made to last! Gold Bell gives a 5% discount on major purchases, and arranges for shipment at an average freight charge of 10,000B. Because it costs little more to send home six items than one, it makes sense to buy big here! **Wamford Antique Furniture**, down Soi 55 Sukhumvit (tel 3900609) makes the same kind of stuff as Gold Bell at half the price, and half the quality. There are some nice Chinese lacquered screens here, and inexpensive blue-and-white china.

For rattan and bamboo furniture, check out **Pippinyo Ltd** on Soi 47, Sukhumvit Rd (tel 2587262). This has delightful patio suites in bamboo—four chairs, chaise longue and coffee table—for just 5000B. There is another factory next door where you can make comparisons in price and quality.

Boutiques, Department Stores & Markets

For jazzy Thai-style clothing (i.e. non-designer outfits), visit the high-fashion boutiques and department stores of Bangkok. If they haven't got what you want in stock, they'll copy it from any design you supply (turn up with a copy of 'Vogue' or 'Elite'), sometimes within hours! They are especially useful for *farangs* with big feet and long legs, who just can't find shoes or trousers to fit in ordinary Thai shops! **Siam Shopping Centre** on Rama IV Rd is 'Boutique City', with four floors of amazing high-fashion clothing, nice jewellery and souvenirs. This is where all the Thai rich kids come—also many backpackers and travellers, determined to buy at least one smart outfit to complement their usual wardrobe of drawstring Banglampoo pants and Samui T-shirts! The nearby **Mah Boohn Krong Centre**, just off Siam Square, on Phyathai Rd, is similar to the shopping centres of Singapore—it has just about everything. Here are clothes, jewellery, hi-fi stuff, 'Dunkin' Doughnut, and a fine exhibition centre.

For readymade clothes, try the 'haute coutoure' boutiques between 31 and 37 Sukhumvit—some of the most fashionable clothes in Bangkok are sold here. The 43-floor **Baiyoke Building**, behind Indra Regent Hotel, is the tallest structure in the city. It has fashion shopping arcades (floors 1 and 2), a cheap food centre, a cinema, a 24-hour snooker club (floor 4), wonderful views from the roof! Below it, the sprawling **Pratunam Market** at the corner of Rajaprarob and Phetburi roads, falls into two sections—a huge covered market crammed with stylish, colourful clothes (*very* cheaply priced!), and an endless street market selling best-deal Ralph Lauren (Polo) sweatshirts at 200B, and copy designer watches at only 200B (steel strap) or 300B (leather strap). Pratunam also has many good tailors and a host of inexpensive *kai yang* and noodle stalls. **Central Department Store**, 306 Silom Rd, is one of the largest and best stores in Bangkok, with smart, casual Thai clothes on the upper floor (where there's nearly always a sale); and an amazing dairy section (fresh yoghurt and Australian cheese!) on the ground floor. Over at Banglampoo, **New World Department Store** offers similar cheap clothing deals, with sales on the fourth floor. **Banglampoo Market**, off Chakrapong, is a buzzing honeycomb of shops, stalls and boutiques selling everything from gold chains and jewellery (almost as cheap as Chinatown), to colourful shirts (100B), smart trousers (from 150B) and summery cotton-print dresses (150B to 250B). **Ko-Sahn Rd**, also off Chakrapong, is good for hilltribe produce, Burmese wall-hangings, fake antiques, and cheap knick-knacks. The **Weekend Market** at Chatuchak Park, behind the Northern Bus Terminal, sells all this stuff—and much, much more—at really low prices. It takes place every Saturday and Sunday (7 am to 6 pm) and is by far the best general shopping market in Bangkok—with everything from quality leather shoes and arty T-shirts to disembered tailors' dummies and old car hub-caps. There's even a pet section, where women squat around offering snakes, irridescent green beetles, and strange squirrel-like things on leads (Thai hamsters?) as pets! The weekend market is a long way to go for your shopping (an hour from town, on bus Nos. 77 or 112) but worth it. Come on a Sunday, when there's more choice of produce—and less traffic!

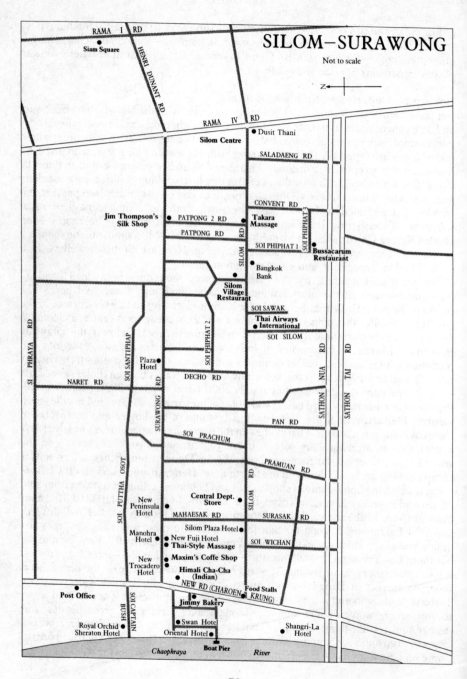

SILOM–SURAWONG

Not to scale

RAMA I RD

Siam Square

HENRI DUNANT RD

RAMA IV RD

Dusit Thani

Silom Centre

SALADAENG RD

CONVENT RD

Jim Thompson's Silk Shop

PATPONG 2 RD

SILOM RD

Takara Massage

SOI PHIPHAT 3

PATPONG RD

SOI PHIPHAT 1

Bussacarum Restaurant

Bangkok Bank

Silom Village Restaurant

SOI SAWAK

Thai Airways International

SOI SILOM

SI PHRAYA RD

SOI SANTIPHAP

SOI PHIPHAT 2

SILOM NUA RD

SATHON TAI RD

Plaza Hotel

NARET RD

DECHO RD

SATHON

PAN RD

SURAWONG RD

SOI PRACHUM

PRAMUAN RD

SOI PUTTHA OSOT

New Peninsula Hotel

Central Dept. Store

SILOM RD

MAHAESAK RD

SURASAK RD

Manohra Hotel

Silom Plaza Hotel

New Fuji Hotel

SOI WICHAN

Thai-Style Massage

New Trocadero Hotel

Maxim's Coffe Shop

Himali Cha-Cha (Indian)

Post Office

NEW RD (CHAROEN KRUNG)

Food Stalls

SOI CAPTAIN BUSH

Jimmy Bakery

Royal Orchid Sheraton Hotel

Swan Hotel

Oriental Hotel

Boat Pier

Shangri-La Hotel

Chaophraya   River

70

Where to Stay & Eating Out

Bangkok is a sprawling capital with no real centre. Instead of one, there are half-a-dozen main shopping/business/tourist areas—each with its own identity, atmosphere and facilities, each offering something different to the foreign visitor. Before deciding which base is right for you, read this section carefully.

Silom-Surawong

If Bangkok can be said to have a centre at all, this is probably it. Silom-Surawong is the city's most important business and financial district, with many airline offices, banks and travel agencies. The huge **General Post Office** on New Road (actually an old road, built 100 years ago!) is a popular meeting-point for travellers—everybody comes here to post parcels or collect mail from home. Conveniently close to the Chao Phya River, Silom is a good base for sightseeing. It also has many shops, restaurants and hotels (including the prestigious Oriental), plus entertainment centres like Patpong and Silom Village. The cost of living is, however, higher here than in other parts of the city.

WHERE TO STAY

The Oriental Hotel, 48 Oriental Avenue (tel 2360400: tx 82997 ORIENTL TH) is one of the oldest and best-known hotels in the East. Over a century old, it has elegant rooms (from 3100B single, 3400B double) luxurious fittings and an unparalleled view across the river. Even if you can't stay here, it's fun to drop in for evening cocktails on the terrace, and watch the sun going down over the Chao Phya. The Oriental is a place that any traveller would like to spend at least one night. There's a choice of rooms either in the new tower block, or (better) in the stylish old building, with suites named after the rich and famous—Noel Coward, James Michener, Joseph Conrad etc.—who have stayed here. One chap reported spending a sleepless night in Barbara Cartland's bright pink suite for a fee of 11,000B. The hotel's **Sala Rim Naam** restaurant is world-famous. Come here either for the Siamese buffet lunch (12 noon to 2 pm daily, 180B), or for the Siamese Dinner & Dance (7 pm to 10 pm nightly, around 500B). Arrive a little early, and go for a leisurely amble through the old building checking out the 'Authors' Lounge', with its Authors' Menu listing the favourite dishes of past literary guests or enjoy the string quartet in the lobby!

The **Shangri-La** at 89 Soi Wat Suan Plu, New Road (tel 2360280; tx 84264/5 SHANGLA TH) is arguably Bangkok's best hotel—brand-new and very impressive. The lobby is so vast, that arranging to meet anybody in it is a waste of time! The whole layout of the hotel, on the river's edge, is superb. It's worth paying 45B for a cup of coffee, just to sit here at sunset, listening to the resident pianist or cellist. Sumptuous suites (all overlooking the river) are offered at 2600B single, 2900B double. Discounts are available in low season, or if booking through a travel agent.

The **Manohra** at 412 Suriwongse Rd (tel 2345070; tx 82114 MANOHRA TH) is excellent value for money. Comfortable rooms from 968B single, 1573 double (best views from 5th floor up), indoor pool, rooftop garden and very convenient location. The nearby **New Fuji** at 299–301 Suriwongse Rd (tel 2345364; tx 84079 PENINHO TH) is a good mid-range bet, with several facilities and amenities, bright, spacious rooms (from

600B single, 700B twin) and personal, cosy atmosphere. Views are best from 3rd-floor rooms and up; guests have use of two swimming pools at nearby associated hotels.

The **Swan Hotel** at 31 Former Customs House Lane (tel 2348594) is central and friendly, just about the best 'budget' buy in Silom. Rooms start at 180B (fan), 290B (air-con), and the quietest ones face into the swimming pool. The Swan also offers a small bar, restaurant and 24-hour coffee shop.

T. T. Guest House, 138 Soi Watmahahrutthanam, Sipraya Mahanakorn Rd (tel 2363053) is ideal for shoestring travellers. Run by three friendly brothers, it has clean rooms (from 80B), a cheap dormitory (50B), a snug TV lounge cum restaurant, good noticeboard and information and a warm, relaxing family-style atmosphere. It's my favourite guest house in Thailand—and a great evening hang-out spot. The middle brother, Sukhum, runs sightseeing trips out to Kanchanaburi—and makes superlative popcorn! Come here on a Saturday night, when the small *wat* behind the guest house holds festive film-show parties (plus market). To get to T.T., go down the small *soi* between Sois 37 and 39, New Rd, and follow the signs.

EATING OUT

For a good night out go to **Silom Village Trade Centre**, near Central Department Store, Silom Road. This has mid-priced Thai, Chinese, European food and seafood in an attractive outdoor setting. Good handicrafts and shopping mall, and live music with classical Thai dancing nightly. Don't pay 280B for the upmarket dance show upstairs (it's a rip-off). Instead, be seated by 7 pm downstairs (by the stage) for traditional Thai music at 7.30 pm, followed by dance extracts at 8 pm. No charge for this show, but you're expected to order a meal. A 3-course dinner (nice dishes are Beef Green Curry, Stuffed Baked Pineapple, Spicy King Prawns or Fried Sea Bass) shouldn't come to more than 220B—if it does, check the bill for padding!

Bussaracum, 35 Soi Pipat 2 (off Convent Rd) offers Thai cuisine at its finest beautifully presented and served. The service is slick and there is live classical Thai music, and great cocktails. Special dishes include *Kao Tang Na Tang* (crispy rice chips with minced pork and mint dip), *Poo Phim* (deep-fried crab meat and shrimp), *Yum Miang Moo* (minced pork, chicken, prawn, garlic and peanuts seasoned with lemon juice) and delicious *Choo Chee Goong Nang* (thick prawn curry with straw mushrooms). Eat well for around 500B per head. Advance-book this place (tel 2358915)—it's very popular.

Rossokul in New Rd (not signed, look for violet building with tiled interior) is an inexpensive Thai-style restaurant with a cafe atmosphere and great food (it's run by the Asst Catering Manager of the Oriental Hotel!). Most dishes are 60 to 80B, and the speciality is duck. **Prakhai**, next to New Fuji Hotel, Surawong Rd, offers good-value Thai/Vegetarian set dinners at 99B, but rather lacks atmosphere. **Buttercup**, c/o Manohra Hotel, Surawong Rd, is a really good Thai-European restaurant, with an all-you-can-eat buffet luncheon at 80B (plus 10% service) from 12 noon to 2 pm daily. **Ring On** restaurant, Silom Rd, does marvellous proper Thai food blowouts at 100B, and **Shangri-La** (above Silom Village) is a Chinese restaurant well-known for its savoury Shanghai-style food, mid-priced. Dress smartly for the trendy **Thank God It's Friday**, at Silom Plaza centre. This is a very select place, serving Thai-European 3-course meals at around 150B. Enjoy live jazz here on Friday and Saturday evenings.

Himali Cha-Cha, off New Road (near Swan Hotel) is an Indian restaurant with a chef who cooks good North Indian food (around 100B a head) and who claims to have been the personal cook of Mountbatten in India. **Whole Earth**, 93/3 Soi Lang Suan, Ploenchit Rd (tel 2525574) is a mid-priced, intimate vegetarian restaurant with acoustic music upstairs, videos downstairs. **Manfred's Bakery**, at Royal Orchid Sheraton Hotel, Siphaya Rd, makes yummy German-style gateaux, chicken croissants, fancy breads etc. **Kwan Nam Hiang**, New Rd, is another good bakery, offering 26B continental breakfasts and lightning-quick service. It's far better than **Jimmy Bakery** across the road. **Kew Gardens Pub & Restaurant**, 311/2 Suriwongse Rd (opposite Manohra Hotel) is a mellow Swedish-run pub with darts, snacks and cheap draught beer. It's open 10 am to midnight.

Sukhumvit

Sukhumvit Road is one of the three longest roads in Thailand, extending right up to the Cambodian border! Only a short stretch of it—from Soi 1 (where it joins Ploenchit Rd) to Soi 63 (the Eastern Bus Terminal)—has really been developed for tourism. Sukhumvit saw its heyday from 1975 to 1982, when it was heavily patronized by oil people on R & R. Since then, the oil crash and the geographical expansion of tourism (mainly to Silom and Siam Square), has led to a swift decline. Today, Sukhumvit is something of a tourist wasteland, occupied mainly by oil-rich Arabs and German businessmen. Noisy and rather impersonal, this area is now geared to the wealthy and powerful, and the lone shoestring traveller may feel out of place. However, very many Western couples and groups have a ball in Sukhumvit—they love its ritzy hotels and restaurants, its fashionable boutiques and tailors, and its raw, vital street action. The busy market between Soi 5 and Soi 7, is a bright, noisy fiesta of food stalls, bars and souvenir shops, and it's fatal to leave your hotel even for a pack of cigarettes—you'll return with a pair of Lacoste underpants instead! Sukhumvit certainly has its seedy side—from Sois 2 to 6 is a maze of massage parlours ('Feeling is Darling'), short-rent condominium apartments ('Cabbages and Condoms'), suggestive bars ('Farang Connection', 'Deep Diggings') and neon-lit brothels—but elsewhere it's quite respectable. Shoppers like this area, but sightseers don't—most of Bangkok's temples are over an hour away by taxi. Best day to visit Sukhumvit is Sunday—when the traffic is less frantic.

WHERE TO STAY
High-class hotels in Sukhumvit are remarkably good value for money. A case in point is the well-established **Ambassador**, 171 Sukhumvit Rd (tel 2510404; tx TH 82910) with rooms at just 1000B single, 1200B twin, and no fewer than 7 restaurants and 5 coffee bars. A vast complex of leisure facilities, shopping arcades and food parlours (with low-fat Bulgarian yoghurt!), many guests need a guided tour to find their room! The **Flamingo Disco** here is just about the best-value nightspot on a Saturday night—full of young middle-class Thais getting their 100B's worth (admission, plus two free drinks). As a single *farang* man, this is one of the few places in Bangkok where you can meet a 'nice' Thai girl (i.e. one who's not there for business!).

The brand-new **Regal Landmark**, 138 Sukhumvit Rd (tel 2540404; tx TH 72341) lacks the Ambassador's character, but has bags of style and class. Rooms start at 1800B single, 2000B double, and the higher you go (31 floors!), the better the views. Numerous facilities (pool, health club, squash courts, sauna, beauty parlour, shopping plaza etc.) and possibly the best Chinese restaurant in town. All this, and the longest escalator in Thailand!

The Windsor, Soi 20 Sukhumvit Rd (tel 2580160; tx TH 82081) is a wonderfully peaceful, personal hotel with nice bright rooms at 1300B single, 1400B twin. The restaurant offers a superior 90B buffet lunch daily (11 am to 2 pm) and the 50B cocktails are memorable. **Park Hotel**, No. 6 Sukhumvit Rd, Soi 7 (tel 2525110; cable PARK HOTEL BANGKOK) is a peaceful European-style haven in the centre of the Arab quarter. Sophisticated too, with polite staff, a select restaurant and plush air-con rooms from 500B. The English-run **White Inn**, Soi 3, is a pleasant family-style hotel with large twin-bedded rooms at 550B and an attractive pool with Tudor decorations. The similarly priced **Quality Inn** on Soi 19 (tel 2535393; tx 21145) fully lives up to its name and is very quiet. **Mermaid's Rest**, down Soi 8, is a small, friendly Scandinavian place with economy rooms from 125B (fan singles) to 375B (air-con doubles). Excellent food and cocktails at the snug bar-restaurant, and Texan-style garden barbecues every Wednesday and Saturday evening. The swimming pool is a real bonus! Equally good value is **Miami Hotel**, down Soi 13, with rooms from 120B (fan) to 450B (air-con), a pool, and a 24-hour coffee shop. Very conveniently located for shopping. So is the **Ruamchitt**, curiously located behind a supermarket on Soi 15. The new wing rooms here (300B single, 350B double) are far superior to those in the old wing (from 120B). **Crown Hotel**, Soi 12 (tel 2580318) is clean, if dilapidated, and has cheap air-con doubles for 279B. The popular coffee shop/bar has a jukebox and offers cheap European-Thai food. **Atlanta**, at the bottom of Soi 2, is another budget option, with a nice pool, pretty gardens, and cleanish rooms from 150B (fan single) to 300B (air-con double).

EATING OUT

The famous **D'Jit Pochana**, 60 Sukhumvit, Soi 20 (tel 3913586) serves genuine Thai cuisine in a pleasant open-air setting. Most dishes are 45–60B, and include *Tod Mon Pla Gry* (a famous Thai dish of minced fish kneaded with chilli paste, deep-fried and served with cucumber sauce) and *Gui Hor Buy Toey* (chicken wrapped in toey leaves). There's a fair choice of German, French and Chilean wines here and also a wide selection of Thai-style desserts and fruits. **Bankeo Ruankwan**, 212 Sukhumvit Soi 12, is another reliable Thai restaurant—rather pricey, but just as popular. Ring 2518229 for a table reservation. At the elegant **Sud Sa-Nguan** on Soi 51, you can either order à la carte at between 35B and 50B per dish (try the Hot and Sour Chicken in coconut milk soup and Shredded Fish with coconut milk and chilli paste) or have the set lunch at 120B. Less spicy fare is served at **Lemon Grass** on Soi 24, and **Laikhram** on Soi 49/2—two other good places to enjoy authentic Thai food at under £5 per head.

Every visit to Sukhumvit should include a meal at **Ambassador City Food Complex**, Ambassador Hotel. Here you can select from over 30 different vendors selling dishes of every nationality—including Thai, Chinese, Japanese, Italian, Muslim, Vietnamese and Korean. Most dishes are around 20B, and you pay by coupon. Look out for the small zoo with flamingoes and mandarin ducks! The upstairs **Bangkapi Terrace** restaurant offers 'Asian Buffet' lunches at 100B, and succulent steaks and grills.

Sukhumvit is well-known for its international cuisine. **Leena Restaurant** (down Soi

74

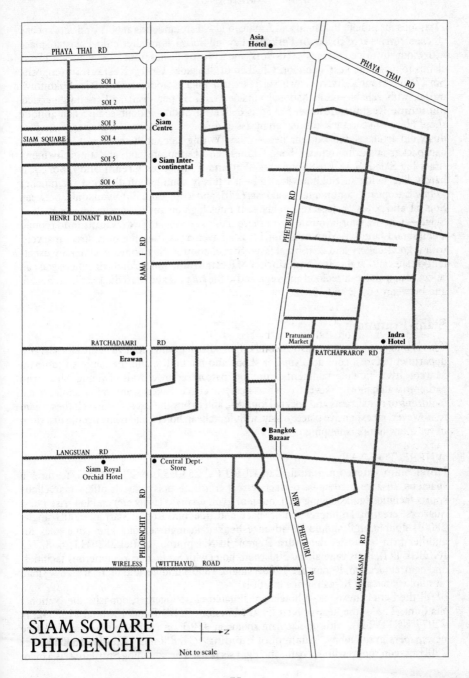

PHAYA THAI RD

Asia Hotel

PHAYA THAI RD

SOI 1
SOI 2
SOI 3
SOI 4
SOI 5
SOI 6

SIAM SQUARE

Siam Centre

Siam Inter-continental

PHETBURI RD

HENRI DUNANT ROAD

RAMA I RD

RATCHADAMRI   RD

Erawan

Pratunam Market

Indra Hotel

RATCHAPRAROP RD

Bangkok Bazaar

LANGSUAN   RD

Siam Royal Orchid Hotel

Central Dept. Store

RD

NEW

PHETBURI RD

PHLOENCHIT

MAKKASAN RD

WIRELESS   (WITTHAYU)   ROAD

SIAM SQUARE
PHLOENCHIT

Not to scale

75

11) is tops for Indian, Pakistani and Arabic food—tasty tandooris at 60B, and very special chicken curries at 55B. **Town Talk,** just beyond Soi 33, is another Indo-Pakistani place with modestly priced set meals (50–90B) and à la carte dishes from 30B. Manager Hassa claims to make the best Tandoori Chicken in Bangkok! **Tiptop Restaurant** (opposite Soi 27) and **Dave's Bistro** (down Soi 4) are two quiet escapes from the noisy Sukhumvit traffic, with reliable multi-national cuisine (50–75B per dish) and friendly service. **Sometime Restaurant** down Soi 55 is delightfully odd—it doubles up as an antique shop! Here you can tuck into Italian pizzas and American burgers, while bargaining for dusty old artefacts and Buddha heads. **New Young Lee,** at the corner of Soi 15, is a backpacker favourite—cheap Thai, Chinese and European food, and a novelty menu (Ears Pig Salad, Sour Lost Soup etc). **Wattana Food & Ice Cream Shop,** Soi 19, is hardly like being in Sukhumvit at all—it's totally soundproofed! Good set lunches (Thai/European), continental breakfasts (28B) and ice-cream. But **Svenson's,** between Sois 51 and 53, is *the* ice-cream palace. It rates high on any ice-cream lover's Richter Scale—'Choose your favourite flavours from this earthshaking extravaganza and rebuild a childhood fantasy!' **Maxim's,** Soi 11, is a haven away from the busy street markets, with a good bakery and 27B breakfasts. **Street food** in Sukhumvit is generally excellent—especially at the **Seafood Market & Restaurant,** 388 Sukhumvit (where you can select your own fresh seafood and veg), and at the *kai yang* and roast duck stalls on Soi 55, and between Sois 2 and 15.

Siam-Pratunam

This is Bangkok's biggest and busiest shopping district, with about 10 of the city's largest department stores, countless smaller shops and boutiques, and the famous Pratunam Market. It's a big entertainment centre too, patronized by crowds of young Thais who gather to watch movies (several cinemas here), to chat in bakeries and coffee shops, to eat in dozens of restaurants and cocktail lounges, and to buy the latest fashion clothes. Siam is, however, an expensive place to stay, with few cheap hotels, and many people just drop in for a few hours' shopping.

WHERE TO STAY
Hotel Siam Intercontinental, Rama I Rd (tel 2530355; tx TH 81155), features a spacious 26-acre garden—a perfect retreat from the noisy city. It offers marvellous sports facilities (golf, jogging trail, outdoor gym, *petanque* lawns etc) and low-rise guest quarters, creating an impression of space and freedom. Rooms start at 2600B single, 2800B double, and should be advance-booked in high season. The same goes for another firm favourite, the **Indra Regent** in Rajaprarob Rd (tel 2520111; tx 82723 INDRA TH). This is a palatial 500-room hotel with exotic decor, numerous facilities, and central location. Rooms are 1700B single, 1800B double, and there are a few small 'studio' rooms at a bargain price of 800B.

All the better inexpensive hotels are situated close together, opposite the National Stadium. Top of the heap is **Krit Thai Mansion,** 931/1 Rama I Rd (tel 2153042; tx 72077 KRIT TH), with immaculate rooms at 450B, an elegant coffee bar, and free newspapers in the lobby. **Muangphol Building,** 931/8 Rama I Rd (tel 2153056), has 280B air-con rooms with *hot* bath, and tight security. The adjoining **Star Hotel** is a bit of a knocking shop, but still the best deal in this area. Run by a friendly Thai family, it offers clean air-con rooms from 250B.

EATING OUT

Hotel Siam Intercontinental has a popular seafood restaurant with special buffet lunch (100B) between 11.30 am and 2.30 pm or order à la carte favourites like the Seafood Basket (feeds three, for 200B). For a big splurge, try the 395B Thai dinner-dance show, commencing 7 pm every Monday and Thursday.

Indra Regent Hotel serves a Thai buffet lunch (in the Garden Bar) from 11.30 am to 2 pm at 150B; the **Indra Grill** features black pepper steak with a glass of red wine at 200B; and the coffee shop serves 'kao tom buffet' (rice porridge to you!) at 70B from 10.30 pm to 2 am. The Indra also does the best hotel-based Thai 'dinner-dance' in Bangkok, recommended by many and a great evening out. It costs 250B if you want dinner (be seated 7.30 pm latest), and 125B if you're only here for the show.

Tokyu Food Centre, at the corner of Rama I and Phyathai roads, has a vast eating area on the 6th floor—hundreds of dishes (mainly Thai, Chinese, Japanese and European) from 15B to 40B. Many travellers end up here—it's pleasantly air-conditioned, and everything is cooked freshly on the spot. **Kloster Bier Garden**, behind Siam Shopping Centre, is a real party in the evenings—draught Kloster beer (20B a glass, 100B a giant flagon), inexpensive Thai dishes, whole suckling pigs roasting on spits, and lots of local atmosphere. Opposite Siam Centre are **Pizza Hut, McDonald's** and, down a side street, two decent Chinese restaurants, both called **Scala**. Nearby, down New Phetburi Rd, some of Bangkok's best seafood restaurants prepare every imaginable fish in the finest Thai and Oriental style.

Banglampoo

This area, near Ratchadamnoen Avenue, started out as a colourful old market: its name derives from its village (*Bang*) origins and the many *lampoo* trees found when the first *klong* was created here. Today, Banglampoo—more particularly, its 'freak street' of Ko-Sahn Rd—is one of the great travellers' centres of the world. This is where most of Bangkok's budget guest houses and cheap flight agencies are concentrated, and it's real backpacker ghetto-land! The main recreations in Koh-Sahn Rd are eating Western food, buying hippy clothes, booking cheap travel, looking out second-hand books and pirated cassettes, checking out guest house noticeboards, watching videos, and meeting other Western travellers. Ko-Sahn certainly isn't Thailand—well, it doesn't pretend to be. It's okay for people with time to hang out, but not really for short-time visitors. After all, if you've only a few days in Bangkok, why spend them sitting with other white faces, eating honey toast, cheese sandwiches and banana pancakes? Still, Banglampoo is cheap, near to the river, just a few minutes' drive from zillions of temples!

WHERE TO STAY

From November to February, Banglampoo's two main guest-house districts—Ko-Sahn Rd and Chakrabongse Rd (Soi Rambutri)—are often packed out. With rooms as cheap as 50B (single) and 80B (double), it's easy to see why. In high season, the best time to look out a room is around 8 am in the morning, when many residents catch early buses out to Samui, Phuket or Chiang Mai.

Places to stay in Ko-Sahn Rd include **160 Guest House** (new and clean), **Bonny's** (a firm favourite), **Top** (behind Bonny's, quiet and secure), **Good Luck** (The family breaks down and weeps when guests try to leave), **C.H.** (friendly, with sun-roof), **Chart** and **Wally's** (both popular, with videos), **Hello** (24-hour restaurant and *loud* video—get a top-floor room!) and **P.B.** (with snooker hall, manic mascot monkey and a manager who trains Thai kick-boxers). One superior place, the **New Nith Charoen** (tel 2819872) has clean, spacious rooms with bath at 140B. Behind this hotel, down a narrow alleyway, are the **Sunee Porn** and **Lek** guest houses. Both have good rooms, laundry service, baggage deposit, and offer river trips. The alleyway leads out to **Viengtai Hotel** at 42 Tanee Rd (tel 2828672). This is a rare luxury option with a pool, a restaurant, and air-con rooms at 520B single, 620B double.

Siam Guest House ('Our rooms are very cosy and bright cos every room has a window') is located just off Koh-Sahn, at 76 Chakrapong Rd. This has a lovely lady owner and good little restaurant. Pity about the noisy traffic! Over the road, behind the temple, is **New Siam** at 21 Soi Chanasongram, Phra Athit Rd. The best rooms here are the 100B doubles, upstairs. Nearby there's **New Apple** (friendly, good roof views), **Ngampit** (quiet, run by friendly family) and **Roof Garden** (the owner, Froggy, is a real travellers' friend!). In this area, most travellers favour **Chusri 1 Guest House** (it's the best of the 3 'Chusris'!) at 61/1–2 Soi Rambutri.

Further afield, two recommended guest houses are **CAC**, just above Wusuk Kasek Rd (homely, with clean 60B rooms) and **K.T.**, off 62/66 Puranasart Rd, off Astandang Rd (five minutes walk from Ko-Sahn; large rooms from 60–90B; dormitory 45B). A couple of upmarket options, with air-con rooms around 500–600B, are **Royal Hotel**, 2 Ratchadamnoen Klang Rd (tel 2229111) and **Thai Hotel**, 78 Prachthipatai Rd (tel 2524967). The new **Youth Hostel**, 25/2 Phitsanoluke Rd (tel 2820950) has huge double rooms at 150B, dorm at 35B, a reading room and cafeteria.

EATING OUT
Choose between cheap Thai snacks down at Banglampoo market, or cheap and rather dull Western fare in and around Ko-Sahn Rd. Most guest houses in Ko-Sahn have restaurants and videos. **Suzi's Bar** doesn't have a video—just great food, and the best banana milkshakes (say some) in the world!

Soi Ngam Duphli—Soi Si Bamphen

These two streets—located off Rama IV Rd, opposite Lumpini Stadium—comprise Bangkok's second cheap guest house centre. Handy for foreign embassies, Patpong, Silom and Siam Square, this area bears many comparisons to Ko-Sahn Rd. It has the same kind of travel agencies, pancake restaurants and hilltribe/hippy clothes, but differs in being noisier (lots of traffic), seedier (drugs, prostitutes etc.) and yet more authentically Thai. Many long-stay travellers hang out here.

WHERE TO STAY
For comfort, stay at **Malaysia Hotel**, 54 Soi Ngam Duphli (tel 2863582). This has air-con rooms at 298B (single), 366B (twin), nice pool and coffee shop, friendly staff and a 24-hour video service. You'll want a room at the back of the building, away from the

traffic. Once popular as a base for American vets, the Malaysia has recently declined—it seriously needs renovation. **Boston Inn**, Soi Si Bamphen, had the same problem, but is currently overhauling itself. By now, it should have new 300B air-con rooms, in addition to the old 150B fan-cooled ones. The Boston has a good pool, with a mysterious sign ('Please do not throw cigarette butts over the other side of the wall'). The nearby **Privacy Hotel** (tel 2862339) has pleasant Thai atmosphere and 210B air-con rooms, but is rather run-down.

The best cheapie is **Sala Thai**, a delightful 'daily mansion' with spotless rooms at 100B single, 150B double. It's down a small alley off Soi Si Bamphen, and is often full. **Madame**, in the same alley, is a cosy, ramshackle place run by a lovely Thai lady with a heart of gold. Rooms here are 60B to 100B. **Freddy 2**, at 27/40 Soi Sri Bumphen, is now one of Bangkok's best guest houses with clean rooms (60–100B), an open-air restaurant, sun-roof, novelty T-shirts, an excellent noticeboard, video and good sounds. Freddy himself is a real gentleman. In Soi Ngam Duphli, worthwhile cheapies are **Anna** (rooms at 80B single, 100B double) and **Sweet House Complex**, which has just about everything—crazy but fun staff, bar-restaurant, pool club, travel agency, hilltribe crafts—even a law office! Only the large 130B double rooms are decent though.

EATING OUT

Blue Fox opposite the Malaysia, is a popular air-con restaurant with Western-style food, groovy sounds, a video, and a well-stocked bar. It closes at 11.30 pm, which is a bit of a drag. Over the road, the **Lisboa** offers reasonably priced Mexican food. Next to the Boston Inn, **T. T. Coffee House** has cheap Thai cuisine at around 30–40B per dish. Try *Pla Tod* (tasty fried fish), *Rad Nah* (fried noodle) and *Kao Tom* (chicken rice soup). For a wide choice of 8B curry and rice meals, walk up Soi Ngam Duphli to the pedestrian bridge on Rama IV Rd.

Chinatown

Bangkok's busy and boisterous Chinatown, around Yaowaraj Rd, has been the main centre for trading by the Thai Chinese (the country's largest minority) for the past 200 years. Few people stay here—it's not really a travellers' centre. Most visitors just spend a morning or afternoon enjoyably exploring its numerous narrow alleyways and neon-lit main streets, overhung by high wooden houses, covered in the grime of decades. The **Thieves Market** of Chinatown sells everything imaginable, from Chinese paper lanterns to birds' nests, from motorbike parts to water pumps, but it's antique-hunting and gold-buying that are the main attractions. Chinatown's atmosphere is frenetic, colourful and noisy (the traffic is quite unbelievable!) but it's got some of the best street life and tastiest cheap snacks in Bangkok.

WHERE TO STAY

Hotels in this area are few, and not geared to Westerners. The **New Empire**, 572 Yaowaraj Rd (tel 2346990), is a clean, comfy place—very popular with Indians and southern Thais—with smart air-con rooms for 250B in the quiet new wing. The **Sineiah** (Somboon) at 415 Yaowaraj Rd (tel 2224716), has clean air-con rooms (220B), a cheap Chinese-Thai restaurant, a small tour agency, and a resident astrologer. Of the many murky Chinese-run cheapies in Rong Muang Rd, adjoining Hualamphong Rd, only the **Sri Hualamphong**, with near-adequate rooms at 100B, merits a mention.

GENERAL INFORMATION

Post Office
The GPO on New (Charoen Krung) Rd is open—along with its Poste Restante counter—from 8 am to 8.30 pm Monday to Friday, and from 8 am to 1 pm Saturday and Sunday. It has a useful parcel-packing service, open 8.30 am to 4.30 pm Monday to Friday, 8.30 am to 12 noon on Saturday. Next to the main building, there's a 24-hour international phone call service (inside the telex building). The post office at Soi Nana, Sukhumvit/Ploenchit, also has a parcel-packing service.

Bookshops
Good general bookshops, with maps and guides, fiction and non-fiction titles, are **Asia Books**, Sukhumvit Rd Soi 15, and **Bookseller**, 81 Patpong Rd, Silom. **Elite Book House**, 3/6 Sukhumvit Soi 24, has used and second-hand books (rare and multi-language). **Chalermnit**, 2 Erawan Arcade, Erawan Hotel, Ploenchit Rd, offers a vast selection of English, French and German books (new and reduced-price) in addition to an extensive collection of travel guides.

Travel Agents
Most hotels have travel agencies, offering set tours of Bangkok. But for major tour or sightseeing deals, contact **Diethelm Travel**, 544 Ploenchit Rd (tel 2524041–9), **World Travel Service**, 1053 New Charoen Krung Rd (tel 2335900–9) or **Sea Tour**, Room 414 (4th floor), Siam Centre, 965 Rama I Rd (tel 2514862–9). Most other arrangements—including visas, cheap flights, cut-price bus/rail travel—are best handled by the bucket-shop agencies of Banglampoo and Soi Ngam Duphli. A typical outfit, like **Ronny's Tour & Travel**, 197 Ko-Sahn Rd (tel 2812556; tx 84482), handles visas (Nepal, Burma and India), cheap bus tickets (Koh Samui, Koh Samet, Phuket and Chiang Mai) and cut-price flights (worldwide). One-way flights from Bangkok are very cheap—to London, £170; to New York, £300; to Bombay, £80; to Kathmandu, £90; to Singapore, £35; to Sydney, £370. Other agencies, like **Gold Travel**, 2/4 Soi Sri Bumphen (tel 2866783), and **Chiangmai First Travel Service** in Ko-Sahn Rd, specialize in cheap domestic bus-tickets—to Samet (and back) for 240B, to Chiang Mai for 160B, to Phuket for 300B, and to Samui for as little as 240B (i.e. 120B cheaper than booking through a hotel!). **STA Travel Office**, attached to Thai Hotel, Banglampoo (tel 2815314), is best for rail tickets, travel insurance, and (they'll sell anybody one!) student cards.

Embassies
Most Bangkok embassies receive visa applications between 8 am and 12 noon only, and may require your passport overnight. If you need a visa for India, Burma or Nepal, you don't have to apply yourself—you can get a travel agent (see above) to do it for you. Addresses of major embassies as follows:

ARGENTINA	20/85 Prommitr Villa, off Sukhumvit 49/1. Tel 2590401–2.
AUSTRALIA	37 Sathon Tai Rd. Tel 2872680
AUSTRIA	14 Soi Nantha, Sathon Tai Rd. Tel 2863011, 2863019, 2863037.
BANGLADESH	8 Soi Charoenmit, Sukhumvit 63. Tel 3918070, 3918069.
BELGIUM	44 Soi Phraya Phiphat, off Silom Rd. Tel 2339370–1, 2332237.
BRAZIL	8/1 Soi 15, Sukhumvit Rd. Tel 2572989.
BRUNEI	14th Flr., Orakarn Bldg, Chitlom Rd. Tel 2501483–4.
BULGARIA	11 Soi Ramkamhaeng 11, Hua Mak, Bangkapi. Tel 3143056.
BURMA	132 Sathon Nua. Tel 2344698.
CANADA	11th Flr, Boonmitr Bldg, 138 Silom Rd. Tel 2341561–8.
CHILE	15 Soi 61, Sukhumvit Rd. Tel 3918443, 3914858.
CHINA	57 Ratchadaphisek Rd. Tel 2457032, 2457037–8.
CZECHOSLOVAKIA	197/1 Silom Bldg, 7th Flr, Silom Rd. Tel 2334535, 2341922.
DENMARK	10 Soi Atthakan Prasit, Sathon Tai Rd. Tel 2863930, 2863942–4.
EGYPT	49 Soi Ruam Ruedi, Phloenchit Rd. Tel 2530161, 2538183.
FINLAND	16th Flr, Amarin Plaza, Phloenchit Rd. Tel 2569306–9.
FRANCE	35 Customs House Lane, Off New Rd. Tel 2340950–6.
GERMANY	9 Sathon Tai Rd. Tel 2864223–7.
HUNGARY	28 Soi Sukchai, off Sukhumvit 42. Tel 3917906, 3912002–3.
INDIA	46 Soi Prasanmit, Sukhumvit 23. Tel 2580300–6.
INDONESIA	600–602 Phetburi Rd. Tel 2523135–40, 2523175–80.

IRAN	602 Sukhumvit Rd (between Soi 22 and 24). Tel 2590611–3, 2589322.
IRAQ	47 Pradiphat Rd, Phayathai. Tel 2785335–7.
ISRAEL	31 Soi Lang Suan, Phloenchit Rd. Tel 2523131–4.
ITALY	399 Nang Linchi Rd. Tel 2864844–6, 2864848.
JAPAN	1674 New Phetburi Rd. Tel 2526151–9, 2590234–7.
KAMPUCHEA	185 Ratchadmri Rd. Tel 2525950.
KOREA (S)	Sathorn Thani Bldg, 90 Sathon Nua Rd. Tel 2340723–6.
LAOS	193 Sathon Tai Rd. Tel 2860010
MALAYSIA	35 Sathon Tai Rd. Tel 2861390–2, 2867769, 2863825.
NEPAL	189 Sukhumwit 71 Rd. Tel 3917240, 3902280.
NETHERLANDS	106 Wireless Rd. Tel 2526103–5, 2526198–9.
NEW ZEALAND	93 Wireless Rd. Tel 2518165.
NORWAY	20th Flr, Chokchai Bldg, 690 Sukhumvit Rd. Tel 2580531–3.
PAKISTAN	31 Soi Nana Nua, Sukhumvit Rd. Tel 2527036–8.
PHILIPPINES	760 Sukhumvit Rd. Tel 2590139–40.
POLAND	61 Soi Prasanmit, Sukhumvit Rd. Tel 2584112–3.
PORTUGAL	26 Captain Bush Lane, Si Phaya Rd. Tel 2337610.
ROMANIA	39 Soi 10, Sukhumvit Rd. Tel 2528515.
SAUDI ARABIA	10th Fl, Sathorn Thani Bldg, 90 Sathon Nua Rd. Tel 2350875–8.

SINGAPORE	129 Sathon Tai Rd. Tel 2862111, 2861434, 2869971.
SPAIN	104 Wireless Rd. Tel 2526112, 2528368, 2535132–3.
SRI LANKA	48/3 Sukhumvit 1. Tel 2512789.
SWEDEN	11th Flr Boonmitr Bldg, 138 Silom Rd. Tel 2343891–2, 2330295.
SWITZERLAND	35 North Wireless Rd. Tel 2530156–60.
TURKEY	153/2 Soi Mahadlek Luang 1, Ratchadamri Rd. Tel 2512987–8.
UNITED KINGDOM	Wireless Rd. Tel 2530191–9.
U.S.A.	95 Wireless Rd. Tel 2525040–9, 2525171–9.
U.S.S.R.	108 Sathon Nua Rd. Tel 2349824.
VIETNAM	83/1 Wireless Rd. Tel 2515835–8.
YUGOSLAVIA	28 Soi 61, Sukhumvit Rd. Tel 3919090–1.

Useful phone numbers

Directory Assistance	13
Long Distance Service	100
Ambulance	25221715
Tourist Police	22162069
Tourist Assistance	2810372, 2232126
Immigration Division	2867003
Police	191

Part IV

AROUND BANGKOK

Elephant Ruins at Ayutthaya

The central region of Thailand offers a number of interesting excursions from Bangkok—palaces and temples to the north (**Ayutthaya, Bang Pa In** and **Lopburi**), islands and beaches to the east (**Koh Samet, Koh Si Chang**, and **Pattaya**), culture and countryside to the west (**Nakhon Pathom** and **Kanchanaburi**) as well as wildlife to the northeast (**Khao Yai National Park**). All of these places can be seen on their own, or, more rewardingly, in combination with each other.

NAKHON PATHOM

Nakhon Pathom lies 56 km west of Bangkok, and is a convenient stopover on the way to Kanchanaburi. It has two main claims to fame—first, it's believed to be Thailand's oldest city, founded around 150 BC; second, it's here that Buddhism was apparently first introduced to Thailand by Indian missionaries, probably during the 3rd century BC. The city is known to have been the centre of the powerful Dvaravati empire, which ruled over several city-states in this region from the 6th to the 11th century.

GETTING THERE

By Bus
From Bangkok's Southern Terminal, buses leave for Nakhon Pathom every 15 minutes from 5.45 am to 9.20 pm. The one-hour trip costs 13B.

From Kanchanaburi, there are regular buses (No. 81) to Nakhon Pathom. It's a 1¹/₂-hour journey, and the fare is 16B.

By Rail
There are six trains daily to Nakhon Pathom from Bangkok Noi station, leaving between 9 am and 6.30 pm. The short 1½-hour hop can be done quite comfortably 3rd class (fare 14B).

WHAT TO SEE
The only real reason for dropping in on this busy, dusty town is to visit the impressive **Phra Pathom Chedi**, said to be the tallest Buddhist monument in the world. Mounted on a circular terrace within a large square park, this landmark *chedi* with a huge bell-shaped dome glittering with orange-glazed tiles from China, rises to a height of 127 metres. The original 6th century *chedi* (a much smaller effort) built on this site was badly damaged when the Burmese sacked the surrounding town in 1057. It was restored and covered over by the present much larger, *chedi*, in the 19th century by Kings Mongkut and Chulalongkorn. At each compass-point in the outer courtyard, you'll find a *viharn* (hall) housing Buddha images in various attitudes—one standing, one reclining, one watched over by the holy serpent, *or naga*, and the last overlooked by a beautiful wall-mural of a Bo tree. A replica of the original Indian-style *stupa* stands to the south of the present *chedi*.

The Phra Pathom is the most venerated *chedi* in Thailand. The constant busy traffic of students, sightseers and pilgrims at this sacred spot gives it a lively, effervescent atmosphere. A leisurely perambulation round the huge base of the *chedi* often turns up all sorts of surprises. On my last visit, I saw a 'Thai Dramatics' show (*lakhon* classical dance-drama) next to a Chinese temple, took part in a Thai action film being shot here, was given a guided tour by a posse of adolescent monks dying to learn English. If you want to meet monks, this is just the place to do it! Just below the *bot*, there's a little museum. This is open 9 am to 12 noon, 1 pm to 4 pm, Wed–Sun. Lots of tat here (seashells, stamps, bits of unidentified rock etc.), but also some nice pieces from Ban Chiang and Ayutthaya.

Many independent visitors to Nakhon Pathom are simply passing through—usually to or from Kanchanaburi. To see the *chedi* unhindered by heavy luggage, take a 2B *samlor* to the railway station, and check it in with the stationmaster (he minds bags for free).

Some people stay overnight at Nakhon Pathom, in order to catch the early morning bus out to **Damnoen Saduak Floating Market**, a 40-minute drive south. This is a whole lot better than the much-fêted floating market of Bangkok which is completely ruined by tourism. Buses go to Damnoen Saduak direct from Bangkok's Southern Bus Terminal (No. 78) every 20 minutes starting at 6 am—you'll want one of the first buses out, to be at the market round 8–9 am when it's at its best. From Nakhon Pathom, take a crack-of-dawn bus (6.30 am latest) to Samut Songkhram, asking to be put off at Damnoen Saduak. The two best markets, **Talaat Ton Khem** and **Talaat Hia Kui** are either side of the Damnoen Saduak canal. Alternatively take a water-taxi south to the less commercialized market called **Talaat Khun Phitak**.

WHERE TO STAY & EATING OUT
To stay, choose between **Mitraworn Hotel**, just outside the railway station, with adequate rooms (with bath) for 100B; and **Nakorn Inn Hotel**, off the northeastern corner of the *chedi* (a 5B *samlor* ride from bus or railway station) with cosy air-con rooms

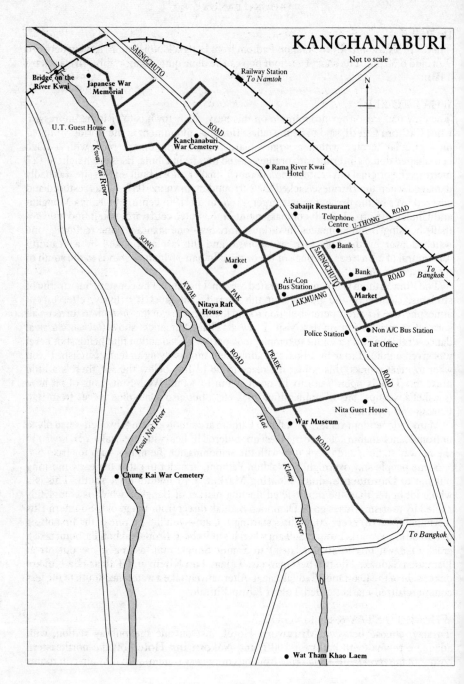

KANCHANABURI

Not to scale

N

Bridge on the River Kwai

SAENGCHUTO

Japanese War Memorial

Railway Station
To Namtok

U.T. Guest House

ROAD

Kanchanaburi War Cemetery

Kwai Yai River

● Rama River Kwai Hotel

SONG

Sabaijit Restaurant

ROAD

Telephone Centre

U-THONG

KWAE

Market

● Bank

SAENGCHUTO

PAK

Air-Con Bus Station

● Bank

ROAD

To Bangkok

Nitaya Raft House

LAKMUANG

Market

ROAD

Kwai Noi River

PRAEK

Police Station ●

● Non A/C Bus Station

● Tat Office

ROAD

● Nita Guest House

Mae Klong River

● **War Museum**

● **Chung Kai War Cemetery**

ROAD

To Bangkok

● **Wat Tham Khao Laem**

at 300B single, 380B double. This place offers 30% low-season discounts, and 6th and 7th floor rooms have the *chedi* views. The Nakorn Inn is also one of the few places in town to enjoy decent food—the pleasant restaurant-cum-coffee shop has good, mid-priced cuisine, with live music thrown in.

For cheap tasty Thai snacks—*kai yang*, satays, spicy sausages on sticks etc—go to the large, sprawling street market between the *chedi* and the railway station. There are lots of inexpensive Thai-Chinese restaurants in this area too.

KANCHANABURI

Some 130 km west of Bangkok, Kanchanaburi is one of the most beautiful provinces in Thailand. If you want to see some real Thai countryside—forests and waterfalls, rivers and mountains, caves and jungles—and don't want to travel all the way to the far north, this is where to come. Kanchanaburi town has a lot to offer in itself, and is also an excellent base for many interesting day-excursions, notably river-rafting down the River Kwai.

The recent discovery of neolithic burial sites in this region has shown Kanchanaburi to be the site of a very ancient civilization. But the present town is of fairly recent origin, having been founded by Rama III in 1833. It lies at the point where two tributaries—the Khwae Noi and the Khwae Yai—meet to form the Mae Klong River. The old town, founded by Rama I as a frontline defence against Burma, is 18 km away.

Kanchanaburi is best known for its associations with the Second World War. It was from here—during 1942–3—that the Japanese army began constructing the infamous 'Death Railway' leading up to Three Pagodas Pass. The idea was to connect Siam with Burma by rail, providing the Japanese with an alternative to their total reliance on sea transport. To carry out this ambitious project—which involved laying 415 km of track over jungle-covered mountains—they put 69,000 Allied prisoners to work and conscripted 200,000 Asians as forced labourers. By October 1943, when the rail link was completed, an estimated 16,000 prisoners and 49,000 Asians had perished, many of them as the result of fearful atrocities.

Today, many of Kanchanaburi's 'attractions' pay tribute to this terrible page in WW II history. Trains still pass across the 'Bridge over the River Kwai', and run up the Death Railway as far as Nam Tok. A War Museum and various cemeteries keep the memory of the heroic fallen alive, and the town itself stands as something of a living reminder of the pointless waste and tragedy caused by war. But this is only one aspect of Kanchanaburi. It doesn't dwell on the past. Rather, it's an extremely friendly and cheerful place—surrounded by breathtaking scenery—which travellers like so much they stay a week or even longer.

Every year, usually at the end of November/beginning of December, Kanchanaburi celebrates River Kwai Bridge Week, commemorating the Allied bombings on the Death Railway in 1945. This festival features a noisy, colourful Light and Sound Show, with lots of fireworks and big bangs. It's very popular, so you'll need to book early. And don't forget the earplugs!

GETTING THERE

By Bus
From Bangkok's Southern Terminal (a 20B *tuk-tuk* ride from Prannok Rd pier on the Chao Rhya river—ask for *either* the air-con *or* the non air-con bus stations—they're separate!), non air-con buses leave for Kanchanaburi every 15 minutes (3-hour trip, fare 23B) and air-con buses every 45 minutes (2¹/₂ hours, 53B). From Nakhon Pathom, buses for Kanchanaburi (No. 81) pick up from the east side of the *chedi*. The 1¹/₂-hour trip costs 22B.

TOURIST INFORMATION
TAT Tourist Office, Saeng Chuto Rd (tel 511200), is next to the non air-con bus station. Good handouts and maps, friendly and helpful staff. Open 8.30 am to 4.30 pm daily.

B. T. Travel Co (tel 511967), just around the corner from TAT, sells daily sightseeing tours by air-con minibus (from 290B). Titinat, the best guide, offers personal tours (only 100B) on a Thursday—her day off. B. T. also have a desk at the Rama River Kwai Hotel.

WHAT TO SEE
There is lots to see and do in Kanchanaburi—allow a minimum of 3 days for sightseeing, and a further day for the river-raft trip. The town and environs invite leisurely exploration by bicycle. There are several hire places (20B a day is average), notably Jakkayanphan shop just below River Kwai 2 hotel. Motorbikes can be hired (200–250B a day) from the Suzuki dealer near the bus station. Short hops around town cost 3B by *samlor*, 5B by *songthaew*. Some *samlor* drivers (e.g. 'Samlor Samsun', who hangs out at the big River Kwai hotel) speak decent English, and offer 'lazy man's sightseeing' tours at 50B for 3–4 hours.

In & Around Town
(by bicycle/*samlor*, 10 km round-trip; full day)

Kanchanaburi War Cemetery – Japanese War Memorial – River Kwai Bridge – Chung–Kai Cemetery – Wat Thum Khao Pun – Jeath War Museum

Kanchanaburi War Cemetery
This suggested tour starts at **Kanchanaburi War Cemetery** in Saengchuto Rd, a 10-minute cycle ride from the town centre. In this cemetery lie the remains of 6982 war prisoners—British, Dutch, Australian and American—who lost their lives building the Kwai Bridge and the Death Railway. The myriad memorial stones, laid out in neat rows within peaceful, well-kept gardens, bear poignant messages ('. . . We think of him still as the same and say—He is is not dead, he is just away') from loved ones who can't forget what happened here 40 years ago. Light relief is provided by the colourful Chinese cemetery next door.

River Kwai Bridge
Cycling 15 minutes further up Saengchuto Rd, turn left (just before the Bridge) down

New Zealand Rd. At the bottom of this is the **Japanese War Memorial**, a rather grim monument erected by the Japanese army to honour the Allied dead. From here, it's only a minute's ride up to the **Bridge over the River Kwai**. This world-famous bridge spanning the Khwae Yai ('large tributary') River, lies some 2 km north of town, and is its main tourist attraction. It's not the original wooden one built by the prisoners which was slightly downstream. This is the later version, assembled from materials brought from Java by the Japanese army (again using POW labour) which had its central spans destroyed by British bombers in 1945. The bridge was rebuilt after the war, and only its curved spans are original. For a real sense of 'atmosphere', be on it when the 10.23 am train passes over on its way to Nam Tok. Post yourself at one of the sentry-points on the bridge, and have your camera at the ready. Listen out for *Colonel Bogey's March* – they sometimes play it on a tinny tannoy as the train passes over! In the evening, return to the bridge for magical sunset views – it really does have a most picturesque location. By the bridge entrance, there's a small Railway Museum, with beautiful old steam engines used during WWII.

Chung Kai Cemetery
From the bridge, take a scenic ride down Patana Rd (parallel to the river) back towards town. Cross the river at the pier below the 'Fitness Park' (a 2B ferry ride), and cycle 15 minutes up the road on the other side—via corn fields and banana plantations—until the **Chung Kai Allied War Cemetery** appears on your left. This smaller, quieter cemetery is built on the site of one of the original POW camps, and is noted for its tranquil, contemplative gardens. Most of the 1750 memorial stones here bear the 'Known to God' inscription for unknown soldiers.

Wat Thum Khao Pun
A kilometre or so above the cemetery—over the railway-line and up the hill—find **Wat Thum Khao Pun**. This is one of many cave temples in the area, and is something of an oddity. On payment of a 5B admission fee, a guide leads you down to a glitzy Buddha image, twinkling with fairy-lights, at the cave entrance. This Buddha encloses a much smaller one found on this spot during a visit by Rama V. The cave is a very sacred spot and there are several reports of local devotees hearing 'ghostly voices' and 'heavenly music' here. As you clamber through the labyrinthine recesses of the cave interior, watch out for gold-prospecting Bangkokites. They turn up every weekend, and ferret around in here looking for the large consignment of gold bars the Japanese army left behind during WWII. Outside the cave, chatty monks play endless games of draughts with bottlecaps.

Jeath War Museum
Back across the river, head right—past floating restaurants and up the hill—until you come to the **Jeath War Museum**. Attached to Wat Chaichunphon, this museum is a replica of bamboo-hut dwellings used by Allied POWs in Kanchanaburi area during WWII. Inside the huts is a rather crude, amateurish (yet curiously effective) exhibition of watermugs, spades, railway spikes, clothing, photographs and sketches which reconstruct various aspects of prisoners' lives, and which give some idea of the suffering they endured. It's a bit over the top, and needs to be viewed in perspective. Whatever, the 20B admission charge levied is excessive—unless you get one of the monks (a friendly lot) to

show you round properly. The name 'Jeath' by the way, is not a misprint for Death. It is made up of the initials of the countries who participated in the building of the Death Railway—Japan, England, America and Australia, Thailand and Holland.

Erawan Waterfall
(by bus; full day)

This is a lovely day-outing, especially between September and November, when the falls are at their best, and the surrounding **Khao Salop National Park** at its most beautiful. Buses go to Erawan every hour, between 8 am and 4 pm, from Kanchanaburi bus station (65 km, 17B). The first bus out is best—you'll want to make a full day of it. Also, lots of local tourists show up mid-afternoon, and then it's definitely a case of paradise lost! Last bus back to Kanchanaburi is at 4 pm.

From Erawan bus station, it's 1¹/₂ km (either walk, or hire a taxi—20B for up to four people) to the foot of the falls. Have the 3B entrance fee to the National Park ready. Erawan comprises seven levels of falls—the climb to the top takes 2 hours, and the scenery gets better and better, the higher you go. Among the attractions are glittering ponds and streams, multi-coloured butterflies, and several species of exotic birds. Bring a good pair of walking shoes for this hike—flip flops or sandals won't do! You'll also need a bathing-suit—each of the lower levels of the falls has a 'swimming pool' (September to December only). Some of the Kwai prisoners were brought to these pools—full of nibbling fish—to have their gangrenous wounds 'cleaned out'! The best swimming is at level 2, an idyllic blue lagoon with a delightful mini-waterfall. Stalwarts who climb all the way up to level 7 get a bonus—the best 'jacuzzi' of their lives!

Death Railway – Nam Tok – Kao Phang Waterfall
(by train and bus; full day)

The 'Death Railway' originally ran all the way from Bangkok to Moulmein in Burma. Today, the only section still in use is the short 50 km stretch from Kanchanaburi to Nam Tok. The two-hour train ride along this route is a fascinating, sometimes nerve-wracking, experience. At certain points, the ground literally drops away beneath the train as it passes over yawning chasms on unsupported wooden sleepers. The story goes that the POWs deliberately made the worst possible job of building the railway. Another story is that the 'Death Railway' is so named because it's such a hazard to travel on. This is, of course, not true. Its title derives from the fact that so many people died making it. Every few yards along its length, a wooden cross marks the last resting place of some unknown prisoner. The sobering statistic is that one person died for each sleeper on the track from Bangkok to Nam Tok. Today, the railway is simply an enjoyable ride through beautiful countryside.

The 10.23 am train for Nam Tok leaves from Kanchanaburi railway station daily (fare 17B). The town of **Nam Tok** ('waterfall') is built on the site of a former POW camp called Tarsau, which was the main jungle base for upriver railway construction camps. From 1943-4, it was also used as a vast primitive hospital, to which tubercular and diseased prisoners were sent by barge from hill camps further up the river. Today, it's a small, sleepy town with nothing worth hanging around for. From Nam Tok station, take a

5B *songthaew* ride (or walk two kilometres) to **Kao Phang Waterfall**. These are very modest falls, nothing to compare with Erawan, but the Thais love it to pieces—splashing about, getting wet etc.

Kao Phang only has enough water to splash about in from June to September. The popular recreation here is to climb up the side of the falls, and make the holy pilgrimage from the top to the elusive **Cave of God**. This cave is a recent archaeological discovery, and is located 2 km behind the falls, down a jungle path. There's a duck up here that's supposed to know the way, but it doesn't. Back on the main road, below the waterfall, you can hitch a bus (15B, 1 hour) all the way back to Kanchanaburi.

River Kwai Raft-trip
(by raft; full day)

This trip is the best thing about Kanchanaburi, and should be booked as soon as you arrive. Several places—including TAT, **Nita Guest House** and **Sunya Rux Restaurant**—offer rafting trips, but they're often heavily subscribed. The best months for river-rafting are November to April, though the season starts as early as September. Trips generally run up and down the Mae Klong River, and include drops at local sightseeing spots. The quality of rafts is very variable, especially if hiring from less reputable places down by the pier. At the time of writing, the best deal is offered by **Sunya Rux**, next to Rama River Kwai Hotel. Sunya offers marvellous one-day trips on his 'houseboat' (actually a 3-section raft—one raft for eating, one for diving, and one for sunbathing) at 200B per person, plus 50B for food. All sorts of fun entertainment is thrown in, including Thai-style water-skiing (i.e. no skis!) hula-dancing, rubber-rings, bongo drums, games, songs and lots of laughs. Worthwhile stop-offs include stunning views over rural Thailand from a hilltop Chinese temple and wonderfully tacky fairground animals at an unusual Thai temple. Sunya also offers 500B two-day trips up to the Burmese border, and four-day 'specials' costing 1000B, which include camping in bamboo forests, expeditions to waterfalls, and visits to remote temples.

RECREATION
Thai-style **massage**—the perfect way to wind down after a hard day's sightseeing—is provided at the parlour just below Kanchanaburi War Cemetery (look out for the modern-style building, with no sign!). Excellent rubdowns are given here, for just 70B an hour.

Thai *lakhon* **theatre**—complete with gongs and xylophones, wistful songs and wild dramatics—is performed most nights (on a small stage mounted on kerosene drums!) in Song Khwae Rd, opposite Nitaya Raft House. Kanchanaburi is one of the few places left on the Thai tourist circuit where this kind of traditional entertainment can still be seen. Don't miss it.

SHOPPING
Best buys in Kanchanaburi are gems—especially blue sapphires from the **Bor Ploy mines** 45 km north of town. Don't shop at the touristy gem shops and jewellers up by the Kwai bridge. Instead, try a reliable backstreet lapidary like **Jumrat Jewellery**, opposite B. T. Travel in the town centre. Blue sapphires sell here from 200B to 20,000B per

carat, depending on cut and quality. Cheaper black star-sapphires (around 400B per carat) make attractive necklaces.

WHERE TO STAY
For luxury, stay at **Rama River Kwai Hotel**, 284/4–6 Saengchuto Rd (tel 511184; tx 78705). This is the only place in town with hot water, and has sombre, but nice air-con rooms at 545B single, 641B double. The disco (the 'Raft') is a big Thai scene on Friday and Saturday nights. **River Kwai 2 Hotel** is a few doors (and a big step) down from its sister hotel. Popular with budget travellers (airy 90B rooms with fan), and with mosquitoes. **Prasopsuk Bungalows**, 677 Saengchuto Rd (tel 511777) is a much better deal, with clean and spacious fan-cooled rooms for 90B, air-con rooms for 250B. Friendly people, good restaurant. **U. T. Guest House**, 25/5 Patana Rd (2 km below the Kwai Bridge) is a pleasant family-style house, with a few cosy 3-bedded rooms (50B per person), motorbike rental, peaceful location and great food (try Briefly Sunny Pork, washed down with Lipton Limited!). Close to Jeath Museum, **Nita Guest House** has clean double rooms at 70B and a popular 25B dorm. Nice garden and cheap cycle hire too. The associated **Nita Raft House** offers peaceful 35B river-raft accommodation. So does **Nitaya Raft House**, at the top of Song Khwae Rd. Living on a raft is okay by day—nice views, romantic atmosphere, sunbathing etc.—but at night you really cook! Superior raft-houses like **Kwai Yai Garden Resort** (tel 511261), 2 km from the Kwai Bridge, are pricey—between 450 and 700B per person. For a full listing of them, contact TAT or B. T. Travel Co.

EATING OUT
The local speciality—*Yeesok* river fish—is best sampled at the **Floating Restaurants** down by the ferry pier. The best of these is **Ruean Ploy** (not 'Rent Boy', as I was first informed!), offering mid-priced Thai/Chinese food, amusing live music ('Elvis rip-offs in Thai' was one description) and effusively friendly doll-like waitresses. Our party took 40 minutes to even place an order! The floating restaurants are particularly good places to watch the sunset.

In town, the travellers' favourite eating place is **Sunya Rux**, next to Rama River Kwai Hotel. Tasty pancakes, great seafood, and cheap breakfasts. The 'Dinner No Spicy' menu offers something called Fried Beef, One Day Light! Sunya is also a cheap guest house, with a mascot monkey who shanghais passers-by in the street. Right next door is **Sabaijit Restaurant**, serving a variety of cheap, palatable Thai-Chinese dishes. Grilled duck and rice, the speciality, is only 10B. The novelty dish is Roast Rib Eye in Sall Crust!

A few people have written in to recommend **Cowboy**, a good little restaurant on the way down to the river from the bus station. Brightly lit and full of Bangkok playboys, it's a popular late-night scene with great live music and phenomenal food and service. Across the road from it, a small Thai food place offers a wide selection of 10B meals, also just about the best seafood in town. **VIP Beer House**, off Patana Rd (1 km below the Bridge), has late-night drinks, a small live band, and a relaxing riverside location. It's the perfect place to round off the evening.

AYUTTHAYA

Just 85 km north of Bangkok lie the stunning ruins of Ayutthaya, Thailand's former capital. Named after the mythical kingdom of Ayodhhya in the Hindu Ramayana epic, Ayutthaya was founded in 1350 by a prince of U Thong (near Suphanburi) who went on to become King Ramatibodi I. Earlier used by the Khmers as a trading outpost, the city's unique situation—on an island at the confluence of three rivers (the Chao Phya, the Lopburi and the Prasak), only 110 km from the sea—soon made it a major trade centre. Over a period of 400 years—from 1350 to 1767—Ayutthaya became one of the greatest and wealthiest cities in Asia. During the 14th and 15th centuries—a period still regarded by the Thais as their Golden Age—the Ayutthayan kings held sway over an empire extending as far north as Vientiane in Laos and as far west as Pegu in Burma. As the capital rapidly outgrew its original 5 × 3 km area, a grid pattern of canals and waterways was dug to enable the incoming armada of boats from China, France, Holland, England, Portugal and Japan to negotiate the city and reach the principal trading points. Astonished European visitors were soon comparing it to Venice. By 1685, when Abbe de Choisy visited with the French embassy, the city walls extended for 10 km and its population exceeded one million. A galaxy of glittering temples had sprung up too, a reflection of the city's burgeoning prosperity. When Glanuis came here in 1682 he found:

> . . .Seventeen hundred temples within Ayutthaya, with at least thirty thousand priests and more than four thousand images of Buddha, all of them gold or gilt . . . The spires of the pagodas and temples were so gilded that in the sunshine they reflected the light so strongly that they disturbed the eyes even from two or three miles away. The King of Siam was indeed one of the richest monarchs of the East.

Ayutthaya was ruled by a succession of 33 kings of various dynasties. The earlier ones were particularly strong, using the new concept of semi-divine kingship to great effect borrowed from the Khmer after the Thais destroyed their capital of Angkhor Thom. Two kings in particular were meticulous law-givers. Ramatibodi excluded practically everybody from giving judgement in court, including:

> Infidels, debtors of the parties, slaves of the parties, diseased persons, children under seven, old persons over seventy, backbiters, covetous persons, professional dancers, homeless persons, the deaf, blind, prostitutes, pregnant women, hermaphrodites, impotent persons, sorcerers, witches, lunatics, quack doctors, fishermen, bootmakers, gamblers, thieves, criminals, and executioners.

And King Trailok (1448–1488) offered death to anyone shaking the king's boat, or allowing stray dogs or love poems into the place. He went easy on anyone who only kicked the palace door—they just lost a foot! Later Ayutthayan kings were less interested in making laws than in collecting white elephants. The more white elephants they accumulated, the higher they were held in esteem. From 1563–4 there was a 'war of white elephants', when an envious Burmese ruler deprived Chakrapat of Ayutthaya of four of his seven prized elephants. It was the beginning of the end. Naruesan the Great recovered Ayutthaya for the Thais a few years later (1587), but it never regained its former power and glory. In 1767, following a series of wars with Burma, Cambodia,

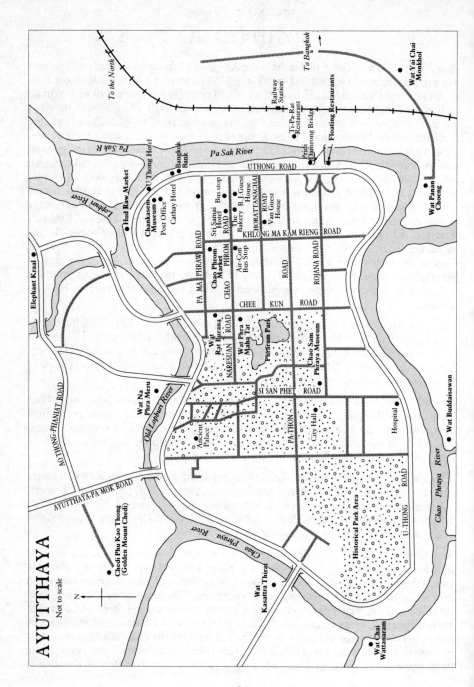

AYUTTHAYA
Not to scale

N

To the North

Pa Sak R.

Lopburi River

Pa Sak River

To Bangkok

Railway Station

To Bangkok

Ti-Pa-Rat Restaurant

Pridi Damrong Bridge

Floating Restaurants

Wat Yai Chai Monkhol

UTHONG ROAD

U Thong Hotel

Hud Raw Market

Chankasem Museum

Bangkok Bank

Post Office

Cathay Hotel

Bus stop

Sri Samai Hotel

The Bakery

B.J Guest House

Van Guest House

HORATTANACHAI ROAD

Wat Panan Choeng

KHLONG MA KAM RIENG ROAD

PA MA PHRAW ROAD

Chao Phrom Market

CHAO PHROM ROAD

Air-Con Bus Stop

ROJANA ROAD

ROAD

Elephant Kraal

CHEE KUN ROAD

Wat Rat Burana

Wat Phra Maha Tat

Phram Park

Chao Sam Phraya Museum

NARESUAN ROAD

Old Lopburi River

Wat Na Phra Meru

SI SAN PHET ROAD

City Hall

Hospital

Wat Buddaisawan

AO THONG-PHANIAT ROAD

Ancient Palace

PA-THON ROAD

Historical Park Area

U-THONG ROAD

Chao Phraya River

AYUTTHAYA-PA MOK ROAD

Chedi Phu Kao Thong (Golden Mount Chedi)

Chao Phraya River

Wat Kasattra Thirat

Wat Chai Wattanaram

94

Luang Prabang and Chiang Mai, the city finally succumbed to its traditional enemy, the Burmese. This time the invaders, determined to destroy Ayutthaya once and for all, razed it to the ground and massacred its inhabitants. When all was done, only 10,000 people were left within its smoke-blackened ruins. The Thais soon regained their independence, but Ayutthaya was never again occupied—its destruction had been so complete.

Ayutthaya today is a small provincial town thinly spread over the vast grid of a once-mighty capital. At one edge lie the temple and the old palace ruins, bleak memorials of a glorious past. A number of temples and towers have been recently renovated, but it's still impossible—surveying the fields of scattered ruins and tumbled buildings—to visualize Ayutthaya's original splendour. Some visitors actually prefer it in its derelict state. 'Ayutthaya was simply *made* to be ruined', is one typical comment, 'you simply can't imagine it being more impressive when it was intact!' Certainly, several of the temples remain majestic in their desolation, and the old city in general exudes a powerful historical atmosphere. This, together with its close proximity to Bangkok, has made Ayutthaya a major tourist magnet.

GETTING THERE

By Bus
From Bangkok's Northern Terminal, non air-con buses leave for Ayutthaya every 10 minutes from 5 am to 7 pm. It's a short 1½-hour journey, costing 17B. From Ayutthaya, buses go right back into Bangkok city centre—very convenient.

By Train
From Bangkok's Hualamphong station, trains leave for Ayutthaya at very regular intervals, from 4.30 am to 11.20 pm. A cheap 3rd class seat (15B) should do for this short 1½-hour hop. Some canny travellers make Ayutthaya the very last place they see in Thailand—Don Muang airport is only 40 minutes down the rail line from here. Ideal, if you don't want to revisit Bangkok!

By River
Bangkok's Oriental Hotel offers a deluxe boat tour to Ayutthaya (600B including lunch). Or you can hire a water-taxi (1500B—you'll need a group!) from the Oriental pier. In either case, it's a long 3-hour trip upriver, another 3 hours back down, and not much time for sightseeing in between.

WHAT TO SEE
The modern town, overshadowed by its neighbouring ruins, is remarkably dull. The only evidence of its 'gangster' reputation is a marked shortage of cheap accommodation and local transport. The local 'mafia' have a monopoly on tuk-tuks, which demand a minimum of 15B for short journeys and 100B for a 3-hour tour of the temples. Fortunately, since Ayutthaya is far too large to explore on foot, there are many *songthaews* and *samlors* prepared to take you from point to point for 5–10B. From the railway station, you can take a 50-satang ferry across the Prasak River into town—far cheaper than a *tuk-tuk*. The station is also a good place to pick up good English-speaking guides. Look

95

out for number one guide, Pock (hairy mole on chin, Philip Marlowe fedora on head, 'silver machine' in the forecourt). Along with other members of the local guide association, he meets tourists off the early trains from Bangkok. It's worth hiring your own guide—you see more and pay less (100B hour) than the standard 600B tours running out of Bangkok hotels daily.

Sightseeing in Ayutthaya can be hot, tiring work—the ruins are very spread out, and are best seen in the cool of the early morning. Certain temple areas, take note, charge 20B for admission (half-price with a student card). Ironically, these are often the ones that have been enclosed in landscaped lawns and robbed of their antique character. Regarding what to see, you can afford to be selective. As Ayutthaya was almost completely levelled, after a while, one chipped *chedi* or mutilated Buddha begins to look just like another. To avoid such repetition, content yourself with seeing half a dozen temples at leisure, and avoid places like the Old Palace and Wat Rajburana where you pay 20B to see hardly anything. Visitors not staying overnight in Ayutthaya can leave their bags in the railway station cloakroom (open 5 am to 10 pm)—useful, if you want to carry on to Bangkok, Lopburi or Sukhothai later in the day.

Temple Tour
(by *tuk-tuk*, taxi; 6–8 hours)

Wat Yai Chai Mongkol – Wat Phra Chao Phanom Choeng – Wat Chai Wattanaram – Wat Buddaisawan – Wat Phra Ram – Wat Mahathat – Wat Na-Phra Mane

Wat Yai Chai Mongkol
Wat Yai Chai Mongkol was built in 1384 and houses the remains of the highest *prang* in Ayutthaya. The famous reclining Buddha left of the entrance has recently been restored, like everything else here. Even the temple's resident community of mangy dogs have been 'renovated'—they're all painted pink with antiseptic! Naruesan the Great erected the impressive *prang*, surrounded by 124 mini-Buddhas, in the 16th century. For good views down over the temple complex, climb the low hill. For self-improvement, study the moral messages ('Loving kindness is personal magnet') pinned to nearly every tree.

Wat Chao Phanom Choeng
Wat Phanom Choeng lies on the Chao Phya river southeast of town and is very old—it was built before Ayutthaya was a capital city. The 19-metre-high seated Buddha (covered in gold leaf) is the largest surviving Buddha image in Ayutthaya, and also one of the very few left intact by the Burmese. On view from 8 am to 5 pm daily, it was built in 1324 by the then king to atone for a terrible crime. He brought the daughter of the Chinese emperor to Ayutthaya for marriage, but unwisely left her down by the pier (below the present temple) to be escorted into the city by soldiers. Assuming he didn't love her, the beautiful princess stayed put in the boat and committed suicide. Wat Phanom Choeng is consequently very popular with Chinese pilgrims, and does a roaring trade in Chinese fortunes. In my case, not so fortunate—'Buddha say', translated my guide, 'you must get sick . . . you must lose money . . . it's not so good, you know!' If you're lucky, you may catch the Khon classical dancers performing here; otherwise, just

soak in the moody, meditative, incense-laden atmosphere. High up on the temple walls, armies of tiny bronze Buddhas can be dimly made out, tucked away in little niches.

Wat Chai Wattanaram

From Phanom Choeng, walk down to the river pier. Here you can liberate a caged tortoise for 10B (i.e. make some merit) and call in on the Chinese Shrine dedicated to the ill-fated princess. From the pier, you can hire boats for river-trips right round the city perimeter. For best use of your time, I would recommend a short 1¹/₂-hour return trip (300B for one to ten people), dropping in on two riverside temples. Ask first for **Wat Chai Wattanaram**, built in 1630 by King Prasad Thong. Recent renovation has deprived this isolated, rarely visited, temple of some of its earlier overgrown charm—but it still has great atmosphere. The Khmer-style central *prang*, together with various smaller *prangs* in the same style, are strongly reminiscent of Anghor Wat (the famous old Cambodian sanctuary). By way of interesting contrast, the frontal *chedis* are Ceylonese-influenced Lanna Thai-style. This is also one of the few extant temples in Ayutthaya were you can still see fragments of original stucco designs clinging to the walls.

Wat Buddaisawan

Returning downriver to the pier, call in on **Wat Buddaisawan**. Built in 1353, this marks the spot where Ramatibodi I resided before founding Ayutthaya. The inner compound is sometimes closed—if so, ask a novice to open it up. It houses a beautiful Cambodian-style central *prang*, with colourful porcelain pieces embedded in its stucco exterior, much like Wat Arun at Bangkok. Eight sets of double boundary stones ring the main *bot*, denoting a major temple under royal patronage. Also known as the 'temple of mangy dogs', Wat Buddaisawan is full of scabby hounds trooping in and out with 'offerings' of dead owls and mice. There's also a glitzy collection of renovated Buddhas, contrasting violently with the surrounding red-brick ruins.

Wat Phra Ram, Wat Mahathat & Wat Na-Phra Mane

Off the boat, take a *tuk-tuk* over to **Wat Phra Ram** on the west of town. This temple marks the site of Ramatibodi's cremation, and was built by his son in 1369. It has twice since been completely restored. Again, there's a nice ancient atmosphere, and you can climb halfway up the main *prang* (adorned with *naga* snakes, *garuda* birds and Buddhas) for good views. Following Ramatibodi's lead, many of Ayutthaya's nobility have been cremated here. Next, take a short ride into the town centre to visit **Wat Mahathat**, built by Ramesuan in 1384. The main *prang*, destroyed by the Burmese, was later discovered to contain a buried treasure chest and a precious relic of Buddha. Look for the famous Bo tree, just inside the gate—it has a stone Buddha's head ensconced in its roots. Then climb the central *chedi* for fine views over to **Wat Rajburana**'s impressive Khmer *prangs*—this saves you paying 20B to see them close up. Finish off at the old 13th-century Wat Na Phra Mane to the northwest of town, overlooking the Lopburi River. This is a real rarity—the only temple left untouched by the Burmese in 1767. They left it alone because, in a previous encounter, one of their kings blew himself up with a cannon here! Inside, you'll find the most beautiful surviving Buddha figure in Ayutthaya. Richly ornamented, and decked out in royal raiment, it looks every inch a king. Nearby, you'll find a large, very serene, granite-stone Buddha. This one is very ancient—some 1300 years old—and was donated to the Ayutthayan kings by the head of the Buddhist order in Sri Lanka. The temple itself has recently been restored, but the main *bot* still has its original wood-roof, the peristyle of which is decorated with Hindu-style *garuda* and Vishnu motifs.

Museums

For those with any remaining time and energy, Ayutthaya also has two museums—the **Chao Sam Phraya** ('National') museum near the centre of town, which bears a charming resemblance to a 19th-century English stately home; and the **Phra Ratcha-wong Chang Kasem** ('Palace') museum to the northeast of town. Both are open 9 am to 4 pm, Wed–Sun, admission 10B. The Palace museum is the more interesting, and sells a decent 20B map-guide of Ayutthaya. The same guide, issued by the Fine Arts Depart-ment, is also sold at Wat Mahathat. All temples sites in Ayutthaya, by the way, are open 8 am to 5 pm daily.

SHOPPING

Fake antiques, synthetic gems and cheap bronze artefacts are peddled (vigorously!) outside the temples. If you do want a cheap *garuda* or Kali figure to put up on your mantelpiece back home, don't pay over 40B for it. For something authentically Ayut-thayan, visit the bamboo and wickerware shops in Wat Phanom Choeng Square. There's a wide selection of attractive bags and baskets here, well-made and very reasonably priced.

WHERE TO STAY

Second-time visitors to Ayutthaya will be glad to know that it finally has a good hotel. This is the new **Sri Samai** in Chao Phrom Rd (tel 251104), with clean, bright rooms at 150B fan, 250B air-con, and a restaurant which is a pleasure to eat in. All rooms have Western toilets too! The **U Thong** and the **Cathay** guest houses on U Thong Rd, by contrast, offer musty, dusty fan rooms at 90B single, 120B double. The U Thong is smellier, the Cathay noisier. At either, *farangs* often end up on the top floor—a wearisome climb after a hard day's *wat*-spotting! Two new little guest houses—**Van** at 51/20 Horattanachai Rd, and **B.J.** at 16/7 Naresuan Rd—get far better mentions. Van is clean and friendly; B.J. has good food, bike rental and a nice family.

EATING OUT

The civilized **Tevaraj** restaurant down by the railway station is the favourite eating place of local Thais. Food is mid-priced (most dishes around 40 to 60B) and superb. Things to try include *Goong Yai Cao* (grilled freshwater lobster), *Gai Poo Kao Fai* (Chicken in Volcano) and—the tour de force—*Kai Dum Toon Yajin* (Black-skin Chicken with Chinese Herbs). Eat in pleasant open-air comfort, amid luxuriant palm gardens, and enjoy impromptu live music performed by 'talented' diners! All this, and unbelievable service too! There's a couple of **Floating Restaurants**, one either side of the Pridi Damrong Bridge on the Pasak River. These are popular, if overpriced. For quick snacks while waiting for a train, there's **Tip-Pa-Rat Restaurant**, just outside the station. It has an English menu, Western-style fare, and ice-cream. The **Bakery House** in Chao Phrom Rd (opposite Sri Samai Hotel) is where to go for continental breakfasts and tasty cakes and pastries. For cheap whip-up wok meals, there's either **Hua Raw market** near the Chan Kasem Palace pier, or the **market by the bus-rank** in Chao Phrom Rd.

Bang Pa In

Bang Pa In is a charming little island in the Chao Phya river, just 20 kms south of Ayutthaya. The summer residence of Thai kings since Ayutthayan times, it's worth seeing for its exquisite assortment of royal buildings in various architectural styles—Thai, Chinese and European—which together make up the **Bang Pa In Palace**. King Chulalongkorn built this turn-of-the-century summer palace after visiting Europe and falling in love with its architecture. He situated it right by the river, providing him and his queen with easy access when they came visiting by royal barge. Sadly, it was whilst on her way to Bang Pa In that Queen Sunandakumaviratn and her children died so tragically when their boat capsized. Chulalongkorn's touching tribute, expressing his inconsolable grief, can be found in the beautiful palace gardens.

GETTING THERE

By Bus
From Ayutthaya (Chao Phrom Rd bus-stop), minibuses run to Bang Pa In at regular intervals, fare 6B. There are also buses from Bangkok's Northern Bus Terminal, every 20 minutes from 5.40 am to 7.40 pm, fare 13B. This is a one-hour trip.

By Train
From Ayutthaya (3B, 3rd class) and from Bangkok (12B, 3rd class) there are regular trains to Bang Pa In. At the station, you'll need a 2B *songthaew* to the palace.

By River
Boats ply back and forth between Ayutthaya and Bang Pa In every half-hour or so. It's a pleasant 40-minute trip, and the one-way fare is 150B. Boats sing out with kitsch tunes like 'Oh, I wish I wuz in Dixie!' when they're ready to depart.

WHAT TO SEE
If visiting Bang Pa In as a side-trip from Ayutthaya (a common option), note that the Palace is open from 8.30 am to 3.30 pm only, and is closed all day on Monday and Friday. However, if you're only coming for the famous Thai-style pavilion in the middle of the lake—the one depicted on so many postcards and posters—then you can see this, and patrol the outer grounds too, till 6 pm daily. Thai picnic people hang out here till late at weekends—buying 8B loaves of bread to feed the 'shadow' fish in the pavilion lake. The larger variety of these fish weigh up to 40 kg, and they're *very* hungry—so don't fall in!

Admission to the palace grounds is 10B. Within, the central attraction is **Phra Thinang Wehat Chamrun**, a Chinese-style building commonly known as the Peking Palace. It's the only building in the compound open to visitors, and is a firm tourist favourite. There's a priceless collection of jade and porcelain (mainly Ming), within, and a twee topiary garden of quaint clipped elephants in the grounds. It's a very romantic spot, much favoured by Thai honeymooning couples. The nearby **Museum** has interesting displays of antiques and ceramics, and is closed on Mondays. Across the river, to the south of the palace grounds, is **Wat Niwega Thamprawat**, a Buddhist temple built in the style of a European Christian church by Rama V. A fascinating blend of English, French and German architecture, this 'church' is situated on a small island, reached by a cable-car ride over the river. Some of the monks give guided tours in English, speaking with pride of their unique *wat*—stained-glass windows, belfry and all. You can swim in the river—at sunset, it's quite a memorable experience!

LOPBURI

Lopburi lies 145 km north of Bangkok, and is one of Thailand's most important historical centres. Recent archaeological finds suggest that the first civilized city here— Lavo—was founded as early as the 4th century AD, though previous to this the area probably received a new Stone Age settlement. The early Dvaravati rulers of Lopburi were replaced in the 10th century by the Khmers, who made it one of their most important capitals. As the old Lavo culture was swept away, the Khmers built an abundance of monuments—the Hindu shrine of Prang Khaek, the Kala Shrine of San Phra Kan, the Triple-spire Shrine of Sam Yot etc—many of which remain near-intact today. In the 13th century, the Sukhothai Thais ousted the Khmers, and the town entered a period of decline. Only 400 years later, when a Dutch naval blockade forced King Narai of Ayutthaya to make Lopburi his second capital (1664), did its fortunes revive. Narai heavily fortified the town, and then brought in French architects to create a beautiful new complex of royal temples, palaces and buildings—in a unique mixture of Thai and European styles. Narai eventually became so enamoured of Lopburi that he spent nine months of every year here and died in the Grand Palace, his finest achievement, in 1688.

Today, Lopburi is rather the 'poor relation' of Thailand's northern temple towns, receiving far fewer visitors than Sukhothai or Ayutthaya. It is not geared to tourism, and people's initial impression of the old fortified town—with its looming Khmer temples employed as traffic islands and its rooftops bristling with TV aerials—is rarely enthusiastic. Nevertheless, it's one of those places which quickly grows on you. Lopburi people are incredibly hospitable and friendly—they'll show you round the sights, they'll point out the best bakeries and ice-cream parlours, and—if you're here in February for the annual 'Beauty Contest for Widows'—they'll probably fix you up with a local bride!

GETTING THERE

By Bus
There are buses to Lopburi every 15 minutes from Ayutthaya, and every 20 minutes (between 5 am and 8.30 pm) from Bangkok's Northern Terminal. From Bangkok, it's a 3 hour trip, costing 32B non air-con, 60B air-con. There are also buses to Lopburi from Kanchanaburi, via Suphanburi (3 hours; fare 21B).

By Rail
From Bangkok's Hualamphong station, there are 7 trains daily to Lopburi—one Express

(leaving 6 pm, arriving 8.26 pm), three Rapid (leaving 6.40 am, 3.45 pm and 10 pm) and three Ordinary (7.05 am, 8.30 am and 8 pm). Basic fares are 111B 1st class, 57B 2nd class, 28B 3rd class. There are also regular trains from Ayutthaya—a 1½-hour journey, costing 13B in 3rd class. If you don't want to stay overnight in Lopburi, come in on an early-morning train from Ayutthaya, look around for a few hours (leave bags in station cloakroom, open 4 am to 9 pm), then hop on a late train (choice of 6.09 pm and 8.26 pm) up to Chiang Mai (arriving 6.35 am and 7.40 am respectively); or, if carrying on to Sukhothai, choose from the 9.10 am, 9.46 am or 11.33 am trains out to Phitsanoluke.

TOURIST INFORMATION
No tourist office, but the **Travellers Drop-in Centre** (cf. Where to Stay) has some maps and printed literature.

WHAT TO SEE
Lopburi divides into the old town, with its Khmer ruins, to the north; and the new town, with its nightclubs and discos (and nothing else) 2 km to the south. *Songthaews* charge 5B for short in-town journeys, and stop running at 8 pm. After that, if you want to take in a club or a restaurant down at Sakeo Circle (in new town) it's a 20B *tuk-tuk* ride from old Lopburi.

Freelance guides hang about outside the major sights—they're an agreeable lot, who don't want money, just perhaps to share a meal or a drink with you afterwards, and to practise their English. Richard, manager of Travellers Drop-in, is working hard towards a proper guide association, with English-speaking guides capable of providing a professional service to travellers.

What Phra Sri Ratana Mahathat
Not that a guide is essential in Lopburi—its few sights can be seen comfortably in a morning and on foot. If you arrive by train, the very first thing you're likely to see is **Wat Phra Sri Ratana Mahathat**, a large 12th-century Khmer shrine right outside the railway station. Many times restored, it's still the most impressive of Lopburi's ruins, conveying a real sense of ruined splendour. Of the three original laterite *prangs*, only the tall central one now stands. It is decorated with beautiful stucco motifs. To the east of it are the large *viharn* and pavilion added in the reign of King Narai. Scattered round the rest of the compound are several interesting *chedis* and *prangs* of different styles (mainly Sukhothai and Ayutthaya), often with niches housing stucco Buddha images. Surprisingly, the rather haphazard restoration achieved here in recent years has done little to diminish the grandeur of this structure, which was created at the height of Khmer power. This aside, the 20B admission fee levied is steep—many travellers just take photos from the roadside!

Phra Narai Ratchanives
Serious sightseeing should start at **Phra Narai Ratchanives**, or King Narai's Palace. This was built over a period of 12 years (1665 to 1677) and was left deserted shortly after Narai's death in 1688. Though restored by Mongkut in the mid-19th century, time has not been kind to this once-majestic structure. Just past the entrance, to the left, you can just make out the king's elephant stables and royal reception hall. Most other buildings

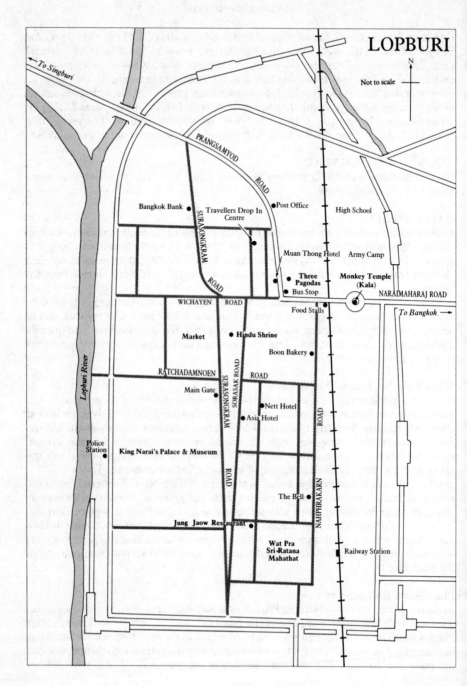

LOPBURI

N

Not to scale

To Singburi

PRANGSAMYOD ROAD

Bangkok Bank

Travellers Drop In Centre

Post Office

High School

SURASONGKRAM ROAD

Muan Thong Hotel

Army Camp

Three Pagodas

Monkey Temple (Kala)

Bus Stop

NARAIMAHARAJ ROAD

WICHAYEN ROAD

Food Stalls

To Bangkok →

Market

Hindu Shrine

Boon Bakery

SOBKRASAB ROAD

RATCHADAMNOEN ROAD

Main Gate

SURASONGKRAM ROAD

Nett Hotel

Asia Hotel

Lopburi River

Police Station

King Narai's Palace & Museum

NAHPHRAKARN ROAD

The Bell

Jung Jaow Restaurant

Wat Pra Sri-Ratana Mahathat

Railway Station

are ruined hulks, and the grounds have been turned into a picnic park. But one section has been set aside for the **Lopburi National Museum**, and this is worth a visit. There's an excellent permanent collection here which describes—via sculpture, art pieces, lintels, votive tablets, etc—the three main cultural periods of Thailand's central plains— Dvaravati (Mon), Khmer (Lopburi-influenced) and Central Plains city-states. All exhibits are well-presented and labelled in English. Outside, there's an odd **open-air museum**, featuring a number of headless and peg-leg Buddhas staked to the lawn and bordered with flowers. Admission to Palace (and museum) is 10B. Opening times are 9 am to 12 noon, 1 pm to 4 pm, Wed–Sun.

Chao Phraya Wichayen

A short stroll away, **Chao Phraya Wichayen** was built for the first French ambassador to Thailand (Chevalier de Chaumont), and later became famous as the residence of Narai's Greek minister, Constantine Phaulkon. The many brick buildings within its walls—a Roman Catholic chapel to the south, the Thai-European-style ambassador's house to the north—are rather too derelict to merit the 15B admission charge.

The landmark of Lopburi, **Phra Prang Sam Yot** (Three Pagodas), lies only 400 metres from the railway station. Constructed in the Lopburi style, its three laterite/sandstone *prangs*—symbolizing the Hindu trinity of Brahma, Vishnu and Shiva—presently decorate the back of the 500B currency note. Converted to a Buddhist temple in Narai's reign, some Hindu motifs can still be made out on the stucco-decorated spires. For some light relief, finish off across the railway track at **San Phra Kahn**, the Kala (Hindu god of death) shrine famous for its hordes of Samae monkeys. These monkeys are held in high regard by local devotees for their human habit of burying their own dead. No one has yet found a dead monkey at this site.

RECREATION

Lopburi is a well-known centre of classical Thai dance and music. **Nartasin School of Art** attracts students from Ayutthaya, Saraburi and neighbouring provinces, training them for professional careers as dancers in big hotels or tourist 'culture shows'. To visit, take a blue *songthaew* (fare 2B) from Three Pagodas bus-stop down to Sakeo Circle in Lopburi new town. From here, it's a 10-minute walk west to a small bridge, 600 metres past which lies the school. Best time of day to show up is mid-morning—if you don't catch a dance class, you'll certainly hear some good live music. Ask permission to use cameras and tape-recorders.

Below Sakeo Circle (ask your bus to put you off there) is a good outdoor swimming pool. On a hot day, well worth the 25B admission. It's open 10 am to 8 pm daily, and women must wear full costumes—and caps! Next to Sakeo Circle bus-stop is **Chao Phraya Nightclub**, with a popular disco on Sunday nights, and good live music every other evening. In the old town, the **Bell** (near station) has a good late-night bar, open till 2.30 am. Behind the Travellers Drop-in Centre, there's a fun snooker club—where smoothie Thais hustle unwary *farangs* at 50B a game.

SHOPPING

There are some good little boutiques, selling fabrics, materials and cheap clothing, opposite the Hindu shrine in Sopasak Rd.

WHERE TO STAY

Lopburi is a low-profile tourist centre, and accommodation is thin. For real comfort, the only option is the new **Teptanee Hotel** near Sakeo Circle. Convenient for nightlife, inconvenient for sightseeing, this offers nice air-con rooms from 200B to 500B. In the old town, the **Asia Lopburi** in Sorasak Rd has fan-rooms from 100B, air-con rooms (with condom dispensers in toilets!) at 200B. This is a clean place, geared mainly to Thais. The **Nett Hotel**, in a small *soi* behind the Asia, has slightly better rooms (at the same price) but is not so friendly. There are several cheap and nasty budget places, mainly in Nahphrakarn Rd—the red-light area. The **Muang Thong**, overlooking Three Pagodas, has adequate rooms at 70B and interesting roof views. The **Travellers Drop-in Centre** at 34 Wichayen Rd, Soi 3 Muang, is the pick of the bunch. It's run by Richard, a young English teacher, who rents out clean, cosy rooms (two only) at 50B and lets guests cook their own food. He invites foreign travellers to make friends with his Thai pupils, and to join in English lessons. This is great fun ('What has Frank been doing in Chiang Mai?' asks Richard. 'Frank . . . has . . . been . . . spending . . . a . . . LOT . . . OF . . . MONEY . . . in . . . Chiang Mai!' chorus the perceptive class). Richard is a mine of local information, and his students enjoy taking foreigners out on sightseeing tours.

EATING OUT

To enjoy quality Thai-Chinese food at under 100B a head, try **Jun Jaow** (corner of Ratchadamnoen and Surasongkram roads) or **Anodard** (south of Sakeo circle) restaurants. The friendly **Phikulkaeo** opposite the station is good for cheap, reliable dishes like sweet and sour pork or fried shrimp with cauliflower (both 20B). There's lots of open-air food stalls in Nahphrakarn Rd, also a number of happy-happy disco cafés. The large market north of the palace, just off Ratchadamnoen and Surasongkram roads, is especially good for inexpensive Thai-style snacks. A small indoor market near Travellers Drop-in, behind Nahphrakarn Rd, has a wide selection of 7B 'meals', also an amazing waffle stand. Just above the good Chinese-Thai restaurant at the Asia Hotel, there's a marvellous **Foremost** ice-cream parlour. **Boon Bakery** in Nahphrakarn Rd offers 25B continental breakfasts, nice cakes and soothing sounds.

KHAO YAI NATIONAL PARK

Khao Yai is the biggest and the best of Thailand's national parks. Set up in 1962, it was also the first. *Khao Yai* means 'big mountain', but actually encompasses three major mountains and numerous smaller peaks. Comprising over 2000 sq km of tropical jungle, dense forest, rolling meadows and green hills, it stretches across four provinces at a cool, refreshing elevation of around 800 metres (2500 feet). Khao Yai's vast acreage of deciduous and evergreen jungle-forest supports nearly all of Thailand's 195 species of protected wildlife—including tigers, elephants, deer, monkeys, bears, wild oxen, silver pheasants, woodpeckers, great hornbills and butterflies—as well as innumerable species of wild flowers, orchids, trees and exotic plants. Honeycombed with hiking trails, it's an ideal spot for naturalists or for anyone interested in seeing Thailand's flora and fauna.

Khao Yai is most pleasant between November and February, when the climate is fairly dry and cool. The banyan tree flowers in this season, attracting a lot of monkeys. And elephants are a common sight, coming down to the saltlick north of the forest for water. However, if you want to see an Amazonian-type rain forest in its full, burgeoning splendour, visit Khao Yai during the rainy months of July to September. Try to avoid weekends—the park is only 200 km from Bangkok, and is very popular as a picnic spot for Thais eager to escape the hot, busy capital. Each Friday and Saturday, they arrive in hordes—they occupy every bungalow, they have a jolly party, they stroll down to the nearest waterfall (rarely further!) and on Sunday night they go home. During the week (your best time to visit), the park is returned to the animals.

GETTING THERE
From Bangkok's Northern Terminal, two air-con buses (7 am and 9 am) leave daily for Khao Yai. It's a 3-hour trip, costing 74B. Returning to Bangkok, there's often only one bus a day from Khao Yai, departing at 3 pm.

WHAT TO SEE
Because much of Khao Yai is damp, dense jungle you can't—unlike say, the open gameparks of Africa—count on seeing anything here. Yes, there are around 200 wild elephants and 20 tigers in the area (plus many bear, gibbon and deer) but if you spot any of these it'll be a bonus. What there *is* to enjoy is a rich variety of birds and butterflies, and the fascinating sights and sounds of an authentic tropical rain forest.

If you're here to spot animals, or simply want to know more about the park, contact Khao Yai's one and only guide—friendly young Po, who has lived and breathed Khao Yai for the past 17 years. He can be contacted at the **Information Centre**, near the visitors' centre, and charges between 100B and 300B a day for guided tours, the price depending on the size of your party.

But the good thing about Khao Yai is that you don't really need a guide. A series of good trails have been marked (i.e. colour-coded trees, set apart at 20–30 metre intervals) which are all easy to follow. Thus, if you walk over 30 metres and can't find a colour marker, you simply return to the last marked tree and try a different direction! All of the four recommended trails can be done in one to three hours, and can be extended or shortened by crossing over from one coded path to another. Trail 1 (red paint) is 4 km long, plus 2 km down the road back to the visitors' centre, and takes 2–3 hours; trail 2 (blue) is a 3.5 km walk through (mainly) grassland, and takes $2^1/2$ hours; trail 3 (yellow) is 2.5 km long and takes around $1^1/2$ hours; trail 4 (also blue) extends 3.5 km, plus 1 km back down to the visitors' centre, and takes around $2^1/2$ hours. The most popular walk starts on trail 1 and loops right onto trail 3. At the junction of these two paths, there's often a group of gibbons high up in the trees—listen out for loud whoops, their way of marking out territory!

An early morning walk is nice and cool, and there are lots of birds to be seen from around 5 am to 9 am. Another good thing about Khao Yai is that several trails lead along the edge of the forest, which makes spotting birdlife quite easy. Gibbons and monkeys are most frisky in the early morning too. A pleasant short outing, if you're staying near the visitors' centre, is down to the small suspension bridge at **Gong Gheow Waterfall**.

Two warnings—*always* keep to the paths, and *never* go off on your own. It's a very thick jungle, and people have wandered off in the past and never returned. The trails are best negotiated in small groups of 2–4 people. Walk slowly and quietly, keeping alert to any sounds or movement and you may be rewarded with sightings of wildlife. During the wet season, take precautions against leeches. These little bloodsuckers lurk on the trails and can be very distracting—all too often, hikers spend more time squinting anxiously down at their feet than admiring the wonders of the forest. For near-total protection, apply a liberal coating of insect repellent to feet, socks and shoes—any leeches that get through this barrier, you can just flick off. There's no need for applications of salt or for smouldering cigarette butts!

Most animal life here is nocturnal and your best chance of spotting elephant, tiger and large game is in the cool of the night, when they are most active. The big thing to do at Khao Yai is a night jeep safari. Armed with a powerful spotlight and a trained guide, jeeps set out from both TAT and Gong Gheow bungalows (around 15B per person in a large group; but 250B if on your own!) and patrol the saltlicks in search of wild elephants etc. Best views are from the jeep roof—you don't see too much down below.

Not everybody comes to Khao Yai for jungle walks and wildlife-spotting. Some play golf. The park offers Thailand's highest golf course—a superb 18-hole links, with club-house. Green fees are 80B (weekdays) to 140B (weekends). To reserve a game, contact TAT (tel 2825209).

There's a moth-eaten museum down at the visitors' centre, with a few stuffed heads and various things preserved in bottles. It's open 9 am to 5 pm every day except Saturday, when it shows an ancient BBC archive film and stays open till 8.30 pm. The small restaurant nearby does reasonable food.

WHERE TO STAY

All accommodation should be advance-booked (especially for weekends), to avoid disappointment. TAT's **Motor Lodge Bungalows** (tel Bangkok 2825209 for reservations) sleep two people and cost 700B. National Park **Gong Gheow Bungalows** (same tel no.) sleep four, and cost 6–700B. There's also some 4-bedded **dormitory** accommodation at Gong Gheow which, at 100B per person, is the best budget option. In the dry season though, you can sleep out with the animals in cheap (10B) and basic jungle huts. To book, contact Po at the Information Centre.

PATTAYA

In just 20 years, Pattaya has mushroomed from a sleepy fishing village to the premier beach resort in Southeast Asia. Today, this wide crescent bay on the Gulf of Thailand, 147 km from Bangkok, attracts thousands of holidaymakers from home and abroad every week. With its high-class Western hotels and restaurants, its discos and bars, its wide range of water-sports and entertainments—not forgetting its miles of clean beaches and pretty offshore coral islands—Pattaya is totally tuned into the package-holiday market. It's hardly like Thailand at all—more like Blackpool or Surfer's Paradise, with its fast-food houses, kiss-me-quick hats and elephant rides up the beach. But if Pattaya is something of a circus, a lot of people do enjoy the show! Especially single men, who constitute some 70% of tourists here. Pattaya is still an international sex capital, with

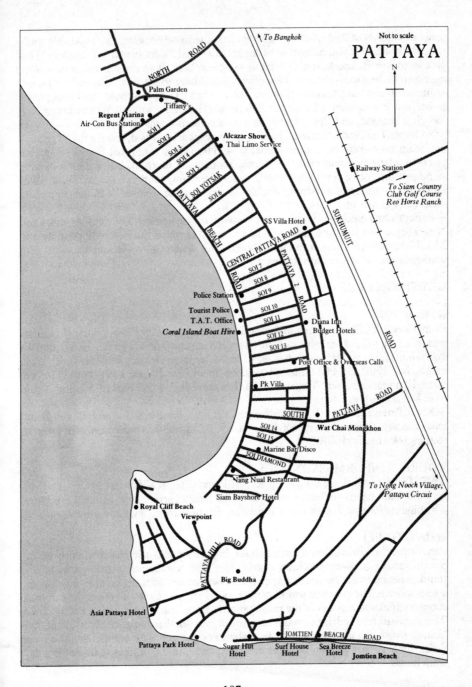

To Bangkok

Not to scale

PATTAYA

N

ROAD

NORTH

Palm Garden

Tiffany's

Regent Marina
Air-Con Bus Station

SOI 1

SOI 2

SOI 3

SOI 4

SOI 5

SOI YOTSAK

SOI 6

PATTAYA BEACH ROAD

Alcazar Show
Thai Limo Service

Railway Station

*To Siam Country
Club Golf Course
Reo Horse Ranch*

SUKHUMVIT

SS Villa Hotel

CENTRAL PATTAYA ROAD

PATTAYA 2 ROAD

SOI 7

SOI 8

Police Station

SOI 9

Tourist Police

SOI 10

T.A.T. Office

SOI 11

Coral Island Boat Hire

SOI 12

SOI 13

Diana Inn
Budget Hotels

Post Office & Overseas Calls

Pk Villa

ROAD

SOUTH

PATTAYA ROAD

Wat Chai Mongkhon

SOI 14

SOI 15

Marine Bar/Disco

SOI DIAMOND

Nang Nual Restaurant

Siam Bayshore Hotel

Royal Cliff Beach
Viewpoint

*To Nong Nooch Village,
Pattaya Circuit*

PATTAYA HILL ROAD

Big Buddha

Asia Pattaya Hotel

JOMTIEN BEACH ROAD

Pattaya Park Hotel

Sugar Hut
Hotel

Surf House
Hotel

Sea Breeze
Hotel

Jomtien Beach

107

some two-thirds of its 55,000 female population currently engaged in 'entertainment'-related activities. If you haven't seen any middle-aged businessmen with teenage Thai girls in tow in Bangkok, you'll certainly see them here. If you're a man on your own, expect to be hassled—the one Thai phrase you'll have to learn is 'May ow' or 'I don't want you/it/anything, thanks'. If you're a couple or a family, you could find better places to be. But if you want a European holiday in Thailand—with all Western comforts, top-class seafood, and Benidorm-style entertainments—look no further.

As befits Thailand's 'Riviera', Pattaya is very expensive. Food, transport and accommodation cost even more than in Bangkok. Here there's not just the usual double price-standard (i.e. one price for Thais, another for tourists), but a double-double standard (one price for high season, another for low), and even a double-double-DOUBLE standard (everything doubles in price at the weekend). Budget travellers often can't afford it!

Pattaya's high season is October to February. It's especially busy over Christmas and New Year, when you'll be lucky to find a sleeping berth on the beach! September and March are quieter, cheaper months—hotels offer generous low-season discounts. But weekends are expensive throughout the year.

GETTING THERE

By Bus
From Bangkok's Eastern Terminal, non air-con buses leave for Pattaya every 35 minutes from 5.25 am to 7.10 pm (plus two late buses at 8 pm and 9 pm). The fare is 29B, and it's a 2½-hour journey. Air-con buses leave at regular intervals daily from major Bangkok hotels, fare 120B. Special transfer buses run direct from Bangkok airport to Pattaya at 9 am, 12 noon, and 7 pm. Tickets are 180B, and are sold at the Thai Limousine desk in Don Muang airport.

From Pattaya (Regent Marina Hotel, N. Pattaya), there are air-con buses to Bangkok's Eastern Terminal every half-hour (fare 50B), and air-con buses at regular intervals to Bangkok airport (100B).

TOURIST INFORMATION
TAT Tourist Office, 382/1 Beach Rd, S. Pattaya (tel 428750) has helpful English-speaking staff, hands out lots of information (including current hotel listings), and issues a fortnightly *Pattaya Tourist Guide* magazine, full of current news and events.

WHAT TO SEE
Pattaya roughly divides into North Pattaya (big hotels, massage parlours, fairly quiet), South Pattaya (mid-range/cheap hotels, bars and restaurants, action-packed), and Jomtien Beach to the far south (expensive resort accommodation, good swimming and water-sports). The cheapest way of getting round are *songthaews*. These make continual counter-clockwise circuits of the main bay area, from Beach Rd round to Pattaya 2 Rd. The standard fare is 5B, but you'll have to bargain very hard to get it! Outside of their 'route', *songthaews* charge more or less what they can get. The same goes for air-con taxis. Many people give up on local transport, and hire motorbikes (150–250B a day) from hotels.

Local sights are few. A pleasant motorbike excursion is up **Pattaya Hill** to visit the Buddhist temple at the top. There's a large seated Buddha here—a recent renovation, nothing special—surrounded by seven quaint mini-Buddhas, one for each day of the week. Nearby, there's a small Chinese temple, decorated with garish carnival figures. The hill provides fine views down over the main bay area.

Inland sights are covered by air-con minibus tours, offered by most hotels and travel agents in Pattaya. These are usually full-day excursions, costing around 250B per person. Attractions visited include **Nong Nooch Village**—a prettily landscaped country resort, 25 km out of Pattaya, with a plastic culture show; **Elephant Kraal**—elephants bathing and doing tourist tricks; and **Pattaya Park** (near Jomtien beach)—with water-slides, whirlpools and family-style frolics.

An hour's drive out of Pattaya (and 100 km from Bangkok), the town of **Chonburi** holds bi-monthly **Water-Buffalo Racing Competitions**. These are great fun, and well worth going out of your way for. Details and dates aren't well advertised, and you'll need to check with the TAT office, or look for clues in the *Bangkok Post* (though some Pattaya hotels are clued into it, with set tours). Coming from Bangkok, it's a $1^1/_2$-hour bus trip from the Eastern Terminal. The event usually runs from 9 am to noon, and features live music, cheap eats, a huge open market with fairground, and a real party atmosphere!

Offshore islands are numerous, and are worth visiting for their amazing variety of tropical fish and beautiful live coral formations. Glass-bottom boat trips run out twice daily—at 9.30 am and 11.30 am—to the coral island of **Koh Larn**. Tickets are sold for 200B from the booth just below TAT office in Beach Rd, or for 280B from large hotels. The cost of the tour includes a good seafood lunch. Snorkelling equipment provided is poor, so it's best to hire some of your own. For less touristy trips to offshore islands like **Koh Sak** and **Koh Pai**, contact View Travel in Pattaya (tel 429976).

RECREATION

Pattaya *is* recreation! There's always something going on here—motorsports events, windsurfing competitions, dove-singing contests, game-fishing tournaments or sand-castle free-for-alls. I arrived during the annual Elephant Fashion Show. This included a tipsy tray-waiters' contest, a bellboy luggage-carrying obstacle course, and one hundred chambermaids making the world's largest bed! TAT carries details of all forthcoming events.

Pattaya's wide range of sports and recreational facilities, are mostly water-borne. The place to go for water-sports is Jomtien Beach, 2 km south of Pattaya Bay, which proudly describes itself as a 'No Tourist Irritation Area'. Here, below Sugar Hut bungalows, you can arrange **Water-Skiing** (800–1000B per hour), **Windsurfing** (100B per hour), **Parasailing** (250B per hour), **Catamarans** (300B per hour) and **Water-Scooters** (200B per hour). The current rage are **Laser Sail-boats** – 'easy man's windsurfing'—at around 200B an hour. All these prices are low season, and can easily double at weekends! Whenever you go, bargain for discounts.

Scuba-Diving takes place at offshore dive sites, and costs between 900 and 1500B a day. Two reliable outfits are **Seafari Sports Centre**, S. Pattaya Beach Rd (tel 429060) and **Dave's Divers Den**, Soi 6 Yodsak N. Pattaya Beach Rd (tel 423286). These offer tuition up to PADI and NAUI licences respectively. Several big hotels offer free scuba-diving lessons in their swimming pools!

Orchids at Nong Nooch

Land-based recreations include **Horse-riding** at Reo Ranch, near Siam Country Club (tel 421188) for 300–400B an hour; **Tennis** at the courts of 14 major hotels (contact TAT for listing) for 100–150B an hour; **Golf** at any of the three good courses here (green fees 150B; contact Mike at Caesar's Bar, nr Beach Rd police station, S. Pattaya, or Brian at California Bar, S. Pattaya, to arrange a game); and **Bowling and Snooker** at Pattaya Bowl, next to Regent Marina Hotel, N. Pattaya (tel 429466). The area round the Regent Marina also has many gyms, saunas and massage parlours.

NIGHTLIFE
After dark, Pattaya offers a different kind of 'recreation' altogether! North Pattaya has two famous nightclubs, presenting extravagant transvestite cabaret shows nightly. Of the two, **Tiffany's**, in Pattaya 2 Rd, is the original outfit—classier and more 'conservative'. The **Alcazar** ('Relief your Tension, and Get Stun to Sensation Spectacular!') offers more racy, topical entertainment. Both clubs charge the same—140B, including one free drink—and have shows at 7 pm, 8.30 pm, 10 pm and (Saturday only) 11.30 pm.

South Pattaya has 'Pattayaland'—a raucous, raunchy collection of brightly-lit bars, animal shows, cabarets, discos and restaurants which commence on the 'strip' in Beach Rd, and go on for as long (and as late) as you want them to. I once asked a tourist official if there was anywhere in Pattaya where a man could enjoy a nice quiet drink without being hassled, and he said 'No'. Cruising down the strip at night—dodging giggling girls trying to drag you into bars, fending off gumless crones hawking sugared candies, and tripping over tiny tots selling weight-readings on the pavement—is quite fun. Everybody's very friendly, and you'll only get into trouble if you want to! An Australian resident commented, 'Pattayaland is called the Big Shop—you can buy anything here, except a heart!' He was referring to Pattaya's bar-girls, a good-humoured lot with hearts of gold—not for sale at any price. They are far less 'professional' than their counterparts in Bangkok's Patpong. Before you pass any judgement, share a few drinks with them, and get to know something of their lives. Most are here, of course, to support large families living on the breadline in the drought-dry northeast or in the slums of Bangkok.

Pattayaland's club action starts at Soi 14, where **Simon's Music Hall** offers Thai boxing at 9.30 pm nightly, plus videos. **Sirens Sea** on Soi 15 offers the full works—**Ladies Thai Boxing** at 8 pm, a Snake Show at 11 pm, and a Crocodile Show at 1 am. Taking the next turning left, Soi Diamond, you plunge into Pattayaland proper—a vast, heaving complex of go-go bars, discos, seafood restaurants, blaring jukeboxes, and neon-lit street markets. At the **Baby Go-Go** bar, drinks are fixed-price (45B) and off-stage antics are even funnier than the floorshow. The nearby **Simon Cabaret** offers the best transvestite show in South Pattaya. You can watch it for free from the opposite side of the road, or pay 50B to watch from the bar, or pay 90B for a front-row seat (and free drink). Showtime is 9.45 pm nightly, and it's a two-hour cabaret. Next to Simon's is **Nang Nual** restaurant, famous for its delicious seafood—around 40–60B per dish—and for its mammoth 'Big Cowboy' steaks (320B). Over the road, you'll find **Marine Bar & Disco Club**. This is *the* bar in Pattaya! At full capacity, there are up to 1000 girls here, with backdrop entertainments of Thai boxing, snake shows and giant wall videos. Most of the girls are freelance—they get up around 9 pm for breakfast, show up here about midnight, and work till 6 am in the morning. Upstairs is the Marine's disco, the hottest scene in Pattaya. The place really jumps! Drinks are 90B, and you're not allowed to stay unless you buy one. Later on, check out the nearby **Plaza**—this is a cheaper disco (drinks only 60B) with a great live band. In between all this boogie-on-down, look in on the small **Saloon Bar**, right next to the Marine. Here you'll find Lam Morrison, a brilliant Thai guitarist, heading up just about the best garage band in Thailand. Heroes of the '60s like Hendrix, Cream, Free and Chuck Berry—he plays them all with the same raw energy, and nearly as well as the originals! He tunes up about 10.30 pm, and plays on till 1 am, or until one of his strings breaks!

SHOPPING

Apart from Bangkok's Chinatown, Pattaya is probably the best place in Thailand to buy gold. Well, there's such a local demand for it. Walking down the strip, you'll notice many of the Thai girls wearing high-fashion gold jewellery. This metal matches their skin texture perfectly. If you see a local girl wearing something you like, it's often worth the price of a drink (20B) to find out where she bought it!

Chanthaburi

A lot of Pattaya jewellery is set with stones from **Chanthaburi**, a 2-hour drive east. This world-famous gem-mining centre is noted chiefly for its star-sapphires and rubies and the whole main street is lined with shops polishing, cutting and weighing out precious stones. You can pick up some real bargains here, especially if you can haggle in Thai! After shopping, visit the gem mines and factory (a 10 minute walk out of the new town), and nearby waterfalls. Chanthaburi also has the biggest church in Thailand. You can also get here by bus from Ban Phe/Samet (1½ hours) and from Bangkok Eastern Terminal (4 hours).

Fashion boutiques and shops selling clothes, silks, handicrafts, coral and shells, jewellery and gemstones, are mostly in the main street of South Pattaya. Many large hotels have shopping arcades.

WHERE TO STAY

Pattaya has no shortage of high-class accommodation. But in high season, and at weekends, it's essential to advance-book—the better hotels quickly fill up! Pattaya caters almost exclusively to the luxury bracket—major hotels often offer swimming pools, tennis and squash courts, jogging trails and watersports, bars and nightclubs, shopping arcades and maybe a private beach. You're lucky if you can find a good double room under 200B here—budget accommodation is in short supply! Room prices fluctuate wildly between high and low season, and between weekdays and weekends. Except where otherwise stated, all prices quoted in this section are 'average' tariffs. Large hotels often offer 30% discounts (or more) during the May to September low season, and several cheaper places discount 50% if you stay a week or more. Bargain hard.

Luxury

Pattaya's most exclusive hotel—actually 3 hotels in one—is **Royal Cliff Beach Resort**, 175 Wisut-kasat Rd, Pattaya Hill (tel 428511; tx 85907 CLIFFEX TH. Superb location, and all of the 700-plus rooms (tariffs start at 1600B) have good views—either of the beach (4th floor), of the coast (from 8th floor), of the mountains (9th floor and up). The Cliff has a private beach, four pools, two restaurants (food could be better), and a host of sports and recreational facilities. Better priced, and just as comfortable, the nearby **Asia Pattaya**, 353 Mu 10, Cliff Rd (tel 428602; tx Bangkok 85902 TH), has rooms from 900B and a lovely pool, popular nightclub and lots of modern charm. The **Siam Bayshore**, S. Pattaya Rd (tel 418679), is well-located for Pattayaland shopping and nightlife. Rooms here start at 900B, and the best ones overlook the beautiful gardens. In North Pattaya, there's the **Montien Pattaya**, Beach Rd (tel 418321) and the **Regent Marina**, N. Pattaya Rd (tel 418015). Both have nice rooms around 900B and top-notch facilities. The Marina has a very popular discotheque. At Jomtien, **Sugar Hut**, 45/4 Moo 12, Sugar Palm Beach (tel 423160), offers exquisite Japanese/Thai-style bamboo huts, set in tropical gardens, at a year-round rate of 650B. The restaurant is famous for its 'Seafood Rendezvous in Basket' meal for 200B (feeds three!). Sugar Hut's water-sport facilities take some beating. Further down Jomtien beach, the **Sea Breeze** (tel 428475) receives consistently good mentions—rooms at around 600B, great food, and very friendly staff. For a full listing of luxury hotels in and around Pattaya, contact the TAT tourist office.

Mid-range

For a luxury hotel at a moderate price, try **P. K. Villa**, Beach Rd, S. Pattaya (tel 418462). This is Pattaya's largest villa, with lovely gardens, a fine pool, and relaxed atmosphere. Rooms start from 400B (low season), and most of them have ocean views. The same goes for **Ocean View Hotel**, Beach Rd (tel 418434), a very comfy place with rooms from 660B. Friendly **Honey Inn**, 529/2 Soi 10, Pattaya 2 Rd (tel 428117), has bright, attractive rooms from 550B, and is so *quiet!* At Jomtien, the **Cobra Cabana** (tel 418079) has a snug location, a good pool, and off-season double rooms as low as 400B.

Economy

Budget hotels are concentrated round Sois 11 and 12, Pattaya 2 Rd. Better ones include **Diana Inn** (tel 429870), with good-value rooms at 175B fan, 275B air-con and a pool, a bar and restaurant; **Pattaya II** which has superior rooms at 150B fan, 300B air-con, a pool, coffee shop, restaurant, car park etc; **Honey House**, down Soi 10, has spacious rooms for 150B fan, 250B air-con and the use of a pool; and finally, **B. R. Inn**, Soi 12 (tel 429449) with large quiet 250B air-con rooms. Other good bets are **U-Thomporn**, **Supin**, **Drop In**, **Tossaporn**, **Malibu** and **Sahasak**. These all have rooms from 100–150B (fan singles) to 200–250B (air-con doubles). The **Seastar** on Soi 10 is a bit of a knocking-shop, but at 80B a room is still the cheapest deal in town!

EATING OUT

Pattaya has some of the choicest seafood in Thailand. It is also the most expensive place to eat in Thailand. Still, there's an amazing range of cuisines. Numerous restaurants, coffee shops, steak houses and fast-food emporia cater for every gastronomic taste— European, Indian, Arabic, Japanese, Chinese, Korean and Thai. But the usual cheap street-snack places are in very short supply here!

Much-copied but never equalled, **Dolf Riks** (in Regent Marina complex, N. Pattaya) is an outstanding restaurant, offering superlative continental dishes in a select setting. The à la carte speciality is Indonesian *Rijsttafel* (a special meat curry) at 185B; also try delectable Fried Prawns at 150B. Riks has a set tourist menu for 220B, and is open from 11 am to midnight. Other good European-style places—all on Beach Rd, South Pattaya—are **La Gritta's**, an authentic Italian restaurant specializing in seafood cuisine: **Buccaneer Terrace** (in Nipa Lodge Hotel), a rooftop restaurant with great bay views and delicious Escargot in White Wine Sauce at 120B, and **Mai Kai** (Hotel Tropicana), a Polynesian restaurant also offering quality seafood and European fare. Several large hotels—notably the **Montien**—offer good evening barbecue buffets.

Nam Nuan, Soi 15, Beach Rd, is tops for Thai/Chinese cuisine, and for steaks. Very pricey though, at around 500B a head. For half this sum, you can enjoy top-quality Thai food at **Dee Proam**, Central Pattaya Rd, with nice gardens and a romantic atmosphere thrown in. Also good are **Somsak** and **Suthep** Thai restaurants on Sois 4 and 5, Beach Rd. For mid-priced Japanese, Thai and European food—helped down by pleasant live music and entertainments—try the **Yume**, close to S. S. Villa on Central Pattaya Rd.

The best places to sample Pattaya's famous seafood are the **Nang Nual** (cf. Nightlife section) and the **Pupen**, just beyond Sigma Resort Club, Jomtien. Local Thais recommend this place—for 600B (the standard four-person meal charge) you get a whole kilo of tiger prawns, two kilos of crab, and lots of amazing extras. For 'novelty' seafood, drop in on the **Sailing Club Restaurant**, next to the tourist office. The menu here is priceless—'Domestic Fowl Pig Vent with Sour', 'Birds in Pepper Curry', 'Fried (?) in Brown Groovy', and (can they be serious?) 'Intermediate Class Curry with Dishcloth'!

KOH SI CHANG

The picturesque island of Koh Si Chang nestles off the east coast of the Gulf of Thailand, about 12 km from the Si Racha shore. Little visited by foreigners—except as a short day-outing—it's a wonderfully secluded island, the ideal retreat from the noise and crowds of nearby Bangkok or Pattaya. Koh Si Chang has fresh, clean air and a relaxing

Mediterranean flavour. Lovely scenery, quiet beaches and pleasant walks make this a perfect place to just switch off. There's a small local population of fishermen and retired government officials. Apart from them, visitors who wisely decide to stay overnight often have the island all to themselves!

GETTING THERE

From Bangkok's Eastern Terminal, buses leave every 15 minutes for the small fishing town of **Si Racha**, 104 km from Bangkok. Fares are 28B non air-con, 44B air-con, and it's a 2-hour trip. Boats for Si Chang island leave from the pier on Soi 14, Si Racha, at 9 am, 11 am, 1 pm, 3 pm and 6.30 pm daily. Boats back to Si Racha from Si Chang leave at 5 am, 6.30 am, 9 am, 12 noon and 4.30 pm. The crossing takes 40 minutes and the one-way fare is 20B.

WHAT TO SEE

Koh Si Chang is encircled by a narrow ring-road, which you can walk round at leisure in 3–4 hours. If you need local transport, there are unique motorized *samlors* which resemble souped-up dragmobiles! These charge 20B for short hops, 80B for round-trips of the island—rather expensive. To tour the island in style, hire a boat (cf. Where to Stay).

Island Tour
(on foot; half–full day)

Chinese Temple – Hin Klom Beach – Tampang Beach – King's Palace – Wat Asdang Nimitr.

The **Chinese Temple** on Koh Si Chang is one of Thailand's finest. From the pier, walk five minutes up the low hill road until you reach the temple staircase. A stiff climb of over 400 steps leads up to a small old *chedi*, where a charming monk (guarding a sacred footprint of Buddha) doles out iced water to overheated climbers. Beautifully located, the temple offers wonderful views down over the island interior and surrounding coastline. From the foot of the temple, another 10 minutes' walk brings you to the north of the island and to **Hin Klom**. This is popularly known as 'Round Stone' beach—its large rocks having been worn to their smooth, round shape by strong westerly winds. Just past this, there's a massive yellow Buddha seated up on the hill. To share its privileged view of the island, walk up the rickety staircase to the small temple at its base. Back on the road, and a kilometre further on, a sign appears for **Tampang Beach**. This is the best beach on the island, but the long 30-minute hike there from the main road tends to put off a lot of visitors! It's apparently not a bad spot to camp out.

Staying on the road, another 10 minutes' walk brings you to the western edge of the island, and to the **King's Palace**. This was the old summer palace of Rama V, left to become derelict after the French took temporary occupation of the island in 1893. Little now remains of the extensive structure, except for the dilapidated wooden summer-house and the rubble-filled swimming pool. The main palace building is now located in Bangkok. Climbing the staircase which once led up to it, you'll find two temples. The one on the left, **Wat Asdang Nimitr**, has a chapel (used by Rama V for meditation) and a pagoda in European architectural style. Also up here is a famous 'bell rock', wrapped in cloth, which produces a bell-like tone when struck with a large stick or stone. The King's Palace area is open from 8 am to 6 pm daily, and there's an admission charge of 4B. It overlooks the small, shallow **Tawang Beach**, a popular Thai picnic spot. Swimming isn't safe here—too many sea-urchins!

In the evening, buy a refreshing pineapple in the town market, and cool off down by the pier. There's a small open-air cinema here, which shows entertaining Thai or Hindi films most nights. Toom, manager of Tiewpai guest house, lets his guests use his schooner to mellow out under the stars.

WHERE TO STAY

Koh Si Chang has three guest houses, all within five minutes' walk from the pier. **Tiewpai Guest House** (tel 272987) is the only one which has got its act together. Toom, the friendly manager, speaks good English (a rarity on this island!) and is a mine of local information. He has rooms from 120B (fan-cooled, but stuffy) to 250B (air-con, better) He also has just about the best dormitory in Thailand—large, clean and well-aired—for 40B per person. Toom offers half-day (9 am to 12 noon) boat trips round the island, with stops for fishing and swimming. At 300B, this is worth doing—if there's a group of you to split costs. Tiewpai's small restaurant serves Thai/European cuisine (nice seafood) and has live music nightly. All the local Thai wide-boys gather here for sing-songs and Mekong parties, and it can get *very* noisy! If it gets you down, move to the quieter guest house just above Tiewpai—it's at the top of the hill, to the right. Otherwise, buy some supplies and camp out on one of the beaches. They're all quite safe.

Si Racha

Si Racha is well-known for its seafood (especially oysters) and for its spicy home-grown *nam phrik si rachaa* sauce. There's good dining at **Seaside** restaurant on Soi 18 pier, and **Chua Lee** next to Soi 10. Both are pricey—most dishes between 40 and 60B—and have 'yuppie' menus (e.g. Crab on Toast, Fresh Oysters On The Rock) but food is superb. While in Si Racha, take a walk (15 minutes, heading north up Chermchormpol Rd, turning left past the Post Office) over to **Koh Loi**. This is a delightful little island connected to the mainland by a long jetty. The attraction here is a pretty set-piece Thai-Chinese Buddhist temple—bring your camera.

Staying overnight in Si Racha (a rather dismal prospect), choose between two 'hotels' on the waterfront pier, opposite Tessaban 1 Rd. These are **Siwichai**, with clean 60B rooms (no bath), and **Siriwattana**, with 100B singles (with bath) and 250B doubles (can sleep four!) with air-conditioning.

From Si Racha, buses leave for Pattaya (30-minute journey; fare 5B) from Sukhumvit Road highway. The bus-stop is a 15-minute walk from town—take the road directly opposite Soi 14, walk down to the highway, cross over, and head right. Pattaya-bound buses often carry on to Rayong for Koh Samet.

KOH SAMET

Samet Island has beautiful beaches, crystal-clear waters and some of the whitest, squeakiest sand in Thailand. Only three hours by road from Bangkok, it was first discovered by young Thai weekenders seeking a quick getaway from the busy capital. Still mainly a Thai resort, Samet has, to date, escaped the eye of the developers. Unlike Koh Samui or Phuket, which are well on their way to becoming *farang* ghettoes, Samet still has no bars, prostitutes or discos to disturb its laidback tranquillity. In the day, people swim, sunbathe and relax. At night, they sit and talk and play music. Boring, say some—but many can't get enough of Samet's simple backwoods charm. Of course, this can't last for long. Two years ago, there was virtually nothing on the island. Now there's windsurfing, jet skiing, motorboats, motorbikes and videos. All it needs is for some bright spark from Pattaya to set up a water-sports centre here, and it'll be the beginning of the end!

Accommodation on the island is mainly cheap, basic bungalows around 50B single, 80B double (twice the price in high season). Huts usually have just a mattress, a mosquito net, and (sometimes) an attached shower. A few bungalows have restaurants, but the fare is unexciting—*khao pat*, pancakes, fruit salads etc. One or two have money-changers and overseas phones (collect calls only). There are no luxury-class hotels on Samet, though a frantic building programme has recently produced a number of new-style bungalows with all mod cons, charging between 350–500B (again, much more in the high season). Visitors can now afford to be selective regarding where to stay. If you don't like one place, move on. The amazing thing about Samet—the one thing everyone comments on—is that every beach has a completely different atmosphere. Some are quiet, some are party-party, one or two are geared to Thais, others have water-sports, some have no electricity and a few are lit up like Christmas trees! Whatever your mood, you'll find something to suit it here. If you're not into bungalows, simply camp out on the beach—the Thais do it all the time, and it's quite safe—except for the mosquitoes!

Samet's mosquitoes are of the malarial kind. Be grateful to them—they're probably the main reason the island is so pleasantly deserted! But be aware of them too—nearly every bungalow-owner on the island has had malaria at one time or another, and there are warning signs all over the place. Even if you're taking malaria tabs, you'll need to take extra precautions—especially after dusk, when malarial mozzies are about. Sleep under a net, cover up with repellent in the open, and have your bungalow sprayed with DDT. While there's no real need for alarm—malaria is pretty difficult to catch—if you do develop symptoms (cramps, fever etc.) contact Sue Wild at Naga Beach bungalows for help. Forget the public health clinic on the island—apart from simple dressings, it's good for nothing. Your best bet is Rayong hospital—the malaria clinic here gives blood tests on the spot and immediate medication. Bangkok also has a good malaria clinic (cf. 'Health', page 21). But first make sure it *is* malaria you've got—it may only be severe dehydration, which is quickly cured by drinking Coke laced with lots of salt and sugar!

Koh Samet is a useful alternative to Koh Samui. It's rainy in May and June (when Samui is still OK) and it's dry in October and November (when Samui is still subject to winds and storms). Samet is very dry from November to February (the official high season), water-shortage problems could leave you paying 20B for a shower! On the plus side, dry weather means relatively few mosquitoes. Christmas and New Year is a big scene on Samet—wild, wild beach parties, after which every bungalow verandah is crammed with sleeping bodies. Avoid coming on weekends and national holidays. Koh Samet is still primarily a Thai resort, and gets crowded at these times. I arrived on a

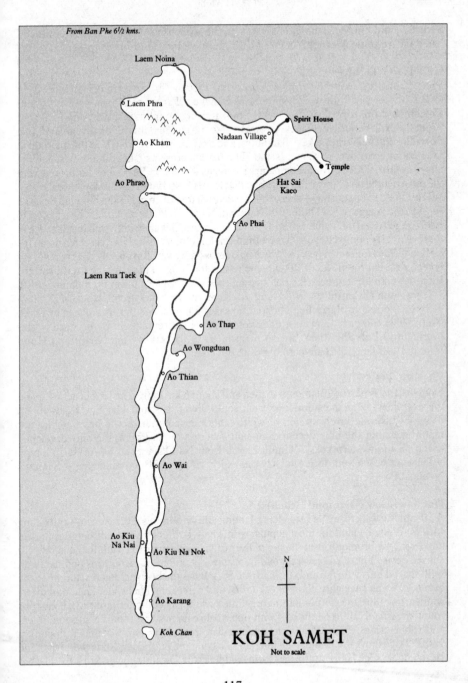

From Ban Phe 6½ kms.

Laem Noina

Laem Phra

Spirit House

Nadaan Village

Ao Kham

Temple

Ao Phrao

Hat Sai Kaeo

Ao Phai

Laem Rua Taek

Ao Thap

Ao Wongduan

Ao Thian

Ao Wai

Ao Kiu Na Nai

Ao Kiu Na Nok

Ao Karang

Koh Chan

N

KOH SAMET

Not to scale

Saturday, and ran the gauntlet of seven separate Thai beach parties (at each of which I had to share some Mekong!) before finally finding a bungalow to collapse in!

GETTING THERE
From Bangkok's Eastern Terminal, buses run at regular intervals from 5 am to 5.30 pm to **Rayong**, a small town 220 km east of Bangkok. Fares are 38B non air-con, 69B air-con, and the trip takes 2½ hours. From Rayong, minibuses leave every half-hour (from the rank behind the Clock Tower, next to the cinema) for the small hamlet of Ban Phe. The 20 km journey takes 40 minutes, and the fare is 10B. From Ban Phe pier, there are regular boats over to Samet Island. The 6.5 km crossing takes 30 minutes, and the one-way fare is 20B. Several companies run boats out of Ban Phe—look for the one with the most people on it: this will be the one that leaves first. But in low season, there's often only a couple of boats a day—then, you just take what you can get! Samet-bound boats go *either* to the village of **Na Daan** (for Diamond, Naga, Ao Phai and Tubtim beaches) *or* to **Ao Wong Duan** (for Tantawan and Ao Tian). All beaches are within walking distance of these two ferry points. Rayong has an Immigration Office, useful for visa extensions. It's a 5B taxi ride from town (ask for *plak nam*), across the river. Rayong also has two decent hotels, with fan rooms for 100B, air-con rooms for 200B. These are the **Otani** and the **Rayong**, both located near the bus station, opposite the clock tower on Sukhumvit Rd.
   If you don't want to go to Rayong at all, there are buses from Bangkok (Eastern Terminal) direct to **Ban Phe**. The journey takes 3 hours, and tickets are sold by **D. D. Tour**. This company, however, does not enjoy a good reputation. If you need to stay overnight in Ban Phe (there are no night boats to Samet), try the **Nuannapa Hotel** (rooms 100B fan, 150B air-con) opposite the pier.

WHERE TO STAY
Samet island is narrow, diamond-shaped and about 6 km long. The best beaches are on the east coast, and the hour-long walk south along it—from Hat Say Kaew to Ao Tian—is just one lovely stretch of white sand after another. Some beaches hire out motorbikes, but the only decent excursion is across to Ao Phrao, the only developed beach on the western coast. Minibuses run from Na Daan as far as Ao Thap Thim. Whichever beach you decide to stay on, expect to pay a 5B 'entrance fee'—Samet is National Park territory.

Hat Say Kaew (Diamond Beach)
A 10-minute walk from Na Daan ferry-landing, this is Samet's nicest beach—and (along with Ao Wong Deuan) the most popular with Thais. It offers silvery-soft sands, calm sea, and (from the promontory at the top of the beach, above the white Buddha) magnificent sunset views. There are several good bungalow operations. **Diamond** is popular, with well-spaced huts with fan and shower from 50B. It has the best seafood restaurant on the beach, offering speciality Tuna Steak (50B) and agreeable Thai wine. Diamond offers windsurfing (80B per hour—but there is little surf till December or January!), boat-trips round the island (100B per head—with stops to dive for oysters!), snorkelling equipment and rubber rings. **Ploy Thaloy** has immaculate rooms (no fan, but linoed floors!) at 100B. **Toy** enjoys the dubious distinction of having the only video (so far) on Diamond Beach. It has nice 100B bungalows (twin-bedded, with fan and shower at 100B). Toy has

118

a good restaurant, with a novelty menu (e.g. Same Noodle served on plate with gravy). **Whitesands** is a place to eat, not stay. Try the 'Curry in Pot' dinner—it feeds three people for just 60B. Glass-bottom boat trips leave from Whitesands at 1 pm daily—the charge is 150B (15B each, if there are 10 of you!). They don't leave at all when the captain has a hangover—very common at weekends!

Naga

Just below Diamond, Naga is a clean secluded cove with a pretty spirit-house and a mermaid on the rocks. Every year, local fishermen turn up with carved wooden phalli for Tuktim, the island goddess, to ensure good luck at sea. Lately, Naga is said to be attracting a lot of graduates and young professionals but I didn't meet any. The beach has two well-run sets of bungalows. **Naga** is run by Sue and Toss—a lovely English-Thai couple—and is famous for its delicious home-made bread, chocolate cake, meat pies and cookies. There's also a shop here—handy for stocking up on mozzie repellent, sun-cream and basic supplies. Sue is a mine of local information, and has a standard year-round price (60B single, 80B double) for her bungalows. Nearby **Nui** has huts at 70B single, 100B double, and makes superlative coconut ice-cream and yoghurt. Just below Nui's, there's a small gaily-painted ashram, run by a friendly lady who puts up travellers for a nominal donation.

Ao Phai (Paradise Beach)

This is a small cosy beach, with pebble-sand and some rocks. There are catamarans (250B per hour) and windsurfers (80B per hour) for hire. **Charlie's** offers well-furnished 'chalet' bungalows at 200B single, 300B double (low season rates). **Ao Phai** and **Seabreeze** have much more basic huts from 50B. **Knop's Kitchen** offers great seafood and nightly barbecues (October to January only).

Ao Thap Thim—Ao Nuan

On Ao Thap Thim, a popular spot, stay at **Tuktim** (lovely new 300B chalets, spartan 50B huts) or **Pudsa** (good-value bungalows at 50B single, 80B double). Ao Nuan is a delightful little cove, down on the rocks below Thap Thim—find it if you can! The single operation here is **Nuan Kitchen** ('Judy's Place') run by an English-Thai couple. It offers tasteful custom-built bungalows from 80B, also hammocks, mellow sounds and good food (try Chicken with Hot Basil Leaf on Rice—the speciality!).

Tantawan (Sunflower Beach)

This is a large, pleasant beach with a pier—handy for boats back to Ban Phe. **Ao Chaw** has 50B huts with fan, shower and mosquito nets—the best budget deal on the island! It also has an overseas telephone (collect calls only—Ban Phe has a proper overseas phone service). **Tantawan** is another good outfit, with comfy huts (100B single, 150B double) and an umbrella-shaded beach restaurant. **Bamboo Restaurant**, set back from the beach, offers boat trips to beautiful **Tha Lu Island** (great for fishing and snorkelling) every Monday and Friday, from October to February, at 100B per person.

Ao Wong Duan (Seahorse Beach)

Ao Wong Duan is a large crescent beach, quickly becoming a yuppie wonderland. Sea views are marred by boats clustered round the pier, and litter clutters the once-virgin white sands. It's all rather tacky, and geared to people with lots of money and no initiative to look elsewhere. The so-called 'luxury resort'—**Wong Duan Villas**—charges 500B for dingy chalets, and 15B for a go on its golf course (actually, a 9-hole pitch and putt). It also hires out noisy jet-skis for 400B per hour. Nearby **Malibu** restaurant serves Fish 'n' Chips, Gordon Blue, and Fillet Steak with Bernie's Sauce! Thankfully, there's **Wong Duan Resort**, with nice 250B rooms (with toilet rolls!), boat-trips to Tha Lu Island, water-sports (windsurfing, scuba, snorkelling), and lovely staff. **Malibu** also has nice bungalows, but at 300B (low season) they're way overpriced. The sole surviving budget outfit on this beach is **Seahorse**, with okay 50B huts and superior food.

Ao Thian (Candlelight Beach)
Despite its motto ('Civilisation Beach—Free is Now!') this narrow, undeveloped beach is strictly for ascetics and nature-lovers. Food and accommodation are depressingly primitive, and there's often a shortage of water. **Lum Dang** has the best stretch of beach, and huts are 50B single, 70B double. Things may improve shortly on Ao Thian. They're building like crazy!

There's little development below Candlelight—if you want to stay further south, it's often a case of camping out on the beach. At the southern tip of the island, a half-hour walk down from Ao Thian, there's some excellent coral-diving and snorkelling to be had.

Ao Phrao (Coconut Beach)
This one is on the western coast—a 20-minute walk across the mainland from the rocks above Ao Phai. Ao Phrao is famous for its amazing sunsets. It's also supposed to be quiet and secluded—but is anything but at weekends when the Thais arrive! Still, it's a nice spot—with a completely different feel to the east coast. Two good outfits, **Ao Plao** and **Coconut**, offer bungalows from 50B to 200B.

Part V

THE NORTH

Wat Prasingh Buddha, Chiang Mai

Bordered by Burma and Laos, the North has been the birthplace of many powerful kingdoms—notably Sukhothai (1238) and Chiang Mai (1296)—and today is a fascinating pot pourri of different peoples, including the exotic hilltribes of its densely forested highlands, and the quixotic travellers who trek out to meet them. There's a lot to be said for the North. It hasn't been jaded by tourism yet (unlike parts of the South) and it people remain the warmest, friendliest and most 'mellow' Thais around. Their laidback quality has less to do with opium (most of which is now gone) than with their long isolation from the rest of the country. Cut off from Thailand proper until the early 1900s, the North still retains much of its distinctive character and culture, customs and dialect. Folk dances and ethnic handicrafts are two big draws of **Chiang Mai** (the capital), which is also a popular base for hilltribe treks. From here, people trek north to the ancient kingdoms of **Chiang Rai** and **Chiang Saen** (part of the opium-producing **Golden Triangle**), or west to the remote hill regions of **Mae Hong Son**, **Mae Sariang**, **Pai** and **Soppong**, which have only recently been cleared of bandits. Alternatively they venture south to visit the historic temple-cities of **Sukhothai**, **Si Satchanalai** and **Lamphun**. Wherever you go in the North, the people are warm, the climate is cool, and the scenery is beautiful!

CHIANG MAI

Chiang Mai, the 'Rose of the North', is many peoples favourite city in Thailand. Beautifully situated in a high valley at the foot of majestic Doi Suthep mountain, it has a refreshingly cool climate and a calm, relaxing atmosphere—the perfect antidote to steamy, frenetic Bangkok, 700 km to the south. A fast-developing tourist centre—famous for its hilltribe treks, ethnic handicrafts, and over 300 temples—Chiang Mai has virtually doubted in size over the past few years, making it Thailand's second-largest city with a population of 150,000. Owing to its mountainous situation, it was virtually cut off from Bangkok until the late 1920s, but is now feeling the full impact of modernization. This is noticeable in the plethora of German beer parlours, European restaurants, trekking agencies and cheap guest houses which have invaded the town centre. Yet Chiang Mai still (somehow) hangs on to its charming 'village' atmosphere, and retains its distinctive culture, customs and cuisine. Wander down any backstreet, and the façade of modern living simply drops away—most of the town's-folk continue to live their lives as in ages past, seemingly unaffected by the bomb of 'progress' exploding around them. They are a happy, easy-going, yet independent people with their own lilting dialect, their own dances and festivals, and (especially in the case of the small hilltribe population) their own colourful costumes and customs. This said, the sight of an Akha girl in full tribal outfit crossing the road (probably on the way home from a Khantoke dinner dance) is today as worthy of comment as, say, a *farang* crossing the same street 20 years ago! Chiang Mai has numerous attractions of its own, but also makes an ideal base for exploring the north of Thailand. It's the kind of place where travellers spend a good deal longer than first planned—or wish they had!

History

Chiang Mai (new city) was built in 1296 by King Mengrai to replace Chiang Rai as the capital of his fast-expanding Lan Na Thai ('One Million Rice Fields') kingdom, which had emerged—along with Mengrai himself—from the old Thai kingdom of Nan Chao in south-west China. From this time on, Chiang Mai remained the principal city of the north, surviving various crises including Burmese occupation and long periods of virtual abandonment. Though the state remained independent for almost 500 years, it was for much of this time vassal to neighbouring powers, such as Ayutthaya, Burma and Luang Prabang.

Every northern Thai kingdom has a legendary background, and Chiang Mai is no exception. Apparently, King Mengrai was out hunting one day, and spotted five mice running down a hole beneath a sacred Bo tree. The appearance of two white sambar deer and two white barking deer clinched it—with three such lucky omens behind him, Mengrai had no real choice but to found a new city! On a more practical level, he needed Chiang Mai as a power-centre to control an empire which was to extend beyond Sukhothai to the south, and as far north as Luang Prabang in Laos. Some 90,000 men working day and night were used to construct the city, and the original walls were completed in just four months. The present siting of the walls and moat, however, date only from the early 19th century—Mengrai's successors altered the city layout and relocated its fortifications on several different occasions.

After Mengrai died in 1317 (reputedly struck by lightning), the kingdom went from strength to strength. It reached the peak of its power and influence under Tiloka Raja (the 'King of the Three Worlds'), whose reigning years—the mid-15th century—are now considered the Golden Age of the Lan Na Thai civilization. In 1556, however, following a period of decline, the kingdom was captured by Burma and became her vassal. For the next 200 years, it was used as a popular base for the Burmese in their wars with the Thais further south. It was only in 1775, in the wake of Ayutthaya's collapse, that King Taksin of Thonburi marched his victorious army north and finally liberated the Lan Na Thai kingdom from its Burmese oppressors. Under the Chakri kings, Chiang Mai remained, at first, semi-autonomous with its own hereditary princes, but then slowly fell under the expanding central control of Bangkok. When the last governor-prince died in 1938, no-one was named to succeed him.

Today, Chiang Mai is two cities in one. The old 13th-century city, with its moat and few remaining sections of thick walls, lies some distance west of the Ping River. The newer city—with its modern hotels and restaurants, rows of shops and handicraft emporiums—is spread all around the old city, between its moat and the river, as well as across the river on the east bank. This area—extending from Ta Pae Gate to Nawarat Bridge—now comprises 'downtown' Chiang Mai. The railway station and the main post office lie on the eastern bank of the river, while the airport is situated to the southwest.

Thanks to its altitude (300 metres above sea level), Chiang Mai is, for much of the year, cooler and less humid than anywhere else in Thailand. Average temperatures are 20°C from October to February (cool season); 30°C from March to May (hot season), and 25°C from June to September (rainy season). For scenery, come in September or October—just after the monsoons—when the valley is at its most beautiful. During December and January, it can get quite cold (an icicle was reported one legendary night) and it's wise to bring a sweater and woolly socks!

Chiang Mai celebrates many joyous festivals—the most notable being the **Flower Carnival** (first weekend of February), the water-throwing festival of **Songkran** (April 13–15) and the candle-floating festival of **Loi Krathong** (Full Moon day of the twelfth lunar month, usually mid-November). They are all exceedingly popular, and it's wise to book transport and accommodation in advance at each celebration.

GETTING THERE

By Air
Thai Airways offer several flights daily to Chiang Mai from Bangkok (standard fare 1275B; night-flight fare, Friday and Sunday, 1020B; it's a one-hour flight). From Chiang Mai, Thai Airways fly to Chiang Rai (300B), Hat Yai (2580B), Phitsanoluke (505B), Phuket (2400B), Surat Thani (2260B) and Udorn Thani (1945B). To book flights, contact Thai Airways (Domestic), Prappoklao Rd, Chiang Mai (tel 211044–6), Thai International, Changklang Rd, Chiang Mai (tel 234150), or one of the town's many travel agents. Advance booking is recommended, especially in the winter high season. Chiang Mai airport is only 3 km out of town, a cheap ride by *songthaew* (15–20B), *tuk-tuk* (30B) or taxi (50B).

By Rail
From Bangkok's Hualamphong station, there are two trains daily to Chiang Mai, both with sleeper facility. The quick, popular Express train leaves Bangkok at 6 pm, and arrives in Chiang Mai at 7.40 am. The (not so) Rapid train leaves 3.45 pm, arrives 6.35 am. Basic fares are 537B 1st class, 255B 2nd class, 121B 3rd class. Most people buy a 2nd-class sleeper seat (add 150B upper berth, 180B lower berth) on the fast Express

train (add another 30B). Lower berth sleeper seats give fine early-morning window views of Chiang Mai valley. Going up to Chiang Mai by train has several advantages—it's safer than the bus, there are great food stops (every station on the way is a bustle of platform vendors running relays of hardboiled eggs, savoury *kai yang*, mango juice and bottled drinks), and, most important, you arrive pleasantly refreshed, after a good night's sleep.

From Chiang Mai, the 4.50 pm Express train leaves daily for Bangkok—making useful stops at Lamphun, Phitsanoluke, Lopburi, Ayutthaya, Bang Pa In and Don Muang International Airport. This train is invariably full, and should be booked 3–4 days in advance. For seat reservations, contact Chiang Mai rail station, Charoenmuang Rd (tel 244795 same-day bookings; 242094 advance bookings). There's a useful baggage deposit (open 6 am to 6 pm) and hotel-booking desk at Chiang Mai rail station. You can also pick up a free city map here.

By Bus

From Bangkok's Northern Terminal, non air-con buses leave for Chiang Mai at regular intervals from 5.25 am to 10 pm (9 hours, fare 133B); four air-con buses leave between 9 am and 10 am, eight more between 8 pm and 9.45 pm (8 hours; fare 242B). Several private bus companies in Bangkok (mainly operating out of travel agencies or guest houses in Banglampoo and Soi Ngam Dupli) and in Chiang Mai (same deal, Moon Muang and Ta Pae roads) offer cheaper tickets, especially for round-trips. Many travellers favour the bus over the train—it's cheaper and quicker. Also, the recent introduction of video cameras on many night buses has greatly reduced the risk of being drugged and robbed—though it's still safer to travel by daylight. Going by night bus, you're not likely to get much sleep. As one couple reported:

We took the overnight bus to Chiang Mai, and at first couldn't get over how civilized it was. As soon as we set off, a smart hostess appeared with a food parcel, containing a chicken drumstick, a piece of cake and an iced Coke. Minutes later, she returned, this time with free toilet paper! This was followed by an issue of paper towels and warm blankets. At the unearthly hour of 2 am, 'lunch' arrived—a bowl of rice with hard-boiled eggs and dried, sickly-sweet fish. Sleep wasn't easy after this, especially when the air-conditioning went into hyperdrive, turning the bus into a fridge! Around 5 am, the hostess whipped our blankets away and we froze to death. She said she wanted to get 'organized' for the next lot of tourists!

Chiang Mai has two bus stations. The **Arcade** terminal services Bangkok, Chiang Rai, Mae Hong Son, Phitsanoluke, Udorn Thani, Korat and all destinations outside the province. The **White Elephant** (Chang Phuak) terminal services Bosang–Sankamphaeng, Lamphun–Pasang, Fang–Tha Ton, and all destinations within Chiang Mai province.

TOURIST INFORMATION

TAT Tourist Office (tel 235334) is at 135 Praisani Rd, just below Nawarat Bridge. Staff are very helpful, and hand out a complete 'tourist information pack' (includes maps, bus/train timetables, hotel listings, photocopied sheets on provincial attractions). They also issue the monthly mag *Welcome to Chiang Mai*, full of current news and events.

Books

D. K. Book House, opposite Suriwongse Hotel, is good for maps (including Nancy Chandler's 60B city map/guide), travel books, dictionaries, English/Thai fiction etc. **D. K. Books**, at the moat end of Ta Pae Rd, has a wide selection of art, history, religious and cultural titles. Both D. K. shops are open 8.30 am to 8 pm daily. For cheap, second-hand maps, guides and fiction books, visit the small **Library Service** at 21/1 Ratchamanka Soi 2 (off Moon Muang Rd, below Oasis Bar).

Post Office

The main GPO, Charoen Muang Rd (east of Nawarat Bridge) has a handy 24-hour overseas phone/telex service (telegrams, from 11 am to 7 pm only). The small post office, just above Warorot market, is open 8.30 am to 4.30 pm only, but is far more central. Travellers come here to buy stamps/aerogrammes, to send parcels (packing service, 6B a kilo, at the entrance) and to queue up for overseas calls (one booth only, open 8.30 am to 12 noon daily). Domestic calls are best made from Lek House, Moon Muang Rd—using public phones in Chiang Mai is a *very* risky business!

Immigration & Banks

Immigration Office, for visa-extensions, is off Highway 1141, near the airport. After the banks close, change money at **Krung Thai Exchange**, Ta Pae Rd (open 8.30 am to 8 pm) or Bangkok Bank Exchange at the Night Bazaar 'Plaza' (open 8 am to 10 pm).

GETTING AROUND

Chiang Mai is a compact city—ideal for exploration **by bicycle**. Several places in town hire out bikes (around 20B a day), but give them a short 'test ride' before paying any money. Cycling 11 km back to town from the Crafts Villages on just one pedal is no joke, believe me! For trips further afield (e.g. to Doi Suthep) consider hiring a **motorbike**. Chiang Mai has such a surplus of motorbikes that rates are very cheap (from 70B a day) and getting a trial run before paying is no problem. Some places (unheard of anywhere else in Thailand) even give guarantees against engine failure and breakdowns. There are many hire places along Moon Muang Rd—or you can enquire at your hotel/guest house. For **car/jeep** rental, contact **Ping Tour & Travel**, corner of Loi Kroh & Khotchasam roads (tel 236310), **Chiangmai Travel Centre**, Rincome Hotel (tel 221692) or **Butterfly Tour**, 82 Samlarn Road.

    Songthaews (red minibuses) are the cheapest form of local transport. They'll take you anywhere on their (more or less) fixed route for only 5B. But you have to know *exactly* where you're going—if you don't, a passenger who does will always get priority. It sometimes saves time to charter a whole *songthaew* for yourself (20–30B). **Tuk–tuks** are a fairly recent arrival in Chiang Mai. Noisy, but quick, they don't cross the street for less than 20B (which is the average short-hop fare). Man-powered **samlors** are useful for getting to certain places (e.g. the Night Bazaar) denied to motorized transport. Average charge is 10B, but they don't cross the street at all during 'siesta' (i.e. most of the afternoon). Most people can walk faster than a Chiang Mai *samlor*.

    For local sightseeing in comfy **air-con buses**, contact well-established travel agents like **Discovery**, c/o Chiang Mai Plaza Hotel (tel 221044), **July**, c/o Suriwongse Hotel (tel 236733) or **World Travel Service**, c/o Rincome Hotel (tel 221692).

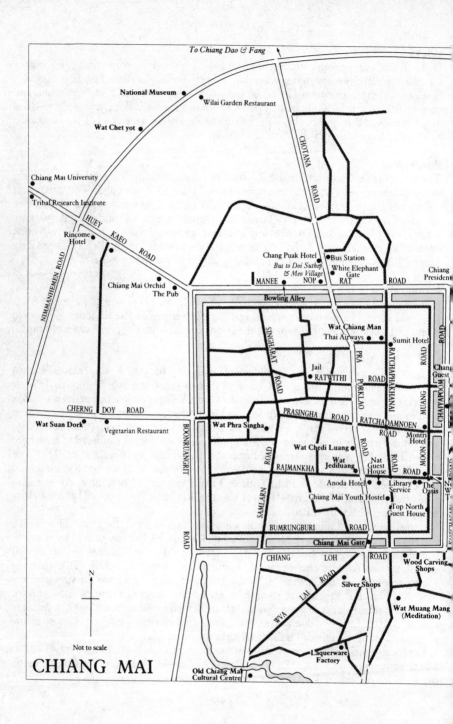

To Chiang Dao & Fang

National Museum
Wilai Garden Restaurant

Wat Chet yot

Chiang Mai University

Tribal Research Institute

CHOTANA ROAD

HUEY KAEO ROAD

Rincome Hotel

NIMMANHEMEN ROAD

Chiang Mai Orchid
The Pub

Chang Puak Hotel
Bus to Doi Suthep
& Meo Village

Bus Station
White Elephant Gate

Chiang Presiden

MANEE
NOP
RAT
ROAD

Bowling Alley

SINGHARAT ROAD

Wat Chiang Man
Thai Airways

Sumit Hotel

RATCHAPHAKHINAI

MUANG ROAD

Chang Guest

Jail
RATWITHI

PRA PORKLAO ROAD

ROAD

CHIAYAPOOM ROAD

CHERNG DOY ROAD

Prasingha ROAD

RATCHADAMNOEN ROAD

Wat Suan Dork
Vegetarian Restaurant

Wat Phra Singha

Montri Hotel

BOONRUANGRIT ROAD

SAMLARN ROAD

Wat Chedi Luang

Wat Jediluang

Nat Guest House

MOON ROAD

N
W
E

RAJMANKHA

ROAD

Anoda Hotel
Chiang Mai Youth Hostel

Library Service
The Oasis

Top North Guest House

BUMRUNGBURI ROAD

Chiang Mai Gate

CHIANG LOH ROAD

Wood Carving Shops

WUA LAI ROAD

Silver Shops

N

Wat Muang Mang
(Meditation)

Not to scale

Laquerware Factory

CHIANG MAI

Old Chiang Mai Cultural Centre

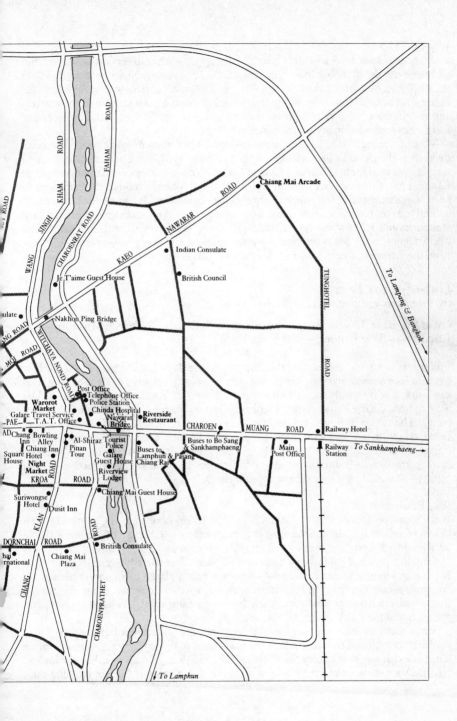

Chiang Mai Arcade

Indian Consulate

Je T'aime Guest House

British Council

Nakhon Ping Bridge

WANG SINGH KHAM ROAD

FAHAM ROAD

CHAROENRAT ROAD

KAEO

NAWARAR ROAD

TUNGHOTEL ROAD

To Lampang & Bangkok

WITCHAYA NOND ROAD

Post Office
Telephone Office
Police Station
Warorot
Market
Galare Travel Service
-PAE— T.A.T. Office
Chinda Hospital
Nawarat
Bridge
Riverside
Restaurant
CHAROEN MUANG ROAD
Railway Hotel

Chang Bowling
Inn Alley
Chiang Inn
Square
House Hotel
Night
Market
Al-Shiraz Tourist
Police
Pinan
Tour
Galare
Guest House
Riverview
Lodge
Buses to
Lamphun & Pasang
Chiang Rai
Buses to Bo Sang
& Sankhamphaeng
Main
Post Office
Railway
Station
To Sankhamphaeng

KROA ROAD

KLAN

ROAD

Suriwongse
Hotel
Dusit Inn

Chiang Mai Guest House

DORNCHAI ROAD

CHANG

ROAD

Chiang Mai
Plaza

British Consulate

CHAROENPRATHET

To Lamphun

ulate

G ROAD

MOI ROAD

AD

WHAT TO SEE

You'll need at least a week to 'do' Chiang Mai properly—it has so very much to offer. Set aside one day for shopping (morning, crafts factories; evening, Night Bazaar), 3–5 days for a hilltribe trek, and 2 days for sightseeing. The first thing to do (if you're here for exercise) is to book your trek. While that's coming together, you can slot in the markets and the temples. Save relaxation till the very end. Chiang Mai's general ambience of inertia has grounded many a good traveller!

Most of Chiang Mai's sights are temples—well, it has an even higher concentration of them than Bangkok! In just one square mile of the old city, there are no fewer than 40 temples, many of them still in use. Chiang Mai temple architecture is a flamboyant mix of Lanna Thai, Burmese, Sri Lankan and Mon styles. There's enough diversity here to keep your interest alive and your camera clicking! As Chiang Mai is an education centre, several temples have schools or universities attached (great for making friends with Thai student monks!). Many also have attractive gardens, full of exotic flowers and plants. But nearly all of Chiang Mai's temples are quiet, spacious and peaceful—a pleasant change from the crowded, touristy *wats* of Bangkok or Sukhothai.

Out-of-town Tour

(by *songthaew*, car, motorbike; full day)

– Wat Phrathat (Doi Suthep) – Tribal Research Centre – National Museum – Wat Ched Yod – Wat Umong – Wat Suan Dork

Full marks to anyone completing this tour in just one day—but it *is* possible! Your best bet is to hire a motorbike or a car for the day. Hopping from sight to sight by *songthaew* can work, but it's costly in time and money. There are regular *songthaews* up to Doi Suthep from Chang Phuak (White Elephant) Gate on Manee Noparat Rd (north wall of moat). The fare is 30B up, 20B down. Going to the Tribal Research Centre, insist on being taken to the *songthaew* rank inside the university campus. If dumped at the university entrance, you've a long, long walk ahead—it's a vast campus. *Songthaew* drivers are presently in a stew about the proposed cable-car construction at Doi Suthep—it would put half of them out of business!

Wat Prathat

Wat Prathat on Doi Suthep mountain is located 16 km northwest of Chiang Mai, at a height of almost 1000 m. It's the most important temple in Chiang Mai, the most visible local landmark, and the one thing that everybody tries to see. The site of Wat Prathat was chosen, in typically Thai fashion, by a royal elephant. The late 14th-century ruler King Ku Na, looking for somewhere to put some holy relics, placed them on the back of his favourite white elephant and let it wander off up the mountain. Near the top, it trumpeted, circled three times, and knelt down—very auspicious. A *chedi* was erected on the spot, and the relics enshrined therein.

Some accounts have the elephant keeling over and suffering a heart attack. Once you've climbed the 306 steps marking the final ascent to the temple, this seems the more likely story! If you don't fancy the exercise, take the short ride up by cable-car instead (10B). Don't show up at the temple in shorts or sleeveless tops ('Dress impolite can't enter this temple'). Entering the inner compound, you'll find the small plated *chedi* housing the Buddha's relics, also a strange little shrine to a sacred chicken, which used to peck the feet of any visitor who strolled in wearing shoes. The present temple—comprising two 16th-century sanctuaries built over the original buildings—is nothing special. But its location, on a clear day, provides splendid views down over Chiang mai and the mountain valley. Try and arrive early in the morning, before the heat (and the mist) gets up. The two big festivals at the temple—Buddha's birthday (Full Moon in May) and Songkran—are especially good times to visit.

Tribal Research Centre
The Tribal Research Centre is located at Chiang Mai University, 5 km west of town. It's a 5-minute walk from the *songthaew* rank within the campus. The centre is worth a visit for its small, fascinating museum of hilltribe artefacts—an excellent introduction to the various peoples who inhabit the highlands of northern Thailand. Come here if you're planning to go on a trek—the centre's small library is a great place to bone up on the hilltribes. Opening times are 8.30 am – 12 noon, 1 pm – 4.30 pm, Mon – Fri.

National Museum
You'll find the National Museum on the Superhighway, northwest of town. It's a small but interesting museum, with a fine collection of Buddha heads and images—mainly bronze and stucco—depicting the evolution of the various architectural styles of north-ern and central Thailand. The ground floor has a massive Buddha's footprint (wood, inlaid with mother-of-pearl), a goliath Buddha's head from the late-15th century, and some beautiful Lanna Thai ceramics. Upstairs, there's the Prince of Chiang Mai's bed (fully mosquito-netted!) and some giant temple drums. Everything, from San Kam-phaeng pottery to the smallest tribal implement, is well-labelled and tastefully presented. Admission to the museum is 10B, and it's open 9 am – 12 noon. 1 pm – 4 pm, Wed – Sun.

Wat Ched Yod
Wat Ched Yod is a short stroll south of the museum. It was probably built by King Tilokaraja in 1455, and its proper name is Wat Photharam Maha Viharn. The *ched yod* refers to the 'seven spires' of its *chedi*—the unusual design of which derives from the Mahabodhi temple in Bodhgaya, India. There's a spire for each of the seven weeks Buddha spent in Bodhgaya after attaining enlightenment under the Bo tree. One of Chiang Mai's most important temples, Ched Yod is also one of the most striking. Instead of the usual bell-shaped *chedi*, here we have a square edifice with friezes of bejewelled, crosslegged Buddhas (very Hindu) running round the base. Some, notably on the northeast corner of the *chedi*, are completely intact. Beyond them are two Bo trees—both descended (via Sri Lankan saplings) from the 'original'. Nearby, there's a smaller *chedi*, built in 1487 to contain Tiloraja's ashes. This is another square structure, with elements of Sukhothai, Lanna Thai and even Romanesque architectural styles. It has floral Renaissance arches and square Doric pillars, and—like every other monument in the compound—is guarded by temple dogs. I asked a monk why there were so many dogs and he said: 'It's very simple—people donate dogs to the temple, because they know we will feed them. The more dogs we have, the easier it is for us to keep our vows of fasting! Apart from its dogs and its unique architecture, this temple has great historical

importance. It was here that the 8th World Buddhist Council met in 1477 to revise the Tripitaka, or Buddhist teachings.

Wat Umong

Returning south down Nimanhemin Rd, turn east up Cherng Doy (Suthep) Rd. About a kilometre past the canal, a sign for **Wat Umong** appears on the left of the highway. If coming from town (5 km away), it's a 10B *songthaew* ride. Wat Umong was founded by Mengrai in 1296, and is a typical example of a forest *wat*—quiet and secluded, with a mirror-calm lake, several meditative walks, and a large park (open 6 am – 6 pm) full of deer, gibbon and exotic birds. The woods are host to a scattering of wooden monks' houses, one of which sells homeopathic medicines (cured my cough!) made from rare plants and herbs grown in the forest. Little remains of the original temple, apart from a large ruined *chedi* with underground chambers where monks once meditated. Some of the niches in the crypt still contain Buddha images. At the top of the steps leading up to the ruins, there's a small pillar—a replica of Emperor Ashoka's pillar in India. Near this is an odd little art gallery full of Dali-esque daubs left behind by monks who've spent time here. For a pleasant woodland walk—and possible wildlife sightings—a path leads off left past the grotesque 'starving Buddha' below the ruined *chedi* to a small gate, giving access to the woods. In the main temple area, all trees have quaint 'moral messages' in Thai, Chinese and English. Some are enigmatic ('Little sacrifice for larger sacrifice is truly dropping a bait'), others are puritan ('A mind without work is most troubled') and one in particular is written for travellers ('To shoulder sufferings, a fool submits himself to the weight of sufferings at the same place. He is seated until his legs become atrophied. He is thus overloaded all his life, being always enslaved by sensual delights'). Every Sunday, between 3 pm and 5 pm, the head *bhikku* gives lectures at the *wat* (in English) on Buddhist meditation. There's a good 5B guide at the small library/museum.

Wat Suan Dork

Wat Suan Dork appears off Cherng Doy Rd, on the way back to town from Wat Umong. This 'Flower Garden Temple' was built around 1383 by King Ku Na. It started out as the pleasure gardens of the early Lanna Thai kings, and later became their permanent resting place. Most of the royals of Chiang Mai are buried in the cemetery adjoining the temple—Indonesian-style *chedis* contain their ashes. The central *chedi* contains a Buddha relic which arrived here on the back of a white elephant, after which the city's White Elephant Gate was named. Of the recently restored temple buildings, the main hall is the largest in the North and houses a sitting Buddha and several smaller images. The *bot* holds the famous Chiang Saen-style bronze Buddha, seated and very large. It was constructed in 1504. Just past the main *viharn*, turn right down a small path to find a small house which gives traditional Thai massage (*nuad*) at 100B an hour. Back on the main road, beside the temple, there's an excellent hilltribe craft shop, selling a lot of weavings that you won't find anywhere else. Prices are very reasonable.

In-town Temples
(by bicycle/*songthaew*; half day)

Wat Chedi Luang – Wat Phra Singh – Wat Chang Man

These three temples are all fairly close to each other, within the city walls. You can see them in a morning, and in any order. If, at the end of the day, you want still more temples, just close your eyes and wander down any backstreet to find some!

Wat Chedi Luang

Wat Chedi Luang is on Phra Pokklao Rd, near the intersection with Rajmankha Rd. It has pleasant gardens, several quiescent dogs, and a massive, partially ruined *chedi*—commenced by King Saen Muang Ma in 1401, completed by his queen, and enlarged to a height of 86 metres by King Tilokaraja in 1454. Damaged by an earthquake in 1545, it is only now being considered for restoration. The eastern niche is reputed to have once contained the famous Emerald Buddha. The *bot* has a gleaming gold Buddha (standing) and 32 *jakarta* story panels. The *nagas* flanking the entrance steps are popularly regarded as architectural masterpieces. And there's a great gum tree with an interesting legend—it's said that as long as the tree stands, so will Chiang Mai. Behind the main *wat*, there's a stunning Buddha cut into the hillside—a dramatic sight indeed, when viewed at sunset.

Wat Phra Singh

Wat Phra Singh, at the intersection of Ratchadamnoen and Singharat roads, is one of Chiang Mai's biggest and oldest temples. The large *chedi* was begun in 1345 by King Pha Yu to hold the ashes of his father. The small *viharn* left of the white *stupa* was erected around 1400, to put up an unexpected guest—the important Phra Singh Buddha, which dropped in on its way to Chiang Mai (the chariot carrying it foundered at this spot) and never dropped out again. This is one of three Phra Singh images (the other two are in Bangkok and Nakhon Si Thammarat). It is in the early Chiang Saen style and—despite losing its head in 1922 (the present one is a replica)—still purports to be the 'original' image. Well, so do the other two. The walls of the *viharn* are decorated with peeling murals, interesting for their portrayals of northern dress, customs, and everyday life. The large compound has several interesting buildings, including a university of 700 student monks—many of them delighted to stop for a chat and a photo. To the right of the *viharn*, there's a small 14th-century scripture repository. Behind this is the *bot* with its large gold Buddha, fine woodcarvings, decorative stucco-work and chandeliers.

Wat Chang Man

Wat Chang Man is on Ratchaphakhinai Rd, near Sumit Hotel. Founded in 1296 by King Mengrai (who used it as his residence while the rest of Chiang Mai was being built), it is the oldest temple in the city. Of the two *viharns* inside the entrance, the one on the right is the more interesting. This houses two venerated Buddha images—one is the tiny Crystal Buddha, said to have been presented to Queen Chamathevi of Haripunchai (modern-day Lamphun) in the 7th century. It is believed to have the power to inspire rain. So does the other image, the diminutive sensuous Buddha Sila (India, 9th century?) which sits alongside it on a raised dais. Outside, the grounds are beautiful—green lawns, tropical fruit trees, oleander and hibiscus bushes etc. This is a real 'farmyard' *wat*, with a twee turtle pond and masses of cats, dogs and chickens. The monks are very friendly—if the *viharns* are closed they'll always be willing to produce a key.

San Kamphaeng & Bo Sang
(by *songthaew*/motorbike; half day)

Chiang Mai is the largest centre for cottage industries in Thailand. The two handicraft villages of **San Kamphaeng** and **Bo Sang**—respectively 13 km and 9 km east of Chiang Mai—produce most of the silk, silver, lacquerware, celadon ceramics, woodcarvings and painted umbrellas found in the street markets of Chiang Mai. Prices aren't necessarily cheaper than in town (indeed, several craft factories are fixed-price) but the quality of goods is generally more reliable—especially silver and lacquerware. Even if you don't intend buying anything, bring your credit card along—you may change your mind! If you don't, there's still much enjoyment to be derived from watching the various craftsmen employing their traditional tools and techniques. Many of the larger factories give interesting English-speaking commentaries, describing the various manufacturing processes. All factories have a showroom (often air-conditioned) and can arrange to send large purchases home for you. There are dozens of craft places lining the famous '13 Kilometre Strip' between Chiang Mai and San Kamphaeng. The places recommended in the sections below are currently those with the best workshop layout, and the best range of fairly priced products.

Don't feel restricted, though—if travellers recommend other good factories, check them out! Buses run up to Bo Sang (4B) and to San Kamphaeng (5B) every 15 minutes or so from Charoen Muang Rd (see map). *Tuk-tuks* can be hired out at 80–100B for a morning—a good option, if there's a group of you. Motorbikes are still the best bet though—very handy for nipping back and forth between the various factories. To save time, it makes sense (as suggested in the order of crafts below) to work your way back to town, having taken the most outlying factory as your starting point.

Silk
Shinawatra Thai Silk, 145/1–2 Chiangmai-Sankhampaeng Rd (tel 331–950; tx 49337 MULBERY TH) is a busy cottage industry where primitive manual handlooms turn out reams of richly-coloured silk cloth. The processes of silk production, well illustrated here, are fascinating—first, the silk-worms are gorged on mulberry leaves; later, the cream-yellow thread is drawn from the cast-off cocoons (just one cocoon can produce 1200 metres of silk thread!) and bleached white or colour-dyed. A single hand-operated loom, working full-pelt, can produce up to 7 or 8 metres of silk material in one day. All prices at the silk factory are *fixed*. If it's just lengths of silk you're after, you'll probably get them cheaper in Bangkok. However, there are some unique colour-combination patterns here which you simply won't find elsewhere—well worth a little extra expense. Standard 2-ply plain silk (suitable for shirts and blouses) sells at 220B a yard; heavier 4-ply cloth (for suits, bedcovers, furnishings etc) at 290B a yard. There's a good range of silk scarves (250B), hankies (70B), shirts (600B), and patterned kimonos (from 2000B). Silk ties, in rather unexciting colours, are around 150B. For men, the best buy of all are double-breasted suits (lined and interfaced) in heavy black silk at only 3600B (£80)—fitted and made up in just three days. Any other items you want tailored (suits, dresses, shirts etc.) will appear at your hotel within 24 hours! But you may well find what you want in the readymade section. Ladies can buy smart, fashionable silk jackets, off the peg, for around 1200B (£25)—about one-third of London prices. Shinawatra also has a wide

selection of cotton fabrics. Thai cotton is extremely well-tempered and high quality. Prices are cheap too—around 70–100B per yard.

Lacquerware

Laitong Lacquerware is at 80/1 Moo 3, Chiangmai-Sankhampaeng Rd (tel 331178; tx 49324 CAC TH ATT T. SANGCHAK, LAITONG). Thai lacquerware is an ancient craft, which actually originated in Burma. In the past, lacquerwork was used to decorate Thai palaces and temples; today, most products are small items aimed at the tourist trade. Lacquer is a thick black resin extracted from the 'lak' tree of the northern forests. The resin is applied to bamboo or teakwood, to create beautiful bowls, boxes, vases, plates and other decorative pieces. Each item is carefully coated and polished at least seven times (and left to dry for a week between each successive coating) before being finished with eggshell, gold leaf, or handpainted decorations. As with silver, the quality of lacquerware is almost impossible to detect on sight: many lacquer pieces sold in the night market, for example, have only two or three coats. Quality at this factory is however, guaranteed. Nice buys include stylish coffee tables (around 11,000B), handpainted tea-chests (around 16,000B) and gold-leaf trinket boxes (500B). Smaller novelty purchases are lacquer ducks and owls (150–200B) and teak elephants (120B).

Teakwood

For teakwood, visit **Chiangmai Sudaluk Co**, 99/9 Ban Nongkhong, Chiangmai-Sankhampaeng Rd (tel 331489; tx SUDALUK TH). This factory is known to take the best care during its teakwood curing process—a vital consideration. Inferior 'green' teak (which looks exactly the same as seasoned woods to the average shopper), splits within a few months. Northern Thailand used to be a paradise for teak exporters, but the forests have now been sadly depleted and good-quality teak is hard to find. Prices are rising 10% each year—making anything you buy a good future investment. All items are made in perfectly interlocking sections, and are superbly carved. Another good reason for buying 'big' is that it costs more or less the same to insure and ship home one teak cabinet as it does six! Smaller teak items, you can buy more cheaply down at the Night Market.

Silverware

Na Na Phan Silverware, 159/1 Chiangmai-Sankhampaeng Rd (tel 331534) produces high-quality silverware and jewellery. Silver generally comes in three grades: 100%, 80% and plated white bronze. Much of the so-called silver sold in the markets of Chiang Mai is plated bronze, which rapidly tarnishes. Na Na Phan sells the real thing—all 'soft' jewellery (bracelets, rings, earrings etc.) is pure silver; more 'solid' stuff (bowls, teapots etc.) are a mix of 80% silver, 20% copper. Very delicate pieces are produced, cleverly blending modern and traditional designs. Prices are very reasonable—on my last visit, I was offered a 50% discount on everything *before* getting down to hard bargaining! Handbeaten silver bowls (made from old Indian rupees!) are offered at a label price of 500B. Silver bracelets go from between 500 and 3000B, necklaces from 1500 to 3000B, and earrings from 250B. If you're into gems, the best purchases are blue sapphires (400B per carat) and turquoise (250B per carat). The factory workshop is a good one, with an interesting new hilltribe jewellery section.

Umbrellas

Bo Sang Umbrella-making Village, 11/2 Opposite of Bosang (tel 331566) started out as a small family collective, but has greatly expanded over the past few years. The craft of umbrella-making, which probably originated in China, was taken up by the Bo Sang villagers some 200 years ago. The gaily-painted parasols they make are usually fashioned from the bark of mulberry trees, which is mashed flat, soaked in a vat of water, and dried (as fine fibres to form a thing paper called '*sa*'. The wafer-thin sheets of paper are applied in layers to the frame of the umbrella which (astonishingly) is cut and formed from a single piece of cane. The finished product is very strong and very practical. Things to buy are brollies (from 120B), lampshades (from 20B), and fans (from 50B)—all attractive little souvenirs. Umbrellas are best bought at this factory where there's a large selection of sunny designs—rather than in Chiang Mai. Prices in the showroom are fixed—but outside in the workshop, it's a different story. Here cheerful artisans will paint just about anything (cameras, wallets, handbags etc.) for as little as 10–20B per piece. A great idea is to turn up with a yard of plain silk, and to ask Chai—the number one artist—to daub it with a dramatic Chinese dragon or peacock. The result is an amazing silk wall-hanging at a (ridiculous) price of 300B—200B for the silk, 100B for Chai's artistry!

Trekking

Trekking out of Chiang Mai is now the major tourist draw of the North. There are over 30 tour companies in town, offering a multitude of treks from 1 to 10 days, usually a combination of walking, elephant-riding and river-rafting. All trekking has to be organized. While people do wander off into the northern hills on their own, they are advised that this is still a very volatile region—bandits, political insurgents, and even suspicious hilltribe peoples, can regard the lone traveller, unescorted by a local guide, as fair game for theft or worse.

The Hill Tribes

What makes trekking in North Thailand so special? The answer must lie in the 500,000 or so highland peoples, members of six major distinct hilltribes, who now inhabit its mountainous valleys and forests. Most of them are relative newcomers, having only arrived in Thailand over the last century, and substantial numbers are still trickling in from Burma and Laos. The hilltribes of Thailand are descended from Chinese and Tibetan Mongols. There are two main lines of descent; first, the Chinese Lolo and Nosu, who descended into Tibeto and Burmano tribes (the Tibetos subsequently became the Akha, Lisu and Lahu tribes); second, the mainstream Chinese, who descended into the Kuomintang, the famous revolutionaries. The Kuomintang later gave birth to the Meo and the Yao peoples. The sixth major line, the Karen, originated in Burma and began settling in Thailand several centuries ago.

Since the hilltribes are such a fundamental part of trekking, it's worth learning something about them before setting out. A few hours spent browsing in Chiang Mai's Tribal Research Centre library always pays dividends, as does a night out at a Khantoke dinner dance. But the best all-round introduction is Paul and Elaine Lewis' *Peoples of the Golden Triangle* (Thames and Hudson, 1984) which sells at D. K. Book Shop, Chiang Mai, at half its London price. You can also find it at Golden Triangle restaurant, Chiang

Rai (even cheaper!), which is near to where the authors live. To start you off, here's a short hilltribe primer:

Karen (Kariang, Yan) are the largest of the tribes of northern Thailand (present population 275,000) though most of the Karen people still live in Burma. They settle at low altitudes, generally around 200 metres, and are heavily engaged in shifting cultivation. The four major sub-groups are: White (Skaw), Red (Kayah), Black (Pa-o), and Pwo (or Plong) Karen. The red and white Karen have a unique language—a blend of Latin (taught them by missionaries in Burma) and northern hilltribe dialect. As a whole, the Karen are a fairly straightlaced lot, often dressed in Western clothes, but their woman (well-known for their weaving, done on a back-strap loom) are often colourfully attired. Karen girls often wear long white tunics, exchanging them for red ones when they get married. In religion, the Karen are mainly animist, though a few are Christian or Buddhist. The best hilltribe crafts come from this tribe—good things to buy (either on trek, or in Ying Ping Bazaar, Chiang Mai) are hand-embroidered jackets, woven baskets, musical instruments, tobacco pipes and animal bells.

Meo (Hmong or Mong) are the most widespread minority group in southern China. The 80,000 or so who live in Thailand settle mainly at high altitudes (1000 to 1200 metres), ideal for the growing of opium, their main cash crop. The Meo probably grow more opium than any other tribe, but also cultivate dried rice and corn.

In appearance, they look very Chinese or Mongolian (hence 'Mong'); in religion, although animist, they practise various Chinese-based rituals, with a strong emphasis on ancestor-worship. Meo huts usually contain an ancestor shrine and are built, unlike Karen stilt-houses, on ground level. The three sub-groups found in Thailand are: Blue Meo (Mong Njua), whose women wear indigo-dyed pleated skirts and keep their hair up in big, puffy buns; White Meo (Hmong Daw), whose women wear turbans and exchange their regular indigo-dyed trousers for white pleated skirts on ceremonial occasions; and the Gua Mba Meo (Hmong Gua Mba) who are recent arrivals from Laos, mostly confined to refugee camps. The clothing of Meo women is particularly ornate, employing decorative embroidery, appliqué, cutwork, pom-poms and batik cloth. Both men and women usually wear silver necklaces.

Lahu (Musuer) probably originated in the Tibetan highlands, and presently number around 60,000 in Thailand. The Lahu divide into four major sub-groups: Black (Lahu Na), Red (Lahu Nyi), Yellow (Lahu Shi) and the Lahu Sheh Leh. The dominant clan, the Lahu Na, have the most interesting traditional dances and have been almost completely converted to Christianity. Partly because opium remains a cash crop, the Lahu are very itinerant. A piece of land on which the opium poppy has grown for four years, is good for nothing. After 20 years, all the land surrounding a village has been exhausted, and the tribe must move on. This is most true of the Lisu (who grow opium for sale) and the Lahu (who both sell it and smoke it). Often, the chieftain or 'shaman' of a tribe will simply drop a raw egg on the ground: whichever direction the albumen flows furthest, the people go! Most Lahu remain strongly animist (despite the Black Lahu defection) and favour swidden agriculture. The women, often heavily adorned with silver medallions, produce unique weaving (notably delicate patchwork trims and fine embroidery) with the pattern appearing on only one side of the cloth. The Lahu are also skilled in basket-weaving and woodwork.

Yao (Yu Mien) are the only tribe to have their own written language. They still use Chinese characters to inscribe Taoist rituals and to keep family records. The Yao are a homogenous group (present population in Thailand 55,000), the only sub-group of their type to migrate to Southeast Asia. Basically animists, with traces of Taoism and ancestor-worship, they tend to settle at opium-producing altitudes. Men traditionally wear black caps. Women often add red-plush collars to their garments. They are noted for their cross-stitch embroidery, and produce richly decorated patchwork clothing. Yao silversmiths are famous for their finely-crafted jewellery.

Lisu (Lisaw) divide into two main sub-groups. The Black Lisu (Ha Lisu) live in China and Burma. The Flowery Lisu (Hua Lisu) live mainly in Thailand, and number around 24,000. They have adopted many Chinese cultural influences, but remain firmly animist in their beliefs. Like most hill people, the Lisu are heavily engaged in shifting cultivation and (along with the Meo) grow opium as a principal grop. They wear lots of coin jewellery, colourful cloth outfits trimmed with rows of appliqued patchwork, tassels and beads, and (at festivals) massive amounts of handcrafted silver ornaments. Of all the tribes, the Lisu are the most visually striking.

Akha (E Kaw, Egor) probably originated in the Tibetan highlands, and currently number around 35,000 in Thailand. The Akha are stubbornly animist, resisting all attempts to convert them to other religions. They place much emphasis on ancestor-worship and erect sacred gates at the entrance to their villages, to safeguard them against evil spirits. The Akha settle at high altitudes and grow opium, in addition to rice and corn. As late-settlers, they've had to make do with the poorest land, and are consequently the most desperate to sell crafts to visitors. Poverty makes the Akha a rather cheerless lot (the men are particularly grim), but they have amazing costumes. Especially the married women, who wear elaborate headdresses (*u-cher*) studded with silver rupees, and lots of showy embroidery. The Akha turn out some nice crafts, including lacquer bamboo baskets, silver ornaments, and scarab-beetle necklaces.

Thailand's half a million hilltribe people are presently in a state of crisis. The problem is opium, or rather lack of it. Opium was first brought to China by Arab traders in the 8th century. By the 19th century, it was seen as a miracle crop—successfully used, along with its derivative morphine, as a medicinal aid in both the East and the West. Encouraged by early traders to grow and consume opium, the hill-tribe farmers adopted it as an integral part of their traditional way of life—it provided them with both medicine and a stable source of income. Later, when the negative, addictive aspects of opium became apparent, the Thai government—under mounting international pressure—officially outlawed the opium poppy (1959). This threatened the hilltribes' whole way of life, and some of them retreated deep into the jungle to circumvent the ban by producing a new, much deadlier opium derivative—heroin. The impact of heroin (80 times more potent than opium) upon the international narcotic market was awesome. In Thailand alone, where heroin addiction was virtually unknown 20 years ago, the authorities are now treating an estimated 300,000 addicts. In February 1988, the Thai government triumphantly announced the seizure of 1.2 tons of raw heroin, their largest haul to date. But this is as nothing to the estimated 100 tons of the death-dealing drug being illegally produced each year in the infamous 'Golden Triangle' area bordering Thailand, Burma and Laos. The legendary opium warlord Khun Sa, forced to limit operations in Thailand and Burma, is now known to have set up heroin refineries in Laos. Few of the profits of the heroin trade make their way into the hilltribes' pockets—they remain, like the addicts they supply, poor and exploited.

Over the last 10 years, the Thai government has made poppy eradication a major priority. Surprise raids on villages and burning of opium crops have been followed by (moderately successful) crop-substitution programmes. With opium-growing land reduced from 3000 'ri' to less than 15 'ri', only 20 tons of opium were produced in 1988, compared with 200 tons 15 years ago. The general effect of all this on the hilltribes, suddenly deprived of opium and encouraged to settle down and grow kidney beans, potatoes, coffee and cabbages instead, is critical. As they struggle to maintain a traditional lifestyle without the poppy—in the face of a growing population, depleted soil, and increasing poverty—what remains of their culture is being exploited for the benefit of tourists form Chiang Mai. Tourism does of course bring some financial benefits—the highland peoples now have a flourishing market for their craft goods—but many sales are conducted through a middleman, and the workers themselves often see little profit. Once dependent on opium and now dependent on tourism to supplement their incomes, these people of the poppy now face an uncertain future.

Going on Trek

Trekking out of Chiang Mai is neither as cheap nor as straightforward as it used to be. There are still some excellent treks to be had, if you deal with the right people. But to

The Opium Poppy

137

deal with the wrong people is to court disaster. Recently, there have been too many cases of over-trekked areas and inadequate service from trek companies. This produces the following kind of situations:

All we got to eat for three days were hardboiled eggs—with baby chicks inside them. They were so well-disguised by the sugar coating that we munched quite a few before realising the truth!

Our guide was out of his head on opium. The village chief gave him a pipe of peace, and the two of them spent the next 36 hours horizontal. Come to think of it, we hardly ever saw the guide in an upright position—even on an elephant!

Our bamboo raft disintegrated in the middle of the river. Our guide and two old ladies were left dangling out of a tree. The next day, our elephants stampeded off into the jungle.

We arrived in a village to find a party of package tourists already there—all clicking away with Nikons and peering into private family huts. It was like a human zoo!

Good trek companies come and go, and your best recommendations will always come from speaking to other travellers. Still, be prepared to spend a day looking round for the right deal, and maybe another day waiting for the group quota to be reached before departure. Choosing a trek is never easy, so here are a few tips. First and foremost, you'll want a company whose guides are registered with the Tourism Authority (ask them to show their badge). This gives you some comeback should your trek hit a major problem. Ideally, your guide should speak good English, in addition to the northern dialect and a couple of tribal languages. If he can cook as well, you're onto a winner! Secondly, it adds greatly to the enjoyment of your trip if the company takes a genuine interest in the welfare of the villages on its route, and doesn't just use them as a circus for tourists. Thirdly, you'll want a guarantee that you're the *only* group travelling on that particular trek circuit. Don't assume that the further north you go, the more remote it's going to be—most of the north is now overtrekked and very touristy. Most treks from Chiang Mai go north to Chiang Rai and the Golden Triangle (very busy) or west to Pai and Mae Sariang (fairly quiet). The virgin territories to the south and east are still being cautiously opened up by company scouts—if you find a trek blazing trails to these regions, or to the southwest of Chiang Mai, take it! Whatever you do, don't ask any trekking agency if it's the 'best'. I did, and the guide said 'No, we are not best. Two companies are better—first one, finished already; second one, doesn't come yet!'

The average cost of a trek is 250B a day—plus another 250B for elephants or river-rafting. A typical 3-day, 2-night trek will therefore cost in the region of 1250B. But there's heavy competition between the various companies, and you can often get cheaper deals by shopping around. At the time of writing, recommended low-price operators include **Aiyeret Tours** (c/o Montri Hotel), **Exotic Tours**, 227 Ta Pae Rd, **Camp of Troppo** 83/2 Soi Lingog, Chotana Rd, **Nat Guest House**, **Folkways** and **Chiang Mai Youth Hostel**. More pricey, but just as good, are **Summit Tours**, 28–30 Ta Pae Rd (tel 232020), **New Wave Service**, c/o Rimping Guest House, Muangsinghkhum Rd (tel 232664), **July Travel**, c/o Suriwongse Hotel (tel 236733), **Lamthong Tour**, 77 Ta Pae

Rd (tel 235448), **Pinan Tour**, 235 Ta Pae Rd (tel 236081), **Top North Tour**, c/o Chiang Mai Hill Hotel, 18 Huay Kaew Rd (tel 221254), **Galare Travel**, 54–56 Ta Pae Rd (tel 236237) and **S.U.A. Tour**, 59–63 Moon Muang Rd (tel 214572).

You won't need to take much on trek—just a change of socks, T-shirts and under-wear, a towel and a swimming costume (for that rare dip in a mountain stream!), a water bottle (fill up before departure), sun-oil, sun-hat and mosquito repellent, a camera and lots of sticky plasters, film (plus a flash), toilet paper, and disinfectant, and a small torch. A couple of plastic bags to hold dirty laundry, or to keep clothes dry (i.e. when it's raining, or when you're fording deep rivers) come in very handy. So do a pair of flip flops—you can't wear shoes in hilltribe huts! People often trek in shorts, but a pair of long pants is a good idea for bristly elephants—one person always rides up front, on the elephant's head, as *mahout*. More often than not, the *mahout* ends up in a ditch or a river. The *mahout* always gets very wet! In the cold season, you'll need to take a sleeping bag and some warm top garments. In the rainy season, a waterproof jacket or a plastic sheet is essential. Small presents to give out at the villages take up little room, and are always appreciated. If you feel (as many do) that doling out lollies, cigarettes and money is like visiting the animals in the zoo, stick to practical gifts like embroidery thread and safety pins (for the hilltribe women), pencils and drawing books (for the kids), and antiseptic or fungal creams (for the head man—his village may only see a doctor once in six months). Only take along antibiotics if you're prepared to administer them. Pointing cameras at villagers is very rude—get them to take a photo of you first, or give them a postcard of your home town. Then they'll be far more likely to pose. Regarding money, you won't need to take much—all meals and accommodation should be included in the price of your trek. But one of the villages might have some nice weavings or jewellery for sale (300B should cover this) and you may want to take along a bottle of Mekong for evening sing-songs (another 100B). For a standard 3–4 days' outing, 500B pocket money should be sufficient. The one thing you *must* take along with you (unless booked in a *very* reliable hotel) is your credit card. If it's lost on trek, well at least you know it's gone. There have been too many cases of cards being duplicated by guest houses while their owner is on trek. The duplicate card goes on a spending spree in Bangkok, and the owner returns home to a massive bill.

Trekking is most enjoyable between October and February—especially in February, when the hills are a riot of blossoming flowers. The rainy months of June to September are not recommended—walking is arduous, river-rafting hazardous, and elephants hide a lot under trees. Even in good weather though, you'll need to be fit—walking 4–5 hours a day along unmarked trails, through deep jungles, and up and down hills, can leave people with sedentary life-styles gasping! So, while you're waiting for your trek to come together, hire a bicycle, see some sights, and get some exercise!

RECREATION

Relaxing 'old style' massage is given at 103 Wangsinghkham Rd, just off Soi Sarkakorn. There are several massage parlours in town (some more dubious than others!), but at 60B an hour, this one has to be the cheapest. It's open 8 am to 7 pm, and you're wise to ring ahead (tel 252663) to make an appointment. If you want to **learn** massage, go to **Old Chiang Mai Hospital**. The teacher here was trained at Wat Po in Bangkok, and he offers excellent 10-day courses (with an examination at the end) at 1200B. Both

Anodard Hotel, 57 Ratchamandkha Rd, and **Prince Hotel**, 3 Taiwang Rd, have good swimming pools. Admission for non-residents is 20B, and you need to bring your own towel. If you want to earn money teaching English (a recreation in itself!), ask a Thai friend to help you place an ad in a local newspaper. The response is always good, and you stand to earn around 90B an hour.

NIGHTLIFE

After-dark action in Chiang Mai revolves mainly around night clubs, discos, bars, cocktail lounges, coffee shops and open-air restaurants. It's all rather intimate, far less boisterous than raunchy, neon-lit Bangkok. Two popular discotheques are **Plaza Disco** (Plaza Hotel) and **Wall Club** (Chiang Inn Hotel). Both are open 9 pm to 2 am nightly, and admission (90B men, 50B women) includes one free drink. Two good night-spots are **Oasis Bar** on Moon Muang Rd, and the **Riverside** at 9–11 Jarernrasd Rd, opposite Chinda Hospital. Both have excellent live music—the Riverside is the main haunt of Thai students, and has a great folk, country and blues band. It is one of the few restaurants to stay open past 10.30 pm (it closes at 2 am). The Oasis has a cosy video lounge and a talented girl singer ('Jim') who comes on at midnight. There's a bowling alley opposite the Chiang Inn Hotel (20B a game). Most balls are chipped, but it works.

SHOPPING

Shopping in Chiang Mai centres on the amazing **Night Bazaar** in Chang Klang Rd. This runs from around 6 pm to midnight daily, and is the place to pick up cheap designer goods, ethnic hilltribe handicrafts, and all manner of low-priced souvenirs. The market itself has a pronounced party atmosphere, jollied along by a booming sound system playing songs like *How much is that doggie in the window?* It's quite a joke trying to bargain down a Lacoste briefcase with Elvis moaning *Hound Dog* down your ear! But everybody hums along to Thai disco hits like *Hi Ho, Hi Ho, it's off to work we go*! By 10 pm, the place is really jumping—the coaxing croons of persuasive street-hawkers ('Herrro! You waaant somethink? Special price for yooou!') float enticingly over the jostling bedlam of package tourists fearfully guarding their wallets, backpackers haggling for hippie hill-tribe jackets, and beggars hopefully rattling tin cups from the pavements. Above it all drifts a variety of aromatic, tantalizing smells from sizzling woks and frangipani stalls, overladen with the less aromatic fumes of beaten-up *tuk-tuks*. From elevated hotel balconies, spent-out travellers looks down in mild wonderment on one of the last great markets of the East building up to its nightly climax of colour, noise, and excitement.

The night market has two focal points—the **Chiang Mai Plaza**, a large 3-storey covered area in mock northern style, and **Ying Ping Bazaar**, an old-style covered market set aside for the hilltribes. The Plaza has the monopoly on fashion clothes and shoes (which are the best buys) and has the cheapest leather-bound fake Gucci/Dunhill briefcases (from 400B). Things to look out for are large patchwork shoulder-bags (120B), tartan-style cotton bedspreads (150B) and appliqué cushion-covers (180B a pair). The Ying Ping by contrast, offers a wide range of traditional hilltribe produce—hand-embroidery, chunky silver jewellery, painted umbrellas, batiks, and musty, dusty 'antiques'. Bargain hard here to get the following prices: Burmese bead-and-embroidery pieces (2 x 2ft size, 500B), opium weights in hand-carved 'pencil boxes' (110B), hippy rucksacks (70B), and beautiful hilltribe jackets (single-sided 250B, double-sided

600 to 100B). Be careful when buying embroidered stuff—some of it is hand-made by villagers and some of it isn't (thinner cloth and bright colours indicate machine-work). For the best bargains, visit the Ying Ping in the early afternoon—this is when the hilltribe folk drop off their best produce.

Outside of the covered markets, there are hundreds of street stalls. Again, bargain hard—for handpainted T-shirts (85B), 'Charles Jourdan' briefcases (1000B), natty 'Gucci' lighters (30B), stylish leather coats (2000B) and jackets (1500B). Don't waste your money on cheap 60B 'Benetton' T-shirts (the only thing that doesn't shrink is the designer label!), or regular 35B T-shirts (even large sizes shrink to super-small after one wash!). The night market also offers the cheapest pirate cassettes in Thailand (from 20B), and some lovely old-fashioned jewellery—e.g. rough-silver necklaces, studded with jade and semi-precious stones, from only 160B

Crowded **Warorot Market,** just five minutes' walk above the night bazaar, is where the locals come to shop. The large covered indoor market isn't up to much, but there are clothing bargains to be found in the side-alley behind it—trousers (for short people only!) around 120B, summery cotton skirts from 90B etc. A lot of the stuff that turns up at the night market apparently originates from Warorot, though you'll have a job finding it! For clothes that don't fade, shrink, or fall apart, shop at **Tantrapantapea** in Ta Pae Rd or **Soakanka** just below Warorot market. These two department stores are where young Thai trendies come to buy the latest fashions.

Chiang Mai's general stores and supermarkets, centred on Ta Pae Rd, are mostly open from 10 am to 8.30 pm. Silk shops are all over town, but **Kinaree Thai Silk,** 40/3 Moo 6, Tonaosankampaeng Rd, gets consistently good mentions. So does the tiny silk shop in Ta Pae Rd, next to 'Hello' money-changer. The best tailors are in Ta Pae Road too—they aren't quite as good as their Bangkok counterparts though. A notable exception is **Seiko Tailor,** just over the Nakhon Ping Bridge on Kaeo Nawarat Rd (tell your *tuk-tuk* driver 'Ran tad pa Seiko'). This is the most respected tailor in town, much used by Thais. Seiko can make up trousers for 80B, shirts for 50B, and a whole suit for as little as 300B!

WHERE TO STAY

Hotels

Three of Chiang Mai's best hotels—all with rooms from 100B (single) and 1200B (double)—are located at the Night Bazaar. **Dusit Inn,** 112 Chang Klang Rd (tel 236835; tx 251037) is the most comfortable. It's a modern 'international' hotel, with two fine restaurants, lifeguards at the pool, and decent views from the 8th floor (and above). The **Suriwongse Hotel,** 110 Chang Klang Rd (tel 236733; tx 49308 HS TH) is well-established and has lots of style, but shows its age. **Chiang Inn Hotel,** 100 Chang Klang Rd (tel 235655; tx TH 43503) is pleasantly sophisticated, with a popular restaurant/coffee shop and half-decent views from 6th floor and above.

Further afield, the up-and-coming luxury hotel is **Chiang Mai Plaza,** 92 Sridonchai Rd (tel 252050) with rooms from 1400B single, 1600B double. Perks here include a smart pool, a swinging disco, and a free American breakfast (10% room discounts too, if booking through Skybird Agency on the first floor). Out of town, **Chiang Mai Orchid Hotel,** 100–102 Huay Kaew Rd (tel 221625) offers classic Doi Suthep views, many facilities and rooms from 1000B. **Chiang Come Hotel**, 7/35 Suthep Rd (tel 211020) is another quiet place, with scenic views. Rooms are very reasonably priced: from 300B single, 380B double.

Guest Houses

There are presently some 80 guest houses in Chiang Mai, most of them charging 50–80B for twin-bedded rooms with fan; 100–120B, with attached bathroom. Three 'superior' guest houses, worthy of special mention are **Srisupan** (lovely rooms from 100B) at 92 Wualai Rd (tel 252811); **Galare** (rooms from 220B) at 7–7/1 Charoenprathat Rd; **Top North** (rooms 100–150B) at 15 Moon Muang Soi 2 Rd (tel 213900); and the new **River Lodge** (rooms around 400B) at 25 Charoenprathat Rd (tel 251109). Galare and River Lodge are both central, with attractive river views. Top North ('We are not fortune tellers, but we know well what you are coming for') is delightfully quiet, and has a good travel agency. In the 70–80B range, there **Nat Guest House**, 7 Prapokklao Rd Soi 6 (tel 212876)— a special place run by a special lady—and the ever-popular **Youth Hostel**, 31 Prapokklao Rd Soi 3 (tel 212863). If these two are full, walk down the small *soi* between them to find friendly **Julie Guest House**. Even cheaper places are **Je T'Aime**, 247–9 Charoenrat Rd (tel 241912), with bicycle hire and riverside situation, and **Peter Guest House**, 46/3 Moon Muang Rd, Soi 9, offering free continental breakfast and toilet paper. Along with Nat and the Youth Hostel, Peter gives excellent service and operates good treks. Travellers have also recommended **Chiangmai Garden**, 82–86 Ratchamaka Rd, and **V. K.** at 22/2 Chang Moi Kao Rd. Though everybody I've ever met in Chiang Mai has been able to recommend a different guest house!

EATING OUT

The best introduction to northern food, largely influenced by Burmese recipes and characterized by its spicy curries, is one of Chiang Mai's famous **Khantoke dinners**. *Khan* literally means 'bowl' and *toke* is a small, low table—usually made of rattan or lacquerware—around which diners sit on the floor and share a succession of tasty dishes accompanied with sticky or plain rice. The principal dishes are *Kaeng Han Le* (pork curry with garlic, ginger and other spices), *Nam Prik Ong* (minced pork cooked with tomato, cucumber, onion and chillies), *Kang Kai* (chicken and vegetable curry) and *Larb* (minced meat mixed with chillies). Today, an intrinsic part of Khantoke dinners are traditional northern dance performances. At **Old Chiang Mai Cultural Centre**, 185/3 Wualai Rd (tel 235097), you can enjoy an endless procession of small-bowl dishes while watching a colourful procession of northern Thai folk-dances. Last on the bill is the popular *Ramwong* (circle) dance, where members of the audience are invited to join in. The second part of the show takes place in an adjoining building, and features hilltribe dances. This is an excellent opportunity to see a number of tribes in rotation, and to note differences in appearance and costume. It's also an excellent photo stop, so bring a flash! Khantoke dinner-dances take place between 7 pm and 10 pm nightly, and 200B tickets (good value – the same show would be 300B in Bangkok) are sold in hotels, at travel agencies, and on the street.

There's a wide range of other places to eat in Chiang Mai. For original Thai cuisine, there's **Baan Suan**, 51/3 Chiang Mai-San Kamphaeng Rd (tel 234116) pleasantly set in a typical northern-style teak house. Most dishes are around 60B, and include 'specials' like Chiang Mai Sausage, Pork Curry Burmese Style, Grilled Black Fish, Grilled Spare Ribs, and Fried Shrimp with Chilli Paste (hot!). There is similar northern-style fare at **Aroon Rai**, 43–45 Kotchasarn Rd (tel 236947). Out of town, the **Galae** restaurant, 65 Suthep Rd (tel 222235) has a romantic atmosphere in a peaceful lakeside setting. Come for the set lunch of spring rolls, pork with honey, chicken satay, shrimp fried rice, chicken in coconut-milk soup, and fresh fruit platter—all for under 200B a head.

China Town Suki, 147/13–16 Chang Klang Rd (tel 235646) does delicious mid-priced Chinese food. If you want to go Indian, **Al-Shiraz**, 123 Chang Klang Rd (tel 234338) serves mouthwatering tandoori, biriani, tikka and kebabs. Seafood (and Japanese food) should be sampled at **Nang Nual Seafood**, 27 Koa Klang Rd, Nong Hoi (tel 235771). This is a delightful restaurant in landscaped grounds with a bird garden, waterfall, shopping arcade, and a selection of dining rooms. Seafood (and Thai/Chinese fare) is cheaper at **Tangsukjai** restaurant, at 98/7 Sridonchai Rd, near Chiang Mai Plaza Hotel. Run by friendly Poo and sister, this is a real 'Thai-style' hangout. For something completely different, there's 'jungle food' including cobra and mongoose! at **Charueng Rueng**, 5 Superhighway (Airport Rd). It's run by an ex-army sergeant, who has 'put his jungle survival-training to profitable use'. Yes, well . . .

Le Coq D'Or, 18–20 Chaiyapoom Rod, is the best for French and Continental cuisine—fireside meals, served in an old-word setting. **Alt Heidelberg**, Huai Kaeo Rd (near Chiang Mai Orchid Hotel) has authentic German food, strong draught beer, and a homely atmosphere. **Bierstube Rest Bar**, Moon Muang Rd, is a cheaper German-style place, with relaxing ambience and Chicken in The Basket. **Garden Cafe** (Dusit Inn Hotel) lays on a lunch-time buffet from 11.30 am to 1.30 pm daily—all the European-Chinese food you can eat for 90B! Back on Moon Muang Rd, **Hungry Horse** (near Ta Pae Gate) and **Peacock Coffee House** (Montri Hotel) cater to Western appetites with steaks, grills, pizzas etc. In between them, **Supun House** does a mean 'Chicken on Fire' for 45B. For good home-style food (mainly French), check out **Times Square** roof-top restaurant, Soi 6 Ta Pae Rd. In the Night Bazaar, find the cheap, **No Name Restaurant** and the **Sala Ice Cream Bar**—two favourite travellers' haunts.

THA TON

Exciting raft or boat trips down the Kok River from Tha Ton—a small village 175 km north of Chiang Mai—are an increasingly popular way of getting to Chiang Rai. The Kok River enters Thailand at Tha Ton from Laos, flowing south past Chiang Rai until it joins with the Mae Khong River in Chiang Saen district. Tha Ton is located just a few kilometres from the Burmese border, and is still used as a (perilous) doorway into Burma.

GETTING THERE
Orange buses (No. 1231) run to Tha Ton regularly from the bus station north of Chang Puak Gate in Chiang Mai. It's a four-hour trip, costing 37B. Alternatively, you could get off at **Fang** (3 hours, 35B) and continue on to Tha Ton (1 hour, 6B) later on.

Fang

Fang is an interesting little 13th-century city, founded by King Mengrai, with a couple of decent hotels—the **Fang** and the **Meta** (rooms for 30B at both)—a nice Thai-Chinese restaurant near the bus station—the **Koo Charen**—and good treks. Local guides meet tourists off the bus, offering cheap 1- and 2-day walks up to the various tribal villages (mainly Karen and Black/Red Lahu) above Fang town.

WHAT TO SEE & WHERE TO STAY

Tha Ton is a scenic little spot, overlooking the Kok River and surrounded by dense jungle and rolling hills. Many colourful hilltribes live in this area, and at the small souvenir shop by the bridge you'll find the cheap, attractive handicrafts which they bring into the village for sale—bright Akha headdresses and anklets, hand-embroidered Karen bags, decorative Lahu ornaments etc. For views down over the winding river and country landscape, climb the steep staircase (just left of the bridge, facing the hills) up to the pretty toybox pagoda, with its huge seated Buddha. At night, the Buddha is eerily illuminated, and the temple compound resounds with strange jungle music, performed by enthusiastic local youths on modern drum-kits. It's quite a party. Another kind of party starts at 4 am every morning, when an immense gong wakes up the monks and everybody else sleeping within a kilometre's radius. If staying overnight here, bring earplugs. Especially if staying at **Thip's Travellers House**, which is situated right at the foot of the temple staircase! Thip's is actually best lodge in town, with clean (if spartan) rooms at 30B a person, a tribe of resident monkeys, lip-smacking chicken curries and banana pancakes, and a relaxing riverside situation. Mrs Thip, the owner, is a bit of an old pirate, but she's red-hot on local information. 'River fed by mountain water', she informs you, 'Good for swimming—no crocodiles!'. While you're thinking about that one, she often dematerialises to watch another Chinese Kung-Fu movie. Her lodge is usually full nowadays, so she's building a new set of bungalows further upriver. Until these arrive, you may have to put up instead at **Jangasem Guest House**, on the far side of the bridge. This isn't half as good as Thip's.

River Trips (Tha Ton – Chiang Rai)

From Tha Ton, you have three choices of river transport to Chiang Rai. First, there's the public river-boat, which leaves Tha Ton pier at 12.30 pm daily and arrives in Chiang Rai 5 hours later (fare 160B). Second, you can hire longtail speedboats—providing an exhilarating 2$^{1}/_{2}$-hour ride through jungle terrain and roaring rapids—from Thip's or Jangasem (160B per head—that is, if you have a group of 10 heads!) Third, and most popular, you can go by river-raft. The rafting season runs from September to February and the best months to hit the river are October and November, when water-levels are highest. Mrs Thip has a virtual monopoly on rafting out of Tha Ton—not altogether a good thing. The trips start out fine: you buy your raft (1600B for two, 2500B for eight) and set off on a 3–4 days *Boy's Own* adventure, stopping for side-treks to Akha, Shan and Lisu villages, perhaps even taking in an elephant safari (250B per day extra). But then you hit the rapids. No problem if you've a guide aboard, or if the river is at high-level. But some people do some to grief on the rocks during the dry season. No marks to Mrs Thip for letting them go out unaccompanied in these conditions. No refund either. And of course no chance of re-selling the raft at Chiang Rai—a thriving business—to other travellers wanting to take it on the much safer ride down to Chiang Saen.

Things to do in Tha Ton include swimming, fishing and canoeing in the Kok River, 'adventure walks' into the jungle (use local guides, 100B per day), and boat-trips *up*-river to the Burmese border, calling in on a Shan village (one-hour ride, 30B). For most of these things, it's back—yes, you guessed it—to Mrs Thip!

CHIANG RAI & THE GOLDEN TRIANGLE

Bordered by Burma and Laos, Chiang Rai is Thailand's northernmost province, a long 785 km from Bangkok. Founded in 1262, it was the first capital of the independent northern Thai kingdom of Lanna Thai. Legend has it that Mengrai decided to build a city here after one of his elephants ran off in a southerly direction, running out of puff at this site on the banks of the Kok River. This auspicious sign (everything a royal elephant did in those days was considered auspicious!) encouraged Mengrai to expand his domain south from his previous power centre of Chiang Saen. Later conquered by Burma, Chiang Rai only became Thai territory in 1786, and was created a full-blooded Thai province in 1910. Today, it's a small, relaxed city of mainly two-storeyed concrete shophouses which give little hint of its former importance. But big changes are on the way. Ever since the province was opened to trekking some 10 years ago, Chiang Rai has become the major destination north of Chiang Mai for hilltribe-spotting tourists. It even has a few trek companies of its own—none of which, in the absence of a TAT tourist office in Chiang Rai, have registered guides or guaranteed service. Chiang Rai has a large highland population of tribal peoples—Akha (who only live in this province), Yao, Meo, Lisu, Lahu and Karen—all attracted here by its eminently suitable terrain: 80% forests and mountains, 20% cultivable valleys. Trekking in this area can be very rewarding—if somewhat overcrowded—and the walks here are far easier than at Mae Hong Son or Pai.

Many travellers use Chiang Rai as a jump-off point for the Golden Triangle—the famous opium-producing centre—and the various places of interest along the Burma/Laos border. Generally the best months to visit are September to December, which have the coolest climate and where scenery is at its most beautiful. By January, the area gets quite cold (around 12°C), and if going on trek, you'll need warm clothing. From March to May, when summer temperatures climb to 35°C, you'll need your hat. Chiang Rai celebrates its lychee fruit 'harvest festival', complete with parades and beauty contests every May. But few foreigners can take the heat!

GETTING THERE

By Air
Thai Airways flies to Chiang Rai from Chiang Mai at least twice daily (fare 300B; flight time 35 minutes).

By River
Boat/raft trips from Tha Ton are a popular way of going to Chiang Rai (cf. Tha Ton section).

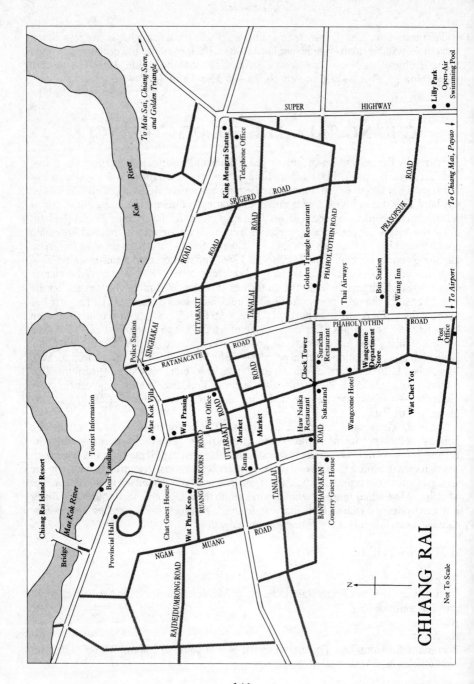

CHIANG RAI

Not To Scale

By Bus
Green buses (No. 166) go to Chiang Rai half-hourly from Nawarat Bridge bus-rank in
Chiang Mai. The 3¹/₂-hour trip costs 47B. There are also a few air-con buses daily
(between 7 am and 3.30 pm), costing 66B and taking only 3 hours.

From Chiang Rai back to Chiang Mai, buses leave every half-hour from 9 am to 5.30 pm.
From Chiang Rai to Bangkok (11 hours), there is one air-con bus (7 pm, 250B) and four
non air-con buses (4, 5, 6, and 7 pm, 150B) daily. Chat House offers buses to Bangkok
too.

TOURIST INFORMATION
The Tourist Information Centre in Singhakhlai Rd (tel 711313) isn't very good. Chat
House gives better local information—and a good trek area map.

WHAT TO SEE
Chiang Rai presents a sharp contrast to busy, burgeoning Chiang Mai, 100 km to the
south. By day, it's quiet, peaceful and easy to get around. At night, all traffic vanishes of
the streets at 10 pm, and it instantly reverts to a sleepy, one-bullock town. To tour around
in style, hire a horse and buggy from the Wangcome Hotel. *Samlors* charge 10B, and
songthaews 5B, for short in-town journeys, but you don't really need them. From the
clock in the town centre (the one with four faces, each giving a different time!) you can
walk to any of Chiang Rai's attractions in under 15 minutes. The provincial capital has a
general feel of total inertia, and few people are into heavy sightseeing. But most people
are content to go for a swim, to have a massage, to wander round the market, and
generally to relax. Then they hire a motorbike (150–250B a day, from Chat House or
Maekok Villa) or hop on a local bus (from the town bus terminal), and travel up to Chiang
Saen and the Golden Triangle, or to Mae Chan, Mae Sai and the border areas. Many
don't come back for a week—most of these places have far more to offer (especially in
terms of atmosphere and scenery) than Chiang Rai.

In & Around Chiang Rai
(on foot, by *samlor*; half day)

This tour is purely optional—Chiang Rai is very thin on 'sights'! The **Morning Market**,
overseen by a large Chinese Buddha, is the place to buy mountain food, wild pig, snake
and iguana ('You can have dead', chirps a cheerful vendor, 'or you can take home and kill
yourself!'). **Wat Phra Keo** used to house the itinerant Emerald Buddha (resident in the
temple of the same name in Bangkok) and now only displays a copy. Nearby **Wat Phra
Singh** probably dates to the 15th century, and used to contain a precious Theravada
Buddha image—but doesn't any more. If you want to see something which hasn't gone
somewhere else, visit the **Temple of the Sleeping Buddha**, about 1 km due east of
King Mengrai's Statue. This has a 17th-century reclining Buddha in the Burmese
style—nothing special, but at least it's original! To finish, walk up the hill to the New
Provincial Hall (Government Offices) for nice views down over the Maekok River. Or
walk left out of Maekok Villa, left again down a small path and across a bridge, to find a
tranquil little park on the riverbank—the ideal spot to watch the sun go down.

RECREATION

The ideal antidote to tiring touring is a relaxing massage at **Wangcome Barber**, over the road from Wangcome Hotel. Massages are given upstairs, and from mid-afternoon onwards. If you bargain a rate of 100B an hour (locals pay only 70B), you've done very well. There's good swimming at **Lilly Park** (tell your *samlor* driver 'Sah why nam Lilly Park'). There's a large clean pool here, open 9 am to 6 pm (for a quiet swim, arrive 3–4 pm); admission 25B. An outdoor pool, a kilometre below Lilly Park (and on the same side of the road) charges only 10B admission. For nightlife, check out **Hill Disco** at Wiang Inn Hotel–it's a big scene on a Friday and Saturday night. Admission is 90B men, 70B women (includes one free drink); 'Happy Hour' is from 9 to 10 pm.

WHERE TO STAY

Chiang Rai has a wide selection of hotels. **Wiang Inn**, 893 Phaholyothin Rd (tel 711543), is a quiet, sophisticated hotel with a definite European flavour. Good pool, useful facilities, and the only deluxe café in town. Air-con rooms start at 500B single, 600B double, and 50% discounts are given June–September. Similar prices and discounts at **Wangcome Hotel**, 869/90 Pemawibhata Rd (tel 711800). This is a modern, chic place with incredibly helpful staff. In the mid-range, there's the old-style **Rama Hotel**, 331/4 Trirat Rd (tel 311344), with rooms from 180B (fan) and 340B (air-con); and **Suknirand**, 424/1 Banphaprakarn Rd (tel 711055), the current Thai favourite (often full) with nice rooms from 140B (fan single) to 300B (air-con twin). **Maekok Villa**, 445 Singhakai Rd (tel 311786), has charming bungalow-style rooms (all with bath, hot water, fresh towels daily) at 120B single, 160B double. It also has a 30B dormitory, and offers good-value sightseeing tours (e.g. to the Golden Triangle, at 600–900B for one–two people).

Budget lodges are generally disappointing. The notable exception is **Country Guest House** at 389 Banphraprakarn Rd. Run by a nice English-speaking family, Country is a delightful ranch-house dwelling, with a lawn and a driveway. Rooms are only 30B and have *solid walls* (remember those?), not the usual paper-thin bamboo partitions. Great facilities include hot showers, free bicycles, free rides round town, darts, volleyball and good information. **Chat House**, 1 Trailat Rd, is the place for 'real travellers' run by personable young Chat. He offers safe, clean rooms at 30B (no fan) and 50B (with fan), also cycle/motorbike rental, trekking, a well-stocked library, information handouts, and an extensive Western-style menu. Chat is a very laidback place, with music, tranquil atmosphere and ethnic decor. It's easy to be laidback here—there's nowhere to sit!

EATING OUT

Best Western-style restaurant is **Golden Triangle**, Phaholythin Rd, offering mid-priced cuisine (steaks, grills etc.) at around 60B a dish. Service is excellent here, and you can eat in air-conditioned comfort. For Thai food, try **Haw Nalika** in Banphaprakan Rd (look for wooden fencing with lights on top). This is where all the locals dine, and the atmosphere is never less than festive. Most dishes cost between 40 and 70B, and specialities include Steamed Fish with Salted Chinese Fruit and Mixed Meat with Cashew Nuts. **Chiang Rai Island Resort**, on the far side of the Maekok River (over the bridge from town) serves delicious Thai food—between 40 and 60B a dish—in a pleasant setting. The **Surachai**, near the clock tower, has inexpensive Thai-Chinese fare and is a big hit with locals. They tuck into 10B bags of crispy locusts, and cram eagerly round trays of dead grubs, beetles and grasshoppers. Most Westerners stick to *kao pat* (fried rice) and Chinese tea! **Chat House** is the place to go for ham 'n' egg breakfasts, yoghurts, fruit salads and muesli. The marvellous **Ice Cream Parlour** at Wangcome Hotel offers 24 varities of Foremost ice-cream, and closes at 9.30 pm. There are also lots of tasty cheap-food stalls near the bus station.

The Golden Triangle

(by bus, boat, motorbike; full day)

From Chiang Rai bus station (rank No. 6) public buses leave for **Chiang Saen**—a charming little town on the banks of the Mekong River—every 20 minutes from 6 am. The 6 km trip takes 1½ hours, and costs 14B. Last bus back to Chiang Rai from Chiang Saen is 4.45 pm, so it's best to make an early start. From Chiang Saen, it's a further 10 km along a flat road (okay for motorbikes) to **Ban Sop Ruak**, the point designated as the **'Golden Triangle'**. You can get there by bicycle hired from a riverside guesthouse in Chiang Saen 15–20B, plus possible 500B deposit; *songthaew* (60B return, if on your own; 150B total, if in a group); by longtail speedboat (200–300B for the 2½-hour round-trip, cheap if there's six of you!) or by public riverboat (80B return). The last method is the most favoured—a very scenic ride up the Mekong and as near as you're likely to get to Burma from here. Public boats allow about an hour for sightseeing at Sop Ruak before returning to Chiang Saen.

Chiang Saen

The once-powerful, fortified city of **Chiang Saen** is now a lively little one-street town, surrounded by ruined temples, crumbling *stupas* and grass-covered walls and ramparts. It's believed to have been built over the ruins of an earlier settlement in 1328 by Phra Chao Saeo Pu, a grandson of King Mengrai—though there's now every indication that the earlier town exercised much power and influence before the 14th century. After the rise of Chiang Mai, Chiang Saen became an associate city ruled over by Lanna Thai princes. Sacked in 1558 by the Burmese, and again in the early 19th century by Rama I, it lay abandoned until rebuilt a century ago by what remained of Chiang Saen's descendants, led by the son of the Prince of Lamphun.

Today, the few skeletal remains of *chedis* scattered around the town are really of interest only to keen archaeological buffs. Many of the old fortifications remain intact, also parts of the old city moat, said to have been scooped out by Naga, the sacred serpent. **Wat Pa Sak**, just left before the city walls, is the oldest *chedi* (20B admission) and **Wat Chedi Luang** is the most impressive extant temple, notable for its 58-metre high octagonal *chedi*. Built around 1390, it is just inside the city walls, to the right. In front of it is the **National Museum**, which houses a fine collection of Chiang Saen artefacts, some dating back to neolithic times. The museum is open 9 am to 4 pm, Wed – Sun (admission 5B), and is primarily of interest for its attractive displays of hilltribe handicrafts and Burmese lacquerware and woodcarvings. Some exhibits (e.g. the 'Wild Cock Trap') have wonderful pseudo-English descriptions! Outside the museum is a bus-stop—handy, if you're on your way back to Chiang Rai.

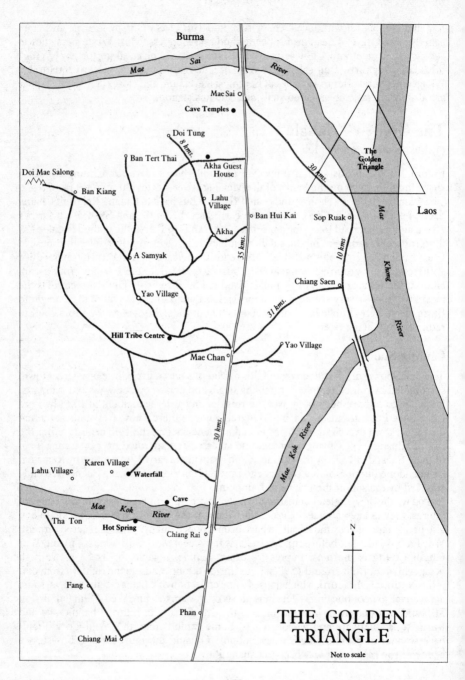

Burma

Mae   Sai   River

Mae Sai ○
Cave Temples ●

○ Doi Tung

Ban Tert Thai ○   *8 kms.*
Akha Guest
House

Doi Mae Salong

Ban Kiang ○   ○ Lahu
Village

○ Ban Hui Kai   Sop Ruak ○

Akha ○

30 kms.

**The
Golden
Triangle**

Laos

A Samyak ○

35 kms.

Mae

Yao Village ○   Chiang Saen ○

10 kms.

Khong

Hill Tribe Centre ●   *31 kms.*

Mae Chan ○   ○ Yao Village

River

30 kms.

Mae Kok River

Lahu Village ○   Karen Village
○   **Waterfall** ●

Cave ●

Tha Ton ○   *Mae   Kok   River*

Hot Spring ●   Chiang Rai ○

N

Fang ○

Phan ○

Chiang Mai ○

THE GOLDEN
TRIANGLE

Not to scale

WHERE TO STAY
Chiang Saen's lovely setting on the Mae Khong (Mekong) River makes it a popular travellers' haunt, and there are many little guest houses perched on the riverbank looking over to Laos. **Gin House** and **Siam Guest House** probably have the best situations. Gin has 30B rooms (with attached showers), good food and cycle/motorbike rental. Siam offers the same deal, but has a better information service. Both places are very friendly. So are **Chiang Saen** (the original guest house) and **Jim's**. For comfort, stay at **Lanna House**, which has clean fan-cooled huts—with shower and sitting area—for only 80B.

Ban Sop Ruak

This village is the focal point of the 'Golden Triangle'—the place where Thailand, Burma and Laos meet at the confluence of the Mae Khong and Ruak Rivers. Until a few years ago, when Thai troops dislodged Khun Sa, the opium warlord, this area was producing three-quarters of the world's supply of opium. Even today it's a popular outlaw sanctuary, with various opium gangs hopping back and forth from one border to the next to escape government suppression. But you won't see any poppy-fields or opium smugglers round Sop Ruak. It's just a quiet, picturesque spot with pleasant views, a few handicraft shops, and a big sign in the main street saying 'Police is Friendly, Ready to Protect'.

Despite its glamorous, exotic image, the Golden Triangle is really just a 'been there, done that' experience. For the best view over the confluence of the rivers (particularly good at sunset) make the 15-minute climb up the hillpath (starts behind the police booth) to the small viewpoint pavilion. In the dry season, there's a small sandbar 'island' in the middle of the river, sometimes with a boatload of sightseers wandering round on it. During September and October, when the river is at its most swollen (and the surrounding scenery at its most lush and green), this is lost to sight. From the pavilion, climb the *naga* staircase to **Wat Phra Thai Pukhao**. This crumbling hilltop temple has a beatific old *maechee* (nun), bags of atmosphere, and mysterious moral messages (Ho! My God! Sightseeing Ruin! Going be memorious, be trustful when Coming. Go forwards, not be Back. He who thinks himself wise, Oh Heaven! is a great fool!'). Recommended.

WHERE TO STAY & EATING OUT
Down in the village, a small guest house called **Pu Kham** has some good hilltribe crafts for sale. Best buys are antique lacquer-bamboo sewing basket and tobacco pouches (100 to 150B)—you won't find original items like these anywhere else. Sop Ruak has a few guest houses—most charging around 50B for spartan cells with 'river views' (i.e. no windows, lots of mosquitoes). Best of a poor bunch is **Sea Wan**, followed by **Golden Triangle** and **Golden Hut**. There's a pleasant riverside restaurant at Golden Triangle, and you can hire out longtail boats there for 2–3-hour trips on the river.

North to Mae Sai
(by motorbike, bus; 1–2 days)

This is a good tour by motorbike from Chiang Rai, with a recommended overnight stay in

Mae Sai. There are several nice places to stay along the way, however, and many travellers work their way slowly north to Mae Sai (or south back to Chiang Rai) by local bus. Pity about the bad road between Mae Sai and Chiang Saen:—the inviting 'triangle' tour (Chiang Rai – Chiang Saen – Mae Sai – Chiang Rai) is presently only negotiable by jeep, not by motorbike.

Mae Sai

Situated right on the border with Burma, 62 km from Chiang Rai, Mae Sai is as far north as Thailand goes. Connected by a concrete bridge to the Burmese village of Tha Khee Lek, it is also the only land-based corridor open between Thailand and Burma. At present, only Thai and Burmese nationals are allowed over the border (from 6 am to 6 pm daily), though from either of the town's two best guest houses, the **Mae Sai** and the **Northern**, you can watch travellers and Burmese braves trying to swim over! Anybody attempting the same thing by raft or boat is politely (but firmly!) dissuaded—part of the Sai River belongs to Burma. Most visitors are content with a climb up to **Wat Phra That Doi**, a hilltop temple affording magnificent views down over Mae Sai and the river. The 207–step staircase up to it starts just before Top North Hotel, just off to the left of Phaholyothin Rd.

Mae Sai itself is famous for its strawberries (which bloom in December) and for its jade-cutting factory, which sells high-quality jade far cheaper than at the tourist shops in the main drag. Mae Sai also used to be a great place to pick up rare gems—aquamarine, sapphires and rubies—brought over the border by Burmese traders. But most of the stuff now hawked on the bridge has actually been bought in Thailand, to be sold back to tourists at inflated prices. For authentic, well-priced gems and handicrafts, check out **Meang Lai Antique Shop**—but remember to bargain hard! Good general buys in Mae Sai are sandalwood, Burmese woodcarvings, Chinese herbs and fresh lobsters. Seafood is good here. Try **Rim Nam** restaurant near the bridge—from June to September, it serves up delicious Mekong river-fish at 100B a kilogram. It also has reliable, mid-priced Thai-Chinese cuisine.

A good side-trip from Mae Sai is to nearby **Cheng Dao Cave Temple**, full of Buddha carvings, huge stalactities and dangerous snakes. A little further on, there's a **Monkey Temple** with a host of lively monkeys, and half a kilometre beyond this you can hire a boat (5B) to visit another cave, housing an enormous reclining Buddha. A short distance south, a junction leads the way up to **Doi Tun**(Flag Mountain), the highest peak in northern Thailand. At the top is **Phra That Chedi** (built in 911), with chanting monks, chiming bells and lots of mystical mist. Doi Tung is best approached by motorbike, or by hiring a truck from **Ban Hui Kai**, halfway down the highway between Mae Sai and Mae Chan. On the way up the mountain (7 km from the main road), you'll find **Akha Guest House**. This offers spectacular views, cheap bungalow accommodation (30B single, 50B double), cosy campfire meals in the evenings, unforgettable sunsets, great hilltribe walks, novelty river-rafting (disintegrating rafts leave people hanging in trees; women travellers get a go on the 'Akha swing' across a ravine, with a choice of potential husbands waiting on the other side!), and an eccentric host named Jiad. People hang out here for weeks—it's so good!

Mae Chan

Mae Chan, 34 km south of Mae Sai, is a small trading town used as a supply-point by local hilltribes. There is not much to see here, except a colourful covered market. From Mae Chan, however, you can hire a pick-up truck (10B, 15 km) to the much-recommended Laan Tong Lodge. Run by two charming ladies (Australian-Thai), this place is set on a scenic little creek, surrounded by seven hilltribes and numerous villages. Bungalows are cheap (30 to 80B) and clean, and every one of them has been constructed in a different hilltribe style! In the evening everyone eats together, and it's good wholesome vegetarian fare. You can walk to at least half a dozen villages (mainly Lisu and Lahu) in under two hours, and enjoy solar-heated showers down by the river. Fishing, swimming, trekking and relaxation—Laan Tong Lodge really does have something for everyone!

Doi Mae Salong

If travelling by motorbike (hire a powerful one: Chat house in Chiang Rai has a couple of nifty 125cc Honda Wings) take a ride up Doi Mae Salong, 36 km northwest of Mae Chan. The scenery along the mountain road is quite spectacular, especially in January when all the flowers are in bloom. Some 20 km out of Mae Chan, you'll pass an interesting Hilltribe Welfare Centre—a good place to pick up handicraft bargains. At the mountain summit, just 3 km from the Burmese border, there's Santi Kiri—a fascinating settlement inhabited by families of the 93rd ('Kuomintang') regiment who fled here from China after the 1949 revolution. Breathtaking views, antique atmosphere (reminded me of Darjeeling), charming locals and 'gourmet' meals at the highest Chinese restaurant in Thailand—this is another reward spot to spend a day or two.

LAMPHUN & PASANG

Lamphun makes a good day-outing, by bus or by motorbike, from Chiang Mai, 26 km to the north. It is the oldest existing city in Thailand, and is said to produce the country's prettiest girls. Both claims to fame derive from the beautiful Mon queen, Chamathevi, who founded the city—then the seat of the Haripunchai kingdom—in the 7th century. She is said to have defeated her main rival, a tribal chieftain with an aggressive desire to marry her, by means of magic picked up from Suthep, the old hermit after whom Doi Suthep is named. Nakorn Haripunchai, as Lamphun was then known, staved off successive attacks from the Khmer and emerged into the 20th century still an independent kingdom. In the process, however, it sustained two major invasions—first by Mengrai, founder of Chiang Mai, later by the Burmese—and little now remains of the original town. One of the few major structures to survive, however, is the beautiful Wat Phra That Haripunchai, a supreme example of classical northern Thai religious architecture.

GETTING THERE
Green buses (No. 181) leave for Lamphun every 15 minutes (6 am to 6 pm) from Nawarat Bridge stop in Chiang Mai. The 1½-hour journey costs 8B. From the same stop, white buses (No. 182) go direct to Pasang.

Wat Phra That, Lamphun

TOURIST INFORMATION

There's a small Thai Airways information desk (oddly situated in a whisky and furniture shop), just round the corner from Lamphun bus stop. Mr Tu, the information officer, goes out of his way to help travellers. He has a small guest house, with a few rooms at 50B, and sometimes takes house-guests out on motorboat excursions down the Ping River, dropping in on Karen tribes. Ask him for directions to **Lamphun Silk Factory**, just below his booth, where special silk is produced for members of the Thai royal family. The weaving processes are worth observing, and there's a small showroom were hand-made ladies' jackets (beautifully embroidered) sell for around 2000B. Stock is limited here—the factory doesn't really deal direct with the public.

WHAT TO SEE

Lamphun is a pleasant, airy little town with some nice bakeries and samosa-snack places. If you're here in August, sample the famous local fruit called *lamyai* (longan). Lamphun's lamyai orchards are said to produce the finest kind of this fruit in the country. You pass the orchards on the bus-ride down from Chiang Mai, and a pretty sight they are too.

From Lamphun bus-stop, it's a 2-minute walk up the road to **Wat Phra That Haripunchai**. Open 6 am to 6 pm daily, this is the main attraction of the city and receives a constant stream of pilgrims and visitors. The outstanding soaring golden *chedi* was originally built in 1064 by King Athitayarat (32nd king of Haripunchai) to house precious relics of the Buddha. This *chedi* is 60 metres high and has a 9-tiered umbrella at the top, gilded with $6\frac{1}{2}$ kgs of pure gold. Behind it hangs the largest temple gong in northern Thailand, made at Wat Phra Singh (Chiang Mai) in the 7th century. In olden days, it used to wake up the heavenly gods (and everybody in town) at 6 am every morning. Nearby, in a small chamber, there's a large gold figure of a pot-bellied monk. This is Sangha Jai, the monk who brought the Buddha's relics here from India. The legend goes that he ate himself into this obese condition deliberately, since—when young and handsome—he was so plagued by women he couldn't keep his mind on the

Buddha's teachings! To get the full effect of this glorious temple, view it from the front, facing the river. For atmosphere, turn up around 11.30 am or 3 pm—at both times, the temple compound is alive with colourful monks and novices walking to or from classes at the monastic college. Viewed against the background of the gleaming gold *chedi*, their yellow and saffron robes make a beautiful sight.

Opposite the temple entrance, the new **Haripunchai National Museum** houses a small, but well-displayed, collection of Lanna antiques found in the region—mainly engraved stones, temple carvings, weapons and amulets. Admission to the museum is 3B, and it's open 8.30 am to 6 pm Wednesday to Sunday.

At **Wat Chama Thevi**, a 15-minute stroll north of town (or a 5B *samlor* ride), you'll find the venerated *chedi* containing Queen Chamthevi's ashes. Probably dating from the 8th century, it has been restored many times but retains the architectural style of the Mahabodhi temple in Bodhgaya. The unusual square shape of this *chedi* has given the temple its more common title of Wat Kukut, or 'wat with a topless chedi'. Four-sided, it has tiered niches containing standing images of Buddha, each row smaller than the one below. All of the stucco figures have one hand raised (though most are armless now) in the gesture of dispelling fear.

Pasang

For good shopping, take a *songthaew* on to **Pasang**, a charming little cotton-weaving village 10 km south of Lamphun. The main street here is lined with shops selling cotton products, batiks, wickerware and other local handicrafts. To see the full range of Pasang produce, visit **Nandakwang Laicum** on the right-hand side of the road. This has lovely batik dresses (320B), shirts (270B) and cushion-covers (80B), also handwoven cotton placemats (200B) and 8-napkin sets (120B). Prices are a little high, but everything's top quality. Nandakwang has a flair for modern, contemporary designs—you won't find anything like this in Chiang Mai. Over the road, Suchada sells more traditional and cheaper stuff: ready-to-wear dresses and nightshirts (150 to 200B), shirts in cotton batik and printed cotton (70 to 100B) and—the best buy of all—litre bottles of Pasang honey, made from the aromatic Lamyai blossom, for 130B. It's delicious! Walk a few hundred yards above Suchada to find a good little bamboo and wickerware shop selling delightful baskets, handbags and furniture at very reasonable prices.

MAE SARIANG

There are several good reasons for dropping in on Mae Sariang (200 km southwest of Chiang Mai) on the way to Mae Hong Son. Within easy reach of several hilltribe settlements, it's a good base for trekking. And close to the Burmese border, it's also an interesting smuggling centre—especially for teakwood from Burma, for which the local Thais pay in rice, cash or gasoline. The town itself has a very scenic location, surrounded by wooded hills, and has become something of a Thai resort. Coffee shops and video parlours now exist alongside tribal mud-huts; painted transvestites and hip young Thais in Levis now stroll the streets with Karen villagers wearing fedoras over traditional costume; barbers administer 'TV tonsures' in modern salons next door to flaking age-old *chedis*. It's a town of stark contrasts—yet the old and the new blend together surprisingly well. The atmosphere is soothingly calm, despite the surface flamboyance, though the nightlife is quite a scene!

GETTING THERE
From Chiang Mai Arcade terminal, buses leave for Mae Sariang (going on to Mae Hong Son) at 6.30 am, 8 am, 11 am, 1 pm, 3 pm, 8 pm and 9 pm. The fare is 50B, and the picturesque journey takes 4 hours. From Mae Sariang, you can pick up buses for Mae Hong Son at 12.30 pm, 10 am, 12 noon, 3 pm, 5 pm and midnight. This is a rather hairy (but scenic) 4 hour journey, costing 52B.

WHAT TO SEE
Mae Sariang is a small town of few streets—you can walk right round it in 20 minutes. There are two Burmese-Shan temples near the bus station. **Wat Jong Sung** and **Wat Si Boonruang**. The larger *wat* has a couple of semi-interesting *chedis* with ornamental spires, and some pagoda-style monks' residences to the rear. To visit the nearest Karen village, 5 km out of town, you can either hire a (rare) *songthaew* for 2B, or walk it. For any local excursions, it's worth calling on Mae Sariang Guest House, which hands out a half-decent map of the area. This lodge also hires out guides (100B per day) for treks to nearby Red Lahu, Karen, Meo and Lisu villages, plus invigorating walks up into the hills. To see wild elephants at work in the nearby teakwood forests (40 km out of the town), contact Pai Toon—a local man with good English—at 217/2 Panit Rd, near the border police camp. Or ask for him at **Sweet Pub**, behind Mae Sariang Guest House. Lek, manager of the Sweet Pub, handles most trekking in the region. He arranges transport to the two tribal centres of **Mae Sam Lap** and **Mae Kong Ka** on the Burmese border. Mae Sam Lap, 48 km due west of Mae Sariang, is of principal interest for the few Pamalaw or 'long-necked' people who live at the Karen village here. Independent travel there is difficult—the roads are very bad. Lek lays on special cars to Mae Sam Lap and back for 100B per person. He also owns two guest houses in Mae Kong Ka, which is a far more pleasant ride—lots of Karen villages to drop into along the way. Mae Kong Ka also has the better shopping—at the village, you can buy beautiful Karen costumes and handicrafts at low prices.

From either Mae Sam Lap or Mae Kong Ka, there are exciting boat trips up or down the Silom River, which separates Thailand from Burma. Going north, you can visit the thriving black-market town of **Joh Ta**, full of smugglers. Here you can buy jade, rubies and sapphires at knock-down prices (haggle hard!), and watch water-buffalo and cows being ferried over from Burma. From Mae Sam Lap, boats normally leave around 8 am and 9 am, arriving in Joh Ta some 4 hours later. It's best to go early, and in a group—the cost of a boat is around 1000B. But you can get there more quickly and cheaply from Mae Kong Ka, on Lek's boat. The alternative trip, proceeding south down the Silom, brings you to the customs point of **Mae Leh Ta**, where some attempt is made to collect taxes from smugglers. This is a scenic and exciting excursion (the river is very fast!) and there's a good chance of seeing elephant-logging along the riverbank.

NIGHTLIFE

There's quite a bit of action in Mae Sariang at night, most of it behind closed doors! Clustered round the small cinema (with its revolving bill of King Kong and Bruce Lee movies) are a plethora of slinky little 'disco cafes' with live music and subterranean lighting. (Some are hostess bars.) **Palace Cafe**, opposite Mae Sariang Guest House, is the red-light venue after dark—very intimate atmosphere, and twangy live music nightly. Best nightspot is the **Black and White** (inside, all black!) opposite the cinema. This has a fun band which invites 'requests' from visiting *farangs*. Whatever you ask for, they play Cliff Richard! Come here in a group—cheap drinks and snacks, lots of laughs. On the way out, watch out for rabid dogs. This town has more mangy, beaten-up and generally done-in dogs than you can shake a stick at.

WHERE TO STAY

The **Mitaree**, in the main street, is Mae Sariang's only hotel. Scruffy twin-bedded fan rooms are overpriced at 150B; the restaurant is mediocre (try 'black rice pudding' for breakfast—it's awful), and the 'English-speaking travel service' comprises one guide, who charges 150B just to see the nearby Karen village. **Mae Sariang Guest House**, near the bus station, is a far better choice—it has comfy fan-rooms at 80B, clean communal showers, friendly (if eccentric) staff, and a good information service. **B. R. Guest House**, right next to the bus station, is run by a friendly family and is immaculately clean. It has just three rooms. At 80B single, 100B double (with fans and attached bathrooms), they are the best deal in town.

EATING OUT

Inthara Restaurant, just beyond Mitaree Hotel, offers a limited range of Thai/Chinese meals, around 30B a dish. The overrated speciality is Chicken in Hot Basil. Try instead Chicken with Ginger and Onions—it's delicious. Across the road, the civilized **Renu Restaurant** offers superior cuisine at 40–60B a dish, and has an air-conditioned lounge. The thing to try here is **Tod Mon Phagay**, or local river fish. Western-style fare—including continental breakfasts, cakes and ice-cream—is served at **Sweet Pub**. Best time to catch manager Lek, by the way, is in the evening. During the day, he's often in the forest.

MAE HONG SON

Long isolated from the modern world by rugged mountains, the mist-shrouded valley of Mae Hong Son has only just emerged into the 20th century. As new roads stubbornly push their way through from Chiang Mai, Mae Hong Son is being touted as the last surviving bastion of traditional culture and customs in the north. Situated on the topmost northwestern border with Burma, nearly half of the province's 150,000 inhabitants are hilltribe people—mainly Karen, Muser, Lisu, Lahu and H'mong. The first settlement was built around an elephant corral site, probably in 1830. The large-scale migrations of tribal clans to and from Burma during the subsequent 40 years led to Mae Hong Son being designated a provincial capital in 1893. Today, while the border to Burma remains closed, the town retains the excitement of a frontier outpost—a modern-day melting pot of old and new civilizations. The surrounding virgin forests and hills—full of caves, waterfalls and hot springs—are a paradise for the nature-lover. Especially during December, when the countryside is ablaze with golden *buatong* (sunflower) blossoms. Lying at high elevation, between two mountain ranges, Mae Hong Son valley is shrouded in early-morning mist throughout the year, and is popularly known as 'The Misty City'. It is also referred to, rather less appropriately, as 'Thailand's Shangri-La'. Whatever, enough of the valley has now been cleared of hill-bandits, and its attractions

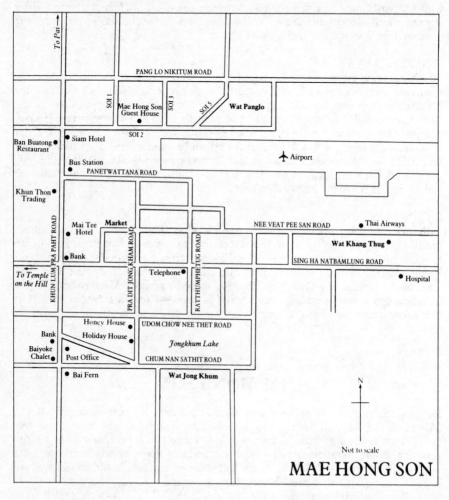

MAE HONG SON

opened to trekking, to pave the way for wide-scale exploration of this beautiful and (as yet) unspoilt province.

Mae Hong Son is at its best—both for trekking and for scenery—from November to February. During these months, the climate is pleasantly dry and cool—cold even, if you're trekking at high altitudes, so take warm clothing and a sleeping bag! In December, the wild sunflowers (*batong*) and the opium poppies come into blossom. Also in December, the town holds it annual 'Miss Hilltribes Contest'—the aim being to give pretty local widows the chance of attracting a new husband! It's a really big event, with a huge fairground, a lively fête and a market that threatens to engulf the entire town! If visiting Mae Hong Son during the rainy months (i.e. up till November) you'll need to take precautions against malarial mosquitoes—they're whoppers! Even in the dry months, it's wise to sleep under a net.

GETTING THERE

By Air
Thai Airways flies twice daily to Mae Hong Son from Chiang Mai (310B, 35 minutes). There's also one flight daily from Bangkok (1350B), with a change of planes in Chiang Mai. Many travellers take the bus to Mae Hong Son, and return to Chiang Mai by air—the glorious mountain scenery is worth the extra expense! Air tickets out of Mae Hong Son are, however, in heavy demand. You'll need to book in advance at Thai Airways on the airport road, leading out of town, immediately on arrival. Some people play safe, and buy a return air-ticket in Chiang Mai.

By Bus
From Chiang Mai Arcade terminal, buses leave for Mae Hong Son (via Pai and Soppong) at 6.30 am, 8 am, 11 am, 1 pm, 3 pm, 8 pm and 9 pm. The fare is 97B, and the journey presently takes around 7 hours. When the new road from Chiang Mai to Mae Hong Son is completed (scheduled for mid-'88) the distance between the two cities will be cut from 350 km to 245 km, allowing a quicker, safer journey. Until then, travel by bus—especially the section between Pai and Mae Hong Son—is a real thrill-a-minute experience. Landslides, floods, yawning chasms, hairpin bends and bulldozers shoving wreckage down the mountain, are all part of the fun. It's best savoured from the bus roof—but make sure you're securely anchored!

From Mae Hong Son, there are three buses daily back to Chiang Mai, leaving at 7.30 am, 10.30 am and 2 pm. They all go via Soppong ($2^1/_2$ hours, fare 30B) and Pai ($4^1/_2$ hours, 50B).

WHAT TO SEE
Not everybody cares for Mae Hong Son town. Ever since it began gearing up for tourism, it's become rather dirty and noisy. Still, many enjoy its raw energy and lively atmosphere—and there are a couple of spots set aside for peace-lovers. The prettiest of these is **Jongkhum Lake** at the south of the town, below the post office. This scenic freshwater lake, with its fountains and exotic gardens (Fitness Park), lies in the shadow of a large mountain and is overlooked by two charming monasteries. It's the place to be with your camera in the early morning when mist still clings to the town, or in the warm glow

of sunset. One of the twin temples here, **Wat Chong Klang**, definitely merits a visit. It houses the oldest, most revered Buddha in the province, said to have been cast in Burma and recovered from the Pai River. It also has 'paintings on glasses' and 'wood carvings old ancient of Buddha'. The former are brilliantly coloured glass paintings of various *jakarta* (life of Buddha) stories; the latter are a fascinating collection of wooden dolls, depicting princes, paupers, beggars and various ascetics. Both attractions were brought here from Burma in 1857. If they're locked up, ask one of the monks to produce the key. The famous Buddha can only be seen at the annual Songkran Festival (mid-April), when it is taken in procession around the town.

The town's principal monastery, **Wat Prathat Doi Khun Mu**, is known locally as the 'Temple on the Hill'. Built 150 years ago to hold some relics of Buddha from India, it sits atop a 250-metre high hill offering fine views down over the capital, and the surrounding mountains and valleys. This *wat* is constructed in the Burmese style with ornately carved, many-tiered roofs, and distinctly Burmese features on the main Buddha image. There are two important *chedis* up here, both of them illuminated at night. The temple has its big annual festival at the Full Moon in October. This marks the end of the rainy season, and the end of a long period of fasting for the resident monks. During the rains, they have to stay put in the temple (by order of Buddha), living on meagre rations. The festival marks their descent from the hill, to resume collecting food daily once more. Its a rich, colourful event, with all the local farmers and town's-folk dressed up in traditional costume, providing some excellent opportunities for photography. To get up to the temple, either hire a motorbike (from Mae Hong Son Guest House or Khun Thou Trading) or climb it. The path starts directly opposite the Mai Tee Hotel in town, and you head up it—keeping left all the way—until the temple entrance appears on your right. After this 10-minute stroll, you can either scale the hill head-on—via the crumbling old staircase beyond the temple entrance—or take the easy hill-road, which starts as a dirt-track some 50 yards *before* the *wat* entrance. In either case, it's about a further 20-minute climb.

Trekking

Ever since Chiang Rai and the Golden Triangle started to become 'overtrekked', adventure-travellers have been drifting over to Mae Hong Son instead. New companies are springing up all over town, offering interesting hill-walks, elephant safaris and river-rafting trips at an average cost of 200–250B per day. Few of them are well-organized—trekking in this region is still very much in the trial-and-error stage—but several people enjoy pioneering unspoilt, sometimes dangerous, trails. Local attractions include **Ban Mai**, a Shan village 3 km south of Mae Hong Son; the **K.M.T.** (Chinese refugee) village at the north frontier, previously the HQ of the opium warlord Khun Sa; the 'Fish Cave' of **Tham Pla**, full of giant catfish and located 18 km out of town; the King's old **Pang Tong Palace** (he still flies in by helicopter every year or two); and the impressive **Pha Sua Falls**, considered by many the best waterfall in the North. Some companies operate longer treks which loop round the Burma border, returning back down the Pai River by raft. Most treks make deliberate detours via opium fields (now very few) and most guides expect you to walk between six and eight hours a day. The scenery is often spectacular, but you have to be fit to enjoy it—the going can get very tough! There's a lot of hill-climbing involved, and the villages visited can sometimes offer only very basic food and accommodation. Even if your trek company provides food, it's wise to bring some supplies of your own. A water-bottle, decent walking shoes, a waterproof (for rainy days) and a sleeping bag (for cold nights) are other useful inclusions.

Independent travel up to the border point of **Mae Aw** isn't as safe as before. Buses no longer run up there (too many have been held up by bandits) and you'll have to hire a jeep. Enquire at the K.M.T. office opposite the old Mae Aw bus-stop in town. Jeep rides cost around 200B return, and you'll need to take a guide along (another 100B) for safety. On the drive up, you can stop off at the King's Palace, the waterfall and an interesting Meo village. At Mae Aw itself, there's a colourful Karen village—but don't go walking about on your own (police and locals aren't always friendly) and keep your camera well out of sight!

The best trek agency in Mae Hong Son is **Don Enterprises**, just up from the post office on the main road. Don were the first team to organize treks to the Burmese border, four years ago, and they've got contacts (even with the Red Karen army) that no-one else has. A very adventurous outfit, they boldly go where other companies fear to tread. Jack, the top guide, knows every village along the border, hardly any of them visited by tourists. Don's standard 2 day 3 night treks cost around 700B, and run up from Soppong to visit Yellow Lahu, Red Lahu, Red Karen and other hilltribe settlements near the Burmese borderline. They also offer elephant treks at 500B per day, and river-rafting up to the border (to visit the long-necked Pamalaw people) at 200B per day. Run by three Burmese guys, Don Enterprises enjoy a particularly good relationship with the various local tribes, and are presently trying to set up a 'Hilltribe Culture Show' with them—this should be interesting. Meanwhile, guide David is planning to run out treks to the newly-discovered Kaiyo tribe, who live—along with other primitive clans—at the river-side village of **Padong**, right on the border. Padong used to be just inside Burma, but the villagers were moved to the Thai side of the border when it was closed. The area around Padong is virgin trekking territory—hardly any of the tribes (mainly Burmese) have yet seen Westerners. Independent travel there is possible, but pricey. Buses run half-hourly from Mae Hong Son market up to the Boat Station on the Pai River. From here, it's a 2–3 hour longtail boat trip (320B one-way, for one to six people) up-river to Padong. Trouble is, there's a 300B charge to visit the village itself—if you can't afford it, stay in the boat! It works out cheaper (around 600B for the whole 'package') to book the Padong trip in town—by now, both **Don Enterprises** and **S & N Tours** (near Siam Hotel) should be handling it. Two other reliable trek places in town are **Mae Hong Son Guest House** (200B) a day, takes out small 3–4 person groups only; Ask for Pang, the best guide) and **Khun Thou Trading**, opposite Mai Tee Hotel. Take note, river-rafting from Mae Hong Son down to Pai is not practical—the water is too shallow.

SHOPPING

Half the school kids in the valley are now busily producing handicrafts for tourists—most of this stuff is attractive and cheap. For authentic hilltribe crafts, try the small shop outside Bangkok Bank in Khunlum Praphat Rd. This has a full range of locally-produced crafts, including rough-cotton Burmese jackets (120B), handwoven Karen tunics (180B) and Burmese printed cotton, plaited with gold and silver thread (120B per

6 × 4 ft length). Prices are a little high here, but the quality of workmanship is generally excellent.

The town's morning market is the place to pick up wildflower honey (delicious), beautiful woven sarongs from Burma, and trek supplies and gear. Novelty buys here include bags of crispy fried pigskin (yes, it keeps) and lung-wrenching Burmese cheroots. Lots of good cheap food too. But arrive at the market early—by 9 am it's all over.

WHERE TO STAY

There are three good hotels in Khunlum Praphat Rd, the main street, offering fan-rooms from 100B, air-con rooms between 240 and 280B. The best is **Siam** (every room has twin beds, soap and toilet-paper), followed by **Mai Tee** (less friendly, but clean) and **Baiyoke Chalet** (nice, if sombre, rooms; popular with Thais).

There's a host of cheap guest houses in Mae Hong Son, most charging 40–50B for one person, 70–80B for two. Check out **Holiday House** and **Honey House**, both beautifully situated overlooking Jongkhum Lake. The Honey is brand-new, and has a cheap dormitory. Two other goodies are **Mae Hong Son Guest House** and **Galare**—both well-advertised (with directions) at the bus station. The Mae Hong Son has the better atmosphere and information service; Galare has the better rooms, with decent mosquito-netting and real beds! **Khun Thou Trading** has amazing rooms, great information, a useful restaurant, and gives the best haircut and massage in town. **New Guysorn**, 5 minutes' walk north of the bus-stop is quiet and clean, and run by friendly people. Pity about the spiders though. . .

EATING OUT

The most stylish place to eat is **Bai Fern**, just below the post office. This has wicker easy-chairs, swiss clocks, exotic plants and bags of period charm. The food's good too—especially Fried Pai River Fish with Pepper and Garlic (40B), Coconut Milk Soup with Chicken and Garlic (35B), and exceptional sweet and sour dishes. There's an amazing selection of coffees (including expresso), and the polished-teak bar mixes a terrific Singapore Sling. It also plays Sinatra and jazz! The nearby **Kai Muk** (Pearl) is another good Thai-Chinese restaurant. Nice things on offer are Fried Chicken with Lemon Juice, and Spicy Catfish Salad. Less appetizing items include Frog Salad and Spicy Pig Intestine Salad, but the standard *kai yang* and *som tam* fare is excellent. Cheaper Thai-Chinese eats are available at the popular open-air **Joke** restaurant, just above Kai Muk. Food here is best in the early morning, when it's fresh. The night market is handy for late snacks—mainly omelettes, soups and 10B meals.

Western-style food is provided at the cosy, friendly **Ban Buatong**, opposite Siam Hotel. It's a good evening hang-out spot, with mellow sounds and friendly staff. Tasty local dishes include Chicken with Fried Cashew Nuts (40B) and Grilled Pork with Honey (30B). The B.B. is famous for its great breakfasts and fruit salads.

Soppong

The small, sleepy market village of Soppong is a popular stop-off on the mountain road between Pai and Mae Hong Son. On first acquaintance, it's hard to see the attraction.

It's even harder when making the 1½-hour ascent up to **Tham Lot Cave** (the main attraction) on foot. Once up there, however, all regrets fade away. The scenery around Tham Lot—one of Thailand's longest-known limestone caves—is quite breathtaking, especially round October and November, when the hills and forests are at their most green and luxuriant. The place to stay is the popular **Cave Lodge**, run by friendly Diu and John, which is within easy walking distance of several intersting hilltribe villages. It is also only five minutes' walk from the cave, and you can hire a guide (30B) plus a lantern (50B) to explore its vast interior, full of fascinating side-chambers and grotesquely-shaped pillars. Be prepared to get wet, though! A stream runs through the cave, and when water-levels are high, the guide often just hands the lantern to the best swimmer and hops it! Travellers also like Cave Lodge for its vegetarian food, its brown bread, and its strawberry and peach wine. All meals are eaten together, so you'll make lots of friends. John himself is an authority on the local hill-peoples, and has written much about Tham Lot and other caves in the region. At present, he only has about 20 rooms for let (30B per person) plus a few 70B two-person bungalows, but will shortly be opening **Cave Lodge 2**, some 25 km from the present lodge, near a checkpoint on the way to Mae Hong Son. There are also plans afoot to run river-raft trips between the two lodges in the not too distant future.

The tiny cafe at Soppong bus-stop—now called **So Cheap Guest House**—has a few rooms for 25B per person. Current bus-timings for Pai, Mae Hong Son and Chiang Mai are posted here. So is a map giving directions up to Cave Lodge. Another place to stay is **Lisu Lodge**, a few kilometres east of Soppong in **Ban Namrin**. Buses go right past it, so you can ask to be put off. Run by a homely Lisu family, this place has rooms for 30B, and good, cheap meals.

GETTING THERE
Buses leave Pai for Soppong (40 km, 2 hours) at 7 am, 11 am and 1.30 pm daily. From Soppong to Pai, there are buses at 8 am, 10 am, 1 pm and 4.30 pm daily. See Mae Hong Son section for bus-timings to Soppong from Mae Hong Son and Chiang Mai.

PAI

People hang out in Pai for weeks on end, and it's easy to see why. Situated midway between Chiang Mai and Mae Hong Son, this restful little town lies in a charming valley completely ringed by rolling hills and mountains. Unlike so-called outposts like Mae Hong Son, it has a genuine pioneer-town atmosphere, and is within easy walking distance of several interesting hilltribe villages, most of them inhabited by refugees from Burma. Pai also offers better and cheaper trekking at present than anywhere else in the North. Rapid development is only a year or two away—already they are planning the new airstrip here—but for the time being Pai remains a tiny one-horse (actually, two-street) town totally geared to relaxation. The standard greeting in these parts is a lazy *Bai nai?* (where you go?), to which the equally laconic response is *Bai eeway . .* (Oh, just cruising . . .). If there's anywhere on earth that invented the word 'laidback', it must be Pai. The only thing that ever ruffles its calm are its dogs. The hounds of Pai are famous.

They come out at night and roam around in packs scaring lone pedestrians witless. You can try pretending to pick up a stone (this is how everybody in Asia tends to move their animals), but if that doesn't work, be prepared to leg it!

The name Pai is actually a corruption of the Shan word for 'refugee'. The original settlers in this region were outcasts from the large Shan state in Burma. They first crossed over the Pai River some 150 years ago, founding Old Pai—still a thriving Shan village—a few kilometres west of the present town, which is only 100 years old.

GETTING THERE
Buses run to Pai from Chiang Mai (3½ hours, 50B) and from Mae Hong Son (4½ hours, 50B). For bus timings from these two points, see relevant 'Getting There' sections.

WHAT TO SEE
There are some beautiful walks around Pai for which you need no guide. Some people hire out motorbikes (20B an hour; contact Pai Cafe, or Duang guest houses), but the dirt-track trails connecting the various hilltribe villages are treacherous. For a safe, relaxing bike tour, contact Joe at Duang Guest House. He'll take you out for a great half-day's sightseeing, including good commentary in English, for only 80B. This way, you can enjoy the scenery, and cover all the local attractions in just a morning.

Pai has some worthwhile temples—there's a nice Burmese-style one above the hospital, and Pai's finest temple just behind the bus station. The most popular, however, is **Wat Mae Yen**—the 'Temple on the Hill'. This is a 30-minute walk (1½ km) east of town—over a bridge, through a Shan village, and up a 350-step staircase. At the top of the shallow steps are a group of three small *chedis*—the central one is the only original thing in the otherwise brand-new temple complex. Twelve years ago, this site was derelict. The present structure—built in mixed architectural style, primarily Lanna Thai—is the work of one persuasive monk, who convinced the town that it was time it made some merit. This little monk, often found seated within the shiny new *bot*, can talk money out of just about anyone. Remember this when he offers you a 'free' banana! The temple has a beautiful situation overlooking a valley—from here you can see across to 'Umbrella Mountain', the highest peak in the province. The views are especially fine around sunset.

The 'road' east out of town, via Kim Guest House, leads to a succession of tribal villages. First, some 3 km from Pai, there's a small K.M.T. settlement. The people here are refugees, forced to flee China after resisting Mao Tse Tung. They only arrived from Burma 10 years ago, and have (a rare phenomena) converted to Christianity. They did so because missionaries said this was their meal-ticket to Taiwan or Singapore. Discovering that they still need a passport (denied to political refugees) hasn't dampened their new faith in the slightest. Now they pray for a passport. Over the road from this village is a small Lisu settlement—the people here are very poor, and the children really appreciate any small presents you may bring. About 2 km further on, there's the Shan village of **Ban Morepang** (Old Pai), where the people still wear traditional Burmese-style turbans and sarongs. The trail comes to an end at **Morepang Waterfall**, some 7 km (two hours' walk) from Pai town. There's good swimming here from September to November—but *kamikaze* slides down the rocks (the popular local recreation) are *not* recommended!

Another pleasant outing is to Pai's famous **Hot Springs**. These are located up in the hills, some 15 km east of town, and are best visited by motorbike (or by cycle—30B day-hire in town). This is a very scenic ride through beautiful woodlands, with the promise of a refreshing mineral-water bath (with a hot tub to soak in!) at journey's end.

Trekking

Pai has densely forested hills, deep jungles, green open valleys and an abundance of lovely natural scenery. Unlike Chiang Rai, this area is almost completely untrekked. Unlike Mae Hong Son, which is still getting its act together, Pai has no less than four good English-speaking guides. They are all cheap (around 100B per day, plus an extra 200B per day for elephants or river-rafting) and they all have independent circuits which don't overlap. The result is inexpensive small-group treks to little-visited villages, and no sight of another *farang* from beginning to end. If anything, however, the Pai trails are hillier and harder going than Mae Hong Son, so you'll need good walking shoes and *a lot* of energy! Again, it can get cold at night (especially October to February) and a sleeping bag, even blankets, may be required. In the rainy months, bring a waterproof or plastic sheet. There's no electricity up in the hills, so a good torch with a powerful beam is a real must.

All Pai's trek guides are attached to guest houses in the town. They are Buffalo Bill and Anan (Pai Guest House), Mr Pong (Cafe), and Jungle Joe (Duang). Of these, the best-known—and the most notorious—is Buffalo Bill. His speciality is the gruelling 7-day trek from Pai up to Mae Hong Son. If you're into walking 6–7 hours a day, and survive days 2 and 3 (a crippling ascent up an 1800-metre mountain), you'll enjoy this one. People trek with B.B. for the 'experience'—wildly eccentric, never less than entertaining, he's a real showman! Of the other guides, only Jungle Joe and Mr Pong are home-grown talents—i. e. born and bred in Pai, with full knowledge of the area. Joe has an especially good relationship with the hilltribes, and is probably the best guide in town—quiet, friendly and reliable. His popular 4-day trek strikes north to visit Lisu, Yellow Lahu, and White Karen villages, and includes an option to river-raft down the Pai River from the Shan village of **Ban Mae Kok** to the Thai settlement of **Sop Kai**. From here, if you don't wish to walk back to Pai, you can take a minibus down to **Mae Malai**, which is only half an hour by bus from Chiang Mai.

Joe also offers a 4-day trek to Soppong's **Cave Lodge**, and (November to February only) 7-day 'adventure' raft trips up the Pai River to Mae Hong Son. The Pai is a narrow, perilous river—non-negotiable before November (too swollen) or after February (too shallow)—but in season, it's an exhilarating experience to travel on it!

SHOPPING
Hilltribe crafts, mainly Karen products, are sold in town at Duang and Cafe restaurants. Prices are okay—hand-embroidered tunics at 200B, handwoven cotton bedsheets around 300B etc.—but you're generally better off buying direct from the villages on trek.

WHERE TO STAY & EATING OUT
Pai has one 'hotel' (the gloomy, Chinese-owned **Weng Pai**) and several cheap, basic guest houses. Best of these is **Duang** ('Your Home away from Home'), right opposite the bus-stop. This has large, clean rooms at 30B single, 60B double; also one special

twin-bedded room, with a swank bathroom, at 150B. Duang herself is a delightful hostess, welcoming guests with free fruit salads, and giving good local information. Her sister, Kim, teaches classical Thai dance at the local school (worth dropping in to see) and runs **Kim Guest House**, 5 minutes' walk up the road. This is another clean place, with rooms from 30B (decent beds) to 40B (attached bathrooms with hot showers!) The back garden is a banana/mango plantation—so more free fruit salads!

Rooms at **Pai** and **Cafe** guest houses (30B single; 40/50B double) are more basic. Thin bamboo partitions give you intimate knowledge of your neighbour's sleeping habits. Large spiders, and other chummy crawlies, are common co-tenants. Still, the food's good. The **Pai in the Sky** (Cafe's restaurant) serves delicious vegetarian meals and is famous for its yoghurt shakes. Try the 18B 'Hotpot'—a wonderful potpourri of chicken, potatoes, tomatoes, onions, garlic and coconut milk, on a bed of rice. Pai guest house, across the road, is the main freaks' hangout, with psychedelic sounds and wacky staff to match. There's a large stuffed eagle in the lobby (rapidly disintegrating) and the special dinner is Elephant Steak with French Freeze. The elephant steaks are really buffalo, but Buffalo Bill (the resident guide) won't admit it. 'I used to have ten elephants', he says, 'but now I have only one. Tourists eat rest!' Actually, B.B. doesn't have any elephants at all, but it's a good story.

The cosy little **P.O.B. restaurant**, just below Weng Pai hotel, offers palatable Thai-Chinese cuisine, and is a quiet alternative to the busy Pai in the Sky. It's run by a friendly Thai lady, and has a useful information board. The best up-to-date trek maps of the area, however, are pinned up at Pai Guest House.

SUKHOTHAI

Birthplace of the Thai nation, Sukhothai lies about 440 km north of Bangkok, and is approached by road from Phitsanoluke. Wrested from the Khmer by two powerful Thai chieftains, Sukhothai ('Dawn of Happiness') was established in 1238 as the first major independent Thai kingdom.

Though its period of power and influence over the Thai states was short—just 150 years—it produced in that time one remarkable ruler, King Ramkhamhaeng the Great. During his 40-year reign, he conquered many neighbouring territories, began direct negotiations with China, invented the Thai alphabet (1283), promoted religion and culture (actively encouraging Ceylonese Buddhist monks and Chinese artisans into the kingdom), and generally paved the way for classic Sukhothai forms of inspirational religious art and sculpture. The Buddha images created in this period possess a distinctive grace and simplicity, a timeless air of serenity, which help to explain why Sukhothai was the spiritual, as well as the temporal, centre of its time. However, a succession of weak kings after Ramkhamhaeng led to the swift decline of this first Thai capital, and in 1365 it became a vassal state of Ayutthaya, the newly-rising star to the south.

An ambitious 10-year project (started 1980) is presently underway, aimed at restoring to their former glory the 70 square kilometres of crumbling brick and stucco ruins comprising Old Sukhothai. Some regret this move, preferring the old walled city in its original derelict state—serene, evocative and lonely. Others cynically remark that the ruins—now renamed 'Sukhothai Historical Park'—are only being restored for the sake of tourism. Most of them have now been made to look as though they were built only last month! The partition of the 'park' into 5 zones—to see each of which you have to pay 20B entrance—and the introduction of eyesore barbed-wire fencing (to stop tourists wandering off into restricted areas) can be off-putting. But in the main, the experiment has been successful. The Sukhothai ruins now make far better viewing than those at Lopburi or Ayutthaya. Visited by busloads of package tourists toting video cameras, this ancient city's original grandeur is slowly, meticulously, being reassembled.

The small town of Sukhothai is a short bus or bicycle ride from the Historical Park, and is an excellent base from which to plan sightseeing. It has good little markets, guest houses, coffee shops and ice-cream parlours, and a wonderfully relaxed atmosphere. Best time to visit is October and November for the annual **Loi Krathong Festival**, celebrated in Sukhothai as nowhere else in Thailand. There's a glorious sound and light show, and the river is packed with myriad tiny boats launching decorative candle-lit floats. As Sukhothai's main event, attended by thousands, advance-booking of transport and accommodation is essential during this festival.

GETTING THERE
Sukhothai is usually reached by bus from Phitsanoluke, which is connected by plane and train to Bangkok and Chiang Mai. Phitsanoluke, 390 km from Bangkok, is a busy, dusty town with little to recommend it except **Wat Phra Sri Ratana Mahathat**, housing the much-revered Jinaraj Buddha. To see this, you'll need to be in town no later than 5 pm—after that time, all you're likely to find are two locked doors and a compound full of saffron-robed monks wandering round in gumboots. Buses run out to Sukhothai from the centre of Phitsanoluke, every half-hour from 6.10 am to 6.10 pm. The fare is 14B, and the journey takes around one hour. If you miss the last bus, or want to stay overnight in Phitsanoluke (really?), try the new **Youth Hostel** at 38 Sanambin (Airport) Rd (tel 242060). It's a converted Thai house, with pretty jasmine gardens. There's a 25B dormitory, rooms from 50B, and a good restaurant.

167

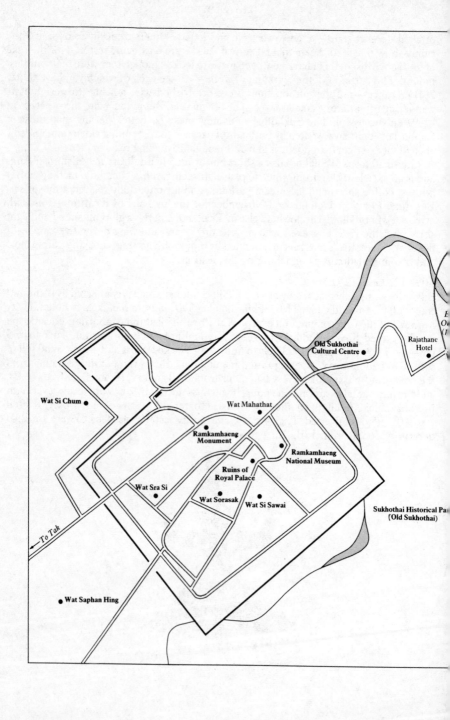

Old Sukhothai
Cultural Centre

Rajathane
Hotel

Wat Si Chum

Wat Mahathat

Ramkamhaeng
Monument

Ramkamhaeng
National Museum

Ruins of
Royal Palace

Wat Sra Si

Wat Sorasak   Wat Si Sawai

Sukhothai Historical Pa
(Old Sukhothai)

← To Tak

Wat Saphan Hing

By Air

Thai Airways flies to Phitsanoluke from Bangkok (daily, 730B, flight time 35 minutes) and from Chiang Mai (four days a week, 505B, flight time 2½ hours). From Phitsanoluke airport, it's a 5B *songthaew* ride into town.

By Train

From Bangkok's Hualamphong station only three trains leaving at 6.40 am (Rapid), 7.05 am and 8.30 am (Ordinary), arrive in Phitsanoluke early enough (respectively, at 1.32 pm, 2.48 pm and 5.15 pm) to carry on to Sukhothai the same day. Basic fares are 292B 1st class, 143B 2nd class, and 69B 3rd class. From Chiang Mai, only the 3.20 pm Rapid arrives in Phitsanoluke at a reasonable time (10.54 pm) to find a hotel for the night.

By Bus

From Bangkok's Northern Terminal, there are three air-con buses to Sukhothai daily at 10.40 am, 10.20 pm and 10.40 pm. The 8-hour journey costs 133B. There are also some cheaper non air-con buses (84B) from the same terminal, but they're far less comfortable.

TOURIST INFORMATION

No tourist office, but good information (and map) from **Chinawat Hotel** in Sukhothai town. Chinawat operates an air-con bus service to Bangkok, via Ayutthaya. So does another decent travel agent, **Win Tours** in Jarodvitheethong Rd (tel 611039).

WHAT TO SEE

Sukhothai Historical Park is studded with wonderful old Buddha images, *wats* and *chedis*, moats and canals, and merits a full day's viewing. To get there from the new town (12 km) hire a *songthaew* (5B) or take a bus from the rank just across the bridge (also 5B). Once there, hire a bicycle—the popular way of seeing the ruins—from outside the Museum (20B per day). Bear in mind, however, that the Park covers a vast area, and that many of the major temples are spaced from 2 to 6 kilometres apart. It can be a long haul by bicycle, and a couple of outlying temples on the suggested route below (e.g. Wat Si Chum, outside the city walls) are probably best excluded from a bike tour! To see all the places mentioned in just a morning—for 80B a person—contact Chinawat Hotel in the new town. This operates worthwhile air-con minibus *tours*, with decent English-speaking guides, from 8.45 am to 12 noon daily. You can find guides yourself in the old city (rates around 100B per hour), but they're purely optional. All the main temples now have detailed information boards in English. To see everything at leisure, and in maximum comfort, hire a taxi (500B for one to five people, for a whole day!) from the rank outside Chinawat Hotel.

Sukhothai Historical Park
(by tour bus, taxi or bicycle; half/full day)

National Museum – Wat Mahathat – Wat Sri Sawai – Wat Sra Sri – Wat Sri Chum – Wat Saphin Hin – Thai Cultural Centre

National Museum

The Park contains a total of 35 important monuments, all scattered over a wide area, so it's necessary to be selective. Half a dozen temples, plus the excellent museum, should be enough for all but the most avid *wat*-spotter! Tours generally start at **Ramkhamhaeng National Museum**, just inside Old Sukhothai city walls. This has a charming scale model of the old city (useful for identifying the various temples you're going to see, and their relative distances apart), also a replica of King Ramkhamhaeng's famous stone inscription, which reads:

> This Muang Sukhothai is good. In the water there are fish, in the field there is rice. The ruler does not levy a tax on the people who travel along the road together . . . Whoever wants to trade in elephants, so trades. Whoever wants to trade in horses, so trades. Whoever wants to trade in silver and gold, so trades.

This Thai-style 'Declaration of Independence' was found by King Mongkut in the 19th century. The museum also houses a fine collection of Sukhothai Buddha images in bronze or stucco, most of them in the attitudes of 'subduing Mara' or 'dispelling fear'. Buddha figures of the Sukhothai style are simple and unembellished, with slim torsos, lotus-bud topknots (*usnisha*), long earlobes, Grecian noses, arched eyebrows and uniformly serene expressions. By way of contrast, you'll also find a few Ayutthayan Buddhas: regally attired, heavily bejewelled, haughtily arrogant. Outside in the grounds, there are a couple of surprised-looking elephants emerging from brick walls. Admission to the museum is 10B, and there's a 5B guide for sale at the entrance. There's no photography (and 'no shouting') allowed inside.

Wat Mahathat

From the museum, people generally move on to **Wat Mahathat**, the largest and (for many) the most beautiful temple in Sukhothai. Probably built in the mid-13th century by Sri Indrathit (Ramkhamhaeng's father), it sits amid a tranquil lotus pond and picnic park in fully restored splendour. Enclosed within its low-walled compound is a tightly-packed maze of 98 small *chedis*, parentally surveyed by a large central *chedi* with a bulbous lotus-bud *prang* and unusual friezes of walking monks circumventing its base. Nearby, a huge black-caped Buddha lurks Dracula-like within a high brick enclosure. One of the larger *chedis*, with a large seated Buddha at its base, can be climbed (be careful!) for good bird's-eye views of the whole compound.

Wat Sri Sawai, Wat Sra Sri & Wat Sri Chum

Wat Sri Sawai, a short distance southwest of Wat Mahathat, is another 13th-century shrine, notable for its three Khmer-style *prangs*, surrounded by a low laterite wall. Traces of Hindu sculpture on this structure suggest that it was not always a Buddhist monastery. Renovation has been kind to this temple, adorning it with a pretty lotus pond and colourful flower gardens. **Wat Sra Sri**, north of Wat Mahathat, is another superb temple. This features a round Ceylonese-style *chedi* within a monastery built on an island in the middle of a pond. The large *viharn* to the front contains a stucco Buddha image, while the small one to the south is constructed in the Ceylonese Srivijaya style. Save a photo for the little black Buddha strutting on the lawn—it's outrageously camp! It's also a classic example of the 'walking Buddha' style initiated by the Sukhothai sculptors. To see perhaps their finest creation, head on to **Wat Sri Chum**, just outside the city walls to the northeast. The awesome Buddha here, housed within a deceptively dull square *mondop*,

THAILAND

measures 11.3 metres from knee to knee, and is said to have once halted a Burmese invasion. The story goes that the intruding hordes took one look at it and fled in terror! Just inside the entrance, a low, narrow passage leads to the top of the *mondop* for panoramic views over pastoral parklands. The passageway ceiling is lined with slate slabs engraved with various *Jakarta* stories, though only a few of them are illuminated.

Wat Saphin Hin & Thai Cultural Centre

About 2 km west of Wat Sri Chum, and situated on a low hill, **Wat Saphin Hin** is a pleasantly remote place to finish off the day. A rough slate causeway leads to the top, where you'll find a small seated Buddha looking serenely over a picturesque landscape. There's a ruined *viharn* up here too, with a 12.5 metre-high standing Buddha. Refreshingly unrenovated, this *wat* retains its age-old sense of tranquility—and for once there's no admission charge! Leaving the historical park, about 1 km out of the old city on the road back to Sukhothai town, look out for **Thai Cultural Centre**. This has a mock Thai village in a pleasant semi-jungle setting, a few 250B air-con bungalows for rent (book in town), a good restaurant, and live music and dance every evening.

Si Satchanalai

(by bus, then by bicycle; full day)

Si Satch is only 57 km from Sukhothai and was, until absorbed into the Sukhothai kingdom, a powerful political, economic and religious centre in its own right. It also had a reputation for producing quality Thai *celadon* and Sawankhaloke pottery, and there are still bargains to be picked up in the town today. Beautifully set between high hills and the river, Si Satchanalai has lovely old ruins which make a good contrast to the renovated temples of Sukhothai.

Local buses run regularly from Sukhothai to Si Satchanalai for 16B. Chinawat Hotel offers a comprehensive 6-hour minibus tour to Si Satch (150B), taking in the old city, the Ko Noi kiln, and the fabric factories of Hat Sieo. Entering Old Si Satch by bus, **Wat Mahathat** and three other interesting hillside temples appear to the right. Off the bus, cross the bridge over the Yom River, and turn right for the ruins. You'll find bicycles for hire on the way, but you don't need them. The best things about this place are the beautiful walks through the hills and woodlands—besides, several temples are inaccessible by bicycle. Si Satch has fewer 'sights' than Sukhothai, but compensates with beautiful scenery in a peaceful countryside setting. There's also good shopping at **Hat Sieo**, a weaving village in Si Satchanalai district which is famous for its fine handmade cotton. The workers are the Lao-Puan people, who originated in Chiang Kwang and who settled in this area, north of old Si Satchanalai, during the early Bangkok period. Continuing their age-old tradition of fabric-making, they turn out beautiful long Thai sarongs (80B for men, 500B for women) and highly ornate material lengths incorporating designs as intricate (and as stylish) as Arabian carpets.

SHOPPING

You can keep your wallet closed in Sukhothai. A tatty souvenir shop called **Choo's** at the Thai Cultural Centre offers antiques at prices you can't afford. A large house opposite new Sukhothai police station sells 'antique' Buddhas and *garudas* you can't take out of the country. Not much of a choice really.

WHERE TO STAY

The new **Rajthanee Hotel**, in Jarodvitheethong Rd, has air-con rooms from 450B, and is friendly and comfortable. But the main travellers' centre is **Chinawat Hotel**, 1–3 Nikorn Kasem Rd (tel 611385). Run by friendly, energetic Lakana ('Slim') and Wijai, it has rooms from 60B in the old building, excellent fan double rooms from 100B and air-con doubles for 140B in the better new block. Useful facilities include cycle rental, currency exchange (cash only), travel agency, postal service, overseas phone, and good information handouts. The nearby **Sukhothai Hotel** at 15/5 Jarodvitheethong Rd (tel 611133) is a reasonable fallback. Rooms here (75B fan, 200B air-con) aren't as clean as at Chinawat, but staff are friendly and guests get a good city map. Travellers also speak well of **Yupa Guest House**, a small lodge overlooking the river (cross the bridge, walk left along the riverbank for 400 metres). This has rooms from 40 to 60B, relaxing swingseats and lovely views from the balconies.

EATING OUT

The **Rajthanee Hotel** has a classy restaurant—eat well here for 100B, with live music thrown in. The **Chinawat** has a decent bakery section, but cakes, ice-creams and continental breakfasts are all better at the **Rainbow Bakery**, just round the corner. **Dream Coffee Shop**, just below Sawatipong Hotel on the road out of town, does the best coffee in town, and is the place to make Thai friends (they love this place!). The small night market behind the bus station does incredible 6B vegetarian and mussel omelettes, plus the usual cheap Thai-Chinese curries and snacks. Similar fare—almost as good—at the municipal market near the town centre.

Part VI

THE NORTHEAST

Rice-workers

Commonly known as *Isaan*, the northeast is the poorest and least-developed part of Thailand. *Isaan* is a derivation of Isana, the old Mon-Khmer kingdom which once flourished in these parts. The name means 'vastness'—which is appropriate, the northeast covering 170,000 square kilometres, or roughly one-third of the country. It also means 'prosperity'—which is far less appropriate. Isaan is a dry and arid plateau which, if lucky, receives only enough rain to produce one crop of rice each year. Recently, successive droughts have triggered off a mass migration of farmers into Bangkok and other major provinces. But if the region is poor in rice, it is rich in history and culture. Folk dances, fairs and festivals go on as in ages past, both delightful and symbolic. Ancient customs and traditions, untouched by the march of progress, continue to charm and fascinate foreign visitors. The northeast is famous for its fine Khmer-style temples, such as those at **Phimai**, and for its *mudmee* silk (much promoted by Queen Sikrit) which is produced at nearby **Pakthongchai**. Further north, the archaeological discoveries made at the small village of **Ban Chiang** suggest that Isaan was the birthplace of the world's oldest Bronze Age civilization. There are some amazing temples—and beautiful cottage industry crafts—up at **Nong Khai** on the Laos border, while at more modern towns like **Nakhon Ratchasima** and **Udorn Thani**, traditional Isaan-style food, like *kai yang* (spicy barbecued chicken) and som tam (spicy raw papaya salad) can be sampled along with delicious Western-style cakes and pastries.

The main attraction of the northeast is its remoteness. People come here to get off the beaten track and to find 'real' Thailand. They are often successful—Isaan is a land of few sights, and very little spoken English. Here, you have to learn some Thai or starve! Every other traveller I've met in the northeast was doing the same as me—peering into a phrasebook and muttering 'Where is the toilet' or 'I want some food without frog in it' in

174

the local tongue. Getting around is a challenge, but never dull! The pace of life is generally slow and relaxed, the people friendly and hospitable, and the old custom of 'wai-ing' (greeting with a bow) observed even during basketball matches! This is the heart and soul of Thailand—spending a week here, you'll learn more about the Thai people (and their language) than a month anywhere else!

The northeast is a large region, best discovered by rail. There are two routes—one running north via Nakhon Ratchasima (for Phimai and Pakthongchai), Udorn Thani (for Ban Chiang), and Nong Khai; the other running south via Buriram, Surin and Ubon Ratchathani. The southern route is not covered in this guide—partly because it has less to offer the general sightseer, but mainly because ongoing border disputes with Kampuchea make this not the safest place to travel at present.

NAKHON RATCHASIMA (KHORAT)

Only 256 km from Bangkok, Nakhon Ratchasima (better known as Khorat) is the popular and convenient 'gateway' to the northeast. Originally, Khorat was two separate towns, Khorakhapura and Sema, which were merged into one during the reign of King Narai (1656–1688). Today, it still has something of a dual identity—the older, semi-rural eastern half of town contrasting starkly with the busy, commercial section to the west. Khorat is an interesting place in itself, but also makes a good base from which to visit the historic site of **Phimai** and the silk-weaving centre of **Pakthongchai**.

During the 1960s, Khorat was used as a major base for American GIs going into Vietnam. This accounts for all the cinemas, Turkish baths, ex-vet clubs and snooker halls you'll find here, together with the town's veneer of Western sophistication. Walking down the street, you'll often be greeted with a lazy 'Hey man, where you go?' by hip young Thais. And as you tuck into your ham 'n' eggs on rye in an American cafe, you may hear nostalgic juke-box standards like *Rum Boogie* and even *In the Mood*! Nevertheless, Khorat remains typically Thai. Only during 1987—the Year of Tourism—did the province begin to attract more than a few Western visitors. Today, it's still common to find yourself the only non-Thai in town. There are a few surviving war veterans—but they rarely surface till the evening, when the bars open!

Visit Khorat between January and March, or in October. Avoid the Thai holiday season of November and December, when every hotel is packed out. Rooms are also scarce from August to early September, when the American army (which still has a base outside town) drops in for military exercises. Khorat has a big 15-day festival—commencing 23rd March each year—in honour of 'Lady Mo', a Thai-style Boadicea who ousted an invading Laotian force from the town in 1826. Her real name was Khunying Mo, and she was the wife of the deputy governor of Khorat. Her statue in the town square—the **Thao Suranari Memorial**—attracts a daily procession of pilgrims. Her festival—one of the best in the northeast—is well worth going out of your way to see and has lots of local entertainments, including traditional folk dances, *likhee* theatre, and *luuk tung*, (children of the fields) music.

GETTING THERE

By Air
A new domestic airline, Bangkok Airways, now operates 3 flights daily to Khorat from

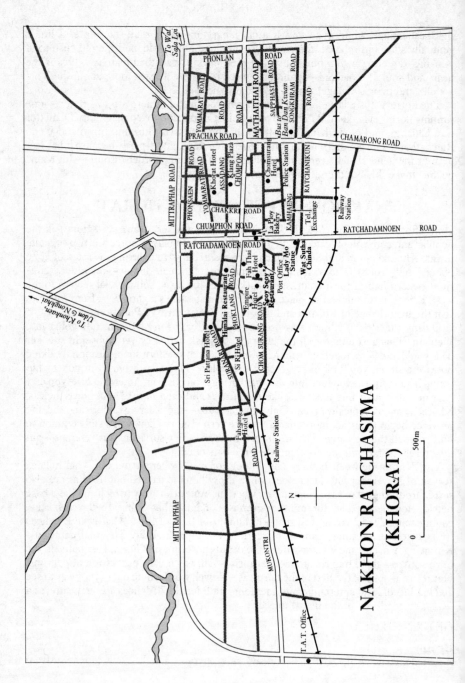

NAKHON RATCHASIMA (KHORAT)

Bangkok. Flight time is 35 minutes, and the fare is 480B (tel 253–4014–5 for further details).

By train
From Bangkok's Hualamphong station, there are two convenient early trains to Khorat—the 6.50 am Rapid (arriving 11.46 am) and the 7.15 am Ordinary (arriving 1.41 pm). After these, no more trains leave Bangkok till 3.25 pm. Basic fares are 207B 1st class, 104B 2nd class, 50B 3rd class.

By bus
From Bangkok's Northern Terminal, non air-con buses leave for Khorat every 20 minutes, from 5 am to 9.30 pm; the fare is 50B, and it's a 4¹/₂-hour trip. There are also some air-con buses, costing 92B and taking only 4 hours.

TOURIST INFORMATION
TAT Tourist office, 2102–2104 Mittraphap Rd (tel 243427) is friendly and helpful, gives out a good town map (with local bus routes) and is open 8.30 am to 4.30 pm daily.

Nida Travel Service, 17 Bouroong Rd, below Himali Hotel (tel 252532) is a useful travel agency, offering sightseeing tours to most provincial attractions.

WHAT TO SEE
Khorat is a small, quiet town at its best after dark. Most of the evening action is around **Chumpon Road**, with its lively, atmospheric night market. Elsewhere, school kids play basketball, adolescents do aerobics and drink beer (not necessarily in that order) and everybody in general is out of doors. The place is ideal for leisurely exploration by bicycle—but there's nowhere to hire one! Local transport is bicycle *samlors* and *tuk-tuks*, charging 5B and 15B respectively for short journeys round town. But you'll have to bargain hard (in Thai!) to get these prices.

In-town Tour
(by *samlor*, *tuk-tuk*, or on foot; 2–3 hours)

Wat Sala Loi – Maha Mirawong Museum
Located northeast of town, 400 metres off the ring road, **Wat Sala Loi** (Temple of the Floating Pavilion) isn't easy to find on foot—local transport is best. This modern temple is highly unusual—the main *bot* or chapel is built in the shape of a Chinese junk. Constructed from local materials, including famous earthenware tiles from nearby Ban Dan Kwian, the structure has won several architectural prizes. The original temple on this site was built in the time of Khunying Mo, and her ashes are still interred here. Within the *bot*, colourful murals depict key events in the life of the Buddha; outside, a tiny mini-Buddha faces into the chapel from a charming pavilion over a lotus pond. Wander round the peaceful garden compound—it's full of curiosities.

The **Maha Mirawong Museum**, attached to Wat Sutchachinda on Ratchadamnoen Rd, is rather small and tacky for a 'national museum', but there is some fine Khmer sculpture and art here—notably a huge Ayutthayan door lintel (beautifully carved) and a brace of fierce Singha lions (at the entrance). Lighting is poor, few objects have English labels, and priceless antiques sit propped up on dusty old fruitboxes. Still, it is worth a visit. The modest *wat* outside has a tranquil lake, pretty gardens, and chatty monks. The museum is open Wednesday to Sunday only (9 am to noon, 1 pm to 4 pm), and admission is 5B.

Phimai
(by bus; full day)

Prasat Hin – National Museum – Sai Ngam
Even if you don't like temples, Phimai is a must. Located 60 km northeast of Khorat, buses go there every half-hour from Khorat (Bus No. 1305, fare 14B, journey time $1^1/_2$ hours). **Phimai Sanctuary** is open 7.30 am to 5 pm daily, and admission is 5B for locals, 20B for foreigners. A useful little 10B guide is sold at the entrance. The **Phimai Hotel**, round the corner from the bus-stop, has reasonable fan-rooms from 80B, air-con rooms from 200B.

Phimai has been dubbed the Anghor Wat of Thailand and it certainly bears many similarities to the famous Cambodian sanctuary, and may indeed have been the work of the same architect. If this is so—and nobody knows for sure—then it dates to the reign of King Surijavarman (1002–1049). It certainly was much added to during the reign of King Jayavarman VII (1181–1201), but was abandoned in the 13th century when the Khmer empire collapsed. In its heyday, Phimai was evidently of great importance being the largest of the dozen or so sanctuaries erected in the northeast during the 11th and 12th centuries—all of them connected by road to Anghor Wat. Today, it stands as a definitive example of Khmer architecture.

Dominating the extensive ruins is the majestic **Prasat Hin** (Stone Castle) shrine. Destroyed some time in the 17th century it has been lovingly restored by the Fine Arts Department, and is now considered one of the most classic structures in all Thailand. Even though all the pieces don't fit together (so complex was the work of reconstruction), the main *prang* (spire) is a model of simple, elegant symmetry, constructed from massive white sandstone blocks. High up, you'll see the large garuda-bird, carrier of Shiva (most Khmer architecture was Hindu); below this, covering the door lintels, there are powerful friezes depicting scenes from the *Ramayana* epic. Many of the best carvings have been removed to the nearby museum, but some beautiful work remains—exquisite lotus blossom motifs over doorways, and the famous panel of elephant/monkey devotees offering sugar-cane and fruit to Buddha, above a lintel in the central chamber.

The excellent open-air **National Museum** (open 8.30 am to 4.30 pm daily) is a short 10-minute walk left out of the sanctuary. All exhibits here—mainly lintels, pediments, and friezes from Phimai (plus finds from other northeastern sanctuaries)—are well-presented and labelled. A group of ghoulish skeletons dating to round 3000 BC, and described as 'prehistoric remains', live in strange 'chicken-coop' coffins.

A kilometre above the museum, you'll come across a reservoir full of 'petrified' stone herons—some of them stationary, some apparently about to take flight, but all of them eerily lifelike. Here you'll find the **Sai Ngam Banyan Grove**—a single immense banyan tree, covering an area of 15,000 square feet. Its many cool, shady arbours make it a favourite picnic spot for Thai families. Locals revere the grove as a shelter for powerful spirits, and the temple to the rear is a popular spot for buying Chinese fortunes, or for making merit by releasing captive birds or fish.

Pakthongchai
(by bus; half day)

Pakthongchai lies 30 km south of Khorat, and produces the best-quality silk in Thailand. The **Silk-Weaving Village** here supplies silk thread for the weaving industry of Bangkok, and is the main supplier of silk lengths and materials to Jim Thompson's. Even if you're not fussed about silk, come to Pakthongchai to see an authentic Thai village, with original wood buildings throughout. The best time to visit is early morning, when all the looms are busily at work and you can see the various silk-weaving processes. Most of the weavers here sell silk direct to the public—it's high-quality stuff, and has unique designs. Opposite the bus-stop, down a side-road, **Pranest Thai Silk** (tel 441173), has a very good range of material. Prices here are fixed, but reasonable: 2-ply silk material is 140B per yard (plain) and 180B per yard (printed); beautiful cushion-covers are 180B each. You'll find many colours and designs here, as well as the bright Eastern colours! Buses leave for Pakthongchai from Khorat bus station (No. 1303; fare 9B) every half-hour. The last bus back to Khorat is at 6 pm.

SHOPPING
You don't have to go to Pakthongchai to find its fabulous silk. Several shops in Khorat sell it too, mainly on Chumpon and Chakkri roads. Try **Tussanee Thai Silk** (tel 242372), facing Lady Mo's statue in the town square. This is a well-established shop, with a wide selection of designs. Again, cheap prices—plain silk from 160B a yard, patterned silk from 200B a yard.

There's also **Sumon Thai Silk**, 2786 Mitraphab Rd (tel 252113), located on the highway leading out of town. Catch a No. 6 bus from Khorat bus terminal—get off at the Esso station, just before the Pakthongchai turn-off. Sumon stocks silks supplied direct from Pakthongchai, and has a better range of fabrics, furnishings, handicrafts and designs than any shop in town. It also has a weaving factory of its own, producing quality-controlled silk of an extremely soft texture. Prices are a little high—plain silk from 200B a yard, patterned silk from 300B a yard—but the same stuff will cost 30% more at Jim Thompson's in Bangkok (where a lot of Sumon's silk ends up). Ask Samat, the pleasant young manager to recommend the best cheap tailor in Khorat!

Best general shopping in Khorat town is at **Klang Plaza** department store, in Assadang Rd.

WHERE TO STAY
The much-rated **Chomsurang Hotel**, 2701/2 Mahat Thai Rd (tel 242940) is an old hotel trying to look new. Gloomy 500B air-con doubles, grim views and a dinky pool. Far better is the **Sripatana**, 346 Suranari Rd (tel 242944); nice rooms from 250B, good pool, and probably the best Thai food in town. Another favourite is the **Empire**, located by the post office (look for the 24-hour coffee shop sign). Rooms here are good value at 140B fan single, 260B air-con double, and the lively restaurant serves good Thai, Chinese, Arabian and European food. But the hotel with character is the **Khorat**,

191 Assadang Rd (tel 242260). Strictly for men, this one—female staff rotate between the lively nightclub and the even livelier massage parlour! The club is a real rage at weekends—admission is 70B; open 9 pm to 1 am. Rooms here are from 150B (single fan) to 230B (double air-con). The Khorat has good information at the front desk.

The inexpensive **Fahsarng Hotel**, 68–70 Mukmontri Rd (tel 242143), has large twin-bedded rooms from 75B fan to 180B air-con. This is a friendly place, with an English-speaking owner—a real rarity! Also in Mukmontri Rd is **Siri**, with fan rooms from 70B, air-con rooms at 200B. The Siri has a 'prepare party place' (a roof with a view) and a bizarre sign in every room, saying it won't accept any guests suffering from 'leprosy or other zymotic diseases'. The **Far Thai**, 35–39 Pho Klang Rd (tel 242533), is a popular Thai hotel, located near the town square. It is friendly and clean, with rooms for 100B fan, 220B air-con.

EATING OUT

Khorat has some really *odd* eating houses! Chinese food is best at the **Seoy-Seoy**, near the post office. It is famous for its frogs. Here you can have Fried Frog, Sweet Battered Fried Frog, and even Tomato Sauce Baked Frog. Other novelties include Goose Legs in Earthen Pot and Sea Leech Cover Pork (?). Most dishes are around 60B, with very nice specialities like Shark's Fin Soup and Oyster Platter at 150B. **Thai Pochana**, at the junction of Mukmontri and Chomsurang roads, has excellent Thai food at under 60B a head.

The weirdest place to eat in Khorat is the **V.F.W. Restaurant**, adjoining Siri Hotel. It's stuffed with American war memorabilia—dusty cups, trophies, plaques and photos donated by American veterans of the foreign wars—the atmosphere is totally unreal. Apart from the odd war veteran (there are 23 left in town) the place is patronized exclusively by Thais (knocking back Mekong, eating T-bone steaks in snug wooden booths, playing endless games of darts and draughts, etc.). Air-conditioned and cheap, the V.F.W. does a wide range of wholesome GI food—burgers, pizzas, spaghetti and Southern Fried Chicken! It's open from 8 am to 10 pm daily, and the 38B special lunches are recommended.

You'll find **La Ploy**, an excellent little bakery, behind Lady Mo's statue in the town square. It's run by a very helpful lady called Nikki, who speaks good English and has cheap Thai, Chinese and Western food. Try the 26B American breakfasts and the marvellous butterscotch ice-cream! Travellers have also spoken well of **Flowers** and **Diamond House**—two more good bakeries, located on Chumphon Road. For cheap Thai/Chinese street food—mainly 10B 'whip-up wok' meals—try the night market off the town square, or the curry stalls opposite the railway station.

UDORN THANI & BAN CHIANG

Udorn Thani, 562 km from Bangkok, is the third-largest province in the northeast. Up until 1893, it was a small village called Ban Markhaeng, but then the prince of Nongkhai moved his HQ here, following Thai-French troubles further north. The village became a province in 1907, by order of Rama V. In more recent times, Udorn Thani became a

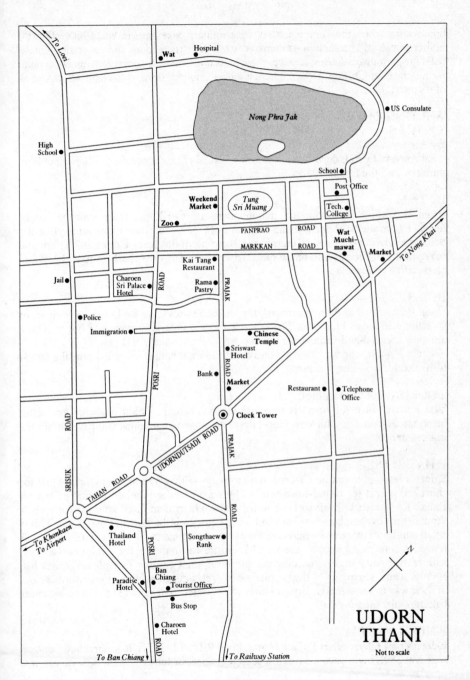

Wat
Hospital

Nong Phra Jak

US Consulate

High
School

School

Post Office

Weekend
Market

Tung
Sri Muang

Tech.
College

Zoo

PANPRAO   ROAD

Wat
Muchi-
mawat

Market

To Nong Khai

MARKKAN   ROAD

Jail

Kai Tang
Restaurant

PRAJAK

ROAD

Charoen
Sri Palace
Hotel

Rama
Pastry

Police

Chinese
Temple

Immigration

Sriswast
Hotel

POSRI

Bank

Market

Restaurant

Telephone
Office

Clock Tower

UDORNDUTSADI ROAD

PRAJAK

SRISUK   ROAD

TAHAN   ROAD

To Khonkaen
To Airport

Thailand
Hotel

POSRI

Songthaew
Rank

ROAD

Ban
Chiang

Paradise
Hotel

Tourist Office

Bus Stop

Charoen
Hotel

ROAD

To Ban Chiang

To Railway Station

N

UDORN
THANI

Not to scale

181

boom-town when the Americans set up a military base here in the 1960s. The GI influence can still be seen in its many Western-style recreations and entertainments—massage parlours, bakeries, ice-cream parlours and discos. A convenient jump-off point for nearby **Ban Chiang**, Udorn Thani is a busy, modern town with a laidback charm all of its own.

GETTING THERE

By Air
Thai Airways fly to Udorn from Bangkok (via Khon Kaen) once daily. Flight time is 45 minutes, and the fare is 1010B.

By Train
From Bangkok's Hualamphong station, there are two Rapid trains daily to Udorn (leaving 7 pm and 8.30 pm, arriving 5.45 am and 6.35 am) and one Express train (leaving 8.30 pm, arriving 6.35 am). Returning to Bangkok, trains leave Udorn at 7.31 am and 6.57 pm (Rapid) and at 7.10 pm (Express) daily. Basic fares are 413B 1st class, 198B 2nd class, and 95B 3rd class.

By Bus
From Bangkok's Northern Terminal, non air-con buses leave for Udorn every hour or so, from 4.15 am to 11.10 pm. The fare is 106B and the trip is around 12 hours. There are also a few (slightly quicker) air-con buses daily, costing 191B.

From Khorat, non air-con buses leave for Udorn Thani every half-hour; the fare is 60B, and it's a 5-hour journey.

TOURIST INFORMATION
The tourist office (of sorts) is opposite the bus station. You'll probably get better information from the **Charoen Hotel** desk-staff—good handouts, and English-speaking assistance.

WHAT TO SEE
Udorn's few sights can be covered in a morning—either on foot, or by *samlor* (5B for short hops; 20B for round-town tour). There's a popular **Weekend Market** just off Prajak Rd, which sells all sorts of weird and wonderful stuff. Strictly for early birds though—it's liveliest between 3 am and 6 am! Close by is the **Zoo** off Posri Road. This is small and nothing special—mid-morning is the best time to find the animals awake. A few quite interesting temples are **Wat Muchimawat** (opposite the Technical College, with rearing naga-snakes guarding the entrance), the **Chinese Temple** off Prajak Rd, and the scenic **shrine** up by the hospital, with a relaxing river setting. Few visitors go out of their way to see sights in Udorn—they often prefer to hang out at the town's yummy bakeries and *kai-yang* stalls.

WHERE TO STAY
Udorn's new **Charoensri Palace Hotel**, Posri Rd (tel 242611), has marvellous air-con rooms at 280B high season, 240B low season. Top-floor suites have the best views. Nice

restaurant, coffee shop and pool. Another goodie is the **Charoen**, 549 Posri Rd (tel 221331), with air-con singles at 280B, doubles at 300B. There's a decent pool (non-residents can use this for a 12B charge), a good information service, and a nightclub called **Ex Calibur** which holds amazing weekend discos (9 pm to 2 am, 80B admission includes one drink). This club is a real scene—cinema usherettes with tiny torches guide guests through the pitch-black gloom to their seats. Single males are instantly joined by a matey Mama-san, who attempts introductions to floppy-eared bunny girls. The best (and safest!) night to come is Tuesday—this is 'Ladies Night' and there's a beauty contest!

The mid-range **Paradise Hotel**, 44/29 Posri Rd (tel 221956), has immaculate twin-bedded air-con rooms at 150B single, 200B double. There are also a few fan rooms for 120B. Decor is a bit tacky, but it's a friendly place, with a twee heart-shaped pool, where people dance to live music in the evening. The nearby **Thailand**, 4/5 Surakorn Rd (tel 221951), doesn't speak English, but does have one regulation in English: 'The guest should not take any disturbing loud noise'. How considerate. Fan-cooled rooms here are 100B single, 120B double. Best budget hotel is still the **Sriswast** in Prajak Road. Friendly family, and large, clean rooms from 80B. If full, you may have to stay at the adjoining **Tokyo**—pretty gross and dirty but very cheap.

EATING OUT

The **Charoensri** Palace does very palatable Thai, Chinese and European food at reasonable prices. Don't confuse it with the similarly-named **Charoen Hotel**, which claims to have the best food in town, but doesn't.

Tasty Isaan-style fare can be found at the top of Prajak Rd—there are three local restaurants here, serving delicious *kai yang* (roast spicy chicken) and *som tam* (grated papaya salad, spiced with garlic, pepper, fish sauce and lime juice). This is eaten with sticky rice, which is moulded into balls with your fingers. These restaurants are open till 10 pm, and the top one has the most going for it: friendly service, a whole barbecued chicken for 25B, and a jukebox which plays the Thai disco version of the *Battle Hymn of the Republic*!

Rama's Pastry, also on Prajak Rd, is a popular air-con bakery and coffee shop. Friendly people, Western-style breakfasts, and exceedingly good cakes and pastries.

Ban Chiang
(by bus, then samlor; half/full day)

This sleepy village, 47 km east of Udorn, is now an important centre of Thailand's past—and an emerging tourist attraction. Up until 20 years ago, archaeologists considered Southeast Asia a cultural backwater—they thought its arts and civilization to have been borrowed from India, China and even Europe. Bronze technology, it was believed, only arrived here from the Middle East around 500 BC.

Then, in 1966, a young Harvard sociology graduate, Stephen Young, literally stumbled on a prehistoric burial site here at Ban Chiang. The first fragments of round-topped pots he submitted were carbon-dated to around 4600 BC, and the village became an overnight sensation. Later excavations, by the Fine Arts Department and the University of Pennsylvania, unearthed a rich collection of iron and bronze tools and utensils, buried alongside human skeletons, which proved that prehistoric man settled in this part of northeastern Thailand between around 3600 BC and AD 200. By around 2000 BC, these men had mastered bronze (and later, iron) manufacture, and developed skills in making pottery and glass beads, in weaving techniques and in the cultivation of rice. Ban Chiang is not alone—many other ancient northeastern village sites are now known—but everything points to it having been the major cultural centre in this region. Much more research is still needed—the prehistory of Southeast Asia being still very much a blank page—but if the Thais can prove it, they may soon find themselves the proud possessors of a civilization predating even those of China, India and Egypt.

Ban Chiang may seem an awfully long way to go and see skeletons, but if you have any interest in history (not only of Thailand, but of mankind) it's worth the effort. On arrival, your first question to locals should be *Yuu thii nai phiphinaphan?* (where is the museum?). Set up by the Department of Fine Arts, **Ban Chiang Museum** is one of Thailand's finest with smart, well-planned displays, well-labelled exhibits. It's open from 8 am to 4 pm Wednesday to Sunday, and the 10B admission includes a useful free handout. The exhibits, all recovered from nearby excavations, feature a collection of WOST ('world's oldest socketed tool'), axes, lozenge-shaped infant burial jars, and round-topped burial pots and jars decorated with distinctive burnt-ochre red 'whorl' designs. These pots have become major collector's pieces. Shortly after Ban Chiang became known as the new 'cradle of civilization', large-scale looting took place at the site and, sadly, few intact pots were retained for the museum. The art of faking pottery has become big business here, so be careful if offered 'antiques'! Remember, even if you did come across an original piece, you'd face a stiff fine if you tried taking it out of the country! Best buys here are embroidered linen jackets and cotton materials, both sold (along with Ban Chiang T-shirts—groan!) at the **Open Museum**, a 10-minute stroll left out of the main museum. This site charges 10B admission, and comprises two of the original ground-level excavation pits—littered with pots, skeletons, supine burials and cord-marked wares. Left exactly as when buried 500 years ago, the skeletons lie face upward, with their heads pointing either northeast or southwest, and their bone arm-ornaments stained green with time. Beside them are placed the weapons and the supply-jars which were to protect and feed them on their journey into the next life.

GETTING THERE

There are two ways you can get to Ban Chiang from Udorn Thani. There are either blue *songthaews* from the rank in Posri Rd, which go all the way to Ban Chiang Museum in 1¹/₂ hours for 10B; or ordinary buses from Udorn's bus station (off Posri Rd), which take you only as far as the highway 6 km out of Ban Chiang. From here to the village is a 10B *samlor* ride. Both buses and *songthaews* leave Udorn regularly. I'd recommend the *songthaew*—great scenery (look out for local fishermen wielding hand-operated Chinese nets in the lush post-monsoon paddy fields) and, if lucky, fascinating co-passengers. I shared a ride with a beaming farmer, proudly holding three muddy bags of fish in the air for everybody to poke and admire, and a young saffron-robed monk in reflecting sunglasses, happily grooving to U2 on his Toshiba ghetto-blaster!

NONG KHAI

This small 'city', 615 km north of Bangkok, has a charming situation on the bank of the Mekong River—right on the border between Thailand and Laos. The town has some delightfully antique wooden houses and buildings of French-Chinese design, and there are some amazing temples and bakeries showing the French-Lao influence. A number of local people in Nong Khai speak fluent French! A popular recreation here is to sit at the restaurant by the pier, and watch boats ferrying folk across the Mekong river into the People's Democratic Republic of Laos. Several travellers entertain notions of crossing over too—the main lure being the famous Lao city of Vientiane, home of the revered Emerald Buddha, which is only 24 km northeast of Nong Khai. You can apply for a visa either at the Immigration Office near the pier, or at the Lao embassy in Bangkok, but it's highly unlikely you'll be granted one. A friend of mine asked an immigration official in Nong Khai 'Can I go to Laos?' And the official replied, 'Oh yes—but you no come back!'

The province is famous for its flora and fauna, best seen at the end of the rainy season. Many people view it in combination with the popular boat race on the Mekong River, held at Nong Khai during the first week of October. But the two most authentic and colourful of the province's many festivals are the **Nong Khai Show**, held the second week of March, and the annual **Seong Bung Fai** (Rocket Festival), which takes place at Wat Pho temple on full moon day in April.

GETTING THERE

By Rail
From Bangkok's Hualamphong station, trains leave for Nong Khai at 6.30 am and 7 pm (Rapid, arriving 5.10 pm and 5.45 am) and at 8.30 pm (Express, arriving 6.35 am). Basic fares are 450B 1st class, 215B 2nd class, and 103B 3rd class.

By Bus
From Bangkok's Northern Terminal, non air-con buses leave for Nong Khai between 5.15 am and 8.29 am (plus two late buses at 8.10 pm and 8.54 pm). The fare is 115B, and it's a long 10-hour journey. Three air-con buses leave daily from the same terminal, at 9 am, 9 pm and 9.30 pm (fare 209B). These are slightly quicker, but most people still prefer to go by train.

From Udorn Thani, it's a short 1½-hour hop to Nong Khai by non air-con bus every half-hour (fare 20B). You can also get there from Khorat, a longer 6–7 hour trip, by local bus (mid-afternoon to early evening service; fare 75B).

WHAT TO SEE
Nong Khai's quaint old-town atmosphere, scenic river location and weird and wonderful temples make it—for my money—the most interesting centre in the northeast. It's a tiny city of just 25,000 inhabitants, with coffee-shops, bakeries, markets and even a small fairground. Though a pleasant place to stroll around by foot, you'll need two separate day-outings by bus to cover the four major temples in the area (they're worth it!). If you're lucky enough to make a local friend—Nong Khai people are *very* friendly—you may find yourself taken everywhere by motorbike, and for free!

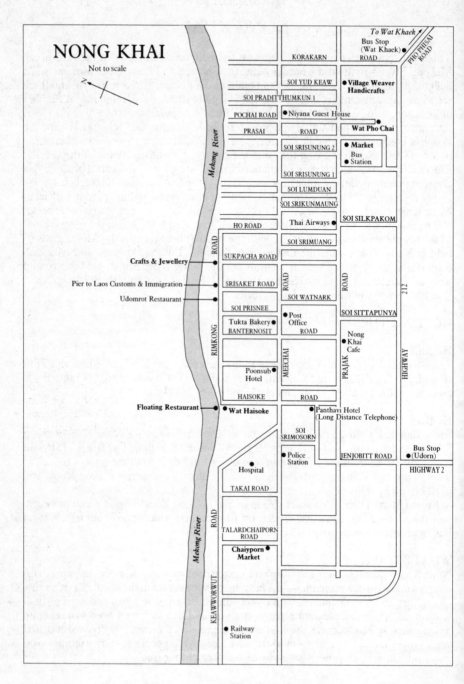

NONG KHAI

Not to scale

To Wat Khaek
Bus Stop
(Wat Khaek)
PHO PHISAI ROAD

KORAKARN ROAD

SOI YUD KEAW

● Village Weaver
Handicrafts

SOI PRADITTHUMKUN 1

POCHAI ROAD ● Niyana Guest House

PRASAI ROAD ● Wat Pho Chai

SOI SRISUNUNG 2 ● Market
Bus
● Station

SOI SRISUNUNG 1

SOI LUMDUAN

SOI SRIKUNMAUNG

SOI SILKPAKOM

HO ROAD ● Thai Airways

SOI SRIMUANG

SUKPACHA ROAD

Crafts & Jewellery ●

SRISAKET ROAD

Pier to Laos Customs & Immigration

Udomrot Restaurant ●

SOI WATNARK

SOI PRISNEE

SOI SITTAPUNYA

Tukta Bakery ● ● Post
Office
BANTERNOSIT ROAD

Nong
● Khai
Cafe

Poonsub ●
Hotel

HAISOKE ROAD

Floating Restaurant ● ● Wat Haisoke ● Panthavi Hotel
(Long Distance Telephone)

SOI
SRIMOSORN

Bus Stop
● (Udorn)

● Police
Station

JENJOBITT ROAD

HIGHWAY 2

● Hospital

TAKAI ROAD

TALARDCHAIPORN
ROAD

Chaiyporn ●
Market

● Railway
Station

Mekong River

RIMKONG ROAD

KEAWWORWUT ROAD

MEECHAI ROAD

PRAJAK ROAD

HIGHWAY 212

Wat Pho Chai – Wat Khaek
(on foot, by bus; half/full day)

Located off Prajak Rd—a short walk to the edge of town—**Wat Pho Chai** houses the major Buddha image of the province, called Luang Pho Phra Sai. Relatively small— 1.5 m high, and with a spread of just one metre across the knees—this beautiful solid-gold figure is believed to have been cast in Lan Chang, and to have spent its early life in Vientiane. The legend is that it came to this spot by 'divine miracle'—General Chakri (later Rama I) was transporting it over the Mekong from Vientiane when the boat sank. But nothing can keep a good Buddha down, and when this one miraculously resurfaced, the *wat* here was built to honour its achievement. The figure receives a personal visit from the King each year, and is taken in glorious procession round the city during the Songram festival. The *wat* itself has been recently renovated—the gleaming new structure is only 10 years old. All the city's major festivals are held here.

From the sublime to the ridiculous, **Wat Khaek** is a fantastic Disneyland of bizarre and spectacular statues—the highlight of many travellers' northeastern tour. It's located 5 km out of Nong Khai, and buses go there from the stop near Wat Pho. Even if you can't face another temple, Wat Khaek is sure to restore your sense of humour! It's a large open compound of incongruous images—towering, beak-nosed Buddhas, nightmarish *nagas*, eight-armed Kalis, and dogs wielding dinner forks and machine guns—reflecting the eclectic philosophy of a Brahmin *shaman* called Luang Pu. He originally studied in Vietnam, then moved to Laos, and was driven here 12 years ago by the Communists. A highly popular local figure, he certainly gets top marks for verve and imagination—as more and more of these Easter Island-like statues go up (the workers inspired by music and sermons from a blaring tannoy) travellers have been moved to increasingly astonished comment! Whatever your reaction, bring lots of camera film. You'll need it!

At the main building, ask for Bhu Lua—the resident 'master'. He's the guy with the dark shades, often dealing out tarot cards under a mountainous sound system. He'll fix you up with a tour round the shrine—a two-storey building choc-a-bloc with Hindu-Buddhist antiques and photos of Luang Pu. Altogether, one of the weirdest collections of 'art' I've every come across! Afterwards, you can feed the giant catfish in the nearby lake. Small 1B bags of popcorn are sold for this purpose at the 'picnic' landing—but don't go dropping in large buns. These attract full-grown catfish—the shark-sized variety!

Wat Prathat Bang Phuan – Wat Hin Maak Peng
(by bus; full day)

GETTING THERE
To get to Wat Prathat, 22 km from Nong Khai, take a bus from the town's southern terminal to **Ban Nong Hong Son**. From the junction here, *songthaews* and buses run the final 10 km up to the *wat*. There's a small restaurant at the junction (opposite the *songthaew* rank) which does just about the best *kai yang* and *som tam* meal I've tasted anywhere, and for only 12B.

To reach Wat Hin Maak Peng, 60 km northwest of Nong Khai, you need a bus to Si Chiengmai from the southern bus-stop in town (20B), followed by a *songthaew*, from Si Chiengmai direct to Wat Hin, or to Sang Khom, which is just past it. Buses for Si Chiengmai pass by Wat Prathat, so you can continue on from here to Wat Hin.

Wat Prathat

The sacred site of **Wat Prathat** is one of the most important in the northeast. Monks from India, it's believed, first came here 2000 years ago and they erected the original Indian-style *stupa*. This was covered over by a taller Lao *chedi* in the 16th century. Shortly after this structure was blown over by heavy rains, the Fine Arts Department stepped in and erected a garish new *chedi*, which stands in stark contrast to the crumbling, atmospheric red-brick ruins elsewhere in the compound. Despite this, the site retains a marvellously dilapidated, overgrown charm. There's a fine collection of mainly 16th-century Lao *chedis* and semi-intact Buddhas, and two impressive seated Buddhas housed within corrugated-roof *viharns*. The larger one was constructed by the Lao people, and was probably the model for the main Buddha image at Phra Pathom *chedi* in Nakhon Pathom. The smaller one overlooks a pretty lotus pond. There's an odd little museum to the rear of the compound with some interesting folk handicrafts, stuffed animals, and boundary stones, but most exhibits lie around on the ground like rubble. Strolling round the compound is fun, but don't sit down—there are a lot of giant ants and crickets around. It's hard to take much in, when you've a three-inch grasshopper up your trouserleg.

Wat Hin Maak Peng

Wat Hin Maak Peng is the most famous meditation temple in Thailand. Set up by an itinerant pilgrim monk called Thet Lang Si, it is known for its ascetic forest-dwelling monks who eat only one meal a day, dress in subdued 'forest-colour' robes made from natural dyes, and don't say a lot. A few monks receive guests, but most are keen meditatives. People accepted for meditation classes at the *wat* get their own little house, and receive a daily group instruction sermon—in Thai. The monastery itself has a wonderfully quiet setting amongst bamboo groves, in a cool forest shelter. Situated at the narrowest point of the Mekong river, you can throw a stone over into Laos during the low-level dry season. On the opposite bank, you'll be able to see a small Lao forest *wat*. The monks of Wat Hin mostly live high up on the cliff above the river, in small cells and huts tucked away between huge boulders. Views up here are spectacular.

SHOPPING

The **Village Weaver Handicrafts** shop, 786 Prajak Rd (tel 411236), is a small self-help project, set up in 1982 by the Good Shepherd Sisters, aimed at giving local villagers a means of supplementing their income—especially young girls who would otherwise be destined for a life of prostitution in Bangkok. Over 200 families now produce goods—mainly high-quality woven fabrics—for the project, which is now making a small yet significant dent in the poverty of the region. Weavers here produce indigo-dyed cotton *matmee* cloth—tie-dyed, mainly with geometric patterns—which is cool, colourfast and very durable. It's an exclusive produce of the northeast, and you can pick it up here at one-third of London prices (the project supplies Oxfam in the UK). Good buys are embroidered jackets, at around 500B; handwoven shirts from 350B, and colourful Cambodian wall-hangings (patterns created in bamboo, then sewn into the cotton cloth) at around 500B. Suvan, the friendly project manager, will discount 10% on most items. All profits go directly to helping the villagers.

WHERE TO STAY

The **Panthavi**, Haisoke Rd (tel 411568), is Nong Khai's only air-con hotel. It has rooms at 100B single, 200B double, good information, and an overseas telephone—but is not too friendly, and often full. Better is the homely **Poonsub** in Meechai Rd—this has bright, comfortable rooms for 80B with fan, 70B without. Ask for one with a view of the river. Less clean, but with large 80B rooms, is the **Pongvichit** in Banterngit Rd.

The **Niyana Guest House**, 239 Meechai Rd (tel 412164), warrants a special mention. Basic rooms (40B), but great facilities: a good library (with information/maps), a TV lobby, laundry service, Western-style food (also something called 'Morning Glory Vine Friend in Garlic and Bean Sauce'!), motorbike and bicycle rental, sightseeing tours, and heaps of back issues of the *Peace Corps Times*. It also operates longtail boat trips on the Mekong River (200B for one to eight people). Advance-book these at the Niyana between 9 am and 4 pm daily, or contact the Chinese manager of the **Sukaphan Hotel** in town.

EATING OUT

Nong Khai has some lively little eating-houses, often with rib-tickling menus. The **Thipros** restaurant, next to Poonsub Hotel, does exceptional *Kai Lao Dang* (chicken cooked in red wine) for 30B, and a galaxy of novelty dishes. You can start with 'Five Things Soup in Firepan' or 'Stewed Deer Gut', and enjoy 'Fried Frog Cutlets' and 'Lucky Duck' as a main course. Well, why not. Down on the river behind Wat Haisoke, the small **Floating Restaurant** has some oddities of its own. Things like 'Duck Eggs preserved in Potash', 'Three Some', and 'Jerked Pork'. Actually, the food (and coffee) is both cheap and good here. For Western-style food, there's the **Udomrot** next to the customs pier. This is on the river, looking over to Laos, and the speciality is Fried Mekong River Fish ('fish you eat today, slept last night at the bottom of the river') for 45B. Whatever you do, don't miss **Tukta Bakery** on Meechai Rd. This is so good that one guy pigged out on seven cakes, five pastries and four milkshakes—and missed his bus back to Bangkok.

There are several cheap Chinese-Thai restaurants down Banterngit Rd—trouble is, not a lot of the food on offer looks edible. Unless, that is, you're partial to skinned frogs floating about in washing-up bowls! In the evening, check out the **Nong Khai Cafe**, in Prajak Road. This is open from 11 am to 2 pm, 5.30 pm to 1 am, and serves both food and (pricey) drinks. Here all the young Thai dudes gather to enjoy a nostalgic live band which plays nothing more recent than 1965. The odd *farang* guest is treated to their 'special medley'—Cliff Richard (*The Young Ones*), Neil Sedaka (*Oh Carol*) and the Everly Brothers (*Wake up, Little Suzie*). They're actually rather good.

Part VII

THE SOUTH

Southern Thailand is a long, narrow peninsula, extending through the Kra Isthmus from Chumphon (460 km south of Bangkok) to the Thai-Malaysian border. Bounded by the Gulf of Thailand to the east, and by the Indian Ocean to the west, both coastlines are dotted with beautiful islands—ideal for scuba-diving, snorkelling, sailing and fishing. The South is geared to total relaxation—this is where everyone comes at some time or other, to swim, to windsurf and water-ski, to laze on dazzling white beaches, and to dine on some of the most delectable seafood in the East. There's a major development programme due here over the next few years, but some of the islands—**Phuket** and **Koh-Samui** in particular—are pretty developed already. No matter—if you're not into beach videos, discos and nightclubs, there's still a wealth of other islands and beaches with hardly a soul on them. Lovely spots like **Krabi** and **Phi Phi Islands** are only just opening up, and tranquil **Koh Phangan** is still a place for beachcombing backpackers. The attractions of the South are extremely diverse. There are spectacular surreal islands at mysterious **Phang Gna Bay**, great shopping and entertainment at busy **Hat Yai**, tasty seafood at historic old **Songkhla**, and Thai-style beach fun at the seaside resort of **Hua Hin**. Overall, the South has a lazy charm, a peaceful, unhurried way of life, and balmy, tropical scenery which acts as an immediate tonic to the hustle and bustle of Bangkok. Southern Thais have their own dialect (a rapid patter called *pak tai*), and their own cuisine, customs and dress. A lot of Chinese and Muslims (ethnic Malays) live down here, and the further south you go, the more polyglot the mixture of peoples becomes. But they all love the sea (which surrounds them) and they all have a fierce sense of independence. Few southern Thais will own allegiance to the central control of Bangkok, and many will ask you what the frantic, busy capital has to compare with their own calm, idyllic way of life. After a few days here, you can truthfully answer 'Nothing!'

HUA HIN

This small fishing port, 180 km southwest of Bangkok, was Thailand's first beach resort and has been the Thai royal family's summer residence since Rama VII (1925–35) built a palace here called 'Klai Kangwon' or 'place free from worries'. Not the most appropriate choice of name, as it transpired. It was while staying at this palace in 1932 that Rama VII learnt of the coup which transformed him overnight from an absolute to a constitutional monarch! Yet the royal family still come on holiday to Hua Hin every April. And, being so close to Bangkok, it remains the favourite resort of Thais in general. The élite of Thailand like to spend the hot months of March and April here, savouring the period pre-War charm and bracing air of this peaceful old seaside resort. Reminders of the past are everywhere: the royal waiting room at the railway station, the king's palace on the northern edge of town, the old-fashioned deckchairs on the promenade, and the clipped topiary gardens in the stylish ex-Railway Hotel.

GETTING THERE

By Bus
From Bangkok's Southern Terminal, non air-con buses leave for Hua Hin every half-hour from 6.40 am to 6 pm (fare 47B). There are also hourly air-con buses, from 6 am to 8 pm (fare 74B). The journey takes 3½ hours.

From Phuket, there are seven non air-con buses to Hua Hin daily, leaving between 6 am and 6.30 pm (fare 129B). Also, one air-con bus (250B) leaving at 3 pm. This is a long 9–10 hour trip, and travelling air-con is a good idea.

By Rail
From Bangkok's Hualamphong station, there are seven trains daily to Hua Hin—one Ordinary (9 am), four Rapid (12.30 pm, 4 pm, 5.30 pm, 6.30 pm) and two Express (2 pm and 3.15 pm). Journey time is 3½ to 4 hours. Fares are 182B 1st class, 92B 2nd class, and 44B 3rd class.

TOURIST INFORMATION
TAT Tourist Office, Damnoenkasem Rd (tel 512120), is small and efficient. Very helpful staff, lots of literature. It's open 8 am to 6 pm daily.

Travel agents like **Tuck's Tours**, 71 Phetkasem Rd (tel 511202) and **Friendship Travel Agency**, c/o Friendship Restaurant (tel 511373), handle worthwhile—if pricey—tours to local sights.

The Post Office is opposite Ralug Hotel, and has an overseas telephone.

Today, Hua Hin is still geared for comfort, not for speed. It's a popular watering-hole for travellers who've become 'templed-out' in Bangkok, and who just want to relax somewhere with no pressure to see or do anything. Hua Hin is wonderfully short on sights. It has a nice 5 km white-sand beach within a wide, curving bay. It has distinctive topography, and is enclosed by two large green hills. It has a fine 18-hole golf course, facilities for several water-sports, and reasonable swimming. It also has delicious Thai and Chinese seafood, served at many places down by the pier. What it doesn't have is temples. You've really got to go out of your way to find one. If you're desperate, head

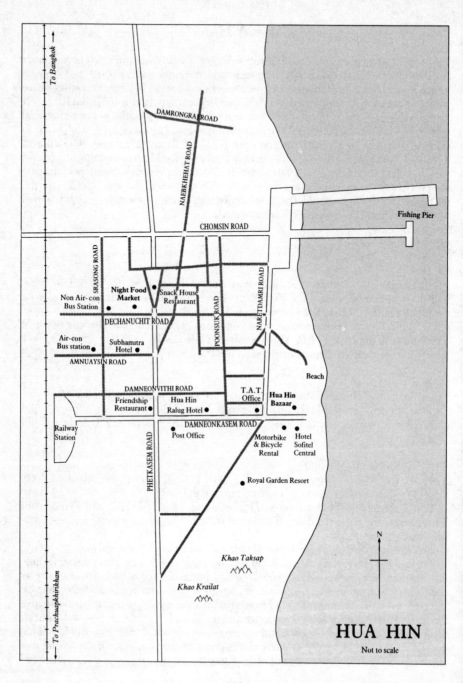

To Bangkok

DAMRONGRAT ROAD

NAEBKHEHAT ROAD

Fishing Pier

CHOMSIN ROAD

SRASONG ROAD

Night Food
Market

Snack House
Restaurant

Non Air-con
Bus Station

POONSUK ROAD

NARETDAMRI ROAD

DECHANUCHIT ROAD

Air-con
Bus station

Subhamitra
Hotel

AMNUAYSIN ROAD

Beach

DAMNEONVITHI ROAD

Friendship
Restaurant

Hua Hin
Ralug Hotel

T.A.T.
Office

Hua Hin
Bazaar

Railway
Station

DAMNEONKASEM ROAD

Post Office

Motorbike
& Bicycle
Rental

Hotel
Sofitel
Central

PHETKASEM ROAD

Royal Garden Resort

N

Khao Taksap
∧∧∧

Khao Krailat
∧∧∧

HUA HIN

Not to scale

To Prachuapkhirikhan

192

south down the beach past an assortment of Thai-style summer houses and climb for 20 minutes up **Khao Taksap** hill. There's a Buddhist temple at the top and spectacular views. In the evening, after a touristy pony-ride on the beach perhaps, it's back to the pier to watch the fishing boats unloading their day's catch. At night, Hua Hin finally livens up, and the town becomes a boisterous buzz of chatty coffee shops, busy seafood restaurants, sizzling snack stalls and lively little markets. This all goes on till very late.

Hua Hin is a small town, ideal for leisurely perambulations. If you need local transport, there are *samlors* for hire (5–10B for short hops). Out of town, there are waterfalls, limestone caves, Karen villages and nice scenery—all worth exploring by bicycle or motorbike. These can be hired from opposite the bazaar in Damneonkasem Rd. For directions, contact the tourist office.

High season at Hua Hin is from October to May. But avoid November to early February—high winds make poor swimming (but good surfing!). March and April are crowded—this is the Thai holiday season. There are a lot of Thais around at weekends too—you'll need to advance-book accommodation if coming then.

RECREATION

The **Royal Golf Course** at Hua Hin—one of the best standard links in the country—has been going strong for 60 years. To arrange a game, contact Royal Garden Hotel. Green fees are 150B—add 100B for caddy, 300B for club hire.

Royal Garden Resort handles all water-sports too—windsurfing (150B per hour), parasailing (350B per hour) and sailing boats (250B per hour). Non-residents can use the tennis courts (90B per hour) and the hotel pool (no charge in low season). You can also slip into the **Sofitel Hotel** pool, provided you buy a drink to justify your presence!

SHOPPING

Check out Hua Hin's famous handprinted cotton at **Khomapastr Textile Shop**, 218 Phetkasem Rd (tel 511250). This has a full range of curtain, upholstery and dress fabrics at reasonable prices—cotton table mats at 600B, printed cotton material around 80B a yard etc. Designs are very attractive, their bright colours deriving from natural dyes extracted from the sea. To visit the fabric workshops and see the various processes, contact the TAT office. Any materials you buy are worth having made up in Hua Hin. Tailors here are cheap and good—they'll make up shirts for 150B, suits from 800B. There's an interesting **night market** running down Phetkasem Rd. This sells a variety of cheaply-priced trinkets—shell jewellery, bone bracelets, bamboo beach-mats etc. It also does a good line in pirated cassettes.

WHERE TO STAY

Hotel Sofitel Central, Damnoenkasem Rd (tel 511012–3), is still *the* classic hotel in Hua Hin, very much geared to rich Thais. An extravagant oddity, with colonial-style architecture, immense landscaped gardens, and quaint topiary, it was used to represent Hotel Le Pnom in the film *The Killing Fields*. Rooms here start from 1200B, though there's some cheaper bungalow accommodation at 550B. **Royal Garden Resort**, 107/1 Phetkasem Rd, is the big European-style hotel. It has less character than the Sofitel, but has better food, recreation facilities and swimming pool. Nice beach-side location too. Rooms cost from 1500 to 7000B, but (as at Sofitel) 10% discounts are offered in low season. Even better discounts (40–50%) are possible at hotels further down the range.

Supamitra Hotel, 19 Amnuaysin Rd (tel 511208), has rooms at 170B (fan) and 300B (air-con) and is a popular mid-range bet. So is **Sailom Hotel**, 29 Phetkasem Rd (tel 511890), with nice pool, tennis courts, and split-rate rooms at 660B (Sunday to Thursday) and 1450B (Friday to Saturday).

The economical **Hua Hin Ralug Hotel**, Damnoenkasem Rd (tel 511940), is a curiosity—quaint bungalows with *vast* double beds, pet eagles 'minding' the tropical-garden restaurant, and illicit couples creeping around in the dead of night. Of the crop of new budget cheapies which have appeared in Naretdamri and Damnoenkasem roads, **Gee Cuisine** and **Welcome Place** get the best mentions. They both have seafood restaurants with Western-style menus and charge between 80 and 100B for rooms.

EATING OUT

Hua Hin is well-known for its fresh seafood, and for delicious fruits and vegetables like pineapple, sugar-cane and asparagus. For seafood, Thais favour the **Saeng Thai** down by the pier. Specialities here are grilled cuttlefish and fresh lobster, and you can dine well for under 100B. Pity about the sewage floating under the pier which tends to overcome Western appetites. Europeans often prefer to eat at the **Sailom Hotel**—good things to try are kingfish (*pla samlee*), crab (*pu*) and mussels (*maleng phu*). Cheap seafood snacks are widely available down at the main market.

Western-style food is great at **Friendship Restaurant**, 112 Phetkasem Rd. Amazing T-bone steaks (150B), ice-cream sundaes and coffee. This also has the most courteous waiter in Thailand—he bows every time you breathe! It is a good evening hangout spot, with jolly live music and entertainments. **Snack House**, further down Phetkasem Rd has a delightful antique flavour—polished mahogany furniture, framed pics of Louis Armstrong's Five Pennies, a massive buffalo's head, and a fun snooker club. This is the place to come for western breakfasts and evening cocktails.

KOH SAMUI

For 15 years or more, the idyllic island of Koh Samui—lying off the western coast of the Gulf of Thailand—was considered the private domain of the shoestring traveller. A tropical paradise of green hills and coconut groves, of towering palms leaning over white-sand beaches, of rustic bungalows serving up delicious seafood, coconut milk-shakes and magic-mushroom omelettes, it was the classic hippy hideaway, far removed from the noisy, expensive package-tourist playgrounds of Pattaya and Phuket.

But all that is rapidly changing. First came electricity, followed inevitably by videos, discos and motorbikes. Today, the major beaches—notably Lamai and Chaweng—have first-class hotels, German beer gardens, and pick-up bars. The final transition from back-pack to Boeing requires only the opening of Samui's elusive airport. The current story is that the runway is now complete, but they've only got a 35-seater plane to put on it! If that's true, the island may yet enjoy a short reprieve from the brutal thrust of progress. Not that progress has been altogether a bad thing—there are now well-surfaced roads around the island, slicker transportation to and from Surat Thani (the nearest coastal town), superior accommodation, and international dining facilities. But as this is Thailand's third-largest island—over 250 sq km in area—many beaches are likely to escape development for some time to come. At present, Koh Samui has something for everyone—which is just as well, since everyone wants to go there!

Samui has periods of bright, sunny weather throughout the year. January to June is dry and hot. July to November is hit-and-miss; sometimes you'll get weeks of perfect weather, other times double-thunderstorms rage and travellers hole up in huts while locals cheerfully wash their cars in the rain. Christmas Day marks the official end of the rainy season, and it's a very big party. Other festivals centre round the island's principal produce—coconuts. Samui's hinterland is one of the largest plantations in the world, and supplies Bangkok alone with millions of coconuts each year. If you're around in mid-October, here's an offer that's hard to refuse:

> The Samui Municipality warmly invite all foreign tourists to watch the yearly monkey competition of the coconuts reaping in the compound of the Customs habitat. We also invite the esteemed tourists to watch the coconut peeling done by islanders in the children's playground near the post office.

GETTING THERE

By Air
Until Bangkok Airways commence direct flights from Bangkok to Samui island (tel Bangkok 253–4014 for further information), the best air-link is from Bangkok to Surat Thani on Thai Airways (one hour flight; fare 1380B).

At Surat Thani airport, you can either pay 150B for a combined bus-ferry ticket to Samui (best), or hire a 35B limo down to Ban Don pier, and pay the boat separately.

By Rail
From Bangkok's Hualamphong station, only two Rapid trains (the 5.30 pm and the 6.30 pm) arrive in Surat Thani at convenient times (4.42 am and 5.59 am) for the early morning ferry over to Koh Samui. Basic fares are 470B 1st class, 224B 2nd class, and 107B 3rd class. Hualamphong's Advance Booking Office sells handy train-bus-ferry combination tickets to Samui—well worth considering. From Surat Thani, trains run back to Bangkok at 5.38 am, 6.10 am, 7.29 am, 10.39 pm (all Rapid), and at 8.22 pm and 10.09 pm (Express).

By Bus
From Bangkok's Southern Terminal, there are four buses daily to Surat Thani—two air-con (8.20 pm and 8.40 pm, 225B) and two non air-con (8 am and 10 pm, 125B). There are also two buses direct to Samui island, via the Don Sak ferry—one air-con (8 pm, 288B) and one non air-con (7 pm, 143B). Several tour companies, in Bangkok—centred mainly in Koh Sahn Rd or Soi Ngam Dupli—operate private buses direct to Samui too. Shopping around, you can buy a bus-ferry combination ticket from them for as low as 240B. Buses to Surat Thani/Samui usually leave Bangkok early in the morning, or late at night, arriving some 11 or 12 hours later.

There are buses from Surat Thani to Phuket (80B, 6–7 hours), and bus/ferry connections from Samui island (book at Songserm, Na Thon) to Hat Yai (200B, 7 hours).

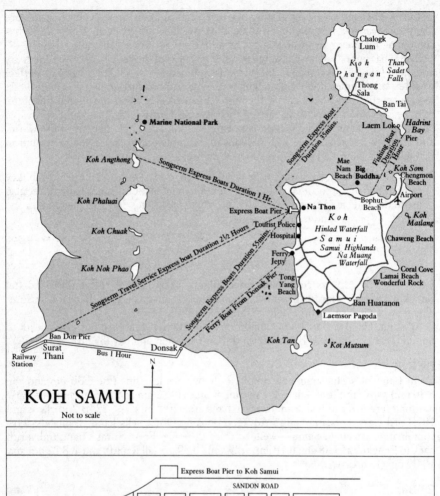

KOH SAMUI

Koh Phangan

○ Chalogk Lum

Than Sadet Falls

Thong Sala

Ban Tai

Laem Loke

Hadrint Bay Pier

Songserm Express Boat Duration 35mins.

Fishing Boat Duration Hour

● **Marine National Park**

Mae Nam Beach

Big Buddha

● *Koh Som* Chengmon Beach

Airport

Koh Angthong

Songserm Express Boats Duration 1 Hr.

Bophut Beach

Koh Matlang

Koh Phaluai

Express Boat Pier

● **Na Thon**

K o h

Hinlad Waterfall

Chaweng Beach

Tourist Police

S a m u i

Koh Chuak

Songserm Travel Service Express boat Duration 2½ Hours

Hospital

Samui Highlands *Na Muang Waterfall*

Ferry Jetty

Songserm Express Boats Duration 35mins.

Coral Cove

Lamai Beach Wonderful Rock

Koh Nok Phao

Tong Yang Beach

Ban Huatanon

Ferry Boat From Donsak Pier

● **Laemsor Pagoda**

Ban Don Pier

Railway Station

Surat Thani

Bus 1 Hour

Donsak

Koh Tan

○ *Kot Mutsum*

N

Not to scale

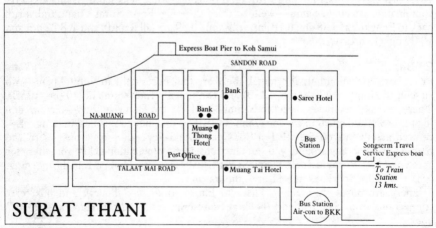

Express Boat Pier to Koh Samui

SANDON ROAD

Bank ●

● **Saree Hotel**

NA-MUANG   ROAD

Bank ● ●

Muang Thong Hotel ●

Bus Station

Songserm Travel Service Express boat

Post Office ●

TALAAT MAI ROAD

● Muang Tai Hotel

To Train Station 13 kms.

Bus Station Air-con to BKK

SURAT THANI

By Boat
From Ban Don pier at Surat Thani, three boats leave daily for Koh Samui (7.30 am, 12 noon and 2.30 pm—timings subject to change!). Fare is 60B one-way, 100B return, and it's a 2¹/₂-hour trip. From Surat's new Don Sak pier, two extra boats for Samui leave daily at 9 am and 4 pm. Fare is 40B, and the journey takes just 1¹/₂ hours. Trouble is, Don Sak is an hour by bus (18B) from Surat Thani. There is also a special night ferry, leaving Ban Don at 11 pm, arriving Samui at 4.30 am. Coming back to Surat Thani from Samui, you've a choice of three boats daily—7.30 am, 12 noon and 3 pm. The later two boats offer free bus transfer to Surat's railway station.

Surat Thani
Surat Thani is a pleasant, unremarkable town 650 km from Bangkok. If you have to stay overnight here, you can dine out on tasty *kao kai op* (marinated baked chicken and rice) at Kaset Market, just above the bus station; look out the excellent Chinese restaurant (try the fresh crab and asparagus) 400 m from Phun Phin railway station, walking into town; get a good night's sleep at either **Wang Tai Hotel**, 1 Talaat Mai Rd (air-con rooms 450B, many facilities) or the cheaper **Muang Tai** (same road, fan/air-con rooms at 150–360B), and take a walk down by the river, dropping in on the several interesting fruit stalls and shops. Buses run every five minutes from Phun Phin station to Ban Don pier (and back), from 6 am to 8 pm. The fare is 5B.

GETTING AROUND KOH SAMUI
A well-paved 50 km ring-road runs around the island, connecting the town (Na Thon), the beaches, and various inland attractions. *Songthaews* are the main form of local transport—they'll take you anywhere on their route for 15–20B. Trouble is, while *songthaews* cover most places of interest, they don't connect the island's two main beaches—Chaweng and Lamai. Half of them ply up the east side of the island, and the other half cover the west side. This means that if you want to go from Chaweng to Lamai, you have to take one *songthaew* into Na Thon, and another one down to Lamai (or vice versa). Another inconvenience is that *songthaews* only run from 6 am to 7 pm—no good at all, if you want to go late-night partying on another beach, or need to get home from a distant disco.

The obvious solution is to arrange your own transport. Many places in Na Thon, Lamai and Chaweng rent out mopeds (100–150B per day), motorbikes (150–200B) and jeeps (400–500B). Insurance is not provided, so it's wise to have a short test-drive before signing any agreement. And always check plugs, brakes, lights, oil and petrol before setting—few of these machines are well-maintained. Be very careful when driving round Samui—the main ring road is very good, but the gravelly dirt-tracks connecting the various beaches with the road are downright dangerous. In 1987 alone, over 30 people died from motorcycle injuries. Your best bet is a good, solid 175cc road-bike which will hold the roads, rather than frail mopeds which won't.

WHAT TO SEE
Samui has much more to offer than beaches. There's some beautiful natural scenery in the interior, worth exploring as a day-tour by motorbike or by *songthaew*. Where you start

your tour is up to you (the suggested route begins at Na Thon, but you can pick it up anywhere). Set out early in the morning (coolest) and bring walking shoes (for Samui Highlands), snorkelling equipment (for Coral Cove), sun-oil, bathing costume and towel. If travelling by motorbike (50B's worth of petrol should see you through the day) you'll also need a sun-hat and sunglasses.

Island Tour
(by motorbike/jeep/*songthaew*; full day)

Hin Lad Falls – Samui Highlands – Na Muang Falls – Wat Laem Sor – Wonderful Rock – Coral Cove – Big Buddha

From Na Thon, head south down the ring-road until a sign for **Hin Lad Falls** appears, 3 km out of town. From here, it's a 2 km stroll inland to the waterfall. No swimming here, but nice scenery. Many people give it a miss, preferring to save their energy for **Samui Highlands**. This pretty hilltop spot is reached via a steep jungle path, leading off the ring-road about 1 km south of Hin Lad. It's a stiff climb, but encouraging signs ('Don't be lazy! Sure! Samui Highland—UP! UP!') and cool drinks served along the way, make it bearable. At the top, friendly Colum provides refreshments and showers for a 20B 'donation', and there are fantastic views. He puts travellers up overnight in his charming bamboo rest-house for a nominal charge of 20B (to book contact him in Na Thon any evening. This lodge has a lovely rock park and flower garden, also a perfect sunset location. Back on the main road, proceed a few kilometres further south (down route 4169) to **Na Muang Falls**. Again, a long 2 km walk inland from the road—though there is access for motorbikes. Na Muang is Samui's best waterfall, especially after the rains when there is great swimming and you can sit beneath the roaring waters and enjoy the best jacuzzi of your life!

Wat Laem Sor is at the southern tip of the island. It's an unusual old pagoda, in a beautiful setting, erected by a venerated monk called Luang Ko Dang. He's dead now, but locals still call his temple a 'very, very magic place'. Stay around until sunset—it really *is* magical then! There's a small beach here, with just one bungalow operation. This is **Laem Sor Inn**, run by an English-Thai couple. It's well known for its Thai fruit wine (highly drinkable) and for its superb food.

Wonderful Rock, just below Lamai Bay, is another 'very, very magic place'. It's actually two rocks—nicknamed Grandfather and Grandmother—which reveal themselves in full phallic glory at low tide. Spotting 'Grandfather' is no problem, but there are numerous candidates for 'Grandmother'. The legend here is that if you don't pray to the resident spirits, you'll get sick and go off your food for days.

Coral Cove lies below the headland separating Lamai and Chaweng bays. It's a small beach, with fantastic snorkelling. You need only go waist-deep into the water to be surrounded by a coral wonderland.

Coral Cove Bungalows, up on the rocks, hire out snorkelling equipment for 20B an hour. They also serve some of the best food on Samui. Delicious 'No Name Mixed Seafood' (30B), chicken salads and fruit salads. Bungalows are marvellous value—particularly the 200B ones right on the beach (these have comfy chairs, flush loos and vast double beds). The coral itself, and the colourful marine life, need no recommen-

198

dation. Wear flippers or flip flops in the water, if possible—if you cut your feet on coral or rocks (and this goes for *anywhere* in Samui), you'll have to take strong precautions against infection. Apply antiseptic and a dry dressing immediately—and stay out of the water for at least four days. Why? Well, there's a chemical quality in Samui's waters which badly aggravates open wounds. Swollen feet are a common sight in Na Thon's hospital (open daily 8.30 am to noon, 1 pm to 5 pm).

Big Buddha lies north of Chaweng bay, up route 4171. This modern Buddha image, 12 metres high and covered with tiny mosaic pieces, sits on a low hill linked by a narrow causeway to the mainland. It makes a beautiful silhouette at sunset—the best time to visit. Below it are seven mini-Buddhas, one for each day of the week. You'll need to dress correctly to visit the temple—the monks are hospitable, but they do turn away people wearing shorts and sarongs.

Ang Thong National Marine Park
(by tour boat; full day)

The beautiful archipelago of Ang Thong ('Golden Tub') lies northwest of Koh Samui, and comprises 40 islands covering 250 square kilometres. Various tour agencies in Na Thon—including Songserm, whose 'big boat' gets there first in the morning—offer good day-trips to the Marine Park. Tickets are 150B, and can be purchased in advance at the major beaches, without having to go all the way into Na Thon.

Ang Thong has several attractions. Tour boats make stops at various coral reefs in the lagoons, where you can go snorkelling. Then there's a longer stop at an island, where you can climb to the top (a gruelling one-hour slog!) for panoramic views of hills and cliffs, lakes and islands. You can stay overnight here, if you make advance arrangements. The next day's boat will pick you up. There's a second island on the itinerary, with a crystal-green saltwater lake, fed by a subterranean tunnel. Ang Thong is, for many, the highlight of their Samui experience—but bring your own food. Meals on board the boat are pretty awful!

RECREATION
Samui's beaches offer various water-sports, many of them yet to be properly organized. There is, for instance, no problem finding **windsurf** boards, but there's often no boat to bring you back if you blow out to sea! This said, Samui doesn't get much surf. Apart from windy November, surfers often find themselves standing on mirror-calm waters. Some of them send back to shore for drinks, while waiting for a breeze to blow up! Two affiliated operations handle **Scuba-Diving** and **Water-Skiing**. These are **Samui Diving School** at the Malibu (tel Na Thon 421273) or **Coco Cabana Beach Club** at Thong Yang Bay (tel 251–4801). These offer diving courses (starting every Tuesday) up to PADI standard, and charge 1100B a day (500B a day for non-divers). Dives commonly take place at **Koh Tao**, one of the best undersea locations in Thailand, or at Ang Thong Marine Park. Both companies are fairly reliable, though scuba-diving on Samui is still rather hit and miss. It's still wise to check equipment before paying over any money.

Several bungalows offer **Fishing** trips—at about 50B a head if there's a group of you. Fishing is said to be best in **Ta Ling Ngam Bay**. A small agency called **Southsea**, in the village just south of Na Thon, goes here—their day trips cost 300B (again, cheap in a group) and call in at **Koh Mudsum**, a lovely little offshore island. For snorkelling, I would recommend **Koh Matlang**, located off the top of Chaweng beach. At low tide, this tiny island is actually connected to the mainland, and you can wade across. Head for the island's point, behind which is a rocky beach. Entering the water here, you'll discover a wonderful underwater world of technicolour live coral and marine life. Look out for pike, angel fish, and giant parrot fish (usually nibbling on the coral), and wear flippers or flip flops to prevent cut feet.

The Beaches

Samui's beaches are famous—long curves of crisp white sand that seem to go on for ever and ever. As someone said, 'Tomorrow is a vision, yesterday is a memory, but today is a beach.' Not a lot happens on the beach. Some bungalows lay on volleyball and beach games, but sun-worshipping and swimming are still the main recreations. For many, the only walk of the day is a leisurely stroll along the sands to see which bungalow is showing the best video, which one is offering the best barbecue or beach party or which had the most amusing menu board. 'Special today!' announced my favourite, 'Magic Mushroom and Barbecued Crap!'

There's a wide range of accommodation available, from basic 50B bungalows with bed, mosquito-net, and (sometimes) an attached toilet, to comfortable 250–500B bamboo dwellings with wood-panelling, ceiling fan and an annexe or balcony. Some beaches now have luxury hotels, with air-con rooms and resort facilities for around 1000B. These low-season prices automatically double in November, when Samui's busy period starts, but you can still get good discounts by renting for a week or more. Outside of the big hotels, food on the island is standard beach fare—banana pancakes, chips, coconut milkshakes etc. Most bungalow operations have their own restaurant, and people generally eat at the one showing the best video.

Each beach has its own scene, and attracts its own devotees. Chaweng is big enough to cater for everyone, but is becoming something of a 'couples' beach. Lamai has a lot of action and boogie-on-down, aimed primarily at the singles market. Maenam and Bophut (Big Buddha) are mellow mushroom-lands, popular with peace-lovers. Laem Sor is where people retreat for total seclusion. And Coral Cove is wonderful for underwater enthusiasts. If you have time, tour them all by motorbike before deciding where to stay. Somewhere out there is a beach just right for you! Once settled, buy yourself a hammock (25B), string it up between two trees, and then just switch off!

Lamai

This is probably Samui's most popular beach. It's rather rocky, and the sand isn't as clean as it once was, but the water's great for swimming. And if its entertainment you're after—discos, bars, parties etc.—there's no need to go any further! Unlike Chaweng, where each set of bungalows has its own restaurant, here at Lamai people often eat at the small 'village', with its several bars and eating-houses. At night, they move on to **Flamingo** discotheque, which is presently Samui's main scene. Of late, it's become something of a pick-up joint for Thai girls, but 'The joint is jumpin' with the hip-hop happening sounds and that sight-sound synchro that you love so much!' And there's a good DJ, who comes on at midnight. Admission is free, and you get a straw with each cheap (40B) drink. The Flamingo rocks up until 3 am. If you don't want Thai rap music and ZZ Top 'happening' inside your head at this late hour, get a bungalow the far side of the beach! Light-sleepers find staying in the 'village' area disturbing—all those motor-bikes revving up in the small hours!

WHERE TO STAY

The 'civilized' end of Lamai begins at **Seabreeze** bungalows (at 100B with fans, good value) and extends north to **Weekender Villa**, around the middle of the bay. Either side of these two operations, accommodation tends to be rather basic. Weekenders is near the village, and is run by 'Big Mama'—a large raunchy Thai lady who fusses over all guests like a broody hen. She offers large, modern bungalows at around 150B (low season), and has an overseas phone and small post office. Similarly-priced operations nearby include **Coconut Villas** (rents out windsurfers and catamarans), **Animal House** (clean place, with a pet gibbon), **Lamai Inn** (everything good, especially the food) and **Mui** 100B huts with twin beds, fan and shower; seafood is superb. All of these operations command the best stretch of beach. A couple—notably Seabreeze and Mui's—are quieter than others.

Chaweng

The largest beach on the island, this divides into Chaweng Yai (to the north) and Chaweng Noi (to the south). The larger bay, Chaweng Yai, is itself divided into two parts by a reef. North of the reef, towards Koh Matland, is quiet and unspoilt—virtually every bungalow up here offers hash cookies, magic mushrooms and other psychedelic mun-chies. Opposite Matlang island, the beach glows green with phosphorescence at night, and it's like walking round in moonboots! South of the reef is the 'original' Chaweng beach. This still has the whitest sand, clearest water and most surf, but is rapidly turning into yuppie resort-land with big hotels and lots of beautiful people posing in dark shades and G-strings. Chaweng Noi, the small southernmost beach, is quiet and good for snorkelling, but is frequented by Thai prostitutes.

The **Chaweng Shop**, set back from the bungalows at the south end of Chaweng Yai, is a useful general store—it saves having to go into Na Thon for supplies, and it has an overseas phone and a Songserm travel office. Close by, behind the new Imperial Samui Hotel, is **Madonna** discotheque. This is tacky, with Thai-oriented music, but can be fun in a crowd. It's open till 3 am nightly, and there are often novelty videos playing at the bar. We saw the porno cartoon version of *Snow White and the Seven Dwarfs*. Unforgettable! So are the 'music parties' which take place at the **Arabian**, south of Chaweng Yai reef, every Saturday, Monday and Wednesday. While you're here, try the Greek food—especially home-made pitta bread and amazing salads. Further south, **Joy** bungalows are building a new 7 million-Baht disco.

WHERE TO STAY

North Chaweng has **Matlang Resort** (nice bungalows for 100B, superb location opposite Koh Matland), **Blue Lagoon** (clean 50B huts, small windsurfing/catamaran school), **Moon** (50B huts with verandah and toilet, fun staff, lots of laughs), **O.P. (quiet 120B bungalows with fans), Lucky Mother** and **Venus** (two late-night hangout places with superior food) and **Marine** (*the* place to eat—tuna salads, fresh yoghurt, fruit salads, and famous 'Bungalow Shakes').

South of the reef, places to stay include **J.R.** (60 to 300B huts, small post office, overseas phone, great breakfasts at **Good Morning Restaurant**); **Liberty** (at 80B, The best bungalows on Chaweng); **Royal Inn** (50B huts right down on the beach); **Magic Light** (250B fan huts; very smart 400B air-con bungalows); **Pansea** (650B fan, 1900B air-con rooms—even smarter); **Imperial Samui Hotel** (1000B air-con rooms—too smart. Who wants a swimming pool on the beach?).

On Chaweng Noi, there are two good budget options—**First** and **Chaweng Noi**. Between them is **Mellow**, where a very mellow Australian lady runs a windsurfing and kayak school.

Bophut (Big Buddha)
This is a smaller beach which is becoming more popular. People come not so much for the sands (which get rather dirty after the rains) but rather for the fishing village, the stunning sunsets and the general air of relaxation. Bophut has a lot of peace and quiet. Places to stay include **Peace** (30B to 150B huts, low-season; friendly 'Mama' offers boat trips, windsurfing, volleyball, table-tennis and gourmet seafood. Peace is *the* night scene on Bophut, with good parties.) The new **Palm Gardens** (40B bungalows right on the beach, great seafood and salads); **Smile House** and **Ziggy Stardust** (200–350B superior shacks. Smile is famous for its beach parties). Eat out at **Ran's** by the pier and enjoy cocktails at the nearby **Oasis** bar.

Mae Nam
Mae Nam is a quiet sandy 5 km beach with calm, clear water (great for swimming), a few fishing boats, and some nice scenery. Ideal by day, it has no electricity at night. After dark, people light small fires on the beach, and play music and munch mushrooms under the stars. There's a small windsurfing school here, and a pleasant little village. Bungalows are mostly basic, but the average charge for two persons is 40–50B (low season). An entertaining place to stay is **Ubon Villas** ('To service with good food. Electric have 24 hour'). Famous for its coconut curries, hallucinogenic mushrooms and 'steamed crap' (crab!), it has delightfully eccentric staff. Other current favourites include **Friendly** and **Happy** (both live up to their names), **Cleopatra Palace** (good information and views of Koh Phangan), **Phalarn** (upmarket 100B bungalows; manager Bo is a gem), and **Rose** and **Rainbow**.

KOH PHANGAN

Ever since Koh Samui began to develop its image as a popular resort, backpackers have been drifting over to Phangan, a short boat-ride away. This is a wonderfully scenic little island, with unspoilt beaches, lovely tropical terrain, and beautiful sunrises and sunsets. Very little development has taken place as yet—the main recreations are coral-diving in the bays and relaxing strolls up into the high forested hills. Most bungalows are simple 30–40B 'dog kennels on stilts', and few of them have electricity, let alone videos. There are only two dirt-track roads on the whole island, and although you can hire motorbikes, there's nowhere of real interest to go.

Koh Phangan is best during November–December (good weather) and March–April (lovely scenery, few tourists). High winds hit the west of the island (including Hadrint) from June to November, and the east (Laem Lok, Thong Sala etc.) from December to June. Swimming and snorkelling are pretty dismal when the wind's up.

GETTING THERE

There are two ways of getting to Phangan from Samui. From Bophut village, there are two boats daily (9.30 am and 3.30 pm) direct to Hadrint Bay. The fare is 50B, and it's a scenic one-hour trip. From Na Thon, there are two boats a day (10 am and 3 pm) to Thong Sala. The fare is 15B (book from Songserm), and the journey takes 40 minutes. From Thong Sala, it's a 5B boat-trip down to Hadrint.

WHERE TO STAY

Most people stay at **Hadrint Bay**—this has a beautiful long stretch of sand, with clear water and good swimming. The top part of the beach is where, as someone said, 'old hippies go to die'. They mostly hang out at **Paradise** and **Palita** bungalows (well-priced at 150B) and have turned hippie sandcastles—swirly, spirally, dreamy creations into a fine art! The Sunrise has adequate 30B bungalows, and a very psychedelic menu. The nearby **Seaview** has hammocks and good 40B huts right on the beach. **Hadrint Bay** bungalows are acceptable, and **Tommy's** are top-notch. Tommy's is another mushroom place, but gets rave reviews for its 'Full Moon' parties and food. Every morning sees a long queue outside **Palita**, which does marvellous cheese buns, and every afternoon there's a crush to get in **Win Bakery** (next to Family House), for its home-made cakes and real Lipton tea (served in earthenware pots!). Win is excellent for seafood too.

If Hadrint has the best sunrises, then **Laem Lok**—a short walk across the narrow peninsula—has the best sunsets. There's no beach to speak of here, but there is an amazing coral cove. Laem Lok is East Hadrint, and has two places to stay—both of them excellent. The **Lighthouse** has the best location, with bungalows 30/40B) imaginatively staggered up the rocks. Guests get free snorkelling equipment, and spend a lot of time in the restaurant. Well, with Mexican tacos, chip butties, vegetarian food, seafood, cakes and cookies on offer, why not? The other outfit, **Sunset**, is just as popular with a friendly family, great seafood and cheap boat-trips round the island. The bungalows are clean as a whistle.

From Hadrint, two boats go up daily to **Thong Sala**, the main town on the island. This has a post office, a few shops, a Songserm travel office, and some fairly basic bungalows. The beaches here are nothing to write home about. From Thong Sala, a couple of taxis run out daily to **Ban Tai**. It's at this small village that you can hire out 200B per day roadbikes to visit **Thansadet Waterfall** (only worth it from September to November, after the rains). If you really want to get away from it all, charter a boat out from Thong Sala to **Koh Tae Nai** a pretty (and pretty remote!) island with a few bungalows for rent.

PHUKET

Popular 'Pearl of the South', the large provincial island of Phuket lies in the Andaman Sea some 891 km south of Bangkok. Once a quiet backwater, now it is developing apace,

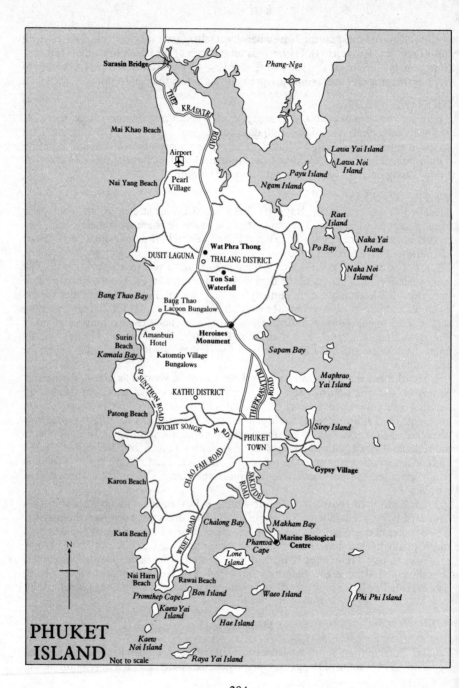

Sarasin Bridge

Phang-Nga

THEP KRASATRA ROAD

Mai Khao Beach

Airport

Pearl
Village

Nai Yang Beach

Lawa Yai Island

*Lawa Noi
Island*

Payu Island

Ngam Island

*Raet
Island*

Po Bay

*Naka Yai
Island*

Wat Phra Thong

DUSIT LAGUNA · **THALANG DISTRICT**

*Naka Noi
Island*

**Ton Sai
Waterfall**

Bang Thao Bay

Bang Thao
Lacoon Bungalow

Surin
Beach

Amanburi
Hotel

**Heroines
Monument**

Sapam Bay

Kamala Bay

Katomtip Village
Bungalows

*Maphrao
Yai Island*

SI SUNTHON ROAD

THEP KRASATRA ROAD

KATHU DISTRICT

Patong Beach

WICHIT SONGK

M RD.

Sirey Island

PHUKET
TOWN

CHAO FAH ROAD

SAKDIDE ROAD

Gypsy Village

Karon Beach

Kata Beach

WISET ROAD

Chalong Bay

Makham Bay

**Marine Biological
Centre**

*Phanwa
Cape*

*Lone
Island*

N

Nai Harn
Beach

Rawai Beach

Promthep Cape   *Bon Island*

Waeo Island

Phi Phi Island

*Kaew Yai
Island*

Hae Island

PHUKET
ISLAND

*Kaew
Noi Island*

Not to scale

Raya Yai Island

and is well on its way to becoming an international resort. Formerly known as Koh Thalang, it used to derive its wealth from tin and rubber. Renamed Phuket—from the Malay word *bukit* (meaning mountain)—it now does just as well out of tourism. The combination of long white beaches, lovely coves and bays, scenic waterfalls and parks, undersea scenery and marine life, superb seafood and resort hotels, calm, clear waters and relaxed tropical atmosphere has made it a natural target for rapid development. A surging tide of tourism is sweeping over Phuket, and the ominous lines of girlie bars are already spreading along the major beaches. 'It's becoming another Pattaya', say some. 'It's not Thailand at all', moan others, 'just an absurdly expensive rip-off'. And it's true, that the prophetic rise of 4-storey hotels on the main beaches spell doom to the old cheap bungalows, striking dismay into the heart of the economy traveller. Phuket is going all out to develop its image as an upmarket family-style resort. In a way, this isn't a bad thing. There's now a full range of water-sports, including scuba-diving and surfing; there's high-class European, Chinese, Thai and Islamic cuisine; there are discos, bars and a lively nightlife; and there are well-organized excursions by boat to nearby attractions like Phi Phi islands, Phang Nga and Ao Luk. Phuket has far more diversity than Koh Samui. Also, being connected to the mainland by a causeway, and with a direct link to Bangkok by air, it is far more accessible. There's really little to complain about. Once you're on a motorbike, and away from built-up Patong and Kata beaches, it won't take long to appreciate how unspoilt the rest of Phuket is. This is Thailand's largest island, and only about 10% of it has been directly affected by tourism. There is nothing one-dimensional about Phuket either. In the hour it takes to drive the length of it, through hills and rubber plantations, running down to coconut groves and white beaches, you'll see no bungalow signs (unlike in Koh Samui, where they appear at every bend in the road!), only some of the most beautiful inland scenery of any island in the country. So, don't be put off by Phuket's yuppie tag—the locals still fish, they still culture pearls, water buffalo still graze the golf course, and the water is as clear as the glass in your diving mask!

Phuket has its high season from November to May. By December, it's really buzzing, and accommodation prices soar. Christmas and New Year have some of the biggest parties in Thailand. September and October are rainy and windy, but there's some great surf. The nine-day Vegetarian Festival, Phuket's main celebration, usually happens at the end of September. This is when the islanders of Chinese ancestry commit themselves to a vegetarian diet, and undergo various painful austerities like fire-walking, climbing ladders with knife-blade rungs and puncturing themselves with pointed sticks. The last day is the best—joyous street-festivals, and lots of firecrackers and rockets.

GETTING THERE

By Air
Thai Airways fly daily to Phuket from Bangkok (1545B, 1 hour 10 minutes) and from Hat Yai (700B, 30 minutes).

By Bus
From Bangkok's Southern Terminal, non air-con buses leave for Phuket throughout the day, from 7.30 am to 10.30 pm (fare 165B). There's also one air-con bus daily, leaving at 7 pm (fare 299B). In both cases, it's a long 13–14-hour journey. Several tour agencies in

Bangkok and Phuket operate private buses—these cost a little more, but are often quicker and more comfortable.

From Phuket back to Bangkok, there are seven non air-con buses daily (leaving between 6 am to 6.30 pm), also one air-con bus leaving at 3 pm.

From Surat Thani, a few non air-con buses go to Phuket each day. The fare is 60B, and the awesomely slow 6-hour journey is made tolerable only by the magnificent scenery.

TOURIST INFORMATION

TAT Tourist Office, 73–75 Phuket Rd (tel 212213), is located near the bus-station in Phuket town. This should be your first port of call on arrival—lots of useful handouts and information; helpful and efficient staff.

GETTING AROUND

From Phuket town, *songthaews* run out to all the major beaches at regular intervals from 8 am to 6 pm. The rank in Ranong Rd (opposite Thai Airways) services Patong, Kata, Karon and Surin beaches (fare 10B), also Kamala and Nai Yang beaches (15B). *Songthaews* for Rawai (10B) and Nai Harn (20B) beaches leave from the circle in Bangkok Rd. A few *songthaews* also go up to the airport, 32 km north of town, for 20B. Taxis and *tuk-tuks* charge a minimum fare of 100B. Only hire taxis or *tuk-tuks* (100B minimum fare from town to beaches or airport) if there's a group of you. *Songthaews* and *tuk-tuks* patrol around Phuket town itself for a standard 5B charge —but you still may need to bargain!

To get around the island itself, consider hiring a motorbike or jeep. These are useful for beach-hopping, exploring the island's hinterland, and for trips into Phuket town. They can be hired, at an average daily rate (low season) of 100B for mopeds, 250B for big police bikes, 550–700B for jeeps, either in town or at the beaches. Hire rates are cheapest at Patong and in Phuket town. As in Koh Samui, there's no insurance provided, but bikes and roads here are in much better condition. A popular outing by bike (or jeep) is north up to the airport, then returning slowly along the coastline, checking out each of the beautiful beaches in turn. There are some especially fine coastal views as you round the headland at Promthep Cape, the southernmost point of the island. But be warned—some of the roads connecting various beaches have been allowed to fall into disrepair. The dirt-tracks between Surin and Patong beaches, and between Promthep and Nai Harn/Rawai, are the main hazards. Tackling these roads by motorbike can be tricky! Casualties should report to **Karon Health Clinic**, located between Kata and Karon beaches. This place gives immediate treatment, and is far better than the hospital in town.

Cars can be rented for about 900B per day without petrol. Contact **Pure Car Rent**, opposite Thavorn Hotel, Rasada Rd, Phuket town (tel 211002); or **Avis** at Phuket Cabana Hotel, Patong (tel 321138), Le Meridien, Karon Noi (tel 321480) or Pearl Village, Nai Yang (tel 311376).

Phuket Town

This compact provincial town is becoming rather too touristy for most tastes. The interesting old Sino-Portuguese residences are being swamped by concrete buildings and souvenir shops, and a lot of the town's earlier charm and character has gone with them. For something to do, visit the Provincial Town Hall, used as the French Embassy in the film of *The Killing Fields*. Or take a walk up **Rang Hill** for a nice view down over the town and island interior. If you need to phone or telex overseas, there's a good service at the modern **Telephone Office**, one block up from the Post Office in Montri Rd. To eat, there's **Mae Porn** at the corner of Phang Nga Rd and Soi Pradit—a good reliable restaurant with unbelievable service; or **Raan Jee Nguat** on the corner of Yaowaraj and Deebuk roads for fresh seafood and tasty curries; or **Mai Ngam** opposite the Post Office for fast-food and ice-creams. Opposite the Pearl Hotel, the best Chinese restaurant in town offers shark's fin soup, birds' nests, and other local favourites. Places to stay include **Pear Hotel**, Montri Rd (tel 211044)—air-con rooms from 702B, pool, restaurant,

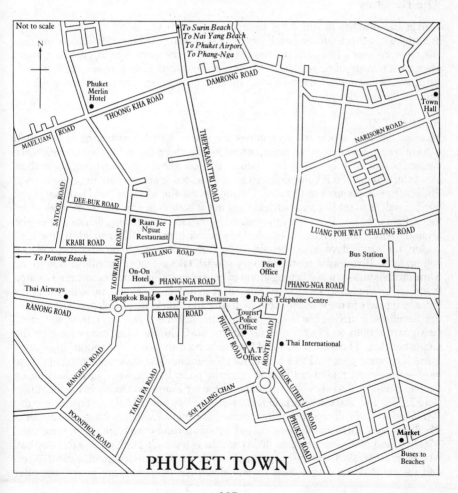

PHUKET TOWN

nightclub; **Phuket Merlin**, 158/1 Yaowaraj Rd (tel 213866)—air-con rooms from 847B, restaurant, nightclub, and 'refrigerator'; and **Thavorn Hotel**, Rasda Rd (tel 2113335)—rooms from 180B to 950B, pool, disco and coffee shop. This is a comfy place.

Accommodation: All prices given in this section for hotels, except where otherwise stated, are 'average'. Even TAT tourist office, which hands out up-to-date hotel lists, can't supply fixed tariffs. Prices vary substantially from high to low season. From November to May, tariffs are often double what they are the rest of the year. But it's still worth bargaining for discounts—especially if you're staying for a week or more.

The Beaches

Phuket has beaches to suit every taste and pocket. If you don't like one, hop on a motorbike and check out another. Every one has its own character and clientele, but they all have white sands, lovely sea and (except Patong) lots of space. The bigger beach hotels offer a wide range of recreations, including water-sports, discotheques, massage parlours, swimming pools, bars and clubs. One or two are so large, you can often wander in and use the facilities for free.

RECREATION
Most of Phuket's sports and recreations are water-related. **Swimming** is best from December to April. At other times, strong winds and powerful undercurrents make swimming out of your depth inadvisable. Bathers should take care not to swallow sea-water—some of it is being polluted by non-treated sewerage. **Surfing** is *the* sport at Phuket from September to October. During storms, the whole of Nai Harn bay is just one big wall of wave! But most surfers hang out at Kata Noi, or at the point break at the top of Patong beach. **Boat trips** to offshore islands (for snorkelling, fishing etc) can be arranged with fishermen on the beach. They charge between 500B and 900B (low/high season) for boatloads of up to 8 people, and will often drop you off on an island, and pick you up later. If you want something very special, take a 3-hour speedboat ride to the **Similian Islands**—an enchanting group of nine islands (Similian means 'nine') located to the east of Phuket. It's widely considered, even by Jacques Cousteau, to be one of the three best places in the world for **scuba-diving** and **snorkelling**. Independent travel to the Similians is tricky, but a few people have hitched a ride over from the small coastguard station on Phuket's northwestern coast, and then just camped out on the empty beaches. The trouble is, you'll have to bring your own scuba/snorkelling equipment. The same goes for **Phi Phi Islands**, the second-best undersea location in these parts—equipment rented out here is generally poor. Fortunately, Phuket itself has a couple of reliable deep-sea-diving outfits. These are **Fantasea Divers** in Patong village (tel 321309) and **Marina Sports** in Kata-Karon village (tel 211432). Both offer 4–5 day *PADI* (open-water diving certificate) courses at around 7500B, and make dives out at Phi Phi, the Similians and the west coast. Fantasea is run by two Dutch guys, Jeroen and Maarten, and offers insurance on diving accidents (the only outfit on Phuket to do so). Marina is a friendly German-run company, with a reputation for exciting night-dives, and for going down deeper than anyone else. Both operations are pricey, but offer

discounts if you advance-book. In addition to diving, they offer **windsurfing, water-skiing, deep-sea fishing, parasailing** (marina only) and **catamarans**. All their equipment is top quality.

WHERE TO STAY & EATING OUT

Nai Yang
Proceeding counterclockwise from Phuket's northern tip, this is the first major beach you'll hit. **Nai Yang** is a secluded half-moon beach with good sand and hardly any people. Set aside as a national park, and fringed by *casuarina* trees, it is short on action and high on relaxation. The Thais like it, and so do retired couples seeking a complete rest. **Pearl Village Hotel** (tel 311376) has 60B tents, 500B fan-cooled bungalows, and 1500B luxury air-con rooms. Also good dining, entertainment and recreation. The Pearl offers discounts of up to 50% in the low season. Prices also come down on quiet weekdays, when you can often have the whole beach to yourself. If at a loose end, take a short hike north to **Mai Khao**, which is Phuket's longest beach. Here, between November and February, giant sea-turtles struggle ashore to lay their eggs. The convenience of Nai Yang is that it is only a five-minute drive from the airport.

Surin – Bang Tao – Cape Sing – Kamala
Surin, 25 km from Phuket town, is another nice quiet spot. It has a lovely long beach (poor for swimming though, owing to strong tides), some excellent seafood-snack places, and a popular 9-hole golf course. For a game, contact **Pansea Hotel** (tel 216137)—green fees are 150B, club hire another 150B. **Pansea** is a good place to stay—for 2050B, you get a lovely 4–person cottage, with all meals and water-sport facilities thrown in. **Bang Tao Bay**, just above Surin, has two decent places to stay—**Bang Tao Lagoon** (cottages from 600B) and **Dusit Laguna Hotel** (tel 311174, air-con rooms from 1815B, lots of facilities). **Sing Cape**, 1 km south of Surin, is famous for its fantastic rock formations, and you can camp out on the beach. It leads down to **Kamala**, a delightful stretch of the sand with one good bungalow operation, **Katomtip Village** (low-season rates, 200B a night). The northern end of Kamala beach is suitable for swimming.

Patong
Patong is 15 km from town, and is Phuket's most developed beach. It has a tacky, action-packed 'village' full of bars, clubs, German restaurants and expensive seafood places. The beach itself is nice – if you don't mind being hassled every five minutes to buy fake diamonds, hammocks or massages. But when the navy rolls in, Patong really earns its title of 'Soho on the Beach'. All prices double, and the place is crawling with pubescent Thai hookers. Bars come and go, but the current favourites include **Kangaroo, Ex-Pat,** and **Lucky Star**. After the bars close, the human zoo migrates to **Banana Discotheque**. This charges 60B admission (one free drink) and is best on a Saturday night. During the day, recreations include water-scooters (300B per hour), jet-skis (1000B per hour), windsurfing (100B per hour), snorkelling (50B per hour) and coral-diving over at nearby Freedom and Paradise beaches (500–800B per day for boat hire).

Patong's rich kids stay at good hotels like **Coral Beach** (tel 321106, rooms from

1500B). **Safari Beach** (tel 321230, rooms from 1320B), and **Seaview** (tel 321103, fan-cooled rooms 500B, air-con 1200B). Recommended cheaper hotels, with rooms between 200B and 300B, are **Club Oasis, Coconut Villa,** and **Thamdee Inn.** Budget places are few and pretty dismal. **Sea Dragon** is okay (rooms 100–200B), and there's a restaurant outside which does roast duck dinners for 25B. There's another place in the village—up a side-road off the main bar street, and past a Mexican restaurant—which has super 80B bungalows. It's run by a French guy, who lets guests do their own cooking. In a place like Patong, where food is so expensive, this is a big plus!

Dining out, try seafood at the **No 1** on Beach Rd (speciality is King Lobster at 400B a kilo) or **Patong Seafood** on the sea-front (recommended dishes include Roasted Snapper-Fish with Brandy, 120B, or Roasted Prawns with Brandy, 180B). European and Thai food is good at the **Orchid** (try the steaks and the lobster) or at **Tums** (the place to go, said one resident, 'when you're fed up of tiger prawns and overpriced steaks'). You can eat well at either place for under 100B.

Karon – Kata

These two long, curving beaches located 20 km out of town are the current favourites. **Karon** is the more peaceful option—a good place to go if you're not into crowds. It has better swimming than **Kata,** and there are windsurfers for hire (100B per hour). Fishermen still cast their nets on Karon, and there's lots of good, fresh seafood available. Places to stay include **Golden Sands** (200–300B), **Ocean View** (200B doubles), and **Karon Beach Seaview** (120B bungalows; best deal on the beach). **Karon Villa** (tel 214820) deserves a special mention for its superb traditional Thai dance shows. These commence 8 pm nightly (turn up 7 pm for music prelude, and a decent seat). No admission charge, but you're expected to at least buy a drink. Many budget travellers hang the expense, and eat here too. Karon Villa has rooms from 1600B, and many facilities.

Kata is actually two beaches in one—Kata Yai and Kata Noi. The smaller beach, **Kata Noi,** has bigger waves, better surfing and one notable hotel—the **Kata Thani** (tel 216632) with rooms from 1200B and a perfect location. **Kata Yai** has better swimming and (in September/October) enjoyable body-surfing. The shallow beach is a popular induction spot for beginner scuba-divers. From here, they graduate to offshore **Koh Pu,** known for its beautiful live coral. Kata Yai hires out windsurfers (100B per hour) and jet-skiers (300B per hour); in the village, you can rent out surf bodyboards from **Chin Cafe** for 100B a day.

Ever since Club Med set up shop at Kata, this beach has been going the same way as Patong. There's now a small 'village', between Karon and Kata, with pizza parlours and coffee shops, noisy videos and motorbikes, and a small street bar with monkeys serving the drinks! The village is quite a scene at night. To eat, try **Marina** restaurant (famous 90B steaks and 120B seafood basket meals), **Pizzeria** (mean 60B seafood pizzas) and snug **Chin Cafe** (ice-creams, shakes and coffee; has the cosiest seats in Thailand). On the way down to the seedy bar street, there's **Sue's Bar & Restaurant** This has a pool, darts, hard-rock sounds, and a wild, wild atmosphere. Nearly anything goes at Sue's— except dancing on the tables! After the bars close at midnight, it's time for late-night boogie at the small **Club 44** disco. This is a small, rather ramshackle affair—but drinks are cheap, and (unlike Patong's 'Banana' disco) there's minimal hassle from the girls.

Club Mediterranee (tel 214830) is at the top of Kata Yai, near the village, and commands a lovely stretch of beach. Rooms start at 2400B, and there's all manner of recreational facilities on offer. Good accommodation in the village itself are **Marina Cottage** (tel 212901; comfy air-con rooms from 540B), **Kata Tropicana** (good-value rooms at 130 to 200B, useful laundry service and restaurant, cheap motorbike rental and sightseeing boat trips), **Kata Villa** (clean rooms from 120B), **Priayung** (nice Swiss-owned bungalows from 70B) and **Fantasea Hill** (bungalows at 50–60B). Travellers also recommend the large well-appointed bungalows opposite Sue's Bar—at 70B a night, probably the best deal on Kata.

Nai Harn

Viewed from the headland above, Nai Harn—just below Kata Noi—looks just about the prettiest of all Phuket's beaches. Its perfect crescent of white sand is ringed by green hills and embraces an idyllic emerald-green lagoon. Then you spot the ugly **Phuket Yacht Club** staggered up the hillside, and the impression is spoilt. Nai Harn now offers sailing, windsurfing and even tennis (swimming is out between May and October), but if you want to get away from beautiful people and beach umbrellas, stay at the southern end of the sands. Here there are two quiet and friendly places—**Nai Harn Bungalow** (Linda Cottage Inn) with cosy huts from 100B to 150B, and its own little beach; and **Sunset Bungalows** with basic, but comfortable, huts at 60 to 60B. You'll find both places off the road leading up to Promthep Point.

Rawai – Chalong

Rounding Promthep Cape at the southern tip of the island, you'll find **Rawai** beach, 17 km from town. Though one of the first beaches to be developed on Phuket, Rawai today is quiet and neglected. This is much to do with its narrow beach, and general lack of atmosphere. Still, scuba-divers like it (many offshore islands here have spectacular underwater scenery) and so do seafood gourmets. Places to stay are limited. Choose between **Promthep Palace** at Laem Ka (tel 212980; rooms from 400B) and **Pornmae Bungalow**, 58/1 Wiset Rd (upmarket bungalows from 300B).

A charming fishing village connects Rawai to **Chalong Bay**. At the pier here, friendly Ruan offers boat-trips over to **Koh Hae** (Coral Island), **Koh Lone** and **Koh Hew**. These trips cost 500B (for one to six people), include stops for fishing, snorkelling and coral-diving, and run from 9 am to 4 pm daily. Chalong Bay itself is a pretty spot at high tide, with many boats moored offshore. You can charter these for fishing trips (around 400B a day), or take the regular 9 am boat to Phi Phi islands (500B, includes meagre lunch).

Chalong Bay is well-known for its seafood restaurants. For around 100B a head, you can eat your fill at **Kaning 1** or **Kaning 2**. These offer a mouthwatering range of crab, prawn and fish dishes (steamed or barbecued), also special *tom yum* seafood soup with lemon grass and chilli. **Pan's Lighthouse** is cheaper and almost as good—this is where all the fishermen and boat people hang out in the evening, and is the best place to charter boats. To arrange overnight stays in a schooner off the bay, contact the agent at Kaning 1 restaurant. He's also the person to see regarding luxury launch trips from the boat club.

Naka Noi

Phuket is world-famous for its fabulous cultured pearls. These come from the small

211

Ko Tapu, Phang Nga Bay

island of **Naka Noi**, off the northeast coast. Several tour agencies in Phuket offer trips there, or you can go independently (30–minute drive up to Po Bay from town, then 20 minutes by boat). Pearls bought at Naka Noi are cheaper even than in the pearl markets of Japan. But don't expect to come away with a pearl necklace. One woman I met has waited 10 years for one of these and still has only 15 matching pearls—she needs 28!

PHANG NGA

Phang Nga lies exactly midway between Phuket and Krabi, and makes a good stop-over from these two more popular resorts. The central attraction here is Phang Nga Bay, an eerie collection of primaeval limestone islands rising out of the sea like grim, forebidding sentinels. The spectacular scenery of this immense bay made it a natural choice of location for the film *The Man with the Golden Gun*. Since then, having captured the public imagination, it has become a big tourist magnet. Every day, an armada of noisy tour-boats invade from nearby Phuket, and there remains only one way to see Phang Nga in its original, timeless splendour—on your own!

Visit Phang Nga between December and April—then, the skies are clear, there is no rain, and the islands are at their most verdant and beautiful. If you want to avoid the crowds, go in October and November—there's often just enough rain to discourage the tour boats!

GETTING THERE

By Bus
From Phuket's Phang Nga Rd terminal, buses leave for Phang Nga every hour till 6 pm. The 85 km journey takes 1 hour 45 minutes, and the fare is 22b.

From Krabi, there are regular buses to Phuket (181 km, 3 hours, 40B), via Phang Nga (88 km, 1¹/₂ hours, 20B). From Phang Nga town, buses leave for Phuket and Krabi every hour, until 5 pm.

By Motorbike
Phang Nga is a popular motorbike outing from both Phuket and Krabi. On a bike, you can really enjoy the scenery.

WHAT TO SEE
The big thing to do here is the spectacular boat-trip round Phang Nga Bay. An enterprising young postman, Sayan Tamtopol, has been offering good, cheap tours for independent travellers over the past seven years. He charges 200B (far less than a tour from Phuket) and throws in a huge seafood supper, overnight accommodation in a Muslim fishing village, and himself as your personal English-speaking guide. The advantage of booking through Sayan is that, because his village is right at the mouth of the bay, you can have the bay all to yourself for hours if you start out early enough. The tour-boats don't roll in till around 11 am. Another bonus for setting out early are the unforgettable dawn views, rather like Chinese paintings. Sayan's tours usually run from 8 am to 2 pm, and he makes stops for snorkelling and swimming. But the scenery is the main event—so bring your camera and lots of film!

Sayan meets travellers off the bus in Phang Nga town (outside Thai Farmers Bank) between 6 am and 8 am daily. This is good if you want free transport to Koh Panyi (the fishing village), but often means a late-start tour. Your best bet is to arrive in town mid-afternoon, and to make your own way to Sayan's place (ring him on 212901–4 ext 089 to let him know you're coming—or just turn up!). To get there, cross over from the town bus-stop and hop in a *songthaew* going to Tha Don customs pier. This short 8 km journey often takes as long as 45 minutes. My vehicle crept around town for half an hour before going anywhere. On the way, it picked up sacks of ice and fish, piles of foam mattresses, shrimp nets and sail rigging, a mountain of egg-boxes, six huge Calorgas drums, a cake trolley, and an outboard engine. Oh yes, and 22 passengers! At Tha Don, look out for the Muslim restaurant by the pier (it's the one with the caged bird over the entrance). Beef and green bean curry is the speciality, and it costs just 10B. From Tha Don, it's a 40–minute boat ride over to Koh Panyi—the correct fare is 10B, but you'll have to bargain to get this!

WHERE TO STAY
Phang Nga town itself is small, and fairly dull. There are a couple of banks, a semi-interesting Muslim market (opposite the bus-stop) and a few cheap hotels. The **Ratapatong**, next to the market, has okay 100B double rooms. A blue building signed 'Hotel', a minute's walk below the Ratapatong, has simpler rooms for 80B. If you want air-con comfort, choose between the **New Luk Muang** on Highway 4 (on the road into town, just below the mediocre tourist office; live music nightly, nice cafe, twin-bedded rooms 230B) or the luxury **Phang Nga Bay Resort** near the pier. This has a scenic setting, rooms at 400B single, 600B double, and there's a little restaurant nearby called the **Jarun**, famous for its cheap, delectable seafood.

Phang Nga Bay
(by boat; 6 hours)

Koh Panyi – Koh Phing Kan – Koh Tapu – Koh Thalu – Koh Hong – Thamlot Cave – Pekinese Rock

Koh Panyi is a fascinating overnight stop. Where else can you stay at a Muslim fishing village built on stilts at the base of a massive limestone island? Koh Panyi means 'flag island', and it was given its name by the first Muslims who arrived here (from Malaysia) over 200 years ago, and planted their flag on its peak. The original settlement of three families is now a thriving township of 1200 people, with its own school, post office and mosque. Colourful exotic birds flutter within wicker cages, cackling elders lull infants to sleep in wooden swing-cribs, the sun sets peacefully against a golden sky, and then everybody vanishes off to prayers in the quaint blue mosque. If staying here, you won't see them again till morning. The evening is spent watching TV soaps and tucking into tasty Muslim pastries with Sayan and his chums. The village generator packs up at midnight and then (provided you've got a mosquito net) it's off to sleep in a comfy bed.

In the early morning, you set off to see the islands. As you approach the centre of the bay, these fan out into a surreal archipelago of tombstone-shaped crags, strongly resembling an ancient stone circle. There are dozens of tiny isles out here, several with interesting shapes which have earned them local soubriquets. **Koh Phing Kan** literally means 'two islands leaning back to back'. Since 007 landed though, it's become more popularly known as James Bond Island. The large pillar of rock in its bay looks like a huge nail driven into the sea—thus its name of **Koh Tapu**, or 'nail island'. **Koh Thalu** and **Koh Hong** are two small rock grottos hollowed out in the base of larger islands by the pounding sea—their names derive from the shape of their interiors (Koh 'Hong' resembles a 'room'). **Thamlot Cave** is the largest subterranean cave on the route, with ghoulish limestone fingers dripping down from its vast ceiling. Just beyond this, returning to base, look out for **Pekinese Rock**. This sits on a low crag, overlooking the mouth of the bay, and bears more than a passing resemblance to a pekinese dog.

KRABI

A spectacular blend of vast limestone cliffs, prehistoric islands and serene white-sand beaches, Krabi is the up-and-coming resort on the southwest coast. It's a lot less developed (and much quieter) than Phuket or Samui, and has just as much to offer. Krabi town, 814 km from Bangkok, is for travellers in serious need of relaxation. They come here to enjoy its famous cakes, pastries and ice-creams, to lie back with the locals, and to languish happily in its mellow, late-night bars and restaurants. Later, they move out to one of the many local beaches, or take a boat over to the glorious **Phi Phi Islands**. Most of the islands in this area were, at one time or other, popular smugglers' hideouts. Krabi town itself—situated close to the mouth of the Andaman Sea—was still doing a brisk trade in smuggled whisky and cigarettes (from Malaysia and Singapore) until a couple of years ago. But that's all stopped now. The local population, mainly Muslims, still do a lot of regular trading by sea—rubber and palm oil are the main exports—but smuggling is no longer necessary. Now they have tourism. In and around Krabi,

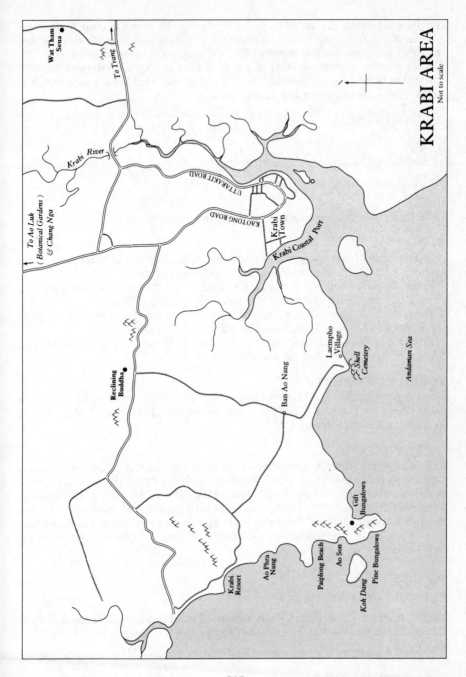

KRABI AREA

Not to scale

Wat Tham Seua

To Trang

Krabi River

To Ao Luk
(Botanical Gardens)
& Chang Nga

UTTARAKIT ROAD

KAOTONG ROAD

Krabi Town

Krabi Coastal Port

Reclining Buddha

Laempho Village

Shell Cemetery

Ban Ao Nang

Andaman Sea

Gift Bungalows

Krabi Resort

Ao Phra Nang

Paiplong Beach

Ao Son

Koh Dang

Pine Bungalows

215

everybody is building like crazy—preparing for the expected tourist boom. It hasn't come yet—the moneyed tourists won't arrive till Krabi gets its airport. Well, it's *got* an airport, and they even opened it. But then they closed it again—the tarmac cracked up!

Krabi province is most pleasant between November and April, the dry months. A bit crowded of late, though. If you don't mind a spot of rain, October is a good month to come—fewer tourists, green and luxuriant flora and fauna.

GETTING THERE

By Air
As soon as Krabi airport is completed, Bangkok Airways will commence operating flights.

By Sea
From Phuket, the *Seaking* boat sails for Krabi at 4 pm daily; fare is 250B.

By Bus
All Krabi-bound buses drop off at Talaat Kao village, 5 km out of Krabi town. From here, it's a 3B (20-minute) *songthaew* ride into the town centre.

From Bangkok Southern Terminal, four buses leave for Krabi daily—two air-con (7 pm and 8 pm, 290B) and two non-air con (7 pm and 9 pm, 161B).

From Phuket's Phang-Nga Rd terminal, two non air-con buses go to Krabi daily (12.50 pm and 2.30 pm, 38B). From Hat Yai—see Hat Yai section.

From Krabi (Talaat Kao junction) there are buses every half-hour to Phuket (181 km, 3 hours, 40B) via Phang Nga (88 km, $1^1/_2$ hour, 20B).

TOURIST INFORMATION
There is good English-speaking information from two reliable travel agencies in Krabi town—**Pee Pee Tours**, c/o Pee Pee Guest House (tel 612155) and **L.R.K. Travel Service**, 11 Khongka Rd (tel 611930).

WHAT TO SEE
Krabi's many attractions require a week or more to appreciate at leisure. Inland sights can be explored by motorbike (hire from Suzuki dealer on Phattana Rd, 175B a day) or by tour-bus (book from Pee Pee Guest House, 150B). If you want to hit the beaches first, touts meet travellers off the bus in Krabi town and provide free transport to various beach-bungalow operations. Arranging your own transport, you'll need a 15B *songthaew* to **Ao Phra Nang Bay**, followed by a scenic 20B longtail boat ride to **Paiplong** or **Ao Son** beaches.

Provincial Sights
(by motorbike/tour-bus; full day)

Shell Cemetery – Noppharat Thara Beach – Than Bokkharani National Park & Botanical Gardens – Wat Tham Seua (Tiger Cave Temple)
The **Shell Cemetery** is 19 km west of Krabi Town, and should be visited early in the

morning. This beach of 75 million-year-old fossilized seashells, forming giant slabs of jutting rock, is a rare phenomenon—something you won't want to miss by turning up mid-afternoon, when the tide is in. Low tide is also a good time to go shell-hunting on the beach. Though if you're out of luck, a few stalls here sell coral, seashell and mother-of-pearl jewellery but prices are not cheap.

Noppharat Thara Beach ('Beach of the Nine-Gemmed Stream') is 18 km northwest of Krabi. This lovely 2 km-long stretch of white sands, lined with casuarina trees, is part of a National Marine Park, and there's nothing on it apart from a few government bungalows. This is another place to come at low tide—good beachcombing for shells, and you can walk over to a rocky island, about 1 km from the mainland. If you want to make a day of it here (avoid weekends—lots of Thai picnic people), catch one of the regular minibuses from Krabi town. Fare is 20B.

Than Bokkharani National Park lies off Highway 4 between Krabi and Phang Nga. If going there by *songthaew* (12B from Krabi), get off at Ao Luk and walk a short way down Route 4039 to find the park entrance. Ao Luk is 46 km north of Krabi town. **Than Bokkharani** is noted for its magical **Botanical Gardens**, aglow with lush, tropical plants and flowers, and completely enclosed by sheer limestone cliffs. Between November and May, you can swim into an illuminated subterranean cave, leading through to a lagoon fed by a waterfall plummetting down from the mountain. During the rainy season, the gardens are at their most splendid, but the emerald-green waters turn muddy-brown, and swimming can be dangerous. Thais arrive in force at weekends (not a good time to come), but the park is generally quiet during the week.

The jungle hermitage of **Wat Tham Seua** is one of the most famous forest *wats* in South Thailand. Here a community of 120 monks and 130 nuns live a spartan, meditative life in a picturesque setting of ancient caves and dense jungle within a secluded mountain valley. The abbot here, a Thai monk called Achaan Jamnien, was prompted to build this temple by a 'heavenly message' to the effect that Krabi was, in olden times, a self-contained island of great spiritual power. Most of his monks eat just one meal a day. Some don't appear to eat at all. Achaan Jamnien's teaching places great emphasis on fasting and meditation, the aim being to cultivate deep insight into the meaning and workings of life. The bodies of local criminals and road-accident victims make their way to this temple, to help the monks who dissect them gain further 'insights'. The horrid photos of these cadavers are hung all around the *bot* as a grisly reminder to visitors of the consequences of an evil life. The *bot* itself is a low-roofed limestone cave, with a number of tiny grottos turned into monastic cells (*kutis*). These are very simple affairs, often containing just a sleeping mat, a couple of books, and a light bulb.

Walking down from the main chapel, a steep staircase appears to the left. This leads up to a high ridge overhung by massive limestone crags. Here nuns live in tiny wooden cubicles, while monks sleep out in the open, on pallet beds at the base of the mountain. Past these, a series of caves appears on the left, each wired up with wall switches to enable easy exploration. First there's the famous **Tiger Cave**—named after the stalactite-like projection from the ceiling which resembles a tiger's claw. Beyond this, you'll find **Bow Cave**, with an interior the shape of a stretched bow, and, right next door, **Eel Cave**,

217

where giant eels (with ears!) lived till some 10 years ago (low water-levels gradually led to their extinction). The plateau path leads on into the jungle, where hardcore ascetic monks live totally at one with nature in huts buried deep in the rainforest. There are two spectacular 1000-year-old sonpong trees here with massive veined trunks resembling giant ducks' feet! A couple of tips: the monks at this *wat* are not allowed to touch women, or the nuns to touch men. Second, don't embark on the (*very* arduous) climb right to the top of the karst hill (directions on map at foot of the ridge staircase) unless you're fit. It's a killer!

Ao Phra Nang

This is a wide, long bay with clean sands, calm waters and good snorkelling. During October and November, there's even some surf. **Krabi Resort** and **Marine Sports Centre** hire out windsurfers (70B an hour) and snorkelling equipment. Get a group together, and hire out a fishing boat (around 250B per day) to the offshore islands. **Koh Dang** has the best deep-sea coral diving, though you'll also find live coral formations off **Turtle Island** and (behind this) **Chicken Island**. Book your boat in advance—owners tend to hide away their outboard engines at night (so many have been stolen) and often need time to 'find' them again!

WHERE TO STAY
The upmarket **Krabi Resort**, at the top of the beach, has superior bamboo bungalows from 500B (20% discounts from June to September), which you can book at its office in Pattana Rd, Krabi town (tel 611389). Budget travellers favour its marvellous bunk-bed dormitory—for 50B, you get treated just like the rich folks, maid and porter service included! Speciality dishes at the restaurant are Steamed Fish with Soy Sauce (75B), Fillet Mignon Steak (55B) and charcoal-cooked prawns. Don't ask for boiled eggs—one guy did, and got two one-minute eggs, scrambled in a tea-cup before his very eyes! Krabi Resort runs out boat trips (250B for 1–8 people), and is building a horrid new concrete hotel, with disco, pool, and 1000B air-con rooms, which will completely change the look of this beach.

At the bottom of the bay, **Ao Nang Villa** ('Be with Nature and Simple be with us') has bungalows from 50B (basic), 150B (with bath, shower and towels) and 190B (new luxury jobs, with concrete floors and Western toilets). Boat trips, motorbike rental, and okay restaurant. Boats over to Pai Plong and Ao Son can be hired here. **Princess Garden**, just up the hill-road behind Ao Nang Villa, is a peaceful, laidback operation run by two friendly Westerners, Larry and Phil. They have the best location in the bay and bungalows here (from 45 to 100B) lie in a quiet and natural woodland setting. Good bar cum restaurant, mellow sounds, and bags of atmosphere. Recommended.

Ao Son

Another nice spot. There are two beaches here, one either side of a tiny promontory circumvented by soaring limestone cliffs. The main beach has **Princess Cave**, a large cleft in the base of one of these mountains. At the start of each fishing season, local men carve wooden *lingams* (phalli) and present them to the resident spirit-goddess. Accord-

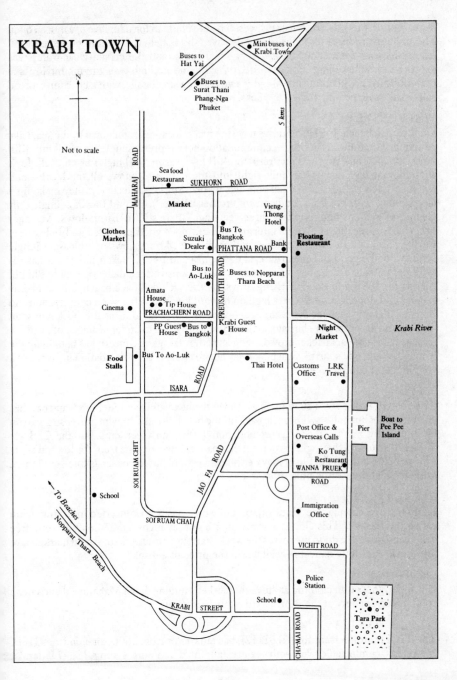

KRABI TOWN

N

Not to scale

Mini buses to
Krabi Town

Buses to
Hat Yai

Buses to
Surat Thani
Phang-Nga
Phuket

5 kms

MAHARAJ ROAD

Sea food
Restaurant

SUKHORN ROAD

Market

Vieng-
Thong
Hotel

Clothes
Market

Suzuki
Dealer

Bus To
Bangkok

PHATTANA ROAD

Bank

Floating
Restaurant

Bus to
Ao-Luk

Buses to Nopparat
Thara Beach

Amata
House

Tip House

PRACHACHERN ROAD

Cinema

PREUSAUTHI ROAD

Krabi Guest
House

PP Guest
House

Bus to
Bangkok

Night
Market

Krabi River

Food
Stalls

Bus To Ao-Luk

ISARA ROAD

Thai Hotel

Customs
Office

LRK
Travel

SOI RUAM CHIT

JAO FA ROAD

Post Office &
Overseas Calls

Pier

Boat to
Pee Pee
Island

Ko Tung
Restaurant

WANNA PRUEK ROAD

School

SOI RUAM CHAI

Immigration
Office

VICHIT ROAD

To Beaches

Nopparat Thara Beach

Police
Station

School

CHA-MAI ROAD

KRABI STREET

Tara Park

219

ing to legend, this was a heavenly princess who took human form for love of a mortal man. She died giving birth to his child in this cave, and is believed to have protected local fishermen ever since. Ao Son is a very scenic spot, and the crystal-clear waters are excellent for snorkelling. For exercise, try a 1½-hour climb over the mountain (take directions from Cliff Bungalows)—this ends up at a small gully, with a charming inland salt-water lake, prettily ringed by rocks.

WHERE TO STAY

On the main beach, **Joy Bungalows** have the nicest location, right down by the sea. Like all other operations at Ao Son, accommodation here is pretty simple—a small hut, with mosquito-net, oil-lamp and mattress, for 40B low season, 60B high season. Rafi, Joy's friendly manager, has a bar built right into the cliff, and knows all the local island legends. Each island, as he'll tell you, has its own spirit—collectively, they make up a large family /e.g. Phi Phi islands mean 'brother brother'). Behind Joy, in a jungle only cleared of pythons and monkeys three years ago, there's **Cliff Bungalows**. Manager Preecha is a reliable source of information, and does good pancakes and bolognese. Further back is the **Pine** operation, with well-spaced bungalows in a pleasant jungle setting. Food is good and cheap here, and Pine's boat trips to Chicken and Turtle islands (50B per person) are the best value in the bay. They also offer a daily trip over to Phi Phi islands for 100B a head. **Gift Bungalows**, on the secluded back beach, attract mainly hippies and dopeheads—it's very high on tranquillity, and very low on conversation. Ao Son has a few seasonal disadvantages—vicious sandfleas during the post-monsoon months and severe water shortage in the dry season. It's also under sentence of death, at least as far as the backpacker crowd is concerned. A Bangkok concern has bought up the whole bay, and will soon be sweeping away all the cheapie accommodation in favour of a yuppie resort complex.

Pai Plong

This relaxed little cove, a 20-minute walk over the headland from Ao Phra Nang bay, has just one set of bungalows. These lie back off the beach in a shady palm grove, and are run by a friendly family. Basic accommodation (70B), no electricity, but the 25B set dinners—usually fish caught fresh from the sea—get rave reports from the few travellers who've made it here. Pai Plong may be short on action, but the beach is fine—and there are often sightings of dolphin offshore.

RECREATION

Krabi has one cinema, the **Maharaj**, part of which has been converted into a nightclub called the **Resort**. This club is a scene on a Saturday night (admission 60B, one free drink) and dead as a dodo the rest of the week. Various bars around the night market have live music and dotty dancers—well worth the price of a drink!

SHOPPING

Cheap, bright cotton clothing at the night market, running down Maharaj Rd and cheap coral/shell jewellery at the nearby **Nid Souvenir Shop**.

WHERE TO STAY

The **Thai Hotel**, 3 Isara Rd (tel 61112), has fan rooms from 160B, air-con from 315B. It's a clean, comfortable place with a fair restaurant. The **Vieng Thong**, 155–7 Uttarakit

Rd (tel 611288), is a reasonable fall-back, with fan rooms from 120B, air-con for 240B. The **New Hotel**, Phattana Rd (tel 611545), is an old hotel, with 120B fan-cooled rooms only.

The cheap **Pee Pee Guest House**, 31 Prachachoen Rd (tel 612155), is going all out to provide a complete travellers' service—sightseeing tours, same-day laundry service, efficient travel agency, economical rooms from 50 to 80B, and a 30B dormitory. Jate, the friendly manager, promises forthcoming attractions of 'American breakfast and video'. He's doing great business, and is opening his 'Pee Pee 2' guest house (Pattana Rd) for the 1988 season. Also the nearby **Krabi Guest House**, in Isra Rd, is a reasonable alternative, with 80B rooms and travel service. The best deal of all though, is **Rong's** at 17 Maharaj Rd, a short five-minute stroll out of town. 'Absolutely Worth a Walk' is its motto, and it is. Run by a gentlemanly local science teacher, this is an incredibly clean and relaxing place, with jungle-setting, twin-bedded rooms for 90B, communal kitchen (you can cook your own food) and tiled bathroom, free bicycles, and homely family-style atmosphere. Recommended.

EATING OUT

Thai Hotel's **Parkway Cafe** is tops for Western cuisine (especially the 60B 'Sizzling Sirloin Steak') and offers soothing live music from 12 noon to 2 pm, from 8 pm to 1.30 am. For seafood, locals rave about **Kotung** restaurant, down by the pier—things to try here include *tom yam kung*, crab balls, and fresh prawns. Cheap Thai snacks and great fruit are sold down at the night market. Krabi town is full of 'tourist informatiuon centres' which are really ice-cream parlours or breakfast places. **Amata House** doesn't have any information at all, but does amazing lassis and yoghurts. Beer is cheap here, and it's a popular late-night hangout, complete with coconut-shell lighting and Dr Zhivago-like classical sounds. Over the road, **Tip House** has scrumptious cakes and ice-creams, and the best continental breakfast in town.

KOH PHI PHI

The twin enchanted islands of Phi Phi Don and Phi Phi Ley lie 40 km offshore from Krabi, in the Andaman Sea. Beautiful beaches, colourful marine life, banks of coral reef and magnificent scenery combine to make Phi Phi just about the best thing in the south of Thailand. Gliding in by boat, escorted by schools of flying fish and dolphin, is like arriving on Treasure Island! Phi Phi Don, famous for its stunning white-sand beaches and excellent snorkelling, is relatively flat. Most of this island is national park territory, so all bungalow accommodation is centred round Ton Sai and Lo Da Ram, the twin crescent bays of the narrow isthmus which connect the two main lands. Phi Phi Ley, the smaller island, is mainly sheer cliffs, inhabited only by the flocks of long-tailed swallows who live on their heights. A few courageous locals regularly risk death climbing precari-ous bamboo ladders to collect birds' nests. The nests of Phi Phi Ley are highly prized for their medicinal qualities, and sell to Chinese restaurants in Thailand, Singapore, Hong Kong and Europe for quite fantastic prices. The Chinese believe that because Phi Phi swallows live at such high altitudes, they can 'drink water from the sky'. When the birds expel (vomit) this heavenly elixir, it's in the form of near-translucent noodles ('king food' to the Chinese) which hardens when exposed to air, to form the nests. The best nests are made from the high-grade white vomit of young birds (yuk), and sell for up to 10,000B a kilo. Low-grade, or black vomit, nests are collected from old birds, and are very cheap. They are apparently good for little else except curing 'loss of appetite'!

Phi Phi has just been discovered by tourism—12 new bungalow operations set up shop in 1987 alone! And every weekend, boatloads of Japanese tourists from Phuket hit the beaches. During the high season (January to March) shortages of food, water and accommodation often mean having to sleep on the beach, bathe in the sea, and live on bananas and coconuts! The best months to come, if you don't mind a little rain, are October and November.

A good alternative to Phi Phi, especially during the overcrowded high season, is nearby **Jum Island**. Good beaches, nice scenery, and, most importantly, hardly any people. The clean, friendly **Jum Island Resort** has bungalows from 50 to 250B, many of them with scenic views. To book, contact Pee Pee Guest House, Krabi town.

GETTING THERE
Boats start running out to Phi Phi from Krabi town in early October. From Krabi town, boats run out to Phi Phi islands from early October through to May. Boats leave between 9 am and 9.30 pm, depending on the tide. They are often full, so you're well advised to advance-book. The 2½-hour trip costs 100B, and tickets are sold at Pee Pee Guest House, Krabi Tours and Travel, and Pee Pee Marine Travel. Marine Travel, near Thai Farmers Bank, offers the best deal—they book you onto a larger boat, with life jackets, lots of room, and insurance for all passengers.

From Phi Phi Don, boats back to Krabi leave from the Cabana pier and from Gift 2 bungalows. Boats to Phuket (at least two daily) leave from the Cabana pier on the Don.

WHAT TO SEE
The big thing to do on Phi Phi is the boat-trip round the islands. For many, this is the highlight of their whole Thailand holiday. Various bungalow operations—notably Andaman and Pee Pee Resort—offer half and full-day boat excursions, and charge 70 or 100B per person. Bring your own snorkelling gear for this trip—equipment supplied is poor. You'll also need your camera, and lots of film. The scenery is out of this world!

From the Don, boats go over to Phi Phi Ley and drop in on its **Viking Cave**—a huge indoor amphitheatre of surreal limestone pillars and plateaus. The cave-drawings of 'Viking ships' are actually quite recent daubings of Portuguese galleons and Chinese junks. Knowing this makes it far easier to refuse the 10B 'admission charge' scam operated by local youths! Hugging the base of soaring cliffs, their sheer faces dripping with limestone cascades, boats move on to **Maya Bay**, a beautifully secluded lagoon with excellent live coral. There's a stop for swimming and snorkelling here, then it's back to Phi Phi Don for **Shark Point**—where you can really swim with the shark! Don't worry—these are small black-finned Leopard Shark, which live mainly on crab, not tourists! At the top of the Don, beyond the sea-gypsy village at **Laem Tong**, you'll come to **Bamboo Island**. This is the best undersea location at Phi Phi. The water's so clear here, you need only lean over the side of the boat for a magical introduction to a wonderland of technicolour coral and exotic fish.

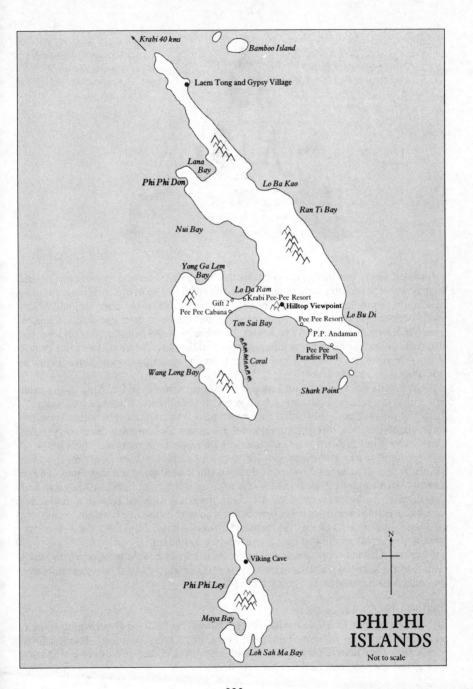

Krabi 40 kms

Bamboo Island

Laem Tong and Gypsy Village

Lana
Bay

Phi Phi Don

Lo Ba Kao

Ran Ti Bay

Nui Bay

Yong Ga Lem
Bay

Lo Da Ram

Krabi Pee-Pee Resort

Gift 2

Pee Pee Cabana

Hilltop Viewpoint

Lo Bu Di

Ton Sai Bay

Pee Pee Resort

P.P. Andaman

Coral

Pee Pee
Paradise Pearl

Wang Long Bay

Shark Point

Viking Cave

Phi Phi Ley

Maya Bay

Loh Sah Ma Bay

N

PHI PHI
ISLANDS

Not to scale

223

Back on Don, you can stroll down to the bottom of Tonsai Bay—below Cabana bungalows—for superb snorkelling. There is over a kilometre of live coral here, running right up to the mouth of the bay. Look out for barracuda, pike, moray eel and (don't touch!) sea-snake. Snorkelling equipment can be hired out from Pee-Pee Cabana or from Mr Jerry just below Pee-Pee Resort. Jerry charges 40B a day for snorkel hire. He also rents out rather tacky scuba equipment at 1500B a day. Better scuba-diving gear is obtainable from the Swedish guy up at Lemhin bungalows, just above Pee-Pee Andaman.

Most people are content with lazing on the silvery sands, and bathing in the calm emerald-green waters. But some wind down with a traditional Thai beach massage. A delightful no-nonsense lady called Suparporn patrols up and down between Andaman and Cabana beaches, offering superior rubdowns for 50B an hour. 'But no Number Ones!', she firmly informs male customers, 'I am respectable married lady!'

A recommended early-morning walk is up to the hilltop **Viewpoint** on the Don mainland. It's an arduous 40-minute climb so you'll need good walking shoes. You're also advised to acquire a local guide—the path up starts from between Andaman and Pee-Pee Resort, but it's easy to get lost! Our bungalow supplied us with a diminutive local lad, wearing enormous wellington boots, who took us up for 5B a head. At the top, enjoy spectacular views down over the twin half-moon bays of the Don. On a clear day, you can see across to Phi Phi Ley, and even over to Phuket.

From the Cabana pier, motorized longboats transport people from beach to beach (10B a trip). Near the Cabana, there's the island's single supply shop—the only place that sells Mekong whisky and mosquito repellent!

WHERE TO STAY
In Ton Sai bay, **Pee Pee Cabana** has the best bungalows (nice 4-person bamboo huts at 500B) but the worst location, right next to the busy, noisy boat jetty. It has a huge restaurant—the **Maya Kitchen**. The Cabana also offers 'choice of Western and oriental toilets' and the food and facilities here are fine.

224

The back bay, behind Cabana, is less clean than Tonsai, but quieter. Stay here at **Gift 2** (basic 50B sheds) or **Krabi Pee Pee Resort** (tasteful, well-spaced bungalows at 500–600B). A new operation, **Charlie's**, has smart, well-appointed bungalows from 100B (no bath, no views, but quiet!) To 300B (with bath, right on the beach).

Further up Ton Sai Bay (a boat-ride from Cabana, or a 15-minute hike east up the beach from the pier) are currently the Don's two best operations. **Pee Pee Resort** is new, clean and friendly, with 100B bungalows (concrete floored!) right on the beach, and 80B ones set back from it. **Andaman Inn** is the pioneer outfit, and still owns much of the land on the Don. Bungalows here are 60B to 150B, and face onto a lovely stretch of beach. Andaman has good food and atmosphere, and is extremely popular. Beyond it—a 20-minute walk over the cliffs—there's Long Beach. This has the best swimming on the island—at low tide, it's the only beach where bathers aren't left stranded in the shallows! Stay at **Paradise Pearl** bungalows—these are 90B to 150B (low season) and have good bathrooms. The Pearl's restaurant is a favourite evening hangout spot, and does marvellous seafood.

HAT YAI

Hat Yai, the dynamic commercial and entertainment centre of the Deep South, started life as a tiny railway junction a few kilometres inside Thailand from the Malay border. Packed full of nightclubs, restaurants, massage parlours, gambling dens and vibrant bazaars, its cheap shopping and wild nightlife now attract over half a million tourists each year—most of them Malaysians who see Hat Yai as the 'one and only fun town' between Bangkok (1298 km north) and Singapore. The town's border situation makes it a real melting-pot of different peoples—mainly Thai, Malay and Chinese—any one of which will be holding a boisterous, colourful street festival any day of the week. Despite frenetic and noisy traffic, Hat Yai is a clean place with a contagiously optimistic atmosphere. Foreign visitors passing through on their way north from Malaysia, or hopping over the border to nearby Pedang Besar to obtain visa extensions for Thailand, often come for the day—and end up staying a week! Hat Yai is also a useful base from which to jump off to nearby Songkhla (a good day-trip), or to other southern centres such as Krabi, Phuket and Koh Samui.

If you're into spectator sports, time your visit for one of Hat Yai's famous Bullfighting Contests. These take place on the first Sunday of every month—between 10.30 am and 6 pm—at the old Stadium on Suppasarn Rangsan Rd, near the Prince of Songkhla University. This is a fun event, with bull fighting bull (there is no matador involved) until one retires to fight another day. You pay 50B per fight, or 200B to stay all day.

GETTING THERE

By Air
Thai Airways fly to Hat Yai from Bangkok twice daily (except Monday, one flight only). The fare is 1760B, and the flight time is 1 hour 15 minutes. You can also fly to Hat Yai from Phuket.

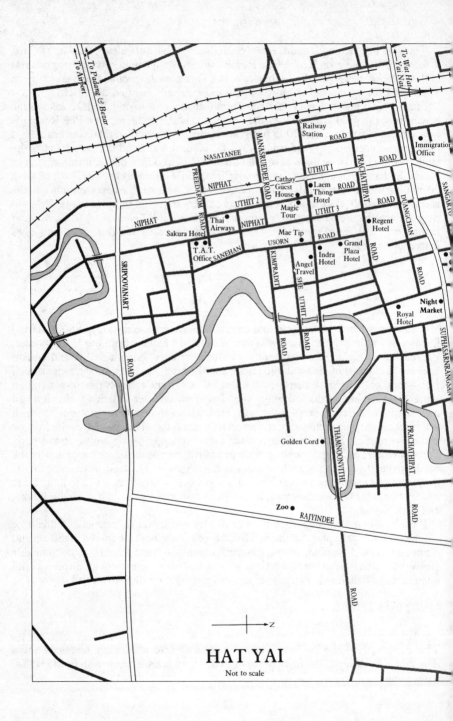

HAT YAI

Not to scale

Hospital

Mosque

MONTRI 1 ROAD

MONTRI 2 ROAD

POONSUWAN ROAD

PRATHAN UTHIT ROAD

Night Market & Bus Station

Plaza Cinema

Arch Travel & Tour

President Hotel

SOI

Boxing Stadium

NIPHAT

SONGKHRAO

Buses & Taxis to Songhkla

Post Office

Stadium

SANG SRI ROAD

Klong Toey

PHETKASEM ROAD

JOOTEEANUSORN

ROAD

Shopping Centre

JB Hotel

ROAD

My House Hotel

Bull Fighting Arena

Golf Course

D

By Rail
Four trains daily from Bangkok's Hualamphong station—two Rapid (leaving 12.30 pm and 4 pm, arriving Hat Yai 4.15 am and 8.50 am), and two Express (leaving 2 pm and 3.15 pm, arriving 5.48 am and 8.50 am). Basic fares are 664B 1st class (Express trains only), 313B 2nd class, and 149B 3rd class.

From Surat Thani, trains leave for Hat Yai at 11.13 pm, 00.36 am, 1.52 am and 3.20 am. The short 5-hour journey is comfortable enough in 3rd class (75B).

From Hat Yai to Bangkok (via Surat Thani), there are three trains daily, at 2.08 pm, 2.47 pm and 4.40 pm.

By Bus
From Bangkok's Southern Terminal, air-con buses leave for Hat Yai every 15 minutes between 5.30 pm and 8.15 pm. The fare is 339B, and it's a crippling 14-hour journey. If you're really into suffering, catch one of the two daily non air-con buses (9.45 pm and 11.50 pm) which charge only 187B, but take 1–2 hours longer.

From Koh Samui (via Surat Thani), a 210B ferry/minibus ticket from Songserm travel agency in Na Thon will get you to Hat Yai in just 7 hours.

From Songkhla, green buses run to Hat Yai every 15 minutes from the rank below the clock tower; or you can pick them up (taxis too) from the Municipal Market. The fare is 7B.

From Hat Yai, non air-con buses leave for Krabi (6 hours, 60B) and Phuket (9 hours, 90B), from opposite the Plaza Hotel. Timings are 5.45 am, 7.45 am, 8.45 am and 10 am daily. Air-con buses for Krabi (5 hours) and Phuket (6½ hours) leave at 8 am and 9.30 am from Hat Yai bus terminal (buy tickets here between 7 am and 4 pm daily, or from a travel agent). The fare is 150B to either destination.

NOTE: The small town of **Phattalung** appears 2 hours out of Hat Yai, on the bus route to Krabi/Phuket (22B). Unless you speak Thai, this is rather a problem place. Travellers come here for the pleasant boat-trip round the lake, and for the tour of the famous caves, but trying to arrange them (or any onward transport) can be a real hassle. Stop off by all means, but if you don't like it, hop on the next bus to Phuket, Hat Yai or Surat Thani from the stop at the post office. If you do like it, and decide to stay overnight, try the **Hotel Thai**—this has clean if overpriced double rooms at 160B.

Visa Renewals – Pedang Besar
Travellers with double-entry Thailand visas visit Pedang Besar, just inside Malaysia, to start off the second half of the visa. Buses run there from Hat Yai bus station, the journey taking one hour (fare 15B). From Bangkok, there's one train daily—the 3.15 pm Express—which carries on beyond Hat Yai to Pedang Besar, arriving here at 8 am. You can pick this train up at 7.20 am, from Hat Yai Junction station. From the Customs Point at Pedang Besar (ask to be put off the bus here), it's a 10-minute walk over the border to Malaysian Immigration. Get your passport stamped both *in* and *out* (two separate desks), and then stroll back into Thailand for another 30 or 60 days stay.

TOURIST INFORMATION
TAT Tourist Office, 1/1 Soi 2 Niphat Uthit 3 Rd (tel 243747), is a friendly, efficient outfit—open from 8.30 am to 4.30 pm daily. Thai Airways (tel 243711) is opposite the Pacific Hotel in Niphat Uthit 2 Road.

Travel agents—useful for transport to Bangkok, Krabi/Phuket, and Koh Samui, include **Magic Tour**, c/o Cathay Guest House (tel 243815) and **Angel Travel Service**, 127 Thamnoonvithi Rd (tel 236184). Both are reliable, and also help with local sightseeing.

WHAT TO SEE
People come to Hat Yai for shopping and recreation, not to see sights. If the two suggested tours aren't enough, there's a pleasant walk down by the riverside to the south of town. Start at the bridge in Thamnoonvithi Rd, and follow the road looping south-west, until you re-enter town at the bridge leading up Niphat Uthit 3 Raod. The river's a bit putrid, but there's much local colour—cows and kids, villages and farms—worth photographing.

Most in-town action—especially at night—centres round Niphat Uthit 1, 2 and 3, and their intersecting roads. Most people get around by foot, but there are *songthaews* if you need them. Their standard charge is 4B.

Wat Hat Yai Nai
(by *songthaew*, 2–3 hours)

This *wat* is located a few kilometres out of town, down Soi 26 Phetkasem Rd. *Songthaews* go there from the town centre for a 5B fare. **Wat Hat Yai Nai** is a real curiosity—there's an enormous reclining Buddha here, recently restored and wearing a big ruby-lipped smile, which mesures 35 metres long, 15 metres high, and 10 metres wide. Beneath it is the subterranean mausoleum cum souvenir shop, where a wily old monk lassoes tourists with wrist cords and invites donations. Elsewhere in the compound, there are many other ways of spending money and making merit—including 8B coconuts and 10B tiles for the new *bot* roof (while stocks last). There's a wonderfully tacky 'merry-go-round' of plaster monks with begging bowls, and an ebullient community of real monks who pounce on *farang* visitors with joyful cries of 'Hey, you!' This is a temple with a difference—lots of jollity and good energy.

Thai Southern Cultural Village
(by *songthaew*; half-day)

This is a fairly typical Thai attempt at 'packaged culture', rather similar to Bangkok's Rose Garden Resort. The 'village' is a large picnic park, with a small zoo (disgruntled eagles, green monkeys, exotic birds etc), located some 3 km northeast of Hat Yai. The culture shows run between 4 pm and 5.30 pm Wednesday to Sunday, and the cost of admission (140B, bookable from several travel agencies in town) should include trans-port there and back. If for any reason it doesn't, you'll have to fork out 20B each way for a *songthaew*. The show ties together a number of things—fingernail dances, wedding ceremonies, Thai boxing, sword-fighting etc.—which, if in the south for only a short time, you might not otherwise see. A couple of turns, like the coconut-shell dance and the cock-fighting, are worth getting a front seat for.

NIGHTLIFE
Hat Yai is a city of the night. After dark, the whole town is one huge, bustling bazaar, overladen with the heady aromas of fragrant frangipani, sizzling *kai yang*, and *tuk-tuk*

exhaust fumes. Stalls around the Regent Hotel and Uthit 3 Road are still serving the south's most delectable street food at 1 am. Night-time Hat Yai is also a continual round of nightclubs, coffee shops, bars, bowling alleys, video houses and cinemas and discos. Every large hotel has its 'Ancient Massage' parlour, usually packed out with rich Malays. For a good straight massage, you're probably safest at the Indra and Sakura hotels, which charge a reasonable 100B an hour. There are several places offering good live music and early-evening cocktails. the **J. B. Hotel** is a goodie—expensive drinks (100B), but a great disco and restaurant. The **My House Hotel**, on the road leading out to Songkhla, has the best live singers (plus popular cocktail lounge), and the **Washington Cafe**, attached to King's Hotel, is a good safe place for the unattached male on the loose—with no-hassle hostesses and live music till 1 am. If you can get a group together, make a night of it at the **Hollywood Nightclub**, opposite Angel Travel in Thamnoonvithi Road. This has a large dance floor, exciting laser show, live band (playing good American copy songs) and a hot DJ pumping out the best in current Thai rap music. Drinks are a bit pricey, but it's fun. Like many similar clubs, the Hollywood opens at 9 pm and rocks on until midnight during the week, and until 1 am on Fridays, Saturdays and Sundays.

The **Post Laser Disc**, opposite the Hollywood, provides more sedate entertainment—this is a cosy little video parlour, showing a selection of popular English-language films from 12 noon to 2 am daily. It is a perfect escape from the heat and traffic, and serves beer and snacks. A few cinemas—the **Siam** and **Hat Yai Ram** in Phetkasem Rd, the **Charloem Thai** in Suppasanrangsan Rd, and the **Colisium** in Prachatipat Rd— have 'original soundtrack rooms' where you can view films in English before they're dubbed over for Thai audiences.

SHOPPING
Full of cheap goods smuggled in from Singapore, Hat Yai has been dubbed the 'poor man's Hong Kong'. At the large **Santisuk Market**, well known as the biggest open black market in Thailand, you can find videos, watches, radios and hi-fi equipment at knock-down prices—e.g. a high-grade portable stereo cassette player, with detachable speakers, for just 1000B! There's also a busy trade in leatherware, batik fabrics, dress materials and numerous other low-priced export or imported goods.

The large shopping area opposite the Chalerm Thai cinema, at the top of Niphat Uthit 2 Rd, is widely considered the best market for fashion clothes in the country—shirts from 60B, summery dresses from 150B—especially if you go hunting amongst the many footpath stalls after dark. For specific electronic bargains—cheap cameras, personal stereos, TVs—try the row of shops alongside the Jomdi Hotel in Niphat Uthit 3. General shopping is good at the **Diana** department store.

WHERE TO STAY
There are dozens of high-class hotels, mostly catering to rich Malaysians and Singaporeans. If coming for the weekend, you'll need to advance-book.

The **J. B. Hotel**, 99 Jootee-Anusorn Rd (tel 244728; tx 62113 JBH TL) is Hat Yai's finest, with all 5-star comforts and air-con rooms from only 567B. Two other good bets in the top range are the **Regent**, 23 Prachathipat Rd (tel 245454; tx 62195), with twin-bedded rooms from 751B, and the **Indra**, 94 Thamnoonvithi Rd (tel 243277), offering rooms from 506B to 1265B. The Regent has an overseas phone service, and the Indra a popular coffee-house with video and snooker. There are good mentions too, for the **Montien**, 120–124 Niphat Uthit 1 Rd (tel 245399). Rooms here start at 506B.

Moderately-priced hotels include **King's**, Niphat Uthit 1 Rd (tel 243966), **Metro**, Niphat Uthit 2 Rd (tel 244422), and **Sakol**, 47–48 Sanehusorn Rd. All three offer good twin-bedded rooms for 160B (fan) and 250B (air-con). The **Laemthong**, 46 Thamnoonvithi Rd, has 160B fan rooms only (large and clean, with bath) and boasts 'the best coffee in Brazil'. All the above offer 20% discounts on weekdays, provided you bargain for them!

The old budget favourite, the **Cathay Guest House** at the corner of Thamnoonvithi and Niphat Uthit 2 roads, has gone into steep decline. It still has a good noticeboard, and still does the cheapest beer and breakfasts in town, but rooms are dirty and way overpriced at 80B single, 120B double. Friendly staff often shout discounts if you walk away (as many do). The nearby **Prince Hotel**, 138/2–3 Thamnoonvithi Rd (tel 232496), is a much better deal—clean rooms here, with bath and balcony, for 100B single, 180B double. Often full—and for good reason—is **Angel Guest House**, 127 Thamnoonvithi Rd, offering pristine twin-bedded rooms (100B for one, 150B for two persons), and a restaurant. Staff are lovely, and Angel herself cooks the best Italian pasta in town.

EATING OUT

The local mix of Thai, Chinese, Muslim and Malay peoples results in an exciting and varied cuisine. Hat Yai is close enough to the fishing port of Songkhla to provide some pretty choice seafood too. Western-style food is on offer at numerous coffee shops, fast-food joints, and hotel restaurants.

For seafood, try **Mae Tip II** restaurant, 190 Niphat Uthit 3 Rd. Open from 10.30 am to 10 pm, this has a choice of outdoor garden or indoor air-con dining. Specialities include Songkhla steamed gray mullet with sour plum (60–90B), famous Pomfret fish with chilli, pepper or garlic (100B), and less spicy-hot dishes like roasted clam or prawn, or sweet and sour sea bass (both 40B). At the **Pata Restaurant**, c/o Kosit Hotel, 199 Niphat Uthit 2 Rd, you can select your seafood from the tank. Popular eats here are raw oysters, baked crab claws, shark fin soup and (for less than 60B) the local favourite, a spicy shrimp soup called *tom yam goong*. Also recommended is **South Thai Bird's Nest Restaurant**, diagonally opposite the Sukhonta Hotel, Sanehanusorn Rd. At this one, you can either play safe with dishes like shark fin soup (200B) or steamed/baked crab, cooked Hong Kong-style (i.e. steamed, then mixed with soya bean sauce, Chinese mushrooms and ginger), or you venture into unknown territory with steamed sea leech ('pure protein!') in red gravy. In a town like Hat Yai, where locals drink cobra blood and eat snake meat, anything goes! The South Thai is also supposed to be one of the best places to sample bird's nest soup. This is mixed in with the dark meat of 'black chicken' (a fowl only found in Hat Yai area), which is supposed to have magical health-giving properties. Diners tend to feel incredibly healthy afterwards or (as soon as they discover what bird's nests are made out of) incredibly ill.

Muslim food is good at the **O Cha**, opposite King's Hotel. Travellers wax lyrical about its superb beef curries. The **Toko Food Centre**, opposite Diana department store, offers an amazing range of fast-foods—from American burgers to Japanese tempura—on a coupon system. Similar quickie fare at the **Noodle Garden**, opposite Odean

Shopping Mall in Sanehusorn Rd. The **Best Burger**, opposite Kosit Hotel in Niphat Uthit 2, serves quality European-style food, while the **Chaw Yang Cafe**, just below Angel Guest House, does cheap Western breakfasts—and excellent *kai yang*. All in all, you're not going to starve in Hat Yai!

SONGKHLA

Once a powerful Srivijaya trading port, Songkhla is now a sleepy little resort-town with a large fishing community and a nice beach. Situated on a tiny peninsula between the Gulf of Thailand and a saltwater inland sea called Songkhla Lake, this is a relaxed mini-city (127 km from Bangkok) with Chinese Portuguese-style houses and buildings (a reflection of early settlers), a hybrid cuisine (from the present Thai-Chinese-Muslim population), a fine National Museum, and some of the best seafood in Thailand.

It's now believed by archaeologists that the area of Songkhla flourished as long ago as the 8th century AD. Both the present centres of southern civilization, Hat Yai and Songkhla, are known to be of very recent origin. The earlier centres, located in the area of Sathing Phra (40 km north of Songkhla), were forced south by commerce. This migration began as early as 1000 years ago, drifting slowly down to the tip of the peninsula at the north side of Songkhla Lake, crossing over via Ko Yo, and settling in the area of present-day Songkhla about 150 years ago. At this point, the old town of Songkhla (Singhorat) which had been founded on the Khao Dang Hill at Ko Yo (probably in the early Ayutthaya period by the Muslim Sultan Suleiman) was abandoned.

The prosperity of the province was ushered in by its first governor, a Chinese merchant called Yieng Hoa, who began his career in modest fashion, collecting birds' nests at the offshore islands of Koh Si and Koh Ha. His family held the governorship of 'new' Songhkla city for the next 129 years. During this period, the port shrugged off its earlier disreputable image as a medieval pirate stronghold and became a major trade centre—sending out mainly rubber and tin to China and India, receiving in return beautiful pottery and ceramics. Examples of these, and other priceless art works, are presently housed in Songkhla National Museum.

GETTING THERE
From Hat Yai (opposite the President Hotel), buses leave for Songkhla every half-hour or so. The 26 km journey takes 30 minutes, and the fare is 7B. If there's a group of you, it's worth getting a shared taxi (12B per person) from Hat Yai. Buses back to Hat Yai leave from Songkhla's Municipal Market, and also from below the clock tower in Ramwithi Rd.

TOURIST INFORMATION
The nearest tourist office is at Hat Yai. For local information, contact Miss Tussanee at the National Museum.

There's a useful travel agency at the Choke Dee Hotel, Vichiangchom Rd. It runs three air-con buses to Bangkok daily—fare 300B, journey time 13 hours.

WHAT TO SEE
Songkhla is a small, quiet and airy town—you can get around by foot, or pay 3B for short-distance cycle-rickshaw rides. Somnolent motorcyclists hang out at the Queen

Hotel, offering 50B return trips to the great white *chedi* on **Khao Noi Hill**, but you don't really need them. You can walk up to this ancient *chedi* (reconstructed by Rama V) in 20 minutes from the museum. Nice views at the top. From the pier below the museum, fishing boats put out to **Yoh Island**, where locals collect birds' nests for soup. Ferries also run across the river to the hill-top city of Old Songkhla, with its crumbling Ayutthayan fortress, famous Black Pagoda, and spectacular aerial views of the whole province. If you're going there, take directions from the museum curator—you'll need them!

The pleasant **Samila Beach**, with its casuarina groves and seafood restaurants, is a 10B *songthaew* ride from the town centre. There's a famous mermaid on the point, and from the white-sand beach you can look over to offshore **Cat and Mouse Islands**, named after their respective shapes. Swimming is rather poor, but there are water-skis, sailboats, catamarans and surfboards for hire below the Samila Hotel. Weekends are busy at Samila beach—this is when the Thais come for picnics. Back in town, the **Waterfront** is worth a visit—this is where all the fishing boats unload their catches, and it's a constant hum of activity. The air hums a bit too—visitors don't linger long here. Walking away from the waterfront, down Nakhorn North Rd, there are many old Chinese, Portuguese and Muslim buildings to be seen. This street retains a lot of original Songkhla architecture.

National Museum – Wat Machimawat
(on foot, by *songthaew*; half day)

The entrance to the **National Museum** is opposite the Queen Hotel. Traiburi Rd. Admission is 10B, and it's open 8.30 am to 4 pm Wednesday to Sunday. Miss Tussanee, the charming curator, speaks good English and is a mine of local information.

Converted from the Old Governor's Palace built in 1878, the museum is an elegant Chinese mansion housing a fabulous collection of Chinese and Thai art treasures—handcarved doors and screens, lacquered furniture (with mother of pearl inlay), Sino-Thai *Bencharong* (five colours) pottery etc. Upstairs, there is King Mongkut's bed, a fine black-stone Vishnu recovered from Sathing Phra, and a Burmese-style Buddha sunning itself on the balcony. Elsewhere, interesting displays of shadow puppets, wooden lintels, abbots' pulpits and garudas. Also, a Dutch cannon, a brace of WWII bicycles (donated by local policemen) and some wooden-dog coconut grinders. The museum has exhibits from all seven provinces of southern Thailand, and is well-labelled in English throughout.

Wat Matchimawat is off Saiburi Rd, to the south of town—a 6B *songthaew* ride from the museum. This is the oldest and the most important *wat* in Songkhla. The *bot* is modelled on that at Wat Phra Keo (Bangkok) and contains beautiful murals, depicting lively scenes of 19th-century Songkhla life and various *jakarta* stories. The venerated marble Buddha within the chapel is 150 years old, and was commissioned by Rama III. If it's closed to view (as it often is) ask the abbot for permission to enter. The outer verandahs of the *bot* are adorned with stone bas-reliefs illustrating the *Romance of the Three Kingdoms*, a famous Chinese epic. In the temple compound, you'll come across the quaint little 'Hermit's Pavilion' (Sala Rishi) commissioned by Rama IV. Murals showing the *rishis* in various yogic postures run round the upper parts of the ceiling and walls. The

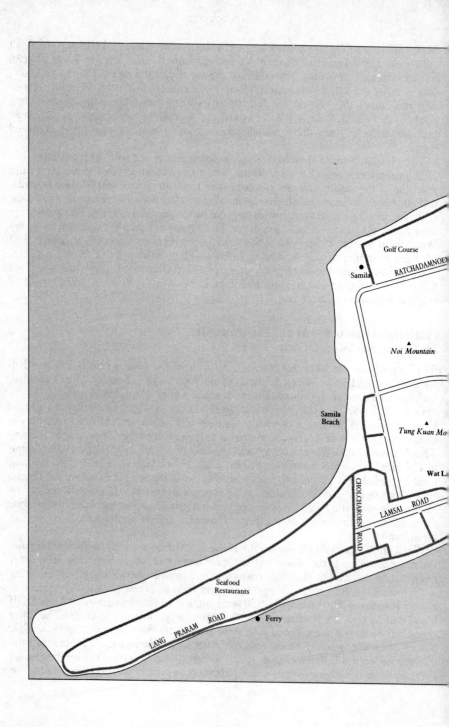

Golf Course

Samila

RATCHADAMNOE

Noi Mountain

Samila
Beach

Tung Kuan Mo

Wat L

CHOLCHAROEN ROAD

LAMSAI ROAD

Seafood
Restaurants

LANG PRARAM ROAD

Ferry

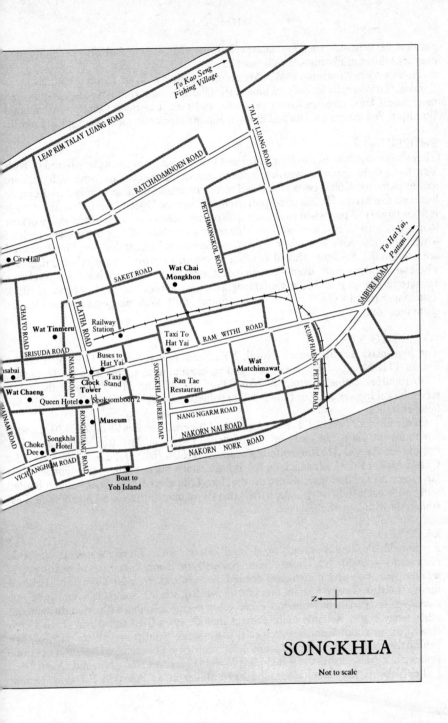

To Kao Seng
Fishing Village

LEAP RIM TALAY LUANG ROAD

RATCHADAMNOEN ROAD

TALAY LUANG ROAD

PETCHMONGKOL ROAD

To Hat Yai,
Pattani

City Hall

SAKET ROAD

Wat Chai
Mongkhon

SAIBURI ROAD

CHAIYO ROAD

PLATHA ROAD

Wat Tinmeru

Railway
Station

Taxi To
Hat Yai

RAM WITHI ROAD

KUMP HAENG PETCH ROAD

SRISUDA ROAD

NASAN ROAD

Buses to
Hat Yai

Wat
Matchimawat

sabai

Clock
Tower

Taxi
Stand

SONGKHLABUREE ROAD

Ran Tae
Restaurant

Wat Chaeng

Queen Hotel

Spoksomboon 2

MAINAM ROAD

Museum

NANG NGARM ROAD

NAKORN NAI ROAD

RONGMUANG ROAD

Choke
Dee

Songkhla
Hotel

NAKORN   NORK   ROAD

VICHIANGHOM ROAD

Boat to
Yoh Island

Z

SONGKHLA

Not to scale

pavilion was originally used for massage. Now, as often as not, local Thai youths use it to play superbowl mini-snooker with marbles.

There's a small museum at Wat Matchimawat, open 8.30 am to 4 pm Wednesday to Sunday. Various exhibits here include early Thai stone and stucco pieces, gas-powered mechanical fans, rare *bencharong* ceramics, and even a couple of diminutive emerald Buddhas. Few pieces are labelled though, and the monk curator doesn't speak English.

SHOPPING

There's not much to buy in Songkhla itself (except fish), but the nearby island of **Koh Yaw** has a thriving cotton-weaving industry producing distinctive fabrics with intricate woven patterns. Koh Yaw is connected to the mainland by a new bridge, and orange buses go there (fare 5B, last one 5 pm) from opposite the Queen Hotel. Best time to visit is from 10 am to 3 pm, when you can drop in on the weavers—mainly young girls working looms made from ex-bicycles! The 'village' is a combine of several families, each of which produces Koh Yaw fabric (*Phaa Kaw Yaw*) in individual designs. The dyes used are quite dark, and gold thread is often woven in to provide light relief. Prices are wholesale, and generally fixed—but there is some leeway for bargaining. Nice purchases are sarong-size (6 ft × 3 ft) material lengths, with complex 'tapestry' designs, at 100B. The longer lengths (12 ft × 3 ft) go for around 160B. Wall-hangings and hankies are quite nice too.

WHERE TO STAY

The high-class **Samila Beach Hotel**, 1 Ratchadamnoen Rd (tel 31130–4; tx 64204 Samila TH), has good beach location, golf course and pool, rooms from 600B (single), 700B (double). Some apartments (Nos. 111–113, 211, and 311–312) have the beach views. Novel topiary gardens ('the result of painstaking tree-bendings') are opposite the hotel entrance.

Of the cheaper hotels, I'd recommend the **Queen**, 20 Saiburi Rd (tel 313072), with fan rooms at 120B, and air-con rooms (with TV) from 280B; or the **Sansabai**, 1 Petchkeree Rd (tel 311106), offering rooms for 150B (fan) and 220B (air-con). The **Choke Dee**, 14–19 Vichiangchom Rd, is rather noisy but has quiet and adequate 120B fan rooms on the 2nd floor. Close by, the **Songkhla** gives free soap, towel and bottled water with each 90B room, and is friendly. Adjoining it, there's a homely little Thai restaurant with lots of character.

EATING OUT

Try Songkhla's famous seafood up at Samila Beach. Here, there are several beachside restaurants—notably **Na Tham** ('Seven Sisters') and **Boonriam**. Both places do excellent *tom yum* soup with prawns and curried fried crab, at around 100B a head. In town, there's the **Ran Tae** restaurant on Nakhon Nai Rd, serving Songkhla's renowned *yum mamuang*—a salad made from thin-sliced green mango, blended with dried shrimps and other tangy items. Reliable main courses include spicy fried squid and curried crab claws. Just as good, according to locals, is the small **Buatip** at 59 Petchkiri Rd, just behind the market. This is noted for its delicious fried sea bass and *sukiyaki* and has some wonderful novelty dishes too—including Walking Deer on Hot Chili, and Deep-Fried Fishes Balls. A few doors along, the **Fern Baker** at 53 Petchkiri Rd, does yummy chocolate cake, coconut macaroons, and cheap American breakfasts. Like the Buatip, it shuts around 9 pm—many local people have to get up very early to go fishing. If you want late-night drinks, there's a cheap open-air restaurant—supplying cheap beer and Thai food till midnight—down Jana Rd, near Queen Hotel. During the day, cheap Thai-Chinese-Muslim fare can be found at the large, interesting town market off Vichiang-chom Rd.

LANGUAGE

In a country like Thailand, where little English is spoken (except in Bangkok and major tourist centres) it makes sense to pick up some of the local language. With a small stock of Thai phrases under your belt, shopping, bargaining, getting round town, and ordering meals suddenly becomes a lot easier. For their part, the Thais are often keen to learn English—especially young students and monks. Walk into any school or temple-university campus, and you'll soon be joined by someone wanting to share a language lesson. For a crash-course in learning Thai, take a long-distance bus journey to somewhere remote like the Northeast. Local buses and 3rd class trains are excellent places for making Thai friends, and for learning the local lingo. As soon as you begin passing round photos of your family, friends and home-town (the perfect way to overcome the language barrier), you'll find a whole busload of people dying to make your acquaintance. In these circumstances, learning to speak Thai is quick, painless and lots of fun!

The Thai language resembles Chinese in that it is tonal, monosyllabic and uninflected. The spoken language has five different tones (mid, high, low, rising and falling), so that any transcription from Thai into romanized alphabets can only be approximate. The written language is something else again—the general traveller simply won't have time to grapple with its complexities! Most visitors are simply grateful that road signs and restaurant menus are often written in English as well as Thai script.

Acquiring a basic vocabulary of Thai can be surprisingly easy—not only do verbs have no tense, but most of the words that you need comprise just one syllable. Many of them sound the same too (e.g. *mai, bai, yai, chai, sai* and *rai*), and can be strung together to produce simple sentences. To avoid the potential minefield of tonal variations (every syllable, depending on how it's pronounced, can have five different meanings!) it's best to say everything in a neutral monotone. The one big exception to this is the word *soway*. Pronounced with rising-tone emphasis (*so-WAY!*), this is a popular compliment mean-

238

ing 'beautiful'. Saying it with down-tone emphasis however, can go down like a lead balloon—you've just wished someone bad luck!

Polite speech requires the addition of the word *kup* (for men) or *ka* (for women) to the end of every sentence. It shows respect for the listener, and is the commonest way of expressing agreement or understanding. The all-purpose word for 'you' is *khun*, while 'I/me' is *pom* (for men) or *Dee-chan* (for women). The word *khun* can also stand for 'person(s)' or 'Mr' (e.g. *saam khun* = three people; *Khun John* = Mr John).

You'll soon notice, when speaking to Thais, their difficulty pronouncing the letter 'r'. It often comes out as 'l'. Thus, *aroi* often becomes *aloi*, and you may be better understood saying you come from *Anglit* rather than from *Angrit*. Confusing? Oh well, *mai pen rai* (or *lai!*). Whether or not you succeed with Thai, it's great fun trying. You'll know you are getting somewhere when your first intelligible Thai remark meets with amazed silence, followed by an excited jabber of super-fast Thai chit-chat. The only polite way I know of halting this rather one-sided exchange is to quickly interject with *Put Thai nid noi—mai geng!* Which roughly translates as 'I'm only a novice—give me a break!'

An important thing to be aware of is regional dialect. The rapid, abbreviated *pak Thai* of the south is miles apart from the clear, more 'correct' speech of Bangkok, and is a completely different language to the relaxed, laidback drawl of the north. This situation can throw many travellers—especially those who arrive in Bangkok from the Deep South, only to find that they've acquired a 'dialect'! Using southern slang like *mabbalai* (*mai pen rai*) or *kup* (*khrap*) simply won't do in Bangkok—here, you'll have to speak proper!

The short vocabulary that follows should be enough to cover most occasions. If however, you're heading into remote provincial areas (e.g. the northeast) where English is hardly spoken at all, Joe Cummings' small *Thai Phrasebook* (Lonely Planet, 1984) is a most useful travelling companion.

VOCABULARY

Hello, goodbye	*Sawadee-kup (ka)*
Good luck, goodbye	*Chock-dee-kup (ka)*
Thank you	*Khop khun kup (ka)*
Pleased to meet you	*Yindee ti-ruja khun*
Sir/Madam	*Khun*
Yes (statement)	*Chai*
Yes (agreement)	*Kup/ka*
No	*Mai* (pronounced 'my')
Good	*Dee*
Bad	*Mai dee*
(Very) beautiful	*SoWAY maak*

Conversation

How are you?	*Khun sabai dee rue (OR sabai-dee)*

I'm fine, thanks	*Sabai-dee, khop khun kap (ka)*
What is your name?	*Khun cheu arai*
My name is John	*Pom cheu John*
My name is Cathy	*Dee-chan cheu Cathy*
How old are you?	*Khun ayuu tao rai*
I'm (30) years old	*Pom/dee-chan ayuu (saam-sip) pi*
I'm from England/USA	*Pom/dee-chan khon Angrit/Saharat Amerikaa*
Do you speak English?	*Put Angrit*
I speak Thai (only) little	*Put Thai nid-noi*
Understand?	*Kao chai mai*
I don't understand	*Chan mai kao chai*
Excuse me	*Khaw thot*
Never mind, no problem, you're welcome, why worry	*Mai pen rai*
Where are you going?	*Bai nai*
I'm going to Bangkok	*Cha bai Bangkok*
I like Bangkok	*Pom/dee-chan chawp Bangkok*
I love Thailand	*Pom/dee-chan raak Muang Thai*
Do you have a room . . .	*Mee hong mai . . .*
for two people?	*song khun*
Do you want (a cigarette)?	*Ao (buri)*
I don't want (it)	*May ao kap (ka)*
I don't have (it)	*May mee kap (ka)*
Do you have a toilet?	*Mee hong-nam mai*
Where is the . . .	*Yu thee nai*
bus-station	*sathanee rot meh*
railway station	*sathanee rot fai*
police station	*sathanee tam-ruat*
boat	*reua*
bank	*thanaakhaan*
restaurant	*raan-aahaan*
doctor	*maw*
hospital	*rohng phayaa-baan*

Food & Drink

Rice	*Kao*
Fried rice with . . .	*Kao-pat . . .*
chicken/pork/crab/shrimp	*kai/muu/puu/kung*
Spicy fried chicken	*Kai yang*
Spicy papaya salad	*Som-tam*
Noodles	*Kuaytiaw*
Curry	*Kaeng*
Fish	*Pla*
Eggs	*Khai*

240

Fruit	*Phon-la-mai*
Sugar	*Nam-taan*
Salt	*Kleau*

Water	*Nam*
Milk	*Nom*
Ice	*Nam-khaeng*
Yoghurt	*Nom priaw*
Coffee, no sugar	*Kaafay, mai sai nam-taan*
Tea, with milk	*Nam-cha, sai nom*
Beer	*Bia*
Whisky	*Mekong*

Let's eat	*Kin-kao*
Delicious	*Aroi*
Enough	*Por Lao*
I'm full up	*Im lao*
I'm not well	*Pom/dee-chan-mai sabai*
What's your special dish?	*Mee arai phe-set*
I'm vegetarian	*Pom/dee-chan kin jeh*

Money

How much?	*Tao rai*
How many baht?	*Kee baht*
Too expensive	*Phaeng bai*
Please discount	*Lot noi*
No way, forget it!	*Ma dai!*

Useful Words

Today	*Wan-nee*
Tomorrow	*Pung-nee*
Yesterday	*Meau wan-nee*
Minutes	*Na-thee*
(How many) hours	*(Kee) chua-mohng*
Year	*Pee*
Big	*Yai*
(Too) small	*Lek (bai)*
Hot	*Rawn*
(Very) cold	*Yen maak*

Numbers

Zero	*Soon*
One	*Nung*

241

Two	*Song*
Three	*Saam*
Four	*See*
Five	*Ha*
Six	*Hok*
Seven	*Jet*
Eight	*Paet*
Nine	*Kao*
Ten	*Sip*
Eleven	*Sip-et*
Twelve	*Sip-song*
Thirteen	*Sip-saam*
Twenty	*Yee-sip*
Twenty-one	*Yee-sip-et*
Twenty-two	*Yee-sip-song*
Twenty-five	*Yee-sip-ha*
30	*Saam-sip*
40	*See-sip*
50	*Ha-sip*
60	*Hok-sip*
70	*Jet-sip*
80	*Paet-sip*
90	*Kao-sip*
100	*Roi*
500	*Ha roi*
750	*Jet roi ha-sip*
1000	*Nung pan*
10,000	*Nung Muen*
1 million	*Laan*

BURMA

by Frances Capel

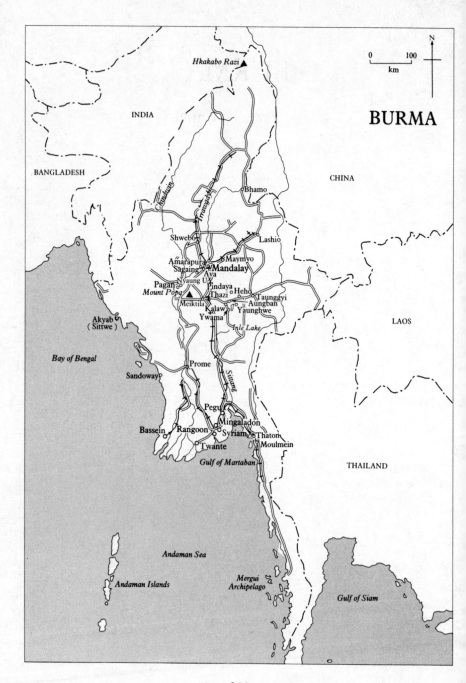

N

0   100
km

BURMA

INDIA

BANGLADESH

CHINA

Hkakabo Razi ▲

Bhamo

Shwebo

Lashio

Amarapura   Maymyo
Sagaing ✦Mandalay
         Ava
 Nyaung U Pindaya
Pagan   Heho
Mount Popa ▲   Thazi   Taunggyi
        Meiktila   Aungban
              Kalaw Yaunghwe
              Ywama

Akyab
(Sittwe)

Inle Lake

LAOS

Bay of Bengal

Prome

Sandoway

Sittang

Chindwin

Irrawaddy

Pegu

Bassein   Rangoon Mingaladon
                Syriam Thaton
        Twante   Moulmein

Gulf of Martaban

THAILAND

Andaman Sea

Andaman Islands

*Mergui
Archipelago*

Gulf of Siam

INTRODUCTION

Burma is a land half-hidden from foreign eyes, whose magic reaches out to enchant those who are not dependent on the comforts of the Western world.

However, dramatic political upheaval in the summer of 1988 is about to cause major changes in government policy. If you want to see Burma as she was, go now before the proposed reforms push her into the twentieth century alongside her sister Thailand.

The country covers 261,789 square miles of forbidding mountain ranges, many sheltering insurgents; wide, fertile river plains; and high plateaux inhabited by hill tribes. The frontiers bord with Bangladesh, India, China, Laos and Thailand, and no tourist is permitted to enter the country overland through any of them.

The capital is Rangoon, and it is through Rangoon's airport that all tourists must enter the country. The main river, the Irrawaddy, (Kipling's Road to Mandalay), with its tributary the Chindwin, is an important waterway navigable by steamer as far north as Bhamo. Other big rivers are the Salween and the Sittang.

Ten degrees north of the equator, cut by the tropic of Cancer, Burma's climate ranges from arid, on the Pagan plain, to tropical monsoon, divided roughly into three seasons with the rains coming towards the end of May.

Of a population estimated at 35,200,000 at the beginning of this decade, about 70% are Burman, the majority of the rest being Shan, Karen, Chin, Kachin, Chinese and Indian, each tribe or race having its own distinctive appearance.

The Burmese are gentle, with dark eyes and hair, and skin that ranges from dark to light. The natural grace of their small-boned bodies is enhanced by the almost universal adherence by both sexes to their national dress, the longyi—a couple of yards of cotton, sewn into a tube, folded across the stomach and tucked at the waist to form a long skirt, a fastening that is endlessly being re-adjusted by men and children, though not by women.

Buddhism touches most aspects of Burmese life. It is reflected in the gentleness and natural courtesy of the people who must always be striving towards their next life. Karma is one of the most misrepresented words of Asia. It means: the sum of a person's actions in one of his successive states of existence, regarded as determining his fate in the next; hence, necessary fate or destiny, following as effect from cause. You cannot change your karma.

Christians, accustomed to the Sunday-best solemnity of their own churches, may be struck by the worldly bustle of Burmese pagodas and temples, where it it not uncommon to find a group picnicking on one of the terraces, laughing, chatting and smoking. But no one can fail to be touched by the tranquillity that seems to pervade even the busiest of Buddhist shrines. You can climb the stairway of a pagoda, your feet weary on the gritty, betal-stained steps, and find, on the cool marble terrace, shaded by jacarandas and tamarinds, scented with jasmine, an old woman, white-haired and wrinkled but still supple, kneeling before a half-smiling Buddha with a devotion that radiates peace.

Until recently, Burma appeared to the visitor as a naive country whose simplicity added charm to its beauty. Today, the lid has been lifted from the cauldron of inefficient government administration, letting out more than a whiff of the crazy turmoil seething within.

After centuries of oppression from despotic kings, foreign traders and British and Japanese occupation, Burma became one of the bloodier theatres of the Second World War. Siding first with the Japanese, she then turned against them and helped the British to subsequent victory, but not without many thousands of deaths on all sides and devastating destruction to both country and economy. Hungry for independence, Burma detached herself from the British Empire in 1948, embarking on a policy that led to complete withdrawal from the world after Ne Win's military coup in 1962. Geographically, this was easy, in a country almost entirely surrounded by mountain ranges and sea. Administratively, with its fertile plains and abundant natural resources, it was possible to live without international commerce. Culturally, perhaps because of the contemplative nature of Buddhism, most Burmese people seemed content to live beyond the stimulation of Western ideas.

For a while Burma cut herself off, closing her frontiers against foreign intrusion, while her leaders tried to establish a viable and totally self-supporting Socialist Union. When foreigners were permitted to enter once more, they found a country where time had stood still while the rest of the world had raced forward in its frenetic pursuit of power and gain.

Today, 26 years later, Burma is bankrupt. In March 1988, student-led protest-riots, quelled by fearful government atrocities, led to the offered resignation in July of Ne Win and some of his ministers. At the time of writing, Reformation is in the air and government policies are in the melting pot: it is impossible to predict the outcome.

At present, (August 1988) land used for industry is nationalised. Agriculture is the principle industry, with teak and rice being the most important export crops, followed by rubber and jute. Almost half the country is covered with these forests. In 1976 the government introduced plans for co-operative farming, mainly on virgin soil, resulting in considerable dissatisfaction among farmers who were paid ridiculously meagre prices for their crops, particularly rice. In September 1987, the rules changed and farmers were allowed to sell non-industrial crops privately, but with complicated export and currency restrictions, this new system has not lessened their resentment.

Sometimes insurgents come down from their mountain camps and sack farming villages, burning houses, taking hostages and occasionally even killing, in an attempt to force the people to rebel against the government. (This is one of the reasons why tourists are restricted to certain areas: no one wants strangers to witness their domestic problems, and no one wants the inconvenience of having to protect visitors from possible danger.)

Burma is rich in minerals, including oil, rubies, jade, zinc and lead. Because foreign firms are not permitted to develop an efficient oil industry, however, much of the oil is untapped and there is a shortage of petrol, which is rationed.

The distribution of wealth is puzzling. Unskilled labourers often earn less than 6 kyats a day. Poverty, or non-materialism, appears at first glance to lie over every household. The home of a family who might once have been considered rich will show little evidence of that former prosperity beyond a few framed photographs and the skeleton of a fine house dying of decay and neglect. These families have been stripped of their ancestral heritage: family treasures have been 'lost' during 'loan' to public departments. If they try to raise a little extra income by letting out their tired but still gracious houses to rich foreigners willing to pay good rents, the government takes most of the profit, making it hardly worth the trouble to administer.

The modest exteriors of other houses, however, conceal the rewards of considerable black-market activity. Although the government officially controls most big businesses it is not impossible to accumulate unofficial profits. While countless truckloads of consumer goods find their way into the country over the mountain passes, Burma's valuable natural assets are smuggled out to lucrative markets in China, Thailand and other countries in ever-increasing volume: jade, rubies and other gems, ivory, teak and gold. The government is broke and unable to buy anything from other countries: every foreign article you see for unofficial sale has been paid for, unofficially, out of Burma's natural wealth. If the reforms that have been proposed during the present unrest materialise, all this will change and foreign developers may help to revitalise the economy. Perhaps it is not surprising that after a quarter of a century of submission to gross political bungling and mismanagement, the Burmese people are in revolt.

Although the penalties are severe, there is now said to be a considerable drug (heroin) trade in Burma, especially in Rangoon. You will hear different opinions as to whether drug addiction is increasing: the official line is that it is diminishing to the extent that drug rehabilitation centres are closing, but this could be from lack of funds. Certainly traffic in drugs is increasing. The US Narcotics Bureau collaborating with the Burmese in an attempt to control the production of the opium poppy. Unfortunately, it grows very easily and there is no other crop so profitable that could be introduced to replace it.

Burma is a country where nothing goes to waste. Litter is harvested with jealous care, paper is recycled in many ways depending on its quality—in the market you may be given your purchases neatly parcelled in bags made from used school exercise books complete with red corrections, or wrapped in palm leaves. Empty tins are sawn down to make serviceable mugs, pots and kitchen implements. Girders and oil-drum lids make garden fences. Stalls display an amazing collection of 'spare parts' from discarded cars, radios and machinery. The life of everything in Burma is as long as the life of the fabric from which it is made.

Clothed in the steam-heat of its monsoonal climate, Burma presents a kaleidoscope of impressions that leave the senses reeling—vibrant street scenes, enriched by the elegance of the people and by relics of fine architecture; markets, with stalls selling exotic and unfamiliar foods laid out as artistically as still-life pictures; railway stations, which offer a vivid microcosm of Burmese life; rural villages with fragile, palm-thatched houses on stilts; a group of people at a communal well, scooping water over themselves, performing their public ablutions with ingenious modesty; a pair of yoked oxen trundling across the skyline pulling a laden cart; river craft, ethereal as Chinese paintings, skimming across the water like butterflies; water buffalo, submerged but for their heads, wallowing in a muddy pool; the silhouette of palm trees against a flaming sunset; the golden dome of a pagoda blazing into life in the first rays of the morning sun.

Part I

GENERAL INFORMATION

Preparing to Go

Tourists in Burma

The Burmese had more than their fill of foreigners in the past. In the 15th century, Western traders were not slow to make fortunes out of Burmese natural resources. Then Burma was annexed three times by the British, who introduced Indians into positions of authority. Finally they were fought over by two countries in the last war. But today they are friendly and interested in foreigners.

The government has been run by one man, Ne Win, from various positions — as a general, as President, as Chairman. He is a man determined to keep the Burmese way of life untouched, and the Burmese Way to Socialism (an odd mixture of Marx and Buddha) uncriticized. This is the reason for the restrictions on tourists, foreign trade etc. However, times are changing with his resignation in July 1988, see page 281.

Burma has its skeletons, like every other country, and it prefers to keep them in the family cupboard. With very active insurgents occupying large border areas beyond the control of the government, tourists are considered to be too much of a responsibility outside the safe wrappings of a Tourist Burma package, or straying from the prescribed tourist trail. There is also, in the eyes of the government, the threat of Western capitalism disrupting the simple lives of the people. If you go into a rural village which has already been 'discovered' by tourists, you are likely to be surrounded by a forest of grasping little hands and a clamour of shrill voices chanting . . . 'one kyat, one kyat, skoo pen, skoo pen', 'lipstik, lipstik', 'bon-bon, bon-bon'.

It is (just) possible to visit all the areas open to tourists within the seven days given to most visitors. Anyone who tries to do so, however, is almost certain to come away feeling frustrated, exhausted and disenchanted, and the kindest advice that they would subsequently hand on, is—don't. It is easy enough (if you have the time and the money) to leave Burma and get another seven-day visa, and another, ad infinitum . . . If you try to cram the whole country into one week you may remember your first visit with gloom! Each place you go to will beckon tantalizingly, as you gallop past, but fear of missing your next connection will speed you on. A great deal of your time will be spent travelling, or waiting to travel, and the not infrequent delays that crop up during your travels will jeopardize your very tight schedule.

Of the people you meet on your travels in Burma, the ones who decided to opt for just a couple, or even only one, of the areas permitted to tourists, will seem far more relaxed and content than the ones who tried to do the lot.

There is a choice of three ways to 'do' the country:

First, there is the **Tourist Burma package** or a package offered by tour operators working from outside Burma in conjunction with Tourist Burma. It must be remembered that it is recent policy that top priority is given to package tourists. If you go under the Tourist Burma mantle you may be allowed to see places that are normally out of bounds. If you decide to put yourself on one of these conveyor belts you will be carried round the country on a carefully controlled itinerary, with assured seats, booked hotels, guided tours in air-conditioned buses and no worries. These packages are not cheap but those who fuss about uncertainties or who worry about tomorrow's plan, may be happiest seeing the country this way.

The second, and most usual, way is to make your own itinerary and your own arrangements to implement it, using the official channels. You will be expected to book your transport and your hotels through Tourist Burma, with all transactions recorded on your currency form. This option means that you can do what you want for as long as you choose and visit only the places and sites that you prefer, but it has to be said that you are liable to suffer many frustrations. Total flexibility of plan and a relaxed attitude are essential.

The third option is to try to defeat the system and see Burma on your own terms, without bureaucratic restriction. You will probably meet battered survivors from this method, with tales of bribery and bravado, of black-market jeeps, journeys on train roofs, avoidence of currency forms, visits to 'Black' areas and illegal currency deals—mostly as exaggerated as fishing stories. You will also meet the victims: those who paid extortionately for a black-market tour, only to be forsaken by their couriers in the night, or to have their transport impounded by the authorities, or who have got within spitting distance of their forbidden destination only to be turned back by one of the many road blocks that lie along all routes.

Although it is possible to visit some of the places that are not on the official tourist list of permitted areas, it normally takes a lot of persistence and perseverence to do so and will probably cost many black-market kyats as well as valuable time. Arrangements must be made without help from Tourist Burma, who will politely assure you that your destination is 'difficult to get to' and will, equally politely, produce obstructions to frustrate you. It is virtually impossible to get to the 'Black' zones along the borders and anyone wishing to do so will find that there are flourishing tourist excursions operating from Thailand that take you up over the passes for a brief look at the thriving Smugglers' Den.

Geography

For those who are honest enough to admit that a glance at the map is necessary before pinpointing Burma precisely, its northwestern boundaries march with Bangladesh and India, while the Bay of Bengal and the Andaman Sea wash its southwestern coast line. To the northeast lies China, and then Laos to the south, with the long mountainous border with Thailand running the rest of the way down to the southern tip. The Irrawaddy, Kipling's 'Road to Mandalay', rises in the Himalayas in the far north and slices its way down for 1250 miles to fan out southwest of Rangoon in a vast, fertile delta, churning its turgid, olive-green water into the Andaman Sea. The other principal rivers are the Salween and the Sittang, running more or less parallel with the Irrawaddy to the east.

As well as the spine of hills that runs down the tail of Burma, mountain ranges encircle the plain that stretches out either side of the Irrawaddy, with the highest mountain, Hkakabo Razi, 5887 m right up on the Chinese border.

Climate

Burma's tropical monsoon climate is divided into three distinct seasons which vary considerably in degree thoughout the regions. It should be noted that while Rangoon and the delta areas have an average annual rainfall of 100 inches, with 90% of the rain falling between May and October, Mandalay has an annual average of only 32.6 inches, and the Pagan plain even less.

When To Go
The most comfortable season is the 'winter' which lasts from November to the end of February with temperatures ranging from 80°F (26°C) by day to 50 or 60°F (10–15°C) at night. It is pleasantly warm but not so hot as to make sightseeing painful. Temperatures in the Shan plateaux can drop to freezing at night and sweaters are needed for Maymyo and the Taunggyi areas.

March, April and May are the hottest months, with temperatures soaring to well over 100°F (40°C), and as much as 115°F (46°C) in Pagan. At this time it is hard to summon enough energy to trail round the sights; the ground burns bare feet; siestas are almost compulsory and the best hours are those before 10 am and after 5 pm. With sunset at about 6.30 pm, this cuts down on the amount you can cram into a day if you don't want to torture yourself.

Some time towards the end of May the monsoon rains begin—four months of deluge that, in the high rainfall areas, can become very monotonous and depressing. There are some compensations during the rainy season, however, apart from the relief of cooling rain after the heat. The whole face of the country changes: great tracts of desert are suddenly transformed into stretches of shimmering water and lush vegetation; dry beds fill with fast-flowing rivers; the skies present a kaleidoscope of dramatic effects. A new landscape emerges to soothe senses that may have become parched by the preceding months.

Getting to Burma

Tourists can only enter Burma by air, arriving at Mingladon Airport just north of Rangoon.

Flights to Burma leave from Bangkok, Dacca, Kathmandu, Kunming and Moscow (via Tashkent and Vientiane). Fares change continually and should be checked at the time of booking.

Airlines serving Rangoon are:

From Bangkok: **Biman Bangladesh Airways, Burma Airways** (only daily flight), **Royal Nepal Airways, Thai Airways International** (three times a week).
From Dacca: **Biman Bangladesh Airways.**
From Kathmandu: **Royal Nepal Airways.**
From Kunming: **Civil Aviation Administration of China (CAAC).**
From Moscow: **Aeroflot.**

Flights go once a week except where stated, and can be unreliable. Biman Bangladesh has a bad reputation for reliability and fleas, but is usually the cheapest—offering London–Rangoon (via Dacca) Bangkok–London round ticket for £500 (April 1988).

Travel agencies that offer good prices include:

Europa Tours Ltd, 3 Wardour St, London W1V 3HE; tel 01 437 2146
United Air Travel, 5/6 Coventry St, London W1V 7FL; tel 01 439 2326

For information on Getting To Thailand see p. 4.

Passports & Visas

Everyone entering Burma must have a valid passport and an entry visa. You can get 7-day visas from a Burmese Embassy. Although the visas are only for 7 days, there is no limit to the amount of times you can apply for another, so long as you do it from outside Burma. They are cheap—£3 (US$5)—and you can usually get them within a few days, or less in Bangkok. You have to fill two application forms and produce 3 passport photographs, and sometimes you must show your return ticket.

Anyone wishing for an extended stay must have a genuine reason. A few foreign students, usually post-graduates, attend the Institute of Foreign Languages to learn Burmese. Go to one of the Burmese Embassies and present your case well and present your case well ahead of when you want to go. It will then be considered on its merits. There are courses at some of the Meditation Centres, for which you can get extended visas. For these, you must apply in good time, giving particulars of your interest and suitability. If you are judged to be a genuine applicant you will then get a letter of sponsorship from the Meditation Centre which you present to the Burmese Embassy, who may or may not grant you the special visa needed. All this can take several months.

If your touring programme gets hopelessly tangled up due to the failure of public transport and you miss your plane out (quite common), the immigration office will not be too difficult about giving you a 24-hour extension, but your reasons must be valid.

You can get visas at any of the following embassies and consulates during your travels:

Australia:
85 Mugga Way, Red Hill, Canberra ACT 2600, tel 95 0045

Bangladesh
Plot 38, Road No. 11, Bamani Model Town, Dacca, tel 30 1915/1461

Canada
116 Albert Street, Ottawa, tel 236 9613/4

China
6 Tung Chih Men Wai Street, Chao-yang District, Beijing, tel 52 1448/1425

Germany
Schumannstrasse 112, 53 Bonn, tel 0228 21 091

Hong Kong
AIA Building, Suite 106, 1 Stubbs Road, Hong Kong, tel 5729241

India
3/50F Shantipath, Chanakyapuri, New Delhi, tel 70251/2

Japan
2–26, 4 chome, Kita Shinagawa, Shinagawa Ku, Tokyo, tel 441 9291

Malaysia
Jalan Taman U Thant 7, Kuala Lumpur, tel 25798

Nepal
Thapathali, Kathmandu, tel 13146/14083

Singapore
15 St Martin's Drive, Singapore 10, tel 235 8763

Sri Lanka
53 Rosemead Place, Colombo 7, tel 91964

Thailand
132 North Sathorn Road, Bangkok, tel 233 2237, or 234 0278

UK
19a Charles Street, London W1, tel 01 629 9531/4486/6966 or 01 499 8841

USA
2300 S. Street NW, Washington DC, tel 202 332 9044/5/6

Currency

The standard unit of currency in Burma is the *kyat*—pronounced chat—which is divided into 100 *pyas*.

It is now compulsory for tourists to change a **minimum** of US$ 100 (or the equivalent) on arrival. Notices are displayed in the airport and Tourist Burma Offices giving currency rules: that further currency can only be exchanged at approved places—Tourist Burma, some hotels and Myanma Foreign Trade Bank; that unused kyats will be reconverted when you go, less the $100 changed on arrival; that kyats are not to be imported or exported. These notices also warn that there is a maximum prison sentence of 3 years for those breaking the currency laws.

Currency is obtainable in 5, 15, 45 and 90 kyat notes: 50 and 100 kyat notes are no longer valid.

Twelve major currencies are accepted, and American Express.

The official rate of exchange (1988)

	Cash	Traveller's cheques
£1	K11.14	11.55
$1	K 5.90	6.11
DM 1	K 3.53	3.66
FF 1	K 1.04	1.70
SF 1	K 4.27	4.43
JY (100)	K 4.73	4.91
HK $1	K 0.77	0.80
Malaysian $1	K 2.35	2.43
Singapore $1	K 3.01	3.14
Australian $1	K 4.55	4.71
Canadian $1	K 4.90	5.08

You are issued with a **currency form** on arrival and all the money you change is supposed to be recorded on this form. All your travel and living expenses are similarly supposed to be recorded on the form, and by the end of your visit the form should balance. Also on the form is a record of all the foreign currency you declared when you came into Burma, and this may have to be accounted for when you leave. You must also enter the number of your American Express card if you have one, though there is no special place given on the form to do so.

A totally unrealistic government ensures a flourishing **black market.** Touts will offer up to five times the official rate for dollars and, less willingly, for sterling. They congregate openly around the main tourist centres—Tourist Burma offices, hotels, taxi ranks, markets and the airport. You don't have to go looking for them—just hang around these places and they will find you. Anyone entering into an unofficial transaction should first discover the best current rate, name it and stick to it. It has been proved wise to count the exchanged kyats before completing the transaction. You will also get from five to

253

seven times the duty free price of any whisky and cigarettes you bring in—Johnny Walker Red Label whisky and 555 cigarettes are the most sought after. Many shopkeepers and stallholders in markets will quote prices in dollars at black-market rates.

Some tourists bring small articles with them to be used for barter at black-market rates. The most eagerly sought are brand-named lipsticks and other cosmetics; brand-named T-shirts and clothes; watches; good pens; calculators; personal stereos; radios etc. It has to be remembered that on arrival in Burma you are asked to fill in a form declaring any 'valuables' you have with you, and that anything you may have 'lost' during your visit will have to be paid for on departure. (This means the more valuable things like cameras, not lipsticks and T-shirts etc.) Overnight demonetization has been known, in order to try to curb the black market. The likelihood of this is extremely small, but it *has* happened, with awkward repercussions for tourists with a horde of unofficial kyats.

Finally, if you are to enjoy Burma to the full, don't let the currency hassle become an obsession. You will see dozens of anxious tourists at the airport and around the tourist centres, furtively negotiating with guilty glances over their shoulders. Decide what you intend to do to make the best use of your dollars and do it. Then forget about money and start enjoying the other, real Burma that manages to shrug off the inconveniences of a ragged economy.

Health & Insurance

You are no longer required to show any health certificates except for Cholera when you come into Burma, unless you come from a zone infected with Yellow Fever. However, you should be up to date on the following immunizations:

Cholera
Tetanus
Polio
Hepatitis
Typhoid

You should also take a course of anti-malaria pills, *starting a week before you go and continuing for 5 weeks after you get home.*

This is very important: malaria is on the increase and the extra weeks either side of your visit are vital.

It is essential to take out comprehensive insurance to cover medical care as well as loss and damage.

What to take

Travel light, preferably with a comfortable back-pack or holdall and nothing else. Clothes dry in moments in the hot season, so you don't need more than one change and a bar of washing soap. *Longyis*, which you can buy on arrival, are comfortable, cool, practical and adaptable, both by day and by night, once you learn to secure them. Pure cotton is the coolest fabric—don't take anything synthetic. You should take a sweater or cardigan in the cool season, or if you plan to go into the hills where it can be cold at night (except in the hot season). You will never want a coat but a light raincoat would be useful in the wet season. One cool, comfortable pair of shoes is all you need, and remember that feet tend to swell to at least a size bigger in the heat. You can buy every sort of sandal and flip-flop very cheaply in the markets. Don't forget, if you plan to wear shorts, to take trousers or a skirt to wear in the temples. Women should avoid vest-shaped and bra-less T-shirts: they cause offence, and light sleeves and skirts are cooler.

Useful additions to your luggage:

Unbreakable drinking mug and water bottle, torch—for frescoes in Pagan and Pindaya Caves, and night visits to the lavatory when electricity fails, sticking plaster, water-purifying tablets, anti-diarrhoea and rehydration pills, sun cream, antiseptic cream, antibiotic spray or powder—any blister or open sore can go bad quickly in the heat, aspirin, bar of washing soap—travels better and lasts longer than powder, toilet soap, mosquito repellent, lavatory paper—not provided in guest houses and many hotels, sticky tape—Burmese airmail letters and envelopes do not normally have gum on them, needle and cotton, as much spare film as you think you will need, biro pens and hard sweets for gifts to children.

For women a thin Indian cotton shawl makes an excellent, easy-to-carry wrap to protect you from the sun and to cover bare shoulders in pagodas. An umbrella is handy in the monsoon, but you can buy them very cheaply in the markets. A small towel makes a good sweat wiper when travelling and, most important, take a very long, very absorbing book—for journeys both to and from Burma and while travelling in the country.

Books

Although there is an enthusiastic second-hand book trade in the towns, you will find prices exorbitant and the range limited. Take what reference books you need with you. Site guides are rare and very dry. You can get the Ministry of Culture's *Pictorial Guide to Pagan*, but a far better one called *Glimpses of Glorious Pagan*, from the Department of History, Rangoon University is easier to get in Bangkok. *Burmese Culture, General and Particular*, from the Ministry of Information is an uninspiring volume that will cost you 20 kyats from the Tourist Burma Office.

Suggested Reading
The Burman, His Life and Notions by Shway Yoe (Sir James George Scott)
Burma As It Was, As It Is and As It Will Be by Shway Yoe (Sir James George Scott)
Buddhism, Art and Faith edited by W. Zwalf
Burma by F. P. S. Donnison
A Wonderland of Burmese Legends by Khin Myo Chit
Burmese Lacquerware by Sylvia Fraser-Lu
Golden Earth by Norman Lewis
The Story of Burma by F. Tennyson-Jesse
In Search Of Burma by Caroline Courtauld
The Union of Burma by Hugh Tinker

The Great Railway Bazaar by Paul Theroux
The Lacquer Lady by F. Tennyson-Jesse
Burmese Days by George Orwell
The Burmese Family by Mi Mi Khaing
Burmese Women by Mi Mi Khaing
Mandalay the Golden by E.C.V. Foucar
The Pagoda War by A.T.Q. Stewart
The Stricken Peacock by Maung Htin Aung
A History of Modern Burma by J. F. Cady
The Making of Burma by Dorothy Woodman
The Road Past Mandalay by John Masters
Defeat Into Victory by Field-Marshal Sir William Slim
The Raiders of Arakan by C.E. Lucas Phillips

If you want to carry one book with you for interesting and pleasant reading, get Shway
Yoe's *The Burman*.

Maps

Good maps of Burma are rare and the ones sold in the country are extremely basic, so
you should try to get one before you go. Good travel bookshops or map centres will sell
the German Nelles Verlag map of Burma, 1:1500 000, which includes city plans of
Rangoon and Mandalay. Otherwise, Tourist Burma will sell you a very inadequate map
of the country or you can pick one up from street vendors or book shops in Rangoon for a
few kyats.

On Arrival

Arrival & Orientation

Whatever uncertainties may shroud your travel itinerary once you get there, one thing is
sure—your visit to Burma starts at Mingaladon Airport, outside Rangoon.

If it is possible to travel so light that your luggage passes as hand baggage, you will have
a head start at the airport. This can make all the difference between getting the last
reclining seat in the Upper Class or a rigid, bolt upright seat in the First Class on the
overnight train to Mandalay, giving you the best range of options for planning the rest of
your stay. So on arrival, don't hang back.

You will be processed through the passport control and immigration counter, to the
customs. If you didn't fill one in on the plane, you will be given a form on which to declare
anything of value in your possession: cameras, radios, etc. as well as jewellery. You will be
expected to account for these on departure, to make sure you haven't sold them:

therefore it is a wise precaution not to set too high a value on them on the form, in case you lose anything and have to pay for it. Don't try to bring in a video camera as it will be confiscated until your departure. Keep the form carefully. If your luggage travelled in the hold of the plane, you must now wait until you are called forward to claim it, when it will be searched. If you have your bag with you, you can go directly to the searching desk.

You will be given a **currency form,** on which you will be asked to fill in all the currency in your possession, whether cash, traveller's cheques or American Express card. This form is as crucial as your passport so don't lose it.

Finally, you must go to the money changing desk, where you will be required to change at least the value of US$ 100—none of which may be re-changed on departure.

N.B. Remember to keep K15, for airport tax on departure.

There is a **Tourist Burma Office** in the airport, but you can't make train bookings here so it is best to get on into Rangoon as quickly as possible. All this procedure can take as much as two hours and needs good humour and patience. Listen to the people around you—many of them may be visiting Burma for the second or third time and will be full of useful tips and the most up-to-date information on how to make the most of your time and your money. It is here that you will hear what the current black-market exchange rate is.

As you leave the airport, touts will approach and ask if you have whisky or cigarettes to sell and many tourists like to get these unofficial transactions over as soon as possible. You should aim to get from five to seven times their duty-free value (1988). You can always get the best rate in down-town Rangoon, so don't be shortchanged at the airport through nervousness. (And don't be too worried about the uniformed officials—they are usually totally unconcerned by your dealings.)

Getting Into Rangoon

By Taxi: The taxi ride into Rangoon costs K60 (1988) and can usually be shared among several people. It takes about half an hour and gives your first taste of Burma, as you rattle through the sprawling shanty-town suburbs of Rangoon.

By Bus: There are buses, which cost only a few kyats, but you must walk for about 10 minutes to the main road to get one (No. 9).

Your first destination must be the **Tourist Burma** office in the centre of Rangoon, open from 8 am to 8 pm seven days a week, unless you have opted to try and beat the system, in which case a guide book will be less use to you than a bottle of tranquillizers!

It is wise to have two possible itineraries before you get to Tourist Burma, in case you can't get seats on trains or planes. All major travel arrangements are made here, so the sooner you arrive the more likely you are to get the seats you want. You can also get all the current information on what is or isn't permitted—things change constantly in Burma.

Tourist Burma

There are Tourist Burma offices in Rangoon, Mandalay, Pagan, Taunggyi, Maymyo and Inle Lake, covering the main tourist centres. There is also a Tourist Burma agent in the Kalaw Hotel, Kalaw, who will arrange travel tickets for you but cannot change money. These offices should be able to give you all the up-to-date information you need to make bookings and reservations. The systems vary, not only from office to office, but from day to day and from official to official. Sometimes the office will handle the whole procedure and you can collect your ticket from them, usually 24 hours later. Sometimes you will have to go and collect your ticket yourself, taking a booking slip with you. The officials are usually friendly and helpful but they are not miracle-workers and they have to deal with archaic communication systems and a great deal of red tape—it will be in the Tourist Burma offices that you are most likely to have to cultivate patience!

Schedules & Prices
Travel times and fares are *constantly* changing and the information in this book is only a guide: all times and prices should be checked. When flying, all flights must be double-checked the day before departure. Planes are liable to leave early if all the seats are taken, so arrive in plenty of time.

Useful Addresses
Aeroflot Airlines, 18 Prome Road, Rangoon, tel 61066
Biman Airlines, 106/108 Pansodan Road, Rangoon, tel 75882
Burma Airways, Strand Road, Rangoon, tel 84566
CAAC Airlines, Mingaladon Airport, Rangoon, tel 40113
Thai International Airways, Mahabundoola Road, Rangoon, tel 75988

Getting Around Burma

Since 1988 there has been considerable tightening up of travel regulations in Burma. If you decide to travel without the blessing of Tourist Burma, you must be prepared for endless frustration.

By Air
There is an air service that connects the four main tourist areas: Rangoon, Mandalay, Pagan and Heho (for Inle Lake). Fares can be booked through Tourist Burma or the airline office.
See below for fares and flights (1988), but check for up-to-date changes.

Fares
Rangoon–Pagan	K532
Rangoon–Mandalay	K588
Rangoon–Heho	K475
Pagan–Mandalay	K193
Pagan–Heho	K386
Mandalay–Heho	K193

Flights
Rangoon–Pagan–Mandalay–Heho–Rangoon—flights on Sundays, Tuesdays, Wednesdays, Fridays.

	dep	arr
Rangoon–Pagan	7.45 am	8.15 am
Pagan–Mandalay	8.35 am	9.05 am
Mandalay–Heho	9.35 am	10.05 am
Heho–Rangoon	10.20 am	11.45 am

Rangoon–Heho–Mandalay–Pagan–Rangoon—flights on Mondays, Thursdays, Saturdays.

	dep	arr
Rangoon–Heho	1.00 pm	2.25 pm
Heho–Mandalay	2.50 pm	3.20 pm
Mandalay–Pagan	3.50 pm	4.20 pm
Pagan–Rangoon	4.40 pm	6.10 pm
Rangoon–Mandalay	6.45 pm	9.05 pm
Mandalay–Rangoon	9.35 pm	11.45 pm

Priority is given to package tourists and you can be turned away even if you have a confirmed seat. It is wise to get to the airport well ahead of time as the planes are known to leave early or change schedules. Always check dates and times ahead.

By Rail

No one should leave Burma without having done at least one train journey in daylight and you should always try to get a window seat. On the whole, the service is reliable, though it does fail from time to time. Fares are cheap: e.g. in 1988 Rangoon–Mandalay cost K110. Tourists are expected to travel Upper or First Class, though you can travel Ordinary if you want to. This is a physical endurance test, but a good way of getting to know the Burmese people at close quarters! The Upper Class seats are the most comfortable. First Class costs more because food is included, but the seats are not nearly so comfortable and are more difficult to sleep in. The overnight trains between Rangoon and Mandalay have extremely comfortable reclining seats in the Upper Class for which it is advisable to book ahead.

For some inexplicable reason, Tourist Burma will only authorize tourists to travel on the trains between Rangoon and Mandalay. Any other route is declared unsuitable and no help will be given. You must, therefore, go to the station and negotiate for yourself: prepare for frustration and you will get there in the end.

The two hour trip between Rangoon and Pegu gives you an excellent taste of rail travel. There is also a circular route round Rangoon, taking about two hours and costing K1, which is fun to do if you have time. Beware as you come into and leave stations; it is becoming good sport among children—and sometimes not just children—to line the tracks and hurl water through the open windows of the trains!

Schedules

Tourist Burma are the first to admit that train times tend to depend on the whim of the driver, and you will find that listed schedules vary from office to office with no one able to tell you which is the right one. The following list, therefore, is only approximate and must be checked.

Rangoon–Mandalay (via Thazi)	Mandalay–Rangoon (via Thazi)
dep 0600 – arr 2000	dep 0600 – arr 2100
dep 1715 – arr 0705	dep 1700 – arr 0730
dep 1845 – arr 0835	dep 1835 – arr 0900

Upper Class costs K110 single, First Class K160 (less comfortable but with food provided). You can get on or off the train at Thazi to connect with the Pagan bus, but it will cost the same.

By Road

Taxis operate in the towns but they tend to be expensive; only those with red registration tags are allowed to carry tourists. You should always negotiate a price before you start.

Jeeps run to certain places, usually departing when they are full—at least 8 people—and picking up more en route. From Mandalay to Maymyo, for instance, costs K30 per head, or K300 for the hire of the whole jeep. These journeys are uncomfortable but fun.

Buses of various sizes run all over the country for miniscule fares. Virtually all motor vehicles except the neat little Japanese taxi pick-ups, are memorably dilapidated—some of the buses are no more than covered lorries with wooden and metal benches down the sides and the middle. When the interior of a bus is packed to maximum capacity, male passengers attach themselves to the outside, hanging on with nonchalant ease as the bus bumps its way over the potholes. Long bus and jeep journeys, such as the 10-hour trip from Pagan to Inle Lake can be an endurance test, though you do stop for refreshment frequently along the route and get to know your fellow passengers very well. It is always worth asking for a window seat if you are booking ahead, as you must on the long-distance trips.

By Pony trap

In the towns you can hire the picturesque pony traps which, shared between up to three people are cheap, about K75 for half a day. The ponies are usually pitifully thin and their drivers urge them along with callous indifference. Negotiate with the driver first and try to get one who speaks a bit of English. He will usually be happy to act as a guide to all the main sights, and will advise on the best eating places and any other local knowledge you require.

By Trishaw

Bicycle trishaws are the cheapest form of transport, just a few kyats for a short journey, or about K50 for half a day. Most drivers will act as guides in the same way as the pony drivers. Trishaws are built to carry two passengers, but as Western bodies tend to weigh more than those of their Eastern hosts it is advisable to take one each. The prices are quoted per person rather than per vehicle.

By Boat

You should certainly try to fit one boat trip into your stay in Burma. The river scenery is more memorable when viewed from a boat than from the shore. Ideally, the trip down the Irrawaddy from Mandalay to Pagan is the one to go for (it isn't possible to do the return journey). The boats go on Thursday and Sunday, except in April and May when the river is too low before the monsoon rains bring the level back up. You book through Tourist Burma and it costs K160 per person, including meals, or K200 with a cabin. Alternatively, there is the 1-hour trip from Mandalay to Mingun, or the 45-minute trip from Rangoon to Syriam. If you go to Bassein from Rangoon it is an overnight journey each way, costing K120, but it takes at least 2 weeks to get permission for this, and so is rarely possible for tourists. An alternative way to enjoy the river scenery is to take one of the two-hour canoe trips in Pagan at sunset.

By Bicycle
You can hire bicycles in various places, including Pagan, Maymyo and Yaunghwe at Inle Lake. It is an excellent way of exploring and gives you maximum independence. Prices vary and are negotiable: e.g. K15 a day in Pagan or K25 in Maymyo.

N.B.
During the Water Festival, in April, schedules are abandoned, many buses don't run and transport can become much more expensive. Double check all departure times and fares. And remember that you are a sitting target for a drenching, which can be extremely chilly if you are in the hills.

Suggested Itineraries

There are many permutations: whichever you choose you must be prepared to change your plans from day to day depending on the complications that may crop up once you start.

If you decide to do a reasonably leisurely tour, and come back for more, then most people would agree that the place where you should try to spend most time on your first visit to Burma, is Pagan.

Day 1: Arrive Rangoon, night train to Mandalay.
Day 2: Explore Mandalay, fly to Pagan.
Day 3: Explore Pagan. (Or, if Sunday or Thursday in right season, spend previous night in Mandalay and catch boat to Pagan.)
Day 4: Explore Pagan and/or Mount Popa.
Day 5: Explore Pagan.
Day 6: Fly to Heho and bus to Yaunghwe for boat tour of Inle Lake.
Day 7: Bus to Thazi for night train to Rangoon.
Day 8: Get off train 2 hours short of Rangoon, early in the morning, to explore Pegu. Catch later train to Rangoon arriving in time to see Shwedagon and catch plane out.

If you can afford it, and if you can get seats, it is obviously more time-saving to fly everywhere. If you do, however, you should try to fit in one day-time train journey, and a boat trip.

Day 1: Arrive Rangoon. Explore.
Day 2: Fly Pagan, 7.45 am. Explore Pagan.
Day 3: Explore Pagan and area.

Day 4: Fly Mandalay, 8.35 am. Explore.
Day 5: Fly Heho, 9.35 am. Bus Yaunghwe. Explore Inle Lake.
Day 6: Fly Rangoon. Boat and bus trip to Syriam.
Day 7: Train to Pegu and back. Sunset Shwedagon.
Day 8: Boat and bus trip to Twante. Back in time to catch plane out.

Fitting in the Whole Circle
This itinerary gives you maximum coverage of the country and no time to enjoy any of the places, most of all, Pagan. It is only feasible if all travel arrangements go smoothly—a rare event in Burma.

Day 1: Arrive Rangoon pm; night train Mandalay
Day 2: See Mandalay, jeep to Maymyo. (Alternatively, on arrival, boat to Mingun for day. Night in Mandalay)
Day 3: Explore Maymyo; return to Mandalay by jeep. Night in Mandalay.
(Or, if still in Mandalay bus to Amarapura, Ava and/or Sagaing. Night in Mandalay.)
Day 4: If day and season permit, dawn boat to Pagan—14 hours. (Worth cutting day 3 programme for.) Otherwise, road or air to Pagan.
Day 5: Fly to Heho and bus to Yaunghwe, on Inle Lake.
Day 6: Boat tour of Inle Lake. Bus to Taunggyi.
Day 7: Fly to Rangoon. Explore town, or take boat trip to Syriam, or Twante. (Or bus from Taunggyi to Thazi then night train Rangoon, breaking journey in Pegu.)
Day 8: Explore Rangoon. Depart.

When you plan your daily sightseeing programme, try to leave time in each place for a leisurely stroll through back streets and alley-ways, and time to explore somewhere away from the main tourist centre.

Where To Stay

By Western standards, accommodation in Burma ranges from mediocre to bad. At the top end of the scale, there are half a dozen or so **hotels** which pretend to compare with 2- or 3-star hotels in Europe, but even these are very lacklustre. Although most will provide private bathrooms and air-conditioning, the facilities are basic, often run-down and the service poor. In cheaper hotels the bedrooms tend to be even more basic and if there is a bathroom en suite, it is likely to have a low-pressure shower rather than a bath.

    Guest houses in the towns are on the whole of a poor standard, but they are extremely cheap. Although the Burmese people themselves are outstandingly clean, their toilet facilities tend to be appallingly squalid. Bedrooms consist of small cubicles often divided from each other by flimsy, woven palm walls, with hard beds, usually a fan, and mosquito nets or mesh over the windows. Only a few serve meals, though most will provide the ubiquitous 'plain tea' on permanent supply.

    The best value for money are the guest houses in Pagan. Somehow the local people here have entered into tourism with more enthusiasm than elsewhere and the comfort of the tourists is given greater consideration. Here you get the feeling that your hosts actually want you to be comfortable and to enjoy your stay and feel welcome. Elsewhere you find a state-controlled, take-it-or-leave-it philosophy that shrugs indifferently at such things as dead light bulbs, cockroaches, no water in the shower, sordid lavatories etc.

Some guest houses live on a knife edge of legality. Those that risk black-market dealings on the side, such as taking a higher rate in exchange for not entering transactions on currency forms, are frequently being banned to tourists for short periods. This can happen overnight so you have to be prepared to find that the one you have selected is temporarily closed, and that others you have not heard or read about have just opened. The newly opened ones are often the best to head for, being keen to win themselves a good reputation on the tourist grapevine. Tourist Burma offices display lists of the guest houses permitted to take foreign tourists.

In short, if you want to enjoy your week in Burma you must forget Western standards of living and accept Eastern standards with good humour and patience!

Because prices change frequently, those given in this book must be taken as a rough guide only. They date from 1988, after a major increase in prices in government hotels.

Eating Out

As a rule you won't find Burma a gourmet's paradise!

You can eat Chinese, Burmese, Indian and European food in Rangoon and Mandalay, and even in the smaller places you will find some European dishes if you want them. 'English Breakfast' is surprisingly common. While menus are printed in English in hotels and larger restaurants, you may have to resort to sign language and a quick inspection of what the other customers are eating in the smaller places. You can get very cheap meals from street stalls, where the ingredients are laid out so that you can choose what you want—these are often delicious.

Unless you have a particular passion for curry, you may find much of the food in Burma disappointingly similar—both the rice and the farinaceous dishes tend to be dominated by spices.

You will find an apparently bewildering range of dishes, the names of which vary from place to place. Rice and noodles form the foundation of most, with every sort of meat, fish and vegetable ingredient and a large variety of seasonings. There are also many kebab-type snacks, as well as fried fritters and pancakes, fruits, and samosas. Fried Rice is usually safe and you can choose the main ingredient of either pork, chicken, prawns, or just vegetables. Fried vegetables are OK and many of the soups, which look watery and insipid, can be delicious. Soup is usually served automatically with the main course.

Drinking in Burma

Buddhists are not supposed to drink alcohol and, although some of them come to terms with their consciences, public drinking is not common, so you won't find many locals in the few 'bars' of hotels. Perhaps it is direct retribution, but on the whole, Burmese people don't carry their drink well.

Except in Taunggyi, where British influence has lingered, there aren't public bars as such, except those in hotels. The atmosphere in the places where you can buy drink

263

tends to be rather seedy: the best solution, if going on the wagon is unacceptable, is to rely on your duty-free during your stay. If you have converted it all into currency, Mandalay Beer, when you can get it, is OK: it is cheap in Tourist Burma approved hotels but otherwise will cost you upwards of K50 a bottle. Rum Sour is another option—Mandalay rum, soda and fresh lime—and not too expensive. Beware Burmese whisky. *And avoid ice at all times.*

A Few Typical Burmese Dishes
Main Courses:
Chicken o no kauk swe—chicken cooked in a coconut soup, with noodles
Chicken si Byam—chicken curry
Sha Nga Boung—fish curry
Balachaung—prawn curry with garlic and ginger
Mohingha—fish soup with noodles, lemon grass, coriander, garlic and chilli
H san Byoke—fish soup
Hingyo—gourd soup

Snacks
Deep-fried white gourds, dried fish chips, corn crackers
Lapet—pickled tea leaf, eaten with fried seeds

Pudding
Kyauk-kyaw—made of coconut
Sa nwin ma kin—coconut cake made with sago

Drink
Todi juice—made from Todi palm: in the morning it tastes sweet and in the afternoon it is fermented, alcoholic, and tastes like yoghurt gone off.
Sugar cane drink—very sweet
Lassi—fruit-flavoured yoghurt drink

Health Precautions

Every country has its indigenous bacteria to which its people have grown immune. This can be disastrous for foreign visitors, particularly as bacteria breed much more quickly in hot countries. With only seven days for your visit, it can be a major tragedy if even as little as 24 hours are wasted in the discomforts and distress of an upset stomach. The unwary visitor can carry bugs home that persist in the system for several months, so it is foolish not to take a few precautions in order to try and stay fit. Ask your doctor to recommend the best pills to take with you in case of upset stomachs.

Don't drink *any* water unless you know for certain that it has been boiled; almost all the hotels and guest houses now supply boiled water, usually in a place where you can help yourself. Ice is rarely made with boiled water, however much you are assured that it has been: bacteria that have been frozen multiply far more rapidly once they are thawed out; this goes for iced lollies, too. One of the main causes of apparently inexplicable gastric upsets is when visitors have had iced drinks. Beware too of bottled water with unsealed caps.

Uncooked vegetables, salads and fruit (unless protected by a skin) should be avoided. There are those who will tell you that water melons are composed of 99% drains.

Cooked food that has been sitting about in the heat for any length of time can be unfriendly to unaccustomed stomachs—resident foreigners will advise you not to be among the first customers in a restaurant or cafe, giving yesterday's leftovers time to be disposed of!

Most hotels and guest houses supply either mosquito nets or mesh over the windows.

The sun can be devastatingly hot, particularly in the middle hours of the day during the hot season, so it is wise to cover your head when you are outside, and to protect your skin if you are at all prone to burning. Dark glasses help to ward off headaches in the intense glare of the sun, and light clothing made of natural fibres (not synthetics) is cooler than bare flesh.

You should always try to carry a bottle of boiled water with you and to refill it whenever you get the chance. A damp flannel in a polythene bag is marvellous on long road and rail journeys.

Medical Care in Burma

Emergencies will be treated in the local hospitals and clinics but stories from those who have had to undergo such treatment are not comforting. Tourist Burma, or your hotel or guest house will tell you the nearest.

A typical experience is that of the tourist who consulted a doctor in Rangoon after a bout of dysentery: he prodded her stomach, gave her a sachet of glucose and charged her K165!

A wander round the General Hospital in Rangoon, Victorian in every way and about to be replaced, will give you an idea of why it is best to try to stay fit. Sick people lie everywhere; there is no privacy, even for the dying. An open drain runs along the back. Relatives throng the beds, bringing food and clean sheets for the patients. A pile of new sheets, donated by one of the embassies, sits untouched in a passage.

The Burmese are desperately short of modern drugs and medical supplies, and when they do manage to install up-to-date equipment, as in a new hospital in Rangoon, no one knows how to use it properly. Anyone wanting serious surgery tries to go to Bangkok—if they can afford it.

Time

The time in Burma is $6\frac{1}{2}$ hours ahead of GMT.

Calendar

The Burmese use a 12-month lunar calendar, so that the dates of festivals and some of the public holidays vary from year to year depending on the phases of the moon. More recently they have also recognized the Gregorian calendar, so other holidays and events are fixed.

Their 'lunar' months are:

Tagu	March/April
Kason	April/May
Nayon	May/June
Waso	June/July
Wagaung	July/August
Tawthalin	August/September
Thadingyut	September/October
Tazaungmon	October/November
Nadaw	November/December
Pyatho	December/January
Tabodwe	January/February
Taboung	February/March

Days of the Week & Names

The Burmese divide Wednesday into two, for astrological purposes only, but otherwise they work on a 7-day week. Each day is represented by an animal or mythical beast which bestows certain characteristics to anyone born on that day. The Burmese take a great deal of care over the naming of their children. Horoscopes are consulted and the time, date and season of the birth taken into account. Certain initials belong to each day of the week and it is considered propitious to chose a name beginning with one of these. Thus:

Monday: *Taninla*—Tiger—calm to angry—K, Kh, G, Gh, Ng.

Tuesday: *Ainga*—Lion—kingly—Z, Zh, Ny.

Wednesday: *Yahu*—Elephant without tusks—peaceful—Ya (Pali R), Ya (Arakanese Ra)—(very unlucky)

Wednesday: *Boddahu*—Elephant with tusks—clever and quick—L, W.

Thursday: *Kya-thabode*—Rat—calm and homely—P, Hp, B, M.

Friday: *Thank-kya*—Guinea pig—garrulous—Th, H.

Saturday: *Sane*—*Ngar* (dragon serpent)—angry—T, Ht, D, Dh, N.

Sunday: *Taninganwe*—*Garuda* (¹/₂ man, ¹/₂ beast)—impetuous, leader of bad and good—A.

You will meet people who were educated in mission schools and convents, and have a Christian name as well as a Buddhist one.

There are a variety of courtesy titles given to people depending on their age, relationship or position:

U, or Uncle, is a sign of respect used when addressing an adult man.

Bo, is used mainly for officers.

Ko, or brother, is used between men who are contemporaries.

Maung, is used to address youths and boys and is how they sign themselves.

Daw, or aunt, is used for all adult women.

Ma, or sister, can be used for any female, but particularly for girls.

Aunty, Uncle, Sister and Brother, in English, are also used between relatives and close friends.

Post

The post in and out of Burma seems to be entirely hit and miss. You can post dozens of cards into the same box on the same day, some even to the same address, and the chances are that more than 50% won't reach their destination. Those that do manage to break through the barrier travel reasonably fast. The blue airmail lettergrammes are fairly reliable and usually take less than a week. (They are not gummed, so you need sellotape or paste.) Airmail to Europe costs K2.25, post cards, K2.

Electricity

230 volts—50 cycle/hertz.

Opening Times

Post offices, airways and most government offices: 9.30 am–4 pm, Monday to Friday. Banks: 10 am–2 pm, Monday to Friday. Tourist Burma: 8 am–8 pm daily.

The Burmese don't keep late hours. Most restaurants are closed by 11 pm, and in many it is difficult to get served after about 8 pm. Some smaller places will stay open as long as they have customers, especially in Pagan.

Shopping

You get good value shopping in markets, if you are prepared to bargain. The vendor may ask you to name a price first but remember that this is merely the launching point for a spirited exchange of bargaining, so you are best to quote about half what you intend to spend. Decide what the article is worth to you, and stick to it.

The Bogyoke (Scott) Market in Rangoon, the Zego Market in Mandalay, and the markets in Taunggyi, Naung-oo, Maymyo and Pegu all offer everything you might want as souvenirs to take home, and you may often be quoted prices in dollars.

Burmese Souvenirs
Souvenirs to take home include: lacquerware, richly embroidered wall hangings, bronze opium weights, carved teak, ivory, Shan bags, *longyis*, umbrellas, jewellery, jade, baskets, pottery.

Tourists are only permitted to buy precious gems from government-approved sources. Beware the many touts who slink up to you and show you a handful of 'gems'—unless you are an expert, you may find yourself buying pretty coloured glass. If you do buy a genuine gem and cannot prove that you bought it from an approved source, it may be confiscated from you when you leave.

Beware also the tout who offers you 'antique' sculpture: if this is genuine it is likely to have been stolen from a ruined temple or even from a state museum. The export of any sort of sacred relic is emphatically forbidden. Such things are not easy to conceal if you are searched and the authorities won't be very friendly if they find anything of this category in your luggage.

Festivals

Burmese people are festive by nature and every full moon in the dry season calls for some sort of celebration. Public events and entertainments are invariably accompanied by the eruption of an instant market. A naked plot of land is suddenly filled with makeshift stalls selling everything from souvenirs to aluminium pots. Food vendors set up field kitchens and cook meals on open fires, with the ingredients laid out for the customers' choice.

Pagodas have their own special **Full Moon Festival,** usually lasting for several days leading up to the night of the full moon.

Pwes are an important part of public festivals. These uniquely Burmese shows are a blend of dance, song and drama with variations that include pantomime, ballet, opera, musical comedy, mime, tragedy and farce. (Their nearest equivalent were the 16th-century masques of Europe.) The enthusiastic audience literally set up camp around the prefabricated stage, sometimes outside, sometimes in a vast palm-woven marquee. A *pwe* can last all night and it doesn't seem to matter if anyone drops off for a quick snooze during the performance.

Major Festivals in Burma

January 4th—Independence Day, celebrated as a major public holiday all over the country.
February 12th—Union Day.
Also in February, around the full moon, there is a **Rice-harvest Festival,** during which an unappetizing looking but delicious tasting concoction called *Htamane* is eaten—a lump of sticky rice mixed with peanuts, ginger, coconut and sesame.
March 2nd—Peasants' Day—anniversary of Ne Win's take-over in 1962.
March 27th—Armed Forces Day—with military parades and tattoos.
April—The Water Festival or *Thingyan.* This takes place some time around the middle of April, to celebrate the Burmese New Year. The old year must be washed away and the new one baptized with water. The exact date of Thingyan must be chosen by astrologers and marks the arrival each year of Thagyamin, the king of the *nats*, bringing peace and prosperity to Burma in the coming year, symbolized by a jar of water.

The whole country greets this visitation with an explosion of celebrations: *pwes*, fêtes, parades and every sort of display. But what lives most in the memory is the deluge of water that makes every outing hazardous during the festival. This was once a symbolic ritual, gently performed for the benefit of the recipient; a grave and deferential pouring of the cleansing stream after permission to do so had been given. Now, it has evolved into a slapstick comedy—no one is immune and permission is seldom requested. Water is hurled from buckets, mugs, bowls, thrown in balloons, squirted from pumps, sprayed from hydrants, and cascaded from balconies and upper windows. Lasting officially for three or four days, it often goes on longer.

May 1st—Workers' Day.

Also in May, the full moon that comes during the latter part of *Kason*, (the division of the Burmese calender that embraces part of April and part of May) is the one that precedes the monsoon rain and is celebrated as a major festival to mark the birth, enlightenment and entry into Nirvana of Guatama Buddha.

July—The full moon in *Waso* (the division of the Burmese calender that includes part of June and part of July), marks the start of Lent for Buddhists, a 3-month period that coincides with the monsoon. Monks must be particularly diligent in their meditation and fasting during Lent and lay people are expected to be extra devout. Marriages are not permitted.

July 19th—Martyrs' Day, to mark the assassination of Aung San and his colleagues in 1947. Wreaths are laid at the Martyrs' Mausoleum in Rangoon.

September—Boat festivals are held throughout the country on every appropriate stretch of water during this season of monsoon rain. Most spectacular is the carnival on **Inle Lake,** where the Buddha images in the Phaungdaw Pagoda are placed in the *Karaweik*, or royal barge, and paraded around the lake with tremendous ceremony.

October—*Thadingyut*. A happy Festival of Light, to mark the end of Lent and all its restrictions and solemnity. For three days, lights blaze out all over the country, oil lamps drift down rivers on floats and fire balloons burst in the sky, in memory of Buddha's return from heaven, illuminated by torches.

November—The full moon of *Tazaungmon* (the division of the Burmese calendar that includes part of October and part of November) is marked by more displays of lights and fire balloons, especially in Taunggyi.

December 25th—Christmas Day is a public holiday.

Sport

Burmese people enjoy football, golf, and many other sports familiar to the West, but it is **Chinlon** that you should look out for—a Burmese game of great skill and grace.

The Chinlon is the hollow, basket-woven ball you see on sale in all markets, larger than a cricket ball with spaces in the woven cane. Six people stand in a circle and pass the ball using only their feet or their legs up to their knees. Points are scored according to the skills of the various passes. You will see it played by youths and men all over the country.

Boxing in Burma is not governed by the Queensberry Rules. Although there are strict rules, all parts of the body may be used and the winner is the first to draw blood—which may be wiped away three times before victory is declared.

People & Language

It is said that there are as many as 67 different races in Burma, as well as immigrants from other parts of Asia, resulting in a bewildering number of completely different languages and dialects. It is therefore foolish to try to identify a Burmese 'type' either in character or physical appearance. The differences are legion—in colour, facial structure and build—and you will quickly notice them as you travel across the country. The main language is Burmese, spoken by almost all Burmese people. It is a member of the Tibeto/Burman group of languages, written in a script derived from *devanagari*—composed mainly of sections of circles. In the towns and larger villages you will usually find someone who can interpret for you—either from the generation which can remember the British occupation, or from the generation which is now at school and college. English has recently been re-established in schools, not only as a compulsory subject but also as a medium of instruction. Many Burmese people who grew up between the '50s and early '80s were not encouraged to learn English. In some of the rural areas you must be prepared to communicate by sign language.

Spoken Burmese is tonal; what sounds like the same word to the Western ear might carry several meanings depending on how you say it. It is therefore dangerously easy to commit a solecism. Very few tourists are likely to have the time, or indeed the incentive, to make a study of the language for a seven-day visit, and you can easily get by without it, though there are inevitable moments of frustration. Sometimes an apparent lack of comprehension when you feel that your meaning must be only too obvious, springs from the *a-na-deh* attitude that is explained under 'Manners' on page 287.

However, it is well worth memorizing half a dozen or so simple and easily recognizable phrases. If you make the effort to express a greeting, request, or a valediction in Burmese, you will win instant rapport and much warmer friendships. You have only to say, for instance, 'please', or 'thank you' in Burmese, to produce delighted smiles and nods of approval, and very often a gentle correction of your pronunciation or inflexion.

Useful Phrases

Please—*che-zu-pyu-ywe*
Thank you—*che-zu-din-ba-deh*
Yes—*houg-keh*
No—*ma-houg-ba-bu*
Hullo—*min-gala-ba*
Good bye—*thwa-ba-oun-meh*
Where is X?—*X-beh-ma-leh?*
Which way to X?—*X-beh-beq-ma-leh?*
The bus stop—*ba-sa-ka mat tain*
The station—*buda-youn-ji*
How much?—*balauq-leh?*
I don't understand—*na-m'leh-ba bu*
Do you understand me?—*na-leh-tha-la?*
Sorry—*saw-ri beh*
Okay—*kaun-ba-bi*
Do you speak English?—*in-gn-leq lo pyaw tha leh?*
What's that?—*da-ba-leh?*

Numerals

The numbers, also formed by a series of curves, are easy to learn and very necessary if you intend to catch buses, or read street numbers:

0—	၀	
1—	၁	*tit*
2—	၂	*nit*
3—	၃	*thone*
4—	၄	*lay*
5—	၅	*ngar*
6—	၆	*chak*
7—	၇	*kun nit*
8—	၈	*shit*
9—	၉	*ko*
10—	၁၀	*ta sair*

271

Part II

BACKGROUND INFORMATION

History

Origins

Most Burmese people are descended from three powerful tribes which invaded the country at different times in the past and struggled between themselves for supremacy.

Like everywhere else in the world, legend and tradition are inextricably woven into Burma's pre-history, and it was not until the 11th century that recorded facts can be added to archaeological research. Parts of Burma and certainly the Irrawaddy basin, were inhabited as far back as 5000 years ago. The aboriginal tribes lived in caves, hunting and harvesting the natural vegetation. They didn't cultivate the land and the only traces they left of their existence were primitive stone implements.

The Mons

The Mons were a Buddhist people from Thailand and what is now Kampuchea. Several centuries before the birth of Christ, they moved west and settled in Lower Burma. These first invaders cultivated and harvested the fertile land, exporting rice, teak, minerals, textiles and ivory to eager markets in China, India, Arabia and today's Indochina.

The Pyus

About 2000 years ago, when Julius Caesar was scooping up his first handful of British soil, Mongol Pyu tribes from southeast Tibet, escaping persecution in their own country, moved down to seek sanctuary in Upper Burma. They made their capital at Sri Ksetra, near Prome, where you can still see traces of Indian architecture in the ruined pagodas, quite different from elsewhere in Burma.

The Burmans

In the 9th century, when Charlemagne was being acclaimed Emperor of the Western world, the Mramma Mongols, from the borders of China and Tibet, moved southwards along the Irrawaddy. (The word *Mram-ma*, pronounced *Bam-ma* by the Burmese, means 'the first people on earth' and it is from this that the word Burman evolved. The Mrammas believed that their kings were descended from Gautama Buddha and were divine.) The Burmans were a pugnacious tribe; they completely annihilated or absorbed the Pyus and then turned their attention to the Mons, forcing them further and further southeast, away from the fertile land around the Irrawaddy into the basins of the Salween and Sittang rivers.

The Shans

Later came the Shans, immigrants from Thailand who, failing to secure land for themselves on the plains, settled in the rugged hills and plateaux in the east.

These three races, the Mons, the Burmans incorporating the Pyus, and the Shans, divided, united, sub-divided and reunited over the centuries in a perpetual struggle for supremacy and land tenure. Immigrants drifted in, too, from India, China, Indochina and Europe. Although several kings tried to unify Burma, their attempts seldom lasted long and it remained divided into rival states and kingdoms, with the centre of power shifting from capital to capital, depending on who was supreme, until the present Union of Burma emerged in this century. Even today, although the government controls the majority of the people, there is a bewildering variety of peripheral groups who live their own lives beyond government control.

From the original trio of immigrant races, Burmans form 70% of today's population, occupying the divisions of Rangoon, Irrawaddy, Pegu, Magwe, Mandalay and Sagaing, as well as the states of Arakan and Tenasserim.

11th Century: King Anawrahta: The New Religion

In 1044, 22 years before the Norman Conquest of Britain, Anawrahta became the 42nd Burman king of Pagan and it is at this point that Burmese history takes over from legend.

The city at the heart of the kingdom of Pagan was traditionally founded by the first Burman king, Thamoddarit, in the 2nd century and established as a walled city by King Pyinbya in 849. Its lifeline was the Irrawaddy and its emmissaries went far afield to establish *entente* with neighbouring countries.

Buddhism flourished; not the pure Theravada Buddhism practised by the Mons but a scrambled amalgamation of the beliefs and practices of the various immigrant races, a

273

religion strongly influenced by spirit and animal worship. King Anawrahta was a religious man as well as an extremely powerful one. In 1058 a young monk called Shin Arahan arrived in Pagan and began to preach Theravada Buddhism to the Burmans. Anawrahta was so impressed that he was converted.

With all the burning zeal of the convert, he thirsted for the Tipitaka scriptures, without which, Shin Arahan assured him, it would be impossible to establish Theravada Buddhism among his people. Discovering that there were no fewer than 30 sets of this scripture in Thaton, Anawrahta dispatched an envoy to the Mon king, Manuha, with generous gifts and with the request that he might be sent a copy. Manuha refused.

Mons Defeated by Burmans

Infuriated by Manuha's rejection, Anawrahta stormed down to Thaton with a powerful army and removed not only the Tipitaka, but also the king, his entire court, his 32 coveted white elephants and a great many useful craftsmen and artisans. (The possession of a white elephant was one of the proofs of the divinity of a king and as such, was every monarch's ultimate ambition. A true white elephant, though not necessarily pure white in colour, must have four toenails instead of five; its skin must show reddish pink rather than black, when wet, and its eyes must have yellow irises ringed with red.)

Ironically, and as a direct result of his conversion, Anawrahta's conquest of the Mons influenced his own people so much that before long the culture, religion, and way of life of the Burmans became distinctly Mon in flavour.

First Union of Burma

Having conquered the Mons, Anawrahta quickly subdued the other states and thus created a united Burma: the first Burmese Empire. Keen to establish Theravada Buddhism throughout his kingdom, he was wise enough to see that it would be impossible to stamp out all the impurities that had coloured the old religion. He somehow established the mixture of Buddhist and animistic belief that is seen in Burma today while gaining himself the reputation for being the upholder of the pure Theravada law. More than anything else it was this revised Buddhism that gave Burma such a unique character. After the 11th century Theravada Buddhism was always the strongest religion in Burma, though there were times of less religious fervour than others.

Pagan's Golden Era: 250 years

Anawrahta's son and successor, Sawlu, was killed in battle trying to subdue a Mon rebellion and was succeeded, in 1084, by Kyanzittha—soldier lord—who subdued the Mon rebels and turned his attention to the reunification of his country. He was a deeply religious man: he built the great Ananda Temple in Pagan and he also sent financial aid to Bodhgaya, in India, to help restore the Mahabodi Temple—the traditional site of Gautama Buddha's enlightenment. Kyanzittha arranged a marriage between his daughter and a Mon prince and appointed their son Alaungsithu to be his successor, thus reuniting Mons and Burmans. So, for 250 years the city of Pagan flourished, the centre of Theravada Buddhism and of power in the East. Pagodas and temples mushroomed all over the country but nowhere so prolifically as in Pagan: it was its golden era.

Seduced by their new religion and cut off, geographically, from the rest of the world, the Burmese concentrated on the life-long struggle to gain merit and attain enlightenment and Nirvana. They formed a strong relationship with Sri Lanka which they looked on as a spiritual Mecca and a source of orthodoxy. While other countries developed, they built temples, confident that Burma was the supreme nation on earth. Pagan gained its revenue from the cultivation of rice, and, when the first fanatic enthusiasm for the New Law of Theravada declined, the people settled down to enjoy their prosperity. But good fortune seldom endures for ever.

The Fall of Pagan

In 1287, when England's King Edward I was trying to conquer Scotland, Kublai Khan, grandson of Ghenghis and emperor of China, decided that his dominance was such that he could demand tribute from the wealthy coffers of Pagan. Not surprisingly, King Narathihapate, refused to contribute and so Kublai Khan marched his huge Tartar army into Burma.

It was the end of Pagan's golden era: tradition holds that Narathihapate had the temples pulled down and the stones used to strengthen the defences of the city. Whatever the truth, Pagan was devastated and the Burmese army annihilated.

14th Century: Fragmentation of Burma

Inspired by the ensuing turmoil, the Mons broke away, moved south and founded a new kingdom of their own in Pegu in Lower Burma. Following this example, the Shans broke away and extended their original territory westwards, establishing a capital at Ava on the Irrawaddy. Meanwhile, the Arakanese spread themselves up the coast of the Bay of Bengal to Chittagong, now in Bangladesh. Thus depleted, the remaining Burmans withdrew to Toungoo on the River Sittang and licked their wounds, dormant but not bowed, for a couple of centuries.

After this reshuffle of allegiance, the waning strength of Theravada Buddhism was suddenly revived by the Mons and Pegu became a place of pilgrimage for scholars and holy men from all over southeast Asia.

15th–17th Centuries: Portuguese Influence

In the 15th century the Western world turned its restless eyes towards the East. In 1497, around the time that Christopher Columbus was busy discovering America while trying to reach the East by sailing west, the Portuguese navigator, Vasco da Gama, discovered the sea route from Europe to India and his countrymen quickly spotted the commercial advantages. They swarmed eastwards in droves and established trade and settlement treaties in and around Burma, enabling them to trade extensively in the East and effectively gain control of many Eastern ports and trade routes for over 100 years.

During this time of Portuguese influence in Burma, a bold adventurer, Philip de Brito y Nicote, who had started life as a cabin boy and quickly found favour for himself in the court of King Razagyi of Arakan, was appointed to Thanhlyn—now Syriam—as head of the Customs. De Brito set about establishing Syriam as a Portuguese stronghold despite native attempts to oust him and then proclaimed himself to be king of Lower Burma.

For 13 years Syriam, policed by de Brito's powerful navy, flourished as a major port, but his flagrant desecration of Buddhist temples and relics so scandalized the Burmese people that they rebelled in force. In 1613, King Anaukhpethlun of Toungoo led an army against Syriam and defeated the Portuguese, after a gruelling 34-day siege. De Brito was captured and condemned to death by impalement, a punishment that was carried out in such a way that it took him three days to die. His followers were exiled and Portuguese power ceased.

The 17th century saw the establishment of British, French and Dutch trading companies in Burma's ports. The capital was moved from Pegu to Ava.

18th Century: King Alaungpaya Reunites Burma

In 1752 the Mons, financed by the French, took Ava as their capital. At the same time the Burman king, Alaungpaya, emerged from the comparative seclusion of tiny Shwebo, where the Burmans had been gathering strength, and swept down on Ava, defeating the Mons once more. He ousted the French, destroyed the foreign trading posts and stormed all over Burma subduing and assimilating the breakaway states until he had reunified the country once more.

Alaungpaya was the founder of the last Burmese dynasty and it was his successors who became overbold in their disregard of national borders and brought about their own eventual demise.

Sacking of Siamese Capital

In 1767, Hsinbyushin, Alaungpaya's son, drove the Siamese out of their capital, Ayutthaya, and returned triumphantly to Ava with many of their craftsmen and scholars who, rather as the Mons had done to the Burmans in the 11th century, injected new ideas into Burmese culture. Hsinbyushin's brother, Bodawpaya, ascended the throne in 1782 and, in the Burmese tradition that a change of reign should be marked by a change of capital, moved the capital from Ava to Amarapura, only a few miles away. He then subdued Arakan, which had remained obstinately separate and united it with the rest of his kingdom, thereby bringing Burma's western border adjacent to India. Many of the Arakanese, however, who had intermarried with Indian immigrants over the years, fled into British-controlled Bengal, in India, and planned to recapture their country.

19th Century: The First Anglo–Burmese War

The Burmese pursued these refugees and bitter border disputes erupted, causing relations between the Burmese and the British to become strained. The British looked for an excuse to rap the knuckles of their troublesome neighbours.

King Bagyidaw, who came to the throne in 1819, was publicly humiliated by the Raja of Manipur, previously an ally, who refused to attend his coronation. Tension increased and when in 1824 the Burmese stormed yet again into India, the British grabbed their chance.

In their isolation from the rest of the world (a political, as well as cultural and intellectual isolation, brought about in part by geography) the Burmese had failed to assess the strength of the British Empire. Their somewhat inflated opinion of their own strength filled them with a confidence that was soon to be shattered. In the First Anglo-Burmese War, the British took Rangoon, but in 1826, in the Treaty of Yandabo, they gave it back and assumed sovereignty only over Arakan and Tenasserim. They also regained those borderlands in Assam and Manipur that the Burmese had annexed in 1819.

Uneasy Peace

Some sort of rapport was then established between the British and King Bagyidaw and the country settled down reasonably peacefully.

Unfortunately, King Tharawaddy, who succeeded Bagyidaw, was a weak man and a bad king. Relations with the British became so strained that the British Resident had to leave Rangoon. The country seethed with unrest. Tharawaddy's son and successor, Pagan, proved to be an even more disastrous king. Because primogeniture—the inheritance of the oldest son—was not practised in Burma, her kings always lived in fear of plots to seize the throne. It was not unusual, therefore, for a new ruler to try to safeguard his position by disposing of all possible rivals. King Pagan, a crazy despot, was responsible for the massacre of literally thousands of his subjects, in his attempt to reign uncontested.

The Second Anglo–Burmese War

As anarchy boiled throughout the country, border disputes between Burma and British India became more frequent and Britain looked for another excuse to regain control. Using a diplomatic incident in 1852, sparked off by the unfair treatment of two British sea captains by the Burmese authorities, the British marched back into Burma to fight the Second Anglo–Burmese War. Determined to prevent further trouble, they annexed all Lower Burma, making it, as well as the states of Arakan and Tenasserim, a province of British India.

King Mindon: The Founding of Mandalay

King Pagan was deposed, much to everyone's relief, in 1853, and King Mindon came to the throne. Mindon was a wise man and, like his predecessor Bagyidaw, he saw that it was prudent to establish good relations with the British. Once again an uneasy peace was restored. With only half a country to rule, Mindon saw the wisdom of looking towards the West in order to try to bring what was left of Burma into line with the modern world.

In 1861, fulfilling a prophecy made by Gautama Buddha 2400 years before, Mindon set about building the magnificent walled city of Mandalay. He moved his court there and in 1872 he presided over the Fifth Great Synod of Buddhism, 2000 years after the Fourth Synod. Mindon was a pious man. He anticipated a severe erosion of Buddhism under expanding British influence and so he called this Synod to try to unify all Burmese people in their faith. The Tripitaka, that Buddhist scripture for which Anawrahta had conquered the Mons in the 11th century, was revised by thousands of scholars to ensure that nothing non-canonical had crept in, and engraved on 729 stone tablets, each of which was enshrined in a separate pagoda at the foot of Mandalay Hill.

King Thibaw: The Last King of Burma

Mindon's successor was one of his sons, Thibaw, the last of Burma's kings. He was a weak man entirely under the thumb of his ambitious wife, Supyalat. Thibaw scrambled to power over the backs of dozens of contenders to the throne and then set about consolidating his position by disposing of anyone whom he considered to be a threat. Appalling atrocities were perpetrated and Thibaw's conscience was stained with the blood of many hundreds of deaths. It is hard to believe that little more than a hundred years ago, when Queen Victoria was pouring respectability over her empire, countless Burmese were consigned to the Irrawaddy, in red velvet sacks to hide the bloodstains, their screams drowned by music and merrymaking as the court participated in entertainments arranged to mask the sounds of massacre.

Once more, anarchy prevailed in Upper Burma, and Thibaw, weakened still further by an excess of alcohol, lost control completely.

The Third Anglo–Burmese War

Now that communication with the rest of the world was improved, news of barbaric behaviour in Burma began to shock Europe. Britain could no longer turn a blind eye to such inhumanity. In 1885, although very reluctant to interfere, they felt obliged to find an excuse to do so. Burma was negotiating with France, to grant the French shipping rights that would have ruined Britain's interests in the valuable teak trade. The British marched into Mandalay, found it virtually undefended due to the corruption of Thibaw's ministers, and within two weeks the whole of Burma was reunited as a province of British India. Thibaw and his queen were exiled.

Burma, freed from tyranny and anarchy, now found itself a vassal of the British Empire, ruled from India.

British Rule

While taking control of the government of Upper and Lower Burma and the Burman population, the British found it prudent, on a divide and rule basis, to allow the minority states, including the Shans, the Kachins and the Chins, to be governed by their own heads of state. Added to this injustice, Burmans were not allowed to serve in the armed forces, while the independent states were heavily recruited.

The Burmese had never been particularly good at managing their own economy but it was humiliating to have it taken over by foreigners who brought in Indians, whom the Burmese had always considered to be inferior, as managers. Nor was it pleasant for them to watch these foreigners grow rich on the revenue gleaned from Burma's extremely profitable natural resources. As the Burmans saw their land slipping further from their control, their nationalist loyalties increased together with their dislike of British domination.

The 20th Century: Rebellion

The imposition of Western government, and British policy towards minorities, as well as encouragement of Indian immigration, sowed the seeds of rebellion.

In the first three decades of the 20th century, the Nationalist movement grew, fed by the YMBA—Young Men's Buddhist Association—which included a number of lawyers who had learnt their profession in English universities and returned to indoctrinate the intelligentsia in Burma. In 1936 students from Rangoon University led strikes against the educational system, winning major reforms and paving the way for subsequent rebellion. Britain was obliged to grant more and more concessions until, in 1937, Burma was officially separated from India.

Aung San: The War Years

Among the leaders of the 1936 strikes was Aung San, an ardent nationalist who dreamed of a totally independent Burma. In 1940, when a number of young men who were considered a threat to the stability of the country were arrested, Aung San, on the hit list, escaped to Japan.

While the war directed British attention to the threat of a Japanese invasion, Aung San turned a blind eye to the incompatibility of Japanese fascism with Burmese philosophy in what he passionately believed to be the interests of his beloved country. Agreeing to collaborate with Japan, he was smuggled back to Rangoon in March 1941 to raise a small band of followers, to be trained in guerrilla warfare by the Japanese. He recruited 30 of his old colleagues from the All Burma Student Movement—a group that became known as the Thirty Comrades.

Nine months later, at the time when America was precipitated into the war by the Japanese attack on their fleet at Pearl Harbour, Aung San and his Burmese Liberation Army helped the Japanese to invade Burma. With the armed forces of the Allies occupied in so many different theatres of the war, those that were left in Burma were not strong enough to withstand the full force of this invasion. Fierce and devastating jungle warfare resulted in the deaths of countless thousands of the British, the Japanese and the luckless Burmese. From this brief and terrible conflict heroes emerged who have almost become household names: Slim, Orde Wingate and his Chindits, Vinegar Joe Stilwell, Old Weatherface Chennault . . .

By the middle of 1942 the Japanese had control of Burma with the full support of Aung San and his Burma National Army. It was not long, however, before the Burmese saw the true nature of the new occupying force; they found they were considerably more oppressed under a Japanese regime than they had been under British rule. Aung San, always wanting what was best for his country, persuaded his 10,000-strong Burma National Army to change sides. Renamed the Patriotic Burmese Forces, they helped the Allies to recapture Rangoon, and by August 1945 it was all over.

After the War

At the cost of hundreds of thousands of lives, war-torn Burma was once more at peace—a battle-scarred wasteland, devastated and impoverished. The economy was non-existent, the political scene chaotic and morale severely bruised. The British wanted to impose direct rule for a few years to try to heal the ghastly wounds left in the aftermath of war, hoping thus to establish a sound government and a healthy economy, but they knew their days were numbered.

Aung San was convinced that only the Burmese people could heal their own wounds. He founded and nourished a strong Nationalist movement and, in September 1946, instigated a national strike that brought the country to a standstill. The British government were more or less blackmailed into granting a list of demands made by Aung San—most importantly promising that Burma should become totally independent at the beginning of 1948. The British were uneasy about granting independence to all the minority states which presented severe threats to unity, being continually at odds with the Burman majority. However, Aung San managed to win a declaration of unity, with each state agreeing to work with the central government on the understanding that any of them could secede from the Union after 10 years if desired.

Assassination of Aung San

A national election was held in 1947 and Aung San and his Marxist-inspired Anti-Fascist People's Freedom League—AFPFL—won a landslide victory.

The world will never know whether Aung San, so single-minded in his pursuit of a Burma for the Burmese people, could have succeeded in solving all his country's problems and creating the utopia of which he had dreamed. Only three months after his election, while the new constitution was still on the drawing board, Aung San and several of his supporters were assassinated during a council meeting. He was 32 years old.

The instigator of this tragic massacre was U Saw, a pre-war prime minister, imprisoned by the British for collaborating with the Japanese. He was executed.

Independence: U Nu

So, when Burma finally became independent, in January 1948, it was U Nu, one of the original Thirty Comrades who was the prime minister of the first of Britain's colonies to separate from the Commonwealth. Almost immediately, the many states and groups within the Union began to raise their individual claims. U Nu's government found itself in conflict with the hill people, who had only paid lip service to unity; with two different communist parties; with the People's Voluntary Organization—PVO (originally founded by Aung San); with the Mons; with the Muslim Arakanese and with a number of small, rebel groups each with a different aim. Civil war raged and insurgent tribes reached the outskirts of Rangoon.

General Ne Win was appointed to be the Commander in Chief of the Armed Forces as well as Minister of Defence.

U Nu and his AFPFL managed to hang onto power in the 1951 elections, but internal schism disrupted his party and paralysed the government. U Nu decided that the only remedy was to appoint a caretaker government with Ne Win as its leader.

Ne Win

For the next 18 months, considerable progress was made in streamlining the government, improving administration, starting an important modernization programme and establishing social services. In 1960 U Nu and his Union Party were re-elected to government but once again the country fell apart. Minority states clamoured for secession and the government lost control.

Military coup: The Burmese Way to Socialism

On March 2nd 1962, while the world concentrated on the Cuba crisis, General Ne Win led a peaceful military coup, took over the Burmese government, imprisoned U Nu and other leading political opponents and appointed a Revolutionary Council. A manifesto was published—*The Burmese Way to Socialism*—renouncing capitalism and proposing an idealistic socialist Union of Burma: a Burma for the Burmese people.

For 12 years Ne Win and the Revolutionary Council sought to reform the country. All businesses and banks were nationalized; foreigners were denied any chance of exploiting Burmese wealth by being limited to 24-hour visas; campaigns were launched to indoctrinate the people in the Burmese Way to Socialism.

U Nu Tries to Intervene

U Nu and the others who had been imprisoned with him were released in 1968. They formed a National Unity Advisory Board and tried to reinstate a parliamentary government. When they were refused, U Nu travelled extensively, trying to raise foreign help for his National United Liberation Front—NULF. He won support from the Mons and the Karens and from some of the hill tribes, but Ne Win was too strong for him and he had to give up. He retired from politics and turned to translating Buddhist texts.

The Socialist Republic of the Union of Burma

On March 2nd 1974, 12 years after the coup, the Revolutionary Council was disbanded and the Socialist Republic of the Union of Burma created, with Ne Win as president of the nation and chairman of the Burma Socialist Program Party.

Ne Win's presidency was not plain sailing: there were riots, demonstrations, attempted coups, punctuated by constant clashes between the government and the border states, with insurgents struggling to disrupt the peace with their various causes, turning sizeable parts of the country into war-zones.

With a state-controlled media, very little official news has come out of Burma until recently: the odd paragraph from Reuters about border fighting; a visit from the Princess Royal; a couple of internal airline crashes. Not much has been said about a government economy that controls the salaries of civil servants, who are paid much the same as they were 25 years ago. Or of government controlled prices for rice, petrol and other necessities, which are immediately resold for 6–700% profit.

In 1981, at the age of 70, Ne Win handed the presidency to U San Yu , seven years his junior. But he retained the party chairmanship and continued to rule supreme. In July 1988, after a quarter of a century of submission to his despotic rule, student-led rebels forced him to propose swingeing reforms and to offer his resignation.

As this book goes to print sixty-four-year-old Sein Lwin, a hardliner (with the same military background as Ne Win) has been elected to succeed him as President and Chairman. The world waits to see whether this political upheaval will result in a sounder, multi-party system; whether bankruptcy can be reversed; whether private enterprise and foreign trade will effectively legalise the black market; and whether Burma can be saved from the death-blow of civil war.

Religion

Buddhism in Burma

Eighty per cent of the Burmese people, including virtually all Burmans, are *Theravada* Buddhists and nowhere in the world will you find a country more influenced by religion than Burma: it is an integral part of its peoples' lives and explains much of their unique character. You will find a Buddha room, or a shrine, or a simple Buddha image high on a wall, in most Burmese homes.

Buddhists believe that there will be five Buddhas in this world cycle; a cycle of countless eons. Each *Sasanna*—law or teachings—lasts about 5000 years, after which the *Dharma*—Buddhist doctrine—is lost. The four who have already passed were:

Kauk-kathan—1st lawgiver
Gawnagong
Kathapa
Gautama

Gautama died about 2500 years ago which means that the present Dharma will last until around AD4500. In some distant time another Buddha (Maitrya) will appear and rediscover the law, just as Gautama and those before him did.

The teachings of Gautama were never recorded and so, inevitably, there arose dispute after his death, resulting in schism. Of the resulting two schools of Buddhist thought, *Theravada*, or *Hinayana*—smaller vehicle—Buddhists believe that it is up to each individual to follow his own path to *nirvana* and that he will only get there by his own effort. *Mahayana*—larger vehicle—Buddhists believe that the strength of their faith will carry all mankind to better rebirth, regardless of personal endeavour.

Lay Buddhists have five precepts to guide them towards enlightenment. They are forbidden to kill, steal, commit adultery, lie, or drink alcohol. For monks there are some 227 rules laid down for them to follow. Gautama Buddha taught **The 4 Noble Truths** in his first sermon:

1. In life there is always suffering.
2. Suffering is caused by desiring things in the fruitless search for happiness.
3. If desire is conquered then suffering will cease.
4. The way to conquer desire is to follow the Noble Eightfold Path.

The Eightfold Path, or the Middle Path, of *Theravada* Buddhists is:

1. Understanding
2. Intention } Wisdom

3. Speech
4. Behaviour, action } Morality
5. Way of life

6. Endeavour
7. Thought } Mental discipline
8. Meditation

These teachings of the Buddha, the *Dharma*, should lead everyone to master their own minds and finally achieve enlightenment.

In its most simple analysis, therefore, the life of anyone aspiring to *nirvana* should be entirely given over to purification of both mind and behaviour, thereby acquiring an accumulation of merit that determines the next incarnation. This dominating aim in every good Buddhist's life can lead to misinterpretation of his actions by Westerners. For example, you will often see and hear a pilgrim striking one of the many bells that stand near pagodas. He is drawing attention to a good act he has just performed: he says '*ah mya*' (please share my merit) and he is answered: '*thardu*' (well done). Thus the merit is shared by rejoicing in another person's good deed. So the bell ringer is not acting out of conceit, but in a desire to give others a chance to share his merit.

Mixed up in this straightforward set of rules there is, in Burmese Buddhism, a strong belief in the power of *nats*, or spirits. This is a hangover from the Hinduism of the Middle Ages, before King Anawrahta was converted to the purer law of *Theravada* Buddhism.

Nats are a class of being, like humans, and are also part of the cycle of rebirth that is governed by good or bad behaviour. Pilgrims pay respect to the guardian *nats* in the pagodas, as to hosts at a party. Wherever you go you will see evidence of this animism, with placatory offerings made to the 37 primary *nats* and to a whole lot of more personal ones as well. There are shrines to the 'outer' *nats* all over Burma: simple huts made of bamboo, coconut shells with strips of coloured fabric attached, and gaudy images, each representing one of the many *nats*, good or bad, that play such an important part in Burmese life. As recently as the middle of the 19th century, people were buried alive under the boundary walls or gates of a new town in the belief that they would be reborn as bad *nats* who would fight off enemy invaders.

Thagyarmin is the king of the *nats* and guardian of Buddhism, promoted thus by Anawrahta when he realized that he must somehow incorporate animism into *Theravada* Buddhism if his new faith was to be adopted by his people, and you will often see images of this *nat* leader, in ornate golden costume. He is custodian of the Buddha's teachings and is expected to participate in all human activities in the cause of Buddhism. Even well-educated Burmese people have a healthy respect for the *nats* and, while joking about them, and telling *nat* stories (as intriguing as ghost stories) they will warn you, in all seriousness, not to mess about with them. Some believe that everybody is inhabited by a good and a bad *nat*, each competing for control of its host, so that when, for example, the person desires a glass of rum, the two *nats* vie with each other until the temptation is either conquered or submitted to. It is this curious mixture of the strict austerity of the *Dharma* and the superstitious practices of animism that plays a large part in making Burmese people so delightfully different. Where else in the world will you find fishermen who gain merit by catching fish and laying them on the bank, thereby 'rescuing' them from drowning? Where else do temple merchants sell caged birds so that pilgrims can gain merit by buying them and setting them free (many of them often returning to the cage for re-sale later).

Pagodas & Temples

A **Pagoda** is a focus for meditation, and a place in which to express devotion and love to Buddha and his teaching. A Buddhist expresses his love for Buddha by building or maintaining a pagoda, reciting the *Tripitaka*, making offerings to the shrines and almsgiving. A profusion of *nat* shrines and images mingle with the Buddhas in cheerful disregard of the pure teachings of *Theravada* Buddhism. You will often see pilgrims pouring water over the image of the *nat* of their choice, to cool it; or even occasionally holding a burning cigarette to the painted lips! The central dome of a pagoda, or *stupa*, is normally solid, and contains a holy relic, such as one of Buddha's hairs. There are terraces around the *stupa* on which stand shrines and temples. Earthquake damage being one of the hazards of Burmese buildings, many have been rebuilt or restored at least once during their lifetime. The earliest domes were generally either perfect hemispheres, of which the Kaunghmudaw Pagoda just outside Sagaing is a good example, or bulbous, like the elegant Bupaya Pagoda and the ruined Ngakywenadaung Pagoda, in Pagan. Later, the domes became more bell-shaped and graceful, like the Shwedagon in Rangoon, and the Shwemawdaw in Pegu. Many *stupas* are gilded and it is a meritorious act to buy gold leaf to enhance a pagoda.

Some of the larger pagodas, such as the Shwedagon, have shrines at the eight main points of the compass, representing the eight sections of the week (in Burma, Wednesday is divided into two) each with its planet and its animal. Here, the faithful can meditate at the shrine representing the day, or that of his own birthday. Thus:

North	Friday	Venus	guinea pig
Northeast	Sunday	Sun	*garuda* (half man, half beast)
East	Monday	Moon	tiger
Southeast	Tuesday	Mars	lion
South	Wednesday am	Mercury	tuskless elephant
Southwest	Saturday	Saturn	*ngar* (half dragon, half snake)
West	Thursday	Jupiter	rat
Northwest	Wednesday pm	Rahu	elephant with tusks

Every major pagoda has its own annual festival, which incorporates a trade fair and a great gathering of clans. Vendors come from all over the country to set up bamboo and thatch stalls for their merchandise. These traders-cum-pilgrims make large contributions towards the upkeep of the pagoda, combining good business with the gaining of spiritual merit. Because of public donations, the state gives very little aid to the maintenance of pagodas.

A **Temple** is a place in which to meditate, worship and pray to Buddha. It contains visual aids to meditation, such as Buddha images and pictures illustrating events in his life.

A **Shrine** is the structure in which the visual aids to meditation are housed, usually surrounded by offerings of flowers and other symbols of love.

Mudras

You will notice that the Buddha images are made in several positions; these are called *Mudras*, and are symbolic of Buddha's life.

Buddha standing represents his descent from heaven, where he had gone to preach to his mother.

Buddha walking represents him taming a rampaging Nalagiri elephant that had been sent to kill him by his cousin Devadatta.

Buddha seated, the most common image, has three positions: legs crossed with the feet hidden; the 'lotus'position—legs crossed with feet resting on thighs; and legs pendant. These represent: Buddha asking Mother Earth to witness his enlightenment; Buddha preaching; and Buddha meditating.

Buddha lying down with his head pointing to the north represents his death and attainment of *nirvana*. Buddha lying down with his head in any other direction represents him sleeping.

There are also symbolic hand *mudras*. The *Bhumisparsa Mudra* is probably the one you will see most: Buddha is sitting cross-legged with his left hand on his lap, palm upwards, and his right hand on his right knee with his finger tips touching the ground. This *mudra* represents Buddha asking Mother Earth to witness his enlightenment.

The *Dhyana Mudra* is that in which Buddha sits cross-legged with his palms together in his lap. This represents a variety of events in Buddha's life, often indicated by whatever he holds or by flanking figures.

The *Dharmacakra Mudra* shows Buddha forming a circle with the middle finger and thumb of his left hand touching the index finger and thumb of his right. This represents his first sermon, preached in India, explaining the Wheel of the Law.

The *Abhaya Mudra* is when Buddha is standing with his right hand raised and his left pointing downwards. It represents Buddha promising his followers serenity, courage and protection if they follow his Law.

The *Varada Mudra* is that in which Buddha is standing with his arms out in front of him, fingers pointing to the earth. Buddha is blessing his followers.

The last of the six hand *mudras* is a combination of the *Abhaya* and the *Varada*, with Buddha standing, right hand raised, left hand pointing downwards. In this *mudra* Buddha is both blessing his followers and promising to protect them. It also represents his return to earth after preaching to his mother in heaven.

Because Burmese culture is founded on Buddhism, you will see these *mudras* re-enacted in the movements and positions of Burmese dancers, and of the marionettes and mime actors at *pwes*.

Shin-pyu

Between the ages of 9 and 13, usually at about 11 (sometimes several brothers do it at once) and when he is able to repeat some Pali phrases clearly, every practising Buddhist boy in Burma is expected to enter a monastery as a novice. Although three months is considered a suitable period for this noviciate, many of the boys stay for only a few days. Later, young men often re-enter for another period, sometimes staying on for life, and it is not uncommon for an older man to leave his wife, who must give her permission, and children to retire permanently into the religious life.

The initiation of the young novice is called *Shin-pyu* and the usual time for it is just before the Buddhist Lent, soon after the harvest when rural families have some money. A *Shin-pyu* is expensive, because not only does it enhance social prestige, according to its grandeur, but also because it offers a means of acquiring merit by feeding as many monks and friends and making as many public donations as possible. Great merit is gained by rich families who sponsor poor novices.

First, the young candidate is dressed up like a pantomime prince, in vivid silks and satins and brocades, with an elaborate headdress, his face transformed by a mask of make-up. He is paraded through the streets, either on a horse, or carried on a litter, or perched up high in a motor vehicle followed by a cavalcade of supporters with music blaring from amplifiers. There is a feast, with entertainment, for guests and monks and family. The boy's head and eyebrows are shaved, the hair falling into a sheet held by his mother and sisters, who later bury it near a pagoda. He now asks to be admitted into the monastery in his carefully memorized Pali phrases, bowing three times to the chief monk, or *sayadaw*. He is dressed in his novice robes, whose colour ranges from saffron, through deep crimson, to maroon; he is issued with his begging bowl and other paraphernalia and so begins his noviciate.

When you see these miniature monks, in and around their monasteries, you will be tempted to suspect that their enforced period of religious detention is not unlike a Western 'summer school' with plenty of games and skylarking and very little austerity. Some monasteries—or *kyaungs*—welcome visitors and you can even go into the living quarters or watch them reciting their lessons.

Only about one eighth of the 800,000 monks—or *pongyis*—in Burma have dedicated their entire lives to monkhood. These have renounced the world and devote their time to meditation and teaching the scriptures. They take 227 vows including those of poverty, chastity and a vow not to hurt or offend any living creature.

Pongyis beg for their food, starting before dawn 'when it is light enough to see the veins in your hand' and they may not eat after noon. They are bestowing merit on those from whom they beg and accept their food without thanks. One of the unforgettable sights in Burma is the silent procession of *pongyis*, ranging from old men to young boys, each with his begging bowl held on his hip, padding barefoot down a dark village street, wrapped against the chill of the pre-dawn. Not all monks beg, however, and those who do, do not necessarily do it every day.

Culture

In prehistoric times, migratory tribes roamed across the face of the earth in every direction, seeking ideal environments. At some moment during those restless migrations, Mongolian and Aryan tribes met and their separate cultures brushed against each other. Buddha was Aryan, but his teachings went to the heart of the Mongolian Burmese. It is often said of the Burmese people that they have a Mongolian heart but an Aryan head. Thought to be descended from the Tibeto-Burmans of Central Asia, their roots probably go back to where the first dinosaurs grazed, not far south of the Tarim Valley where the earliest Chinese civilization was born. While Alexander, Xerxes, Caesar and Pompey were busy with their campaigns, writing familiar chapters into Western history books, equally stirring events were happening in the Far East, of which few Europeans were aware.

The first Burmese Empire was built during the Pagan period, between the 11th and 13th centuries, but excavations prove that Burmese culture was established at least five centuries before that, having evolved from the beginning of Buddhism.

It is Buddhism, above all else, that has shaped Burmese culture. Pagodas, temples, monasteries and their satellite buildings and shrines are the vehicles for almost all visual cultural expression in Burma. Acres of frescoes, sculpture, wrought gold and silver, bronze and ivory, intricate carved wood and stucco work, as well as the many styles of architecture, were all inspired by, and fashioned for, spiritual rather than material reward. You will even see reflections of Buddhism in the movements and positions of dancers, actors, and puppets, based on the positions or *mudras* of Buddha images.

In spite of the kitsch and glitzy gold that seem wholly artificial, many of their designs are inspired by nature: flowers, leaves, buds, birds, animals, and fish. Even the shape of a *stupa* is modelled on such things as lotus petals, banana buds, cones, and pineapples as well as the Buddha's begging bowl. If you let your eyes and ears sift out the touches of Western influence—the plastic, chrome and formica, the blaring transistorized music, the strident motor horns—what remains gives a clue to what has inspired Burmese culture. The simple line of the earthernware water jars, the delicate structure of the bamboo and palm-thatched houses, the fragile beauty of the river boats, the gentle sound of bells stirred by the wind in a pagoda *hti*, the silhouette of a bullock-cart, seen against a sky at sunset, the supple grace of a woman kneeling to make obeisance to a Buddha image, the soothing chant of *mantras*, intoned by a monk in a temple (now too often distorted by the installation of a Western amplifier.)

If you can find some, listen to the freedom of improvised Burmese music. Notice the innocent humour in Burmese drama, as well as the enthusiastic sense of theatre. Read Burmese poety—even in translation it is pure and simple:

A'po gyi oh ka kone gon
M'they ba nai ohn
Nauk hnit ka T'zaungmon pwe
Kyi ba ohn

Don't die yet
Bent-backed old man
Wait until next year
And see again
The Tazaungmon Festival

Anyone looking for a European type of culture—secular paintings, sophisticated theatres, weighty literature, melodious music—will be disappointed. They will find the antithesis in Burma: an entirely different form of culture that has developed from the inner calm that stems from the tranquillity of Buddhism.

Manners

The Burmese are so courteous that they will not reveal their feelings, however much a foreigner may unwittingly cause offence, so it is a good idea to have some knowledge of their codes of behaviour. Sometimes called the Celts of the East, Burmese people don't get impatient. Unnecessary displays of emotion are repugnant to them therefore to show anger, irritation or excessive affection is not good manners. In other words, when you turn up to claim your seat on a plane, only to find it has been given to someone else, or your jeep breaks down miles from shade at noon, or your hotel has run out of Mandalay beer—keep smiling.

Perhaps the best-known taboo in Burma is wearing shoes in holy places including those in ruins. You will see notices posted at the entrances of most pagodas asking you to remove footwear, and very soon this becomes instinctive.

Immodesty and the display of flesh, particularly legs, are offensive to the Burmese: on the footwear notices you will also see a request for visitors not to wear shorts or T-shirts without bras, within the holy places. Usually someone will politely tell you if you forget to take your shoes off, but they are less likely to tell you if your dress offends them. Their reticence does not lessen their distaste: if you go into a pagoda in the sort of scanty clothing that Westerners tend to wear in hot places you are committing a serious religious and cultural offence.

In Burma, feet are considered to be the meanest part of the human body and heads the most noble. Feet must *never* be pointed at people and are kept firmly tucked away out of danger whenever possible. You will notice that if a Burmese person walks past you, or crosses between you and someone else, he will duck his head below the level of yours as a mark of courtesy and respect.

The Burmese use the right hand for eating and the left for personal hygiene; the right hand is therefore used whenever possible for contact with other people—to give with the left hand would be insulting. But often, both hands are used together, or, when the right hand presents you with something, the right elbow is cupped in the left hand—a gesture of warmth that means you are being given the world!

Whatever your belief, or non-belief, you can give great pleasure at no cost to yourself by honouring the Buddha images in the temples. The simple act of kneeling and bowing your head over your clasped hands will open the way to friendship with the people around you. Similarly, if you buy one of the flower offerings that are sold in the pagodas and place it at one of the shrines, the attitude of the people around you will change—you are no longer a mere foreigner.

A-na-deh is a complicated and probably unique Burmese sentiment best described as a reluctance to give someone unpalatable news, or to ask a favour for fear of refusal, or even to warn someone of imminent peril. In the West, it looks very much like taking the line of least resistance. It also covers the more familiar Asian reluctance to say no. To give a direct refusal or to put someone else in the position of having to receive a direct refusal constitutes a loss of face and a lack of taste: to avoid such a situation a great deal of circumlocution sometimes has to be employed in order to arrive at a compromise where both parties accept that the desired object is in fact not worthy of desire. The process of *a-na-deh* can involve a certain amount of prevarication and half-truth and can prove extremely frustrating to foreigners trying to arrange schedules. It is important to be aware, therefore, of the motives that lie beneath an apparent inability to make firm arrangements, and to know that what may seem stone-wall obstinacy is in fact to do with a reluctance to lose, or make you lose, face.

Part III

RANGOON

Spires at Shwedagon Pagoda

All visits to Burma begin at Mingaladon airport, just north of the capital city of Rangoon. The half-hour taxi ride into the city takes you through rich jungle, interspersed by sprawling shanty towns, communal wells at the ends of the streets, decaying pagodas in dusty compounds. You catch your first glimpse of the golden dome of the Shwedagon and then you rattle on down Sule Pagoda Road into the heart of the city where Tourist Burma basks in the lee of the Sule Pagoda on its traffic island.

HISTORY
The history of Rangoon goes back more than 2000 years, beyond the days when it was called Dagon, to the beginning of this Buddhist world cycle, and the events that led to the foundation of the Shwedagon on Singuttara Hill (see Shwedagon history).

Travellers from the west wrote of Dagon, with its golden pagoda, in the 16th century but it was not until 1755 that it was founded as a city. King Alaungpaya captured what was then the village of Dagon from the Mons and renamed it Yangon, meaning 'safe place' or 'end of strife', from which the name Rangoon evolved. It became a thriving port a year later when Syriam fell.

The fortunes of Rangoon fluctuated: in British hands it became a major trade centre, until it was virtually destroyed by fire in 1841. It was rebuilt, only to be devastated in 1852 during the Second Anglo-Burmese War. It became the capital a hundred years ago: The 'Queen of the East' it was called and people said that by the 20th century it would rank with the most booming of American cities. Thanks to the *Burmese Way to Socialism* as administered by Ne Win's government, this prophecy remains unfulfilled.

Rangoon is a decaying memorial to British colonialism. The wide, tree-lined main streets are lined with once-gracious buildings, little changed or maintained since the

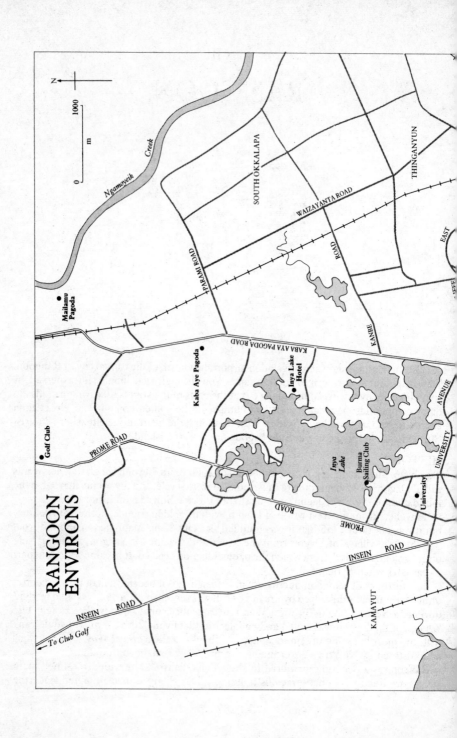

RANGOON
ENVIRONS

N

0 1000

m

Ngamoyeik Creek

Mailamu
Pagoda

Golf Club

PROME ROAD

PARAMI ROAD

KABA AYE PAGODA ROAD

Kaba Aye Pagoda

SOUTH OKKALAPA

WAIZAYANTA ROAD

THINGANYUN

Inya Lake
Hotel

KANBE
ROAD

Inya
Lake

Burma
Sailing Club

PROME
ROAD

University

UNIVERSITY
AVENUE

EAST

INSEIN   ROAD

INSEIN   ROAD

To Club Golf

KAMAYUT

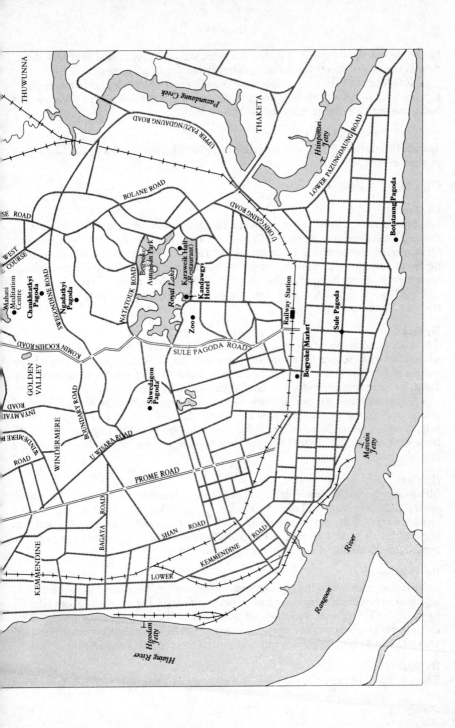

British departed, laid out on a grid system that makes it easy to find your way about, though few of the streets are named—certainly not the smaller ones.

As Rangoon has to be every visitor's first impression of Burma, it is unfortunate that it is probably the dirtiest, smelliest town in the country. It still has a large population of Indian origins so racial appearances will be misleading.

TOURIST INFORMATION
Tourist Burma is located beside The Sule Pagoda in the centre of Rangoon. Open 8 am to 8 pm every day.

GETTING AROUND

On Foot
You can explore the heart of the city on foot and, as long as you take it slowly, this is by far the best way to see and appreciate Rangoon. Taking the Sule Pagoda as your starting point, it is only a short walk south to the river and the teeming waterfront, and then east to the Botataung Pagoda; or north to the Scott Market and the food markets, through the narrow back streets between Anawrahta Street and Mahabandoola Street.

To get to the Shwedagon, the Zoo, the lakes and anything else in the suburbs you should go by bus, taxi, or trishaw.

By Bus
There are frequent buses from the city centre to all parts of the suburbs. These are often so crowded that the men travel clinging to the outsides. If you can get a seat, you can go anywhere for just a few kyats, but you must learn to read the Burmese numbers. Passengers are friendly and will generally tell you where to get off.

A few useful buses are: No. 37 to the Shwedagon, No. 46 round the Royal Lakes (any going down Signal Pagoda Road pass the Royal Lakes), Nos. 51 and 9 to the airport (51 is quickest—1 hour), No. 3 to Kyauk Htat Gyi and Nga Htat Gyi Pagodas, (or No. 47 from Shwedagon), No. 38 to Thida (or Htinbonseik) Jetty for Syriam, Nos. 14 or 5 are best for Peace Pagoda.

By Taxi
Much more expensive, but better if you want to see something of the city as you travel, are the taxis. Negotiate with the driver before you start: for several people, the hire of a taxi for a tour of the city is not prohibitively expensive—K60 per hour is quoted as reasonable by Tourist Burma. The fare from Tourist Burma to the Shwedagon would be about K25-30 (1988). A taxi from the airport costs K60.

By Trishaw
Trishaws are cheap, plentiful and excellent for sightseeing. Your driver will usually act as a guide and you should negotiate a price before you start. Expect to pay about K50 for half a day, or K5 for a short journey, i.e. from Tourist Burma to the museum. Although they are designed to carry two people, you pay per head rather than per vehicle and you are less likely to have to get out and help push if there is only one of you.

By Rail
There is also a city circular rail route that takes about 2 hours. If you have time this is

worth doing, but avoid the rush hour! Tourist Burma will tell you that it is not possible for tourists to do this so you must deal with the station direct. For K1 you can sit back and enjoy a microcosm of Burma displayed in suburban communities as the train trundles from station to station. The names of the stations are in Burmese so if you want to break your journey at any of the stops, you must either commandeer an English-speaking fellow passenger or get someone to write down the characters for you before you start. The carriages are very basic.

By Boat
Ferries and riverboats depart frequently from various piers and are ridiculously cheap i.e. K1 for a 45-minute trip to Syriam.

WHAT TO SEE
In the frantic rush of trying to fit in all that there is to see, you should take time to wander in the narrow back streets linking up the main boulevards. Here, where there is little traffic, you will see kaleidoscopic impressions of the Burmese people. Tall buildings seem to be only just standing with balconies clinging miraculously among fluted columns and balustrades; the graceful architecture can still be seen, its crumbling stucco shrouded in washing draped from windows. Faded canopies shade doorways and always a colourful crowd presents a shifting foreground.

If you intend to use your seven days in seeing as much of Burma as possible, then you will not be able to explore Rangoon completely. If your itinerary allows only a few hours, your first priority must be a visit to the Shwedagon, which is about 3 km northwest of Tourist Burma. On the way back go to the Scott Market, little more than half a kilometre northwest of Tourist Burma, and then wander down through the back streets in a southeasterly direction, taking in the Sule Pagoda and a quick visit to the museum before reaching the waterfront. Here you can stop off at the Strand Hotel for a fresh lime soda or a Mandalay beer. If there is time, walk 1 km east to the Botataung Pagoda.

The Shwedagon Pagoda

History
At the end of the last Buddhist world cycle, five lotus buds were seen on Singuttara Hill on which the Shwedagon now stands. As each bud unfurled it released a bird carrying in its beak a saffron robe—the symbol of sanctity. These signs were interpreted to prophesy the coming of five Buddhas in the next world cycle—that is, this one. Coming at approximately 5000-year intervals, four of these Buddhas have now passed, Gautama being the most recent, 2400 years ago. Each of these four left behind him a relic to be enshrined on Singuttara Hill: Kaukathan, the first, left his staff; Gaunagon, the second, left his water filter; Hathapa, the third, left a piece of his robe, and Gautama left 8 hairs from his head. These hairs were given by Gautama to two merchant brothers who honoured him after his enlightenment. He ordered the brothers to take them to Singuttara Hill and build a shrine for them. The brothers had great difficulty finding the hill and during the process they were robbed of four of the precious hairs. Finally, with the help of the king of the *nats*, they found the hill and the relics of the previous three Buddhas, and they began to build a suitable *stupa* to enshrine them. When it was finished

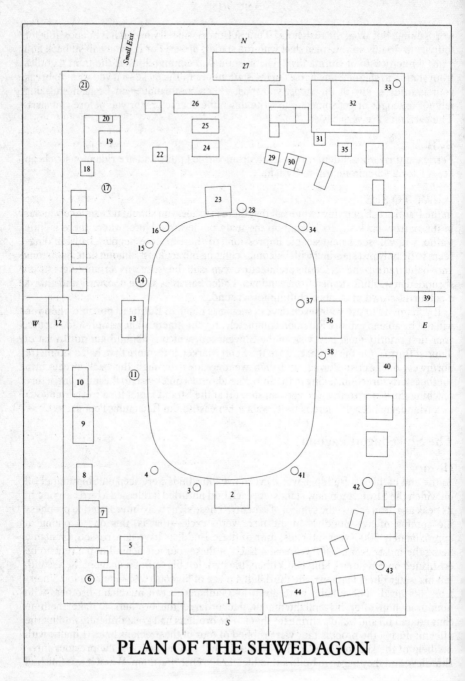

N

Small Exit

27

21

26

20
19

25

24

22

18

17

23

28

16

15

14

13

33

32

31

35

29 30

39

W 12

E

11

10

9

8

7

5

6

4

3 2

1

S

37

36

38

40

41

42

43

44

PLAN OF THE SHWEDAGON

a great ceremony was organized for the actual enshrinement. The casket holding the remaining hairs was opened and to everyone's incredulous joy, the four that had been stolen were found to have been replaced. A series of miracles then happened—the hairs rose into the sky, shedding a dazzling light over all the world. People were cured of chronic disabilities, the earth shook, barren trees blossomed and jewels rained from the heavens.

So the Shwedagon was born. A series of *stupas* made of various metals and marble were built one over the other, like Chinese boxes. Over the centuries, successive kings, queens and rich benefactors have added to, repaired, and replaced the main structure, sometimes offering their own weight in gold-leaf for gilding. Today, it stands nearly 100 metres tall on the hill-top, its golden dome dominating the landscape for miles around.

Over the years, earthquake damage has been devastating—there were eight earthquakes in the 17th century alone and, in 1768, one which destroyed the whole of the top of the pagoda. This was rebuilt by King Hsinbyushin and its present height and shape date from then.

When de Brito was in power in Syriam in the 17th century, he raided the pagoda and, among other things, carried away a great bell given by King Dhammazedi 200 years before. (He planned to melt it down to make canons, but dropped it in the river on the way back to Syriam.) British soldiers occupied the Shwedagon in 1824 for 2 years, having taken Rangoon without resistance in the First Anglo–Burmese War. It provided the ideal vantage point from which to dominate the city. They occupied it again in 1852 in the Second Anglo-Burmese War and retained control of it for 77 years until 1929. (On this occasion, the admiral commanding the British fleet carrying the conquering army was Jane Austen's brother.)

Inevitably, there was looting and desecration. Surrounded by so many treasures, members of the invading army succumbed to temptation. A tunnel was dug into the heart of the main *stupa* 'to make an ammunition store'. The vast pagoda bell was stolen too, but as with the one de Brito stole, it fell into the river. This time, it was salvaged and returned to the Shwedagon.

Two years after the British relinquished control, a fire severely damaged the western staircase, part of the north side of the pagoda and part of the eastern staircase.

The following plan of the Shwedagon is not drawn to scale. The numbered shrines are those mentioned in the text. Some of the others have been put in, to help orientation, but there are many more.

A Tour of the Shwedagon
(See plan for numbers referred to in text.)
There are four stairways to the main plateau and two lifts. The **southern stairway** (1), from which one of the lifts also goes, leads up from Pagoda Road and is probably the busiest. Its entrance is guarded by an ogre and a massive *chinthe*, the half-lion, half-griffin temple guardian you will see all over Burma. These stairs were rebuilt after the Second Anglo-Burmese War and you can still see some of the pre-war teak beams overhead. A little way up on the left there is a platform where pilgrims can gain merit by buying food and feeding the very prosperous-looking pigeons. About halfway up you cross a bridge, replacing a drawbridge across the old moat. As you climb barefooted up 104 gritty steps, you pass stalls selling pagoda ornaments, offerings and souvenirs. The

secular nature of much of the merchandise is less unsuitable than it may seem at first, when you consider that the stallholders all contribute to the upkeep of the pagoda, so that plenty of merit is earned, both by them, and by their customers.

When you reach the main terrace, you will see more than a hundred lesser buildings, small shrines, halls and miniature pagodas, clustered apparently at random, round the base of the main dome.

The huge golden *stupa* of the Shwedagon is solid. It rises 98 m from a square base into octagonal terraces from which circular bands graduate upwards into the traditional bell shape. Above, a double wreath of lotus petals supports the smooth curve of a banana bud topped by the seven-tiered *hti*. Gold leaf covers the lower parts and gold plate adorns the lotus petals, banana bud and *hti*. The 5 m-high vane and flag are encrusted with thousands of diamonds, rubies, emeralds, sapphires and other gems, all flashing in the sun, surmounted by an orb inlaid with more than 4000 diamonds tipped by one of 76 carats. Gold and silver bells tinkle melodiously in the wind.

It is customary for pilgrims to keep a pagoda always on their right, giving their most important side to Buddha. You will find that few people adhere to this practice now, but as a gesture of courtesy visitors should turn left and go clockwise round the marble walkway.

Facing you at the top of the southern stairway is (2) the **Temple of Konagamana,** the second Buddha. The many Buddhas in this shrine are among the oldest you will see here. Immediately to the left is the **Planetary Post for Mercury** (3) (see Religion, page 282 for the planetary posts with their associated days, directions and signs). **The Planetary Post for Saturn** (4) is on the southwest corner and the **pavilion** opposite (5) has 28 images in it depicting the 28 *avatarsor* incarnations of Gautama Buddha.

Tucked into the southwest corner of the platform there is a **column** (6) inscribed in Burmese, English, French and Russian, commemorating the student riot in 1920, a forerunner to Independence. A little further on, to the left of the marble walk, a glass case (7) encloses **The Guardian Nat of Shwedagon,** Bo Bo Gyi, on the right, with Thagyamin, **King of the Nats,** on the left. Next to this is the **Arakan Tazaung** (8), a carved wooden prayer pavilion with nothing in it, donated by the Arakanese. The head of the 3-m-long reclining Buddha in the adjacent carved **pavilion (9)** points north, showing that he has attained enlightenment. His favourite disciple, Ananda is at his feet. Beside this the **Chinese Merchants' Tazaung** (10) contains a number of Buddha images. The two figures under the white umbrella opposite, on the right of the marble walkway (11), are **Mai La Mu** and **Sakka,** the legendary parents of King Ukkalapa who founded the Shwedagon.

The landing at the top of the western stairway is the **Two Pice Tazaung,** so called from the daily donation of 2 pice (copper coins) from businessmen and stallholders, towards the rebuilding of the stairs after the fire in 1931. With 166 steps, this is the longest of the four stairways. Opposite on the right is the **Temple of the Kassapa Buddha** (13), also destroyed in the fire, with the **Jupiter Planetary Post** (14) beside it. The man under the white umbrella a bit further on (15) is **King Ukkalapa,** founder of the pagoda.

On the northwest corner of the main *stupa* is the **Rahu Planetary Post** (16), and north of this, beyond the marble walkway, is a small, golden-spired, **octagonal pagoda** (17), the **Pagoda of the Eight Weekdays**. The eight creatures, each associated with a day of the week and a planet, face the eight cardinal points, interspersed with Buddha images in eight niches.

Behind this, in a pavilion to the northwest, is the **Maha Gandha Bell** (18), cast and donated by King Singu in 1779. This was the bell the British stole in 1825 and dropped in the Rangoon River. Weighing 23 tons it was later raised and restored. The inscription in Burmese asks that Singu may attain *nirvana*. Just past the bell is an **Assembly Hall** (19) with a 10 m-high Buddha image presiding over erudite lectures on Buddhist teaching that are given here to monks from all over Burma.

Among the jumble of small shrines in the northwest corner, there is one (20) that stands out as being more than usually decorated with offerings, and well-attended by people. This is the **Wonder Working Buddha,** known to work miracles for the faithful.

Right in the corner (21) are two **Bodhi Trees**. The smaller one grew from a cutting of the tree in Bodhgaya under which Gautama Buddha attained enlightenment. It was planted by Burma's first Prime Minister, U Nu. Going on round the main *stupa*, there is a star-shaped inset on the ground in the open (22) called the **Wish Fulfilling Place,** always well populated by kneeling pilgrims, facing the *stupa* in earnest supplication.

In the middle of the northern base is the **Temple of Gautama Buddha** (23), with Gautama as the main image. Opposite, facing north, the **Sandawdwin Tazaung** (24) stands on the spot where Gautama's eight hairs were washed in a well fed by the Irrawaddy before being enshrined. The building north of this (25) is the **Library of the Zediyingana Society,** with more than 6000 books on religion and Burmese culture.

North of the Library, **Statues of Indians** guard a pavilion (26). Here, a dragon guards Buddha and an imprint of his foot. At the top of the **northern stairway** (27), a battle took place in 1824 between Burmese soldiers, who had fought their way up the 128 steps, and the British, who repulsed them.

The **Planetary Post for Venus** (28) stands just beyond the Temple of Gautama Buddha and opposite, noticeably Indian in design, is a **replica** (29) **of the Maha Bodhi temple** in India. Beyond the Maha Bodhi to the east, the **Kannaze Tazaung** (30) is said to be where King Okkaoapa prayed to be given relics of the Buddha. This Buddha image is called *Sudaungbyi*—Buddha who grants the King's Prayer. The stone in front is a Wish Granting Stone—if it feels light to the supplicant, then his wish is granted!

The Buddha in the **Shin Itzagona Tazaung** to the northeast (31) has eyes of different sizes. Meaning Monk Goat-bullock, it commemorates a monk-alchemist who, trying to discover the Philosopher's Stone, poked out his eyes when his final experiment failed. His assistant rushed to the slaughter-house and brought him an eye from a bull and an eye from a goat, in order to try to restore his sight.

Just to the north, is the **Naungdawgyi Pagoda** (32), the golden replica of the Shwedagon *stupa*, on the site where the eight hairs of Gautama were originally kept, awaiting their final enshrinement. Women are not allowed to climb onto the platform here.

Right in the northeastern corner (33) the **Dhammazedi inscription,** tells the story of Shwedagon in Pali, Mon and Burmese. Originally on the eastern stairway, it dates from 1485.

The **Planetary Post for the Sun** is on the northeastern corner of the main *stupa* (34) with the **Maha Tissada Bell** (35) in an ornate pavilion opposite. Donated by King Tharawaddy in 1841, it weighs 42 tons.

The **Temple of the Kakusandha Buddha** (36), opposite the eastern stairway, was originally built by Ma May Gale, wife of King Tharawaddy. It was destroyed by the fire in 1931 and this replica was built in 1940. The image of Kakusandha, the first Buddha, and those of three others in the temple have their right palms turned upwards—an unusual pose. Up on the terrace of the main *stupa* behind the Kakusandha Temple, in a niche, is the miracle-working **Tawa Gu Buddha** (37). Women are not allowed onto the upper terraces and men must first get a ticket from one of the pagoda officials.

Beside the Kakusandha Temple is the **Planetary Post for the Moon** (38). A little way down the 118 steps of the eastern stairway are the **Dhammazedi Stones** (39), whose temple was the last thing to be destroyed by the 1931 fire before it was stopped. There are tea shops on the stairs, as well as the usual stalls.

On the south side of the eastern stairway is **U Nyo Tazaung** (40) with carved panels illustrating the life story of Gautama Buddha. The **Planetary Post for Mars** (41) is on the southeast corner of the main *stupa* and the pillar opposite it (42), is a **Hamsa Tagundaing**—a prayer pillar said to bring favours to the founder. These pillars are often surmounted by the sacred *Hintha* or *Hamsa* bird.

The **Bodhi Tree** in the southeastern corner (43) is another said to be grown from a cutting of the one at Bodhgaya.

On the left, as you come back to the landing of the southern stairway there is a **Curio Museum** (44) with a collection of statues and models. Opposite, just to the right of the Konagamana Temple, is the stairway to the upper terrace, for men only.

Full Moon Festival

During the Full Moon Festival in March, people come from all over Burma and beyond, to visit Shwedagon. For the week of the festival you will find the pagoda *en fête*, with an eruption of stalls and sideshows clustered at the foot of each stairway. At this time the always busy terraces will be crowded, day and night, and on the final night when the moon is full, many hundreds of people sleep up on the platform, or keep vigil at their own special shrines throughout the night. If you are lucky enough to be in Rangoon during this festival, get up before dawn and climb one of the stairways on the final day. It can be a moving experience to step out onto the terrace in the grey pre-dawn and find a ceaseless perambulation of people, walking, sitting and praying before the shrines. Tables of offerings are laid out in front of many of the images, bearing bowls of rice, fruit, drinks and pastries.

Bats

There is a natural phenomenon that occurs regularly during the dry season as the sun sets. To witness it you must go to the foot of the steps at the western entrance to the Shwedagon, just before the sun goes down, some time after 6 pm, but varying slightly throughout the year. To begin with, you will notice the sky above the stairway beginning to fill with bats, flying apparently at random from out of the pagoda. Then, suddenly, there will be an explosion of bats from the turret eaves—they will pour out in an endless great black rope of swirling bodies which will set off across the twilight sky, pouring over the city towards their feeding grounds in the paddy fields. This amazing spectacle lasts for about 6 minutes and oddly enough, very few of the residents of Rangoon seem aware of this nightly miracle. Do try to see it if you can.

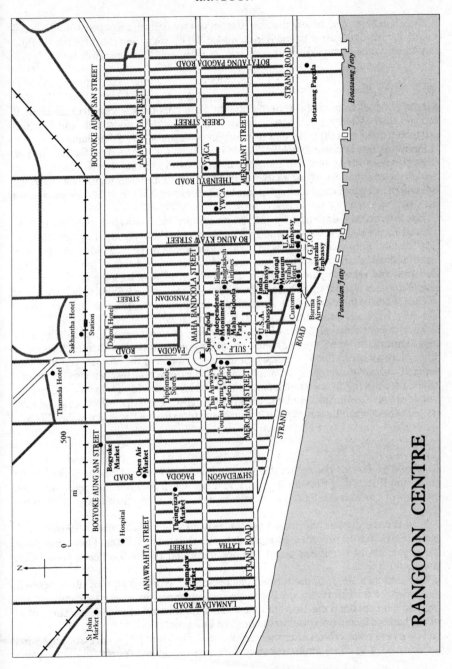

RANGOON CENTRE

Once you have spent time at the Shwedagon, you are likely to get pagoda-indigestion if you try to visit all the other pagodas in Rangoon. Of the many that exist, the two that you should try to see if you have time, are Sule Pagoda, and Botataung Pagoda.

Sule Pagoda

Rising as it does from the heart of the city, the **Sule Pagoda** is an excellent landmark if you get lost. Wherever you are, keep walking across the grid system and you will eventually come to an intersection from which you can see its golden dome.

Paradoxically, because the Sule Pagoda is right on the doorstep of Tourist Burma, many people never get round to going into it. It stands on an island, surrounded by a busy road, its four entrances so unremarkable that they are almost indistinguishable from the workshops, watchmakers, photographers and tailors that have their businesses around the base.

The original pagoda dates from the 3rd century BC, when two Indian monks went to Thaton to preach and were granted permission to build a pagoda near the fabulous Shwedagon. They had brought with them a hair from Gautama Buddha and this was enshrined within the *stupa* which was called *Kyaik Athok*—Shrine of the Sacred Hair. Repaired and rebuilt many times over the years, the present building is 48 m high, a conventional octagonal shape surmounted by a golden dome, surrounded by a cluster of shrines. Each of the eight sides is dedicated to the eight divisions of the Burmese week, with its own planet and animal. (See 'Religion', p. 282.)

After the dazzling splendour of the Shwedagon, the Sule pagoda has a delightfully cosy atmosphere, with its rather haphazard arrangement of satellite shrines. It is one of those places where, if you sit quietly on the steps of one of the shrines, you may find yourself with an unassuming companion, a bank clerk or school teacher, curious about a tourist who has the time and inclination to sit and let the world pass by. Most Burmese people are only too happy to practise their rusty English, learnt in the days of British rule, and talk about what life is really like in Burma today, and what it was like in the old days.

Botataung Pagoda

Southeast of Tourist Burma, on the waterfront about one kilometre east of the Strand Hotel, the **Botataung Pagoda** is unusual in that you can go inside the *stupa*. Normally, the heart of a pagoda is solid and its essence is more of a concept than a tangible or visible reality.

Two thousand years ago Indian monks brought relics of Buddha to Burma to be enshrined where the present pagoda stands beside the Rangoon River. They came under the protection of a military guard of honour formed by 1000 officers: *bo*—leader, *tataung*—1000.

In November 1943, in the turmoil of the Second World War, a bomb completely destroyed the original Botataung Pagoda, revealing among the ruins a miniature golden *stupa* which contained the Buddha relics, and a great hoard of pagoda treasure, all of which had been contained within the original building.

The pagoda was rebuilt after the war, almost a replica of its predecessor but with a hollow *stupa*. You climb some steps from the entrance and find yourself in a honeycomb of cells with walls made of mirror mosaics. The effect is dazzling as you walk through the maze of little chambers and alcoves, past glass showcases full of some of the treasures from the first pagoda—a vast collection of gold, silver, bronze and terracotta images, displayed as if in an antique shop window.

In a long hall behind the main *stupa* you will see a row of Buddhas, monks and wealthy benefactors, staring ahead with vapid smiles while mechanized figures jerk through scenes from Buddha's life, fuelled by pilgrims' kyats, on a platform in the corner. (These kitschy contraptions crop up all over Burma, side by side with the sacred images.)

The huge bell in the forecourt is for anyone to strike, drawing attention to a merit-gaining act, not in order to boast but so that those who hear can rejoice and thus gain merit for themselves.

Rangoon National Museum

Even if you are short of time, it is worth paying a visit to the museum. It is in Pansodan Street, within easy walking distance of the Tourist Burma office, *en route* for the Strand Hotel.

Open every day, except on Mondays and public holidays, from 10 am to 3 pm, 1 pm to 3 pm on Saturdays, it costs 1 kyat to get in and you must leave your bag inside in a drawer for which the key costs another kyat. The first thing you see as you enter is the magnificent **Lion Throne,** a vast gilded wooden structure inlaid with lacquer work. King Thibaw, last of Burma's reigning monarchs, sat on this splendid throne when it was housed in the Royal Palace in Mandalay.

Fortunately for posterity, the British stole the throne when they annexed Mandalay and sent it to Calcutta—an act of greed that saved its life when the Royal Palace was burnt down in 1945. It was returned by Lord Mountbatten after Burma became independent in 1948, and gives an impression of the sumptuous flamboyance of the old Burmese court. The museum holds many memorials to the final chapters in the bloody history of Burma's monarchy. Showcases contain elaborate inlaid gilt betel-containers, goblets, platters and boxes, encrusted with semi-precious stones. There are also displays of state clothes, some so thick and stiff, sewn with braid, jewels, beads, cords and sequins, padded and winged, that it must have been torture to wear them in the tropical heat. King Thibaw's state clothes show just how tiny he was.

On one wall there are photographs of the Royal Palace in Mandalay, poignant evidence of the beautiful walled paradise that existed before it was razed to the ground by fire during the retaking of Mandalay in 1945. Look out for the photograph of King Thibaw and his Queen Supyalat—he looks bored and she rather bad tempered. You can also see a collection of models of some of the buildings in the Royal Palace, further evidence of the tragedy of the fire, and gilded furniture and palanquins conjuring up ghostly echoes of splendid state processions.

Upstairs there are reproductions of prehistoric cave drawings, relics from Pagan, musical instruments, puppets, and many other artefacts from Burma's past. On the top floor there is a model exhibition of working people and their crafts, with an unrealistic aura of prosperity and contentment. Beyond, you will find an interesting show of paintings ranging from traditional Burmese to those of international schools.

Other Sights Around Rangoon

Martyrs' Mausoleum
On the hill just north of the Shwedagon, off Transport Road, you will find the mausoleum containing the tomb of Aung San and the seven ministers of his cabinet who were assassinated on July 19th 1947. Overlooking Rangoon, it is a fitting memorial to the passionate single-minded devotion of the man who dedicated his short life to founding an independent Burma, but who did not live long enough to put his ideals into practice.

Kyauk Htat Gyi Pagoda
Northeast of the Shwedagon, on Shwegondine Road, you can see the **Kyauk Htat Gyi pagoda**. A No. 3 bus from the city centre will get you there, or a No. 47 from Shwedagon. An airy metal and corrugated iron pavilion houses a vast reclining Buddha. Although the statue is modern and not much venerated, at 70 m it is larger in length than the more famous reclining buddha in Pegu, and is very fine, if somewhat gaudy. Draped in a golden robe with braid edges, the recumbent Gautama stares out with brooding calm, head propped on hand, the soles of his feet engraved with whirling prints and sacred symbols. This pagoda is a centre for the study of Buddhist manuscripts, with about 600 monks living in the monastery studying ancient Pali texts. A strangely somnolent bell peals at sunset.

Nga Htat Gyi (or Ngadatkyi) Pagoda
Just south of the Kyauk Htat Gyi pagoda, in the Ashay Tawya Monastery, in Campbell Road, you can see a huge sitting Buddha, known as the 'Five Storey Buddha' for obvious reasons. You approach along a covered walkway, lined by ramshackle wooden houses on stilts, up to the usual clutter of temple stalls. Look out for the **Abbot's House**, beside the pagoda—an ornate, brightly painted Chinese-style building, donated by China.

Kaba Aye Pagoda
Off the northeast corner of Inya Lake, and reached by Kaba Aye Pagoda Road, this is the 'Peace Pagoda' built in the early '50s by U Nu, the first prime minister of independent Burma after the assassination of Aung San.

The story is told that a monk, Saya Htay, was meditating one day and received a vision of an old man in white who gave him an inscribed bamboo pole and told him to take it to the prime minister and tell him that he must do more to strengthen the Buddhist faith in Burma. U Nu, being an extremely pious Buddhist, obeyed this supernatural order and built the pagoda for the Sixth Buddhist Synod, which was due to start in 1954, and dedicated to World Peace.

It isn't a beautiful building but it has some good gold images inside and a silver Buddha in the inner chamber weighing 500 kilograms. Lovely pink marble colonnades lead up to it. There are five entrances, each adorned by a standing Buddha nearly 3 m tall. After the Sixth Buddhist Synod, an Institute of Advanced Buddhist Studies was founded in the grounds, called the **Maha Pasan Guha**.

Maha Pasan Guha
Just north of Kaba Aye Pagoda is the Maha Pasan Guha, a huge artificial cave built for

the Sixth Synod, modelled on the Satta Panni Cave in India where the First Buddhist Synod took place three months after the death of Gautama Buddha.

Not long after his inauguration as prime minister, U Nu led a pilgrimage to visit the major Buddhist sites throughout the East. It is believed that he had a vision while meditating under the Bodhi tree in Bodhgaya, India, where Gautama received his enlightenment. U Nu foresaw an international gathering of Buddhists in Burma, dedicated to seeking peace in a world plagued by wars.

Such was U Nu's enthusiasm, that when he returned to Burma and proposed the building of this cave for the coming Synod, he inspired devout Buddhists to create it, without pay. It took 14 months, measures 139 by 371 metres and has an assembly hall big enough to hold 10,000 people. It was finished only 3 days before the Synod opened on May 17th 1954, the day on which *Theravada* Buddhists celebrate the birth, enlightenment and death of Gautama Buddha.

Because the present government is against fervent Buddhism, the religious purpose for which this hall was intended is played down. As a compromise, it is now used as an examination centre for monks.

Mai La Mu Pagoda
Near the airport, in the south of the suburb of Okkalapa, is the Mai La Mu Pagoda. Named after its founder, the mother of King Okkalapa who founded the Shwedagon, it was built to cheer her up after the death of a grandson. It is known as the 'Disneyland Pagoda' because its life-sized figures depicting scenes from the *Jataka* are as glitzy as any from Disneyland.

Rangoon Zoo

The Zoo is about 2 km north of Sule Pagoda, just south of the Royal Lakes, little more than half an hour's walk from the city centre, or, if it is very hot, the girls in the Tourist Burma office will write down the bus numbers for you. Alternatively, a trishaw will cost about K10, or K25 in a taxi. The entrance fee is 1 kyat.

For those who enjoy zoos it is well laid out in attractive grounds with a lake and plenty of paths flanked by flower beds and shaded by trees and shrubs. A miniature train runs through the grounds which are usually crowded with groups of people in exuberant holiday mood. There is a good map of the lay-out on a board and you will find most of the usual zoo animals and birds there.

Anyone who does not like to see wild animals in captivity, however, should be warned that the living quarters of some of the larger animals are distressingly cramped. Elephants huddle in a dusty compound, tethered by their hind legs, all dignity gone. On certain Sunday afternoons, the elephants are paraded, the bears dance and visitors can handle the cobras—if they want to!

Royal Lakes

Just north of the zoo the Royal Lakes are an attractive stretch of ornamental water, with inlets and creeks. This is a favourite picnic spot for locals, some of whom swim in the rather muddy pools. On the northern shore is the **Bogyoke Aung San Park** with a compelling bronze statue of Aung San as the focal point—which conveys the dynamic personality of the man who did most to gain Burma her independence.

The Karaweik

One of the main attractions of the Royal Lakes is the **Karaweik**—just off the eastern shore and visible from several points round the lake. Built in the 1970s, it is a huge concrete replica of the old Royal Barges used by Burmese kings—an endearing example of the contradictions that seem to epitomize Burma. Seen from afar it is a magnificent folly, exuding echoes of the good old days; inspected more closely, it is tawdry and sadly lacking in the style and elegance that would have clothed it had it been built and still used by King Mindon.

With twin hulls, like the mythical Indian *karaweik*, or water bird, it is surmounted by an elaborate tiered pagoda, and squats on the lake like a puffed up broody hen. It is well worth the 1 kyat entrance fee to go inside, where the halls within the hulls are linked by a central chamber. Although rather dingy, with a canteen-like restaurant, the original decor is enhanced by fine lacquer and marble with glittering glass mosaics inset with mother of pearl. The food is not remarkable for its quality or its value but there are traditional Burmese Dance and Puppet Shows, to go with the dinner, which you can book at the Tourist Burma Office. These will give you some idea of the national dance style, even if rather more influenced by the rewards of tourism than by local culture.

You can walk right round the outside of the building and there is one of the best views of the Shwedagon to the west, especially at sunset.

Inya Lake

Further north, halfway to the airport, Inya Lake, another favourite picnic spot, is larger than the Royal Lakes and very popular with sailors and wind-surfers. Few tourists have time to spare for sailing, but you can become a temporary member of the Rangoon Sailing Club. Dotted with islands and indented with creeks and inlets, Inya Lake is a good place for swimming. On the northeastern shore is the Inya Lake Hotel, opened in 1961 and listed as a Luxury Hotel. It is an ugly, functional-looking building with uninspiring interior decor, but it offers more facilities than you will find in most Burmese hotels and has a swimming pool, tennis court and putting green as well as a view over the lake. There are often exhibitions of local art in the hotel, and in the foyer the shop is one of the state-approved outlets for Burmese gems, silver, ivory, and other national specialities. Every February there is a great gathering of dealers in gems and pearls, for the Gems and Pearls Fair, where invited guests can trade leagally in Burma's valuable natural products.

SHOPPING & MARKETS

The Bogyoke Market (or Scott Market)

Northwest of Sule Pagoda, with its main entrance on Bogyoke Aung San Street the **Bogyoke Market** is a vast covered market with hundreds of stalls laid out along a grid system of passageways. Here you will find every sort of Burmese souvenir: lacquerware, ivory, teak, Shan bags, *longyis*, mother-of-pearl, jewellery etc. Easy to miss, on the right-hand (eastern) side, across an uncovered intersection, is the art section of the market. Here, as well as good local watercolour and oil paintings, you will find charming hand-painted watercolour greetings cards, depicting local scenes, selling for as little as 4 kyats each. There are produce stalls on the perimeters of the market where you can buy fruit etc. Bargaining is a must and some vendors may offer you (illegally) prices in dollars.

Open-Air Market
Across the road from the Bogyoke Market on the south side, there is an open air market, with local produce, where you see the local population going about their daily affairs.

The Indian Market
Another vivid microcosm of Burma is in the Indian Market, south across Anawrahta Street, where you see all the unfamiliar spices, seasonings, fruit and vegetables of the East, laid out with natural artistry.

The Chinese Market
The Chinese Market is a few blocks west of the Indian Market, opposite the General Hospital. Again, this is a place where it is a delight to wander, even if you don't want to buy anything. There is a distinctly Chinese flavour to the atmosphere, bright with flowers and vibrant with noise.

The Diplomatic Shop
On the west side of Sule Pagoda Road, just north of the pagoda, is the Diplomatic Shop. Here you can buy a variety of Burmese specialities such as ivory, lacquerware, teak etc; you must pay in foreign currency and the prices are not cheap. Tourists are limited to certain counters only, the rest being for diplomats. There is a Complaints/Suggestions Book in which a generation of tourists have expressed their frustrations, but there is no evidence of reaction by the authorities!

The Rangoon Glass Factory
Not far from the university in Yogi Kyaung Street, just off Insein Road, west of Inya Lake, you can visit the private enterprise **Glass Factory**. Ask Tourist Burma to write down the bus number for you.

In the shade of trees there is a teeming hive of activity here, where you can watch the manufacture of glass from the molten stage to the delicate crafting of intricate ornaments and utensils. Stacks of bottles and lamp glasses and unfamiliar shapes lie under layers of dust; the furnaces glow with fierce heat and a pair of girls demonstrate the creation of an exotic fish or a long thin glass stick that they draw out between them like toffee. There is a stall where you can buy the finished products very reasonably.

Mme Thair
Mme Thair holds court in 220 Edwards Street. In her apartment you will find stacks of antiques, lacquerware, beads, carvings and other curios she buys and sells, some genuine, some dubious, all as intriguing as their owner. A huge tulle-trimmed brass double bed dominates one room, a swinging chaise longue another: an endless trail of people come and go bearing packages. This is undoubtedly the top place in Rangoon for

305

antiques and particularly lacquerware, but it is best to be taken there by someone approved by Mme Thair: if she doesn't like the look of you she may be uncooperative. It is her house, rather than a shop, and you should behave as if you are her guest.

WHERE TO STAY

Hotels

The Inya Lake Hotel, Kaba Aye Pagoda Road (about 9 km out of the city centre), tel 62858. Listed as one of Burma's top hotels, this one belongs to a spy film, set behind the Iron Curtain. Opened in the early '60s, its design reflects that unfortunate chapter in architectural history. Perhaps the fact that the Russians paid for it explains the dreary, soulless atmosphere and the drab, institutional atmosphere of the public rooms. It has over 200 rooms, costing from $26.50 for a standard single, $40.50 double, to $174 for a de luxe suite. Add 10% to all prices. The service is grudging, the food uninspired and the numerous facilities second rate. There is a swimming pool, tennis courts, a putting green and a view over Inya Lake.

The Kandawgyi Hotel, Kennedy Road (about 4 km from the centre, on the shore of the Royal Lakes), tel 80412. Also listed as a luxury hotel, the Kandawgyi is a much nicer place to stay than the Inya Lake Hotel. After an exhausting day's sightseeing you can flop down on the verandah and watch the sun slip down in the western sky, throwing a crimson path across the lake to the Karaweik. The atmosphere is relaxed and friendly and you do feel the staff are pleased to help you. A room with a bathroom en suite and a view over the lake costs from $27.50 single, $33.00 double. There are also self-catering chalets in the grounds, with two double bedrooms, costing $75.

The Thamada Hotel, 5 Signal Pagoda Road (about 1 km north of Sule Pagoda, and very handy for the station), tel 71499. There is a pleasant, convivial feeling in the Thamada, and the rooms are comfortable with air conditioning and bathrooms en suite. A single room costs from $22.00, doubles, $33.00.

The Strand Hotel, 92 Strand Road (on the waterfront only a short walk from the city centre), tel 81533. The Strand is one of Rangoon's legacies from the days when the British clapped their hands and called: 'Boy—bring me a whisky and soda!' Ghosts of Somerset Maugham's characters haunt the faded, rather seedy halls and passageways, wringing their hands over the slipped standards! An economy single costs from $11.50 without bath, and a superior single with bath costs from $23.00. Add 10% to all prices. Somehow you can forgive the decay, the lethargy, the dinginess and imagine yourself back in time among palm court orchestras and solar topees. Staying at the Strand is 'an experience' and the food isn't that bad. You can often see a Burmese wedding party being photographed in the foyer.

The Sakhanta Hotel, Rangoon Station, tel 82975. Although situated, literally, on the station, the Sakhanta is surprisingly quiet, and very convenient if you plan an early start or late arrival. The rooms are airy and comfortable with air conditioning and bathroom. Single from $12.00.

The Dagon Hotel, 256 Sule Pagoda Road, tel 71140. Hardly qualifying as a hotel, the Dagon is reached up a steep stairway past a noisy restaurant. The rooms are small cells (very basic) from $10 single, and the public bathrooms are of dubious cleanliness. All right if you are with friends, not much fun alone. The food in the restaurant is quite good and cheap.

Guest Houses

YMCA (men and women), 263 Maha Bandoola Street (a short walk east from Sule Pagoda). This is fairly spartan, with a range of accommodation from single rooms at K60, to doubles with bathroom at K75. There are men-only rooms also and the Asian plumbing leaves much to be desired. The food is reasonable and there is a warm kindred spirit atmosphere in the public areas, where tourists of all nationalities meet to swap and share up-to-the minute information about travelling in Burma.

YWCA (women only), 119 Brooking Street (a few blocks closer to the Sule Pagoda than the YMCA). Here there is a clean, airy feeling to the 2- and 3-bedded rooms with mosquito nets. Prices for one person range from K24 to K36. The zinc-tub washrooms are reasonably clean and the Asian loos are a better bet than the European ones. No restaurant but a friendly atmosphere.

The Garden Guest House, South Block, Sule Pagoda Road (round the corner from Tourist Burma Office), tel 71516. Small, cleanish rooms with fans and nets, no windows, set round a big, airy landing. Plumbing is passable, and the restaurant unremarkable. Single accommodation ranges from K70 and you can have an extra bed in your room for $2.50, though no bedding is provided.

Other guest houses come and go on the Tourist Burma approved list, and you will find an up-to-date list of them in the Tourist Burma office. The simple truth is that if you are doing Burma on a tight budget, you can't be too fastidious about where you stay.

EATING OUT

Apart from the hotels and guest houses mentioned, the Karaweik, and the many roadside stalls where the food can be delicious, Rangoon has little to offer the gourmet. The following restaurants and cafes are passable.

Karaweik, on the Royal Lake. Mediocre Burmese food with dancing or puppet displays. See p. 304.
Yankin, off Gubar Pagoda Road. Good Chinese food.
Ruby, 50 Spark Street. Good Chinese food.
Mya Kan Tha, 70 Natmauk Lanthwe. Smart Chinese, very good food, probably the best in town.
Shwe Ba, near Resistence Park. Good Burmese food.
Sule Restaurant, near Diplomatic Stores. Good Bengali food.
For cheap out-of-door Chinese food in the evening, there's a nice atmosphere at the **Maha Bandoola Street** end of 20th Street where there are lots of tables outside.

Cafés

Nilar Win, between 37th and 38th Streets on south side of Maha Bandoola St. Good for cold drinks and yoghurt, especially fruit lassis.
Gold Cup Cafe, Sule Pagoda Road, for tea and pastries.
Shwe Lain Maw, between 38th and Lewis Streets. Cold drink shop, good for milk shakes.

Part IV

AROUND RANGOON

The Golden Rock

Depending on which itinerary you chose, you may have time for one day trip from Rangoon and, if so, you have a dilemma: if you want to include a boat trip, then you should choose Syriam or Twante; if you have no other train journey in mind, then you should go to Pegu. In all three cases, the journey is half the fun and the destination the icing on the cake.

PEGU

HISTORY
Once upon a time, so they say, Pegu was a minute island in the Gulf of Martaban. It was so small that there was only room to hold one *hintha* (or *hamsa*) bird—the mythological sacred duck whose image you often see in Burma—so its mate had to cling to its back. Because of this, Pegu used to be called Hamsawaddy, and even today its women are said to be very possessive about their men! Over the years, silt from the rivers that flowed into the bay built up until Pegu was joined to the mainland. It became a great seaport and city, and its golden era, which started in 1365 when it became the capital of lower Burma, lasted for 270 years. The silt that had made it part of the mainland, however, continued to build up and by 1635, when the capital moved to Ava, the Pegu river was so shallow that the town could no longer be used as a seaport. It was briefly re-established as a capital in 1740 by the Mons but it was destroyed 17 years later by King Alaungpaya. King Bodawpaya ordered a certain amount of restoration during his reign at the end of the 18th

century, but by this time the river had changed its course and the town became a backwater. Now, its unimposing streets and muddy river make it difficult to visualize how this simple little town could once have been such a mecca.

GETTING THERE
Although Pegu is one of the places you *are* allowed to visit, Tourist Burma seem determined to make your journey as complicated as possible. They will tell you that it is no longer possible to go by train, and will advise you to go to the bus station in Latha Street. When you get there, however, none of the drivers will agree to take you, even when you flourish your passport. They say that they will be stopped at the checkpoints and you won't be allowed through. Recent complaints to the Tourist Burma office produced the assurance that the matter was about to be reviewed—meanwhile, be patient.

By Rail
The 2-hour train journey to Pegu takes you through a variety of scenery that gives an excellent impression of rural Burma. Book a K15 Upper Class window seat through Tourist Burma, or go direct to the station and struggle with rail officials. There are plenty of trains, but the one that leaves at 5 am has the advantage of giving you an armchair view of the sunrise and glimpses of kerosene-lit villages coming to life. And you can explore Pegu before it gets too hot.

By Bus
Buses leave from Latha Street every half hour, costing K10 and taking about 2 hours. You may need a certain amount of cajolery to get on board and it helps if you have a Burmese friend.

By Taxi
You can hire a taxi but with the shortage of petrol you must expect to pay many hundreds of kyats—the price will vary from day to day. If money is not a problem and there are several of you, going by car gives you much more flexibility if you want to stop off en route.

GETTING AROUND
You will find **taxis, pony carts** and **trishaws** parked outside the station. Negotiate with your driver before you start. The trishaws and pony carts are the most fun, and much cheaper (from K50 for three hours) and if your driver speaks English you will get a good guided tour of the sights. **Taxis** are expensive, from at least K60 an hour. Although you may choose to plan your own route through Pegu, you are best to let your guide dictate: he knows the best circuit and you won't miss anything.

GETTING BACK TO RANGOON
The same problems exist when you try to go back to Rangoon. Again, you have to be patient and persevere.

By Bus
If you want to get back by bus, you should go to the bus station when you arrive and book

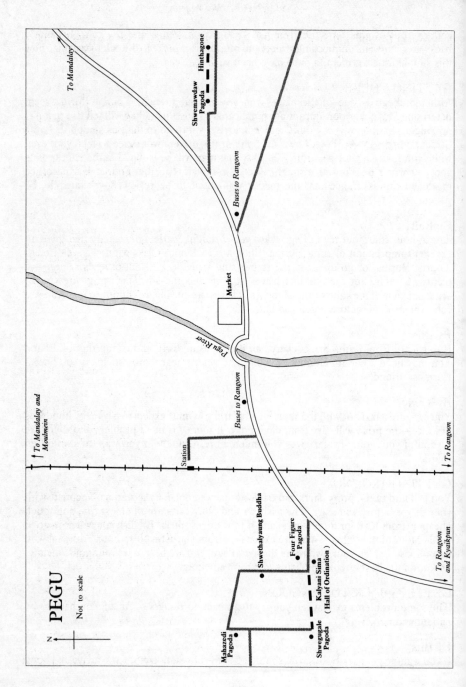

PEGU

Not to scale

N

To Mandalay

Shwemawdaw Pagoda
Hinthagone

Buses to Rangoon

Pegu River

Market

Buses to Rangoon

To Mandalay and
Moulmein

Station

To Rangoon

To Rangoon
and Kyaikpun

Shwethalyaung Buddha

Four Figure
Pagoda

Kalyani Sima
(Hall of Ordination)

Mahazedi
Pagoda

Shwegugale
Pagoda

a place. If you leave it to the afternoon you won't be able to get a ticket and all the buses will be full.

By Rail

The last train back to Rangoon leaves at 8 pm and you should check this on arrival. Go to the station master who will arrange a ticket for you and don't be deterred if he can only offer you an Ordinary Class seat—for just two hours, the discomfort is well compensated for by the experience as you crush in with livestock and baggage, sharing your metal seat with any amount of friendly locals, monks, nuns, babies and sacks of this and that. Trains in the afternoon are much livelier than the dawn one.

As your train approaches Rangoon, don't be surprised if your fellow passengers suddenly become very active and start to throw sacks and packages out of the window. The train has come down from the north and some of its passengers have had access to black-market goods that have slipped into the country over the Thai border. To avoid embarrassment at Rangoon Station it is often considered sensible to deliver goods to friends at a pre-arranged track-side rendezvous. Others, however, wait until the train stops at the station. They then shoulder their sacks of goods and charge out through the barriers like human battering rams, streaming across the forecourt into the rows of dilapidated vehicles that await them, roaring away out of range of an authority that appears totally unmoved by this blatant display of smuggling.

WHAT TO SEE

The Shwemawdaw Pagoda

You won't easily forget that early morning drive or ride from the station to the Shwe-mawdaw Pagoda: with its golden dome standing out in dramatic relief between you and the shimmering sky. Your guide/driver will relieve you of your sandals at the bottom of the steps leading up to the pagoda and you should allow yourself a good hour if you are to absorb the unique atmosphere of the pagoda and also the Hinthagone Temple beyond.

Shwemawdaw means 'Great Golden God', and the 114 m-high *stupa* is visible for miles, taller by 14 m than the Shwedagon, and of the same style, though less imposing. Its history goes back more than a thousand years to when two merchants brought two of Gautama Buddha's hairs back from India and enshrined them here in a small *stupa*. The *stupa* was enlarged and embellished several times over the years—a sacred tooth was added to the collection in 982 and another in 1385. King Bayinnaung gave the crown jewels to make a new *hti* in the 16th century and in 1796 King Bodawpaya restored the *stupa*, giving a new *hti* and raising the height of the dome. Earthquakes, as was so often the case in Burma, were the cause of several disasters that damaged the pagoda and in 1930 a serious quake almost completely destroyed it, leaving only the mound on which it stood rising from the rubble. Restoration work began in 1952, funded by voluntary donation and implemented by free labour and the new, diamond-studded *hti* was raised in 1954, only two years later.

There are four stairways up to the pagoda and you are likely to approach it up the western flight, past the usual collection of stalls, decorated with pictures of the aftermath of the last earthquake. The terrace is shaded by trees in some parts and dotted with pavilions and temples. As you walk slowly round, you pass faithful Buddhists, praying at their special shrines or at one of the eight planetary prayer posts around the *stupa*, now and then scooping up pitchers of water to pour over the Buddha to cool him. There is a **museum** containing relics rescued from earthquake destruction and a hall where you can see photographs of the restoration. Families of dogs lie on the marble flags, while their puppies squabble for scraps at the foot of the shrines. As you walk round you will see a piece of the pagoda that was damaged by the 1917 earthquake built into the rock at the base of the new one as a sort of memorial to the past.

Although similar in style to the Shwedagon, the Shwemawdaw is much less elaborate and the atmosphere more rural and comfortable, making you feel more inclined to settle down in the shade of one of the trees to relax for a while.

Hinthagone Hill

It would be very easy to miss what is almost the highlight of a visit to the Shwemawdaw Pagoda—the walk through to the Hinthagone Hill beyond. Still barefooted, you descend the steps on the eastern side, opposite the ones by which you arrived. A covered way leads through a delightful community of shanties and up the hill beyond. Groups of men, squatting on their haunches, mouths stained dark red with betel juice, call out friendly greetings: 'Hullo, where you from? What your country? What your name?' Girls in bright *longyis* pose in front of you, asking to be photographed. You catch glimpses of family life as you pass each simple home—children playing on the hard-baked mud, women crouched over fires, men sitting in doorways smoking. Chickens and dogs scratch about under the stilted huts and the air is pungent with the smell of cooking mingled with scented jasmine flowers that are sold as offerings to the pagoda shrines.

You come first to a ruined pagoda perched on the hillside, unimpressive except for its position overlooking the town and the surrounding plain, but full of atmosphere. It was built by U Khanti, a hermit who also built on Mandalay Hill. From here you climb a flight of steps to a more recent, jerry-built construction—a vast, open-sided temple, roofed in corrugated iron, on a frame of iron girders, decorated with paintings. Brick seats line the perimeter, from which you can gaze down on tumbled stones, relics of the last earthquake, and far out across the plain. This Hinthagone Hill is said to be the rock on which the original pair of *hintha* birds perched, far out in the Gulf of Martaban.

You can buy a bunch of flowers for K3 at the top of the steps and lay them on the offering table, near the gold statue of the *hintha* birds. If you kneel and bow to the Buddha in the way the Burmese do, palms touching, forehead to the ground, you will be rewarded by delighted smiles and murmurs from other pilgrims.

Return to the western entrance of the Shwemawdaw, and retrace your route, back through the town, past the market which it is more sensible to visit at the end of your tour, so you can dismiss your driver before you explore it. To see the remaining sights your guide should continue west, over the railway lines, and then branch right down an unmetalled track.

Kalyani Sima

The Kalyani Sima, about 1 km west of the station, is a **Hall of Ordination** originally built in 1476 by King Dhammazedi. When the first Burmese Empire crumbled, Buddhism was severely threatened by schism and Dhammazedi made it his ambition to restore the faith to the pure *Theravada* law. He sent monks to be taught and ordained at the

Mahavihara Monastery on the Kalyani River in Ceylon, which was then the centre of *Theravada* Buddhism. When they returned he built this Hall of Ordination, the first of 397 similar halls around the country, in which the monks could ordain novices into the newly purified faith. The original building was destroyed in 1599 by de Brito, the Portuguese adventurer, and thereafter fires, plunder and earthquake destroyed several reconstructions, until the 1930 earthquake razed it to the ground. The present building was finished in 1954 and is still used for ordination today.

There is a cool tranquillity about Kalyani Sima, in no way spoiled by the knowledge of its recent construction. The grounds are shaded by trees, and dotted with the dwellings of the monks who go about their daily life with impassive serenity. It would not be hard to lead a contemplative life in such peaceful surroundings.

The 10 stone tablets that you can see just beyond the Hall are inscribed with the history of Buddhism in Burma, and that of Burma's trade with Ceylon and south India in the 15th century. Three are in Pali and the rest in Mon.

Just opposite the Kalyani Sima there is a large column with four Buddhas standing back to back in front of a ruined temple. One of them is decorated with an inverted swastika, representing the perpetual wheel of life in Buddhist theology.

The Shwethalyaung Buddha

A few hundred yards northwest of the Kalyani Sima, your driver will deposit you at the entrance to the temple that houses the **Shwethalyaung Buddha,** one of the largest and, purportedly, most lifelike images in Burma, which is the focus for many faithful Buddhists. King Migadippa I built it in 994, when the Mons were still powerful—a vast reclining Buddha on the eve of his entry into *Nirvana*. It suffered from total neglect for 500 years, was then restored several times before being forgotten again after the destruction of Pegu in 1757. The jungle moved in and completely obliterated all trace of the statue and it lay undisturbed for 125 years. Then, during the British domination of Burma, an Indian contractor dug into what he assumed to be useful hard core for the railway he was building, and unearthed the Buddha.

You approach along a covered arcade lined with plenty of stalls, through a glittering glass-mosaic hall and up a flight of steps guarded by two vivid *nagas*—mythological serpents. There he lies, all 180 feet of him, a vast white figure in a gilded robe, smiling his passionless smile, his head propped on a pile of bejewelled caskets. An open-sided pavilion shelters him, with a corrugated roof on meccano girders, spacious, airy and surprisingly dignified in spite of its lack of sophistication. You can see a list of the dimensions of the statue displayed on a board, right down to the size of his nose. Don't miss the intricate carvings on the soles of his feet, or the painted glass panels showing scenes from his life in the wall below his head, set in mosaic and enamel. The Buddha is flanked by guardian *nats* and surrounded by pleasant trees and shrubs.

There are food stalls opposite the Shwethalyaung where you can sit in the shade and drink plain tea.

The Mahazedi Pagoda

Not far beyond the Shwethalyaung is the **Mahazedi Pagoda,** which is still being restored. Meaning 'great *stupa*' the Mahazedi has external stairways and walkways, like many of the pagodas in Pagan, and you can climb up for good views of Pegu and the plain.

King Bayinnaung built this pagoda in 1560 to enshrine one of Buddha's teeth. Bayinnaung was a man of great ambition—he could boast 11 white elephants to confirm his sovereignty and he coveted a Buddha's tooth to guarantee him a place in history and a quick path to enlightenment. He heard that the Portuguese had looted such a relic during their sacking of the Buddhist Jaffna, in Ceylon, and it was rumoured that it was the most sacred of all Buddhist relics, The Tooth of Kandy. Bayinnaung offered the Portuguese a fortune in gold for this tooth, but, frightened of the Inquisition, the governor of Goa decided it would be safer not to trade with pagan relics and had the tooth publicly crushed and thrown into the sea. It was then put about that the miraculous tooth had materialized again, this time in Colombo, in Ceylon. Once again Bayinnaung negotiated, and this time he won both the tooth and one of the king's daughters to replace one of his wives who had recently died. There was a tremendous reception at Bassein to receive the tooth and the princess—Bayinnaung had achieved his goal and at the same time had set himself above Anawrahta, and Alaungsithu, both of whom had tried, but failed, to acquire a Buddha's tooth. The triumph was soon blighted when news came that the Tooth of Kandy was still in Ceylon. Bayinnaung refused to believe in this new rumour and had his tooth enshrined in the Mahazedi Pagoda with a begging bowl also ascribed to the Buddha.

Ten years after Pegu was conquered in 1599, Anaukhpetlun moved the sacred relics to his capital in Toungoo, and from here they were transferred to the new Burmese capital in Ava. King Thalun built the Kaunghmudaw Pagoda (see Sagaing p. 340) near Ava, and the relics, whatever their real origins, are still enshrined there today, while the real Tooth of Kandy remains in Ceylon.

The Mahazedi was frequently destroyed or damaged during Pegu's turbulent history. The 1930 earthquake reduced it to a pile of rubble, from which the building you see today was lately restored.

The Shwegugale Pagoda

Not far south of the Mahazedi you will come to the Shwegugale Pagoda, where a cool chamber runs around the *stupa*, inhabited by 64 seated Buddhas.

Now is the time to ask your driver to return you to the centre of Pegu, to the market.

The Kyaikpun

The Kyaikpun is about 3½ km south of Pegu on the road back to Rangoon. If you can get into one of the overcrowded buses it only takes a few minutes to get there, but you may then find yourself unable to get into another bus. If you have time, and if your driver is willing, it is not too uncomfortable to do it in a trishaw or a pony trap; otherwise, you will have to take a taxi—buses to Rangoon are difficult to get onto, and it would be risky to hope for a later connection.

King Dhammazedi built this huge construction in 1476, a giant version of the four Buddhas in Pegu opposite the Hall of Ordination. These four, each 30 metres high, sit round a central column, back to back, facing the four cardinal points of the compass. They are the last four Buddhas of this world cycle: Gautama faces north, Kakusandha, east, Konagamana, south, and Kassapa, west. Legend tells of four sisters who had sworn a pact of chastity, and gave donations for the building of the Kyaikpun. It was said that if any of them broke the pact, then one of the Buddhas would be destroyed. You will notice that there isn't much to be seen of Kassapa, facing west, but if this was indeed due to the marriage of one of the sisters, retribution was not immediate—Kassapa was a victim of the 1930 earthquake.

It is hardly worth going on a further kilometre or so to **Payathonzu** to the 15th-century Shwegugyi Pagoda and its satellite buildings. These are virtually in ruins, although this site, being more remote, has a marvellously tranquil atmosphere. The pagoda was modelled on India's great Bodhagaya Temple and the surrounding buildings each represent one of the seven stages through which Buddha passed during his seven-week meditation after his enlightenment.

Pegu Market

The market is in an angle between the main road and the river, an enormous spread, both indoors and out, with stalls selling everything from fresh fruit and vegetables, spices, fish and meat, to every sort of household requirement, many of which have found their way here along the well-worn smugglers' path to the black market. You can buy Shan bags, *longyis*, sandals and souvenirs. You must bargain. Buy fresh fruit and go over the bridge and along the western bank of the river, where you can sit in the shade of a tree, looking down on the muddy water and watch frail rafts and craft being poled downstream. It is hard to believe that this was once a major sea-port.

WHERE TO STAY

There is no official hotel or guest house for tourists in Pegu (1988). If you wish to stay unofficially, hang about the station or the bus depot and you will probably be approached by a youth who will offer to find you somewhere to stay. Sometimes you may be offered free hospitality in exchange for English conversation, but with the short time at your disposal it is almost impossible to fit in such a bonus.

EATING OUT

There are plenty of food stalls in the town and in the market, where you can get the usual range of curries, noodles and fried snacks.

Sights on the road to Pegu

If you get a group together and travel to Pegu by road there are several interesting things to see along the way. A No. 9 bus from Rangoon will take you as far as the first one for just a few kyats.

The British War Cemetery, Htaukkyan

About 30 km north of Mingaladon Airport the road forks, northwest for Prome and northeast for Pegu and Mandalay. The cemetery is to the right of the fork, a beautifully kept memorial to the 27,000 Allied servicemen who died in Burma and Assam during the Second World War. This very different corner of Burma is well worth a visit. Beautifully kept, it is peaceful and extremely moving, with a central colonnade flanked by row upon row of simple grave stones surrounded by flower beds. The cemetery, maintained by the Imperial War Graves Commission, is still visited by many people every year.

315

The Naga-Yone

A short distance past the cemetery on the Pegu road you come to a long monastery wall beside a military checkpoint. Within this enclosure you can see the eight planetary posts with their guardian animals, as at the Shwedagon, and a Buddha wrapped round by a cobra, whose hood forms an umbrella for the figure. You will see dozens of these *Naga-Yones* around Burma. Their origin stems from when Buddha was meditating, after his enlightenment. His life was threatened by a storm and the *Naga*, half snake, half dragon, protected him with its body. These statues are a typical example of how the pure *Theravada* Buddhism has been tempered with an enduring belief in *nats*.

The Shwengungpin—The Golden Banyan Tree

Beside the road to Pegu is an ancient **banyan tree** believed to be the home of powerful *nats* who are the guardian spirits of the highway. Buses and cars stop here to make offerings to these *nats*. There is a brick shrine and a small market where the offerings can be bought. New cars are brought here to receive the blessing of the nats. With the bonnet of the car towards the shrine, the car is driven backwards and forwards three times! Scent is then sprayed on the bonnet and prayers are chanted. The 'mediums' who perform this ceremony receive a large fee from the car owner, who is presented with a garland of ribbons to tie onto the car to protect it from accidents.

Kyaikkaloh Pagoda

Well beyond Mingaladon, on a hill a few yards off the highway in a pretty leafy grove by a small lake, is the **Kyaikkaloh Pagoda** which was allegedly built in 426 BC, when eight missionary monks came from India with relics of the Buddha. A powerful and very ferocious ogre once lived on this hill. Proud of his supernatural power, he had challenged Buddha to hide from him. Buddha hid in the ogre's hair; the ogre failed to find him and had to concede victory. He then became a devout Buddhist, called the hill *Kyaikkaloh*— the Place where the Buddha was Hidden—and the pagoda was built later.

Syriam & the Kyauktan Pagoda

GETTING THERE

As is often the case in Burma, the journey to Syriam is at least half its attraction. Take your passport as the police have a habit of waylaying you in Syriam and if you can't produce identification you will be taken to the Police Office where you can be kept hanging around for hours. From Rangoon take a No. 9 bus from the market, or a No. 38 bus from Sule Pagoda Road to Thida Jetty, where you catch a ferry down the Pazundaung Creek and across the Rangoon River. Apart from a 2-hour gap at lunch time, boats leave every hour on the hour from the bustling, vibrant jetty and cost only K1. You can buy all sorts of refreshment during the 45-minute crossing and there is plenty to see as the boat churns its way down the muddy creek, past anchored craft of all types, sampans, sailing junks and motor boats. Gulls squabble for scraps thrown by passengers and all around you is a babble of voices and the nasal chant of vendors. Check before you leave the jetty when the last boat leaves for Rangoon—the time varies.

GETTING AROUND
Pony traps, trishaws and taxis congregate at the ferry terminus. Prices are much the same as in Rangoon and you should negotiate first.

HISTORY
Hard as it may be to believe when you get there, Syriam was once the main port and trading centre for this part of Burma, long before Rangoon superseded it. Here the swashbuckling Portuguese de Brito set up his headquarters at the end of the 16th century and set about trying to dominate Burma. He gave his allegience to whichever of the conflicting races suited his purpose, commanded his own private army and sacked Pegu in 1599. He allowed his followers to commit appalling sacrilege in Buddhist shrines and thus earned for himself the worst sort of death, by impalement, when he was finally conquered by the Burmese in 1613. The town continued to thrive as a port with Portuguese, British, French and Dutch trading posts until it was sacked by King Alaungpaya in 1756. Rangoon then became the centre of trade in Burma.

Today Syriam's economy is based on the largest oil refinery in Burma, a brewery, and rice from the surrounding delta. The small town is a delightful cameo of Burmese life, colourful, noisy and busy with a thriving market. Here and there you can still see the ruined walls of the houses built and occupied by foreign traders, particularly Portuguese. It is quite a walk from the jetty to the town centre—a trishaw costs about K10.

Kyaik Khauk Pagoda
The Kyaik Khauk Pagoda stands on a little hill about 3 km outside the town, on the way to Kuauktan. Its golden *stupa* rises like an echo of the mighty Shwedagon a few miles away to the west. This pagoda has its own special atmosphere—a sort of calm benevolence that makes you want to sit on a step in the shade and watch the graceful homage of the faithful pilgrims around you as they make their offerings to the shrines. The two tombs in front of the pagoda are those of two Burmese writers, Natshingaung and Padethayaza.

GETTING TO KYAUKTAN
Jeeps and buses to Kyauktan await ferry passengers arriving at Syriam jetty. Jeeps will quote you about 300 kyats. Buses don't always connect with the ferry times and wait till every seat and space is full before they depart. They range from small pick-ups to large ramshackle trucks and sometimes seem reluctant to take foreigners. The fare varies from about K3 to K5 for the 45-minute journey through settlements and plantations. Kyauktan lies at the end of the road, about 20 km from Syriam.

Because the bus service is not very regular, you should allow yourself plenty of time to get back to Syriam to catch the last boat back to Rangoon.

Ye Le Paya Pagoda
From where the bus stops walk along the river bank to your right for a couple of hundred yards. You pass through a colourful straggle of shops, stalls, houses and cafes with an attractive, village atmosphere. Ferries run more or less continually from the landing stage, across to the Ye Le Paya Pagoda, meaning the 'Pagoda in the Middle of the River', a five-minute journey that costs K1.

People throw food into the water from the steps as you approach the island and you will see the blunt noses and gaping mouths of large catfish churning the murky water. These ugly fish look evil, but they are quite harmless. Some grow to over 1 m in length, and you can buy balls of bread for them on the island and gain yourself some merit by feeding them. The pagoda itself is an apparently random group of buildings with ornate, pinnacled spires and turrets covering the whole of the tiny island—a hotch potch of shrines around a gilded temple containing four alabaster Buddhas. In one of the pavilions you can see paintings of the principal pagodas in Burma and other Buddhist countries.

Twante

GETTING TO AND AROUND TWANTE
Tourist Burma will tell you that you can only go to Twante on a day trip, arranged by them, in a group of not less than 10 people, costing $81 each.

It is not, however, impossible to make your own arrangements, and it is much cheaper.

By Boat
A canal links Rangoon with the Irrawaddy to the west, and the two-hour boat trip to Twante, along its banks, is well worth doing if you have time.

Boats leave from a jetty about 2 km west of the Strand Hotel, deep in the heart of dockland. As there are no approved tourist boats, you may need local help. Ask a trishaw driver to take you to the Twante Jetty. He will show you which boat to catch and may help you to get your ticket. The boat goes to Dalla, where you catch a bus for the 15-minute journey to Twante.

By Bus
Catch one of the sampans that depart frequently from opposite the Strand (costs K1, or K6 for the whole boat) across the Rangoon River to the entrance of the Twante Canal, where buses depart every hour for Twante.

The pottery town of Twante straggles around dusty tracks deep in lush jungle. The flimsy buildings are made of split cane walls woven in checkered patterns and palm-thatch. Dogs bask in the sun, women gather at a communal well to do the family washing watched by enchanting, solemn-faced children. Youths play Chinlon, passing the hollow cane ball with supple skill, using only their feet and knees.

The pottery itself is under a huge canopy of thatch, dim and cool, in spite of the ancient brick kilns where the fires reach hellish temperatures. In the entrance, potters sit on the baked-mud floor turning wheels with their feet, while their hands shape the clay into jars, bowls and jugs ranging in size from miniature cups to vast Ali Baba vats. The pottery is stacked in all its various stages of manufacture, and English-speaking women will tell you anything you want to know. A short walk through the village takes you to the pottery shop where you will be torn in two between the wonderful collection at incredibly low prices, and the thought of the size of your luggage and the flight out of Rangoon.

Bassein

Bassein, the largest town in the Irrawaddy delta, is about 190 km west of Rangoon and is one of Burma's major ports. You have to get permission to go there from the Ministry of Trade. This takes at least 2 weeks, so at present few tourists manage to get there. Those that do have to take a guide.

GETTING THERE

By Boat
Given permission, the only way you would be allowed to go is by boat. An overnight boat which allows you plenty of daylight and sunset leaves Rangoon at 3 pm–5 pm, depending on the tide, stopping at villages on the way where you can buy baskets, fruit and woven mats and arriving at about 8 am. Another boat leaves at 5 pm and goes direct. The journey costs about K110 and you have to pay the guide.

GETTING AROUND
You have the usual choice of expensive taxis, or trishaws and pony carts which are cheap and provide you with a guide. There are also buses, but you will need local help to catch the right ones.

Deep in the heart of the delta paddy fields, Bassein exports mountains of rice every year, together with raw jute. Bassein has given its name to the hand-painted umbrellas for which it is famous, and you can go to the factory where they are made. It also produces a large quantity of pottery which you can buy in the market.

The history of Bassein goes back a long way, to when the Mons and the Burmese fought to gain control of the Irrawaddy basin. King Alaungpaya sacked the town during the 18th century in his attempts to establish a united Burma and in 1852 the British established a garrison here and began to cultivate the delta for rice.

The population of 140,000 includes many Indians, descended from Indian traders who settled in Bassein centuries ago, as well as Karens and Arakanese. The word 'Bassein' is derived from the Burmese word for Muslim.

The Shwemokhtaw Pagoda
The focal point of the town is the golden *stupa* of the Shwemokhtaw Pagoda, banded with concentric rings, soaring to an elegant *hti* and spire. It was built at the command of the Muslim princess Onmadandi, a pious lady who, having three contenders for her hand, ordered each one to build a pagoda. The **Tazaung Pagoda** and the **Thayaunggyaung Pagoda** were the other two. History doesn't relate whether the princess married any of the competitors.

WHERE TO STAY
If you travel by overnight boat each way, you won't need to stay in Bassein.

EATING OUT
There is a good Chinese restaurant two buildings beyond the jetty on the river.

Part V

MANDALAY

The Chinthe at Mandalay Hill

Mandalay lies about 580 km due north of Rangoon, on the Irrawaddy. It is more typical of Burma than the capital and many tourists prefer it. First impressions tend to be of a broken-down, sprawling town with no obvious centre and a great deal of neglect and decay. A closer inspection shows it to be cleaner than Rangoon, and more prosperous. Its markets are better stocked, its bicycles newer and its guides more obliging.

HISTORY

The history of Mandalay is little more than a century old and it concludes with the fall of the last Burmese dynasty, the Konbaung Dynasty, founded by King Alaungpaya who reunited Burma in the 18th century. In the endless scramble for power that dogged the reign of every monarch in Burma, Alaungpaya's successors rose and fell with blood-stained frequency until Mindon ousted his useless brother, King Pagan in 1853.

Mindon was a very religious man and he knew of the ancient tradition that Buddha had visited Mandalay Hill with one of his protégés, Ananda, and had prophesied that a city would be built there 2400 years after his death which would be a sacred centre of Buddhist teaching. Mindon saw himself as the destined vehicle by which this prophecy could be fulfilled. He set about the creation of the new city in 1857 and, in 1861, he moved his court and government and about 150,000 people from the previous capital in Amarapura. Mandalay's brief period as the Golden City had begun. Most of the buildings that had formed the Royal Palace in Amarapura were taken to Mandalay and re-erected within the walled palace—a splendid array of elaborate carved teak pavilions generously decorated with gold, gems and glass mosaic. Twenty-four years later the British took over and Mindon's son Thibaw was exiled. The magnificent palace became a barracks for the British army and Mandalay's golden promise was violated. On

320

20 March 1945, as the Second World War rumbled to an end, the Allies shelled the Japanese headquarters inside the palace walls and all the teak buildings were burnt to the ground.

Mandalay is built on a grid system, with numbered streets running north to south, and numbered roads running east to west, making it simple enough to find your way around, though not all the numbers are clearly displayed. The separate trade guilds tend to stick together in the same quarter, many of them in private-looking houses and huts so it is not easy to find them without a guide.

A devastating fire in 1981, which started in a black-market petrol store, raged through the northwest quarter of the city along the banks of the Irrawaddy, gutting over 6000 buildings and leaving 35,000 people homeless. As a result you will find many modern buildings, some finished, some under construction, often of garish ugliness, with a disregard for style and a preponderance of crude decorations in neon colours. But there are still plenty of the more traditional buildings and, miraculously, none of the important sacred buildings were destroyed.

GETTING THERE

By Air
The flight from Rangoon to Mandalay takes about two hours and costs K588 (1988). See page 258 for details. As in all Burmese flights, check times well ahead of departure. An airport bus will take you to the Tourist Burma office in the Mandalay Hotel.

By Rail
The train from Rangoon to Mandalay is the only rail route authorized for tourists. The journey takes 14 hours and you book seats through Tourist Burma. There are three Express trains a day on which tourists are allowed to travel. The service is fairly reliable although there are occasional stories of long delays with passengers stuck on board for hours. Travelling overnight is a great advantage—you save time and get enough daylight to appreciate the journey. Taxis, trishaws and pony carts can be hired from the station on arrival.

See pages 259–260 for details of fares and schedules. It is worth noting that the First Class seats are upright, hard, and impossible to sleep in.

By Road
You can get to the centre of Mandalay by bus or pick-up from Pagan and from Taunggyi—an uncomfortable 10-hour journey that is hell for sufferers from bad backs, but a great experience if you are fit and don't mind discomfort.

GETTING AROUND

By Taxi
Taxis, jeeps and pick-ups are as expensive as anywhere else, and you should always negotiate first. K60 an hour is average, but the price goes up when petrol is scarce. It is obviously always best to get a party together if you want to hire something for the day. Expect to pay anything upwards of K300.

By Bus & Truck

There are plenty of buses around the town and journeys seldom cost more than a couple of kyats. They are always crammed full and, if you manage to squash into one, difficult to see out of. For longer journeys, to Sagaing for example, there are trucks as well as buses. Get a local to direct you to the right departure point as these vary from company to company.

By Pony Cart or Trishaw

Far the best way to do your sightseeing is by pony cart or trishaw. Fares are cheap and you negotiate for a day—about K75 for half a day. Most of the drivers speak passable English which they are keen to practise, and will be happy to act as guides. If you use the same driver/guide for your whole stay he will conduct you round and help with language problems. He will also advise on the best place to go if you need to sell whisky, cigarettes or dollars. The pony carts take up to 3 passengers (4 Western-sized bodies are too much for the wretched pony). Although trishaws are built to carry 2 passengers, the fare is per head and you will be less likely to have to get out and push if you have one per person. Many of the trishaw drivers have a part share in a pony, so your guide is liable to turn up in either a cart or a trishaw. A single short journey, station to hotel for instance, costs about K5-8—you have to bargain every time, stating your price.

TOURIST INFORMATION

There are Tourist Burma desks in the station and at the airport where you can make bookings for approved hotels and guest houses. The main office is in the Mandalay Hotel, about 1¹/₂ km northeast of the station. You must go here for all travel bookings and up-to-date information and for official currency exchange. They will also look after your luggage, at your own risk.

Mandalay In a Day

If you have stamina, it is possible to see most of the main attractions in Mandalay between your arrival in the morning by air or on the overnight train and your departure at dawn the next day.

Suggested Morning Tour

The Mahamuni Pagoda
Tapestry, Gold Leaf & Ivory Workshops
Zegyo Market
Shwekyimyint Pagoda
Lunch (Let your driver/guide advise you on which is the best restaurant. He will probably be delighted to come in and sit with you and talk, and help you with the menu.)

Suggested Afternoon Tour

Silk-Weaving Workshop,
Shwenandaw Pagoda
Atumashi Monastery
Kuthodaw Pagoda

Sandamuni Pagoda
Kyauktawgyi Pagoda
Mandalay Hill in time for sunset

Morning Tour

The Mahamuni Pagoda

Tradition holds that the Mahamuni Buddha was created during Buddha's lifetime, with the help of the king of the gods, and that Buddha was so pleased with the likeness that he said it would retain his essence for the 5000 years decreed for the present Buddhist world cycle. The image, originally cast in huge sections of brass and coated in layers of gold leaf, was enshrined on a diamond and gold throne on Sirigutta Hill in Arakan, and the story of its subsequent history can be seen in a series of paintings in one of the pavilions at the pagoda. Hungry for the merit gained by acquiring the image, various kings tried to remove it. Looters stripped it of its gold, one of its legs was stolen, diamonds were prised from the throne. The ship that carried away these treasures sank and the jungle rose up and covered the vandalized image, hiding it from greed for centuries. The Arakanese found and restored it and it remained in Arakan until 1784, when King Bodawpaya's troops carryed it to Amarapura. Here the Mahamuni Buddha stayed, much venerated until, in 1884, a fire destroyed the pagoda that housed it. It was then moved to its present site within a replica of Bodawpaya's pagoda.

The Mahamuni Pagoda is likely to stay in your memory long after you leave Burma—it combines the babble of a milling crowd, the worldly clatter of the temple market and the deep peace of Buddhism. An arcade of colourful stalls leads to a golden archway and there, seated below the biggest diamond in Burma, is the Buddha. He is nearly 4 m high. His great face is lumpy and distorted from the thick coating of gold leaf that is added daily in K5 sections, donated by pilgrims seeking merit. Nearly 30,000 kyats' worth of gold are said to be added every day. At 4 o'clock every morning the overloaded face is washed and polished watched by the faithful. There is always a crowd, sitting, kneeling or standing around the shrine.

The rest of the Mahamuni complex is like a museum with displays of the stone slabs inscribed with religious texts collected by Bodawpaya; life-sized statues of past monarchs; pictorial histories and Buddha images from all over Asia. Look out for six bronze sculptures in a building of their own, all that remain of 30 looted from Cambodia by the Thais in 1431. These were looted again, by the Mon King Bayinnaung in 1564, and taken to Pegu, whence they were looted by the Arakanese, to be finally snatched by Bodawpaya together with the Mahamuni Buddha in 1784. Of the six that survived this series of raids, two are *dvarapalas*—warriors who guarded the temples—and are believed to hold supernatural powers of healing. The patient must rub the part of the statue that corresponds to his affliction. If their burnished bellies are anything to go by, the Burmese are as prone to upset tummies as tourists.

Tapestry, Gold Leaf & Ivory Workshops

It is probable that your driver will have his own favourite workshops to take you to, where you can watch the craftsmen at work and buy the finished products. If not, there is a splendid group on 36th Road, between 77th & 78th Streets, about $1^1/2$ km northeast of the Mahamuni Pagoda, only a slight detour on your way to the Zegyo Market.

Tapestry: here you can watch children and young women sewing sequins and braid onto enormous, commissioned tapestry wall hangings that will take more than two months to finish and sell for nearly K3000. Incomplete works lie on frames, sometimes outside, waiting to be padded and finished. The designs range from religious and mythical to naturalistic and you can buy the smaller ones from about K300.

Gold Leaf: There is an unlimited demand for gold leaf in Burma for the decoration of pagodas and Buddha images. However poor a man may be, he will never grudge the purchase of a K5 slip of gold to put on his chosen Buddha. Here, in the workshop, you can see the enormous amount of energy that goes into producing each sweet-paper-sized leaf. Flowers propitiate a *nat* image in the corner, while a sweating labourer pounds the raw fragments of gold, trapped between sheets of leather in a wallet. He bashes them with a hammer for five hours, the time carefully counted by a primitive water-clock consisting of a perforated coconut shell floating in a dish of water—five sinkings to the hour!

Next door, in a separate workshop, the gold is made up into dainty packets, to be sold for K5 at the pagoda stalls. If you are lucky, your guide will casually appropriate one of these gossamar-thin leaves and press it to your hand 'now you are gilded like the Buddha'.

Ivory: Almost next door, you can watch craftsmen carving intricate designs in ivory, brought down from the jungle by trackers and sold for large sums of money. You can see the raw ivory waiting to be worked, and in the front shop there are show-cases of the finished products for sale. You can buy anything from large set pieces for many thousands of kyats, to tiny exquisite elephants that are reasonable enough in price to offer temptation. Although trading in ivory is legal in Burma, it is extremely expensive and you are supposed to get permission to take it out of the country.

Zegyo

The Zegyo Market, on 84th Street about 3 km north of the Mahamuni Pagoda, is one of Burma's biggest and most vivid markets, designed by an Italian, Count Caldrari in 1903. Here you can see the hill tribes—Shans, Chins, Kachins in their colourful costumes—as well as people from the plains. Built around the Queen Victoria Diamond Jubilee Clock, it is an enormous spread of stalls, both inside and out, divided by lanes and passages, with each category of merchandise in its own section. You will find plenty of black-market stuff here, smuggled in from Thailand, openly displayed and openly bought. There is food of every possible sort—spices, herbs and flowers as well as cloths, *longyis*, hats, shan bags, sandals, household goods and hardware. Everything is overlaid with the pungent smell of *ngapi*—a compressed fish-paste used in Burmese cooking.

Shwekyimyint Pagoda

Due north of the Mahamuni Pagoda, on 24th Road between 82nd and 83rd Sts, the Shwekyimyint Pagoda appears delightfully random, as if each new chamber and shrine were tacked on in a moment of religious impulse with no particular design, and then furnished with a clutter of offerings and images. The various courtyards are clean, shady and very peaceful. There is a recumbent Buddha with a cosy, kind face and another, also lying down, which is uncharacteristically elegant and frail-looking, surrounded by figures acting out scenes from his life.

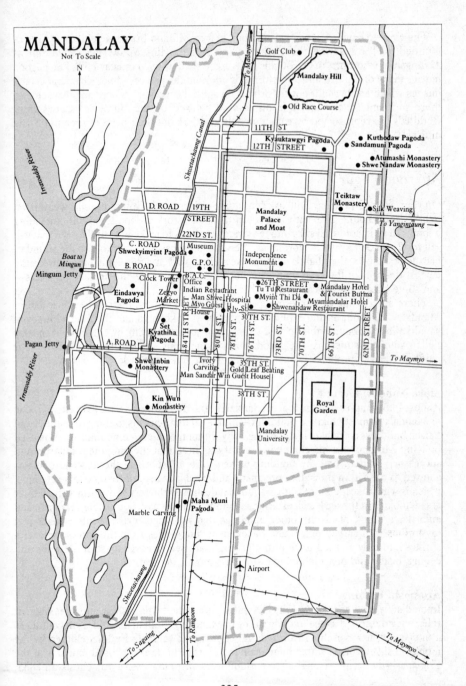

MANDALAY

Not To Scale

N

To Irrawaddy River

Golf Club

Mandalay Hill

Old Race Course

Shweetachaung Canal

To Madaya

11TH ST

Kyauktawgyi Pagoda
12TH STREET

Kuthodaw Pagoda
Sandamuni Pagoda
Atumashi Monastery
Shwe Nandaw Monastery

D. ROAD 19TH STREET

22ND ST.

Mandalay Palace and Moat

Teiktaw Monastery

Silk Weaving

To Yangintaung

C. ROAD
Shwekyimyint Pagoda

Museum

G.P.O.

Independence Monument

B. ROAD

Clock Tower

B.A.C. Office

Indian Restaurant

Boat to Mingun

Mingum Jetty

Eindawya Pagoda

Zegyo Market

Man Shwe Myo Guest House

Hospital

Rly. St.

26TH STREET
Tu Tu Restaurant
Myint Thi Da
Shwenandaw Restaurant

Mandalay Hotel
& Tourist Burma
Myamandalar Hotel

30TH ST.

A. ROAD

Set Kyathiha Pagoda

84TH STREET
80TH ST.
78TH ST.
76TH ST.
73RD ST.
70TH ST.
66TH ST.
62ND STREET

Pagan Jetty

Shwe Inbin Monastery

Ivory Carving
Man Sandar Win Guest House

35TH ST.
Gold Leaf Beating

To Maymyo

38TH ST.

Royal Garden

Kin Wun Monastery

Mandalay University

Marble Carving

Maha Muni Pagoda

Shweetachaung

Airport

To Sagaing

To Rangoon

To Maymyo

The Shwekyimyint Pagoda existed long before Mindon built his golden city: it was founded in 1167 during the Pagan era by Prince Minshinzaw, the exiled son of Alaungsithu who came to live out his exile in the shadow of Mandalay Hill. The pagoda houses many of the treasures that formerly adorned the palace—gold, silver and crystal images which are brought out for display on special occasions. There are also some of those mechanical, slot-machine displays so beloved by the Burmese: scenes from Buddha's life represented by garish models who jerk out their parts in time to blaring music!

Afternoon Tour

On your way to Mandalay Hill, ask your guide-driver to take you to the silk-weavers on 62nd Street. Young girls with flowers in their hair work at looms, skilfully threading bobbins of vivid coloured silks into the stretched warps to make beautiful *longyis* that will sell for 2 or 3000 kyats, for formal and ceremonial occasions. Working to the sound of blaring pop music, their hands never pause in their work and they earn only a few kyats a day. At the back of the shed there is a shop where you can buy the finished products—and some cheaper things as well.

There are a group of interesting pagodas clustered around the southeastern foot of Mandalay Hill and, having explored as many as your stamina and the time allows, you should aim to conclude this second half of your tour of the city by climbing Mandalay Hill to watch the sunset. All the pagodas are within a stone's throw of each other and your guide-driver will probably take you to them in the following order:

Shwe Nandaw Kyaung
Almost 1 km southeast of the foot of Mandalay Hill, this 'golden palace monastery' is one of Mandalay's most poignant buildings—for it is all that remains to show what the Royal Palace buildings were like. It stood originally within the palace compound and was used by King Mindon and his chief wife, and it was here that the king died. His son and successor, Thibaw, had the building moved to its present site (because no one was allowed to die within the palace precincts) and used it as his private meditation temple, which is why it escaped the conflagration that destroyed the rest of the palace in 1945. It is sad, looking at the dark teak exterior, elaborately carved with figures, flowers, fruit and animals, to think of all the other buildings that no longer exist. Inside is dark and mysterious with carved pillars and panels depicting scenes from the *Jataka*, colourful shrines and only a faded trace of the gilding that used to cover most of the walls and ceiling, inside and out, highlighted with glass mosaic decoration.

Atumashi Kyaung
Immediately next door to the Shwe Nandaw, the ruined Atumashi is another poignant relic, once described as the finest building in Mandalay. Built in the mid-19th century as a monastery, it was richly furnished and contained a valuable Buddha clothed by the monks in silken robes, with a huge diamond in its head. It also housed four sets of the *Tripitaka*—the scripture of *Theravada* Buddhism—kept in massive teak chests. In 1885,

during British occupation of the city, the Buddha disappeared. In 1890 a disastrous fire gutted the building, with all its contents, including the *Tripitaka*, leaving the shell you see today, rather like a dramatic stage setting with arches, turrets, broken columns, wooden stumps and stairways leading to the stars. Some of the stucco carvings remain.

Kuthodaw Pagoda
The Kuthodaw Pagoda is half a kilometre due north of Atumashi Kyaung. Massive red wooden doors open into a cool arcade roofed with corrugated iron, flanked by meditation couches and paintings, leading to a small, rather cosy *stupa* guarded by ochre *chinthas*. Rows and rows of dazzling white miniature pagodas in the grounds house pairs of marble slabs, 729 in all, inscribed with the entire *Tripitaka* in Pali script. King Mindon convened the Fifth Buddhist Synod in 1872 and arranged for scholars to carve out these massive pages of what is called 'The World's Biggest Book'. He then commissioned a relay of 2400 monks to read the whole work without a pause—a recitation that lasted for nearly 6 months! It may be the influence of so much scholarship, or the spacious lay-out of the pagoda, or the unusually elegant Buddha image at the entrance, but the Kuthodaw has a profoundly soothing effect on the mind, especially after a marathon of sight-seeing.

Sandamuni Pagoda
Half a kilometre west of the Kuthodaw, the Sandamuni was built as a memorial to King Mindon's brother, Kanaung, who was assassinated here on the site where the King's temporary palace stood while the walled palace was being constructed.

It would be easy to confuse the Sandamuni with the Kuthodaw pagoda because it, too, is surrounded by carved marble tablets, standing in rows like tombstones. These are erudite interpretations of the *Tripitaka*, said to have been composed by the hermit monk U Khanti, who was responsible for much of the building on Mandalay Hill. As in the Kuthodaw, the *stupa*, approached through a simple entrance, is small and simple and the atmosphere very peaceful. A gilded Buddha smiles kindly from a small chapel; a boy strikes the bell four times and the echo goes on and on, harmonizing with the sing-song chant of a monk reciting scripture.

Kyauktawgyi Pagoda
Another half a kilometre to the west, the Kyauktawgyi is the final pagoda before you climb the hill for a splendid finale.

When King Mindon conceived this pagoda in 1853, his idea was to have it modelled on the Ananda Temple in Pagan, perhaps in honour of Buddha's disciple, Ananda, who was with him when he prophesied the building of Mandalay as a centre for the Buddhist faith. But a rebellion in 1866 disrupted his plans and the present pagoda was the result. The Buddha is carved from a single block of marble from the quarry at Sagyin nearby; it is said to have taken a team of 10,000 men 13 days to transport it to the site.

The long, pillared entrance arcade is flanked by stalls and booths and the cool cloisters are lined with stone seats and decorated with paintings arranged in pairs, each pair representing dreams and reality. In the shrine sits an enormous marble Buddha with richly jewelled cross belts, a gilded headdress and anklets. He is backed by a wrought screen under a gilded ceiling, set with red whorls. Electric fans stand on the dais cooling the Buddha among offerings of bananas, melons, and flowers.

Mandalay Hill

Allow an hour for an easy climb, with plenty of stops to explore the many shrines on the way, and to rest and enjoy the view. The actual climb of 236 metres (and an estimated 1,729 steps) is not strenuous, except in really hot weather, even in bare feet, and the path is roofed in corrugated iron the whole way up. There are two flights of steps on the south side of the hill, which meet some way up, and a steep stairway up the west slope. A hermit monk, U Khanti, is said to have designed many of the buildings on the hill, as well as others in Mandalay, during the construction of King Mindon's new city.

If you take the main entrance, guarded by two ferocious *chinthes* (half-lion, half-griffin temple guardians), you come almost at once to a special *nat* temple where you can often see an elaborately dressed *nat* woman performing sinuous symbolic dances, accompanied by a twanging, plink-plonk orchestra, surrounded by crowds of applauding onlookers.

Stone seats line the stairways, inscribed with the names of their donors, and the struts of the roofing are similarly inscribed. The steps, stained with splashes of red betel juice, are gritty under your bare feet; friendly people greet you as they go down: 'Hullo, where you from?' The hillside is desert-dry and there are snakes among the scrub. Enshrined in the first big pagoda you come to, about half way up, are three of the bones of Gautama Buddha, retrieved from his funeral pyre when heavy rainfall extinguished the flames during his cremation. These and other of his bones were enshrined in Peshawar, in what is now Pakistan, until they were discovered during excavation work in 1908. Unappreciated by the Islamic people who by then predominated, they were presented to the Burmese Buddhist Society by the British government.

About two-thirds of the way up the hill you come to a temple in which a giant, golden-draped Buddha stands, pointing imperiously towards the walls of the ruined palace, with a smaller, bronze figure, kneeling at his right side, gazing out in the direction indicated by the Buddha. Called the *Shweyattaw*, this reminds us that Buddha climbed this hill with his disciple Ananda and prophesied that a great city would be built, 24000 years after his death, and that it would become a centre of Buddhist teaching. If you follow the direction of the outflung arm and look down into the walled, moated palace, filled now with trees, you can try to imagine it as it was—an inner city composed of carved and gilded teak buildings, water gardens and flowered walks. This is the only Buddha known to be in existence that does not use one of the conventional *mudras*—symbolic positions of the Buddha's arms and body.

Near the top, in a huge hanger-like construction called **Sawnyinaung Pagoda,** you will find a gruesome tableau in a cage. (There is another of these, about 9 levels from the top.) The four plaster figures represent those who drove Buddha to leave his family and seek enlightenment in meditation and solitude. There is an old man, a sick man, a dead man pecked by carrion crows and a monk—reminders to us mortals that all life is transitory until one reaches *nirvana*. (Sometimes one or more of the figures are removed for cleaning.)

From this pagoda follow the notice that reads 'To the Two Big Snakes', climbing the only very steep face of the hill on deep stone steps until, at last, you approach the summit. On the last terrace before the top, look out for the statue of a woman, kneeling in front of one of the Buddha shrines on the east side of the pagoda, offering in her hands her two breasts. This is Sanda Moke Khit, an ogress who was converted by Buddha's teaching and who cut off her breasts as a gesture of humility. In return, Buddha told her that in her next incarnation she would be so elevated that she would return as Min Done (Mindon) and be the king who would found Mandalay.

At the top there is a terrace, wide and pillared, where you are cooled by a gentle breeze. The Two Great Snakes rear up at you from a cage just below the top on the far side. They are the snakes who were charmed into docility by listening to the preaching of the hermit U Khanti, who designed so many of the sacred buildings of Mandalay.

The views on all sides are magnificent, and you can hear the chanting of soldiers, as they drill in their camp far below. In the near distance, you can identify all the pagodas you have visited in the city. The pavilions on stilts, with red roofs, close to the foot of the hill are communal shelters donated by King Mindon for the outlying communities when they came in for the pagoda festivals. You can see the Shan Hills, dark against the eastern sky, and in the west beyond the Irrawaddy, the sun slides down behind the Sagaing Hills.

Other sights

If time and enthusiasm permit, there are several more pagodas to visit in the city.

Eindawya Pagoda
About a half kilometre west of Zegyo Market (cross the canal on 26th (B) Road, and then turn left), the richly gilded Eindawya Pagoda gleams in the sunlight. Built in 1847 by King Mindon's crazy predecessor, Pagan Min, the pagoda contains an unusual Buddha carved out of the grained, silica mineral called chalcedony, which came from Bodhgaya, in India, where Gautama Buddha attained enlightenment.

Set Kyathiha Pagoda
Not far south of Zegyo Market, between 30th and 31st Roads, Set Kyathiha Pagoda was almost entirely rebuilt having been severely damaged during the Second World War. Inside you will see a magnificent 5 m seated bronze Buddha, commissioned by King Bagyidaw in 1823. It was cast in Ava, moved to Amarapura in 1849 and finally brought here in 1884. The Bodhi tree that you will see at the entrance to the pagoda was planted by U Nu, the man who became the first prime minister of the Union of Burma after the assassination of Aung San. After a somewhat turbulent political career, U Nu, a deeply religious man, now translates Buddhist scriptures. The Bodhi is sacred, in honour of the one which Gautama Buddha was sitting under when he was enlightened.

Shwe Inbin Kyaung
The Shwe Inbin Kyaung is about half a kilometre southwest of Set Kyathiha Pagoda (cross the canal on 35th (A) Road, take the first left and it is on your right). Here you can see intricate 13th-century wood carving in an atmosphere of meditative calm, as the monks go quietly about their daily tasks.

The Mandalay Museum
On 80th Street, located just outside the southwest corner of the palace walls, is the museum with its rather random collection of artefacts. Here you can see fossils and

neolithic relics, palm-leaf manuscripts, carvings, costumes, photographs, models, implements and ornate craftsmanship. There is even a sample of the handwriting of Queen Supayalat, the ambitious wife of Burma's last King, Thibaw. Perhaps the most entertaining of the exhibits is the display of puppets, so popular at puppet shows and *pwes*. All the favourite characters are represented, from the Votress, who usually starts the performance, to Thagyarmin, king of the *nats*, with other *nats*, political ministers and royalty.

The Royal Palace

Like Mandalay Hill, the Royal Palace dominates the city. Wherever you go you seem to follow the course of one of its walls; whichever street you look down, there is the palace at the end. Only from the top of the hill can you appreciate its full size and design. All the original teak buildings were destroyed by fire during fighting between the Allies and the Japanese in 1945. An aerial view reveals mainly trees and a few roofs within the walls. (The Museum in Rangoon has photographs and models of some of the main buildings which, with the Shwe Nandaw Kyaung, are all that are left to indicate the splendour of the palace.)

King Mindon wanted it to represent Mount Meru, the Hindu centre of the cosmic universe, through which all knowledge and wisdom is drawn. The massive crenellated walls, facing north, south, east and west, each nearly 2 km in length, form a square, flanked by a moat that is 70 m wide and about 3 m deep. The walls are 8 m high and taper from a width of 3 m at the bottom to 1.5 m at the top. Each wall has 3 gateways, marked with signs of the zodiac. These impressive fortifications were not so much defensive, but rather an example of the *Theravada* Buddhist practice of protecting a sacred spot. In the very centre of the palace grounds stood the throne room containing the **Lion Throne,** now on display in Rangoon's museum, topped by a soaring gold-plated tower, through which knowledge and wisdom were supposed to descend directly to the king on his throne.

The palace is now an army headquarters and only the Burmese are allowed in. Tourists are unlikely to get permission to enter, but if you do manage to slip through the south gate you will find trishaws whose drivers will show you all that there is left to see—little more than a clock tower and a model of the palace as it was, with some photographs.

The Waterfront

Anyone who is fascinated by riverside life should visit the waterfront. Go west along 35th or 26th Roads, not far beyond the canal. There is much to see: boats out on the river or moored along the mud banks, loading and unloading; bullocks standing patiently between the shafts of their carts; men carrying great loads that dangle from poles across their shoulders; women balancing baskets on their heads with effortless grace. The smell of the river is a mixture of the tang of mud, the stench of old fish and the acrid fumes of diesel. Wharves and insubstantial warehouses reverberate with the babble of voices and the clatter of activity; frail shanties line the banks and the turgid water of the Irrawaddy surges past in its everlasting journey to the sea.

WHERE TO STAY

Mandalay has two hotels and several guest houses that are approved for tourists, but frankly, the standard of accommodation is not great. As guests houses can be black-listed overnight for currency fiddles, no list can be guaranteed to be up-to-date. Tourist Burma will be able to tell you which are currently in favour.

Add 10% to all prices given: where kyats are quoted they are as calculated at the exchange rate in 1988.

Mandalay Hotel overlooking the south moat on 26th street, tel 22499. This is Mandalay's so called 'first class' hotel. Set back from a well-kept garden, it is too far to walk to from the town centre—a double annoyance as it houses the main Tourist Burma office. The service and accommodation are not impressive. Single rooms from $25, double from $30. The rooms are small, with air conditioning and bathrooms. There is a large canteen-like dining room where the food is uninspired. A set dinner, often English, costs K33. A breakfast of nasty coffee and 2 pieces of toast costs K15 and an extra K2 for more toast but no more butter and jam. Service is slow and grudging, particularly in the bar upstairs, where non-residents are liable to be refused a drink if there is one of the frequent shortages, and an air of melancholy hangs over the moist-eyed regulars. There are special tables with 'Foreign Guests Only' on them. Rum Sour, for K9, is excellent.
Mya Mandalar a block south and a block west of the Mandalay Hotel, on 26th Street, tel 21283. Better value than the Mandalay, especially if you go for the two cheaper rooms in the old block.

Old block: single $8, double $10.50 (only one of each).
New wing: single $21, double $27.

The new rooms are quite comfortable and modern, but for less than half the price, the two old ones are adequate though shabby and dirty, with unreliable fans and air-conditioning and bathrooms that leave much to be desired. The dining room, which includes tables in the garden, serves dull, sometimes uneatable food at snail pace in a dingy atmosphere. Continental breakfast costs K10, and a mediocre plate of fried rice costs K20. There is a swimming pool, but it is usually empty. The reception staff are extremely friendly and obliging.

Guest Houses

There is no doubt that your impression of a guest house is dependent to a large extent on your mood. If you are with friends, then primitive lodgings and unhygienic sanitation can be endurable; if you are on your own, or irritated by your companions, or unwell, then the same conditions can be a nightmare. Standards are all fairly similar: you will get a cubicle room with two beds, a fan and a mosquito net; communal plumbing, free plain tea and, sometimes, meals can be bought. They all charge K21 for a single room and K36 for a double. Most of them will expect you to take your shoes off before going upstairs.

Most of the approved guest houses are in the middle of the town, not far from the station, with the exception of the **Myint Thi Da** on 29th Street between 73rd and 74th Streets, and this is probably the best. The rooms are reasonably clean, though small and airless, and there is a convivial atmosphere in the reception area. There is no dining room but **The Shwenandaw restaurant** is just round the corner.

The **Man San Dar Win** is on 31st Street between 80th and 81st Sts. The staff are friendly, the accommodation cramped but reasonably clean. Opposite the Man San Dar Win is the **Man Shwe Myo**, and the **Aung Nawayard** and **Aung Thiri** are also in the same block, all very similar.

The other four listed guest houses in this area are more expensive because they have, or say they have, air conditioning. At K54 single, and K108 double, they are hardly worth the extra. The **Sabai Phyu,** in this group, offers a cubicle, no shower and no air conditioning, whatever they may advertise. The other three are: **Taung Za Lat, Tokyo** and **Wa Than oo.** There are a large number of other guest houses not officially approved and if you find everything is full, ask your driver-guide to take you to one that he recommends.

EATING OUT

There are dozens of eating places around the city, and where ever you go the menu tends to be variations on a theme of rice and noodles. Establishments rise and fall in popularity and your driver-guide will suggest the one that is currently in fashion. If you prefer to be independent, the following will give you a reasonable meal. **Htaw Yin,** on 81st Street between 30 and 31st Sts. A simple Chinese restaurant where the food isn't too bad and the proprietor will advise you in your choice. You can get a good meal from K20. **Shwenandaw,** on 73rd St between 28th and 29th Streets. A very popular Chinese restaurant which seems more clean and organized than most. There is always a cheerful atmosphere here, and a large choice of dishes. You can eat well for K50. Try their 'rum sour', and their delicious fried prawns and vegetables. **Tu Tu,** on 27th Street between 74th and 75th Streets. Here you can get Burmese food. Don't be too disappointed: more variations on a similar theme.

There is an Indian restaurant with an indecipherable name on the corner of 27th and 81st Streets, where, again, the menu looks depressingly familiar.

Snacks

Nylon Ice Cream, on 83rd Street, between 25th and 26th Streets is good for ice cream, milk shakes and yoghurt drinks. **Olympia Cafe,** next door, has delicious spring rolls and other snacks. **Flowers World Ice Cream,** on 84th Street near the Mahamuni Pagoda, is clean and modern and has delicious ice cream and milk shakes (K4) and cold boiled water.

Part VI

AROUND MANDALAY

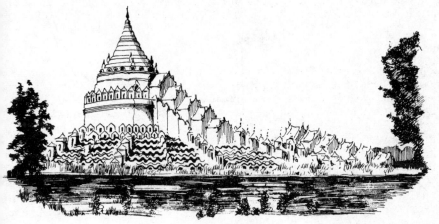

Hsinbyume Pagoda, Mingun

Mingun

If you can possibly fit it in, you shouldn't miss a visit to Mingun, particularly if you are not able to do the Mandalay to Pagan boat trip. It is a delightful place and the 1-hour boat journey is idyllic.

GETTING THERE
Tourist Burma include organized tours to Mingun in some of their packages and you must ask on arrival about which days they go and the current cost. They normally take about 5 hours in all and cost about K100.

More fun, and a lot cheaper (K4 each way) is to arrange for your pony cart/trishaw guide to collect you early in the morning and take you down to the boat that leaves roughly every hour from the jetty at the end of 26th Street. You clamber over several craft and settle down on the deck and wait for the boat to fill up. In the early morning it is a joy just to sit there and watch the river, before the heat of the day, while more and more people pile into the boat. Finally, when every square inch of deck space is taken up , the boat chugs out into the main stream and churns its way up river against the current, past every sort of craft. Palm-thatch dwellings cluster on the sand banks beside the water— temporary structures on stilts that are moved as the river contracts and expands with the seasons. These are the homes of the fishermen who harvest the river and you see their boats drawn up on the sand.

When the river is low, they test the depth with poles as the boat approaches land.

333

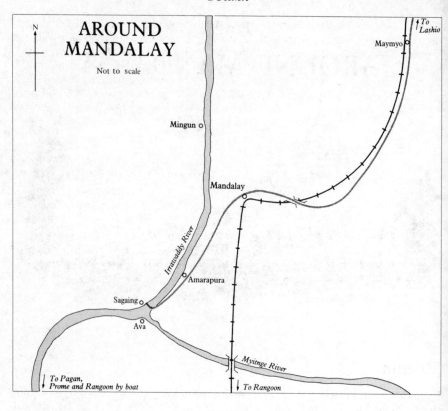

AROUND
MANDALAY

Not to scale

N

To Lashio

Maymyo

Mingun

Mandalay

Irrawaddy River

Amarapura

Sagaing

Ava

Myitnge River

To Pagan,
Prome and Rangoon by boat

To Rangoon

There are two places to land at Mingun. If you get out at the first you have a walk of about 15 minutes, across a field from the jetty, then to the right, down a dusty track through the outskirts of Mingun—a delightful rural community. Alternatively, you can stay on the boat and get out at the final landing stage, right in the middle of the village. After Mandalay, first impressions of Mingun are of peaceful and orderly simple homes.

Mingun Pagoda

You will have seen the massive bulk of the Mingun Pagoda long before the boat put you down, but it becomes lost in the trees as you walk down the track until you come out into a clearing and see it on your left, guarded by two gigantic *chinthas* on the right of the track, ruined by earthquake in 1838 but full of grandeur. (Two large chunks of stone nearby were the eyes of one of the *chinthas*.)

King Bodawpaya conceived the idea for this pagoda at the height of his power in 1790. He was one of Burma's more ambitious rulers and he believed that it was in his destiny to become a Buddha. With such an ambition, it was necessary for him to gain a great deal of merit and when he was presented with one of Buddha's teeth he decided to enshrine it in the largest pagoda in the world, to be called **Mantara Gyi.** With literally thousands of slaves he set about the construction of a pagoda that was to be 150 m in height. The base alone took more than 15 years to build and long before he achieved his aim, Burma's economy crumbled and he had to abandon the project, hoping that he could go back to it later. He died in 1813 and none of his hundreds of descendants was inspired to finish the work. An earthquake in 1838 tumbled the upper sections and the great pinkish-ochre slab that you see today is all that remains of Mantara Gyi, overgrown, riven with cracks and broken walls, and yet still strangely impressive. It is possible to scramble up the crumbling corner, onto the platform and get a wonderful view from the top.

Pondawpaya Pagoda

If you go towards the river and then turn right on the lower track, you come to the Pondawpaya Pagoda, a small working model of what the Mantara Gyi Pagoda was to be like. It is only 5 m tall, and you can imagine King Bodawpaya standing here, magnifying this miniature in his mind's eye and dreaming of the fulfilment of his grandiose plans.

Settawya Pagoda

To the south of the Mingun Pagoda and next to the Pondawpaya Pagoda, with steps running down to the river, the stark white Settawya Pagoda has a hollow vault in which a marble footprint of the Buddha was enshrined, during the building of the Mingun Pagoda.

Mingun Bell

If you walk on a little way past the Mingun Pagoda you come to the Mingun Bell, hailed as 'The Biggest Ringing Bell in the World' i.e. the biggest uncracked bell. It hangs from a metal arch on a giant shackle beneath a corrugated roof set into carved wood supported on pillars. This bell was meant to adorn the Mantara Gyi Pagoda. Bells are struck to proclaim merit: the bigger the bell the further the proclamation is carried. Bodawpaya had it cast in 1790 and then executed the craftsman who created it so that he would never be able to duplicate such a fine piece of workmanship! It weighs about 90 tons and it is a miracle that when it was thrown from its original moorings in the 1838 earthquake it was not damaged. It hung at an angle for 65 years, until the Irawaddy Shipping Company made its present frame. Anyone who doesn't suffer from claustrophobia can climb under the rim and stand inside while someone outside gives it a bang—the effect is rather eerie.

Hsinbyume Pagoda (or Myatheindan Pagoda)

Don't be lured back to the jetty and the tea shops before you have gone to the far end of Mingun, to the Hsinbyume Pagoda, up on the left. It is a delicious dazzling white icing-sugar concoction, the only one of this design in the whole world, charged with a very special atmosphere. It was built in 1816 by Bagyidaw three years before he became king, in memory of his favourite wife Hsinbyume. It is designed to resemble Sulamani Pagoda, which stands on Mount Meru, the Buddhist (and Hindu) centre of the universe, home of the king of the gods, through which all wisdom and knowledge is channelled. The undulating lines of the seven terraces represent the seven mountain ranges round Mount Meru, leading to the central *stupa* which is guarded by five mythical beasts, now sadly vandalized. The stairs are steep and narrow, the wind on the upper terraces cools you after your climb and at the top a monk meditates beside the Buddha.

Buddhist Infirmary

In a compound on the opposite side of the track from the bell, there is a Buddhist-run Infirmary which you can visit. Founded in 1915, it was Burma's first old people's home. Ancient Burmese lie on pallets in bare rooms, and a Mr Sing dispenses tea, accompanied by biscuits that could be as old as his charges, to weary visitors.

If you have time before the last boat back to Mandalay, which goes at 3 pm, the foothills around Mingun are lovely and you can wander along shady paths and visit some of the many monasteries and pagodas that litter the slopes. Look out for the **Ngwe Zedi,** with a maze-like entrance to a dark tunnel. The boat goes from the central jetty and you can sit on the terrace above, drinking refreshing plain tea, waiting for someone to ring a bell and announce its departure. The voyage back downstream to Mandalay is quicker, going with the current.

Amarapura, Ava & Sagaing

If your programme allows you one full day out from Mandalay, then the trip to Sagaing is certainly the most rewarding. There is time to include a stop either in Amarapura or Ava on the way. If you try to do both, you will cram the day too full and spoil it. Of the three, Ava is probably the one to leave out—alternatively you could do Amarapura and Ava in one day, and Sagaing separately but few tourists can afford the time for this. Apart from the many interesting and beautiful things to be seen in and around these three towns, they represent a large section of Burmese history.

As if to emphasise the Buddhist belief that all life is ephemeral, many newly established kings of Burma found it propitious to found new capitals, often encouraged by astrologers. After the fall of Pagan, the power centres shifted restlessly between Sagaing, Ava, Shwebo and Amarapura, until King Mindon decided to establish his palace in Mandalay in 1857. It is fascinating to contemplate the amazing energy and inititiative that must have gone into each removal. The new capital had to have a suitable palace with temples and pagodas and all the fine buildings necessary for court life. Only the religious buildings were constructed from masonary—everything else was made of wood. If the wooden buildings were still servicable they were often dismantled and moved to the new capital. Today, you must use your imagination to refurbish these ancient capitals and try to see them as they were.

GETTING THERE

For about K300, you can hire a 3-wheeler tourist cab for the day. It takes up to 4 people in some discomfort but gives you maximum flexibility and a guide.

Alternatively, arrange for your pony trap/trishaw driver-guide to meet you very early in the morning and take you to the bus for Sagaing. Don't admit that you are getting off in Amarapura or Ava because there is a mysterious demarcation ruling that passengers for places en route must go in a different, less frequent bus. If you prefer to be your own guide, buses leave roughly every half hour from the corner of 84th and 29th streets.

Amarapura

Less than 11 km south of Mandalay, Amarapura—The Immortal City—is the most modern of the abandoned capitals. It was from here in 1861 that King Mindon moved to the last of the royal palaces, at Mandalay. Although there is little trace of its former glory, established for 40 years between the 18th and 19th centuries and then for less than 20 years until 1860, it has managed to retain a very special atmosphere and it is worth taking time to wander through it.

GETTING AROUND

It is rather spread-out and straggly, so you should hire a pony trap to take you round.

To see everything, you must get off the bus on the outskirts, by the old palace wall, opposite an unremarkable pagoda guarded by painted elephants. If you don't want to cram the day too full, you will find more than enough to see if you get off in the middle of the town where you can pick up a pony trap.

WHAT TO SEE

The old city walls were pulled down and recycled into roads and railways and some of the secular wooden buildings were transferred to Mandalay: only the pagodas that marked the corners of the one mile of wall still stand, together with a few tumbled ruins, overgrown with creeping jungle and linked by dirt tracks.

Patodawgyi Pagoda

The Patodawgyi Pagoda is down a track to the left, just past the old palace walls, on the far side of the railway line. It was built by King Bagidaw in 1820, with a traditional bell-shaped *stupa* and five terraces, giving excellent views from the top across the paddy fields and away towards Ava and the Sagaing hills. There is a stucco Buddha here overgrown with lush vegetation and you can see examples of *Jataka* marble reliefs on the terraces—illustrations of scenes from the Buddha's life. The large inscribed tablet tells the history of the pagoda.

Taungthaman Lake

You can either meander on through the tracks beyond the railway line, quite a distance, to the Bagaya Kyaung (monastery) and its surrounds, or go back to the main road and take the left turn in the middle of the town. Whichever way you choose, the skeleton of U Bein's Bridge is the landmark to head for. The lake is a vast area of water for part of the year, drying out to become fertile arable and paddy fields in the dry season, cut by a network of tracks. The bridge, built 200 years ago by U Bein, the mayor of Ava at the time when the capital was transferred, is partly constructed with teak from the abandoned palace in Ava. It is somewhat rickety these days with a few yawning gaps, but still servicable for most of its 1 km length.

Bagaya Kyaung

You will see plenty of activity around the Bagaya Kyaung, one of the largest monasteries in Burma, with about 700 monks and novices living in a spacious compound with strange shaped living quarters (paddle-steamers). There are usually groups of novices by the well on the edge of the lake and you may hear the sound of their chanting voices, inside the compound, reciting the scriptures by rote.

Wander round outside the walls, through ruins of temples, where crumbling plaster Buddhas look out from corrugated shelters, and where oleanders and lilies fight for survival amoung the encroaching jungle. The monastery extends beyond its compound and you can go into some of the wooden buildings. Take off your shoes and climb the steps: if you are lucky, and are prepared to pay your respects to the monk presiding by one of the Buddha shrines you are likely to win a warm welcome and English conversation from the older monks, who enjoy answering your questions.

Kyauktawgyi Pagoda

South of the U Bein bridge, the Kyauktawgyi Pagoda stands within a walled enclosure among old trees and bougainvillea, overlaid by an atmosphere of peace enhanced by the meditative calm of the monks who come to pay homage to the large seated Buddha, made of greenish Sagyin marble. The pagoda was built by King Pagan in 1847, to the same design as the famous Ananda Temple in Pagan, though not nearly so elaborate. It was re-roofed in 1979 and you can still see, under the white paint, traces of a startling blue colour-wash that dates from the same time. Look for the intriguing paintings on the entrance walls. They illustrate life in Burma in the mid-19th century, with some European faces in the crowds. They also dwell on the generosity of King Pagan towards his people, which must have brought some secret derision from the artists as Pagan was one of the cruellest of all the kings, responsible for the deaths of many thousands of his subjects.

Weaving

The main industry of Amarapura today is weaving cotton and silk and more than half the houses of the 10,000 inhabitants own at least one loom. You will see trays of spools spread out on the ground and hear the rhythmic rattle of the shuttles if you walk through the back lanes, and most of the weavers are only too delighted to demonstrate their skills if you go into one of the houses. Their main product is the *acheithtamein*—the ceremonial *longyi*—and there is a central shop in the middle of the town, controlled by the government.

Bronze Casting

Amarapura is also renowned for its bronze casting. Many famous pagoda bells came from here as well as the remarkably life-like statue of Aung San that stands in the Aung San Park in Rangoon.

Ava Bridge and Ava

The Ava Bridge is the only bridge over the Irrawaddy and is located about 20 km southwest of Mandalay. It was built by the British in 1934, an elegant 16-arm span of girders, more than 1 km in length. In April 1942, the British were forced to demolish part of it to try to hold back the Japanese, after the last train crossed carrying evacuees from the British General Hospital in Maymyo. It was not repaired until 1954. There are check-points at either end and drivers must pay a small toll. **Thabyedan Fort,** on the left, on the Ava side, was built by the Burmese before the Third Anglo-Burmese War, and captured by the British. It formed one of a triangle of forts, thought to be invincible: the other two are **Ava Fort** and **Sagaing Fort**. With a few brief gaps, Ava was the capital for nearly 400 years from 1364, after Sagaing's brief ascendancy following the fall of

Pagan, until Amarapura took over in 1841. It was founded by King Thadominbya on a man-made island, created by the digging of a canal from the Irrawaddy to the Myitnge.

GETTING THERE
Any bus from Mandalay to Sagaing passes through Amarapura and Ava. Get your driver/guide to take you to one of the several departure points in the centre of Mandalay (K4 each way). If you stop in Amarapura, resume your journey on any of the frequent buses that pass the same stop. Get off just before the Ava Bridge, after less than half an hour's journey. Or hire a 3-wheeler cab for the day (see Getting to Amarapura). Take the track on the right down to where the ferry (K1) fords the Myitnge River, just before it flows into the Irrawaddy. You can then hire one of the pony traps that wait on the far side. During the rainy season you must take the ferry from Thabyedan Fort.

Ava, also called 'Ratnapura'—City of Gems—was a name that embraced the whole of the Burmese empire as late as the 19th century and even in the dying years of the Konbaungset dynasty in Mandalay the government was called the 'Court of Ava'. Now a ghost city of romantic ruins encompassing several contemporary villages, the name Ava is translated as 'entrance to the lake', referring to the confluence of the two rivers. This was the centre of the rice trade that built the economy of the area when Ava was the capital.

WHAT TO SEE
Before the walls of the city fell into ruin, an aerial view would have revealed that they were built in the shape of a *chinthe*, the mythical lion that guards the entrances to so many of Burma's pagodas and temples. Little can be seen now: there are still remains around the north gate—the **Gaung Say Daga** (Gate of the Hair-Washing)—where the king used to have his hair washed in a ceremony of public purification during the Thingyan Festival in April. Near the north gate you can see the **Nanmyin Watchtower,** all that remains of the palace built by King Bagyidaw after he moved the capital back here from Amarapura in the 19th century. It earned its name Leaning Tower of Ava after the earthquake in 1838, a catastrophe that dealt the final blow to Ava's supremacy.

Within the walls you will find the **Htilaingshin Pagoda,** built by King Kyanzittha during the Pagan era. The **Bagaya Kyaung,** also within the walls, is a wooden monastery that was built after the Maha Aungmye. On the southern side, away from the river, is the **Leitutgyi Pagoda,** notable for its four storeys, and the **Lawkatharaphu Pagoda.**

Maha Aungmye Bonzan, or Ok Kyaung
The brick monastery near the north gate is the Maha Aungmye Bonzan, built in 1818 by Bagyidaw's chief wife, Nanmadaw Me Nu, for her favourite abbot, Sayadaw Nyaunggan, with whom she was believed by many to have had more than just a spiritual relationship. The elaborate plasterwork on the outside was designed to imitate the more common wooden monasteries which were so vulnerable to fire. It is intriguing to stand looking at the aloof Buddha inside, on a glass mosaic plinth, and speculate on the true story that lies behind the creation of this frivolous building and on the actual relationship between a woman whose husband was shortly to become king, and a man dedicated to the stringent vows of Buddhist monkhood. As you enter the monastery, look for the marble plaque engraved in English, telling of the life of the Burmese wife of an American missionary.

The large white stone memorial near the monastery stands on the site of the Let Ma Yoon—no-holds-barred—prison, and was erected in memory of an American missionary, Dr Adoniram Judson, who wrote the first Anglo-Burmese dictionary. Unable to distinguish between British and Americans, the Burmese imprisoned Judson for a year during the First Anglo-Burmese War, subjecting him to harrowing torture.

There are many pagodas, temples and shrines to be seen in and around Ava and the temptation is to wander among them, through attractive farming communities, in the shade of trees, with the river sparkling in the background. But, if you are to include Sagaing in your day, you should not linger too long.

About a kilometre south of the city is Ava Fort, one of the trio of forts including Thabyedan and Sagaing, mistakenly thought to be invincible.

Sagaing

Seen from a distance, especially from the Irrawaddy, Sagaing must be one of the most beautiful sights in Burma. It has a mystical aura that may stem from Sagaing's reputation for being the heart of Buddhism in Burma today. The modern part of the town is spread out below a backcloth of hills to the north, where *stupas* and spires and turrets rise from the trees, dazzling white and glinting gold; an ethereal kingdom shimmering like a mirage.

GETTING THERE

There are a variety of buses from several different stops in the middle of Mandalay, K4 each way, and you should get your driver/guide to take you to the best one. Whichever one you catch, you can break your journey in Amarapura and/or in Ava, and catch any later bus on the same route. There is a ferry from Ava that will take you across the Irrawaddy, where you can then get a pony cart or taxi into the centre of the town. If you are in Ava, you must go back up to the Ava Bridge and catch the next bus into the centre. Neither should cost you more that a couple of kyats. Or you can hire a jeep for the day (see 'Getting to Amarapura').

To visit the Kaunghmudaw Pagoda, 10 km west of Sagaing, a taxi will cost anything from K60, a pony trap anything from K35 or a bus only a couple of kyats.

If you take the road through the valley between the two main ridges, towards the river, you can get a boat back to the market for K1 and from here you can get the bus back to Mandalay. Alternatively, you can get a boat from Sagaing, south across the river to Amarapura where you can pick up the bus. If you have time, this one-hour trip, costing only a few kyats, gives you the best view of Sagaing, across the olive-coloured Irrawaddy.

Sagaing was the first capital after the fall of Pagan, founded in 1315, its supremacy only lasting until 1364 when King Thadominbya moved to Ava. Those 50 years, so long ago, have cast an undiminished spell over this magical place.

WHAT TO SEE

Today there are over 600 monasteries and nunneries dotted over the hills to the north of the modern town, with more than 5000 monks, nuns and novices living there. If only there was sufficient time, you could wander through the hills to discover them.

Kaunghmudaw Pagoda

Before you are captivated by wandering in the hills, you should make the 10 km journey out to Kaunghmudaw Pagoda to the west, passing lots of ruined pagodas on the way. You can do this by taxi, pony trap or bus, the bus costing only a couple of kyats, the pony trap anything from K35, and the taxi anything from K60.

The pagoda was built in 1636 by King Thalun, to house the holy relics that he had transferred from the Mahazedi Pagoda in Pegu, including the coveted 'Tooth of Kandy' and Dhammapala's miraculous begging bowl (see Pegu, page 308). The perfect hemisphere of the *stupa* is reputed to represent the breast of the king's favourite wife. More prosaically, it was modelled on the Mahaceti Pagoda in Ceylon. If you walk round the lowest of the three terraces below the 46 m-high *stupa*, you will find dozens of shrines housing an assortment of *nats* and *devas*—goddesses—each embellished by placatory offerings, and most attended by kneeling supplicants. The niches in the 812 pillars that surround the *stupa* are for oil lamps that are lit at the **Thadingyut Light Festival** during the October full moon, to celebrate the end of Lent. If you can read Burmese, the great marble slab in the grounds tells you the history of the pagoda. Look out for the sacred pool where an old crone summons a sacred turtle from the depths with an eerie ululation. You can buy a bowl of little fish to set free in the pond and gain yourself some merit.

The village of **Ywataung** that you pass on the way to the pagoda is a centre for silversmiths, and if you have time to stop you can visit the workshops and watch the craftsmen who are only too pleased to demonstrate their skills.

The Hsinmyashin Pagoda
Also on the way back, you will see the Hsinmyashin Pagoda, known as the 'Pagoda of Many Elephants'. Built in 1429, it was destroyed by an earthquake in 1482, rebuilt, and destroyed by another earthquake in 1955. You can still see two of the elephants that gave it its name, large and brightly painted at the entrance.

Other Pagodas
There are plenty of other pagodas to be seen in Sagaing, but none of especial interest unless you are a pagoda addict. If this is the case, get one of the English-speaking pony trap drivers to take you round and be prepared to run out of time before even a brief exploration of the hills. **The Htupayon Pagoda** in the town, was built in 1444, destroyed by the earthquake that did so much damage in this area in 1838, and only partly rebuilt by King Pagan before he was ousted by Mindon in 1853. You can see the rather unusual style of the three layers of the base, bordered by arched recesses.

The Aungmyelawka Pagoda, also called the Eindawya Pagoda, stands on the banks of the Irrawaddy, near the Htupayon. It was built in 1783 by King Bodawpaya in an effort to earn merit to atone for the appalling atrocities that marked his scramble to power and his reign. The design is a sandstone replica of the Shwezigon Pagoda near Pagan.

The Ngadatgyi Pagoda, near the Htupayohn, dates from 1657 and houses a very large seated Buddha. King Pindale who endowed this pagoda was subsequently drowned with all his family which cleared the way for his ambitious brother.

The Datpaungzu Pagoda, also in the town, was built to house relics from other pagodas that had to be demolished during the building of the Myitkyina railway.

Sagaing Hills
Hermits lived in the many hills around Sagaing centuries before history was written,

when primeval forests covered all the land. There are trees whose trunks and roots are
gnarled and twisted like massive snakes writhing on the rocks. You could spend days
happily wandering here, shaded by trees and vines and intertwining creepers, fragrant
with the scent of flowers. Paths, steps and covered ways twist and climb, diverge and
meet, leading you from one monastery to another, from pagoda to temple, from shrine to
simple dwelling. Great earthenware jars tempt you to ease your thirst, but you should
resist and stick to your own water bottle. Far from the babble of life in the town, these
hills have a magic that makes it easy for the non-believer to understand the lure of a
contemplative life. It was here that a recent traveller from Europe, seeking a particular
Buddhist nun, was taken ill and collapsed on the threshold of a convent. She came to her
senses lying on a bamboo mat on a platform in a cool timber-framed room; nuns in pink
and yellow robes knelt beside her, massaging her aching limbs, holding pungent
tamarind bark to her face, offering a black, tepid liquid for her to drink. She slept
through the hot hours of the day and awoke again to find the nuns sleeping beside her.
They had no language in common but the nuns had known instinctively how to restore
her so that she was able to go out and resume her journey.

There are too many pagodas and temples on the crests of the hills to describe each
one: you must choose your own favourites. No one minds if you go into the monasteries,
so long as you show respect. The golden dome of the **Sun U Ponya Shin Pagoda**
dominates the western ridge, and you get glorious views from here. It is possible to drive
to the top, and it is here that you will be taken if you are on a conducted tour, but it is
much nicer to walk if you have time. There are four covered flights of steps that zig-zag
up the hill, the most popular being the one which ascends from **Thayetpinseik**—
Mango Tree Port—where all public transport terminates, including boats. There is no
mango tree now, but a solitary *chinthe*, mourning the demise of its mate. Taking these
steps, you get to a large, airy pagoda at the top from where you can look across the valley
to **Sun U Ponya Shin Pagoda** on a ridge the far side. A lovely way back to Thayetpinseik
from here is to take the steep steps down towards Sun U Ponya Shin Pagoda and then
branch downhill on a narrow, steep track through the valley, keeping left and wandering
through villages to the river, where you can catch a sampan back to the town.

Part VII

MAYMYO

Mindlay

It is a curious thing, but Burmese people believe that foreigners, or certainly British foreigners, should go to Maymyo because it will remind them of home: one even went so far as to liken it to the Sussex Downs. If you are feeling homesick and do indeed pine for a familiar landscape, then you would be best to take the next flight home: certainly you won't find a substitute in Maymyo. Perhaps they think that, as the British used it as a hill resort in the 19th and 20th century, it must be like Britain.

Maymyo was a hill station garrisoned by the British who called it Maytown after a Colonel May who was stationed there and who squashed a rebellion in the area in 1886 after the British had annexed Upper Burma. British colonials escaped to Maymyo from the heat of the plains during the hot season and it is reputed to be a good example of a typical Colonial hill resort like those in India during the Raj. Standing on a plateau over 1000 m up in the Shan Hills, it is cooler than the plains in the hot season but less so today because massive deforestation has caused a change in the climate. Whatever people may say, it is hard for even the most fertile imagination to see it as anything but Burmese in character. The most obvious sign of British influence is that most of the houses are built of brick, or solid wood, with chimneys, unlike the flimsy buildings in Mandalay and elsewhere.

GETTING THERE

It is possible to get there by train from Mandalay but this is not encouraged by the authorities and if you do it is a tortuous, hair-pin route into the hills taking several hours. The train goes on to Lashio, way up in the Shan Hills towards the Chinese border and emphatically a black area for tourists because of insurgents.

The best way to go is by jeep from Mandalay and your driver/guide will take you to one

343

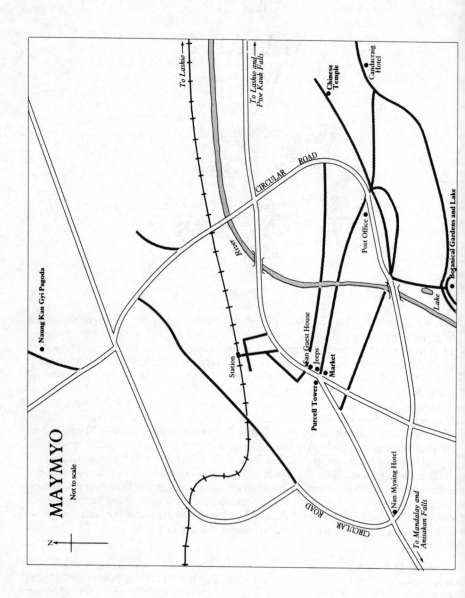

MAYMYO

Not to scale

N

To Lashio

To Lashio and
Pwe Kauk Falls

Chinese
Temple

Candecraig
Hotel

Naung Kan Gyi Pagoda

CIRCULAR ROAD

River

Post Office

Botanical Gardens and Lake

Lake

Station

San Guest House
Jeeps
Market

Purcell Tower

Nan Myaing Hotel

CIRCULAR ROAD

To Mandalay and
Anisakan Falls

344

of the departure points where the jeeps wait until they have a full load, the last ones leaving around 3 pm. The cost is K30 per passenger, or K300 if you want to hire the whole vehicle. (The return trip, downhill, costs only K10!) The official capacity is 8 people but, though you may start with this number, you are likely to pick up several more on the way, who cling to the outside and the back of the jeep. As long as you aren't a nervous passenger, the journey is fun. The jeep stops frequently; sometimes to satisfy the needs of passengers who may wish to buy a snack from a roadside booth; or, having taken a deviation into a mysterious back yard, to fill up with black-market petrol from an illicit store of jerrycans, a transaction that includes the handing over of a fat roll of banknotes; and several stops are made to fill a thirsty radiator. There is also a scheduled rest stop, about half way, where everyone climbs stiffly out and goes into a cafe for refreshment until the driver gets bored and blows the horn. The route runs east along a plain and then climbs steeply, zig-zagging, through scrub and jungle, past vivid blossoms and plantations, with panoramic views down to the plain.

The jeep takes anything from 2 to 3 hours, depending on its performance and the whim of the driver. It will drop you in the centre of Maymyo where you can hire one of the distinctive miniature 'stage coaches' called *mindlays*, that are a feature of Maymyo.

GETTING AROUND
The trim, brightly painted *mindlays* are fun to travel in for short distances, or you can negotiate for a day's hire from about K100. The trip from the town centre to the Candacraig costs from K8-K10.

The best way to get about, if you are energetic, is by bicycle, which you can hire from various places in and around the town including the Candacraig, for about K25 per day. It is wise to have a trial ride before you agree to the deal.

WHAT TO SEE
Naung Kan Gyi Pagoda
Bicycle north over the railway line on Circular Road, to Naung Kan Gyi Pagoda, which you see on a hill ahead of you. It is less than half an hour's ride from the centre of the town, out past army barracks and a Catholic seminary.

Leave your bicycle at the foot of the hill and climb the track to the covered steps that lead to the pagoda, remembering to remove your shoes. It is an easy climb and well worth doing at sunrise or sunset. The octagonal pagoda is delightful, on a terrace surrounded by the living quarters of monks and the novices, who you may see sitting on the floor chanting their scriptures in unison. The views all round are lovely and a light breeze cools you as you gaze down through mist and the smoke from fires, to the sound of distant bells. Paintings of the Buddha's life decorate the roof of the pagoda terrace, where dogs lie sleeping among floral offerings to the shrines.

The Botanical Gardens
The Botanical Gardens, a 20-minute bicycle ride to the south of the town centre, are a rather soulless arrangement of formal flower beds planted with military precision, and neat sandy paths round a lake, dug by Turkish prisoners in the Crimean War. Nasturtiums and pansies add an English touch, to the vivid cannas and hibiscus and the beautiful old trees. At the entrance there is a group of food and drink stalls under shady canopies where you can revive yourself before the ride back and buy seeds to take home.

345

Maymyo Market

The Market is right in the middle of the town, an enormous spread of stalls, shops and booths where you can buy every sort of article from food to souvenirs. The stalls that cater especially for tourists will quote prices in dollars at a favourable rate of exchange and there are some excellent bargains to be had if you want to take home embroidered wall hangings, teak and ivory, opium weights, Shan bags, old silk *longyis* etc. Beware of the tout who creeps up and whispers that he has 'precious gems' and shows you a few samples, surreptitiously hidden in his hand: it is extremely difficult for the layman to differentiate between gems and coloured glass, especially in a shady corner. You will often see people from the hill tribes in the market, with their colourful costumes, more strident voices and sturdier figures.

The Station

The train from Lashio to Mandalay stops at Maymyo and the station is a gold mine for anyone whose hobby is people-watching. Young men and women throng the platforms in trendy Western denims acquired over the Thai border, very conspicuous to the eye that has grown accustomed to *longyis* and demure blouses. The train, waiting to depart, is full to bursting with people packed tight on the roof, reaching down to haul up more and more friends and luggage. Noise and excitement charge the air and you are tempted to investigate ways and means of getting into the next train up to Lashio, in spite of the emphatic out-of-bounds ban for tourists, and the lack of time.

Pwe Kauk Falls

The Pwe Kauk Falls are 8 km out of the town on the Lashio road—about 45 minutes in a *mindlay*—quicker on a bicycle. The ride is attractive, though hilly and quite tiring in the heat and passes through villages and fertile farmland with lots of shady trees. The falls themselves are not especially spectacular. They were a favourite picnic spot for the British in the early days and it is amusing to sit by the muddy water and picture those intrepid ladies under their parasols, laying out their sandwiches and tea and refusing to wilt under the midday sun.

Anisakan Falls

About 8 km southwest of Maymyo, at Anisakan, the falls are more splendid but you must abandon your bicycle or *mindlay* beyond the railway line and walk and it is uphill all the way back! The river cascades in five steps, hurling up spray when there has been rain. Follow the falls down along the path and then look back. You can swim here and it is said that there are no mosquitoes, so it would be an ideal place to camp.

WHERE TO STAY

The Candacraig Hotel

It is fashionable to refer to the Candacraig Hotel as a typical British country house, offering typical British-style hospitality, and indeed many people go to Maymyo just to go to the Candacraig. Perhaps in colonial days it may have lived up to its reputation but standards have slipped since the days when it was the quarters, or 'chummery', for bachelor employees of the Bombay Burma Trading Company at the beginning of this century. You will find tourists who rave about the Candacraig, and its nostalgic atmosphere: you will find others whose memories are not so happy.

It stands above the town in a nice garden looking a little like an ivy-clad villa in Sunningdale, with a balcony and octagonal turrets. Inside, an air of lethargy prevails. There is a Tourist Burma desk, a broken fridge, a seedy, institutional dining room and a distinct lack of maintenance. An impressive stairway leads to bedrooms that are certainly furnished in colonial style, but lacking the comfort one associates with colonial living. Walls are paper-thin; nights are full of the noise of voices and dogs, and of lizards rootling in your luggage. Apart from turret room 104, with its large private shower room, sanitation is basic: one dismal shower/lavatory for women, and one for men. The water is often turned off during the day; you can only use the showers between 6 and 7 pm, if they are working. The blazing log fires and traditional roast beef and Yorkshire pudding that are spoken of in some of the guide books may be laid on but somehow you need to rely heavily on your imagination to summon up echoes of the past. In spite of all this, the Candacraig has an appealing atmosphere! Single rooms for K70, double for K170, a bed in a 4-bedded room for K60 per person. You can hire bicycles for K3 per hour or K25 per day.

Nann Myaing Hotel
You will find better service and comfort at the Nann Myaing Hotel, an old British building, done up, which you see on your right as you come into Maymyo from Mandalay. For K96 single, K161 double, you get air conditioning, bath en-suite and an excellent cook who was trained at the Inya Lake Hotel in Rangoon. To stay here, get off the jeep just after the police check point.

Guest Houses
Although there are several guest houses in and around the town, none are authorized by Tourist Burma. Rules have tightened up recently and you are unlikely to find any that will risk taking you in.

EATING OUT
Maymyo has plenty of small cafés and restaurants where you will get the usual choice of rice and noodles. The chef in the Nann Myaing was trained in the Inya Lake Hotel which, he will be the first to tell you, sets his food above any other you will find in Maymyo. If you are nostalgic and go for the roast beef and Yorkshire pudding at the Candacraig, don't expect too much.

You can buy strawberries in season, in punnets around the market: they are cheap and delicious, but you should wash them. You can also get strawberry lassis (yoghurt drink) which are excellent, but can be a cause of upset tummies.

Part VIII

PAGAN

Ananda Temple

It is almost unthinkable to plan a tour of Burma without including a visit to Pagan, the extraordinary, ruin-scattered plain from which so much history stems. It covers 40 square km on the eastern shore of the Irrawaddy, southwest of Mandalay in Central Burma. The village of Pagan lies within a bend of the river, about 5 km southwest of Nyaung-oo, the main town and ferry terminal. Two kilometres south of Pagan is Myinkaba, where lacquerware is made, with the village of Thiripyitsaya a further 3 km to the south. Taking Pagan as the centre, the sacred buildings and ruins lie within a 5 km arc from Nyaung-oo, clockwise to Thiripyitsaya.

GETTING THERE

By Air
You can fly from Rangoon, from Mandalay, or from Heho via Mandalay. See page 00 for details of fares and schedules.

The airport is about 6 km east of Pagan village, 2.5 km southeast of Nyaung-oo. An airport bus takes passengers to Pagan village.

By Road
You can take a pick-up truck or bus from Mandalay, costing K88 and taking about 7 hours; or from Taunggyi, costing K143 and taking a good 10 hours. Book your ticket through Tourist Burma, who will tell you where to catch your transport (sometimes they are not very helpful about the Mandalay–Pagan bus). You will be delivered to the Tourist Burma office in Pagan village. It is possible to go from Rangoon but this is is an unendurable journey and unthinkable with the present time limit.

By Train

You can combine train and pick-up or bus using Thazi station, on the Rangoon-Mandalay route, as your junction. The full fare for this is K225, Upper Class from Rangoon. The bus from Thazi to Pagan costs K115. Buses connect with the three express trains a day each way, though you may have to wait some time. The nearest railway station to Pagan is Kyaukpadaung, about 50 km to the southeast from where you would have to catch a bus. To get here from Mandalay or Rangoon, you would have to change at Pyinmana. From Taunggyi you could go by train to Taungtha, about 60 km northeast of Pagan and catch a bus. As none of these options are geared for tourists, you would have no co-operation from Tourist Burma, no reliable schedules or connections and almost certainly unaffordable delays, given the present time limit.

By Boat

If you can possibly manage it, go on the boat from Mandalay—a 12-hour journey of enchantment you will never forget. Boats leave at 5.30 am every Sunday and Thursday, except during the dryest season just before the rains begin, around the end of May when the river is too low. Tickets cost K160 (K200 with cabin, but you will be far too engrossed by the scenery to wish to waste a moment inside). Book through Tourist Burma. Breakfast and lunch are included in your ticket, as well as transport to and from the boat. This is the one package that it is well worth doing through the official channels: the non-tourist boats are photogenic and delightful to observe, but, like some of the scenes on station platforms, perhaps best appreciated as a spectator. Tourists on the upper deck are kept very separate from the lower deck passengers. Although Tourist Burma insist that it is impossible to spend the previous night on board, and the cabins are locked, there are those who have managed to get onto the boat and sleep on deck.

HISTORY

Pagan's history began as early as the 2nd century AD, in the days when the Pyus were settling in Upper Burma, and tradition attributes its foundation to the Pyu king Thamuddarit, in AD107. The early chronicles list 55 Kings of Pagan from this date but a certain amount of legend dilutes the known facts until the 11th century when Pagan entered its 'golden era'. It is certain, however, that in 849, King Pyinbya established a walled city with 12 gates and a moat and it is from this time that the earliest monuments date.

It was Anawrahta, the 42nd king of Pagan, reigning from 1044 to 1077, who was responsible for the birth of its 250-year era of greatness. During this time, the kingdom of Pagan reached as far north as Bhamo, east across to the Salween River and to the west of the Chin hills. The Irrawaddy was its lifeline, bringing in rice and linking it to the trade routes of the Indian Ocean. Irrigation was improved, making it possible to grow more rice and crops locally. The economy flourished. When Anawrahta first came to the throne, the religion that prevailed in Burma was a mixture of animism, and several different forms of Buddhism and Hinduism—which explains some of the frescoes depicting such figures as Shiva and Vishu. But then came a young monk, Shin Arahan, possibly from the Mon capital Thaton, who converted Anawrahta to the pure law of *Theravada* Buddhism, and thus changed the course of Burmese history (see History, page 272). In a fever of religious zeal, the new converts started on an orgy of building,

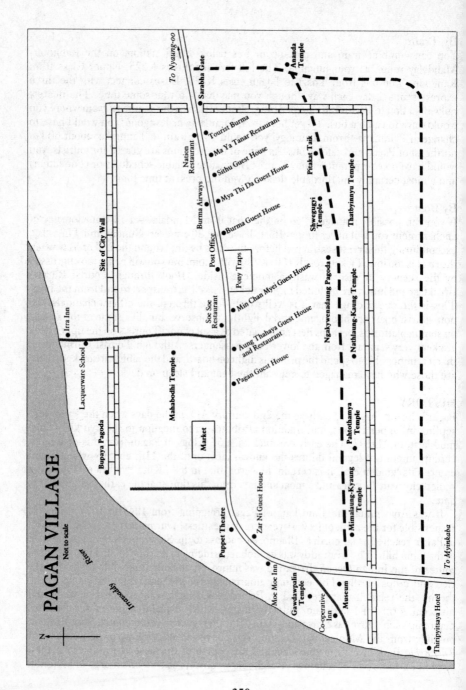

PAGAN VILLAGE

Not to scale

Irrawaddy River

Bupaya Pagoda

Lacquerware School

Site of City Wall

Irra Inn

Mahabodhi Temple

Market

To Nyaung-oo

Sarabha Gate

Ananda Temple

Tourist Burma

Nation Restaurant

Ma Ya Tanar Restaurant

Sithu Guest House

Burma Airways

Mya Thi Da Guest House

Pitakat Taik

Burma Guest House

Post Office

Pony Traps

Shwegugyi Temple

Thatbyinnyu Temple

Soe Soe Restaurant

Min Chan Myei Guest House

Aung Thahaya Guest House and Restaurant

Ngakywenadaung Pagoda

Nathlaung-Kaung Temple

Pagan Guest House

Puppet Theatre

Zar Ni Guest House

Pahtothamya Temple

Mimalaung-Kyaung Temple

Moe Moe Inn

Gawdawpalin Temple

Co-operative Inn

Museum

To Myinkaba

Thiripyitsaya Hotel

350

throwing up temples, pagodas and shrines in a mad struggle to gain merit, until, by the time Pagan finally fell to Kublai Khan's forces in 1283, many thousands of sacred buildings enhanced the plain, of which 2250 can still be seen. According to tradition many of the buildings were demolished by the Burmese in an attempt to fortify the city against the invading Mongols. Subsequent neglect, aided by the elements, earthquakes and vandalism, has reduced Pagan to what you will see today. Earthquake damage has been horrendous, the last major 'quake having been as recent as 1975, but it is a sad fact that vandals have been almost as destructive, greedily tearing out the entrails of images in an attempt to find the treasures enshrined, and stealing vast amounts of carved ornamentation. Only a small proportion of masonry buildings survived. The secular buildings—houses, palaces, offices, shops—were made mostly of teak, as were almost all the monasteries. They have all gone now.

Looking down from a high terrace of the Thatbyinnyu Temple, or the Gawdawpalin, it is hard to visualize how Pagan looked in its golden era. Where oxen plod on sandy tracks between fields of stunted vegetation there stood a city seething with the trappings of wealth and poverty, of spiritual fanaticism and worldly intrigue. A maze of streets and squares were lined with elaborately carved teak buildings, rich in colour, vibrant with noise. Among the jostling crowds were merchants, politicians, housewives, servants, farmers, fishermen, as well as pilgrims and holy men. Wharves and landing stages lined the banks of the Irrawaddy, where fleets of merchant ships loaded and unloaded in ceaseless trade with other ports of the East.

Today, the whole area is an intriguing combination of past and present; of ruined temples adjacent to others that are still thriving; of archaic agricultural methods and transistor radios; of indigenous people, elegantly and discreetly clothed in *longyis*, and foreigners in brief shorts and sun-tops, clanking cameras and sweating under their back-packs.

Pagan Village
Although the name Pagan embraces the whole plain, it focuses on the village of Pagan which is the centre. Here, the guest houses are far and away the best you will find in Burma; there is a so-called luxury hotel and the cafe food is excellent. There are a number of souvenir shops, with lacquerware as the main attraction, and a puppet theatre at the far end of the village where you can watch a half-hour show (very bad) for K10.

The local inhabitants are more blatantly materialistic than elsewhere in Burma: as you walk down the street you will be surrounded by gangs of children, asking for pens, sweets, lipsticks—'for my sister'—and money. Men will approach you stealthily from the shadows and offer you stolen 'antiques'—carved statues and reliefs allegedly from the ruined temples but not always genuine. If you show an interest, the ensuing bargaining can go on for the whole of your visit: don't forget that the penalties for trying to smuggle sacred relics out of the country are severe.

TOURIST INFORMATION
Open from 8 am to 8 pm, the Tourist Burma office is the first building on your left as you enter Pagan village through the Sarabha Gateway. As well as travel information, they will have a list of the current approved guest houses. You can change money here and there is a machine that dispenses iced boiled water—when it is turned on and someone has remembered to fill it up.

The Burma Airways office is a short distance further on, on the other side of the road, with the post office beyond.

GETTING AROUND
You can explore the immediate surrounds of the village on foot or by bicycle, which you can hire from several centres for K15 a day or by pony cart for K50 for half a day. The advantage of the latter is that if you get an English-speaking guide he will tell you far more than any guide book can, and will negotiate for keys to locked buildings (and many of the ruined buildings *are* locked in an attempt to halt vandalism). Once you get off the tarmac roads, a bicycle becomes a severe burden in the loose sand.

Itineraries
You can cram a lot into a couple of days in Pagan. Three days would be ideal and give you a chance to see Mount Popa. One day, alas, is not enough, but with careful planning you can cover a fair range of sights and experiences. It is undoubtedly preferable to explore only a few of the pagodas or temples than to try and gallop round the lot. You will enjoy them almost as much, if not more, by climbing to the highest point of one of them—the Thatbyinnyu, for instance, or the Gawdawpalin—particularly at sunrise or sunset, and look down over the plain and see them all spread out below you. The market at Nyaung-oo is worth a visit, not more than half an hour's bicycle ride to the northeast, and so is the lacquer-making village of Myinkaba to the south, 15 minutes on your bike but the track is sandy and hard-going. Some of the guest houses will arrange two-hour canoe trips up river to a monastery where you can explore and watch the sun setting in the company of friendly young novices. The cost is usually K10 per person.

WHAT TO SEE

In & Around Pagan Village

The Sarabha (or Tharaba) Gateway
You will go through this massive gateway, all that is left of the great city wall built by King Pyinbya in 849, as you come into the village from Nyaung-oo. Stop and look for the Mahagiri Nats, Golden Face and Mr Handsome, the brother and sister guardian spirits of Pagan, who beam out at you from behind screens of floral tributes on the outside of the wall. (See Mount Popa for their story.)

Pagan Museum
Open every day except Mondays and holidays, from 9 am to 4.30 pm, the museum is a modern building in the lee of the Gawdawpatin Pagoda. Although small, it has an interesting collection of archaeological exhibits: pottery, terracotta, bronze, glazed *jataka* plaques showing scenes from Buddha's life, stone reliefs, statues and fragments of painted cloth, all dating from Pagan's golden era between the 10th and 14th centuries.

Look out for the section that gives details of the UNDP/UNESCO project to restore national monuments and artefacts at selected sites in Burma. There is a covered annexe in the vividly planted garden where you can see many ancient stone images from the temples, as well as plaques recording fascinating details of the donations of slaves and land to religious buildings and temple records.

Ananda Temple

For those who like wedding-cake architecture, the Ananda must take the prize. Just to the east of the old city wall, it was built in 1091 by Kyansittha, one of Anawrahta's sons, when the passion for merit-gaining endowments was at its height. The name, which was also the name of Buddha's cousin and disciple, stems from *Anandapynnya*—Burmese for the Infinite Wisdom of Buddha. Legend tells of a vision, granted to Kyansittha by eight saints whom he had succoured, of a sacred grotto in the Himalayas, which he used as his model for the Ananda. It is an excellent example of the Early Style of temple architecture. The ground-plan is of a Greek cross, the arms formed by the four entrances, lined with booths; the centre is a massive cube, each face of which enshrines a 9.5 m high standing Buddha, richly coated in gold. These four images are the four Buddhas of this world cycle who have already achieved enlightenment: Kakusandha in the north, Konagamana in the east, Kassapa in the south and Gautama in the west. The two figures kneeling before Gautama are Shin Arahan, the monk who converted Anawrahta, on the left, and King Kyansittha on the right. The north and south Buddhas are original, the other two are replacements. Two parallel vaulted passages surround the central block, cool and cave-like, the walls pierced by dozens of niches holding images, lit by rows of small lancet windows. The green glazed terracotta tiles are the largest collection in a single building, telling stories from the *Jataka*, or Life of Buddha. At the western entrance there are two of the Buddha's footprints, divided into 108 sections.

Outside, two tiers of sloping roofs, and then four receding terraces form a base for the pineapple-shaped dome and golden spire and *hti*. The Ananda is very much a living temple, full of pilgrims, temple merchants and tourists.

The Thatbyinnyu Temple

Thatbyinnyu means omniscience, one of Buddha's attributes. The temple was built in the mid-12th century by Kyansittha's grandson and heir, Alaungsithu, and is not unlike the Ananda. It is square with four projecting entrances, but the eastern entrance is longer than the others. The Thatbyinnyu represents the transitional style of architecture, between the Early Style of the Ananda, and the Late Style of the Gawdawpalin, located 1 km to the northwest. It is one of the earliest double-storied temples with the main Buddha image seated on the upper floor. This is the highest temple in Pagan and one of the favourite places for tourists to watch the sun rise and set. Narrow, steep stairways built into the thickness of the walls and equally steep external steps take you up through the terraces towards the soaring spire. From the top you get glorious panoramic views of the whole of the plain—the green and terracotta landscape, the vast spread of ruins, the undulating snake of the Irrawaddy and the distant hills. The small white pagoda that you can see just to the northeast was the 'tally pagoda'—to keep count of the number of bricks used, one out of every 10,000 was set aside and used to build this miniature.

You can take an aerial tour of the following seven buildings from the terraces above the Thatbyinnyu.

The Pitakattaik

Just to the north of the Thatbyinnyu, and surprisingly small, you can see the Pitakattaik or Library, said to have been built by Anawrahta during the 11th century to house the 30 sets of the *Tripitaka* which he captured from Thaton and brought to Pagan on the 32 white elephants of Manuha, the deposed Mon king. It is a 17 m-square brick building, topped by five receding roofs like a temple, decorated with stucco carving. Inside there is a central hall surrounded by a passageway, dimly lit from perforated windows. It is fascinating to stand in the cool interior and try to picture what it must have been like, all those years ago: did Anawrahta come here to browse among his captured scriptures? Did he study them to improve his faith and gain merit, or did he merely regard them as loot?

The Shwegugyi Temple
To the west, or left of the Pitakattaik as you look down from the Thatbyinnyu, is the Shwegugyi, or Golden Cave, Temple, an elegant little building, transitional in style, built in 1131 by Alaungsithu. It stands on a high brick platform, with a hall and passageway round a central block and receding terraces on top rising to the dome and spire. The stucco ornamentation is in excellent condition and there is a rather charming black Buddha. Among the inscriptions inside is one that says the temple took seven months to build. It is said that Alaungsithu was brought here from the palace by his ambitious son when he was ill, who then smothered him and grabbed the throne.

The Thandawgya Image
Between the Thatbyinnyu and the Pitakattaik, you can see this large seated Buddha Thandawgya, meaning 'within hearing of the royal voice' because it was close to the palace. Built in the 13th century by King Narathihapate, it has lost its stucco coating but there is still something imposing about this 6 m-high image constructed with greenish sandstone bricks.

Nathlaungkyaung Temple
Looking just southwest from the Thatbyinnyu Temple, you see a crumbling brick building that is the only example of a Hindu temple in Pagan, probably built for the use of Indians who came to help in the building of other temples in the 11th century. There is a central pillar inside and the fragments of carvings are of the Hindu trinity: Vishnu, Brama and Shiva, and the cosmic serpent Seesha. The name of the temple means 'temple where the spirits are confined' suggesting that *nats* were supposed to be housed here.

Ngakywenadaung Pagoda
Looking down from the Thatbyinnyu, to the west just beyond the Nathlaungkyaung, you see this curious bulbous *stupa* held together with metal straps, on a tapering base. Green glazed tiles still cling to the terracotta bricks. The name means 'ear ornament of Ngakywe'—Ngakywe having been a strong man of Pagan.

Pahtothamya Temple
Just beyond the bulbous Ngakywenadaung *stupa*, looking down from Thatbyinnyu to the southwest, is the Pahtothamya, meaning 'temple of great fruitfulness'. Traditionally it was one of five temples built by Nyaung-u Sawrahan (also called Taungthugyi), a 10th-century usurper. In these temples he 'set up what were neither spirit-images nor images of the Lord, and worshipped them with offerings of rice, curry and fermented drinks, morning and night'. This intriguing hint at some sort of Bacchanalian cult is

counterbalanced by the more sober theory that the temple was built during the 11th century under the reign of Anawrahta's son, King Sawlu, and that its name refers to the blossoming of *Theravada* Buddhism. It is built in the Early Style, with a main block, a vaulted entrance hall, perforated stone windows and a terraced roof, topped by a bulbous dome. Inside, there are splendid murals with scenes from Buddha's life, at present being restored.

Mimalaungkyaung Temple
Completing the aerial tour from the Thatbyinnyu, a little further west the Mimalaung-kyaing Temple or 'temple which fire cannot burn' is believed to date from the reign of Narapatisithuy at the turn of the 12th century. The actual temple is small with ornate roofs, and stands on a large solid base approached up a flight of steps guarded by two *chinthes*. Fire was one of the chief hazards of this parched land when almost all secular buildings were made of wood, bamboo and thatch. A great fire in 1225 reduced most of the city to ashes.

Gawdawpalin Temple
Another of the wedding cake temples, the Gawdawpalin, almost 1 km northwest of Thatbyinnyu, was started in the early 13th century by King Narapatisithu, in order to try to win merit after causing hardship to the builders of the Sulamani temple at Minnanthu. He died before it was finished and his son Htilominlo completed it. It suffered badly in the 1975 earthquake, but has been skilfully restored. Designed in the Late Style, it is double-storeyed, square in plan with entrances on all four sides. Receding terraces, with crenellated parapets and corner *stupas* lead up to an elegant tower and spire. A vaulted passageway runs round the central block on the lower floor, with Buddhas on each face. You can climb up narrow stairs to the upper floor where a seated Buddha faces east. Continue on up to just below the tower, to another favourite viewpoint for watching the sun rise and set over the plain.

Bupaya Pagoda
One of Pagan's most attractive buildings, the Bupaya stands on a cliff on the edge of the Irrawaddy on the northwestern corner of the old city wall, a striking landmark for seamen. Legend attributes the Bupaya to Pyusawhti, whose father-in-law, Thamudarit, founded Pagan in the 2nd century. Pyusawhti, it is said, rescued Pagan from The Five Great Menaces—tiger, flying squirrel, boar, bird and gourd plant—which threatened its existence. He built pagodas on the site where he defeated each of the menaces. The Bupaya was built where he overcame the gourd whose tenacious roots and branches were about to engulf the land. It was completely destroyed in the earthquake in 1975 but has been rebuilt exactly as it was, with wide crenellated terraces leading to the bulbous *stupa*, crowned by a gilded finial and *hti*. You get marvellous views of river life from the terraces and the atmosphere here is not unlike that of an English seaside promenade.

Mahabodhi Temple
Completing those buildings that you can easily explore on foot from the village, the Mahabodhi stands back north of the road behind the Burma Airways office. Built in the 13th century by Htilominlo, it was inspired by the Mahabodhi temple in India, where

Gautama Buddha gained enlightenment under the bodhi tree, and is the only temple of its kind in Burma. A large prayer hall with a sanctum is crowned by a pyramid-like spire, divided into horizontal shelves with many niches holding seated Buddhas. Above this is a slender *stupa*. If you climb to the roof you get a good view of Pagan Village.

All these buildings lie within the old city wall.

Northeast of Pagan, Around Nyaung-oo

Nyaung-oo is the little town northeast of Pagan village, where the boat from Mandalay puts in, and close to the airport. It is an attractive place with a thriving market in the centre. If you sit down at one of the open cafes near the quay you may be joined by one of the older generation of Burmese, anxious to practise their English, who will tell stories of the past and give opinions of the present.

There are a number of interesting buildings but if you are pressed for time, you should concentrate on the **Shwezigon Pagoda** and the **Kyansittha Umin** 'tunnel', taking in the **Htilominlo Temple** which stands back to the right (south) of the road about a third of the way from Pagan to Nyaung-oo.

Thetkyamuni Temple
East of Nyaung-oo, the Thetkyamuni is a compact brick temple surrounded by greenery. Probably dating from the early 13th century, it has wall paintings of scenes from the *Jatakas*, four entrances, three receding terraces and a tower on top.

Kondawgyi Temple
Just south of the Thetkyamuni Temple, the Kondawgyi is another 13th-century temple, its name meaning 'Great Holy Mound'. It is a small ochre brick building with plenty of stucco remaining.

Kyaukgu Umin Temple
Moving east, the Kyaukgu Umin—rock cave tunnel—is built into the side of a ravine, dating back to the 11th century. This is a splendid temple with a great hall on the ground floor. Two massive pillars support the roof and the terraces above, with doors on either side leading into a maze of tunnels that run back into the cliff, from which little cells and caves branch off, where the monks used to pray and meditate. In the hall there is a big seated Buddha on a lotus throne and paintings on the walls. Unlike the more common stucco carvings, those that decorate the pillars, windows, doorway, pilasters, frieze and dado are of stone and there are stone reliefs in niches illustrating the life of the Buddha. There is something very tranquil about this temple which grows out of the side of the cliff.

Thamiwhet Umin & Hmyaatha Umin
Almost a kilometre southeast of Nyaung-oo and close to each other, these are two tunnels with cells branching off them cut into the sides of sandstone hills. Their purpose was to provide cool, peaceful cells where monks could pray and meditate, like the Indian cave-temples.

Traditionally, these buildings go way back to before Pagan's golden era, and perhaps there were caves here as early as the 1st century, but the present structures date from the 13th century.

Sapada Pagoda

On the southern outskirts of Nyaung-oo the Sapada was built in the 12th century by The Venerable Sapada, who came from Sapada village, near Bassein. He went to Ceylon as a novice, lived there for some years studying the *Pitaka*, and then returned to Burma in 1191 as an ordained monk, and founded a Sinhalese Order of Buddhism in Pagan. Modelled on a Sinhalese pagoda, it has a box-like relic chamber between the *stupa* and its finial.

Shweizigon Pagoda

On the southwest corner of Nyaung-oo as you come in from Pagan, the golden dome of the Shweizigon glitters dramatically in the sun. It is said that King Anawrahta, who regarded himself as being far above all other mortals, collected a tooth, the collar bone and forehead bone of the Buddha and put them on a sacred white elephant. 'Let the white elephant kneel where these holy relics shall rest,' he said. It knelt where the Shwezigon now stands. Anawrahta started building at once, but only completed three of the terraces before he was killed in 1077. It lay abandoned until Kyanzittha, the second of his sons to succeed him, came to the throne in 1084. Shin Arahan, the monk who converted Anawrahta to *Theravada* Buddhism, now old and much venerated, urged Kyanzittha to finish the pagoda. Great teams of builders were pressed into action, quarrying local rock, and the Shweizigon was finished in seven months and seven days. Like his father, Kyanzittha had an inflated idea of his own importance over other men. If you look at the two stone pillars at the eastern entrance you can see a lengthy inscription: this recalls a prophecy made by the Buddha that there would be a great king of Pagan whose reign would see the blossoming of Buddhism, and goes on to say that Kyansittha was that king.

The structure of the Shweizigon became the prototype for later Burmese *stupas*: three receding square terraces, topped by an octagonal base on which stands the golden dome, ringed finial and *hti*. Green glazed tiles on the terraces illustrate scenes from the Buddha's life.

There is something very jolly about this pagoda, its precincts cluttered with shrines and small *stupas* and kitsch mechanical dioramas of Buddha's life. Perhaps the reason is the presence of the 37 traditional *nats* carved from wood, now in their own special temple beside the main pagoda, but originally used to decorate the terraces in the hope that people would come to worship them and then be converted to the more pure *Theravada* Buddhism that Anawrahta was trying to establish. The Shwezigon Pagoda Festival, during the November/December full moon, is particularly well attended because of the continuing popularity of those *nats* today.

Kyanzittha Umin

Take the sandy track to the left of the long colonnade entrance to the Shwezigon— south—a short distance, to this cave temple, named after Anawrahta's son, Kyanzittha (1084–1113). Built with a large forecourt, the dim interior has long corridors, cells and some wall paintings. Ask the guide who lets you in to show you the fascinating pictures of

AROUND PAGAN

Mongol soldiers, done during the Mongol occupation of Pagan under Yesu Timur, Marco Polo's grandson. Some of the faces seem like modern etchings.

Gubyaukgyi (or Kubyauk-gyi) Temple—Wetkyi-in Village

Leaving Nyaung-oo to return to Pagan, take the sandy track to the left (south) just past the fork in the road. The Gubyaukgyi Temple still has some fine frescoes of scenes from Buddha's life: sadly, most of the panels were removed in 1899 by Dr Thomann, a German who has a lot to answer for in his desire to collect Burmese antiquities. The gate is locked, and though you can look through, you won't see much unless you go with a guide who can let you in. The temple was built in the 13th century, with the pyramid-type top inspired by the Mahabodhi Temple at Bodh Gaya in India, where the Buddha gained enlightenment. On the other side of the road there is another cave temple down some steps where the passages and cells lead off a sunken courtyard.

Htilominlo Temple

About 1.5 km short of Pagan on the left, as you return from Nyaung-oo, the Htilominio is one of the bigger temples—a great terracotta brick pile from which you get marvellous views, especially as the sun rises or sets. Although ruined, it is sufficiently impressive to attract a number of temple-merchants selling souvenirs at the entrance.

Built by King Htilominlo in the 13th century, the name—'favoured by the umbrella, favoured by the king'—refers to the method by which he was chosen to succeed his brother Narapatisithu in 1211: the king summoned all five claimants to his throne and stood them round a white umbrella—the symbol of kingship. The umbrella bowed towards Htilominlo, thus indicating his suitability and giving him his name.

There are four entrances, one of which is a big vestibule, leading to four Buddhas on the lower floor. Claustrophobic stairways lead up through the thickness of the walls to the upper storey where there are four more Buddhas. Receding terraces with steep stairs lead on up to the tower. Some stucco carvings can be seen and if you look up high on the inner walls you will see horoscopes of important people that were written up there out of reach of vandals.

Upali Thein

Slightly nearer Pagan than the Htilominlo, on the other side of the road (north) the Upali Thein is marked by a sign in English. As Buddhism flourished, so did the need increase for ordination halls, used not only for ordaining monks but also for religious ceremonies such as confessions by monks of offences against the faith. Upali was a monk who lived during the reign of Htilominlo and this building is one of the best-preserved examples of the *thein* or ordination halls of the Pagan period. It is small, braced inside with metal girders and although you can't get in, you can see through the grid some fine painting on the ceiling and walls.

South & East of Pagan Village

Still close to the village, but best visited by pony trap with a guide who can get keys to the locked temples, there are a number of interesting ruins to see as well as the village of **Myinkaba** which is the centre of the lacquer industry. (If you don't want to go into locked buildings, you can easily get to Myinkaba by bicycle, though some of the track is soft sand.)

Shwesandaw Pagoda

Just southeast of Pagan village, the Shwesandaw, meaning 'Golden Holy Hair Relic' takes its name from a hair of the Buddha that was enshrined here by Anawrahta, having been given to him by the King of Pegu in thanks for help in a battle against Khmers. Plain and unpretentious, this pagoda is a forerunner of the familiar style of the Shwezigon and its successors: receding square terraces, divided from the dome and *hti* by an octagonal base. Because of its combination of simplicity and grandeur, this pagoda seems to embody the ambivalence of the Buddhist faith. It is also a marvellous platform from which to witness the dawn.

Shinbinthalyaung Temple

Like a long, elegant coffin, the Shinbinthalyaung lies in the lee of the Shwesandaw and contains Pagan's biggest reclining Buddha. So closely entombed that you can hardly appreciate his beauty, he is 18 metres long and wears a face of infinite calm. Although the head points to the south (traditionally the position of the sleeping Buddha) this Buddha, lying on his right side, cheek on right hand, represents the dead Buddha, but is so placed to face the Shwesandaw Pagoda.

Dhammayangyi Temple

Not far southeast of the Shwesandaw, the Dhammayangyi Temple broods over the plain of Pagan like a massive toad, shrouded in the macabre legends of its past. Being more remote, and therefore less crowded, it is a good one from which to watch the sunset. Beware, if you do this, however: there is only one stairway which is very easy to miss if you linger until darkness before you descend!

Of similar style to the Ananda, a square with four projections forming a Greek cross, it is less elegant than its predecessor. It was built by King Narathu in the 12th century. Legend holds that Narathu smothered his father—a popular way of gaining the throne—and murdered his Indian stepmother whom, in keeping with custom, he had taken on as one of his own wives. Worried about his chances in the quest for *nirvana* he quickly ordered the building of this temple in order to win merit. He threatened torture and death to any mason who left a crack big enough to insert a needle between the bricks, which explains the exceptionally fine brickwork. He never finished the temple, however—the father of the murdered wife sent eight of his soldiers disguised as Brahmins to avenge the death of his daughter. They stabbed Narathu in his throne room and then stabbed each other in a pre-arranged plot to avoid further recrimination and bloodshed.

Two vaulted passageways run parallel round the four sides of the temple but the inner one is bricked off preventing access. It is intriguing to speculate why this is so—could the victims of the bloody retribution have been interred within . . . ? Whatever the answer, it is the best brickwork in Pagan.

Sulamani Temple

Not far to the east of the Dhammayangyi, the Sulamani Temple was built by King Narapatisithu at the turn of the 12th century, on the site where he found a magnificent ruby on the ground. Large and solid, with two storeys and receding terraces, it has a vaulted passage around the lower floor and four seated Buddhas. Steep steps lead up through the walls to the upper storey and then on up to the terraces. There are good views from the top.

Minnanthu

The village of Minnanthu, 3 km southeast of Pagan village, has a remote, almost biblical atmosphere. Oxen wait patiently in the shade of scrubby trees, surrounded by the various processes of cart and cart-wheel making, an industry that supports the village. Sandy tracks lead to the four main temples here and you are best to go with a pony trap guide because keys and local knowledge are needed. (You pay a few kyats for the key.)

Lemyethna Temple

Going north on the track from the village, the Lemyethna is a dazzling white building, rather elegant, built in the Late Style of the 13th century. It is square, with porches on each side, receding terraces above with crenellated parapets and miniature *stupas* below a pineapple dome crowned by a *hti*. The holy relics enshrined within the *stupa* lie in a series of caskets of sandalwood, crystal, gold, silver and stone. It is difficult not to be aware of the extremely crude, modern murals that have replaced the original ones: as if an infant school class had been let loose with pots of poster paint.

Payathonzu Temple
Next up the track from the village you come to the Payathonzu and you should take a torch to appreciate this fascinating trio of small, square temples linked by narrow, vaulted passages. Each of the three is of identical design outside, thought to date from the late 13th century. Inside, the walls, pilasters and ceilings of the eastern and part of the central temples are richly decorated with paintings, while the western part is unadorned except for a few tentative sketches. The paintings are amazingly vivid and modern in execution, so much so that it is tempting to suspect they have been touched up—in fact the only restoration work so far is not in retouching the artwork but in filling some of the cracks and crevices left by earthquakes. The paintings include flowers, mythical monsters, animals, birds and people, as well as Buddhas and scenes from the life of Gautama Buddha. Intriguingly, some of the figures do not depict orthodox Buddhism but hint at a more orgiastic form of worship, which could possibly be attributed to a 13th-century sect of 'forest dwellers' who were not averse to taking alcohol and other stimulants. So calm and innocent looking now, the Payathonzu sets the imagination racing.

Thambula Temple
Just beyond the Payathonzu, the Thambula is another Late Style, single-storey temple, built in 1255 by Queen Thambula, wife of King Uzana. It is of no special interest, but has some frescoes inside.

Nandamannya Temple
Not far on up the track to the north, the Nandamannya is a small square temple uninteresting outside but decorated inside with a glorious array of frescoes, elaborately embellished with scrollwork and depicting many aspects of Buddhism. Look out for the panel on the west wall where a procession of rather under-dressed women seem to be making all sorts of improper proposals. They are probably meant to represent the daughters of Mara, the Evil One, sent to tempt Buddha. Some of the paintings here are so clear you feel they could have been done yesterday. Until 1987, pilgrims came from all over Burma to visit an old monk who withdrew from the world into one of the tunnel cells when the Japanese occupied the country in 1941. He never emerged. People brought offerings and processed through the candle-lit passageways, to kneel around the old hermit on his litter and listen to his feeble voice intoning mantras and prayers and offering advice to his followers.

Dhammayazika Pagoda
Standing rather isolated, 3 km southwest of Minnanthu, the Dhammayazika Pagoda is often ignored by tourists who are pressed for time: this is a pity because it is of unusual design. A conventional bell-shaped dome is surmounted on receding terraces that are

pentagonal, with a small temple built on each of the five sides enshrining a Buddha image. Most temples have the four Buddhas of this world cycle who have already attained Enlightenment facing the cardinal points; the fifth image in the Dhammayazika is Metteyya, the final Buddha of this cycle who is a *bodhisattva*—an embryo Buddha still on the path to enlightenment—currently residing in celestial Tushita. An inscription in the pagoda records that King Narapatishithu built it in 1198 to enshrine four holy relics he had been given by the King of Ceylon. Some of the stucco relief on the walls is still very clear.

Myinkaba

Two kilometres south of Pagan village and accessible by bicycle, though some of the track is soft sand, the village of Myinkaba is worth a visit not only for its buildings, but for its own charm and because it is the centre of the lacquer industry. It was the site of the temple-prison built to house the Mon king, Manuha and his court, after Anawrahta had swept them all into his kingdom in the wake of the captured *Tripitaka* (see 'History' p. 272). Here, the exiled Mons occupied themselves with the delicate crafts they had practised for centuries in their own land, crafts unknown to their barbaric captors. The making of lacquerware was one; it became their livelihood and so it is today. The quality of the products varies enormously, depending on the material used and on the time spent on each article—some can be bought for just a few kyats, others will cost thousands. As you walk through the village you can see all the processes of production, and you are always welcome to stop and watch. In some dwellings the bamboo is split with knives, to be woven into various shapes and then lacquered. You will see the lacquering, and the teams of girls scratching out the designs on green, orange and black surfaces. Piles of articles lie waiting to be finished: top-quality lacquerware can take more than one generation to complete.

The village is delightful, a maze of sandy tracks links frail wooden houses and huts on stilts from many of which you hear drifts of music from transistor radios. Monks walk slowly in the shade of jacaranda trees and palms; children play in the dust while their mothers do the washing at the communal well. You may be disappointed to find that the children in Myinkaba tend to be materialistic and greedy: it is alas we, the foreign tourists, who have made them so.

Mingalazedi Pagoda

Half way between the villages of Pagan and Myinkaba, just after the turning to the Thiripyitsaya Hotel, the Mingalazedi—meaning Auspicious—was the last of the great pagodas to be built before the fall of Pagan in 1284. It is told that King Narathihapate, who started building it in 1268, heard of a prophecy that when the pagoda was finished, Pagan would be destroyed. He stopped building at once, but a few years later was reprimanded by a monk for failing to complete a work of merit. Frightened for his *karma*, he quickly completed the work in 1274. Ten years later, the Mongol army of Kublai Khan, under the command of Yesu Timur, swept down from the north and that was the end of Pagan's golden era.

The pagoda is very splendid and well proportioned, rising majestically from a hem of trees close to the shores of the Irrawaddy. It is the final flowering of the design first established by the Shwezigon, with three receding terraces, a bell-shaped dome on an octagonal base and a tapering finial. Small *stupas* stand at the corners of the terraces and you can climb steep stairways to the base of the dome. Features to look out for are the large terracotta tiles illustrating scenes from Buddha's life, around the terraces. To protect these tiles from further vandalism, the pagoda is one of the many that are kept locked: if you are not with a guide, you must contact the current 'pagoda warden' for the key.

Kubyaukkyi, or Gubyaukgyi Temple

On the left just as you come into Myinkaba village from Pagan, the Kubyaukkyi Temple stands back in a tranquil glade, as if veiled in the romance of its history. Currently (1988) in the process of complete restoration, it is closed to the public, but once it is reopened it will be one of Pagan's greatest treasures.

The story is told that Kyansittha fell in love with beautiful Thambula who conceived his child. Recalled to the court of his father, Anawrahta, Kyansittha gave his lover a ring, telling her that if she bore a girl, she was to sell the ring for its upkeep, but that if she bore a boy she was to bring both child and ring to court. Seven years later, when Kyansittha had succeeded to the throne left vacant by his brother Sawlu, Thambula turned up at court with her son and the ring. Kyansittha was delighted: he made her his queen and showered gifts on her and on the boy, Rajakumar. Years later, in 1113, when Kyansittha was dying, Rajakumar remembered all the favours he had received from his father and commissioned a splendid golden Buddha to be made and enshrined in the dying king's honour.

The single-storey temple of typical Mon design has some marvellous stucco carvings outside. There is one entrance, through a vaulted passage which leads to the inner chamber in which niches used to contain sacred images, before temple thieves removed them. The interior is dimly lit by perforated stone windows, and strong artificial light is needed to appreciate the full magnificence of the frescoes. Skilled restoration work has already revealed a wealth of them, now almost as clean and clear as the day they were painted more than 800 years ago: pictures of all aspects of Buddhism, scenes from Buddha's life, myths and legends, with Mon inscriptions. You could spend many hours marvelling over these remarkable paintings and when the restoration work is finished the Kubyaukkyi will surely become a favourite among scholars, artists and pilgrims.

Until recently, the Myazedi Stone stood in a cage next to the temple, inscribed by Rajakumar in the four languages of his time—Mon, Burmese, Pyu and Pali. It records the dates of succession of some of the kings of Pagan and its discovery in 1887 was of particular importance because it is one of the earliest known inscriptions in Burmese, and the longest in Pyu, providing a vital clue in the deciphering of that lost language. It is now in the museum.

Myinkaba Pagoda

Going a short way towards the centre of the village from the Kubyaukkyi you come to the Myinkaba Pagoda, a simple brick bell-shaped *stupa* standing on an octagonal, crenellated base. Anawrahta had this built to try to attone for having scrambled to power by killing his half-brother King Sokkate. (They fought on horseback: Sokkate, mortally wounded, fell into the stream here on his horse and died—Myinkaba means 'brought on

BURMA

the horse's saddle'.) Because this pagoda was built before Anawrahta's conversion to *Theravada* Buddhism, its design is much less elaborate than the architecture that developed under the influence of the Mons.

Manuha Temple

Standing on the crossroads in the village centre, the Manuha has a somewhat seedy air of neglect, its walls patchy and stained. Manuha, the captured Mon king of Thaton, who was exiled in Myinkaba, sold what was left of his treasures in order to build this temple in the hope of earning enough merit to get a better deal in his next incarnation. The huge images inside, so cramped that you can barely squeeze past them, are said to symbolize Manuha's captivity. The temple has two storeys, the upper being smaller than the lower, with pinnacles on the corners and a stepped roof from which you get splendid views. Three of the Buddhas are seated, but in the confined space it is impossible to see them properly. You can, however, climb to a window high in the wall to inspect the rather smug smile that one of them wears. The reclining Buddha, 30 m long, is also hemmed in by walls so that you cannot see him in true perspective. He is in the *Parinibbana* position, representing that moment when Buddha attained *nirvana*, lying on his right side with his head pointing to the north. In the 1975 earthquake, the top storey fell in, severely damaging the largest of the seated Buddhas, whose head was remade during repair work in 1981.

A short way along the path you can see statues of Manuha and his queen, Ningaladevi, wearing surprisingly worldly smiles.

Nanpaya Temple

Along a path from the Manuha temple, the Nanpaya is believed to have been the temple-prison used to house King Manuha during his captivity. Built in the 11th century in the Early Style, with an eastern entrance hall and a hollow interior, it has four square stone pillars supporting the roof, decorated with carvings of Hindu deities.

It is intriguing to speculate on what the quality of life must have been like for the captive Mon king and his family and court. If this modest building was indeed the quarters of the king and his attendants, they must have been rather overcrowded. But the fact that the king was allowed to build his own temple, the Manuha, indicates that he was given some measure of privilege.

Thiripyitsaya

Few tourists have time or the energy to explore the remaining temples on the road to Thiripyitsaya, nor those in the small village of Thiripyitsaya itself, 3 km to the south. Some of them are very fine and you will need a guide or keys to see inside most of them. Taking them in order as you come to them:

Apeyadana Temple is said to have been built by Kyanzittha in honour of his wife Abeyadana.

Nagayon Temple was built by Kyanzittha and foreshadows his triumph—the Ananda—being of the same design but less elaborate. A Buddha image inside stands protected by the hood of a *naga* or snake, that favourite Buddhist creature who sheltered Gautama Buddha from a storm and, in this instance, was said to have protected

Kyanzittha on this site from the wrath of his predecessor and brother, Sawlu. Frescoes inside are of Hindu gods as well as of scenes from Buddha's life.

Pawdawmu Pagoda is beside the Nagayon, a simple brick *stupa* that was built in the 11th century. It was later encased in a larger *stupa* which was removed 50 years ago.

Somingyi Monastery is just past the Pawdawmu, on the other side of the road; a ruin of one of the more elaborate of the many monasteries that were built during Pagan's glory. Because most monasteries were built of wood, there are few left, making this one of interest.

Seinnyet Ama Temple & Seinnyet Pagoda are known as the Seinnyet Sisters, standing side by side within a brick enclosure. The Ama, or older sister, is the temple, attributed to the 11th century though its design is more typical of the 13th, and must once have been very richly decorated. The Nyima, or younger sister, is the pagoda, with an unusual bowl-shaped disc on top of the dome, topped by a finial deeply cut with rings.

The small village of Thiripyitsaya was the site of a royal palace in the 4th century, long before Pagan became great. During the golden era it was a port for trading ships from India and Ceylon. There are three pagodas worth looking at.

Ashe Petleik (eastern) & Anauk Petleik (western) Pagodas just south of the village date from the 11th century, and are thought to have been built by Anawrahta. They are fairly similar in design; the eastern one is larger and the western better preserved, with unusual niches in the dome for Buddha images. Originally vaulted corridors ran round the base of each pagoda with an eastern entrance, protecting unglazed terracotta tiles illustrating scenes from the life of the Buddha.

Lawkananda Pagoda stands on the bank of the Irrawaddy, its name stemming from a Pali word meaning 'joy of the world'. A dazzling white *stupa* with a gilded *hti* rises from a carpet of trees with views over the river which, before the monsoon rains, seems to be miles of sand banks. It was built by Anawrahta in the 11th century to enshrine a holy tooth, sent by the King of Ceylon and carried ashore by Anawrahta himself, wading neck deep through the water, the tooth in a jewelled casket on his head.

WHERE TO STAY

Hotels

The Thiripyitsaya Hotel, built to pagoda design and listed as one of Burma's few First Class hotels, stands by the river south of the village. Accommodation is in comfortable chalets, set in attractive grounds planted with vivid clumps of oleanda, bougainvillea, colleus, cannas and hibiscus. There are fountains and a swimming pool (with water not entirely transparent). A somewhat institutional dining room serves edible food for around K29 for a set menu. You can buy lacquer, ivory, silver and teak in the souvenir shop, and there is an extensive verandah bar. Although it lacks character, it is undeniably good value for those who are concerned with modern comfort, at $24 for double rooms with bathroom, air conditioning and fridge, $18.50 single.

The Irra Inn, on the northern edge of the village overlooking the river, is less modern and has a more Burmese atmosphere. The balcony rooms are cool, cleanish and airy, costing from K128 for a double room, K96 single, to K235 for a double suite. All rooms have bathrooms en suite. The service is friendly but slow and the food unremarkable.

Guest Houses

Regulations have become a lot stricter recently. You are unlikely to find a guest house willing to risk losing their authorized status by bending currency rules. You must book and pay through the Tourist Burma office, who have a list of all establishments currently in favour.

Except for the Co-Operative, all the guest houses charge a set K12 per person per night. They are of a high standard compared with other tourist areas, generally clean, comfortable and friendly, with a sitting/dining area and plenty of free tea. The plumbing is of a higher standard than you will find in other places, with showers and refreshing water tanks from which you can bale water over yourself. The rooms are mostly two-bedded, with woven palm walls, sheets, mesh over the windows and/or mosquito nets. The staff will arrange bicycle hire, canoe trips, puppet shows, laundry and massage sessions, and most of them sell souvenirs.

The Co-Operative, down past the museum on the right, is a fairly ramshackle place in a large garden, but cheap at K16.80 for a single and K27.40 for a double room, and full of atmosphere. The 12 rooms open onto a verandah, all rather airless, with fans and nets, and there is a large dining area where the food is good and cheap.

The Sithu, first on the left after the Tourist Burma office, is one of the most popular and so is often full. The rooms are arranged round a compound beyond the reception area.

The Mya Thida, next to the Sithu, deserves equal popularity. Its owners make a great effort to see that their guests are comfortable and well served. There is a clean eating area hung with tapestries; the sanitation is reasonable, the atmosphere peaceful. They serve good, cheap breakfasts and their pancakes are excellent.

The Burma Guest House, further down, also on the left, has recently opened after a brief closure. The atmosphere is nice here, with rooms opening off a central, cane-work sitting area. They serve very good lassis (a delicious yoghurt drink) and the staff are obliging.

The Minchan Myei, The Aungthahaya, The Pagan and The Moe Moe come in that order as you continue down the street and are all adequate.

EATING OUT

The Ma Ya Tanar Restaurant immediately next door to the Tourist Burma office will give you excellent food very cheaply, with friendly service. Their 'Special Burmese Dish' is delicious, as are their fried vegetables.

The Nation Restaurant opposite, also has good food very cheap, especially the Chinese dishes, and a variety of fruit lassis.

The Soe Soe Restaurant further down on the right has a lively atmosphere and good food.

Marie Min. opposite the Tourist Burma office, is a good vegetarian restaurant, particularly popular for its milk shakes and lassis.

The Aye Yake Thar Nar, off the road to the Irra Inn, serves good Burmese food.

Otherwise, you will eat well and cheaply in most of the guest houses, where other tourists are keen to swop valuable travel experiences. Try the guacamole in the Mya Thida. You will find that, though there may be more variety of menu, and formality, you won't eat any better in the hotels but you will pay more.

Mount Popa

If you have time, a visit to **Mount Popa**, about 50 km southeast of Pagan, is well worth the effort of arranging to get there. The journey across the plain and up into the hills is half the fun.

GETTING THERE
Tourist Burma will arrange an official jeep for you costing K770 for 8 people. It is a 2-hour drive and you can go whenever you choose. Alternatively, you can find a private jeep for $300 and no entry on your currency form. Staff in the guest houses usually know someone who will oblige. If you do this you run the risk of being stopped because unofficial jeeps are not allowed to carry tourists. Take a damp face cloth in a polythene bag as the roads are extremely dusty. You will be put down in the centre of the village, oposite the **Hall of 37 Nats**, at the foot of the stairway up the hill.

Mount Popa was thrown up out of the plain almost 1600 m above sea level by an earthquake in 442 BC. This cone of rock later erupted and gushed out a stream of lava, creating a fertile bed for the lush vegetation that gave the mountain its name—*Popa* being the Sanscrit word for 'flower'. Mount Popa is the traditional home of the *nats*—in particular the **Min Maha-Giri Nats** (Lords of the High Mountain) and it is to their shrine that thousands of pilgrims come every year, particularly during the May/June full moon Festival of the Spirits.

The Min Maha-Giri Nats were the Mr Handsome and Golden Face whose images guard the Sarabha Gate into Pagan village, a powerful blacksmith and his beautiful sister. The king of their region grew jealous of the blacksmith's amazing strength so he seduced and married Golden Face and used her as a decoy to lure her brother into his territory. Mr Handsome was captured and burnt at the stake and Golden Face leapt into the flames and died with him. The spirits of these two became mischievous *nats*, living in a saga tree and tormenting anyone who came near. The king had the tree felled and thrown into the Irrawaddy from which it was retrieved by King Thinlikyaung of Pagan, transformed into carved images of the brother and sister, and enshrined where you will see them today on Mount Popa. Covered steps lead up past very expensive souvenir stalls to a random conglomeration of shrines, pagodas and temples at the top. It only takes about 15 to 20 minutes and your progress is watched eagerly by the tribe of monkeys which swarm over the steps and railings. There is a cooling breeze at the top and a panoramic view down over the plain for miles. Several chambers lead one from another, each with glitzy Buddha shrines, *nats* and offerings.

Get the driver to stop at the village half way back down the mountain, where you can buy coconuts with a straw through a hole in the top, giving you a delicious and refreshing drink.

WHERE TO STAY
There is no approved tourist accomodation, though you could find a room if you wanted for about K12. The stall holders on the steps will tell you where to go. However, having paid for your jeep, it makes better sense to return in it to Pagan.

Part IX

INLE LAKE

Ceremonial Barge

The Shans are Burma's largest ethnic group after the Burmans. The Shan States cover a vast area of mountains and plateaux east of Mandalay with China, Laos and Thailand as their eastern neighbours. They contain most of the Golden Triangle, notorious for its flourishing crops of *papaver somniferum*, better known as the opium poppy. When the Shans first settled here in the 16th century, having been pushed out of Central Burma, they were divided into 34 princedoms, ruled by *Sawbwas* who were of royal status. In the days of the British Raj the Shan States came under the jurisdiction of a governor, the first of which was Sir George Scott, the author of *The Burman, His Life and Times*. When Burma was granted independence in 1947, the Shan States joined the Union with the promise of secession in 10 years if they wanted. But in 1958, with Ne Win in power, this promise was revoked. The Shans rebelled but were suppressed. Many of them went into hiding in the hills, forming terrorist groups, financed by the opium poppy. The government has little control over these heavily-armed insurgents. Now and then rumours of 'incidents' leak out, but with a state-controlled media it is difficult to find out the extent of the fighting. For this reason, most of the Shan States are out of bounds for tourists, except for the area around Inle Lake.

The hill people are noticeably different from those in other parts of Burma: they come down to sell their wares in the picturesque markets that travel round the towns in the Inle area, and you should certainly try to go to one. Physically, the Shans are more substantial and less elegant than their neighbours from the plains; their voices are more strident and they exude a raw earthiness you don't find elsewhere. Their clothes are different, too. Some wear headdresses of lengths of cotton wound like turbans, or hanging down and secured round the brow with cord. Ordinary patterned towels are often worn, both as

368

turbans and as neck-cloths. Colours tend to be stronger and less subtle than in other parts of Burma—vermilion, egg-yolk yellow, magenta, electric blue. Black velvet jackets are traditional, decorated with sequins and silver embellishments. Materials vary from ordinary cotton to thick, padded cloth with quilting and braid, and rich wool. Kachins wear pantaloons under mid-length *longyis*. Shans wear conical hats made of split bamboo and Shan men wear baggy trousers.

GETTING TO INLE LAKE, KALAW & PINDAYA

By Air

The airport is at Heho from where an airport bus will take you to Taunggyi—40 km to the east, or Yaunghwe, 35 km to the southeast. See pages 258–259 for fares and schedules.

From Pagan you fly via Mandalay.

By Train

From Rangoon or Mandalay, to Thazi, costing K110 Upper Class, and then by jeep, costing about K60. You could go all the way to Shwenyaung, the junction for local connections, by train—a spectacular journey through the mountains, but it takes at least eight hours and is not authorized by Tourist Burma.

By Road

Pick-up from Pagan (10 hours) costing K143, leaves the Toyota garage beside the pony cart park, in the middle of the village around 3.30 am. It stops at Meiktila, Thazi, Kalaw and Heho. If you have time to explore Kalaw and Pindaya you should break this journey to do so.

Pick-up from Mandalay (10 hours) costs K143, leaving around 5 am. Book in advance through Tourist Burma who will tell you where to catch the truck. Pick-ups leave from the station in Thazi when they have enough passengers. All schedules change frequently: check before you book.

If you are going to Inle Lake first, change pick-ups at Shwenyaung and go straight down to Yaunghwe, about 11 km, rather than on into Taunggyi.

As for everywhere else in Burma, if you can afford to hire a taxi or jeep for your own use, you will be more flexible: but the prices are astronomic and you run the risk of being stopped by the authorities.

GETTING AROUND

Shwenyaung is the railway terminal and road junction for Inle Lake and Taunggyi, from Thazi. You can pick up a bus or truck here, to take you to your destination.

In Yaunghwe, the village from which you explore Inle Lake, you can hire bicycles, trishaws or pony carts. But the village is not large and you can easily walk from one end to the other. The lake itself must be explored by boat, and your boatman will take you to all the interesting places.

Yaunghwe, Inle Lake & Ywama

Yaunghwe

On the 11 km drive down from Shwenyaung, look out for **Shwe Yan Pwe,** a magnificent teak monastery dating from 1870.

When you arrive in the middle of Yaunghwe you may wonder if you've come to the wrong place. There is no sign of the lake which, you discover later, is to the south, hidden from sight by an apparently endless spread of vegetation flanking the canal.

Yaunghwe is a delightful rural town in a valley surrounded by ranges of hills that elevate the horizon wherever you look. Paddy fields stretch away in all directions. There are a number of pagodas and temples, some dilapidated and overgrown with weeds, and a museum.

Until recently, most tourists gravitated towards **The Friendship Restaurant** in the centre of the small town, not just to eat, but because it was the headquarters of Yaunghwe's Mr Fix-it, a multi-lingual entrepreneur whose camp mannerisms hide a talent for slicing through red tape and a brain divided into cash deposits. With the help of his brothers, all made in his image, he can get you anything, from an upper-class railway seat to a black-market boat. With a flick of his long, curved finger nails he will accept any currency from whisky to dollars. Rumour has it that he is temporarily out of circulation. Look out for him: he will undoubtedly return.

TOURIST INFORMATION
The Tourist Burma office is on the track that borders the canal leading to the lake, 10 minutes' walk west from the main street, beside the tourist-boat moorings.

Yaunghwe Haw, marked on the map in the Inle Inn, is the town's museum, with displays relating to the area. This building was the palace of the last of Yaunghwe's *sawbwas*.

Wandering through the back streets you may be lucky and pass a *shin-pyu* procession led by a percussion band, on its way to the **Golden Pagoda**—Yat-amamanaung—at the southern end of the village. This pagoda is full of tarnished gold and dusty paper offerings, with the ubiquitous reminder, in garish plaster statues, that 'You will grow old'. A column of girls in brightly coloured *longyis* carrying flowers and offerings that include bundles of kyat notes, escort the novice in his pantomime suit of embroidered golden satin, his face a mask of cosmetics.

Walk down to the canal and watch the sun dipping below the hills beyond paddy fields. You can hear the murmuring of voices of the workers, coming home in single-file along the banks, the throb of an outboard engine returning from the lake, and the contented blowing of water buffalo, taking an evening wallow.

WHERE TO STAY
There are two guest houses, under the same management, **Inle Inn,** K25 single, K40 double, and **Bamboo House,** which acts as an annexe when the Inn is full, at the same price. Bedrooms in Inle Inn are clean with woven walls and brick-hard beds; the plumbing is not perfect, and an air of despairing lethargy hangs over the place.

The Inn organizes gala evenings for its guests, with special Burmese food and puppet shows. You are given a candlelit Shan meal, carefully prepared, for K40, followed by an excellent puppet show, and they sell puppets very reasonably.

There are government plans to build a Spa Hotel on the west side of the lake and you may even see signs to it, but it has not yet got beyond the drawing board.

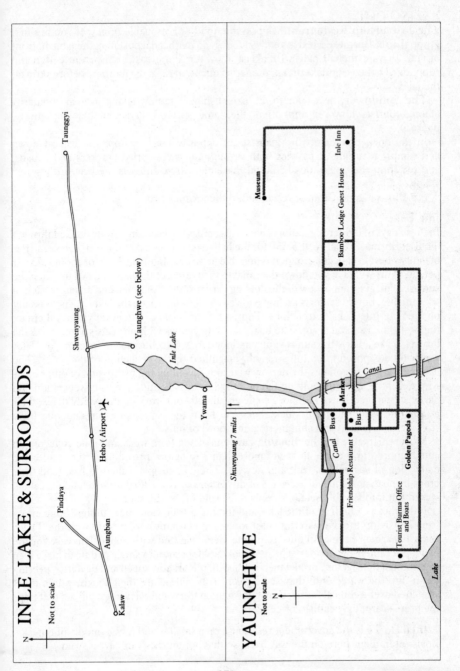

INLE LAKE & SURROUNDS

Not to scale

Kalaw

Pindaya

Aungban

Heho (Airport)

Shwenyaung

Taunggyi

Yaunghwe (see below)

Inle Lake

Ywama

YAUNGHWE

Not to scale

Shwenyaung 7 miles

Canal

Canal

Bus

Bus

Market

Museum

Bamboo Lodge Guest House

Inle Inn

Friendship Restaurant

Tourist Burma Office and Boats

Golden Pagoda

Lake

EATING OUT

The Friendship Restaurant has passable food at reasonable prices. If you are in a group the set Burmese Meal is good value at K35 per head, cooked on the table in front of you. Beware their 'English Breakfast' however: limp toast, transparent coffee and rubberized boiled eggs take on a nightmarish quality at six in the morning before a trip on the lake.

The Sunflower, next door to the Friendship, is rapidly taking over in popularity among tourists however and offers the same sort of service in a jollier atmosphere.

In the open market off the main street opposite the bus stop, you can sit down and sample a variety of pastries both savoury and sweet, fried crackers and kebabs, and tea from the ubiquitous kettle on the table. **Shwe Inlay** is the best of these tea shops.

Hu Pin is a good Chinese restaurant in the town centre.

Inle Lake

In these days of tighter regulations, boat trips across the lake can only be booked through Tourist Burma. A boat costs K550 for the half-day trip and takes up to 10 people, so it is obviously best to collect a group. It is possible to hire an unofficial boat for about K75 per person. This will take you down the canal to the mouth of the lake at dawn to watch the sunrise. You get a good view of the floating gardens, the fishermen and an impression of lakeside life, but these boats are not allowed to take you across the lake, so you miss out on much of Inle Lake's attractions. Tourist Burma boats go whenever you ask them to: the best time is about 7 am. The boats are long canoes with no seats so you sit on the boards. Take a hat—the sun is young and tender as you chug down the canal, but later you will be exposed to its full strength, magnified by the reflection of the water. The boatman-guide negotiates the narrow waterway, avoiding the procession of other boats with deceptive ease, flipping up the outboard to miss floating lumps of vegetation and partly submerged water buffalo. People are already out working the paddy fields, their *longyis* hitched up to form knickerbockers. Then the canal opens up and Inle Lake stretches away, calm and shimmering, in a bowl of hills.

Most remarkable are the **'floating gardens'** made from weed and mud collected up and anchored to the lake floor not more than 3 m below, providing fertile soil for the cultivation of vegetables, fruit and flowers. The lake people, called Inthas, tend their crops by boat, and you will see acres of this *kyunpaw*, as the floating vegetation is called, staked out into towable sections ready to be sold off by the state.

Intha means 'children of the lake' and the Intha tribe came here in the 18th century from Tavoy on the Tenasserim coast to escape constant border wars with the Thais. Intha fishermen have a unique technique, demonstrated with nonchalant ease for the benefit of camera-laden tourist boats. Hooking a foot round a single paddle to make it an extention of the leg, they propel their boats with remarkable speed and dexterity, peering down into the water until they see signs of fish. These are then caught within a net stretched over a conical frame, thrust down upon them and releasing a gill net that traps the prey—carp, ugly catfish, or eels.

Inlai Bo Te is the government rest house on a small island in the middle of the lake. Boats often moor here on the way back, so that hot tourists can have a swim.

Ywama
The boat takes you to the daily floating market (biggest day, Monday) at Ywama where all the streets are canals.

Dozens of vendors congregate in the liquid market place, their boats full of fresh fruit, vegetables and flowers, fish and meat, clothes, hats, and souvenirs. Some even carry cooking fires and provide instant meals, passed from hand to hand across the water, wrapped in parcels of palm leaves. For just a few kyats you can buy a bunch of bananas, a bag of orange-coloured raspberries or a pumalo, whose flesh, if you can break through the outer skin, is sharp and thirst-quenching.

If you go ashore, walk through to the monastery temple behind the stalls. You may find a funeral wake, gathered round an open coffin containing the waxen corpse of a monk in his robes awaiting the procession to his funeral pyre. The people are not sad, they sit round laughing, chatting and smoking: death, to a Buddhist is the beginning of a new life, and for a monk, an almost guaranteed step up on the ladder towards enlightenment. After the market your guide may take you to a weavers' shed, where you can go ashore and watch ceremonial longyis in bright coloured silk being woven on looms.

Your next stop will be the **Phaungdaw U Pagoda,** on the canal bank. Like a New Testament temple, the precincts bustle with commerce. Pilgrims and tourists eat and drink at trestle tables round a central courtyard, and there is a covered market packed with stalls. Steps lead up to the temple where a collection of what look like rounded lumps of gold sit on a dais. These are, in fact, Buddhas that have been so overlaid with gold during their 800-year lives that they have lost their original shapes completely. King Alaungsithu brought them from Malaya in the 12th century and they are so revered by Buddhists that the Phaungdaw U Pagoda is one of Burma's most popular shrines. Once a year, during the September full moon festival, four of the five Buddhas are rowed round the lake in a replica royal barge, to visit all the other pagodas. In the past, all the Buddhas went on this annual outing, but one year the barge capsized and only four could be found on the lake floor. At the end of the day, when the procession returned to the Phaungdaw U, the fifth Buddha was found, back on the dais, wearing an enigmatic smile. Ever since then, he remains at home to guard the pagoda. If it is a sunny day—it can be quite cloudy and cool, even in the hot season—persuade your boatman to stop on the way back near one of the floating islands, or at the **Inlai Bo Te** island, so that you can swim in the lake. In the hot season there is no need to take swimming things—dive overboard in your clothes! You will be dry in minutes when you come out, much refreshed.

Taunggyi

GETTING THERE
See 'Getting to Inle Lake'. If you want to go to Taunggyi first, the jeep from Thazi costs about K60.

Buses from Yaunghwe to Taunggyi depart from outside the Friendship Restaurant until about 9 am, and then from opposite the market. The fare is K10 for an hour's drive switch-backing through the hills on precipitous roads with dramatic hair-pin bends.

Taunggyi, meaning 'big mountain', is the capital of the Shan States, a busy commercial

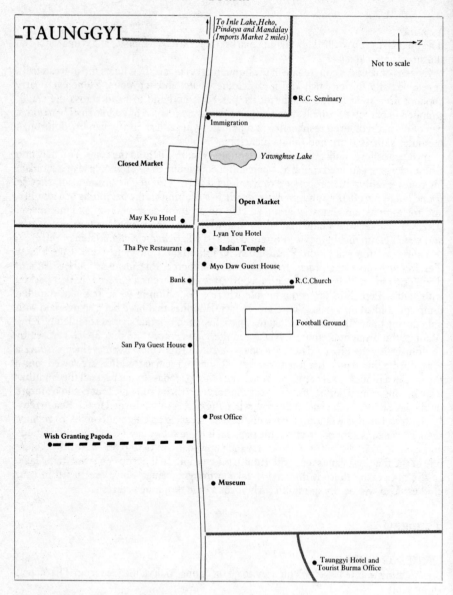

town on the lower slopes of Mount Taungyyi. Goods in the markets reflect its strategic position on the main road to the mountain routes into Thailand. Tourism plays little part in Taunggyi's economy: you are less likely to be bothered by the outstretched hands and demands of children here than in other towns and it is hard to find English-speaking locals. The cafes and guest houses are fairly basic and, strung out down the busy main road, extremely noisy.

WHAT TO SEE
The **Museum** is small but well organized, open 9 am–4 pm except at weekends. You can see displays of traditional costumes, indigenous birds and animals, vegetation and crops. Most interesting is the anthropological section, with cultural, social and political displays showing the struggles of the Shan States, generation by generation, in relation to Burma as a whole. Look out for the typewriter with keys in Shan characters!

The **market** is Taunggyi's throbbing heart, a kaleidoscope of colour and chanting voices, pungent with the smell of spices, tobacco and durian fruit. Here, you will see the variety of dress and physique that sets the hill tribes apart. The food stalls are on your right as you walk down the hill, and household and non-perishable goods are opposite.

Three kilometres out of Taunggyi going towards Mandalay there is an 'imports' market, crammed with stuff smuggled in from Thailand. Just above the central market there is a **mosque** on the right where there always seems to be some sort of ceremony going on. If you go in you will probably be befriended by one of the Indian Moslems and even invited to share a meal. The large **Catholic Church** is down a side road above the mosque and alongside playing fields. Here nuns and novice priests shepherd in orphans and school children, leading the Mass in sing-song, chanted, English.

Climb the main road out of town leaving the museum on your left, and take any of the several turnings to the right, through a residential area and up the hill to the monastery and temple at the top. This is called the **Wish Granting Pagoda**. Whether your wishes will be granted or not, it's an easy climb with cameo glimpses of family life through open doors and windows. A tall, rather solemn Buddha guarded by *nagas* stands in the pavilion at the top behind a row of white umbrellas. The wind whispers over the corrugated roof, chasing lizards into cracks in the breeze-block and brick walls. It is cool in the shade of pines which overlook the town and the hills beyond.

WHERE TO STAY
The Taunggyi Hotel, once called the Taunggyi Strand, incorporating the Tourist Burma office, is up the hill beyond the museum on the left. It stands among pines, shrubs and flowers and you catch faint echoes of its colonial past, though the government rest house just beside it, once the quarters of the British Superintendent of the Shan States, is a far more telling relic from the British Raj.

The hotel is rated Second Class. A certain faded style makes up for its air of dilapidation and it is among the nicest of the authorized hotels. The rooms are comfortable and carpeted, with bathrooms and there is a bar and the usual institutional restaurant where you can choose English, Chinese or Burmese food from a large menu, reasonably priced. Single rooms cost K130, double, K171.

Guest Houses
There are a number of guest houses, and you must consult the Tourist Burma list for those currently in favour. The standard is not great: small rooms, hot and noisy, with very primitive and often sordid plumbing. Single rooms K25, double, K40.

The **San Pya Guest House** is perhaps the pick of the bunch, but it has a television lounge that attracts a vociferous audience throughout viewing time. The plumbing is poor and the locks on the loo doors are not to be trusted.

The May Kyu Hotel, further down, serves food, but is rather chaotic with its plumbing downstairs through the kitchen, and small rooms without much ventilation.

The Myo Daw Guest House, almost opposite the May Kyu, is barely adequate.

WHERE TO EAT
The **Lyan You Hotel** doesn't take foreigners overnight, but is an excellent restaurant, both for food and for atmosphere. Because Taunggyi has rather more liberal drinking laws than elsewhere in Burma, a legacy of British influence, there is a completely different atmosphere in the licensed eating places. In the Lyan You, wooden tables in separate booths are crowded with customers exuding uncharacteristic ribaldry and laughter, lubricated with Rum Sours, Shan whisky and Mandalay beer.

The **Tha Pye,** opposite, has not quite the same atmosphere of bonhomie, but the food is good and cheap.

En Route to Inle Lake

If you have time, it is well worth breaking your journey to Inle Lake and exploring Kalaw and Pindaya, both of which are on the way, after Thazi.

Meiktila

Meiktila is about 20 km west of Thazi, and is the junction of the Rangoon-Mandalay and Pagan-Taunggyi roads. Like Thazi, it hasn't much to tempt you to linger, but there are plenty of places where you can get a meal if you are changing trucks.

Thazi

Thazi is a busy railway junction where you change from train to pick-up and vice versa. There are plenty of places where you can get a meal while you are waiting but nothing of enough interest to detain you.

From Thazi, the last part of the journey is well worth the discomfort of a crowded pick-up. The zig-zag road climbs to over 1300 m through jungle and plantation, with frequent vistas across valleys to distant hills. In the hot season, there is the added excitement of the frequent fires that race up the parched hill-sides and leap the road so that your truck, with its tank full of black-market petrol, must drive through the flames!

Kalaw

GETTING THERE
You can either get off the bus/pick-up from Thazi, or take the bus from Taunggyi. It costs about K15, either way.

The train journey, through the hills from Thazi or from Shwenyaung, is spectacular but takes up to four hours, and is not authorized by Tourist Burma.

About 70 km west of Taunggyi, Kalaw, 1320 m up on the edge of the Shan plateau, gives a welcome respite from the heat—even in the hot season it feels cool. A popular hill station during British rule, it retains its colonial atmosphere, albeit somewhat decayed. It blazes with blossoms and bougainvillea and you can walk for miles among pine woods and orchards and explore the market teeming with hill people in colourful costumes. There is a picturesque circular 'park road' which takes you round the fringe of the hills, past the old British houses and steps lead up to a number of temples and a monastery.

Well worth it if you have a spare day, is to get a guide to take you from Kalaw to one of the **Palaung tribe villages** in the hills. They all wear marvellously flamboyant costumes and the whole village comes out to welcome you as if you were royalty. It is a 2-3 hour walk each way through glorious hill scenery and your guide/interpreter will cost about K200 for the day.

At present you can't visit the Padaung village, near out-of-bounds Loi Kaw 150 km away, where it is still posssible to see the 'giraffe' women wearing rings round their necks and ankles. The practice is illegal now, but older women must still wear their rings because their muscles have no strength.

WHERE TO STAY
The Kalaw Hotel, in a beautiful setting, with tennis court and lots of flowers costs K150 single, K190 double, or K75/K115 in the annexe. The food is the same as in all other government hotels.

The **Thin Yu Mying,** in the middle of Kalaw, is the only approved guest house for tourists, a dismal place costing about K20 per person. It also serves as an annexe to the hotel. Its Chinese restaurant is the only one worth trying in the the town.

Pindaya

About 45 km north of Kalaw, Pindaya is a prosperous agricultural town in the hills, situated beside a lake. It is famous for its caves where countless numbers of golden Buddhas crowd the dimly lit interiors, many of them hundreds of years old. For some, a visit to this charming town is one of the highlights of a holiday in Burma, not so much for the caves as for the atmosphere and setting, rural but not scruffy and dirty. And for the fact that few other tourists find time to visit it.

GETTING THERE
Take the bus from Thazi, Kalaw or Taunggyi and get out at Aungban. From here you take another bus north to Pindaya. In all it costs about K25 each way.

The drive there is almost the best part, taking you through open hill country with plantations of beautiful green crab apple trees, pines, tea, coffee and cabbages.

The town clings to the shores of the lake with hills rising from one end, richly studded with pagodas. Beyond the hotel, the road runs along the lake past groups of ruined pagodas and a remarkable avenue of 200-year-old banyan trees, to the foot of the cliffs where there are a couple of cafes and a cluster of ancient ivy-clad pagodas. You can either walk to the caves from here, a steep climb up covered steps that is more fun but fairly exhausting, or you can continue on the road which zig-zags to the top. Either way, the views are magnificent.

In the reception chamber you can see holy texts, translated into English—daunting exhortations to 'shun evil ways', 'avoid wicked companions', 'think holy thoughts'.

King Anawrahta visited these caves in the 11th century and you feel that nothing much has changed in the subsequent 900 years. The extent of the main cave with its chambers and secondary caves is not immediately apparent, and it is large, dark and awe inspiring. Rough walls soar upwards towards ceilings lost in the dimness, lived in by pigeons and bats. You can see the secondary caves opening out if you walk round behind the Buddhas. Among the many huge images in the main cave, look out for the one with a distinctly Hindu style. Each cave contains groups of Buddhas in different attitudes, with smaller ones in niches and on shelves around the walls. Water drips from lime-encrusted stalactites, making the floor wet and slithery. The last gallery slopes downwards and legend has it slicing its way westwards below the earth's crust as far as Pagan, only 120 miles as the crow flies. Unromantic archaeologists pour cold water on this tradition.

There is another shrine built into the cliff off the walkway to the cave, with more Buddhas, and several pagodas and monasteries nearby.

There is a story told of seven 'Kain ya' princesses who left their home in Kayah State, to the south, to swim in Pindaya Lake. The Kain ya were mythical creatures with human bodies on bird legs: *kayah* means 'land of the Kain ya'. As the princesses played in the lake, a monstrous spider emerged and captured them. They were imprisoned in the caves for many years and you can still see their stalactite loom. Then a Prince Charming came to their rescue, slaying the spider and setting them free. The water in the lake is muddy with the blood of the spider. The name Pindaya comes from *Pin-gu-ya* meaning 'got the spider' and a spider is Pindaya's symbol.

Pindaya town was once a popular holiday resort for the British who appreciated the invigorating air and the good walking country around.

WHERE TO STAY
The Pindaya Hotel overlooks the lake on the road to the caves. The rooms are clean and reasonably comfortable, with hot showers; K20 double and K15 single, plus 10%. The food is adequate and the staff very friendly. Don't rely on the electricity supply!

The **Sen Lin Yaune** is a guest house in the town centre, costing K35 per person.

WHERE TO EAT
If you don't eat in the hotel, the **Mg Mg Lay** is a simple and good Chinese restaurant just off the Main Street at the town end of the lake.

There is another Chinese restaurant on the south (left) side of the road heading towards Kalaw.

Two more Chinese restaurants in the town are the **Kyanlite** and the **Mi Khine**.

Part X

'OUT OF BOUNDS'

A Padaung 'giraffe woman'

Things change continually in Burma, as in the rest of the world. At the time of writing, it is not possible for tourists to visit vast areas of the country, unless in exceptional circumstances. Some places could become accessible in the future particularly to visitors on Tourist Burma packages if restrictions were to relax. The following are a few of the many places that it would be worth visiting if the opportunity arose.

The information given about getting to these places cannot be used except as a general indication: if they open up, then access for tourists will become authorized. At present, you would be stopped if you tried any of these journeys.

Prome

Prome lies on the eastern bank of the Irrawaddy, about a third of the way upstream towards Mandalay. Not, strictly speaking, out of bounds—but you must get special permission from Tourist Burma to visit it.

GETTING THERE

By Boat
If visa restrictions relax, the ideal way to visit Prome is by boat, from Pagan, but the journey takes two days going with the current, with an overnight stop at Magwe, and so is not feasible at present. It would cost about K200.

By Train
There are trains from Rangoon taking about 9 hours, K50 Upper Class.

By Road
It would be possible to go by bus from Rangoon or Pagan, but it would take forever and the journey would be unendurable.

Prome is a pleasant little town dominated by the golden *stupa* of the **Shwesandaw Pagoda,** surrounded by elegant pinnacles, standing on a hill overlooked by a vast Buddha who stares at it with rather vacant eyes. The pagoda attracts many pilgrims during the **Tazaungdaing Festival** every November. The area is an important archaeological centre, with **Sri Ksetra** as the main attraction.

Sri Ksetra

The area around Prome is an archaeologist's paradise, with remains dating back to the Pyus who settled in Burma about 2000 years ago and made their capital at Sri Ksetra not far to the southeast of Prome. Excavation work in modern times has uncovered many prehistoric artefacts among the brick ruins, some of which prove that *Theravada* Buddhism was practised in central Burma long before Anawrahta's time. The ancient city is scattered with pagodas and temples, many of which are unusual shapes, their *stupas* being conical or cylindrical like great terracotta rhubarb-forcing jars, or cube shaped with soaring arched doorways. There is a small museum with some of the excavated artefacts, and with plans and details of the lay-out. Sri Ksetra was built, so it is said, with the help of Thagyarmin, the king of the *nats* and several others, including Naga, the snake-dragon.

Thagyarmin took Naga by the tail and swung him in a circle, to define the limits of the city, but, looking at the ruined walls today, Naga must have been of a considerable length! The strategic position of Sri Ksetra, close to the Irrawaddy in central Burma, made it a valuable city and there was continual conflict between the early tribes as to who should own it. Sri Ksetra finally collapsed in the 9th century and fell into ruin. Two hundred years later, in his quest to set up the greatest city and centre of *Theravada* Buddhism, Anawrahta removed all the sacred relics from the temples and had them installed in his magnificent Pagan.

Today the railway runs through the ruins of the old city, so pilgrims can get out of the train at Hmwaza to see it before going on to Prome.

WHERE TO STAY
There is no approved accommodation for tourists so you will have to persuade one of the hotels or guest houses to let you stay. The **People's Hotel** and the **Saw Pya Hotel** are both pretty basic, costing around K30 for the night.

EATING OUT
There are a number of cafés where you can get a meal, but nowhere remarkable.

Moulmein

Moulmein is a 'brown' area because of its proximity to insurgents in the hills to the east, who make random raids on the farming communities, burning villages, taking hostages, sometimes even killing, in their attempts to kindle rebellion against government policies. Only in very special circumstances would tourists be allowed to go there.

GETTING THERE

By Air
It is less than an hour by air from Rangoon, costing about K500.

By Train
Leaving Rangoon at 6 am it is a most enjoyable 9-hour journey—through lovely and very varied scenery—to Martaban, followed by a half hour ferry over the Salween River to the town. The fare is K50, Upper Class.

GETTING AROUND
You will have the usual choice of pony traps and trishaws, with driver/guide, for about K50 for half a day, or a taxi, for about K60 an hour.

Moulmein, deep in Mon territory, is spread along the southern banks of the Salween River, below a long ridge of hills. It is Burma's third-largest town and was once a major port until silt made the river unsuitable for big ships. Teak was the main product and you will still see the forests and timber stacks in the surrounding countryside, interspersed with rubber plantations and other crops. The Japanese started their invasion of Burma through Moulmein, having come over the mountains on the Thai border. The British used the town as an administrative centre for 25 years until the middle of the 19th century and you will see ample evidence of their influence in the architecture of houses, churches and municipal buildings. The town has a pleasant, rather sleepy atmosphere, and there are attractive cameos of Burmese life in the back streets and along the water-front. Boys take their ponies down to bathe in the river in the evening, letting them submerge until only their noses show above the murky water.

Moulmein has a thriving University and a teacher training college, where English has recently been reinstated as a compulsory subject. Dominating the town from the hill behind is Kipling's 'old Moulmein Pagoda, lookin' lazy at the sea'—the **Kyaikthanlan**, with wonderful views across the river and away to the distant hills. The **Uzena Pagoda** is memorable for the three figures that depict the ephemeral nature of life—the old man, the sick man and the corpse, followed by the holy man whose teachings will point the way to enlightenment. As you climb the steps to the pagoda, look out for an unremarkable, recumbent plaster Buddha on the right, rather unkempt and seedy, stained by bird droppings and cloaked in dust. The walls of this Buddha's shrine are decorated with remarkable murals, clean and clear, showing everyday life in Moulmein in the last century. Look to the left and you will see a splendid portrayal of a British couple in the process of moving house, with all their belongings around them and their furniture being lowered or hoisted on ropes.

The **market** in Moulmein is a treasure trove, stacked with every sort of thing to buy including not a few black-market goods.

You would have to hire a jeep or taxi to take you to the **caves** in the hills nearby, probably having to pay more than K60 an hour. These are gloomy caverns full of stalagmites and stalactites, where Buddha images have been set up in shrines over the years. One of them, the **Kawgaun Cave,** is known locally as the Cave of Ten Thousand Buddhas.

About 60 km south of Moulmein, at **Thanbyuzayat,** there is a huge and beautifully kept War Cemetery, the burial ground for thousands of Allied prisoners of war, most of whom died building the 'death railway' to Thailand under the Japanese in the Second World War.

A few kilometres south of the cemetery, at **Setse,** there is a glorious beach—a long white sweep of sand, fringed with palm trees and washed by the Andaman Sea. The University of Moulmein have a marine research department here, funded by foreign aid. The British used to use this attractive seaboard as a holiday resort in the days of their administration.

WHERE TO STAY
Because Moulmein is a brown area, there is no approved tourist accommodation. There are a number of places to stay in if you can persuade them to have you: ask in the market.

EATING OUT
There are a number of cafés where you will get the usual rather indifferent Burmese, Chinese and Indian dishes.

Thaton

Thaton is about 140 km due east of Rangoon across the gulf of Martaban.

GETTING THERE

By Train
It is about 7½ hours by train from Rangoon, on the Moulmein train leaving at 6 am and costing about K35 Upper Class.

GETTING AROUND
There is the usual choice of taxi, pony cart or trishaw.

The Mons called the rich, fertile land between the Sittang and the Salween rivers Suvannabhumi—The Golden Land—and made Thaton their capital. East of Rangoon across the Gulf of Martaban, southeast of Pegu on the way to Moulmein, Thaton was the womb that gave birth to *Theravada* Buddhism in the 3rd century BC. Two missionaries, Sona and Uttara, were sent to Burma by India's King Ashoka, to convert the Burmese to the pure *Theravada* law. In those days, before silt closed the waterways, Thaton was a major port, trading with India and China, and so it was natural that the mission should start here. It was also from here, in the 11th century, that the monk Shin Aran went north to Pagan, converted King Anawrahta and set in motion the chain of events that led to the conquest of the Mons by Anawrahta and their subsequent influence over the culture of their captors. (See 'History' p. 272.)

Thaton's importance waned after Anawrahta's conquest of the Mons in his efforts to gain the *Theravada* scriptures, and today you must search carefully for the few medieval remains that are still visible. Traces of the city walls can be seen and the **Shwezayan Pagoda** dates from the 5th century BC when the Mons were still animists, and is thought to enshrine five of Buddha's teeth.

WHERE TO STAY
As in other non-tourist places, there are no approved hotels or guest houses, but if you ask around, you will be directed to someone who will turn a blind eye to authority and accommodate you.

EATING OUT
There are plenty of cafés where you will get the usual rather unexciting curry and noodle dishes.

The Kyaiktiyo Pagoda, Golden Rock

The Kyaiktiyo Pagoda, on its gilded rock, is one of the most fascinating buildings in Burma and well worth a visit if tourist restrictions are relaxed. At present it is out of bounds, due to its proximity to the hills in the east where insurgents present a threat to safety. A recent Karen attack has strengthened this ban. As it takes at least two days and nights, if not three, to go and see it and return, and you are likely to be turned away by a road check on the way, it could be a very frustrating waste of precious time to try and beat the system only to be turned away at the last minute.

GETTING THERE
The pagoda is midway between Pegu and Thaton, near the town of **Kyaikto** where there is a station. Trains from Rangoon via Pegu take about 4 hours. It is also possible to get there by bus from Rangoon or Pegu, or to hire a jeep, but this is expensive.

If you get to Kyaikto early enough to catch a bus that will take you the 15 km out to Kinpun by noon, it is worth trying to do the 10 km climb in time to watch the sunset from the top; it is a fairly strenuous haul, taking about 5 hours, but wonderfully satisfying and you should be able to stay in the monastery at the top. Take a sleeping bag if you do this and don't oversleep and miss the sunrise. Otherwise you must spend the night at the monastery in Kinpun.

Legend has it that in the 11th century, King Tissa, the son of a sorcerer and a *naga* princess, was given one of the Buddha's hairs by an ancient hermit. The hermit told the king that he could have the hair if he could enshrine it in a pagoda built on a rock the exact shape of the hermit's head. Tissa searched in vain until Thagyamin, king of the *nats*, gave a hand and found just the rock for him, at the bottom of the sea. A miraculous ship carried the rock to the top of the mountain and then turned to stone nearby, where it can still be seen—the **Kyaukthanban** or 'stone boat' pagoda. The rock was balanced on the edge of a sheer cliff, so precariously perched that you feel you could almost push it off: it would be no use to try, however, although it is said that you can move it slightly—its position is secured by the precision with which the Buddha's hair was placed, enshrined within its tiny 5½-metre golden pagoda!

383

After the long climb through thick jungle, up the zig-zag path and along the ridge, past shrines and Buddhas and pilgrims' halts, opening up wonderful far views, your first sight of the great shining rock with its elegant spire is awe-inspiring and very moving. You will be in company with many faithful pilgrims who make the journey as often as possible to gain great merit and you may even see people being carried up in litters.

Sandoway

West of Prome on the coast, Sandoway is one of Burma's main seaside resorts, accessible to tourists only at certain times. With glorious white sandy beaches and clear water, Sandoway is a good place for anyone who prefers sunbathing and swimming (rather a waste of precious time in Burma) to the more rigorous pastime of sightseeing and exploring pagodas. At present tourists are not normally allowed to go there, though you do hear of people who have managed to get there with help from a Burmese friend.

GETTING THERE

By Air
The only way is to fly in over the great range of mountains, the Arakan Yoma, to the east. The fare is $100. An airport bus takes you to your accommodation.

There are no cultural sights in and around Sandoway but the hinterland is very beautiful, with rich farmland, and the beaches are the best in Burma. Look out for the unusual shells in the sand.

Seven kilometres inland, the market town of Sandoway has attractive wooden houses with verandahs, and a good market where you can get Arakan *longyis*. There is a mosque, and you can watch weavers at their looms.

WHERE TO STAY
The **Ngapoli Hotel**, 8 km from the airport, is clean and pleasant, with small chalets, water and (unreliable) electricity. About $20 per head. The food is simple though adequate: fish is plentiful and good. The **American Club**, in Rangoon, has 2 bungalows in Sandoway taking 6 people, sometimes available to non-members for about $10 per night. Apply through the US Embassy.

Guest houses cost $5 per head.

Loikaw

Loikaw is the capital of Kayah State, south of Shan country, too close to the lawless tribes on the Thai border to allow tourists to go there at present.

If you were able to get there, you would go by road from Taunggyi.

The interest here is that the Padaung tribe live around Loikaw, much publicized because of their 'giraffe women'. Before the practice was banned by law, the girls of the tribe, from the age of about 6, had gold rings fastened round their necks and ankles, one each year, until the neck was stretched to as much as 12 inches. This ghastly fate, which kills the muscles in the neck, was meant to so deform the women as to deter would-be kidnappers! Today, although you will not see girls and young women ringed, you can still see older women in their awful bondage, unable to hold up their heads without support.

INDEX – THAILAND

Page references in *italics* refer to maps

INDEX – BURMA

Page references in *italics* refer to maps